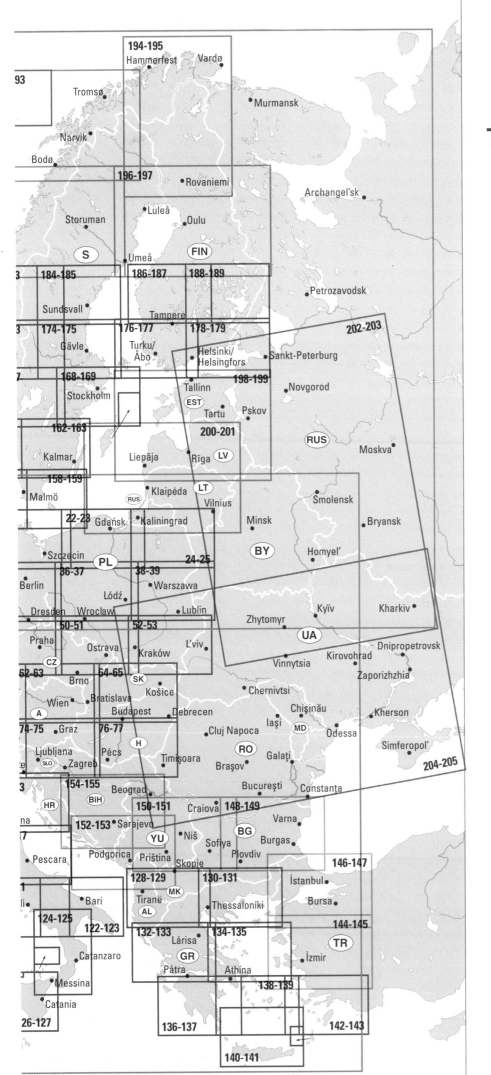

CW00370076

NE

TABLEAU ... BLAGE
KARTENÜBERSICHT

Scale-Scala-Escala
Échelle-Maßstab
1 : 8 000 000

1 cm = 80 km   1 inch = 126.26 miles

0   100   200   300   400   500 km
0   50   100   150   200   250   300 miles

Scale-Scala-Escala
Échelle-Maßstab
1 : 3 000 000

1 cm = 30 km   1 inch = 47.35 miles

0   50   100   150   200 km
0   25   50   75   100 miles

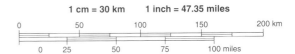

Scale-Scala-Escala
Échelle-Maßstab
1 : 1 500 000
*(Is. Canarias, Madeira,
Açores 1 : 2 000 000)*

1 cm = 15 km   1 inch = 23.67 miles

0   25   50   75   100 km
0   20   40   60 miles

Scale-Scala-Escala
Échelle-Maßstab
1 : 1 000 000

1 cm = 10 km   1 inch = 15.78 miles

0   10   20   30   40   50   60 km
0   5   10   15   20   25   30   35 miles

Scale-Scala-Escala
Échelle-Maßstab
1 : 800 000

1 cm = 8 km   1 inch = 12.63 miles

0   10   20   30   40   50 km
0   5   10   15   20   25   30 miles

		GB	I	E	F	D
A	Österreich	Austria	Austria	Austria	Autriche	Österreich
AL	Shqipëria	Albania	Albania	Albania	Albanie	Albanien
AND	Andorra, Andorre	Andorra	Andorra	Andorra	Andorre	Andorra
B	België, Belgique	Belgium	Belgio	Bélgica	Belgique	Belgien
BG	Bălgarija	Bulgaria	Bulgaria	Bulgaria	Bulgarie	Bulgarien
BiH	Bosna i Hercegovina	Bosnia and Herzegovina	Bosnia ed Erzegovina	Bosnia-Herzegovina	Bosnie-Herzégovine	Bosnien-Herzegowina
BY	Belarus'	Belarus	Bielorussia	Bielorrusia	Biélorussie	Weißrußland
CH	Schweiz, Suisse, Svizzera	Switzerland	Svizzera	Suiza	Suisse	Schweiz
CZ	Česká Republika	Czech Republic	Repubblica Ceca	República Checa	République Tchèque	Tschechische Republik
D	Deutschland	Germany	Germania	Alemania	Allemagne	Deutschland
DK	Danmark	Denmark	Danimarca	Dinamarca	Danemark	Dänemark
E	España	Spain	Spagna	España	Espagne	Spanien
EST	Eesti	Estonia	Estonia	Estonia	Estonie	Estland
F	France	France	Francia	Francia	France	Frankreich
FIN	Suomi, Finland	Finland	Finlandia	Finlandia	Finlande	Finnland
FL	Fürstentum Liechtenstein	Liechtenstein	Liechtenstein	Liechtenstein	Liechtenstein	Liechtenstein
FR	Føroyar, Færøerne	Faeroe Islands	Isole Fær Øer	Islas Feroe	Îles Féroé	Färöer
GB	Great Britain and N. Ireland	Great Britain and N. Ireland	Gran Bretagna e Irlanda d. Nord	Gran Bretaña e Irlanda del Norte	Gr.-Bretagne et Irlande du Nord	Grossbritannien und Nordirland
GBG	Guernsey, Guernesey	Guernsey	Guernsey	Guernesey	Guernesey	Guernsey
GBJ	Jersey	Jersey	Jersey	Jersey	Jersey	Jersey
GBM	Isle of Man, Mona	Isle of Man	Isola di Man	Isla de Man	Île de Man	Insel Man
GBZ	Gibraltar	Gibraltar	Gibilterra	Gibraltar	Gibraltar	Gibraltar
GR	Hellas	Greece	Grecia	Grecia	Grèce	Griechenland
H	Magyarország	Hungary	Ungheria	Hungría	Hongrie	Ungarn
HR	Hrvatska	Croatia	Croazia	Croacia	Croatie	Kroatien
I	Italia	Italy	Italia	Italia	Italie	Italien
IRL	Ireland	Ireland	Irlanda	Irlanda	Irlande	Irland
IS	Ísland	Iceland	Islanda	Islandia	Islande	Island
L	Lëtzebuerg, Luxembourg	Luxembourg	Lussemburgo	Luxemburgo	Luxembourg	Luxemburg
LT	Lietuva	Lithuania	Lituania	Lituania	Lituanie	Litauen
LV	Latvija	Latvia	Lettonia	Letonia	Lettonie	Lettland
M	Malta	Malta	Malta	Malta	Malte	Malta
MC	Principauté de Monaco	Monaco	Monaco	Mónaco	Monaco	Monaco
MD	Moldova	Moldova	Moldova	Moldavia	Moldavie	Moldau
MK	Makedonija	Macedonia	Macedonia	Macedonia	Macédoine	Makedonien
N	Norge	Norway	Norvegia	Noruega	Norvège	Norwegen
NIR	Northern Ireland	Northern Ireland	Irlanda del Nord	Irlanda del Norte	Irlande du Nord	Nordirland
NL	Nederland	Netherlands	Paesi Bassi	Países Bajos	Pays-Bas	Niederlande
P	Portugal	Portugal	Portogallo	Portugal	Portugal	Portugal
PL	Polska	Poland	Polonia	Polonia	Pologne	Polen
RO	România	Romania	Romania	Rumanía	Roumanie	Rumänien
RSM	San Marino	San Marino	San Marino	San Marino	Saint-Marin	San Marino
RUS	Rossija	Russia	Russia	Rusia	Russie	Rußland
S	Sverige	Sweden	Svezia	Suecia	Suède	Schweden
SK	Slovensko	Slovakia	Slovacchia	Eslovaquia	Slovaquie	Slowakei
SLO	Slovenija	Slovenia	Slovenia	Eslovenia	Slovénie	Slowenien
TR	Türkiye Cumhuriyeti	Turkey	Turchia	Turquia	Turquie	Türkei
UA	Ukraïna	Ukraine	Ucraina	Ucrania	Ukraine	Ukraine
V	Città del Vaticano	Vatican City	Città del Vaticano	Ciudad del Vaticano	Cité du Vatican	Vatikanstadt
YU	Srbija i Crna Gora	Serbia and Montenegro	Serbia e Montenegro	Serbia y Montenegro	Serbie et Monténégro	Serbien und Montenegro

ROAD ATLAS
ATLANTE STRADALE
ATLAS DE CARRETERAS
ATLAS ROUTIER
STRASSENATLAS

EUROPE
EUROPA

Contents

Sommario

Sumario

Sommaire

Inhaltsverzeichnis

GB Legend — I Legenda

GB Legend	I Legenda
Toll motorway, dual carriageway	Autostrada a pedaggio a doppia carreggiata
Toll motorway, single carriageway	Autostrada a pedaggio a singola carreggiata
Non-toll motorway, dual carriageway	Autostrada senza pedaggio a doppia carreggiata
Non-toll motorway, single carriageway	Autostrada senza pedaggio a singola carreggiata
Interchange; restricted interchange; service area	Svincolo; svincolo con limitazione; area di servizio
Motorway under construction	Autostrada in costruzione
Motorway in tunnel	Autostrada in galleria
Number of motorway; european road; national road; regional or local road	Numero di autostrada; itinerario europeo; strada nazionale; strada regionale o locale
National road, dual carriageway	Strada nazionale a doppia carreggiata
National road, single carriageway	Strada nazionale a singola carreggiata
Regional road, dual carriageway	Strada regionale a doppia carreggiata
Regional road, single carriageway	Strada regionale a singola carreggiata
Local road, dual carriageway	Strada locale a doppia carreggiata
Local road, single carriageway	Strada locale a singola carreggiata
Secondary road	Strada secondaria
Road under construction	Strada in costruzione
Road in tunnel	Strada in galleria
Motorway distances in kilometres (miles in United Kingdom and Ireland)	Distanze in chilometri (miglia nel Regno Unito e Irlanda) sulle autostrade
Road distances in kilometres (miles in United Kingdom and Ireland)	Distanze in chilometri (miglia nel Regno Unito e Irlanda) sulle strade
Gradient 14% and over; gradient 6%–13%	Pendenza maggiore del 14%; pendenza dal 6% al 13%
Panoramic routes	Percorsi panoramici
Pass with height and winter closure	Passo di montagna, quota e periodo di chiusura invernale
Toll point	Barriera di pedaggio
Railway and tunnel	Ferrovia e tunnel ferroviario
Ferry route (with car transportation) and destination	Linea di traghetto (con trasporto auto) e destinazione
Transport of cars by rail	Trasporto auto per ferrovia
National park, natural reserve	Parco nazionale, riserva naturale
International boundaries	Confini internazionali
Internal boundary	Confine interno
International airport	Aeroporto internazionale
Religious building; Castle, fortress	Edificio religioso; Castello, fortezza
Isolated monument	Monumento isolato
Ruins, archaeological area	Rovine, area archeologica
Cave	Grotta
Natural curiosity	Curiosità naturale
Panoramic view	Punto panoramico
Other curiosities (botanical garden, zoo, amusement park etc.)	Altre curiosità (giardino botanico, zoo, parco divertimenti ecc.)
Town or place of great tourist interest	Città o luogo di grande interesse turistico
Interesting town or place	Città o luogo interessante
Other tourist town or place	Altra città o luogo turistico

	E Leyenda	F Légende	D Zeichenerklärung
	Autopista de doble vía de peaje	Autoroute à péage et chaussées séparées	Zweibahnige Autobahn mit Gebühr
	Autopista de una vía de peaje	Autoroute à péage et chaussée unique	Einbahnige Autobahn mit Gebühr
	Autopista de doble vía sin peaje	Autoroute sans péage à chaussées séparées	Zweibahnige Autobahn ohne Gebühr
	Autopista de una vía sin peaje	Autoroute sans péage à chaussée unique	Einbahnige Autobahn ohne Gebühr
⦾⑫⦾⑬⦾Ⓢ	Acceso; acceso parcial; estación de servicio	Échangeur; échangeur partiel; aire de service	Anschlussstelle; Autobahnein- und/oder -ausfahrt; Tankstelle
	Autopista en construcción	Autoroute en construction	Autobahn in Bau
	Túnel en autopista	Tunnel autoroutier	Autobahntunnel
A11 E50 N13 D951	Número de autopista; carretera europea; carretera nacional; carretera regional o local	Numéro d'autoroute; route européenne; route nationale; route régionale ou locale	Straßennummer: Autobahn; Europastraße; Nationalstraße; Regional- oder Lokalstraße
	Carretera nacional de doble vía	Route nationale à chaussées séparées	Zweibahnige Nationalstraße
	Carretera nacional de vía unica	Route nationale à chaussée unique	Einbahnige Nationalstraße
	Carretera regional de doble vía	Route régionale à chaussées séparées	Zweibahnige Regionalstraße
	Carretera regional de vía unica	Route régionale à chaussée unique	Einbahnige Regionalstraße
	Carretera local de doble vía	Route locale à chaussées séparées	Zweibahnige Lokalstraße
	Carretera local de vía unica	Route locale à chaussée unique	Einbahnige Lokalstraße
	Carretera secundaria	Route secondaire	Nebenstraße
	Carretera en construcción	Route en construction	Straße in Bau
	Túnel en carretera	Tunnel routier	Straßentunnel
▼ 63 ▼	Distancias en kilómetros (millas en Gran Bretaña e Irlanda) en autopista	Distances autoroutières en kilomètres (miles en Royaume-Uni et Irlande)	Autobahnentfernungen in Kilometern (Meilen in Großbritannien und Irland)
▼ 23 ▼	Distancias en kilómetros (millas en Gran Bretaña e Irlanda) en carretera	Distances routières en kilomètres (miles en Royaume-Uni et Irlande)	Straßenentfernungen in Kilometern (Meilen in Großbritannien und Irland)
»»	Pendientes superiores al 14%; pendientes entre 6%–13%	Pente 14% et outre; pente 6%–13%	Steigungen über 14%; Steigungen 6%–13%
	Rutas panorámicas	Routes panoramiques	Aussichtsstraßen
Col d'Izoard 2360 10-6	Puerto de montaña con altura y cierre invernal	Col avec altitude et fermeture en hiver	Pass mit Höhe und Wintersperre
	Peaje	Barrière de péage	Gebührenstelle
	Ferrocarril y túnel	Chemin de fer et tunnel	Eisenbahn und Tunnel
Bastia	Línea marítima (con transporte de coches) y destino	Ligne de navigation (bac pour voitures) et destination	Schiffahrtslinie (Autofähre) und Ziel
	Transporte de coches por ferrocarril	Transport de voitures par chemin de fer	Autoverladung per Bahn
	Parque nacional, reserva natural	Parc national, réserve naturelle	Nationalpark, Naturschutzgebiet
	Límites internacionales	Frontières internationales	Staatsgrenzen
	Límite interno	Frontière intérieure	Verwaltungsgrenze
⊕	Aeropuerto internacional	Aéroport international	Internationaler Flughafen
♠ ♜	Edificio religioso; Castillo, fortaleza	Édifice religieux; Château, château-fort	Religiösgebäude; Schloss, Festung
▲	Monumento aislado	Monument isolé	Alleinstehendes Denkmal
∴	Ruinas, zona arqueológica	Ruines, site archéologique	Ruinen, archäologisches Ausgrabungsgebiet
∩	Cueva	Grotte	Höhle
✳	Paraje de interés natural	Curiosité naturelle	Natursehenswürdigkeit
☼	Vista panorámica	Vue panoramique	Rundblick
★	Otras curiosidades (jardín botánico, zoo, parque de atracciones etc.)	Autres curiosités (jardin botanique, zoo, parc d'attractions etc.)	Andere Sehenswürdigkeiten (Botanischer Garten, Zoo, Freizeitpark usw.)
LONDON	Ciudad o lugar de gran interés turístico	Localité ou site de grand intérêt touristique	Ortschaft oder Platz von großem touristischen Interesse
NORWICH	Ciudad o lugar interesante	Localité ou site remarquable	Sehenswerte Ortschaft oder Platz
BIRMINGHAM	Otra ciudad o lugar turístico	Autre localité ou site touristique	Andere touristischen Ortschaft oder Platz

EUROPEAN ROAD NETWORK
RETE STRADALE EUROPEA
RED EUROPEA DE CARRETERAS
RÉSEAU ROUTIER EUROPÉEN
EUROPÄISCHES STRASSENNETZ

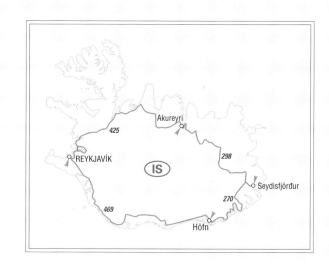

LEGEND - SEGNI CONVENZIONALI - LEYENDA - LÉGENDE - ZEICHENERKLÄRUNG

Motorway and road with motorway characteristics
Autostrada e strada con caratteristiche autostradali
Autopista y autovía con calzadas separadas
Autoroute et route de type autoroutier
Autobahn und Schnellstraße mit getrennten Fahrbahnen

Other roads
Altre strade
Otras carreteras
Autres routes
Sonstige Straßen

E15
M1
Road number
Numero di strada
Número de carretera
Numéro de route
Straßennummer

169
Distances in kilometres
Distanze in chilometri
Distancias en kilómetros
Distances en kilomètres
Distanzen in Kilometern

Distances in Great Britain and Ireland are expressed in miles.
Nel Regno Unito e in Irlanda le distanze sono espresse in miglia.
Las distancias en Gran Bretaña e Irlanda son expresas en millas.
Les distances en Grande-Bretagne et Irlande sont exprimées en miles.
Entfernungsangaben in Großbritannien und Irland sind in Meilen wiedergegeben.

Scale - Scala - Escala - Échelle - Maßstab
1 : 8 000 000 (1 cm = 80 km   -   1 inch =126,24 miles)

| 0 | 100 | 200 | 300 | 400 km |

| 0 | 50 | 100 | 150 | 200 | 250 miles |

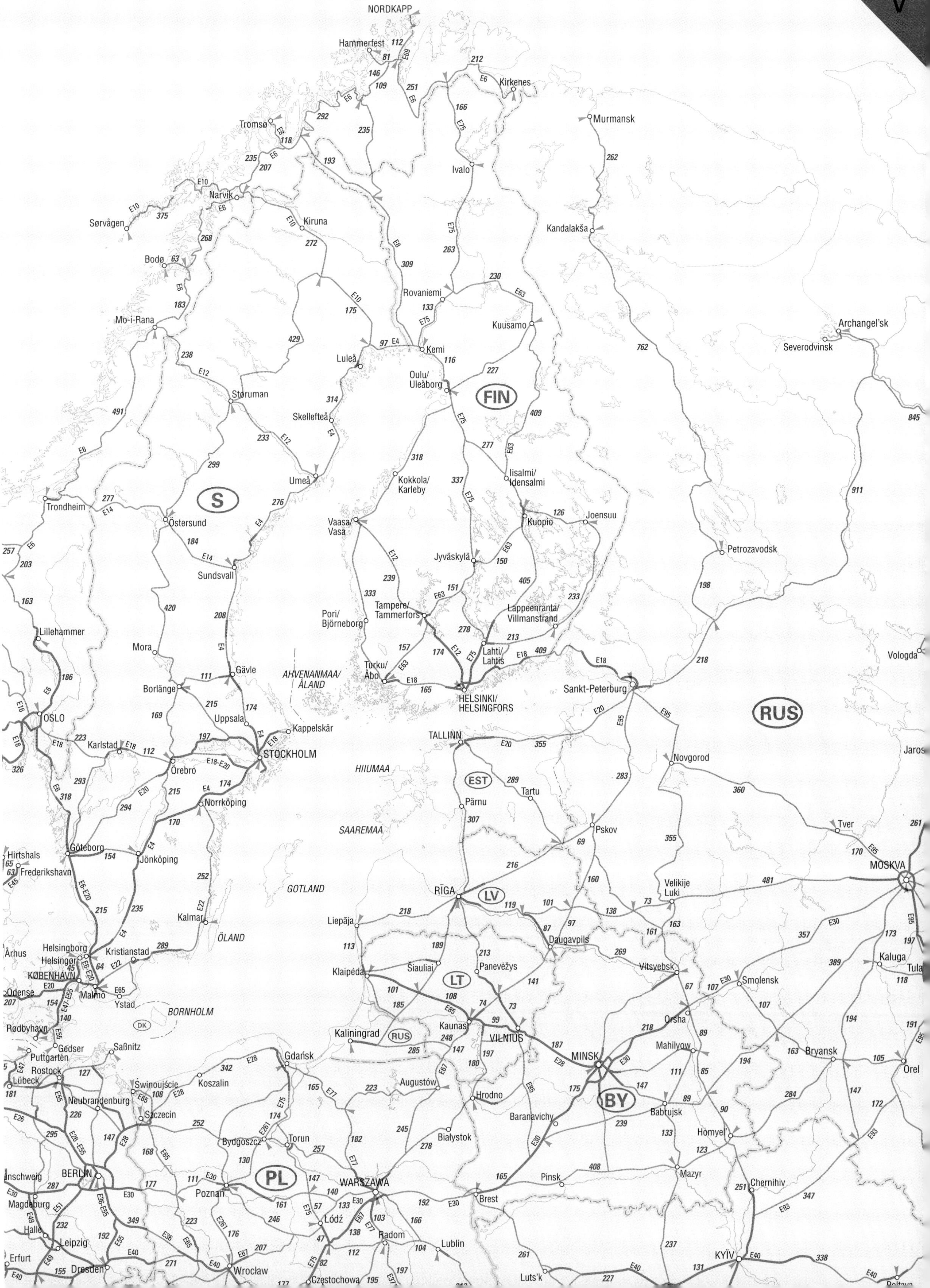

NORDKAPP

Hammerfest 112
81 E69
146
109 251
Tromsø 292
E8 235
118
235
207 193
E10
Narvik
E6
Sørvågen 375
268
Kiruna
Bodø 63
E10
272
E6
Mo-i-Rana 183
238
E12
429
Storuman 314
491
Skellefteå
E6
233 E4
299
E12
Umeå
Trondheim 277 276
E14
Östersund 184
E14
Sundsvall
E6 257
203
163
420 208
Lillehammer 186
Mora
E4
111 Gävle
Borlänge 215 174
E5
169
OSLO Uppsala
E18 223 197
Karlstad E18 112
326 Örebro E18-E20
293 215 E4 174
318 294
Norrköping
170
Hirtshals 65 Göteborg 154
63 Frederikshavn Jönköping
E45 252
215 235
E22
Kalmar
ÖLAND
Helsingborg
Århus Helsingør Kristianstad 289
45 64 E22
KØBENHAVN
Odense E20 Malmö E65
207 154 Ystad
140 BORNHOLM
Rødbyhavn DK
Gedser Sassnitz
Puttgarten
Rostock 127
Lübeck 181
E55 342 Gdańsk
Neubrandenburg 226 Koszalin
E26 Świnoujście 165
295 Szczecin 252 E77
147 174
168 Bydgoszcz Torun
BERLIN 130 257
287 177 111 147
Magdeburg E51 Poznań 140
232 161 57 133
Halle 349 223 246
192 E36 176 Łódź 103
Leipzig 138
Erfurt E40 207 Radom 104
155 Dresden 271 Wrocław 112
177 Częstochowa 195

FIN
Ivalo
Murmansk
262
Kandalakša
Kirkenes
E6
166
E75
E8 263
309
Rovaniemi 230
133 E63 Kuusamo
97 E4 Kemi 227
Luleå 116 762
Oulu/Uleåborg
314 409
E4 277
E63
318 845
Kokkola/Karleby 337
Vaasa/Vasa Iisalmi/Idensalmi
E12 126
Jyväskylä 150 Joensuu 911
239 151 Kuopio
333 E63 405
Pori/Björneborg Tampere/Tammerfors 233
157 278 213 Lappeenranta/Villmanstrand
174 E12 Lahti/Lahtis E18 409
Turku/Åbo E63 218
165 Sankt-Peterburg
HELSINKI/HELSINGFORS E20
TALLINN E95 E95
E20 355 Novgorod RUS
EST 289
Pärnu Tartu 283 360
307 Pskov Tver 261
69 355 170
216 Velikije Luki 481 MOSKVA
RĪGA 160 73
LV 119 101 138 163
Liepāja 218 87 97 357 173 197
113 189 269 161 Kaluga
Klaipėda 213 Daugavpils 389 Tula
Šiauliai Panevėžys 67 107 Smolensk 118
101 LT 141 107
185 108 74 73 218 Orsha 89 194 191
Kaliningrad 99 Vitsyebsk Mahilyow 163 Orel
RUS 248 VILNIUS 187 111 85 194 105
285 147 MINSK 147 89 147
180 175 BY 239 90 172
Augustów E30 133 Homyel
Hrodno 165 123
Białystok Baranavichy Babrujsk
245 Mazyr 251 Chernihiv 347
278 408 Pinsk
WARSZAWA Brest 261 237 KYÏV E40 338
192 Lublin Luts'k 227 131
166
Archangel'sk
Severodvinsk
Vologda
Petrozavodsk
198
Jaros

IRL 134 ISLE OF MAN
Galway/Gaillimh N1 116 upon-Tyne
136 102 A66 96
N18 65 N6 GBM A1 M6
Limerick/Luimneach N7 124 N7 DUBLIN/BAILE ÁTHA CLIATH GB York
N21 N8 161 102 58 Leeds Kingston-upon-Hull
N25 124 Holyhead A55 Liverpool 60 M62
124 N22 Rosslare 108 Manchester M180
N25 Waterford/Port Lairge A5 144 75 M1 167
Cork/Corcaigh 156 Birmingham M6 197 A1 A17
Fishguard 84 A14 A47 Norwich
A40 146 M5 M40 M1 Cambridge 79
Cardiff M4 Bristol Oxford 120 125 A14 Ipswich
Penzance A30 A30 117 M4 LONDON 72 Harwich
76 Plymouth A38 124 M5 80 75 Harwich
149 Southampton M20 Dover
Portsmouth 147 Folkestone Calais

Wilhelm-
Groningen E22 197 Emden 200
NL E22 E232 E233
AMSTERDAM E30 226
Den Haag E204 Arnhem E37
Rotterdam E25 208 Duisburg Dortmund
Oostende E19 172 243
Antwerpen E40 E42 215 Düsseldorf
Lille E17 E313 E314 69 Köln
BRUSSEL/BRUXELLES B 198 Bonn E40 209
170 E42 215 Liège Koblenz E35
287 E25 E421 E44 289
Amiens E19 L E37 265
295 E44 E17 LUXEMBOURG E50 Mannheim
Le Havre E44 242 123 55 E25 Saarbrücken
CHANNEL 230 Caen E46 Reims 323 Metz Karlsruhe
ISLANDS GBG Cherbourg E46 239 Rouen 215 E54 Nancy 168 102
Brest E50 120 E15 E50 Strasbourg
GBJ E3-E46 183 PARIS E50 E54 134 E35-E52
237 St-Malo E3 Troyes E21 192
E50 E401 144 E50 316 283 E531 E41
296 Rennes E50 E402 202 E54 E23 E35 211
107 Le Mans E5 120 E17 E35 E54
182 Angers E501 Orléans E60 Dijon E21 Besançon Basel Zürich
Nantes E502 E5 Tours E604 247 E54 BERN
179 E62 208 Bourges E62 193 195 E27 CH
E3 E601 Poitiers E11 304 E607 E62 E62 Genève Lausanne 360
La Rochelle 254 214 F 346 E15 148 E612 E25
319 E603 E602 E606 Limoges 346 Clermont-Ferrand E62 E70 254 328 E35
Bordeaux E70 186 191 E70 184 Lyon E611 296 139 E64
337 E72 Brive-la-Gaillarde E11 251 Grenoble E712 Torino
243 399 E15 294 214 185 E62
257 Pau Toulouse 394 Nîmes 128 Sisteron 130 Genova
188 146 E80 137 E712 Nice 195
AND E9 E15 Perpignan Marseille 211 MC
349 E80
CORSE
Bastia 155
Ajaccio 159
Bonifacio
Porto Torres 122 Olbia
229 285
SARDEGNA
Cagliari

A Coruña/La Coruña
Santiago de Compostela E70 321 E70 Gijón
158 Oviedo Santander
Vigo E1 Orense 305 E70 Bilbo/Bilbao Donostia-San Sebastian
158 140 León 260 E804 E70
Porto E82 427 Burgos 312 E5-E80 Pamplona/Iruña
120 E80 E802 Valladolid E804 306 270 Zaragoza
Coimbra 429 Salamanca 214 Soria E804 E7 Lleida/Lérida
Óbidos P E1-E80 370 E803 Ávila Segovia E5 314 317 Girona/Gerona
192 Abrantes MADRID E90 E15 Barcelona
LISBOA E802 345 E90 378 370
279 Badajoz Toledo E901 E15
E90 E1 E802 Mérida E30 266 358 E901 Valencia
Sines E102 200 E803 294 Albacete E15
270 249 E1 Córdoba 245 145 260
Lagos Huelva E1 E5 243 135 Murcia Alicante/Alacant
Faro Sevilla E5 258 E92 E92 273 Cartagena
Cádiz 256 250 Granada Murcia
Algeciras E5 E15 Málaga E15 Almería
Gibraltar GBZ
Ceuta E
Melilla E

Palma Cala Rajada
ILLES BALEARS / ISLAS BALEARES

DRIVER INFORMATION - INFORMAZIONI UTILI
DIRECCIONES ÚTILES - INFORMATIONS UTILES
NÜTZLICHE AUSKÜNFTE

A	Österreich	A, C, D	0043	112	130	100	50	0,5 ‰
AL	Shqipëria	B, C, E	00355	a 19; 17	-	80	40	0,0 ‰
AND	Andorra, Andorre	A, C, D	00376	112	-	60-90	30-50	0,5 ‰
B	België, Belgique	A, C, D	0032	112	120	90	50	0,5 ‰
BG	Bălgarija	A, C, D	00359	166; 150	120	90	50	0,5 ‰
BiH	Bosna i Hercegovina	A, C, D	00387	92; 94	120	80	60	0,5 ‰
BY	Belarus'	B, C, E	00375	02; 03	110	90	60	0,0 ‰
CH	Schweiz, Suisse, Svizzera	A, C, D	0041	112	120	80	50	0,8 ‰
CZ	Česká Republika	A, C, D	00420	112	130	90	50	0,0 ‰
D	Deutschland	A, C, D	0049	112	130	100	50	0,5 ‰
DK	Danmark	A, C, D	0045	112	110	80	50	0,5 ‰
E	España	A, C, D	0034	112	120	90-100	50	0,3-0,5 ‰
EST	Eesti	A/B, C, D	00372	112	-	90-110	50	0,0 ‰
F	France	A, C, D	0033	112	130	90-110	50	0,5 ‰
FIN	Suomi, Finland	A, C, D	00358	112	120	80-100	50	0,5 ‰
FL	Fürstentum Liechtenstein	A, C, D	0041	112	-	80	50	0,8 ‰
GB	Great Britain and N. Ireland	A, C, D	0044	112	112 (70 mph)	96 (60 mph)	48 (30 mph)	0,8 ‰
GR	Hellas	A, C, D	0030	112	120	110	50	0,5 ‰
H	Magyarország	A, C, D	0036	112	130	90	50	0,0 ‰
HR	Hrvatska	A, C, D	00385	92; 94	130	80-100	50	0,5 ‰
I	Italia	A, C, D	0039	112	130	90	50	0,5 ‰
IRL	Ireland	A, C, D	00353	112	112 (70 mph)	96 (60 mph)	48 (30 mph)	0,8 ‰
IS	Ísland	A, C, D	00354	112	-	80-90	50	0,5 ‰
L	Lëtzebuerg, Luxembourg	A, C, D	00352	112	120	90	50	0,8 ‰
LT	Lietuva	A, C, E	00370	112	-	90-110	60	0,4 ‰
LV	Latvija	A, C, D	00371	112	-	90-110	50	0,5 ‰
M	Malta	A, C, D	00356	191; 196	-	64	40	0,0 ‰
MC	Principauté de Monaco	A, C, D	00377	112	-	50	50	0,5 ‰
MD	Moldova	B, C, E	00373	902; 903	-	90	40	0,0 ‰
MK	Makedonija	A, C, D	00389	92; 94	120	80-100	50-60	0,5 ‰
N	Norge	A, C, D	0047	112; 113	90-100	80	50	0,2 ‰
NL	Nederland	A, C, D	0031	112	120	80-100	50	0,5 ‰
P	Portugal	A, C, D	00351	112	120	90-100	50	0,5 ‰
PL	Polska	A, C, D	0048	112	130	90-110	60	0,2 ‰
RO	România	A/B, C, D	0040	112	120	90	50	0,0 ‰
RUS	Rossija	B, C, E	007	02; 03	-	90-110	60	0,0 ‰
S	Sverige	A, C, D	0046	112	110	70-90	50	0,2 ‰
SK	Slovensko	A, C, D	00421	158; 155	130	90	60	0,0 ‰
SLO	Slovenija	A, C, D	00386	112	130	90-100	50	0,5 ‰
TR	Türkiye Cumhuriyeti	A, C, D	0090	112	120	90	50	0,5 ‰
UA	Ukraïna	B, C, D	00380	02; 03	130	90-110	60	0,0 ‰
YU	Srbija i Crna Gora	A, C, D	00381	92; 94	120	80-100	60	0,5 ‰

UE
UE → 01/05/04

a Tiranë

-	+1	Euro (€)	(43) 1 5872000
-	+1	Lek (ALL)	(355) 4 240955
-	+1	Euro (€)	(376) 827117
-	+1	Euro (€)	(32) 2 5138940
-	+2	Lev (BGN)	(359) 2 9879778
-	+1	Konvertabilna Marka (BAM)	(387) 33 532606
-	+2	Belarus Rouble (BYR)	(375) 17 2269840
-	+1	Schweizer Franken (CHF)	00800 10020030
[b]✓	+1	Koruna Česká (CZK)	(420) 2 21580111
-	+1	Euro (€)	(49) 69 21238953
✓	+1	Danske Krone (DKK)	(45) 33 111415
-	+1	Euro (€)	(34) 913 433 500
✓	+2	Kroon (EEK)	(372) 645 7777
-	+1	Euro (€)	(33) 8 92683112
✓	+2	Euro (€)	(358) 9 4176911
-	+1	Schweizer Franken (CHF)	(423) 2396300
-	0	Pound Sterling (GBP)	(44) 020 8846 9000
-	+2	Euro (€)	(30) 210 3271300
✓	+1	Forint (HUF)	(36) 1 488 8700
-	+1	Kuna (HRK)	(385) 1 4556455
✓	+1	Euro (€)	(39) 06 49711
-	0	Euro (€)	(353) 1 6024000
✓	0	Íslensk Króna (ISK)	(354) 5355500
-	+1	Euro (€)	(352) 42828210
[b]✓	+2	Litas (LTL)	(370) 2 622610
✓	+2	Lats (LVL)	(371) 7044377
-	+1	Maltese Lira (MTL)	(356) 224444
-	+1	Euro (€)	(377) 92166166
-	+2	Leu (MDL)	(373) 2 210825
-	+1	Denar (MKD)	(389) 91 118498
✓	+1	Norsk Krone (NOK)	(47) 24144600
-	+1	Euro (€)	(31) 202018800
-	0	Euro (€)	(351) 21 3466307
[b]✓	+1	Zloty (PLN)	(48) 22 827 7173
-	+2	Leu (ROL)	(40) 1 3145160
✓	[c]+3	Russian Rouble (RUB)	(7) 95 7530003
✓	+1	Svensk Krona (SEK)	(46) 8 7255500
-	+1	Slovenská Koruna (SKK)	(421) 48 4136146
✓	+1	Tolar (SIT)	(386) 1 5891840
-	+2	Türk Lirası (TRL)	(90) 312 2128300
-	+2	Hrivna (UAH)	(380) 44 2124215
-	+1	Yugoslav Dinar (YUM)	(381) 11 3612754

[b] winter-inverno-invierno-hiver-Winter   [c] Moskva

Key to table
Legenda
Leyenda
Légende
Zeichenerklärung

Required driver's papers
Documenti di guida richiesti
Documentos requeridos para conducir
Papiers de conduire requis
Erforderliche Fahrzeugpapiere

A Driver's licence
   Patente di guida
   Carné de conducir
   Permis de conduire
   Führerschein

B International driver's licence
   Patente di guida internazionale
   Carné de conducir internacional
   Permis international de conduire
   Internationaler Führerschein

C Log-book
   Carta di circolazione
   Carné de circulación
   Permis de circulation
   Kraftfahrzeugschein

D Green card
   Carta verde
   Carta verde
   Carte verte
   Grüne Versicherungskarte

E Special insurance
   Assicurazione speciale
   Seguro especial
   Assurance spéciale
   Spezialversicherung

International code
Prefisso internazionale
Prefijo telefónico internacional
Indicatif international
Internationale Vorwahl

Emergency numbers
Numeri d'emergenza
Números de emergencia
Numéros d'urgence
Notrufnummern

Tourist offices
Uffici turistici
Oficinas de turismo
Bureaux de tourisme
Touristenämter

 (km/h)

Speed limit on motorway
Limite di velocità in autostrada
Límite de velocidad en autopista
Limite de vitesse sur l'autoroute
Höchstgeschwindigkeit auf der Autobahn

 (km/h)

Speed limit outside the towns
Limite di velocità su strade extraurbane
Límite de velocidad en carreteras extraurbanas
Limite de vitesse sur les routes extra-urbaines
Höchstgeschwindigkeit außerhalb der Städte

 (km/h)

Speed limit in towns
Limite di velocità nei centri abitati
Límite de velocidad en ciudades
Limite de vitesse dans les villes
Höchstgeschwindigkeit innerhalb der Städte

Maximum permitted alcohol level
Tasso alcolemico massimo tollerato
Límite alcohólico màximo consentido
Taux d'alcoolémie maximum admis
Höchsterlaubte Blutalkoholgehalt

Lights on during the day
Obbligo luci accese di giorno
Encender los faros durante el dia
Feux allumés obligatoires de jour
Licht einschalten während des Tages

Time zone from Greenwich
Fuso orario da Greenwich
Huso horario de Greenwich
Fuseaux horaires de Greenwich
Zeitzone mit Bezug auf Greenwich

Local currency
Valuta locale
Divisa local
Devise locale
Lokalwährung

note: the table is indicative; it is advisable to check the information before leaving.
nota: la tabella è indicativa; si consiglia di verificare le informazioni prima della partenza.
nota: el prospecto es indicativo; se aconseja verificar las informaciones antes de partir.
nota: le tableau est indicatif; il est conseillé de vérifier les renseignements avant de partir.
Notiz: Die Informationen sind als Hinweis gedacht; es empfiehlt sich,
*   die Auskünfte vor der Abfahrt zu überprüfen.*

 1

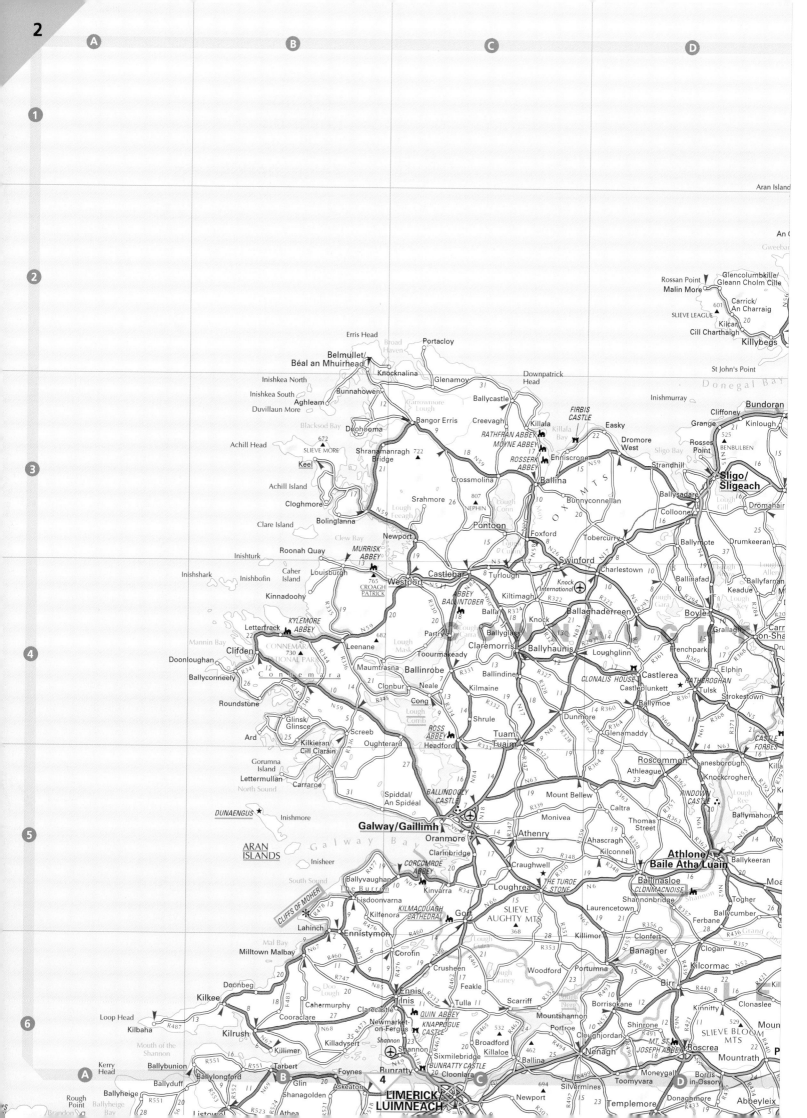

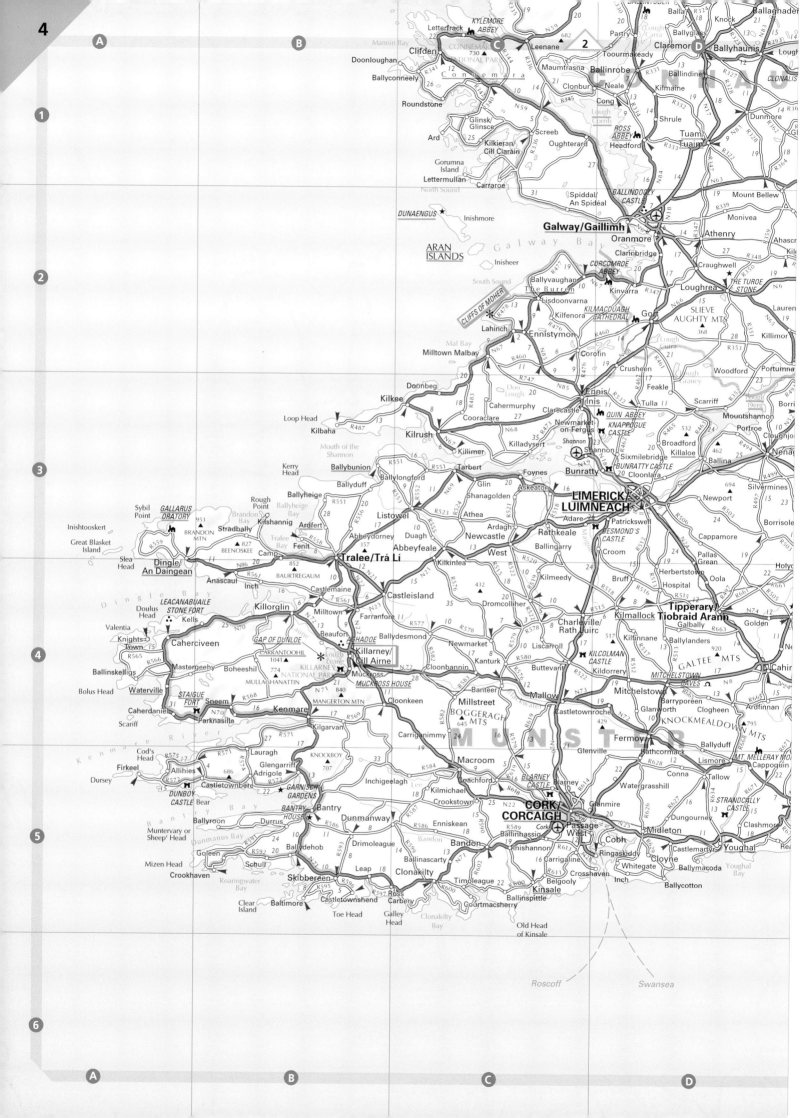

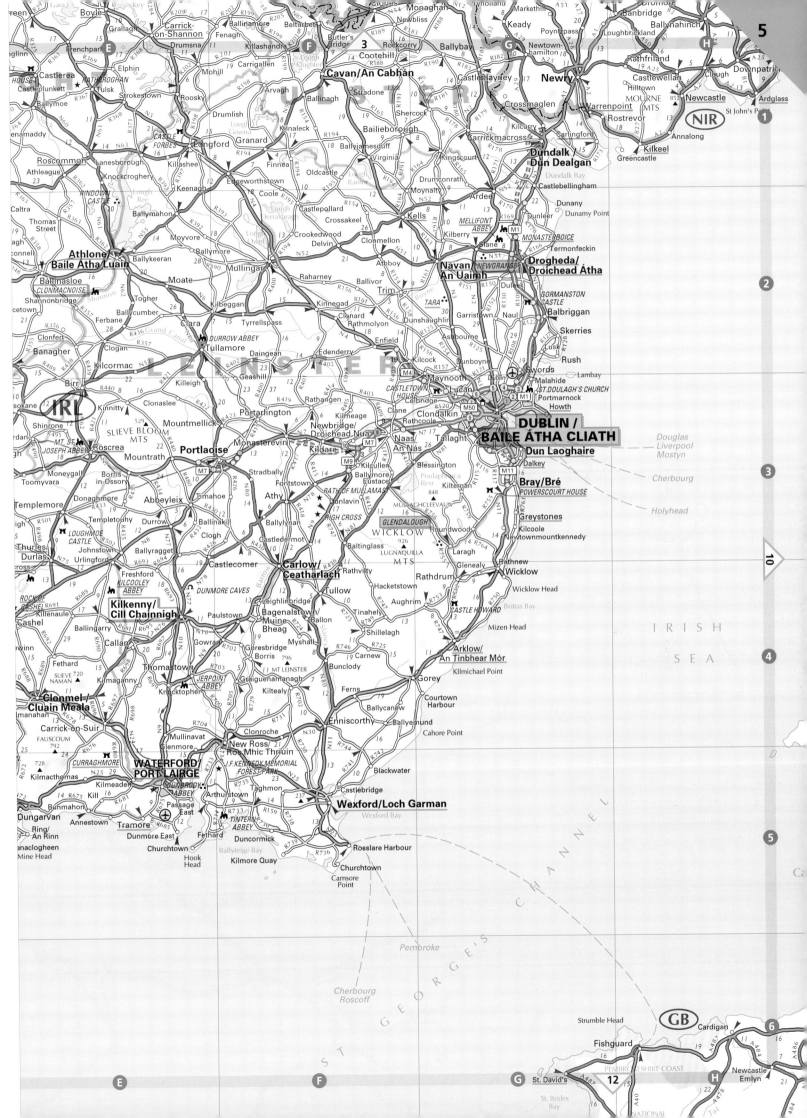

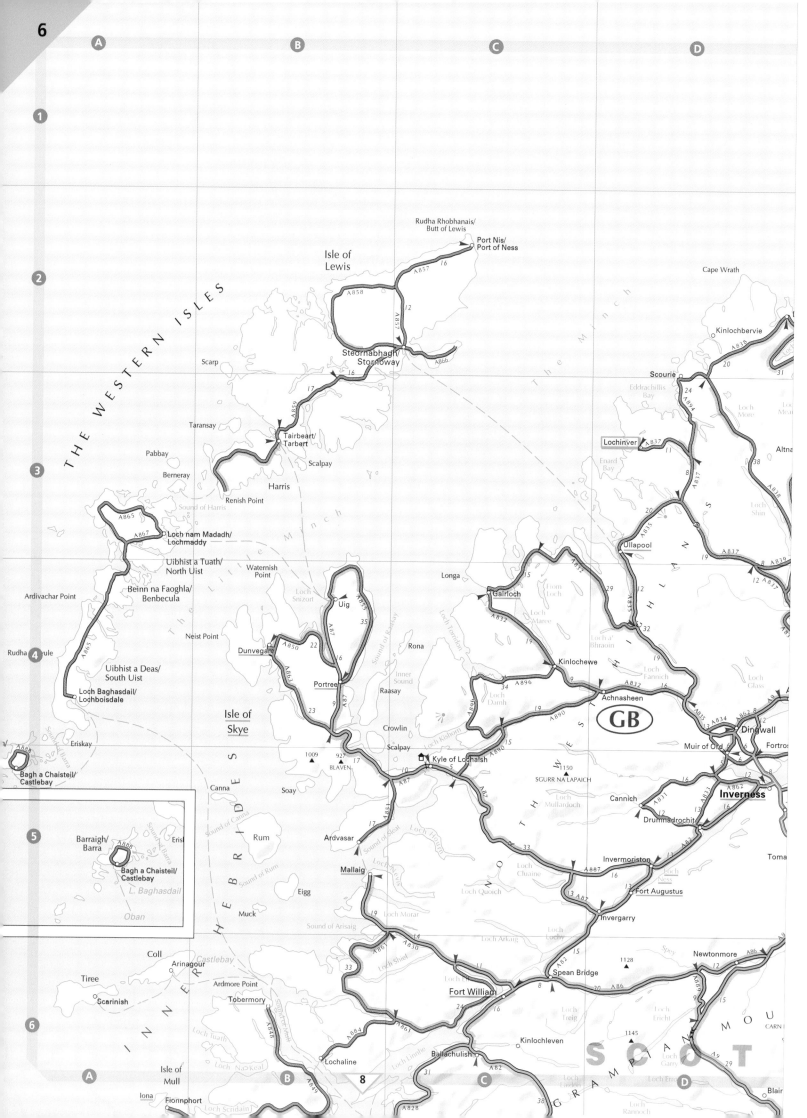

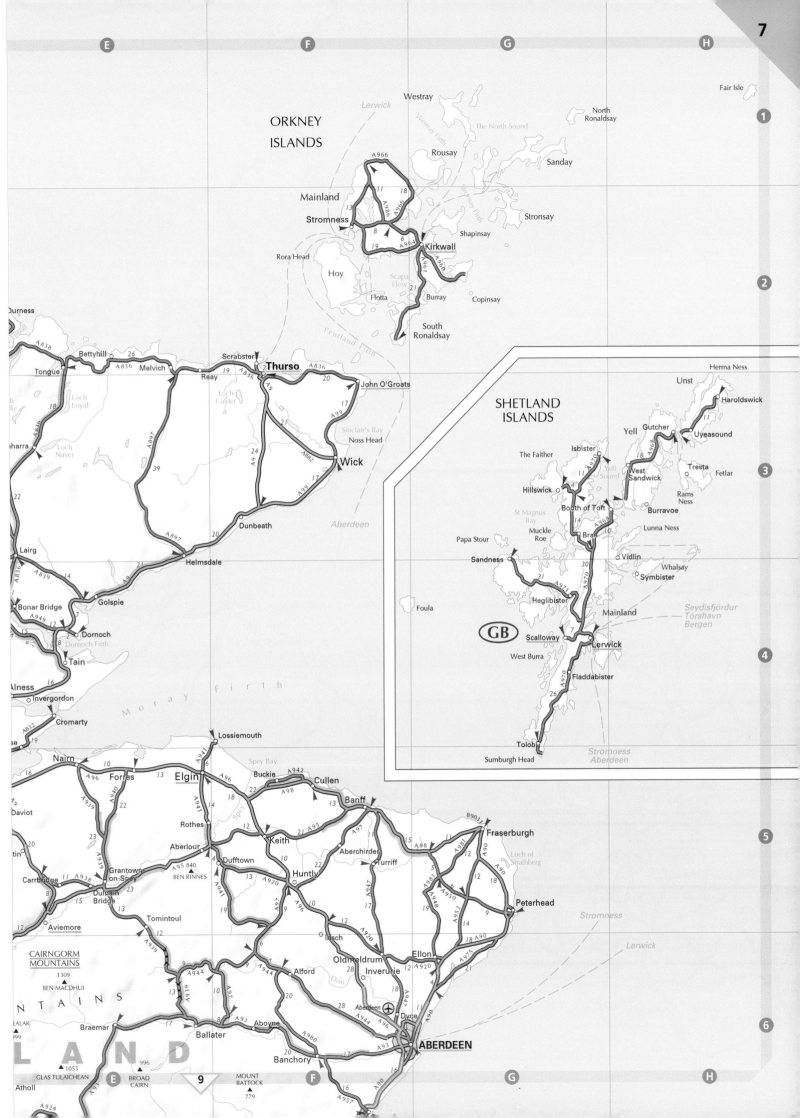

ORKNEY ISLANDS

Fair Isle

Westray

North Ronaldsay

Lerwick

Rousay

Sanday

Westray Firth

The North Sound

A966

Mainland

Stronsay

Stromness

Shapinsay

Kirkwall

Rora Head

Hoy

Scapa Flow

Flotta

Burray

Copinsay

South Ronaldsay

Pentland Firth

Aberdeen

SHETLAND ISLANDS

Herma Ness

Unst

Haroldswick

Yell

Gutcher

Uyeasound

The Faither

Isbister

Tresta

Fetlar

Hillswick

West Sandwick

Rams Ness

St Magnus Bay

Booth of Toft

Burravoe

Papa Stour

Muckle Roe

Lunna Ness

Brae

Sandness

Vidlin

Whalsay

Heglibister

Symbister

Foula

Mainland

GB

Seydisfjörður
Tórshavn
Bergen

Scalloway

Lerwick

West Burra

Fladdabister

Tolob

Stromness
Aberdeen

Sumburgh Head

Durness

Bettyhill

Scrabster

A838

A836

Tongue

Melvich

Reay

Thurso

A836

Loch Loyal

Loch Calder

John O'Groats

A9

Sinclair's Bay

Noss Head

Loch Naver

Loch Naver

Wick

A897

A9

A99

Lairg

Dunbeath

A897

Helmsdale

Bonar Bridge

Golspie

A949

Dornoch

Dornoch Firth

Tain

Alness

Invergordon

Cromarty

A832

Moray Firth

Lossiemouth

Nairn

Spey Bay

Forres

Elgin

Buckie

A96

A942

Cullen

A98

Banff

Daviot

A939

A941

Rothes

Spey

A95

A97

B9031

Fraserburgh

Aberlour

Keith

Aberchirder

A98

A981

A90

Loch of Strathbeg

Carrbridge

Grantown-on-Spey

A95 840

BEN RINNES

Dufftown

Huntly

Turriff

A947

A981

A90

Peterhead

Dulnain Bridge

A939

Tomintoul

A97

A96

Insch

A920

Oldmeldrum

Ellon

A950

A952

A90

A975

Aviemore

CAIRNGORM MOUNTAINS

1309

BEN MACDHUI

A939

Alford

Inverurie

A944

Don

Stromness

Lerwick

MOUNTAINS

A944

A97

A93

Braemar

A939

Ballater

Aboyne

A980

Banchory

Aberdeen

Dyce

A947

ABERDEEN

LAND

1055

GLAS TULAICHEAN

996

BROAD CAIRN

MOUNT BATTOCK
779

A957

A93

A96

Atholl

A924

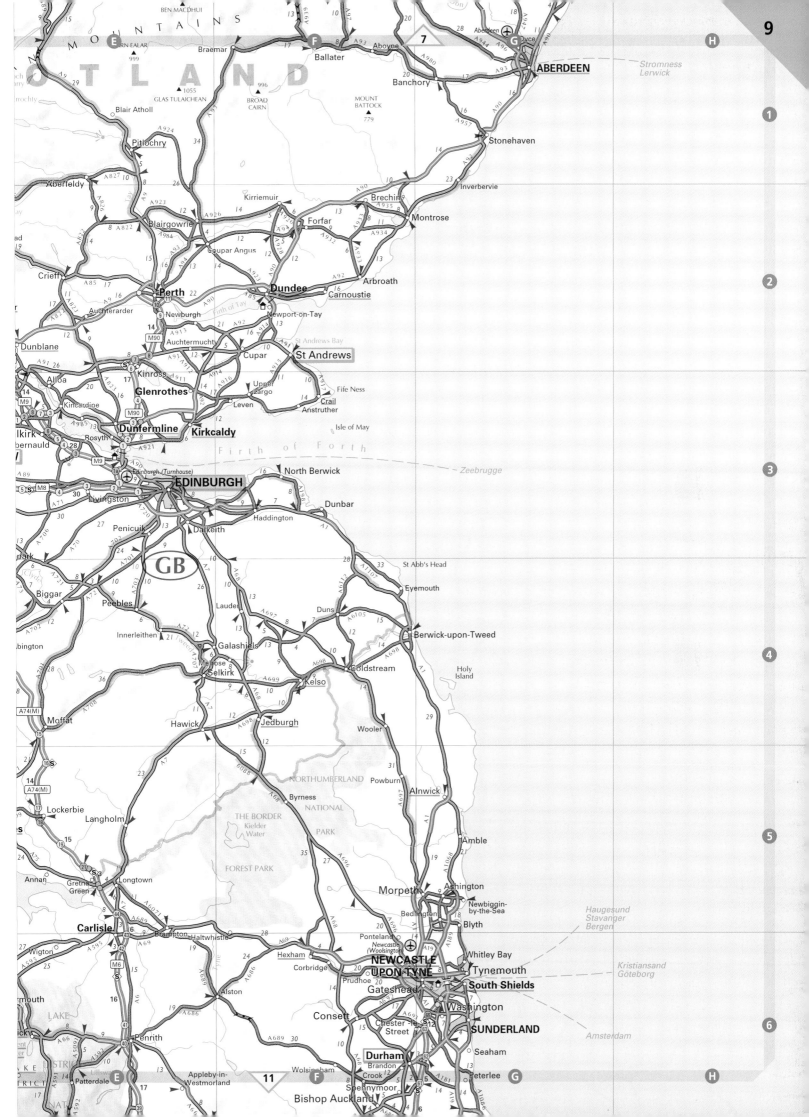

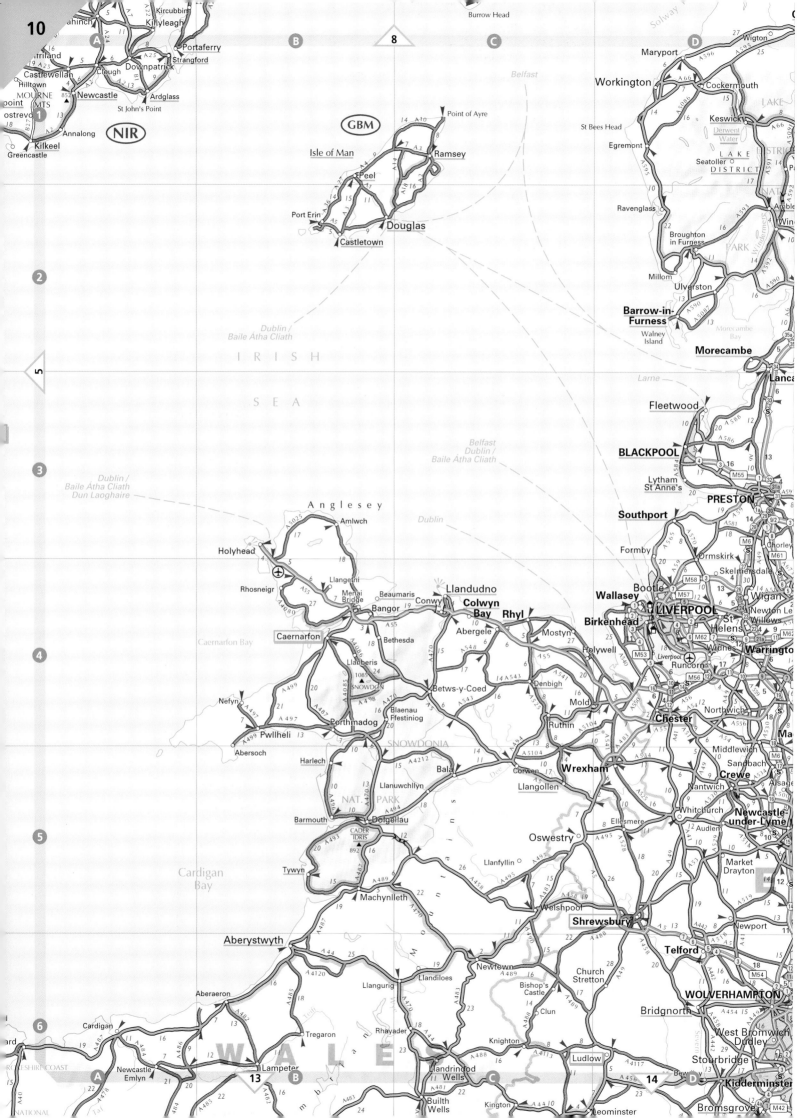

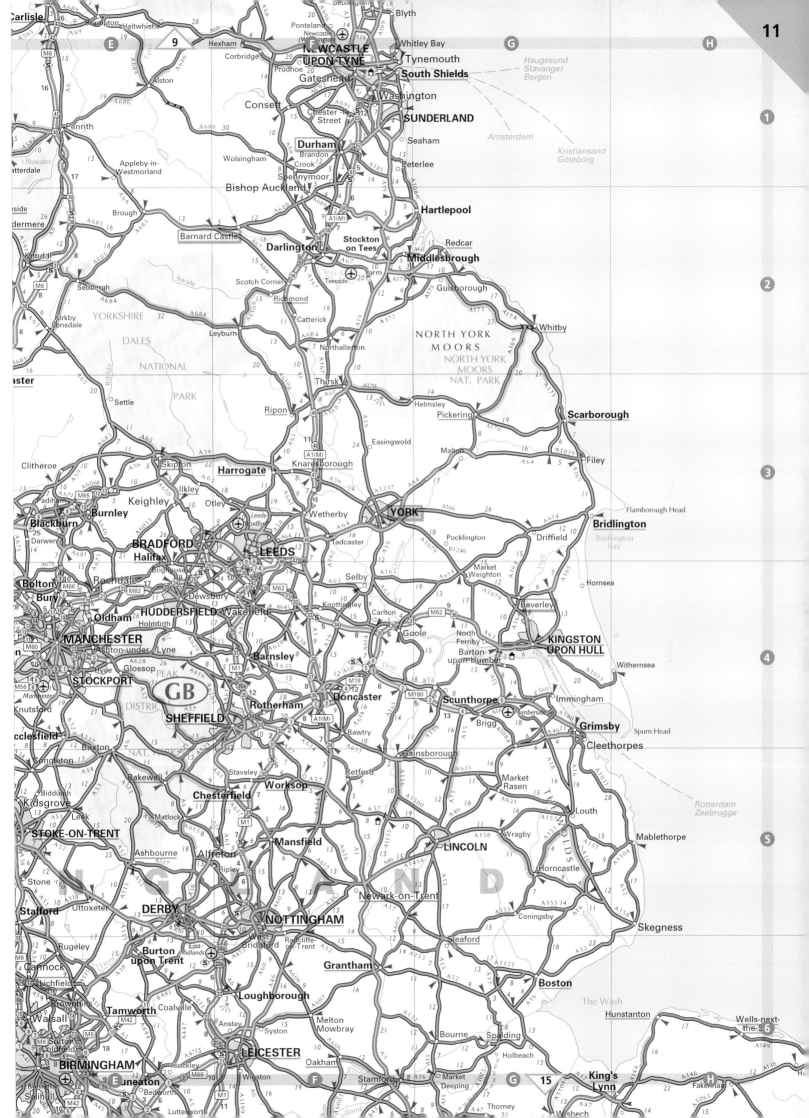

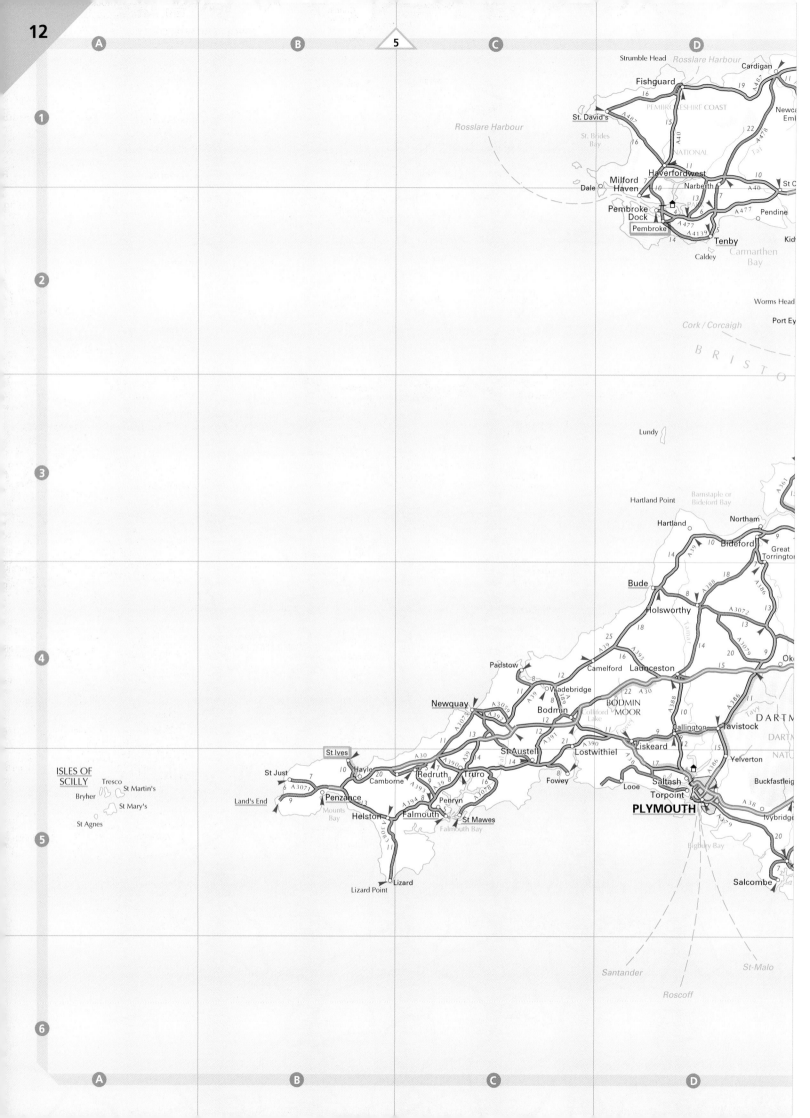

5

A · B · C · D

Strumble Head · Rosslare Harbour · Cardigan
Fishguard
Rosslare Harbour
St. David's
PEMBROKESHIRE COAST
Newca
Emli
St. Brides
Bay
NATIONAL
Haverfordwest
Dale · Milford
Haven · Narberth · St C
Pembroke
Dock
Pembroke · Tenby
Caldey · Carmarthen
Bay
Pendine
Kid

Worms Head
Port Ey
Cork / Corcaigh
BRISTO

Lundy

Hartland Point · Barnstaple or
Bideford Bay
Hartland · Northam
Bideford
Great
Torringto
Bude
Holsworthy
Tamar
Padstow · Camelford · Launceston · Oke
Wadebridge · BODMIN
MOOR · DART
Newquay · Bodmin · Colliford
Lake · DART
NATU
St Austell · Lostwithiel · Liskeard · Tavistock · Yelverton
St Ives · Hayle · Redruth · Truro · Fowey · Looe · Saltash · Buckfastleig
St Just · Camborne · Penryn · St Mawes · Torpoint
Land's End · Penzance · Falmouth · Falmouth Bay · PLYMOUTH · Ivybridge
Mounts
Bay · Helston · Bigbury Bay
ISLES OF
SCILLY · Tresco · St Martin's
Bryher · St Mary's · Salcombe
St Agnes
Lizard
Lizard Point · Santander · St-Malo
Roscoff

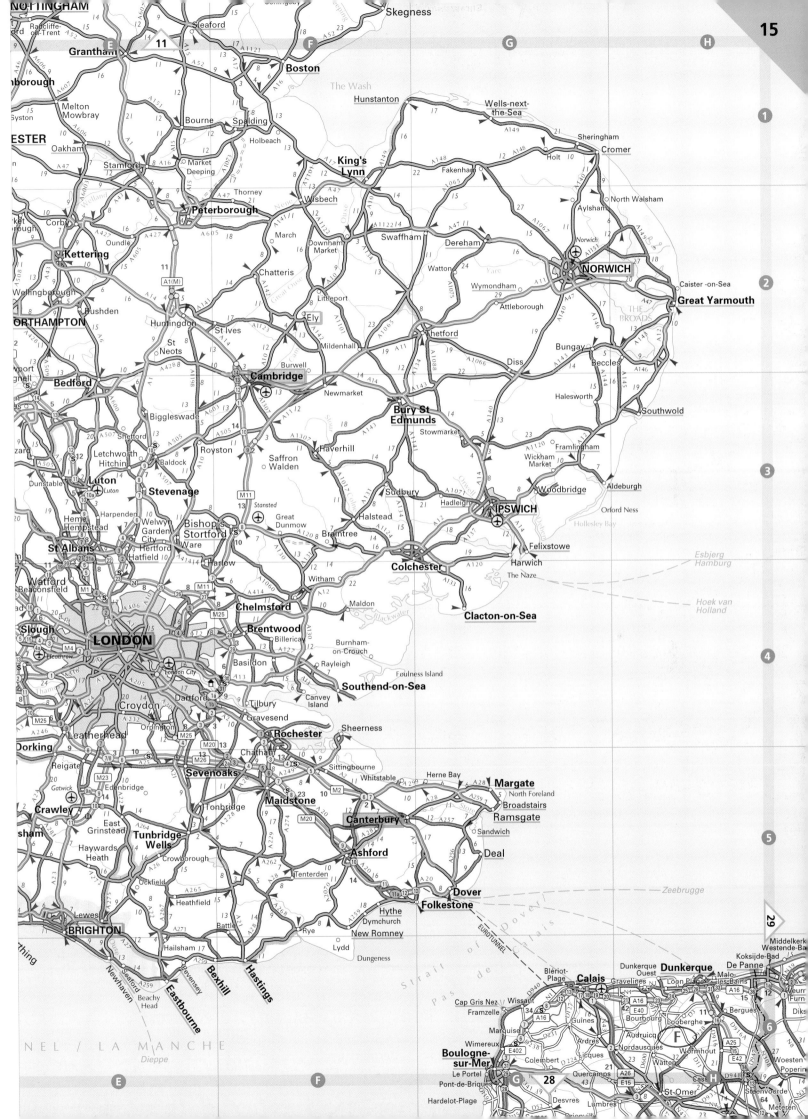

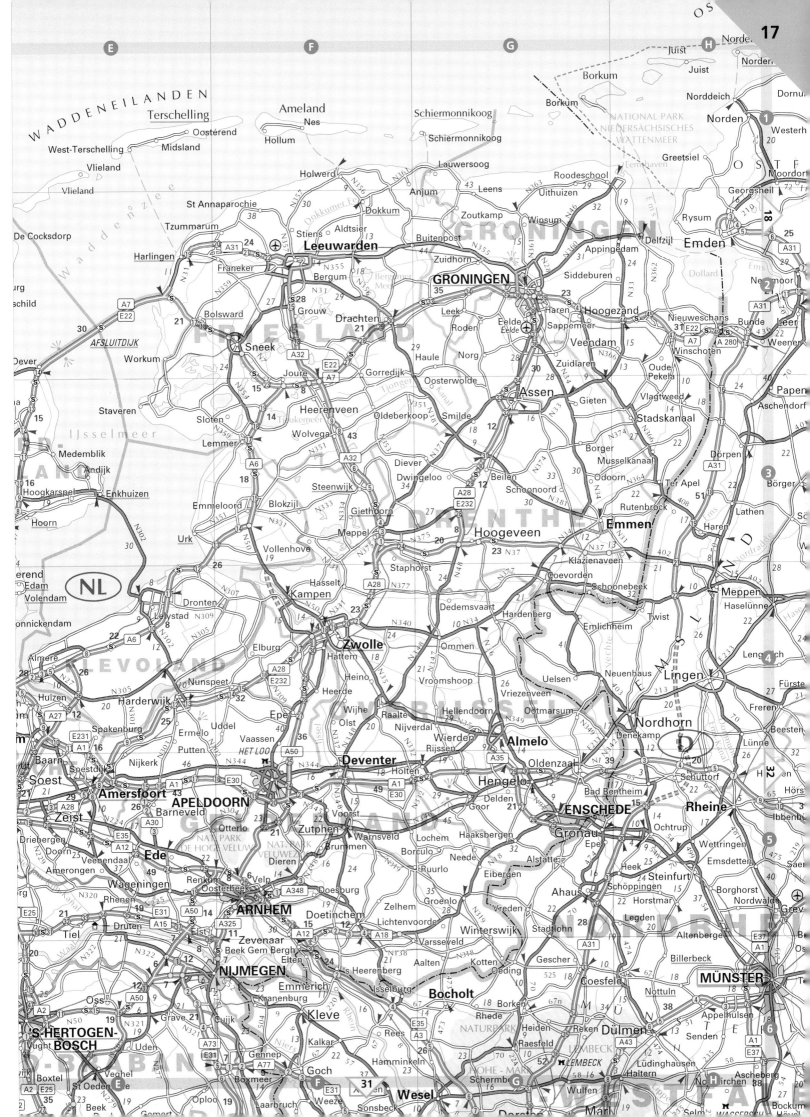

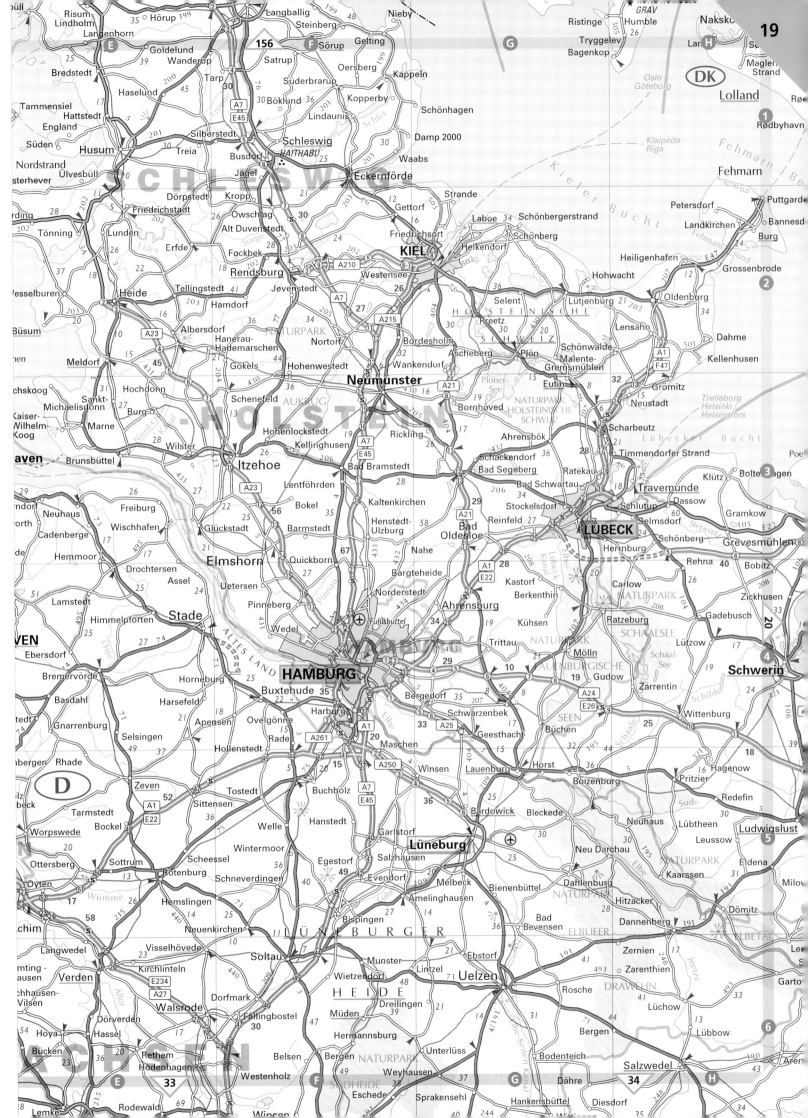

A B C D

1
2
3
4
5
6

NADMORSKI PARK KRAJOBRAZOWY
Karwia
Wierzchucino 213 25 215
Krokowa Władysł
SŁOWIŃSKI PARK NARODOWI
Łeba Ulinia 43 Choczewo Swarzew
Jezioro Łebsko Żelazna Mierzyno 15 Puck
Jezioro Gardno Kluki 10 Zamostne Celbowo
Rowy Smołdzino Wicko 218 10
Objazda Gábino Bolszewo Reda
Ustka 213 50 Głowczyce 35 Wejherowo Rumi
Jarosławiec 203 18 Żelkowo Nowa Wieś Lęborska Godętowo 18 20
Jezioro Wicko 39 203 Lubuczewo Damno Lębork Osowo Lęborskie Koleczkowo
Postomino Słupsk Rędzikovo 211 26 Łebno Chwaszczyno
Darłówko Mianowice 51 E28 Oskowo Kartuzy Miszewo
Dąbki Darłowo 205 Staniewice 27 Dębnica Kaszubska Czarna Dąbrówka 54 Sierakowice 211 12 Rębiechowo
Bukowo Morskie Sławno Warszkowo 34 Budowo 211 Rokity 228 329 Żukowo
Łazy 34 42 Korzybie Barcino 21 Kołczygłowy Klukowa Huta Egiertowo
Mielno Malechowo Ostrowiec 24 Suchorze Unichowo Jasień Sulęczyno 228 21 Nowa Karczma
Będzino Niemica 6 E28 30 Kępice 209 Pomysk Wielki Bytów Półczno 20 Kościerzyna Skarszewy
Koszalin Sianów 205 Borysław 21 Łubno Bytów 228 9 Lipusz 214
Biesiekierz 206 37 Polanów 28 Tuchomie Starogard Gdańsk
Niedalino 168 Mostowo Dretyń Lipnica Dziemiany Wdzydze Kiszewskie 35 Bytonia Zblewo
Białogard Rosnowo 168 205 206 Piaszczyna 43 Wiele 16
Wełdkowo Głodowa Drzewiany 17 Miastko Zielona Chocina Brusy Osowo Leśne Lubic
Stare Dębno Bobolice Biały Bór Koczała 236 212 Męcikal BORY Czarna Woda Wda
Nw. Ludzicko Wierzchowo Grzmiąca 19 Brzezie Konarzyny Rytel Czersk
Połczy drój Kołacz Barwice 26 Gwda Wielka Rzeczenica Przechlewo 42 Legbad Śliwice Luby
Ostrowice Szczecinek Czarne 201 202 Człuchów 14 Chojnice Tlen
Zarańsko Łubowo Jelenino 201 Barkowo 19 12 Silno Tuchola
Czaplinek 22 Debrzno 188 Zamarte Pamiętowo Ostrowite
Złocieniec Okonek 48 Lędyczek Kamień Krajeński 19 Gostycyn PL
Machliny Podgaje Radawnica 27 Lipka Lułowo 38 44
Mirosławiec Iłowiec Jastrowie Górzna Sępólno Krajeńskie 13 Mąkowarsko Św
Bronikowo Byszki Złotów Sypniewo Więcbork Koronowo Chełmno
Kalisz Pomorski Kłębowiec Szwecja Rudna Wierzchucin Królewski Pruszcz WISŁA
Tuczno Płytnica Krajenka Mrocza Tryszczyn Dobrcz
Rusinowo Wałcz Skórka Łobżenica Nakło nad Notecią Bydgoszcz
Gostomia Piła Wysoka Kosztowo Sadki Ślesin Wybcz
Szydłowo Śmiłowo Wyrzysk Paterek Rynarzewo Brzoza
Trzcianka Ujście Szamocin Smogulec Kcynia Szubin Łabiszyn
Stare Osieczno Siedlisko Margonin Morakowo Gniewkowo
Człopa Sarbia Chodzież olańcz Budzyń
Czarnków

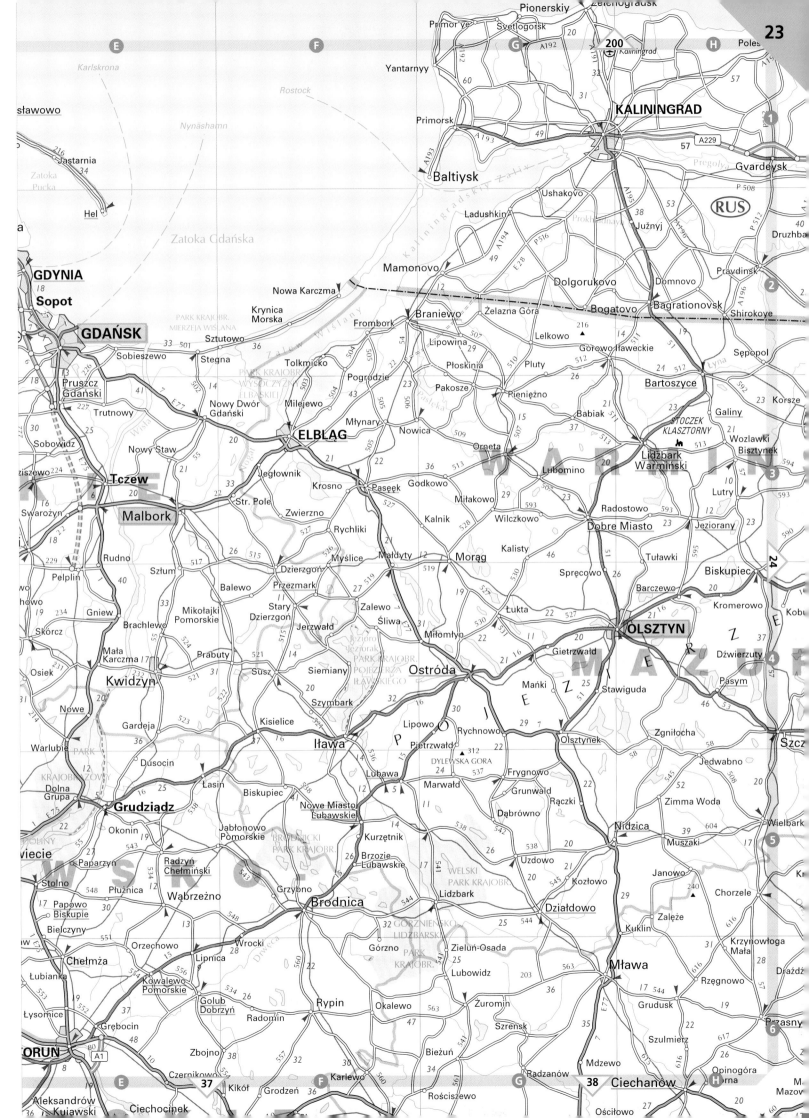

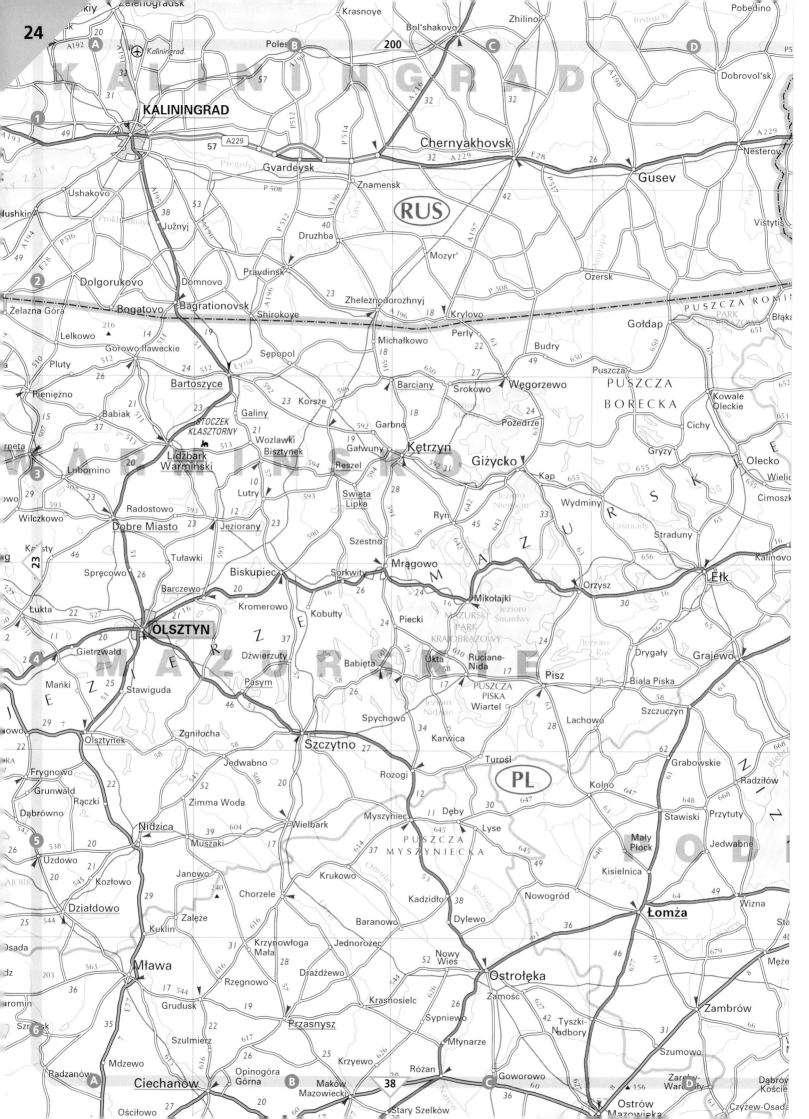

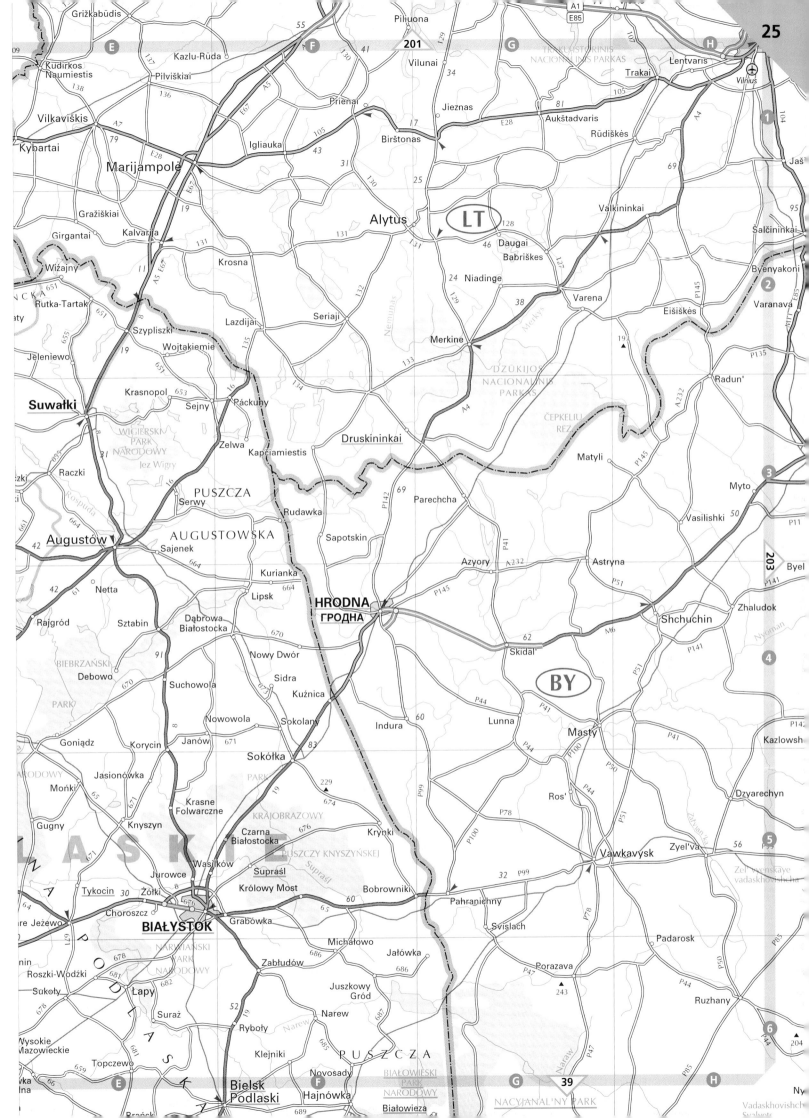

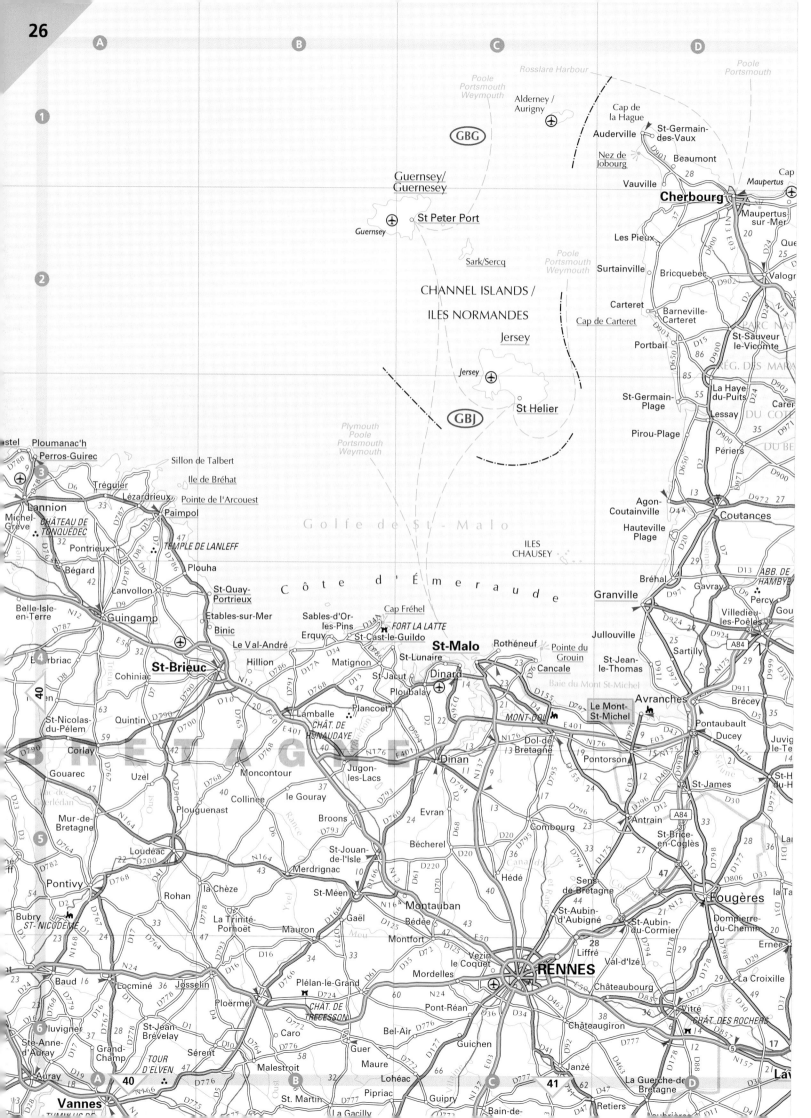

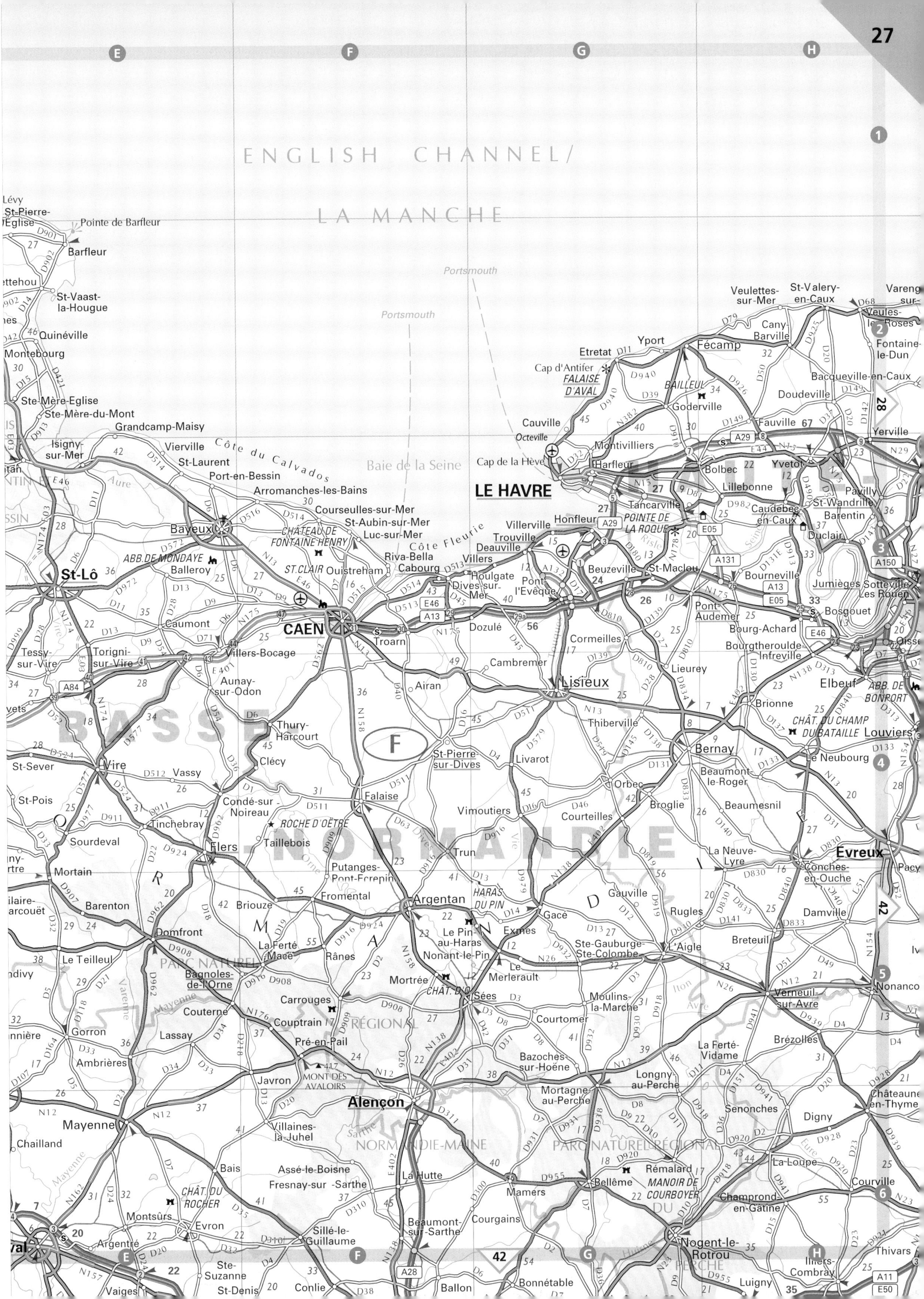

E F G H

1

ENGLISH CHANNEL /

LA MANCHE

Portsmouth

Portsmouth

Lévy
St-Pierre-Eglise
Pointe de Barfleur
Barfleur
2

St-Vaast-la-Hougue

Quinéville
Montebourg
Ste-Mère-Eglise
Ste-Mère-du-Mont
Grandcamp-Maisy
Isigny-sur-Mer
Vierville
Côte du Calvados
Baie de la Seine
Cap de la Hève
St-Laurent
Port-en-Bessin
Arromanches-les-Bains
Courseulles-sur-Mer
St-Aubin-sur-Mer
Luc-sur-Mer
Bayeux
CHÂTEAU DE FONTAINE HENRY
Riva-Bella
Cabourg
Côte Fleurie
Villers
Villerville
Honfleur
Trouville
Deauville

LE HAVRE
Harfleur
Montivilliers
Octeville
Cauville
Cap d'Antifer
FALAISE D'AVAL
BAILLEUL
Goderville
Fécamp
Yport
Etretat
Veulettes-sur-Mer
St-Valery-en-Caux
Veules-les-Roses
Varengeville-sur-
Fontaine-le-Dun
Cany-Barville
Bacqueville-en-Caux
Doudeville
Fauville
Yerville
Yvetot
Bolbec
Lillebonne
Tancarville
Caudebec-en-Caux
St-Wandrille
Barentin
Pavilly
Duclair
Jumièges
Sotteville-les-Rouen
Bourneville
Bosgouet
Bourg-Achard
Bourgtheroulde-Infreville
Elbeuf
ABB. DE BONPORT
CHÂT. DU CHAMP DU BATAILLE
Louviers
Le Neubourg
Bernay
Beaumont-le-Roger
Brionne
Lieurey
Cormeilles
Pont-Audemer
St-Maclou
Beuzeville
Pont-l'Evêque
Pont-Audemer
POINTE DE LA ROQUE

St-Lô
ABB. DE MONDAYE
Balleroy
Caumont
Tessy-sur-Vire
Torigni-sur-Vire
Villers-Bocage
Aunay-sur-Odon
CAEN
ST. CLAIR
Ouistreham
Troarn
Dozulé
Cambremer
Lisieux
Thiberville
Airan
Livarot
St-Pierre-sur-Dives
Orbec
Broglie
Beaumesnil
La Neuve-Lyre
Conches-en-Ouche
Evreux
Damville
Rugles
Breteuil
Verneuil-sur-Avre
Nonanco

BASSE-NORMANDIE

Vire
St-Sever
St-Pois
Sourdeval
Mortain
Barenton
Domfront
Le Teilleul
Gorron
Ambrières
Mayenne
Chailland
Tinchebray
Flers
Taillebois
ROCHE D'OËTRE
Thury-Harcourt
Clécy
Condé-sur-Noireau
Falaise
Vimoutiers
Courteilles
Trun
Putanges-Pont-Ecrepin
Argentan
HARAS DU PIN
Le Pin-au-Haras
Nonant-le-Pin
Exmes
Gacé
Gauville
Ste-Gauburge-Ste-Colombe
L'Aigle
Moulins-la-Marche
Courtomer
Brouze
Fromental
Rânes
La Ferté-Macé
Bagnoles-de-l'Orne
Carrouges
Couterne
Lassay
Couptrain
Pré-en-Pail
Javron
MONT DES AVALOIRS
Mortrée
CHÂT. D'O
Sées
PARC NATUREL RÉGIONAL
NORMANDIE-MAINE
Alençon
Villaines-la-Juhel
Bais
Assé-le-Boisne
Fresnay-sur-Sarthe
Sillé-le-Guillaume
Le Merlerault
Bazoches-sur-Hoëne
Mortagne-au-Perche
Longny-au-Perche
La Ferté-Vidame
Brézolles
Senonches
Digny
La Loupe
Courville
Châteauneuf-en-Thyme
Rémalard
MANOIR DE COURBOYER
Bellême
Mamers
Courgains
Beaumont-sur-Sarthe
Nogent-le-Rotrou
Illiers-Combray
Thivars

Mayenne
Montsûrs
Evron
Argentré
CHÂT. DU ROCHER
Ste-Suzanne
Conlie
Ballon
Bonnétable

PARC NATUREL RÉGIONAL

NORMANDIE

F

42

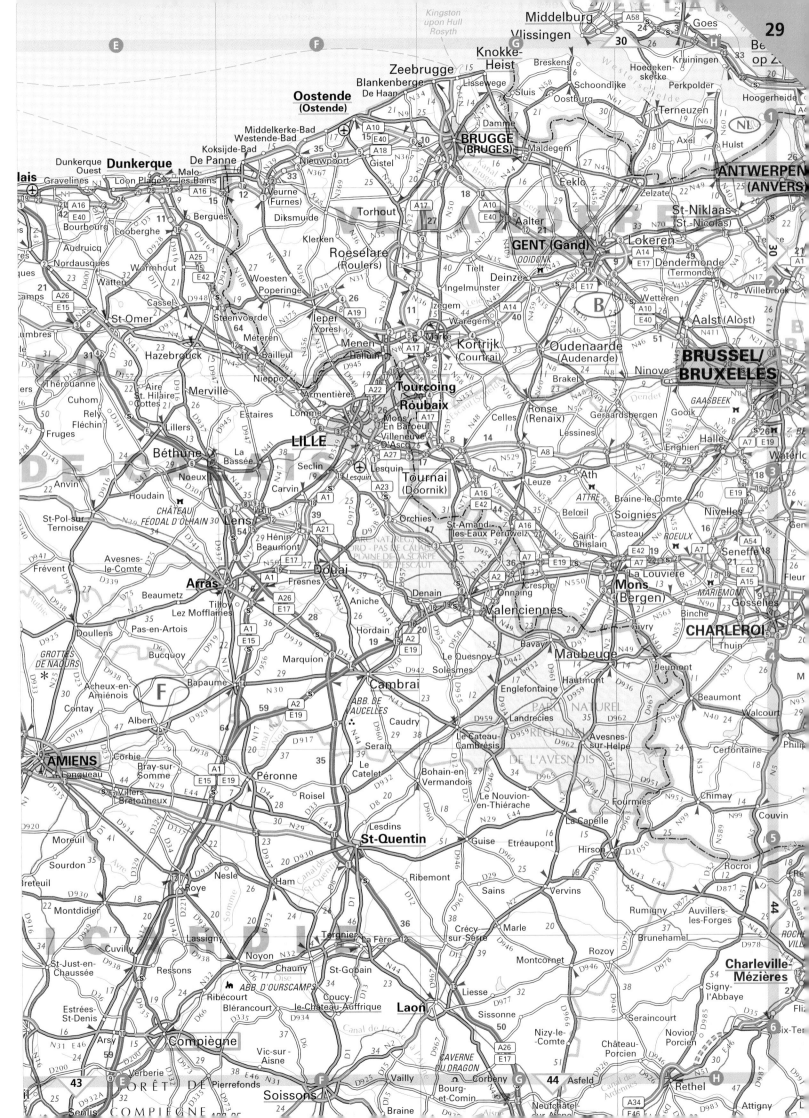

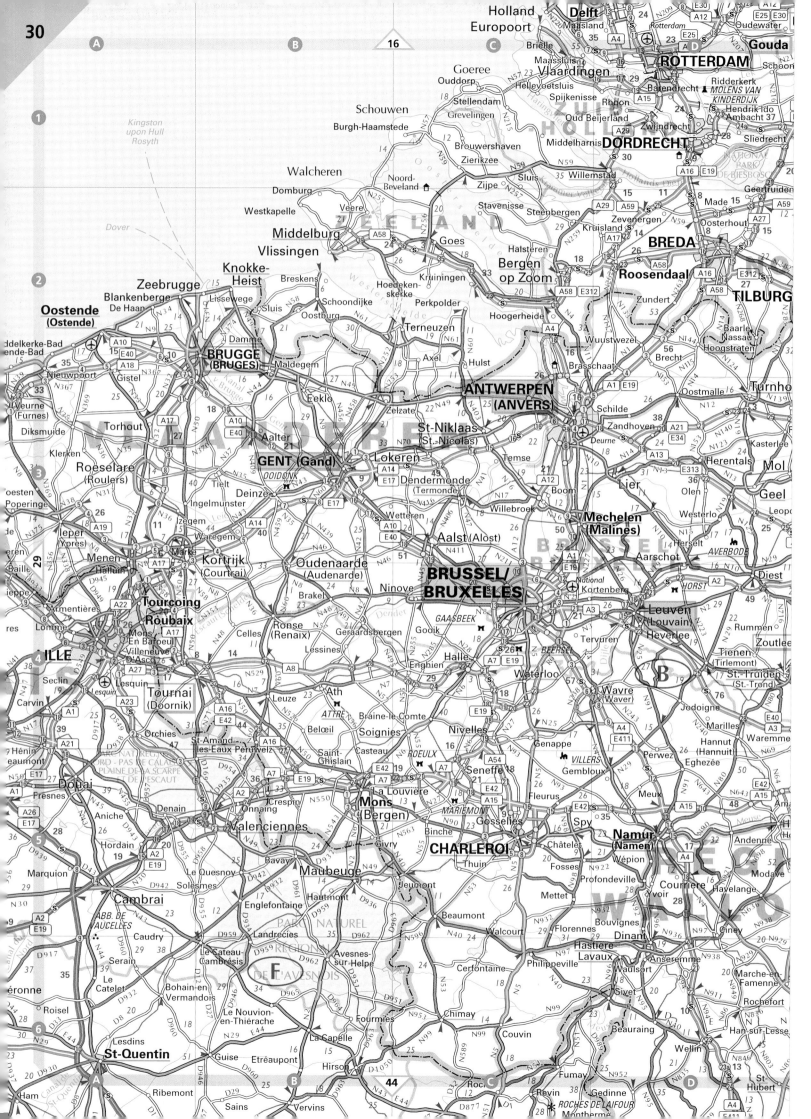

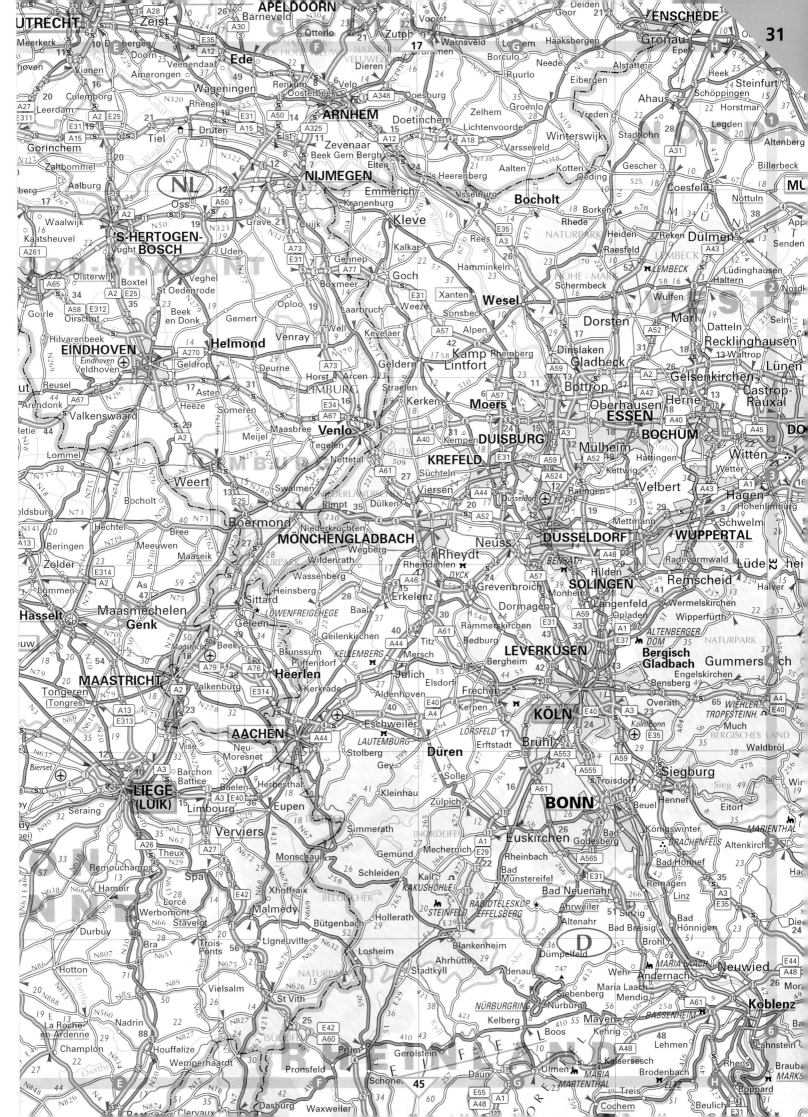

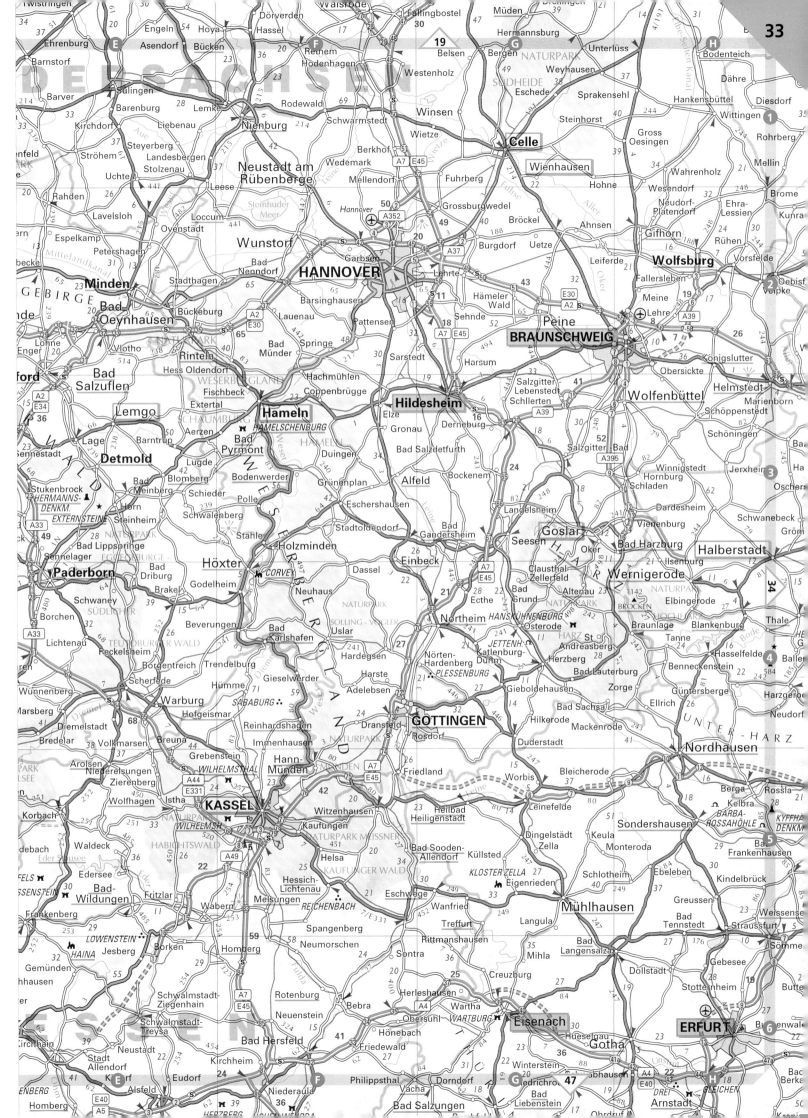

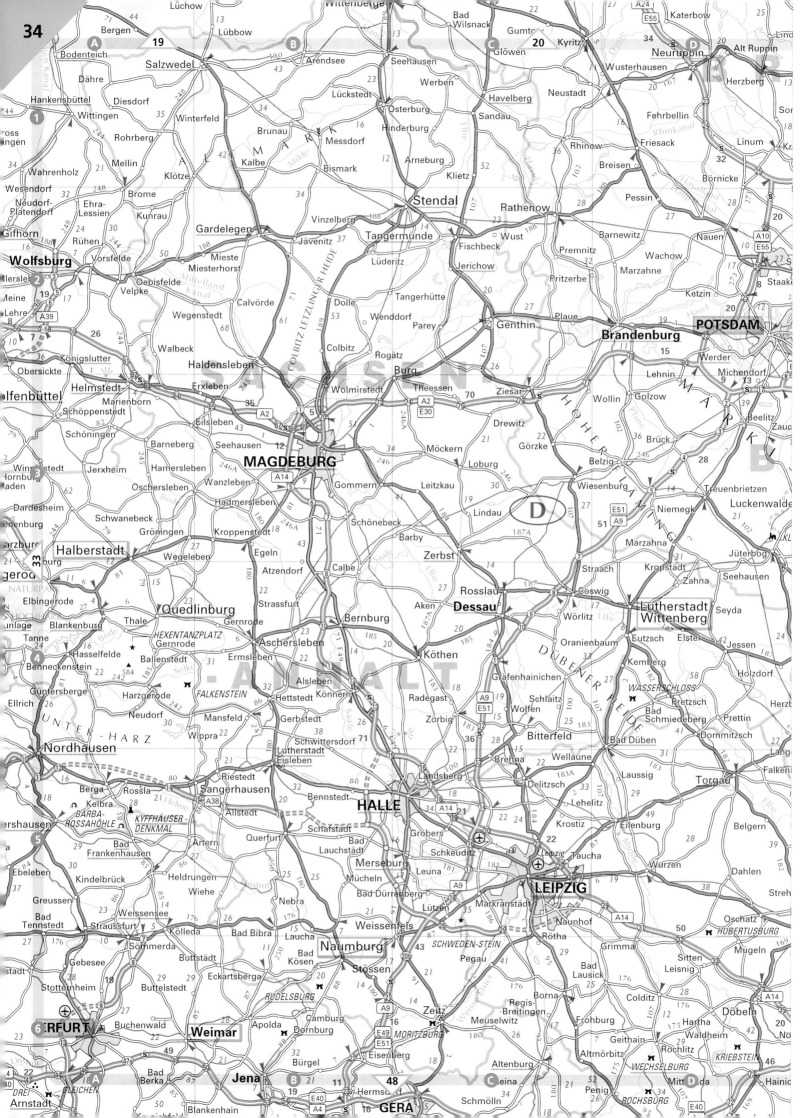

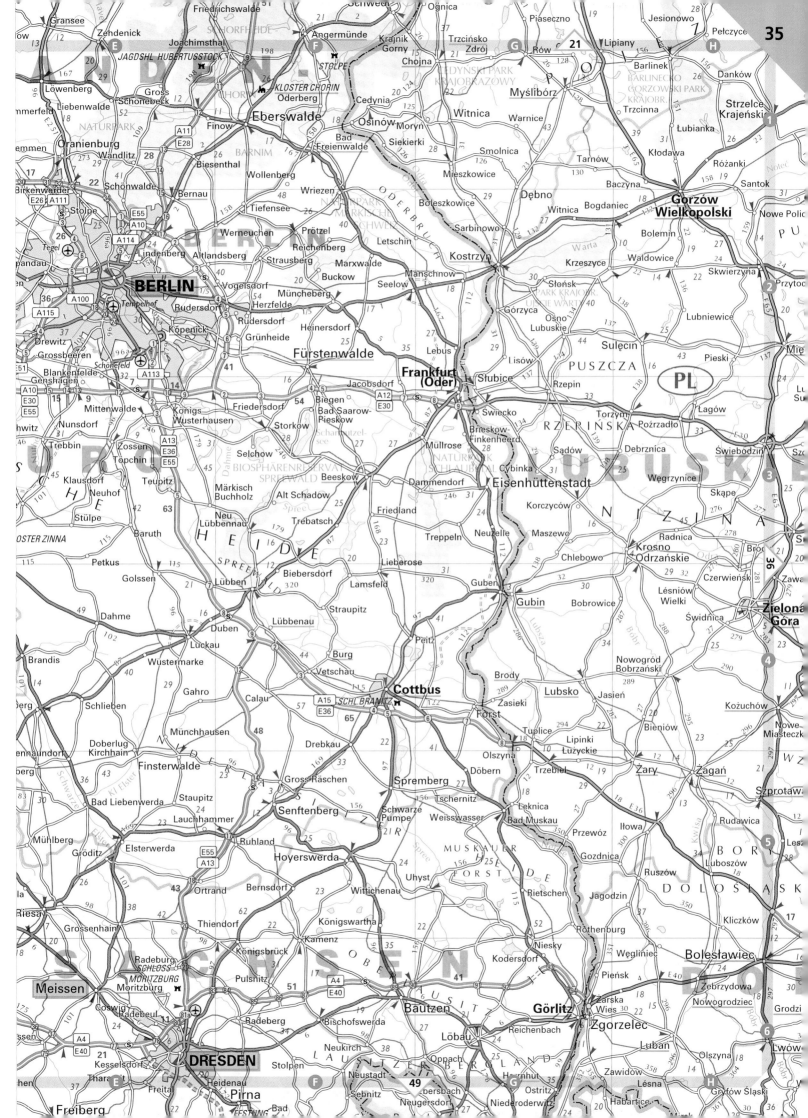

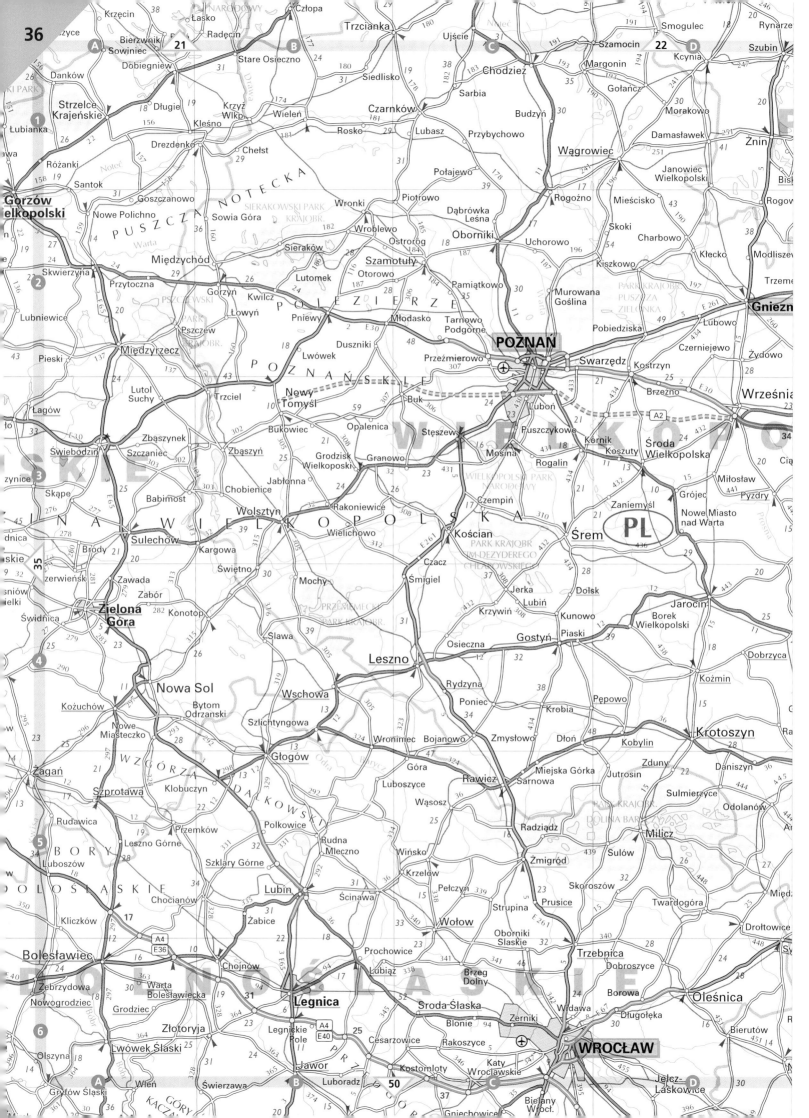

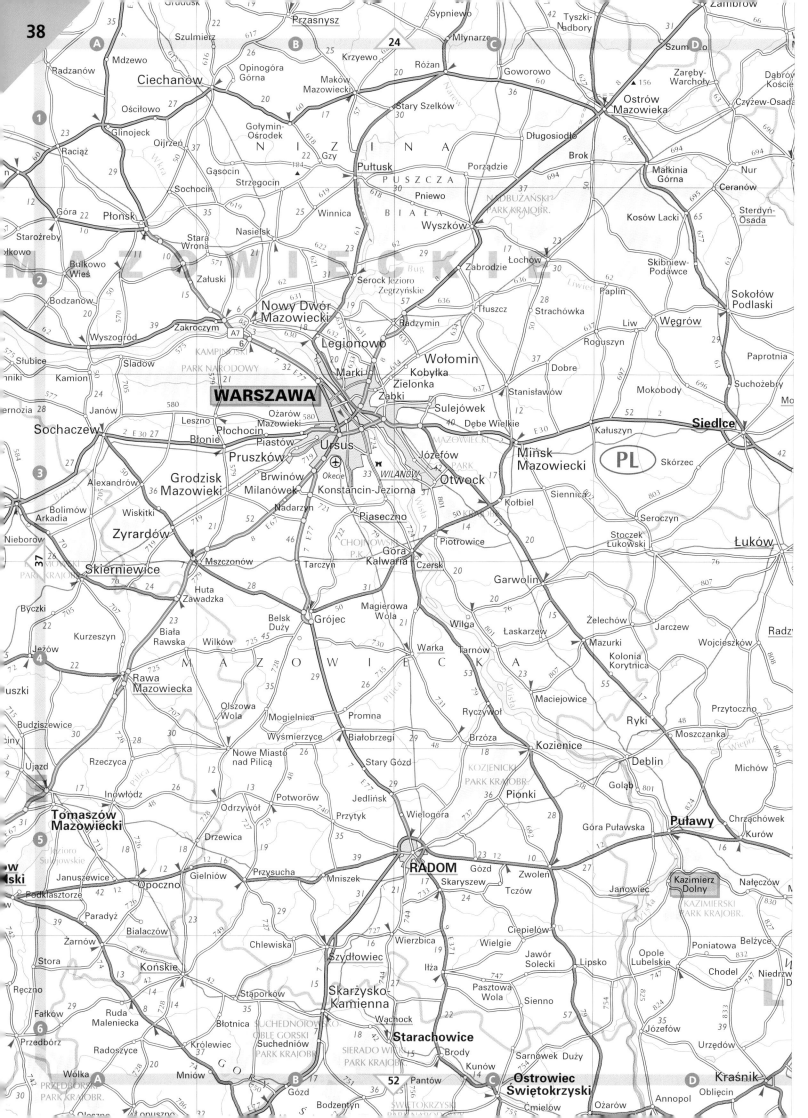

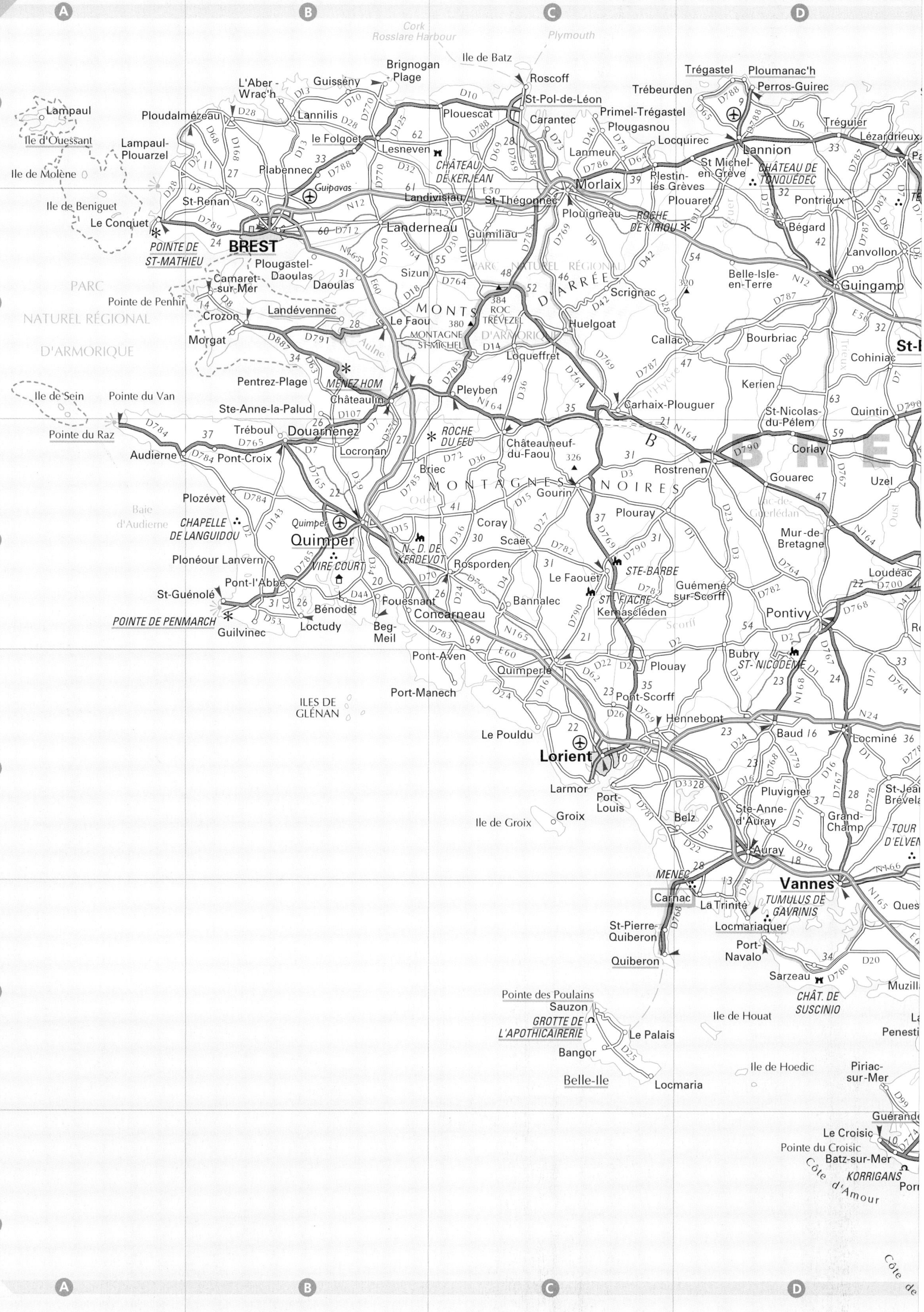

A B C D

Cork
Rosslare Harbour
Plymouth
Ile de Batz

1
Lampaul
Ile d'Ouessant
Ile de Molène
Le Conquet
Brignogan
Plage
L'Aber-Wrac'h
Guissény
Ploudalmézeau
Lannilis
le Folgoët
Lesneven
Plabennec
St-Renan
Guipavas
Landivisiau
Landerneau
Guimiliau
St-Thégonnec
Plouigneau
Morlaix
Plouescat
St-Pol-de-Léon
Carantec
Plougasnou
Lanmeur
Locquirec
Plestin-lès-Grèves
Plouaret
St Michel-en-Grève
Roscoff
Primel-Trégastel
Trébeurden
Trégastel
Ploumanac'h
Perros-Guirec
Tréguier
Lézardrieux
Lannion
Pontrieux
Bégard
Lanvollon
Belle-Isle-en-Terre
Guingamp
St-I
CHÂTEAU DE KERJEAN
ROCHE DE KIRIOU
CHÂTEAU DE TONQUÉDEC

2
Pointe de St-Mathieu
BREST
Plougastel-Daoulas
Camaret-sur-Mer
Daoulas
Pointe de Penhir
Landévennec
Crozon
Morgat
Le Faou
MONTAGNE ST-MICHEL
Sizun
ROC TRÉVEZEL
Huelgoat
Scrignac
Callac
Bourbriac
Kerien
St-Nicolas-du-Pélem
Quintin
Cohiniac
Loqueffret
Carhaix-Plouguer
PARC NATUREL RÉGIONAL D'ARRÉE
MONTS D'ARRÉE
PARC NATUREL RÉGIONAL D'ARMORIQUE

3
Ile de Sein
Pointe du Van
Pointe du Raz
Audierne
Pont-Croix
Tréboul
Douarnenez
Locronan
Plozévet
CHAPELLE DE LANGUIDOU
Ploméour Lanvern
Pont-l'Abbé
St-Guénolé
POINTE DE PENMARCH
Guilvinec
Bénodet
Loctudy
Baie d'Audierne
Quimper
VIRE COURT
N.-D. DE KERDEVOT
Briec
Pleyben
Châteaulin
ROCHE DU FEU
MÉNEZ HOM
Pentrez-Plage
Ste-Anne-la-Palud
Châteauneuf-du-Faou
Gourin
Coray
Scaër
Rosporden
Bannalec
Le Faouet
STE-BARBE
ST-FIACRE
Kernascléden
Guéméné-sur-Scorff
Plouray
MONTAGNES NOIRES
Rostrenen
Gouarec
Corlay
Uzel
Mur-de-Bretagne
Loudéac
Pontivy
ST-NICODÈME
Bubry

4
ILES DE GLÉNAN
Fouesnant
Concarneau
Beg-Meil
Pont-Aven
Port-Manech
Le Pouldu
Lorient
Larmor
Port-Louis
Ile de Groix
Groix
Quimperlé
Plouay
Pont-Scorff
Hennebont
Baud
Locminé
Pluvigner
Grand-Champ
St-Jean-Brévelai
TOUR D'ELVEN
Belz
Ste-Anne-d'Auray
Auray

5
Pointe des Poulains
Sauzon
GROTTE DE L'APOTHICAIRERIE
Le Palais
Bangor
Belle-Ile
Locmaria
Ile de Houat
Ile de Hoedic
MÉNEC
Carnac
La Trinité
St-Pierre-Quiberon
Quiberon
Locmariaquer
Port-Navalo
Sarzeau
Vannes
TUMULUS DE GAVRINIS
CHÂT. DE SUSCINIO
Penesti
Piriac-sur-Mer
Ques
Muzilla
La
Guérande
Le Croisic
Pointe du Croisic
Batz-sur-Mer
Côte d'Amour
KORRIGANS

6

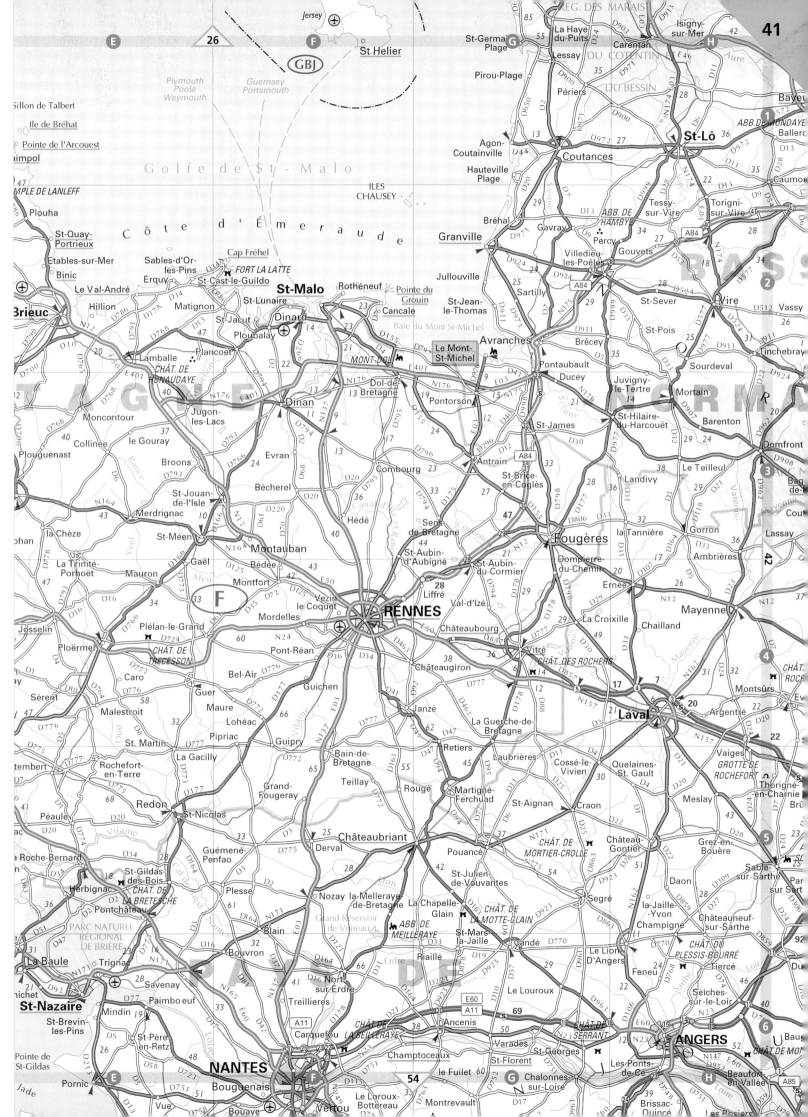

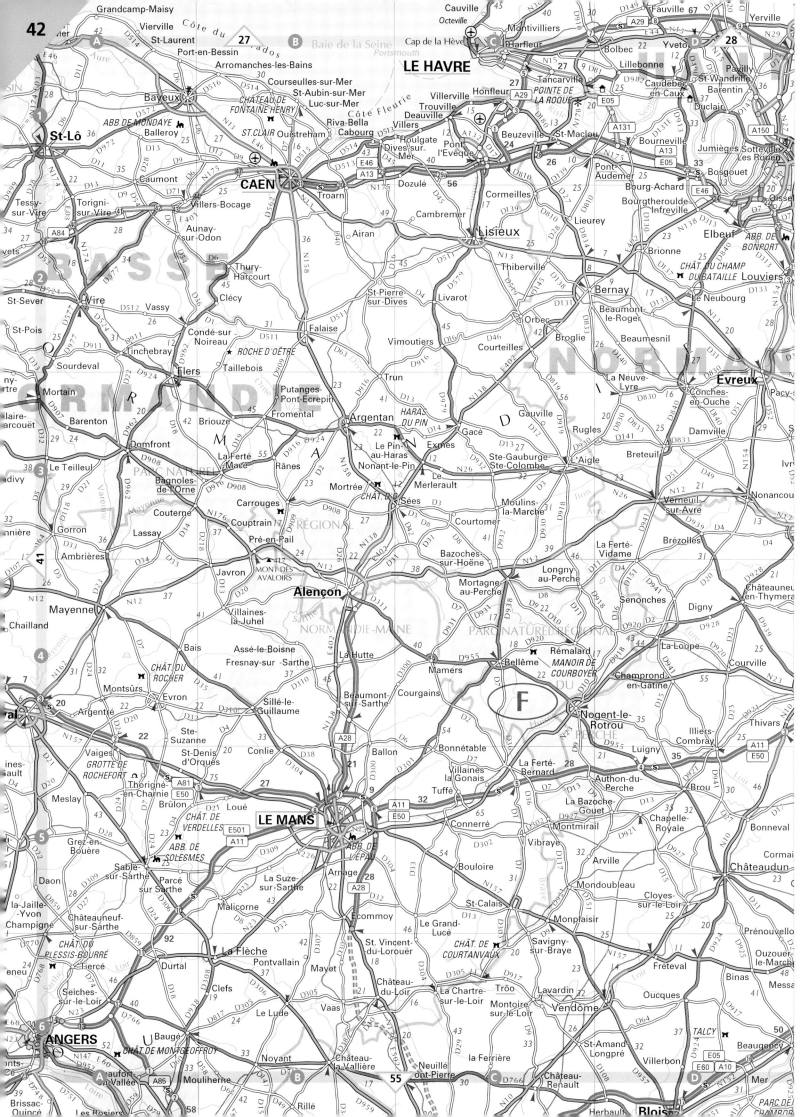

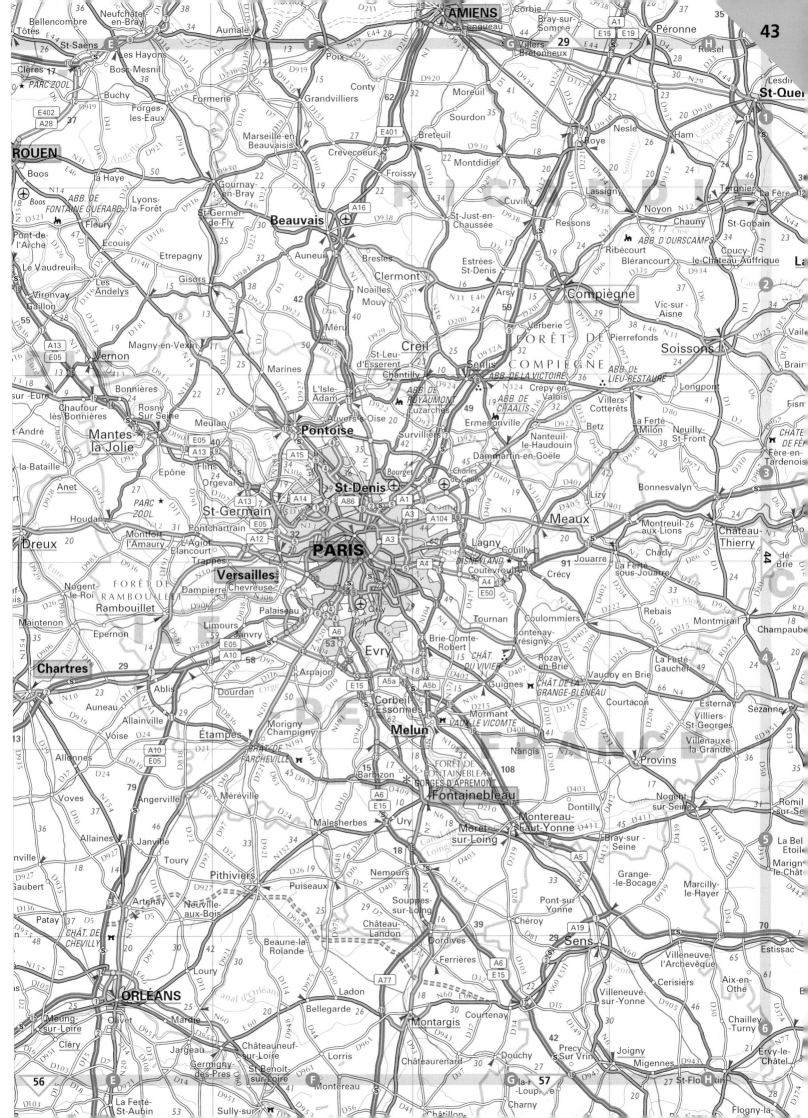

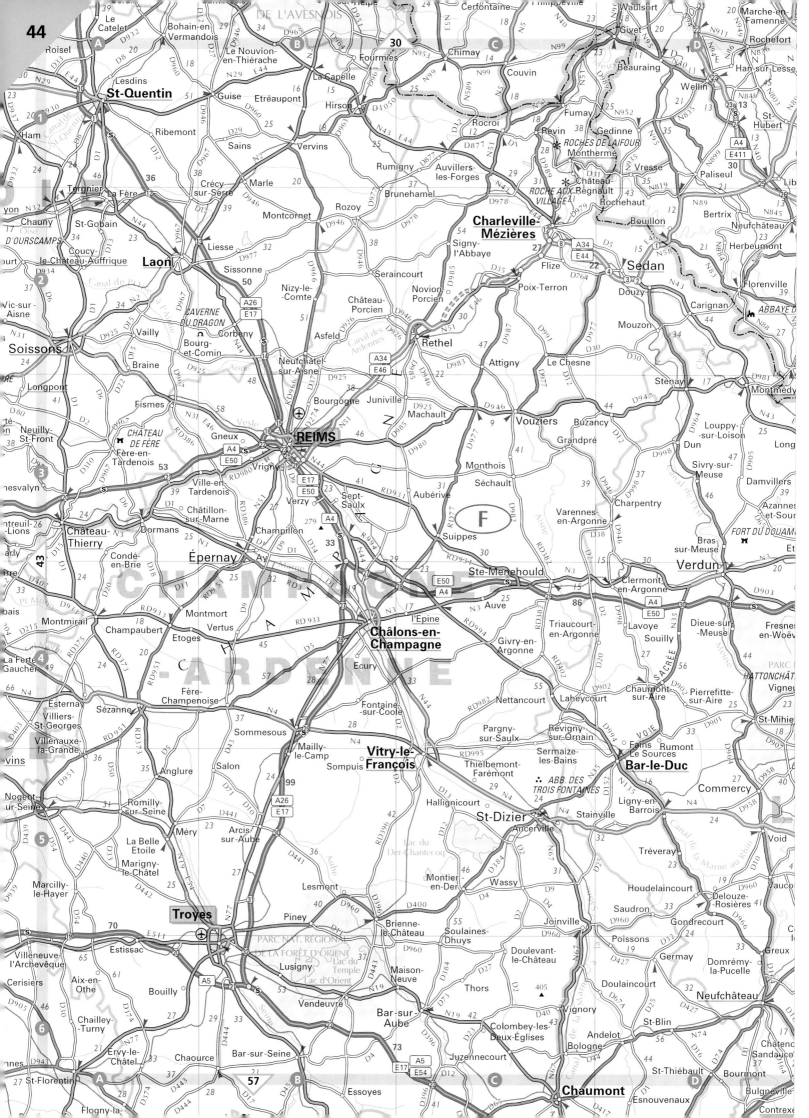

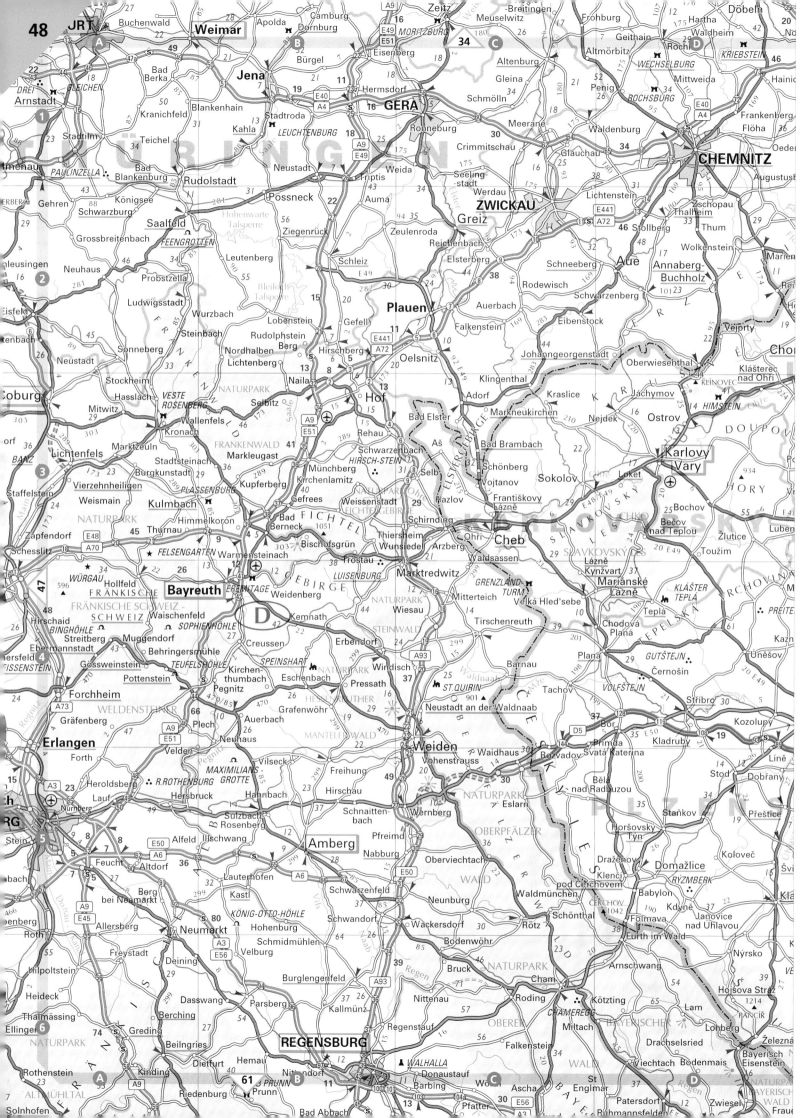

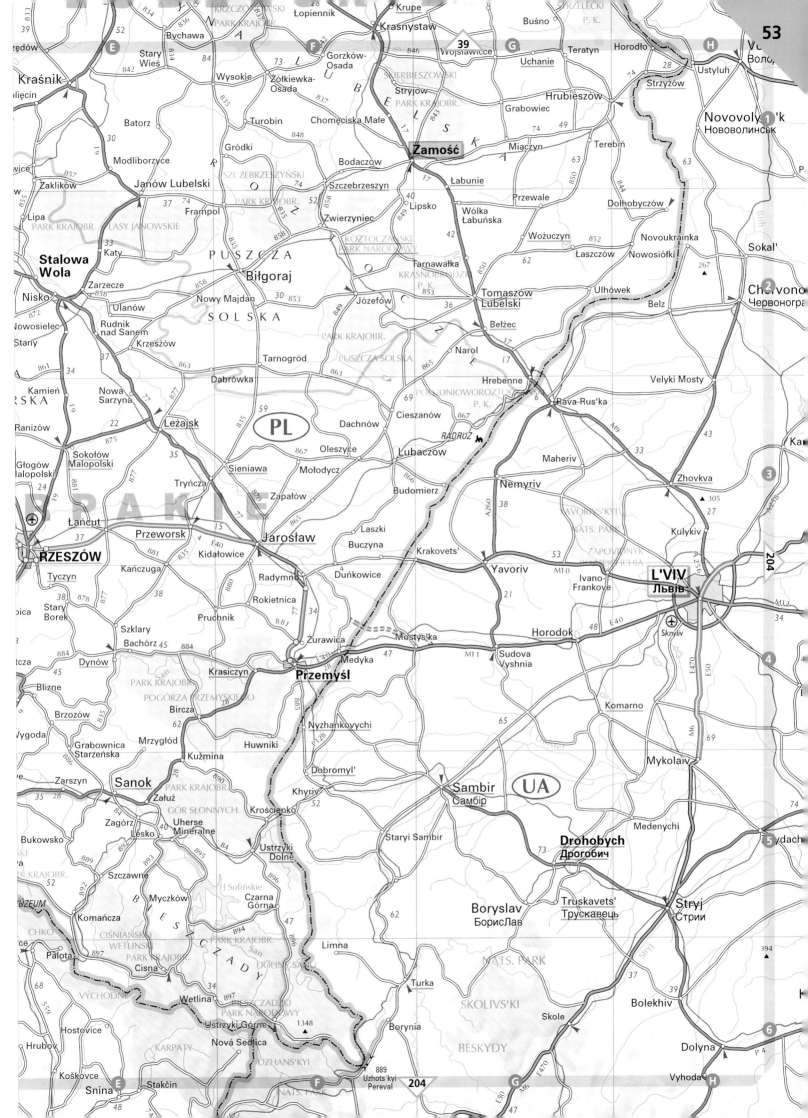

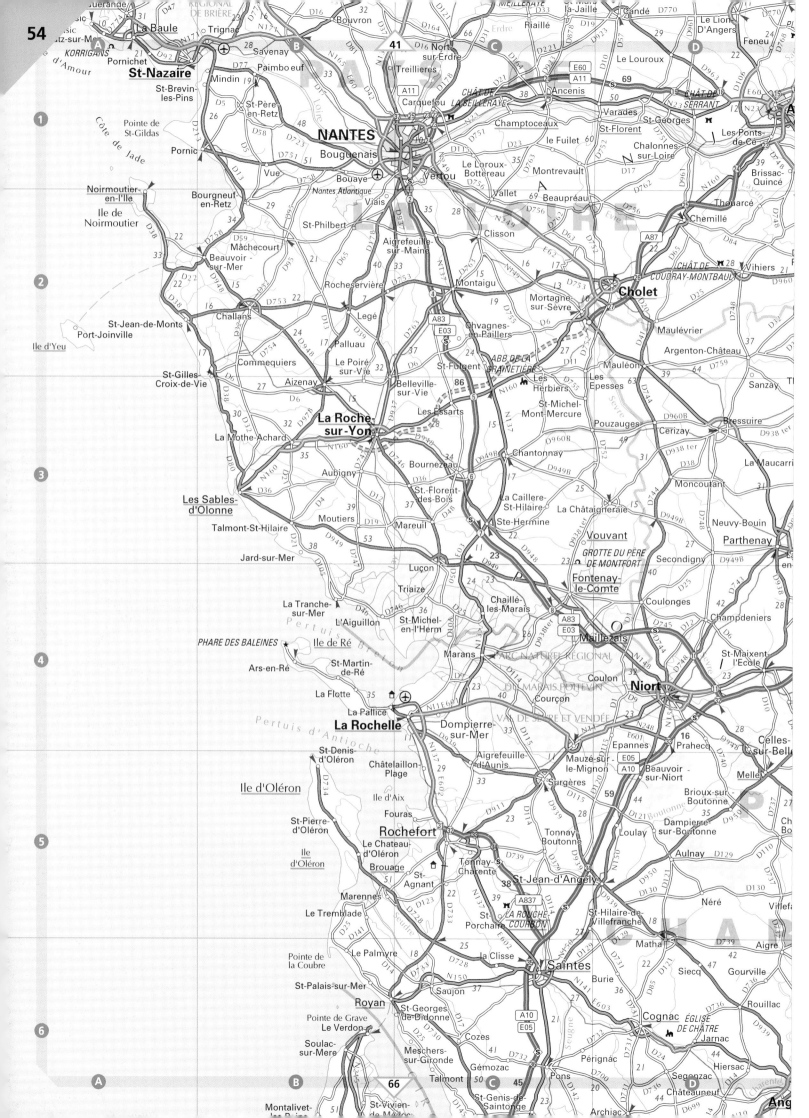

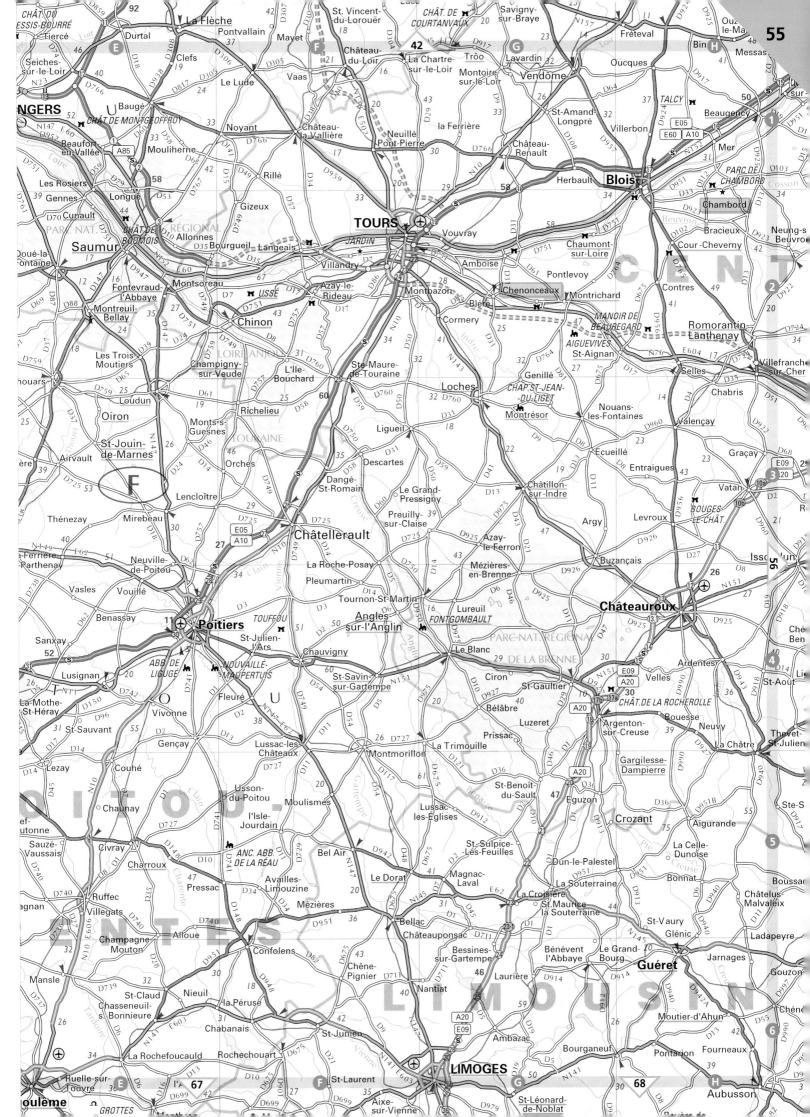

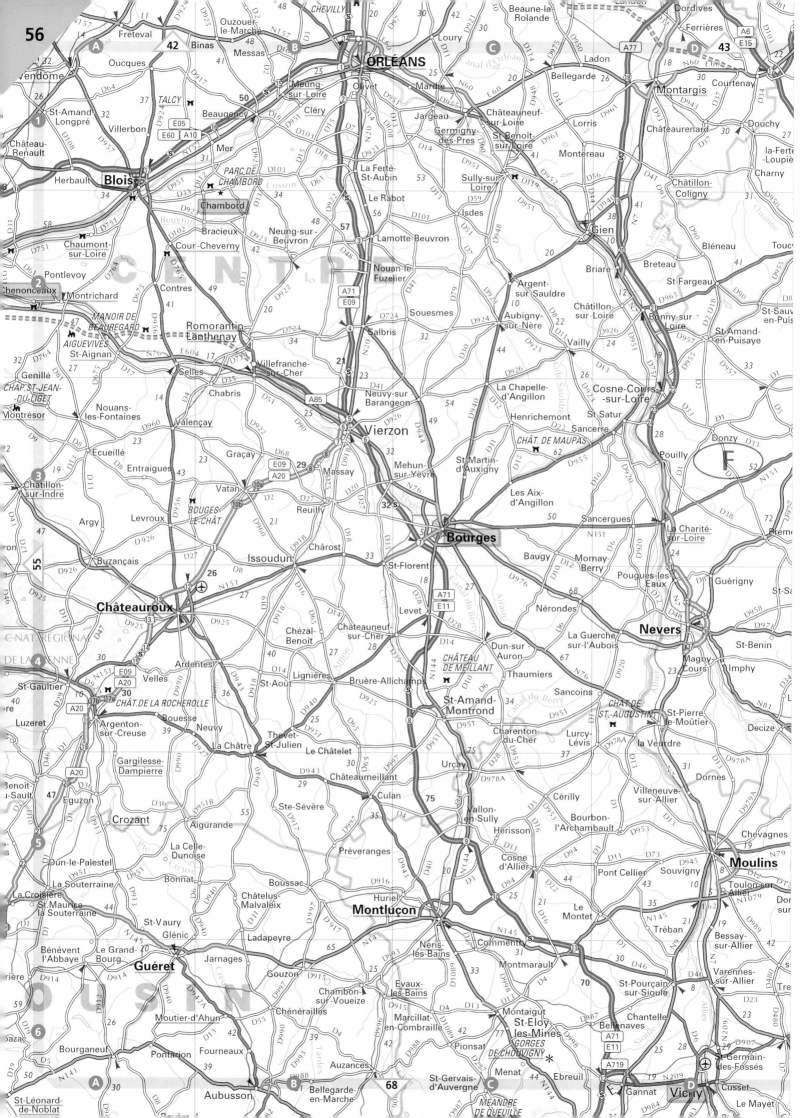

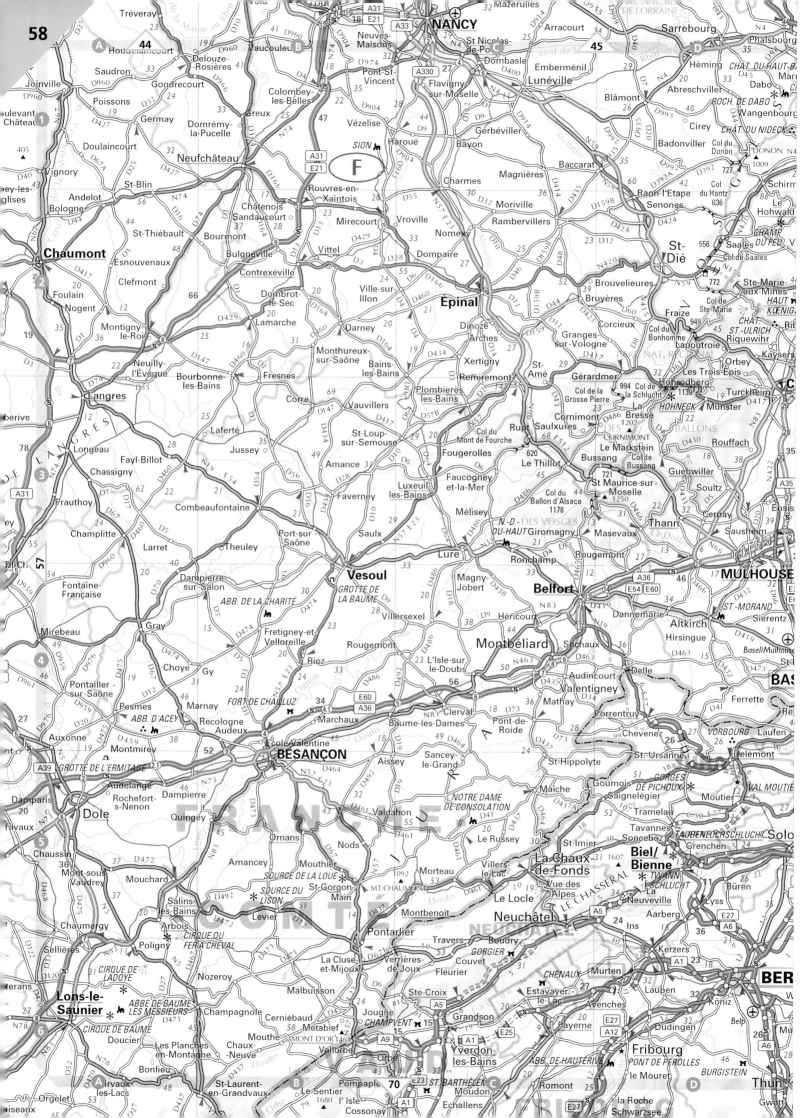

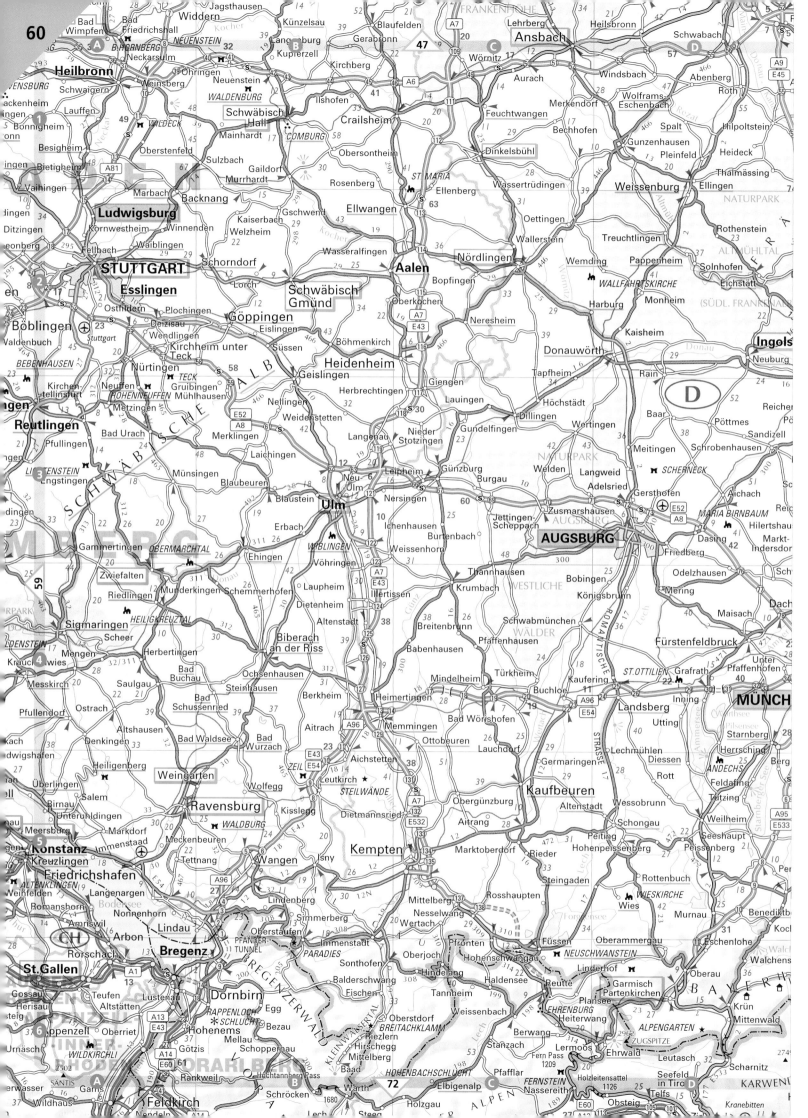

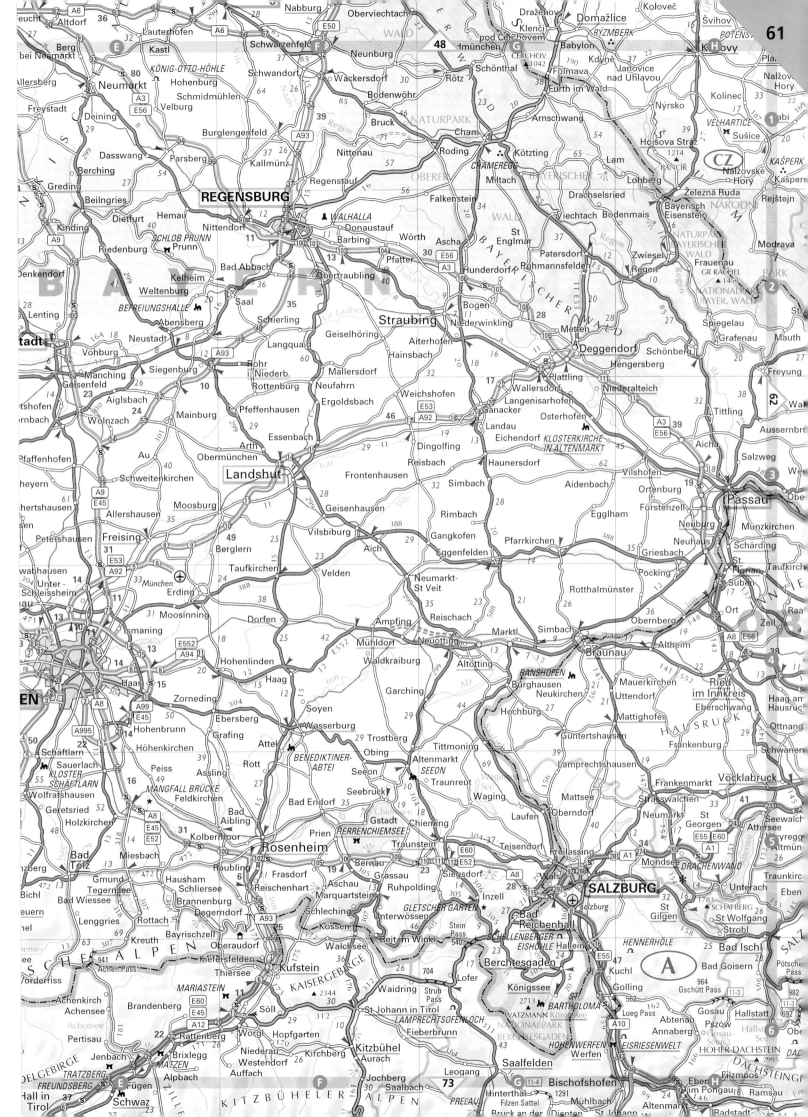

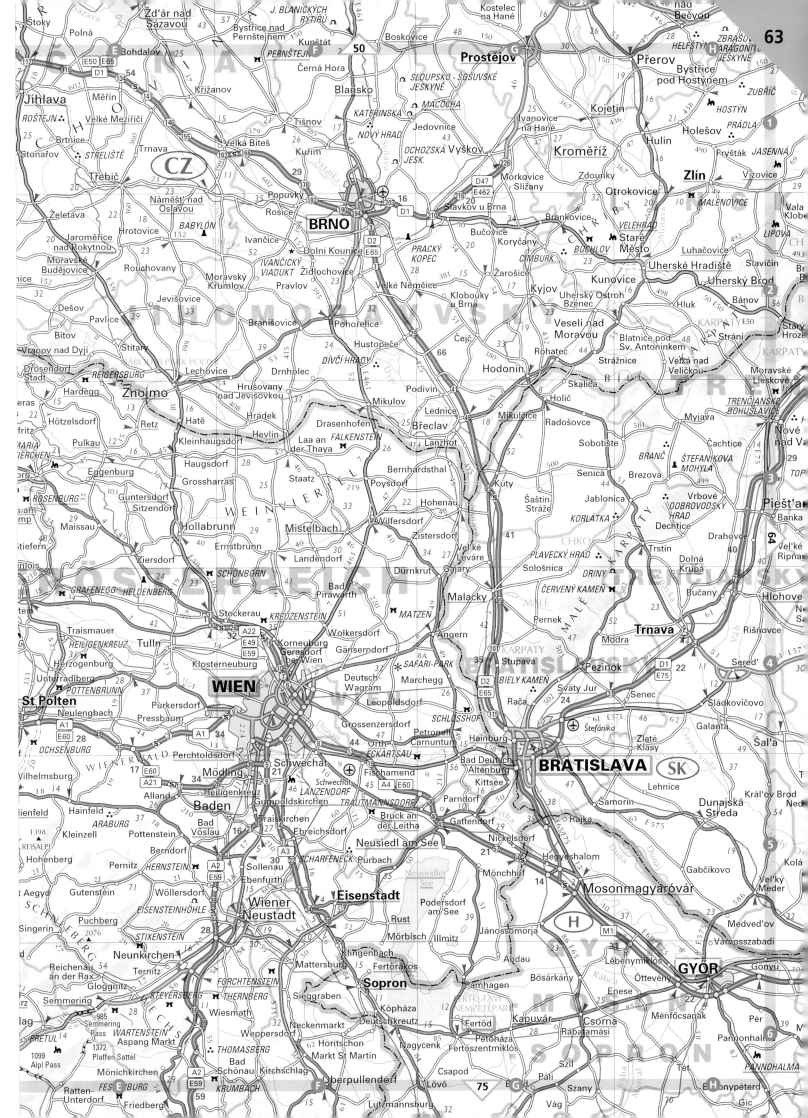

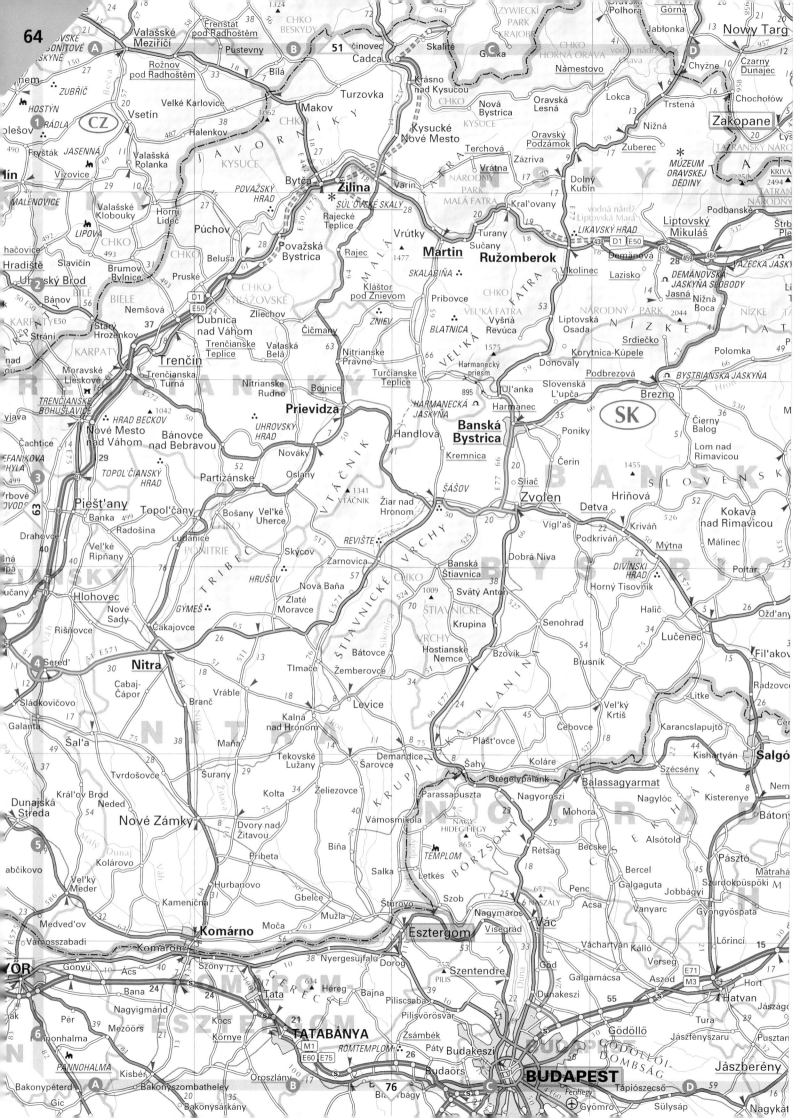

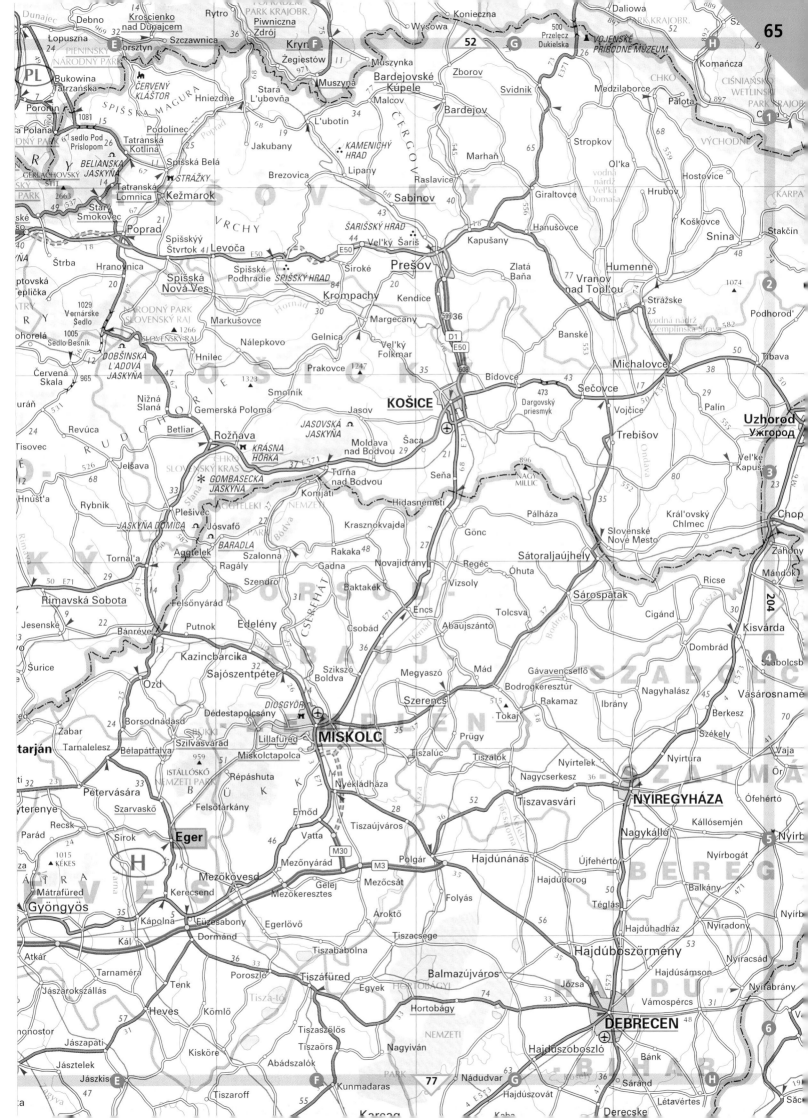

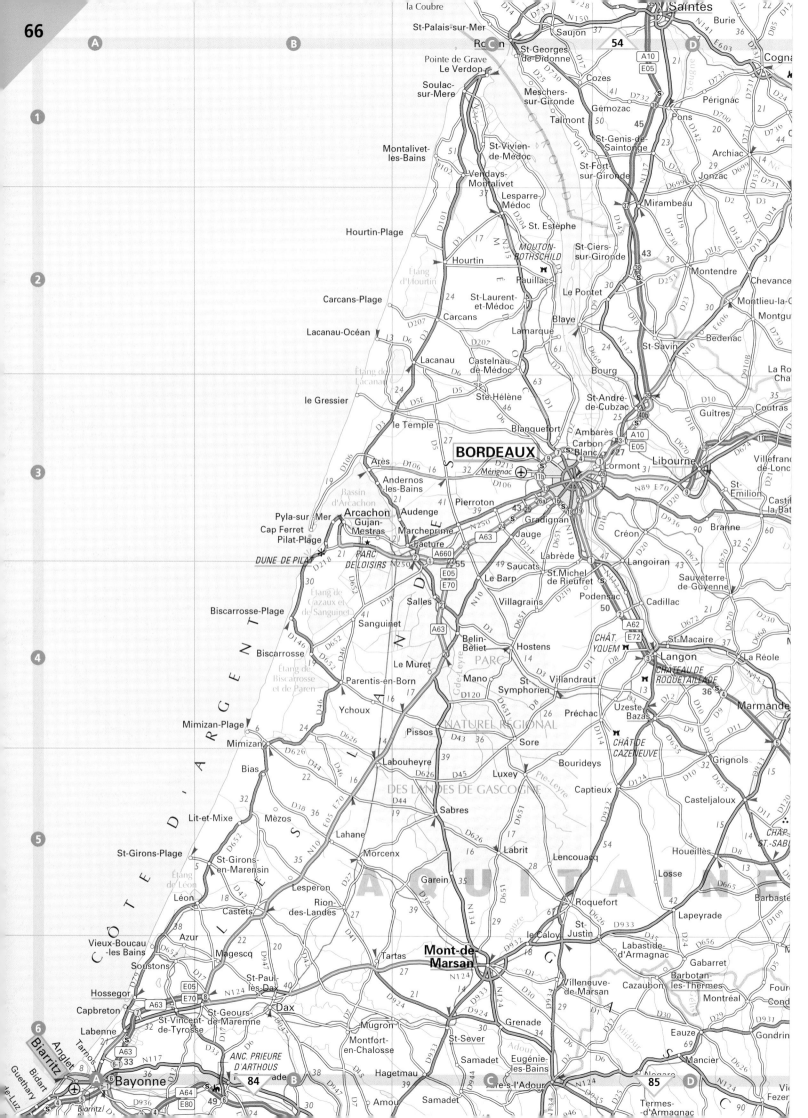

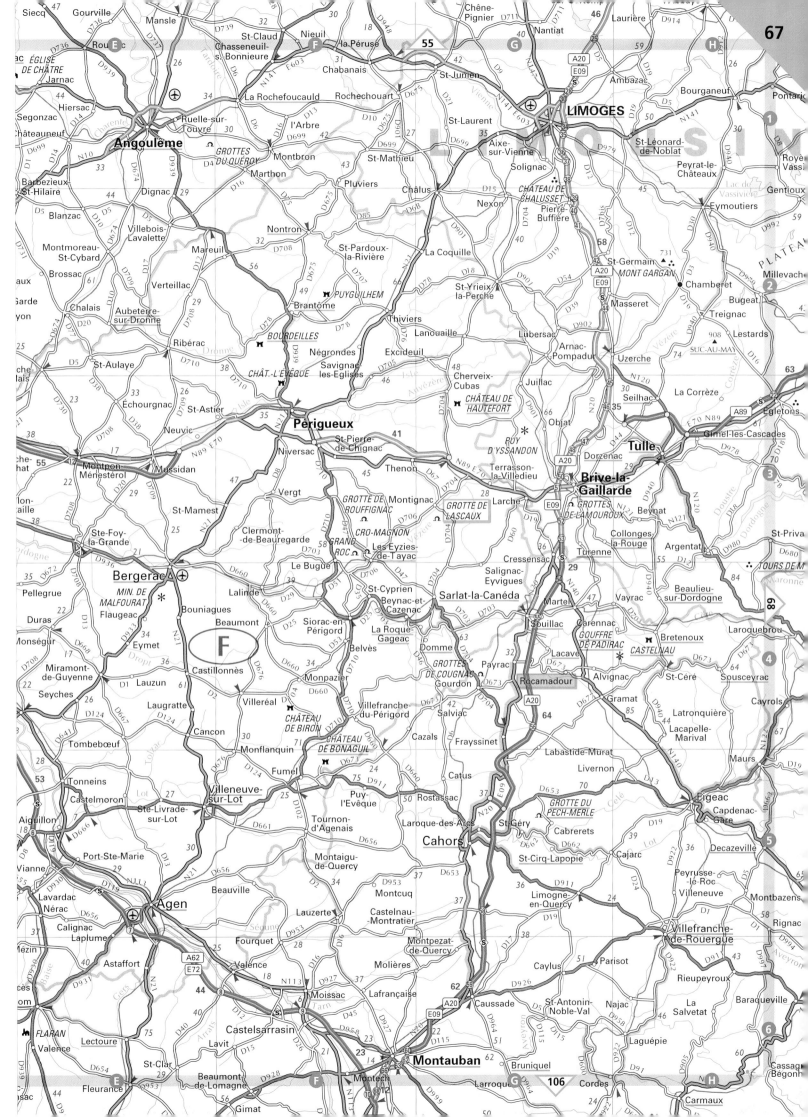

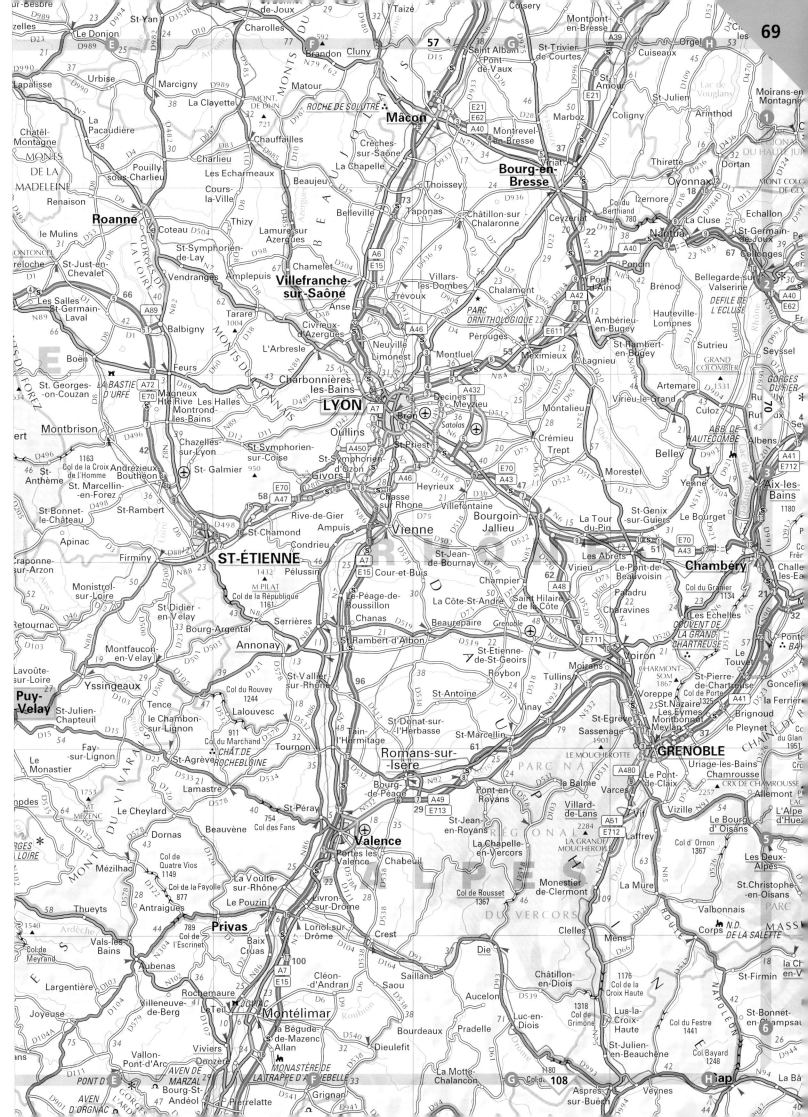

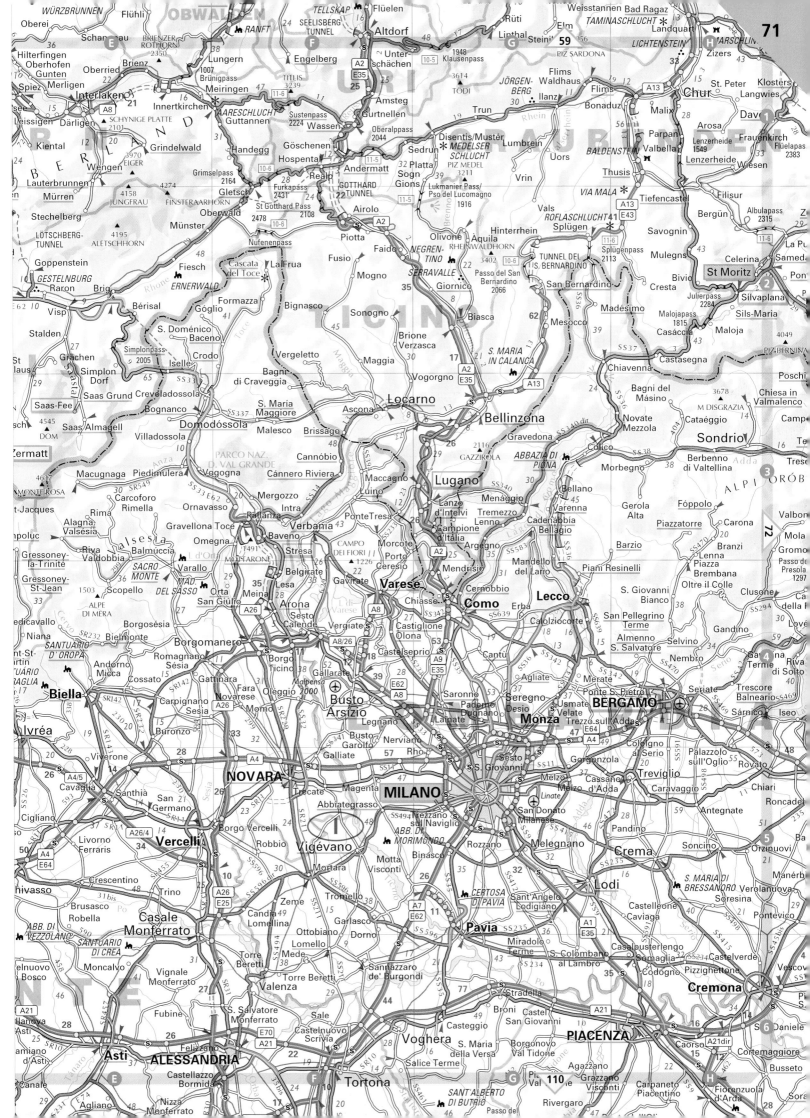

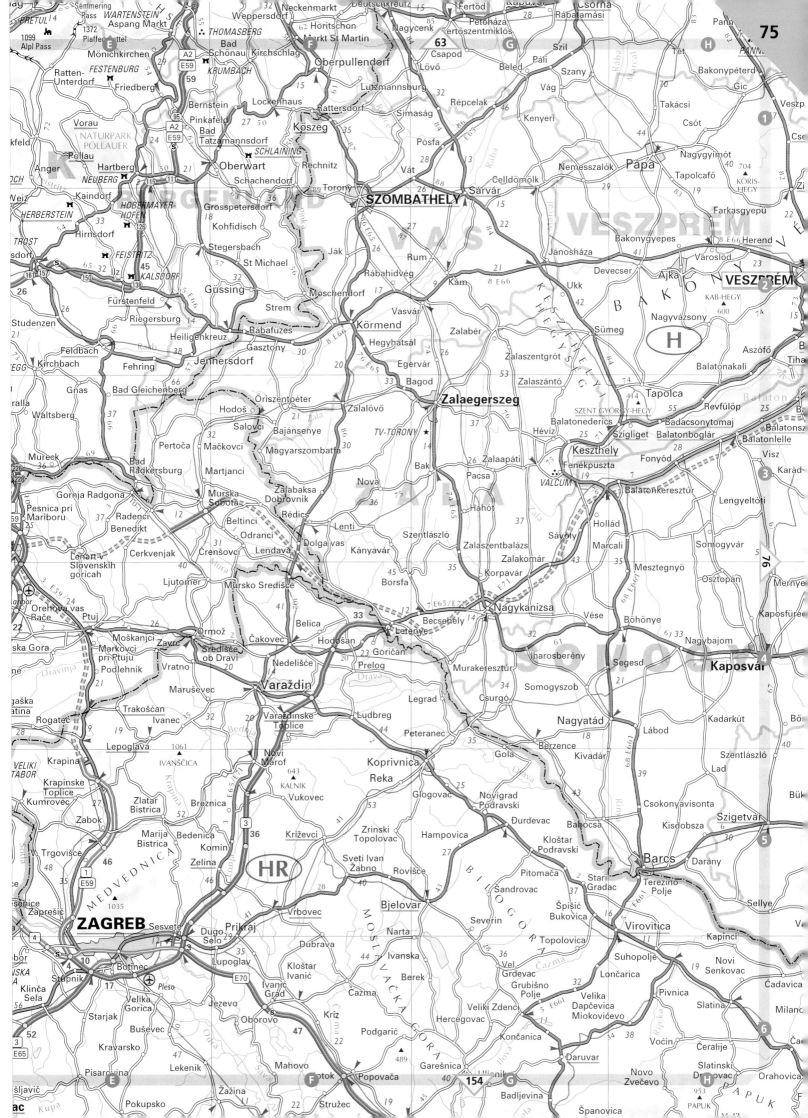

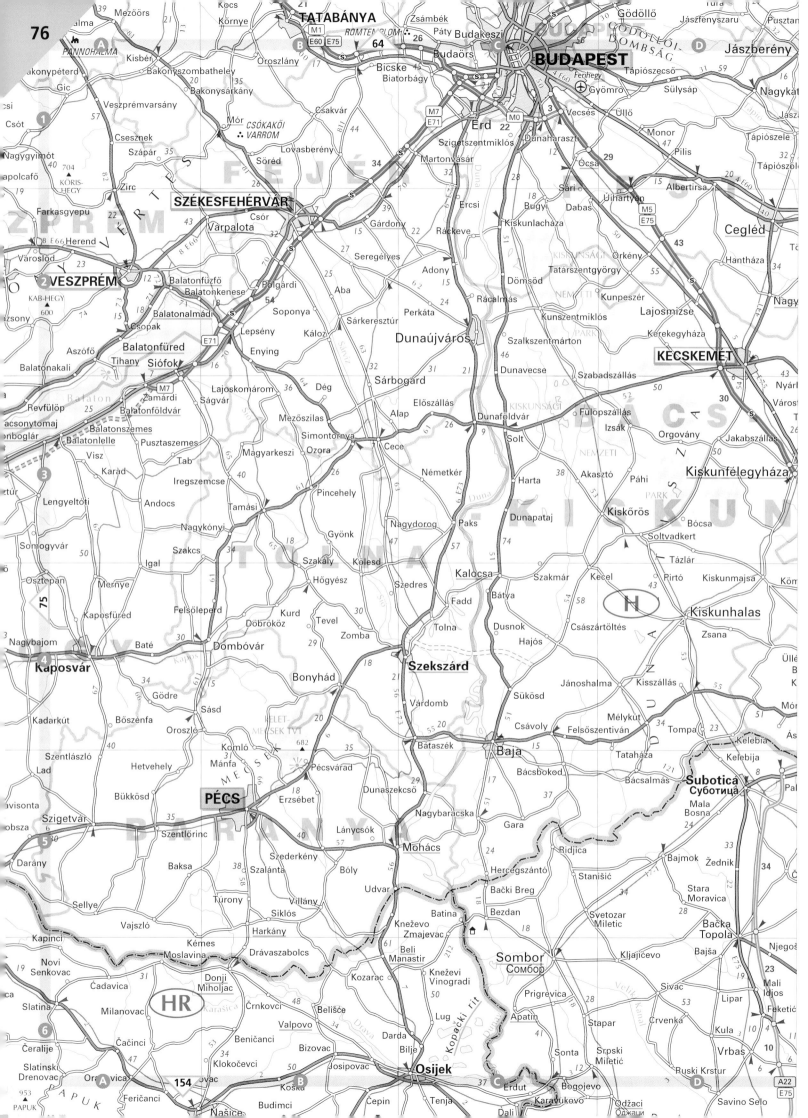

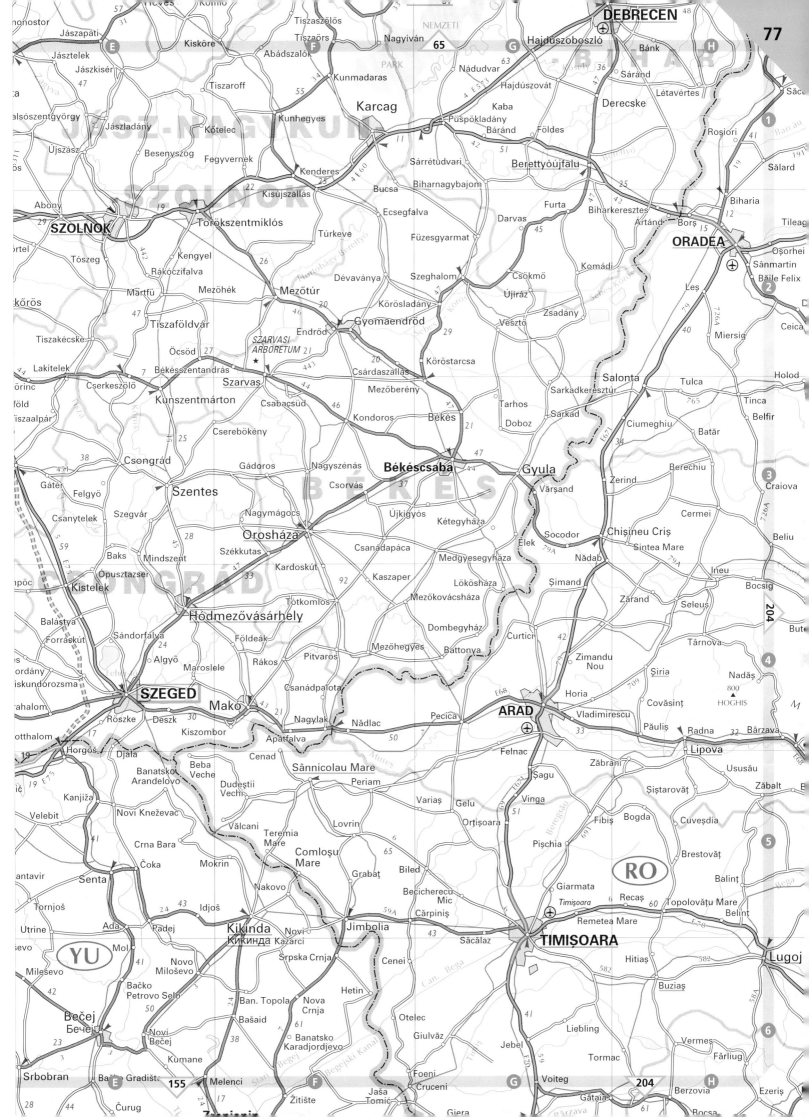

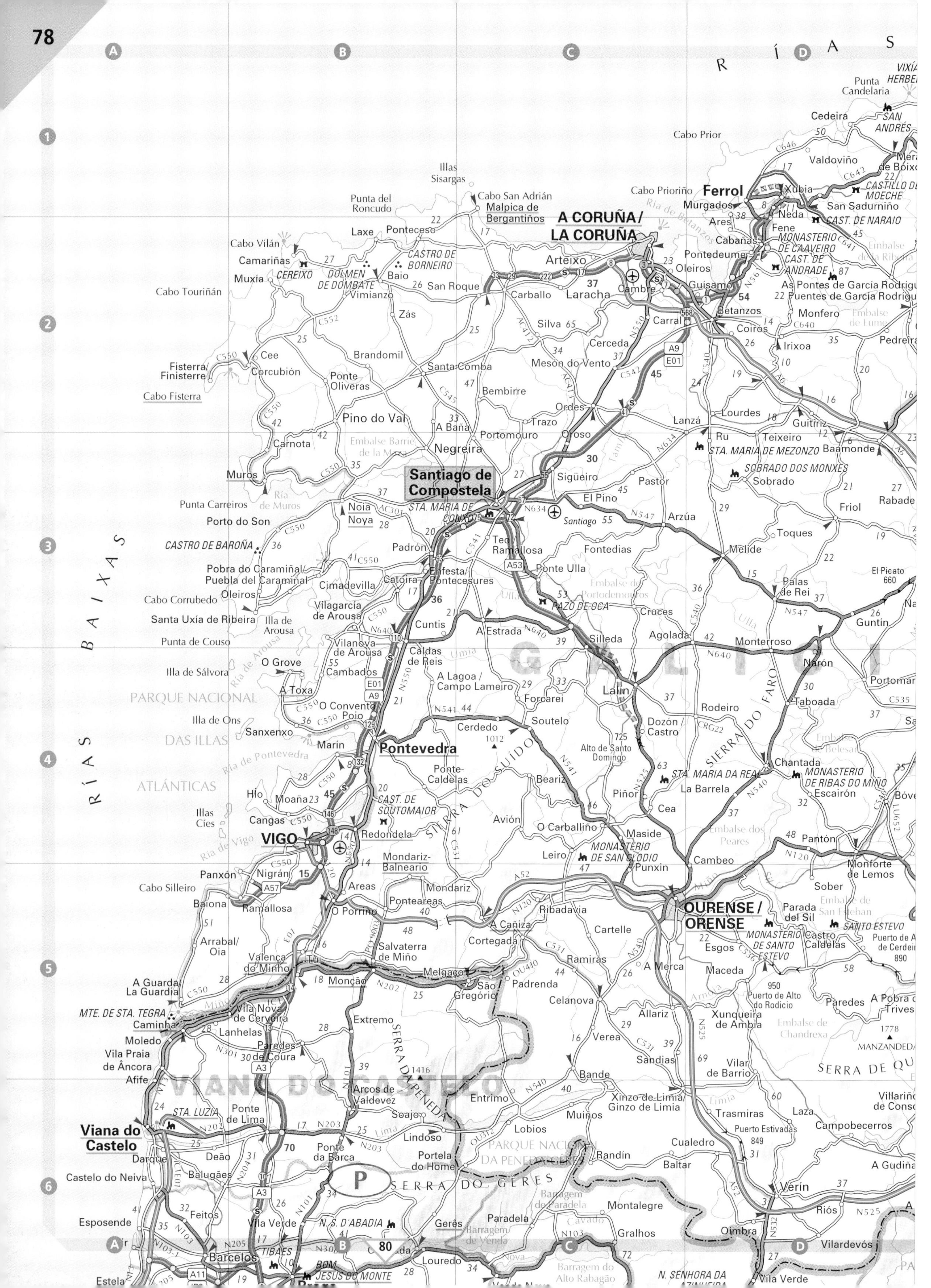

RÍAS

A   B   C   D

1

Cabo Prior
Cedeira
Valdoviño
Punta Candelaria
Vixía Herbeira
Punta Herbeira
SAN ANDRÉS
CASTILLO DE MOECHE

2

Illas Sisargas
Punta del Roncudo
Cabo San Adrián
Malpica de Bergantiños
Laxe
Ponteceso
Cabo Vilán
Camariñas
Muxia
Cabo Touriñán
CEREIXO
DOLMEN DE DOMBATE
Baio
Vimianzo
Zás
San Roque
CASTRO DE BORNEIRO
Carballo
Larcha
Silva
Cerceda
Arteixo
A CORUÑA / LA CORUÑA
Cambre
Oleiros
Guísamo
Ferrol
Murgados
Ares
Cabanas
Neda
Fene
Pontedeume
MONASTERIO DE CAAVEIRO
CAST. DE ANDRADE
As Pontes de García Rodríguez
Puentes de García Rodríguez
Monfero
Betanzos
Coirós
Carral
Xubia
San Sadurniño
CAST. DE NARAIO
Meirás
de Boixo

3

Fisterra / Finisterre
Cabo Fisterra
Cee
Corcubión
Brandomil
Santa Comba
Ponte Oliveras
Bembirre
Mesón do Vento
Ordes
Oroso
Trazo
Pino do Val
A Baña
Portomouro
Negreira
Carnota
Muros
Punta Carreiros
Porto do Son
Noia
Santiago de Compostela
STA. MARÍA DE CONXO
Sigüeiro
El Pino
Santiago
Pastor
Sobrado
Arzúa
Melide
Toques
Palas de Rei
Friol
Rabade
El Picato 660
Lanzá
Lourdes
Guitiriz
Ru
Teixeiro
STA. MARÍA DE MEZONZO
Baamonde
SOBRADO DOS MONXES

4

CASTRO DE BAROÑA
Pobra do Caramiñal / Puebla del Caramiñal
Oleiros
Cabo Corrubedo
Santa Uxía de Ribeira
Punta de Couso
Cimadevilla
Catoira
Enfesta / Pontecesures
Padrón
Teo
Ramallosa
Ponte Ulla
Fontedias
Vilagarcía de Arousa
Illa de Arousa
Cuntis
A Estrada
Silleda
Agolada
Monterroso
Narón
O Grove
Vilanova de Arousa
Caldas de Reis
A Lagoa / Campo Lameiro
Forcarei
Lalín
Rodeiro
Dozón / Castro
Taboada
Chantada
PARQUE NACIONAL DAS ILLAS ATLÁNTICAS
Illa de Sálvora
Cambados
A Toxa
O Convento Poio
Sanxenxo
Illa de Ons
Cerdedo
Souteiro
Bearíz
Piñor
Cea
STA. MARÍA DA REAL
La Barrela
Escairón
MONASTERIO DE RIBAS DO MIÑO
Pantón
Marín
Pontevedra
Ponte-Caldelas
Alto de Santo Domingo
Avión
O Carballiño
Maside
MONASTERIO DE SAN CLODIO
Cambeo
Punxín
Monforte de Lemos
Sober

5

Hío
Moaña
Cangas
Illas Cíes
Redondela
CAST. DE SOUTOMAIOR
Mondariz-Balneario
Leiro
VIGO
Panxón
Nigrán
Mondariz
Areas
O Porriño
Ponteareas
Ribadavia
Cartelle
Cortegada
OURENSE / ORENSE
Esgos
MONASTERIO DE SANTO ESTEVO
Castro Caldelas
Cabo Silleiro
Baiona
Ramallosa
Salvaterra de Miño
A Cañiza
Ramirás
A Merca
Maceda
Arrabal / Oia
Valença do Minho
Tui
Melgaço
São Gregório
Padrenda
Celanova
Allariz
Xunqueira de Ambía
Paredes
A Pobra de Trives
A Guarda / La Guardia
MTE. DE STA. TEGRA
Caminha
Moledo
Vila Praia de Âncora
Afife
Vila Nova de Cerveira
Lanhelas
Paredes de Coura
Monção
Extremo
SERRA DA PENEDA
Arcos de Valdevez
Soajo
Bande
Verea
Sandias
Vilar de Barrio
Villarino de Conso
MANZANEDA
SERRA DE QUEIXA

6

STA. LUZIA
Ponte de Lima
Viana do Castelo
Castelo do Neiva
Darque
Deão
Balugães
Ponte da Barca
Lindoso
Portela do Home
SERRA DO GERÉS
PARQUE NACIONAL DA PENEDA-GERÊS
Randín
Baltar
Muíños
Lobios
Xinzo de Limia
Ginzo de Limia
Trasmiras
Cualedro
Puerto Estivadas
Laza
Campobecerros
A Gudiña
Esposende
Feitos
Vila Verde
N.S. D'ABADIA
Gerés
Paradela
Barragem de Venda
Montalegre
Oimbra
Verín
Ríos
Barcelos
TIBÃES
BOM JESUS DO MONTE
Louredo
Vila Verde
Vilardevós

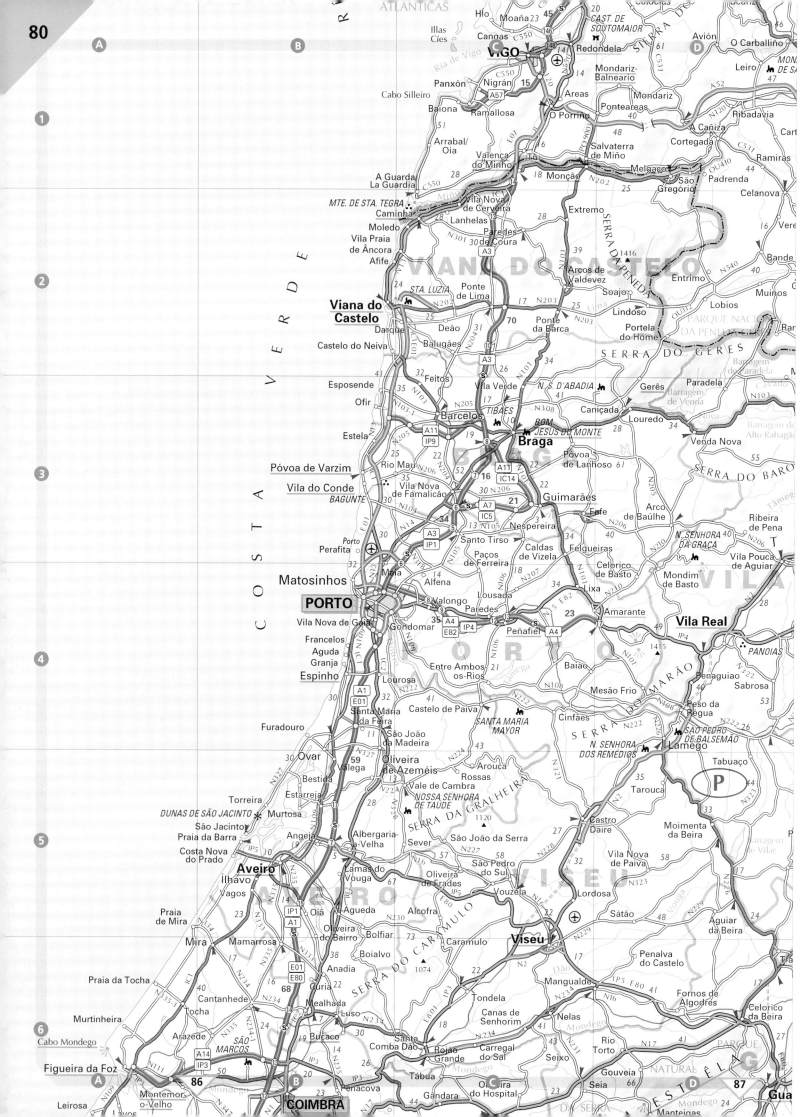

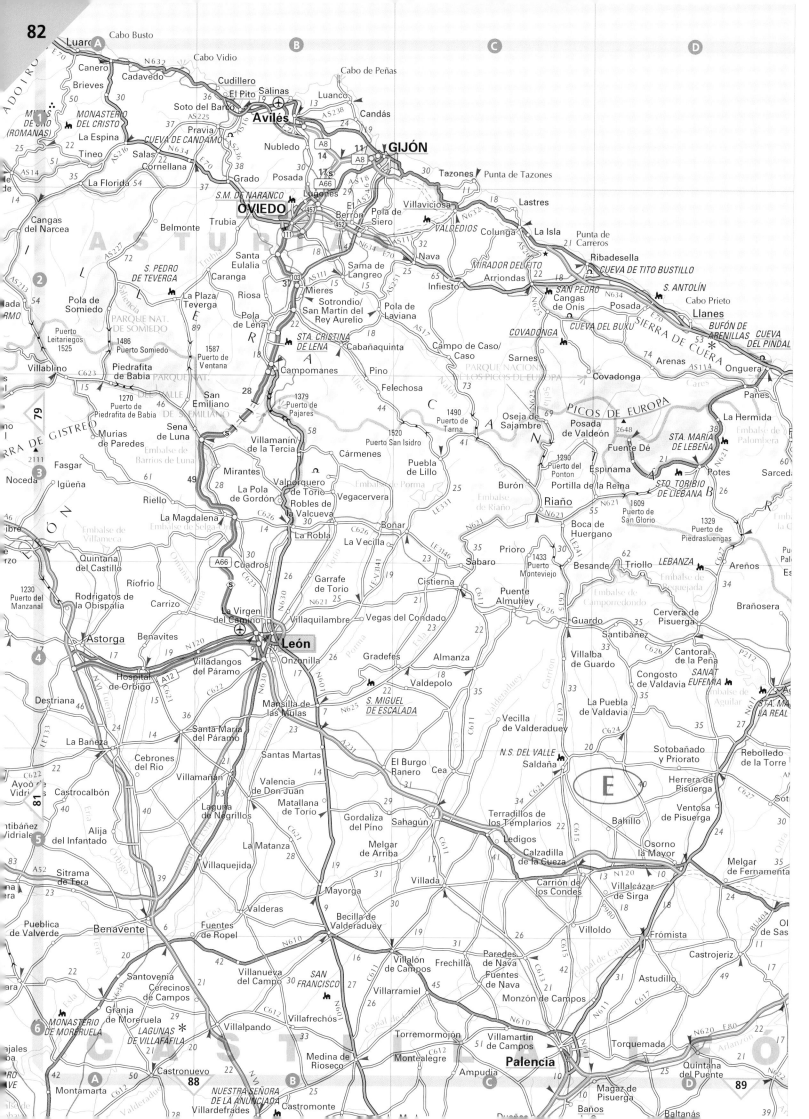

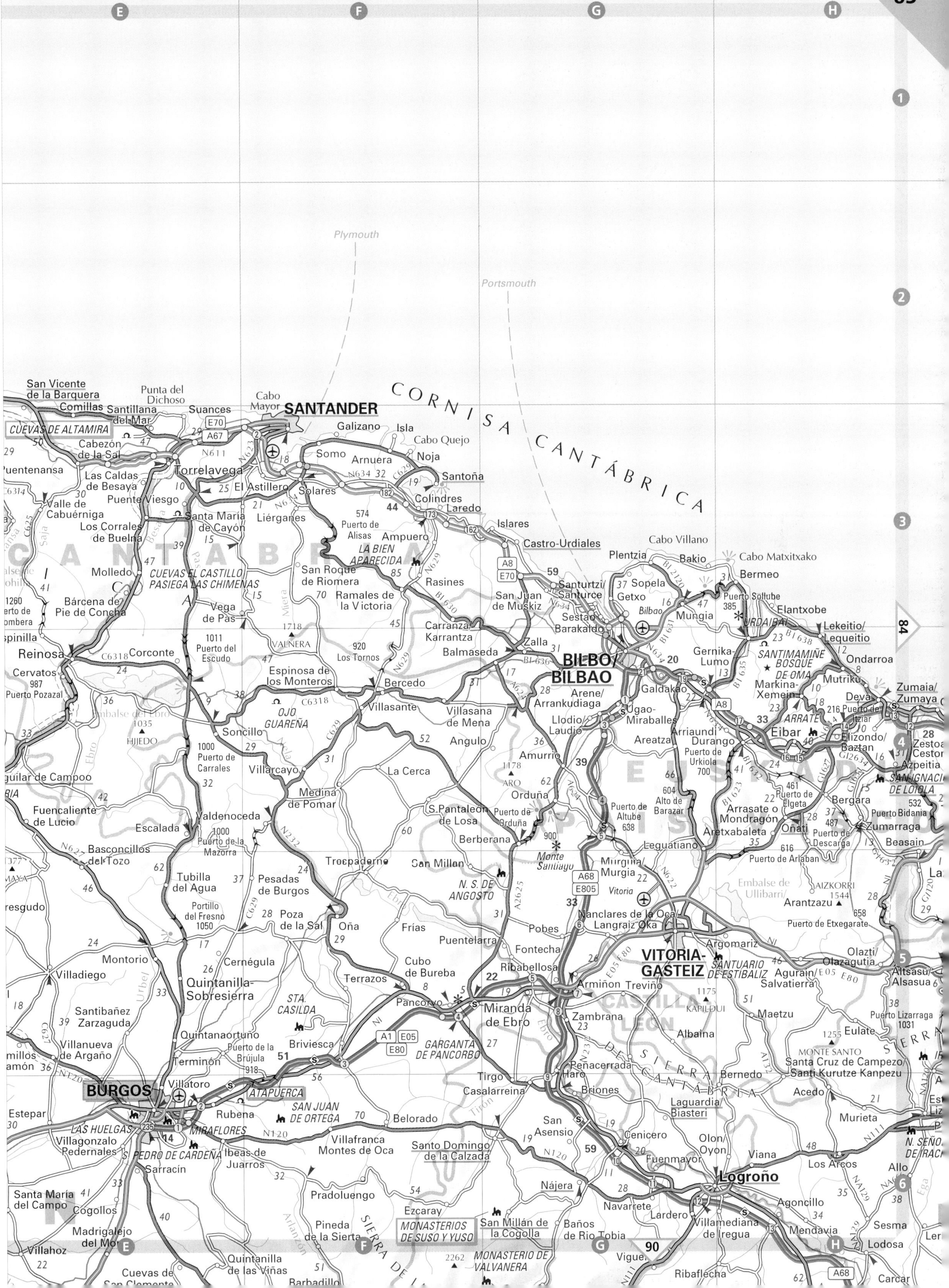

E F G H

1

2

3

84

Plymouth

Portsmouth

CORNISA CANTÁBRICA

San Vicente de la Barquera
Comillas
Santillana del Mar
Suances
Cabo Mayor
SANTANDER
Galizano
Isla
Cabo Quejo
Noja
CUEVAS DE ALTAMIRA
Cabezón de la Sal
Torrelavega
Somo
Arnuera
Santoña
Colindres
Laredo
Puentenansa
Las Caldas de Besaya
El Astillero
Solares
Islares
Valle de Cabuérniga
Puente Viesgo
Santa María de Cayón
Liérganes
Castro-Urdiales
Los Corrales de Buelna
574
Puerto de Alisas
Ampuero
Plentzia
Bakio
Cabo Matxitxako
Bermeo
Molledo
San Roque de Riomera
Rasines
Cabo Villano
LA BIEN APARECIDA
Santurtzi/Santurce
Sopela
Getxo
Puerto Sollube
Elantxobe
Reinosa
CUEVAS EL CASTILLO PASIEGA LAS CHIMENAS
Vega de Pas
Ramales de la Victoria
San Juan de Muskiz
Bilbao
Mungia
URDAIBAI
Lekeitio/Lequeitio
Ondarroa
Cervatos
Corconte
VALNERA
Carranza/Karrantza
Zalla
BILBO/BILBAO
Gernika-Lumo
Markina-Xemein
Mutriku
Deva
Zumaia/Zumaya
Espinosa de los Monteros
Bercedo
Balmaseda
Galdakao
Arene/Arrankudiaga
Ugao-Miraballes
Eibar
Elizondo/Baztan
Zestoa/Cestona
Villasante
Villasana de Mena
Llodio/Laudio
Areatza
Arriaundi
Durango
ARRATE
Azpeitia
OJO GUAREÑA
Soncillo
Angulo
Amurrio
Arrasate o Mondragón
Bergara
Zumarraga
Villarcayo
La Cerca
Orduña
Aretxabaleta
Oñati
Beasain
Medina de Pomar
ARO
Puerto de Urkiola
Puerto de Elgeta
Valdenoceda
S. Pantaleón de Losa
Puerto de Altube
Puerto de Barazar
Escalada
Berberana
Monte Santiago
Leguatiano
Puerto de Arlabán
Basconcillos del Tozo
Trespaderne
San Millán
Murgia/Murguia
AIZKORRI
Arantzazu
Aguilar de Campoo
Tubilla del Agua
Pesadas de Burgos
N. S. DE ANGOSTO
Vitoria
VITORIA-GASTEIZ
Puerto de Etxegarate
Olazti/Olazagutia
Altsasu/Alsasua
Fuencaliente de Lucio
Poza de la Sal
Oña
Frías
Pobes
Nanclares de la Oca
Langraiz Oka
SANTUARIO DE ESTIBALIZ
Agurain
Salvatierra
Montorio
Cernégula
Terrazos
Cubo de Bureba
Puentelarra
Fontecha
Armiñón
Treviño
Maetzu
Villadiego
Quintanilla-Sobresierra
STA. CASILDA
Pancorbo
Ribabellosa
Argomariz
KAPILDUI
Puerto Lizarraga
Quintanaortuño
Briviesca
Miranda de Ebro
Zambrana
CASTILLA LEÓN
Albaina
SIERRA DE CANTABRIA
Eulate
BURGOS
Villatoro
ATAPUERCA
Puerto de la Brújula
Terminón
GARGANTA DE PANCORBO
Tirgo
Casalarreina
Haro
Peñacerrada
Bernedo
Santa Cruz de Campezo
Santi Kurutze Kanpezu
Acedo
Estepar
LAS HUELGAS
Rubena
SAN JUAN DE ORTEGA
Belorado
Briones
Laguardia/Biasteri
Murieta
Villagonzalo Pedernales
STO. PEDRO DE CARDEÑA
Ibeas de Juarros
Villafranca Montes de Oca
Santo Domingo de la Calzada
San Asensio
Cenicero
Olon/Oyon
Viana
Los Arcos
Allo
Sarracín
MIRAFLORES
Cogollos
Pradoluengo
Ezcaray
San Millán de la Cogolla
Baños de Río Tobia
Fuenmayor
Logroño
Agoncillo
Sesma
Lodosa
Santa María del Campo
Madrigalejo del Monte
Pineda de la Sierra
MONASTERIOS DE SUSO Y YUSO
Nájera
Navarrete
Lardero
Villamediana de Iregua
Mendavia
Villahoz
Cuevas de las Viñas
Quintanilla de San Clemente
Barbadillo
MONASTERIO DE VALVANERA
Vigue
Ribaflecha

4

5

6

90

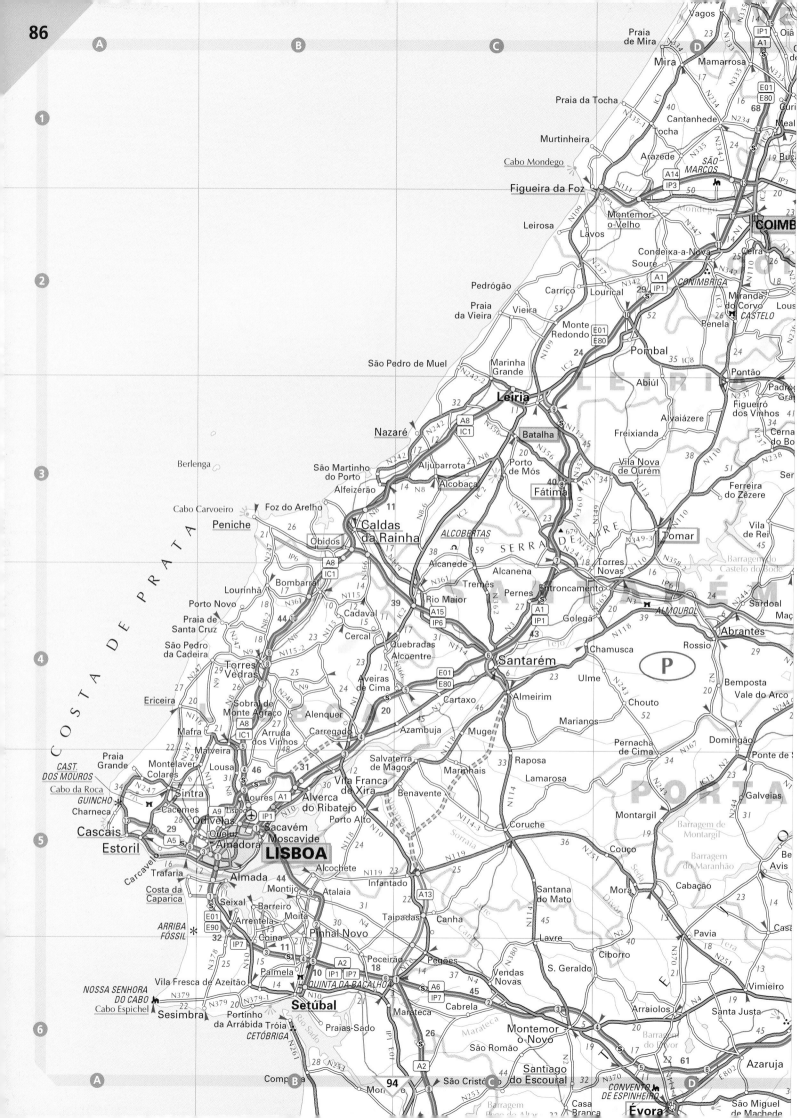

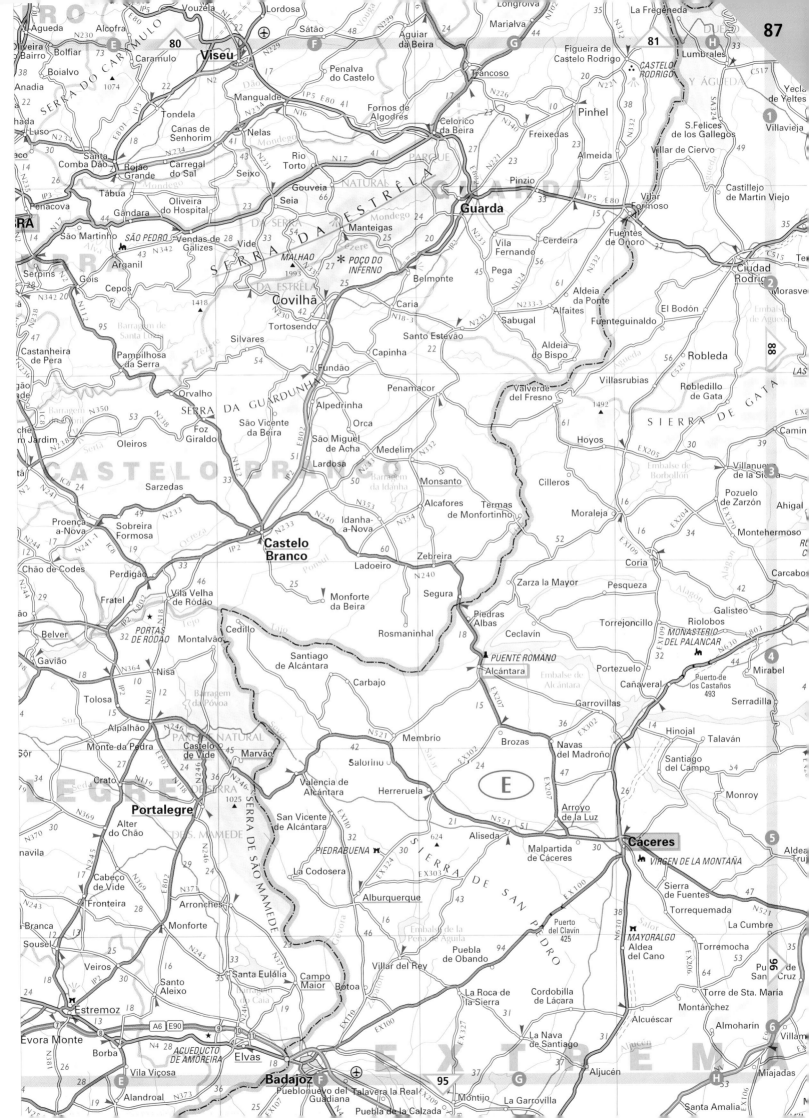

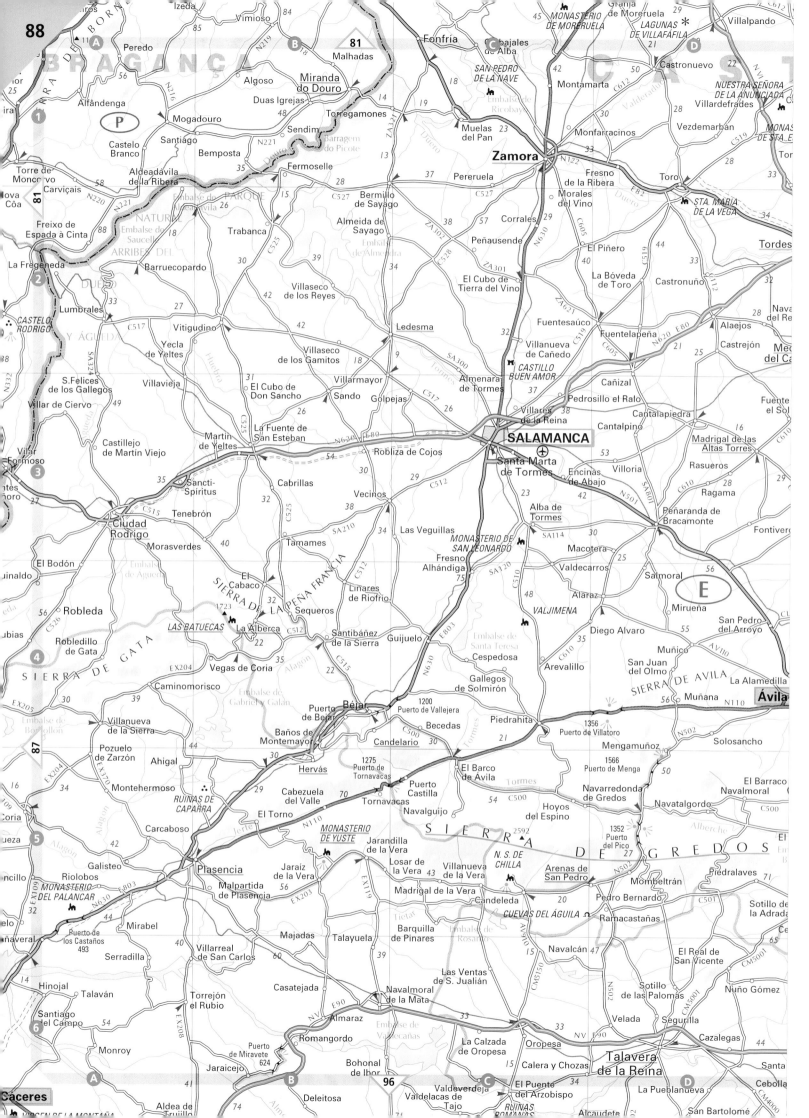

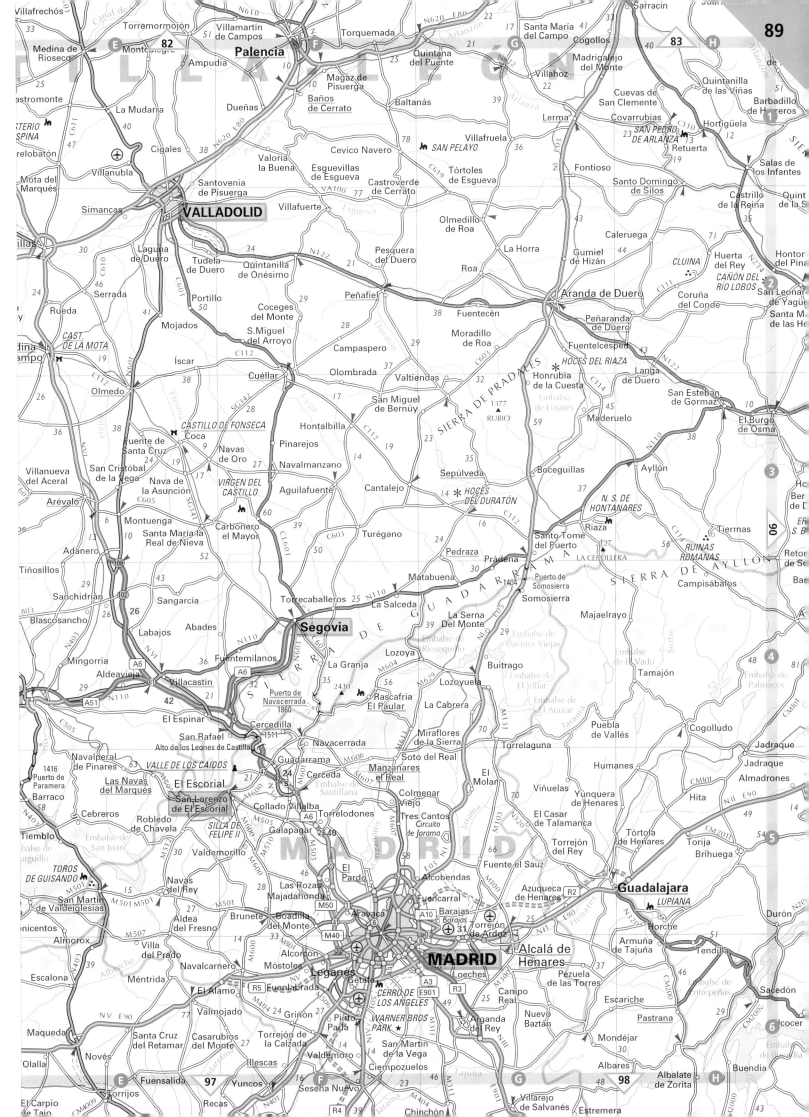

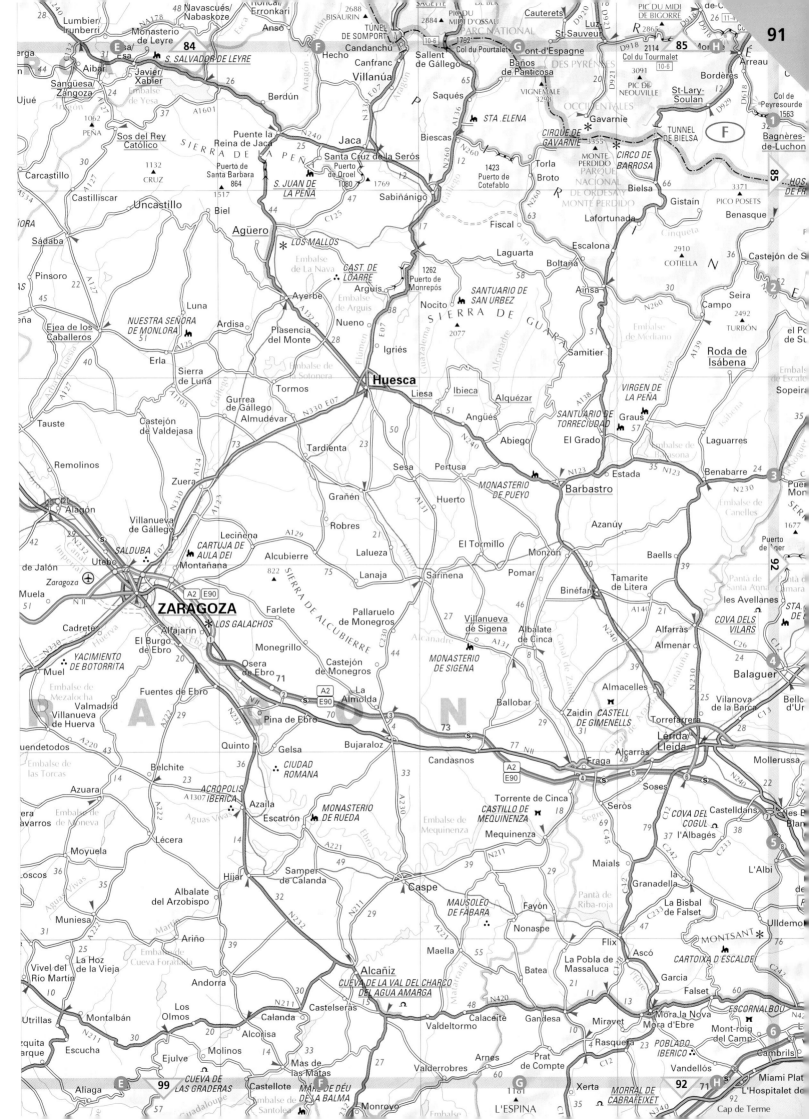

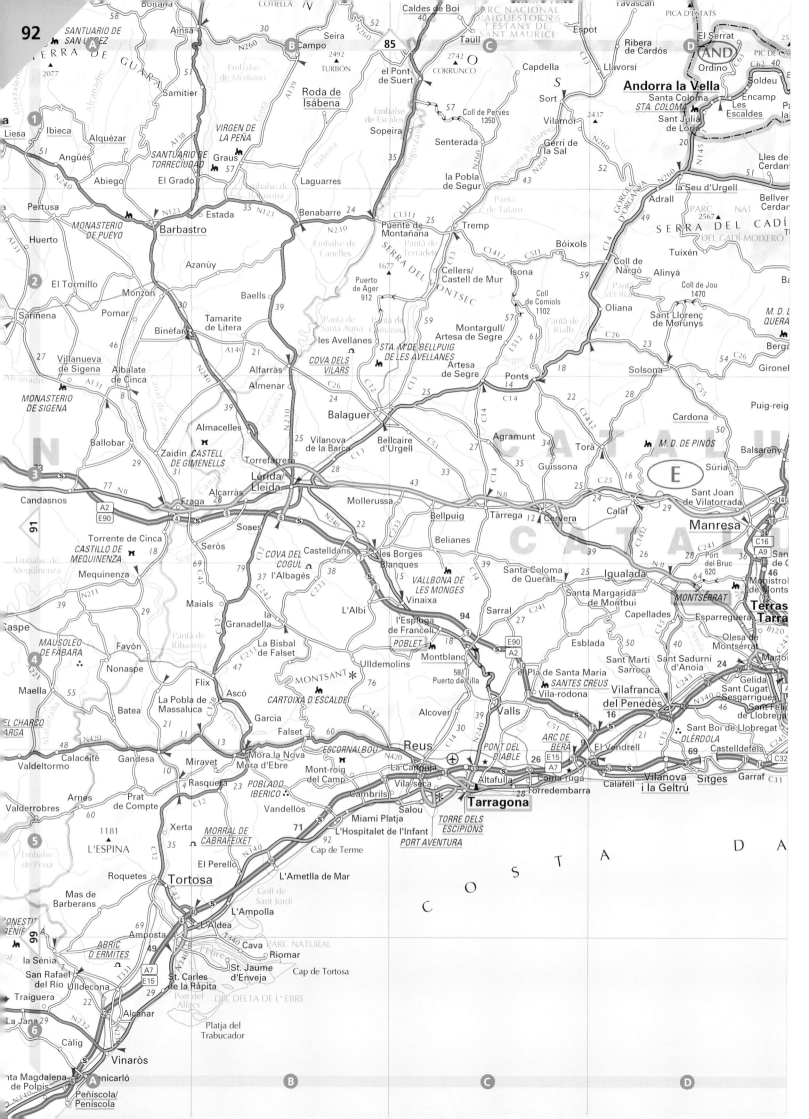

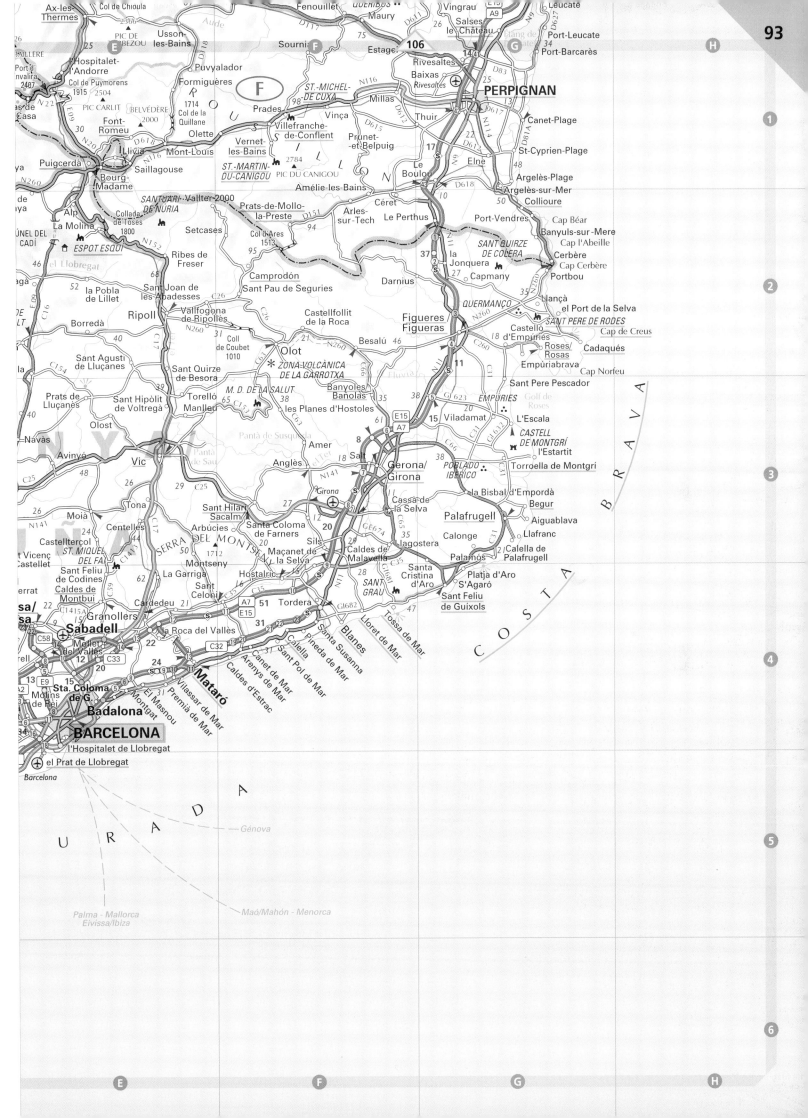

A B C D

1

NOSSA SENHORA DO CABO
Cabo Espichel
Sesimbra
Vila Fresca de Azeitão
N379
N379-1
Portinho da Arrábida
Tróia
CETÓBRIGA
Setúbal
Palmela
QUINTA DA BACALHOA
Poceirão
Pegões
S. Geraldo
Ciborro
Vendas Novas
Cabrela
Marateca
Praias-Sado
Rio Sado
N10
N252
IP7
A2
IP1
86
10
18
A6
IP7
N4
45
2
Arraiolos
Montemor-o-Novo
São Romão
São Cristóvão
Santiago do Escoural
CONVENTO DE ESPINHEIRO
Évora
Casa Branca

COSTA AZUL
Comporta
Montalvo
Alcácer do Sal
NOSSA SENHORA DA CONCEIÇÃO
Barragem Pego do Alto
Casa Branca
Alcáçovas
Xarrama

2

Casa Branca
Melides
Lagoa de Santo André
São Francisco da Serra
Santo André
Grândola
São Romão
Torrão
Barragem de Vale de Gaio
Viana do Alentejo
Alvito
Barragem do Alvito
SERRA DE GRÂNDOLA
SETÚBAL
N261
N5
N383
N257
N254
São Mar

Cabo de Sines
Sines
Santiago do Cacém
MIROBRIGA
Abela
Azinheira dos Barros
Santa Margarida do Sado
Odivelas
Barragem de Odivelas
Ferreira do Alentejo
Cuba
Matos
Vidigu
SERRA
RUÍNAS ROMANA

3

Porto Covo
São Domingos
Alvalade
Ermidas-Aldeia
Beringel
Pedrógão
N121
N261
Vila Nova de Milfontes
Derreada
Bicos
Cercal
Torre Vã
Aljustrel
Santa Vitória
Beja
Baleizão
Salvada
Serpa
Santa Iria
N260
Almograve
São Luis
Santa Luzia
Garvão
Carregueiro
Trindade
Albernoa
N389
N262
N263
BEJA
N261-4
N123
N122

4

Zambujeira do Mar
Odemira
Telheiro
São Martinho das Amoreiras
Ourique
Entradas
Castro Verde
Vale de Açor
Vale do Po
São Teotónio
Santa Clara-a-Velha
Santana da Serra
CASTRO DA COLA
São Marcos da Ataboeira
Alcaria Ruiva
São João dos Caldeireiros
Mértola
Praia de Monte Clérigo
Rogil
Nave Redonda
Gomes Aires
Semblana
N120
N393-1
N123
N266
Odeceixe
Arrifana
Aljezur
Alfambras
SERRA DE MONCHIQUE
Marmelete
Monchique
Almodôvar
São Pedro de Solis
São Miguel do Pinheiro
Espírito Santo
Santa Ana de Cambas
Carrapateira
Bordeira
Bensafrim
São Marcos da Serra
São Barnabé
Dogueno
N267
N122

5

Castelejo
Vila do Bispo
FOIA 902
Barragem da Bravura
Barragem do Funcho
Ameixial
Martim Longo
Pereiro
Cachopo
Barragem de Odeleite
Cabo São Vicente
Salema
Burgau
Lagos
Alvor
Mexilhoeira Grande
Silves
Portimão
Lagoa
Messines de Baixo
São Bartolomeu de Messines
Salir
Querença
Barranco do Velho
Odeleite
S. Silv de Gu
Sagres
Ponta de Sagres
PONTA DA PIEDADE
Vau
Carvoeiro
PONTAL
Armação de Pera
Albufeira
Paderne
Loulé
São Brás de Alportel
Portos dos Fusos
SERRA DO CALDEIRÃO
N268
N125
N124
N264
N396
N270
Castro Marim
Ayamon
Monte Gordo
Vila Real de Santo António
Isl Cr

FARO
Vilamoura
Quarteira
Vale de Lobos
MILREU
Estoi
Moncarapacho
Tavira
Olhão
Fuzeta
Faro
RIA FORMOSA
Cabo de Santa Maria
N125
N198
N125

6

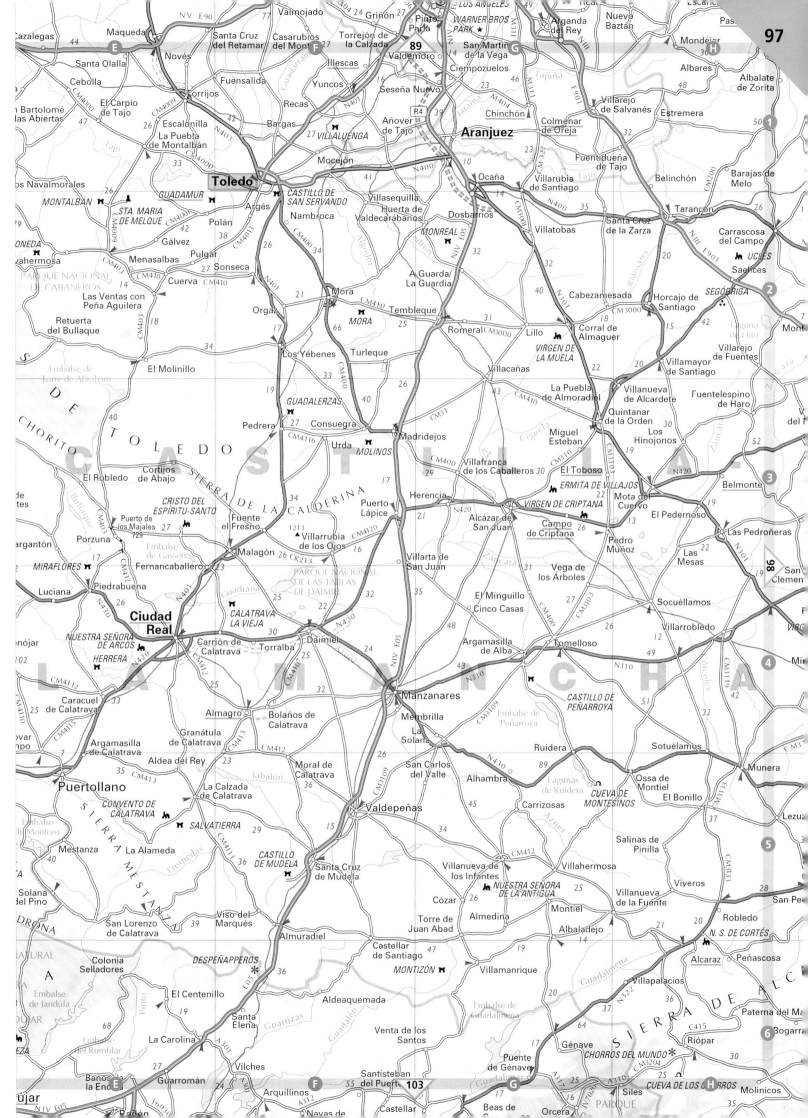

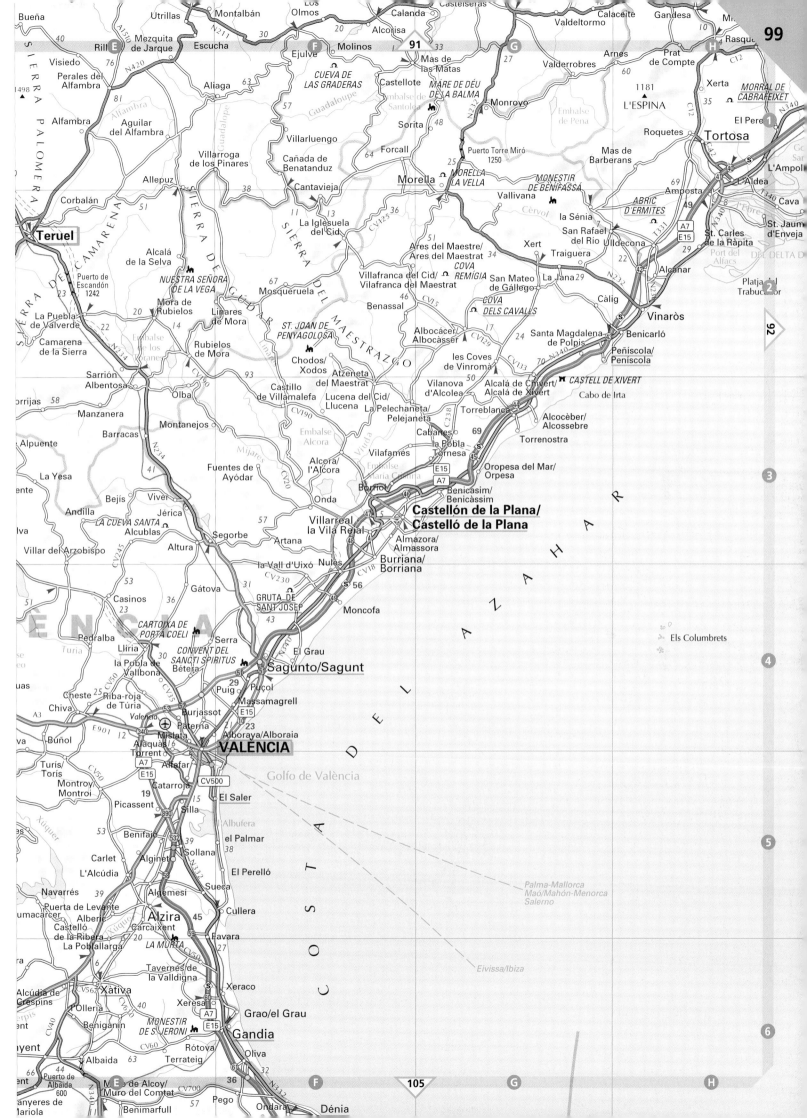

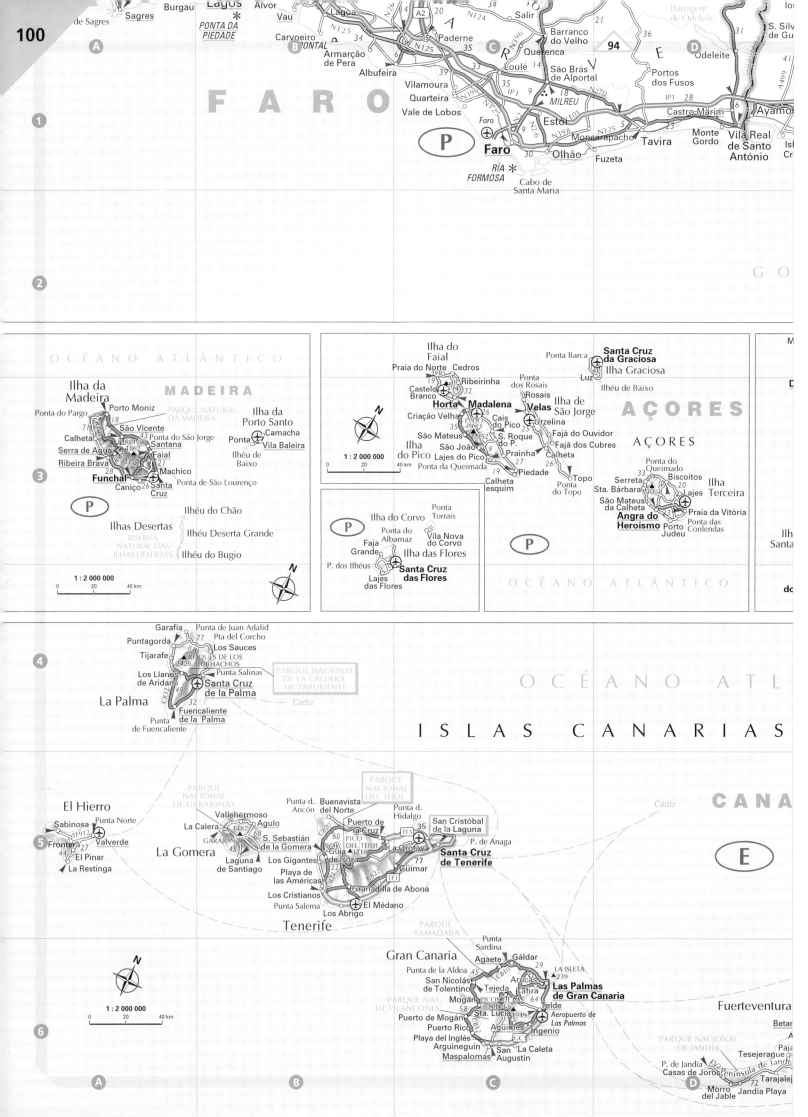

FARO

Burgau · Lagos · Alvor · Lagoa · N26 · A2 · Salir · Barranco de Odeleite

de Sagres · Sagres · PONTA DA PIEDADE · Carvoeiro · N125 · Paderne · N396 · Barranco do Velho · S. Silv de Gu

PONTAL · Armação de Pera · Albufeira · N125 · Loulé · São Brás de Alportel · Portos dos Fusos · Odeleite

Vilamoura · Quarteira · Vale de Lobos · São Brás · MILREU · IP1 · Castro-Marim · Ayamo

Faro · Estói · Monte Gordo · Vila Real de Santo António

Faro · Olhão · Tavira · Fuzeta · Moncarapacho

RÍA FORMOSA · Cabo de Santa Maria

OCÉANO ATLÂNTICO

MADEIRA

Ilha da Madeira · Porto Moniz · São Vicente · Santana · Ponta do São Jorge · Ilha da Porto Santo · Camacha · Vila Baleira

Ponta do Pargo · Calheta · Serra de Água · Ribeira Brava · Faial · Machico · Ponta de São Lourenço · Ilhéu de Baixo

Funchal · Caniço · Santa Cruz

Ilhas Desertas · Ilhéu do Chão · Ilhéu Deserta Grande · Ilhéu do Bugio

RESERVA NATURAL DAS ILHAS DESERTAS

1 : 2 000 000 · 0 · 20 · 40 km

AÇORES

Ilha do Faial · Praia do Norte · Cedros · Ribeirinha · Ponta Barca · **Santa Cruz da Graciosa** · Ilha Graciosa · Luz · Ilhéu de Baixo

Castelo Branco · **Horta** · **Madalena** · **Velas** · Ilha de São Jorge · Rosais · Ponta dos Rosais

Criação Velha · Cais do Pico · Urzelina · S. Roque do P. · Fajã do Ouvidor · Fajã dos Cubres

São Mateus · São João · Prainha · Calheta

Ilha do Pico · Lajes do Pico · Ponta da Queimada · Piedade

AÇORES · AÇORES

Ponta do Queimado · Serreta · Biscoitos · Ilha Terceira · Sta. Bárbara · São Mateus da Calheta · Lajes

Calheta Nesquim · Ponta do Topo · Topo · **Angra do Heroísmo** · Porto Judeu · Praia da Vitória · Ponta das Conlendas

1 : 2 000 000 · 0 · 20 · 40 km

Ilha do Corvo · Ponta Torrais · Vila Nova do Corvo · Faja Grande · Ponta do Albarnaz · Ilha das Flores · P. dos Ilhéus · **Santa Cruz das Flores** · Lajes das Flores

OCÉANO ATLÂNTICO

ISLAS CANARIAS

Garafía · Punta de Juan Adalid · Pta del Corcho · Puntagorda · Los Sauces · Tijarafe · ROQUES DE LOS MUCHACHOS 2426 · Punta Salinas · PARQUE NACIONAL DE LA CALDERA DE TABURIENTE · Cádiz

Los Llanos de Aridane · **Santa Cruz de la Palma** · **La Palma** · Fuencaliente de la Palma · Punta de Fuencaliente

OCÉANO ATL

CANA

El Hierro · Sabinosa · Punta Norte · Valverde · Frontera · El Pinar · La Restinga

PARQUE NACIONAL DE GARAJONAY · Vallehermoso · Agulo · La Calera · GARAJONAY 1487 · **La Gomera** · S. Sebastián de la Gomera · Laguna de Santiago · Los Gigantes

Buenavista del Norte · Punta d. Ancón · Punta d. Hidalgo · Puerto de la Cruz · San Cristóbal de la Laguna · P. de Anaga · PARQUE NACIONAL DEL TEIDE · PICO DEL TEIDE 3718 · La-Orotava · **Santa Cruz de Tenerife** · Guía de Isora · Güímar · Playa de las Américas · Los Cristianos · Granadilla de Abona · Punta Salema · El Médano · Los Abrigos · **Tenerife**

Cádiz

CANA

E

Gran Canaria · Punta Sardina · Gáldar · Agaete · Punta de la Aldea · LA ISLETA · San Nicolás de Tolentino · Tejeda · Tafira · Arucas · **Las Palmas de Gran Canaria** · PARQUE TAMADABA · Mogán · PICOS DE FAS · Telde · Puerto de Mogán · Sta. Lucía · Aeropuerto de Las Palmas · Aguimes · Ingenio · Puerto Rico · Playa del Inglés · Arguineguin · La Caleta · San Augustín · Maspalomas

Fuerteventura · PARQUE NACIONAL DE JANDÍA · Tesejerague · P. de Jandía · Casas de Joros · Morro del Jable · Jandía Playa · Península de Jandía

1 : 2 000 000 · 0 · 20 · 40 km

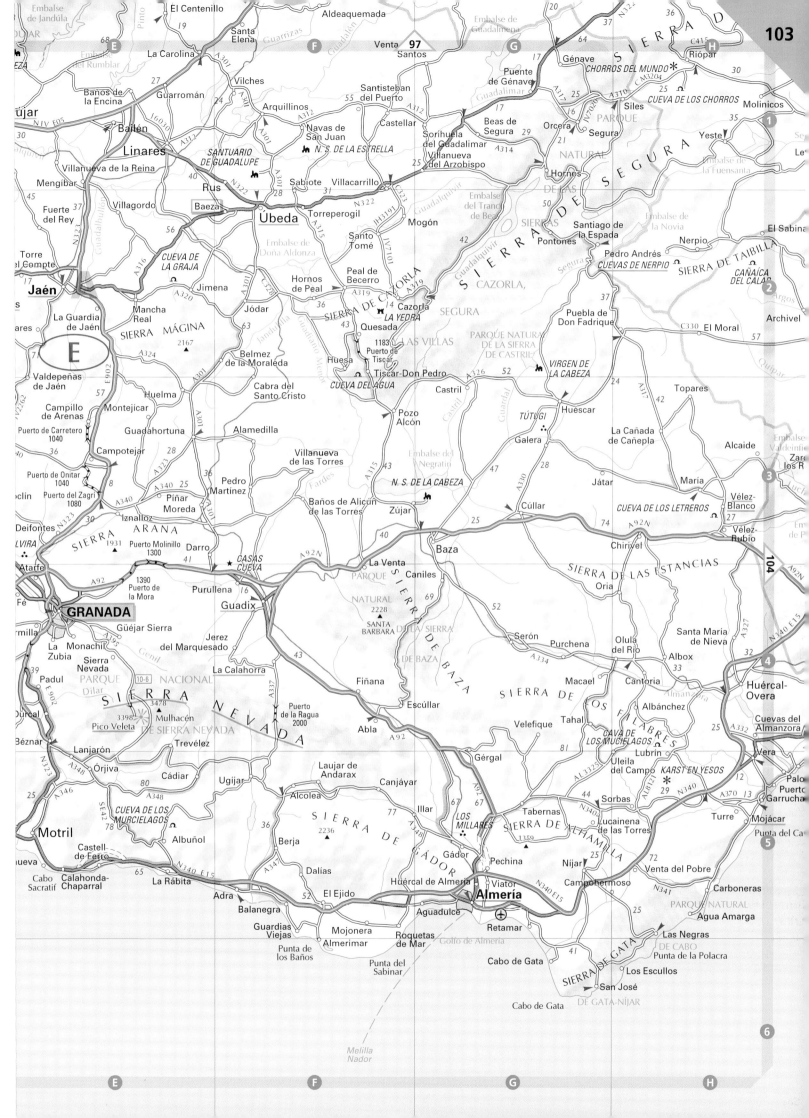

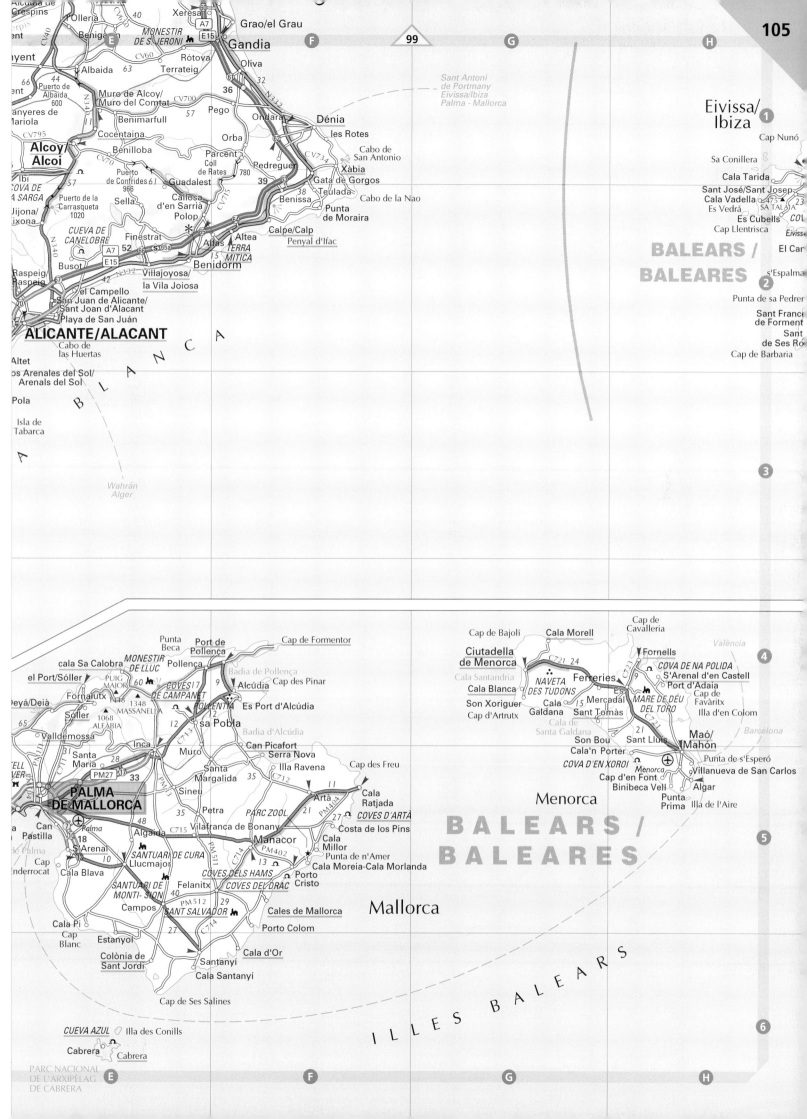

Alcúdia de Crespins
l'Olleria
Benigà
MONESTIR DE S'JERONI
Grao/el Grau
Gandia
99
Sant Antoni de Portmany
Eivissa/Ibiza
Palma - Mallorca

Eivissa/ Ibiza
Cap Nunó
Sa Conillera
Cala Tarida
Sant José/Sant Josep
Cala Vadella
Es Vedrá
Es Cubells
Cap Llentrisca
El Car
s'Espalma
Punta de sa Pedren
Sant France de Forment
Sant de Ses Ró
Cap de Barbaria

Ròtova
Terrateig
Oliva
Albaida
63
Muro de Alcoy/
Muro del Comtat
CV700
Pego
Ondara
Dénia
les Rotes
Puerto de Albaida
600
36
N332
anyeres de Mariola
Cocentaina
Benimarfull
57
Orba
Parcent
Cabo de San Antonio
Xàbia
Alcoy/ Alcoi
Benilloba
CV70
Coll de Rates
780
Pedreguer
Gata de Gorgos
Ibi
COVA SARGA
Guadalest
39
Teulada
Cabo de la Nao
Puerto de Confrides
966
Callosa d'en Sarrià
Benissa
Punta de Moraira
Jijona/ ixona
Sella
Polop
Calpe/Calp
Penyal d'Ifac
Puerto de la Carrasqueta
1020
Finestrat
Altea
Alfas
CUEVA DE CANELOBRE
52
TERRA MITICA
Busot
Benidorm
Villajoyosa/ la Vila Joiosa
el Campello
San Juan de Alicante/
Sant Joan d'Alacant
Playa de San Juán
ALICANTE/ALACANT
Cabo de las Huertas
Altet
os Arenales del Sol/
Arenals del Sol
Pola
Isla de Tabarca

BALEARS / BALEARES

Wahrān Alger

A B L A N C A

Mallorca

cala Sa Calobra
MONESTIR DE LLUC
el Port/Sóller
PUIG MAJOR
60
COVES DE CAMPANET
Deyá/Deià
1348
Fornalutx
MASSANELLA
Sóller
1068
ALFABIA
Valldemossa
Santa María
PM111
Inca
C713
PALMA DE MALLORCA
PM27
33
Palma
Can Pastilla
18
S'Arenal
Cap Enderrocat
Cala Blava
SANTUARI DE CURA
Llucmajor
SANTUARI DE MONTI-SION
Felanitx
Campos
SANT SALVADOR
Cala Pi
Cap Blanc
Estanyol
Colònia de Sant Jordi
Santanyí
Cala Santanyí
Cap de Ses Salines

Punta Beca
Port de Pollença
Pollença
Cap de Formentor
Badia de Pollença
Alcúdia
Cap des Pinar
POLLENTIA
Es Port d'Alcúdia
sa Pobla
Badia d'Alcúdia
12
Muro
Can Picafort
Serra Nova
Santa Margalida
Illa Ravena
35
C712
Sineu
Petra
PARC ZOOL.
Vilafranca de Bonany
21
PM40A
Artà
Cala Ratjada
COVES D'ARTÀ
Costa de los Pins
Manacor
27
Cala Millor
Punta de n'Amer
PM402
Cala Moreia-Cala Morlanda
13
COVES DELS HAMS
Porto Cristo
COVES DEL DRAC
Cales de Mallorca
Porto Colom
Cala d'Or

Menorca

Cap de Bajolí
Cala Morell
Cap de Cavalleria
València
Ciutadella de Menorca
C721
24
Fornells
COVA DE NA POLIDA
Cala Santandria
NAVETA DES TUDONS
Ferreries
S'Arenal d'en Castell
Port d'Adaia
Cala Blanca
Cala Galdana
Mercadal
Sant Tomàs
MARE DE DÉU DEL TORO
Cap de Favàritx
Son Xoriguer
Cap d'Artrutx
Cala de Santa Galdana
Son Bou
Sant Lluís
21
Maó/ Mahón
Cala'n Porter
Barcelona
COVA D'EN XOROI
Punta de s'Esperó
Villanueva de San Carlos
Menorca
Cap d'en Font
Binibeca Vell
Algar
Punta Prima
Illa de l'Aire

BALEARS / BALEARES

ILLES BALEARS

CUEVA AZUL
Illa des Conills
Cabrera
PARC NACIONAL DE L'ARXIPÈLAG DE CABRERA

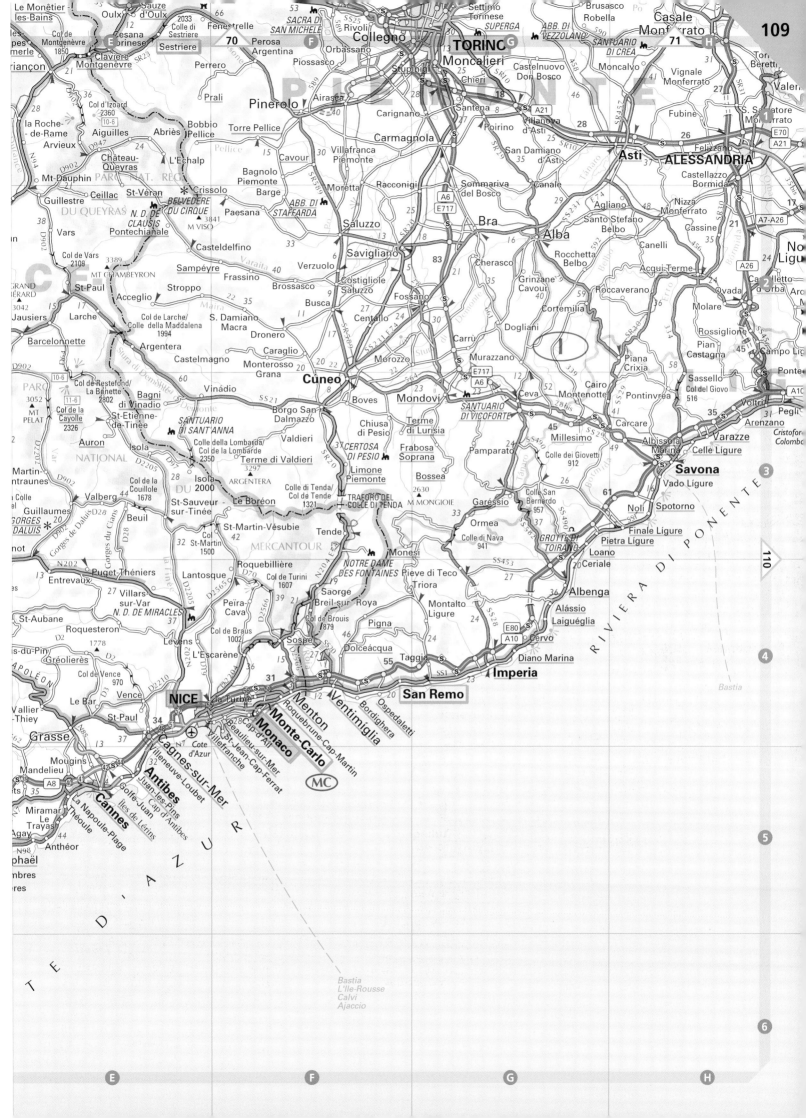

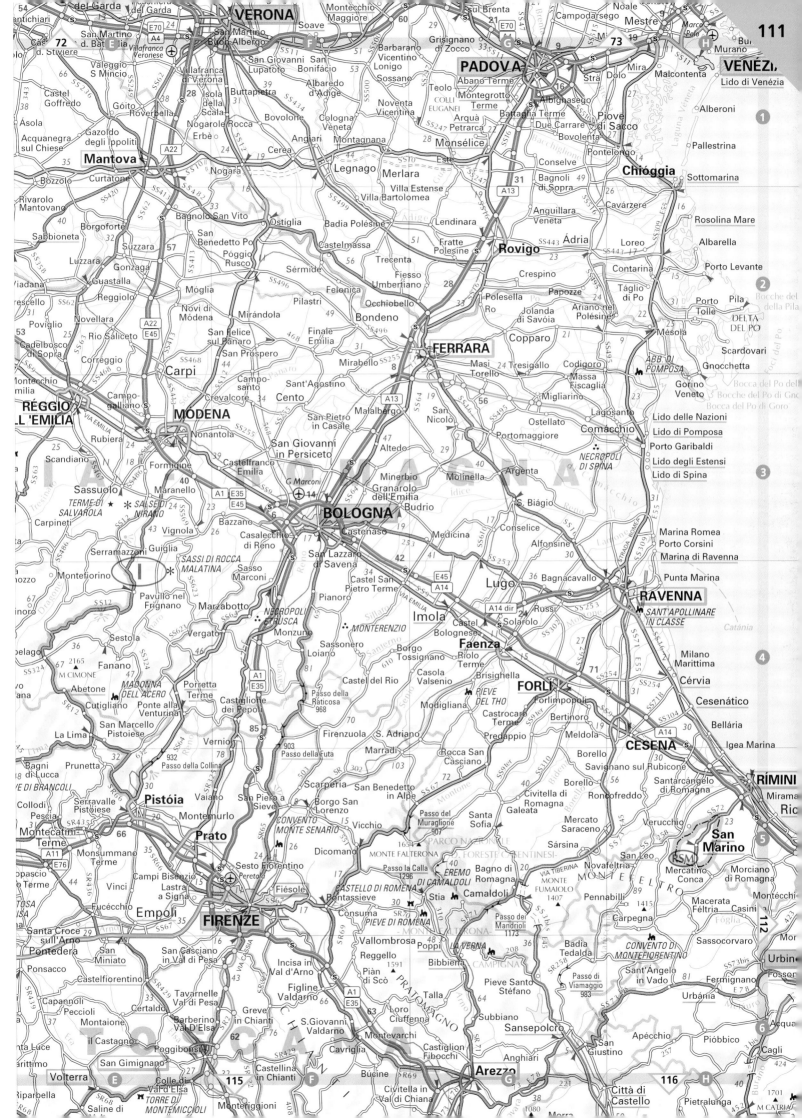

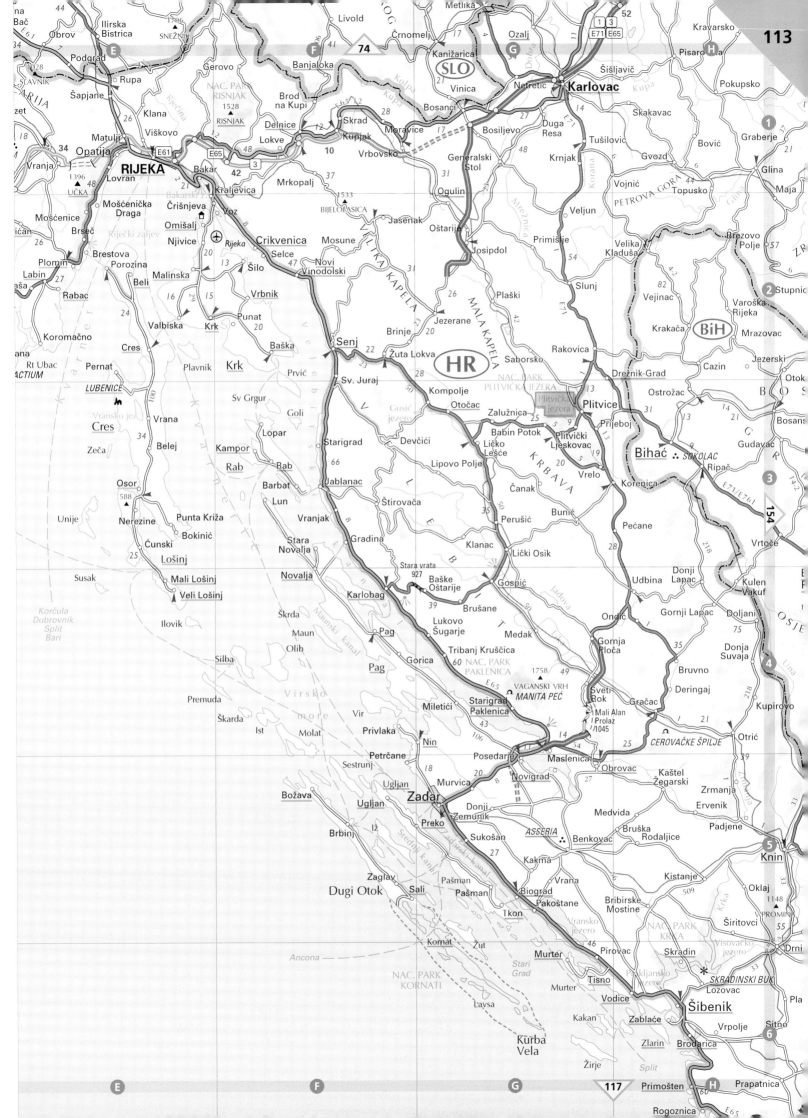

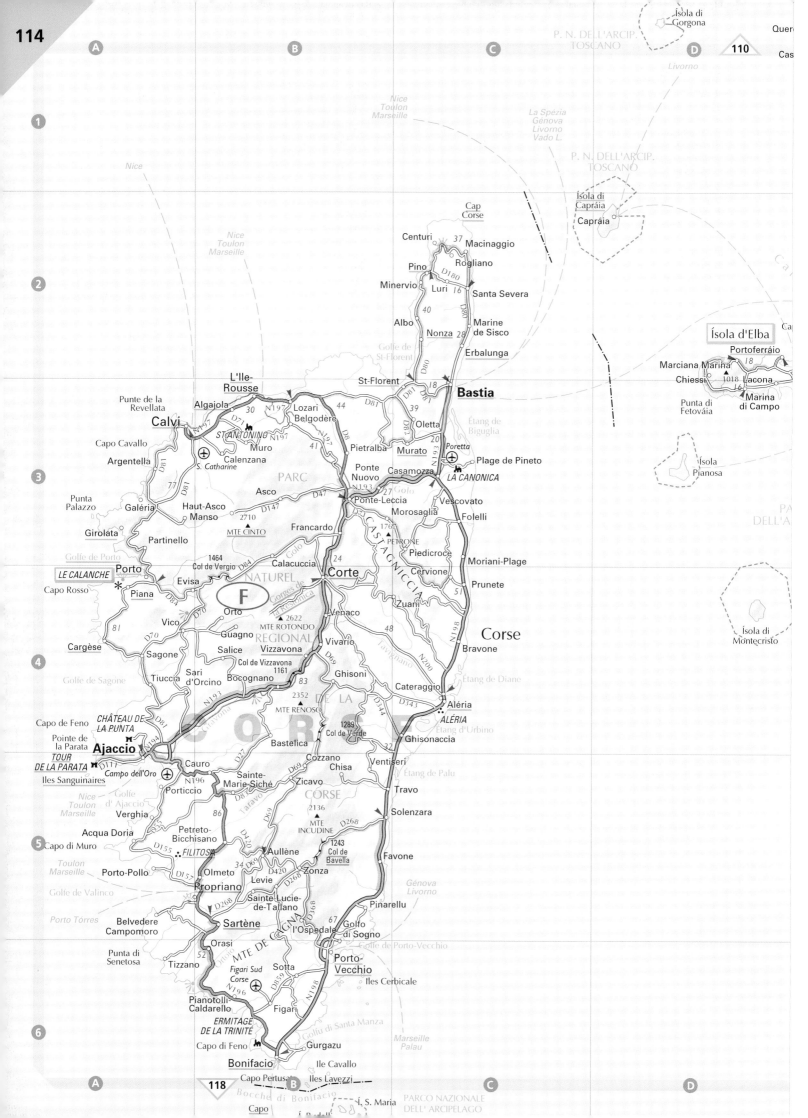

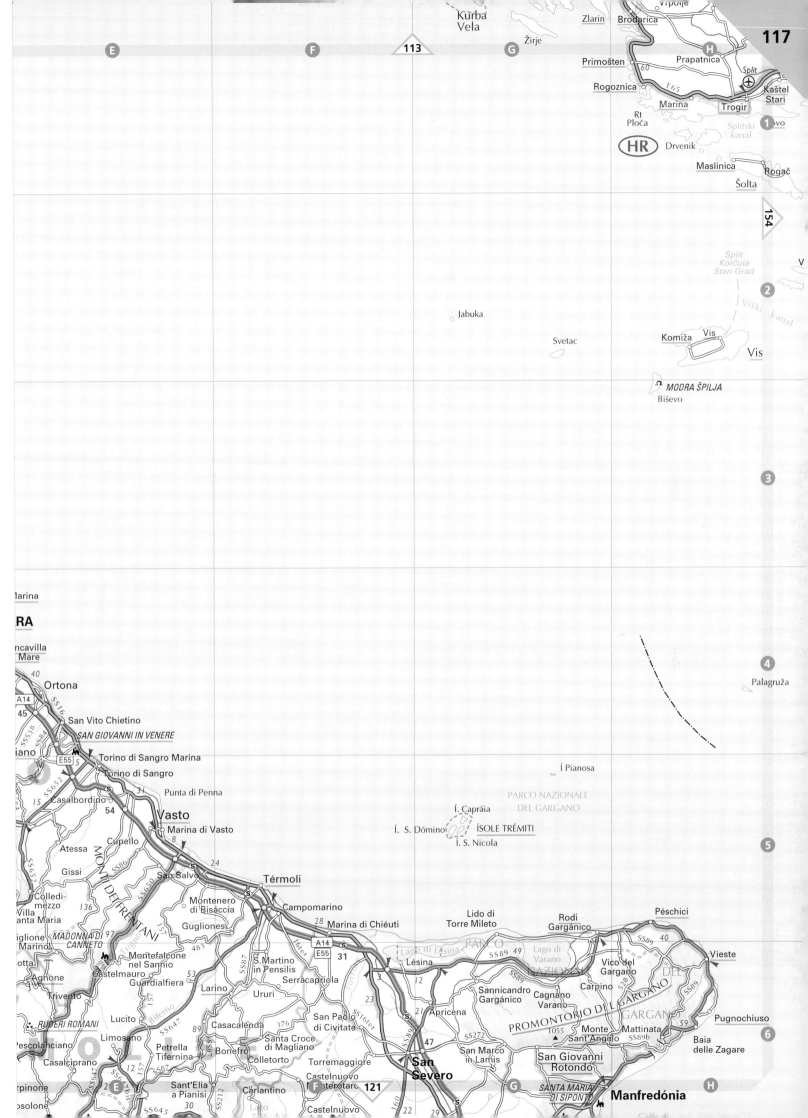

Kūrba Vela

Žirje

Zlarin
Brodarica

E
F
113
G

Primošten
Prapatnica

Rogoznica
E65
Split

Marina
Trogir
Kaštel Stari

Rt Ploča

Splitski kanal

1

HR
Drvenik

Maslinica
Rogač

Šolta

154

Split
Korčula
Stari Grad

V

Viški kanal

2

Jabuka

Komiža
Vis

Svetac
Vis

MODRA ŠPILJA
Biševo

3

4
Palagruža

Marina

RA

ncavilla
Mare

40

Ortona

A14

45
SS16

SS538

San Vito Chietino

SS84

SAN GIOVANNI IN VENERE

iano
E55
5
Torino di Sangro Marina

SS652

Torino di Sangro

Í Pianosa

s
31
Punta di Penna

15
SS80

Casalbordino
PARCO NAZIONALE
DEL GARGANO

54
Vasto

Í. Capráia

Cupello
Marina di Vasto

Atessa
8
Í. S. Dómino
ÍSOLE TRÉMITI

SS86
Í. S. Nicola

Gissi
SS652

24

SS650
San Salvo

Colledi-
mezzo
Montenero
di Bisáccia

Términi

Villa
anta Maria

136
Campomarino

iglione
MADONNA DI
CANNETO

s

Lido di
Torre Mileto

Rodi
Gargánico

Péschici

Marino
157

28
Marina di Chiéuti

SS89
40

ottal

483
Lago di Lésina

PARCO

Lago di
Varano

Vieste

Agnone
Montefalcone
nel Sannio

SS87

S.Martino
in Pensilis

A14
E55
31

Lésina

SS89
49

NAZIONA

Vico del
Gargano

DEL

Trivento
Castelmauro
Guardialfiera

53

Serracapriola

12
SS89

Carpino

Larino

Ururi
23

Sannicandro
Gargánico
Cagnano
Varano

RUDERI ROMANI
Biferno

Lucito

SS647
89

Casacalenda

376

San Paolo
di Civitate

SS161ter

21
Apricena

PROMONTORIO DEL GARGANO
GARGAN

59

Pugnochiuso

escolanciano

Limosano

Santa Croce
di Magliano

47
1055
Monte
Sant'Angelo

Mattinata

SS89b

Petrella
Tifernina

Bonefro
Colletorto

Torremaggiore

San Marco
in Lamis

San Giovanni
Rotondo

Baia
delle Zagare

Casalciprano

Castelnuovo

E
F
121
G

SANTA MARIA
DI SIPONTO

H

rpinone

Sant'Elia
a Pianisi

Cárlantino

30

Castelnuovo

Manfredónia

Sardegna

Corse

Costa Smeralda

PARCO NAZIONALE DELL' ARCIPELAGO DE LA MADDALENA

SASSARI

Nuoro

Alghero

Porto Torres

Olbia

Castelsardo

Santa Teresa Gallura

Palau

La Maddalena

I. S. Maria

Isola Maddalena

Isola Caprera

Baia Sardinia

Capo Ferro

Porto Cervo

Porto Rotondo

Capriccioli

Golfo di Olbia

Capo Figari

Golfo Aranci

Costa Smeralda

San Teodoro

Budoni

Posada

La Caletta

Cala Liberotto

Capo Comino

Isola Tavolara

Isola Molara

Capo Coda Cavallo

Suaredda

Siniscola

Orosei

Cala Gonone

Dorgali

Galtelli

Oliena

Orgosolo

Mamoiada

Onani

Bitti

Lodè

Lula

Buddusò

Alà dei Sardi

Pattada

Ozieri

Oschiri

Berchidda

Monti

Telti

Loiri

Padru

Cuzzola

MONTE NIEDDU

MONTE ALBO

GALLURA

NURAGHE MAJORI

Tempio Pausania

MONTE LIMBARA

Calangianus

Sant'Antonio di Gallura

Bassacutena

Arzachena

Luogosanto

Aggius

Bortigiadas

Perfugas

Martis

Chiaramonti

TERME DI CASTEL DORIA

Viddalba

Valledoria

Trinità d'Agultu e Vignola

Vignola Mare

Portobello

Capo Testa

Santa Teresa Gallura

Sèdini

SAN PIETRO DI SIMBRANOS

Sorso

Sennori

Osilo

Nulvi

Ploaghe

S.S. TRINITÀ DI SACCARGIA

Codrongianos

Mores

Ardara

Ittireddu

Nughedu San Nicolò

Bultei

Bono

Bottidda

Benetutti

Orune

Osidda

Pattada

Buddusò

LOGUDORO

NUR. S. ANTINE

Torralba

Giave

Cossoine

Bonorva

Semestene

Pozzomaggiore

Padria

Mara

Montresta

Bosa

Suni

Tinnura

Tresnuraghes

Cuglieri

Santa Caterina di Pittinuri

Scano di Montiferro

Sindia

Macomer

Silànus

Bolòtana

Lei

Birori

Borore

Dualchi

Noragugume

Aidomaggiore

Abbasanta

Ghilarza

Sèdilo

NURAGHE SANTA SABINA

Santu Lussurgiu

ABBAZIA DI SANTA MARIA DI CORTE

MONTE FERRU

Villanova Monteleone

Ittiri

Thiesi

Uri

Olmedo

SANTUARIO DI VALVERDE

NECROPOLI ANGHELO RUJU

Alghero

Fertilia

Maristella

Capo Caccia

GROTTA DI NETTUNO

Tramariglio

Porto Conte

Argentiera

Palmadula

Pozzo S. Nicola

Stintino

Capo del Falcone

Fornelli

Cala d'Oliva

Isola Asinara

PARCO NAZIONALE DELL'ISOLA DELL'ASINARA

Punta Caprara o dello Scorno

Capo Càccia

Platamona Lido

SAN MICHELE DI PLAIANU

Golfo dell'Asinara

Capo Marargiu

Bonnànaro

Mannu

Coghinas

Lago del Coghinas

Lago Omodeo

Costa Paradiso

Corse

MTE DE L'OSPEDALE

Sartène

Porto-Vecchio

Bonifacio

Figari

Sotta

Pianotolli-Caldarello

ERMITAGE DE LA TRINITÉ

Capo di Feno

Capo Pertusato

Iles Lavezzi

Ile Cavallo

Gurgazu

Iles Cerbicale

Golfo di Sogno

Colle de Porto-Vecchio

Pinarellu

Sainte-Lucie-de-Tallano

Orasi

Tizzano

Belvedere Campomoro

Punta di Senetosa

Sardinia

Bocche di Bonifacio

i. Budelli

i. Razzoli

i. Spargi

Costa Smeralda

TOMBA DI GARIBALDI

L'ORSO

NUR. RUJU

NUR. PALA E RUGHES

NUR. S. SABINA

Grotta del Bue Marino

PARCO NAZ. GOLFO DI OROSEI

Golfo di Orosei

Serra Orrios

Genova La Spezia Livorno Civitavecchia Piombino

Genova Livorno

Civitavecchia Livorno

Napoli

Propriano Genova

Toulon Marseille

Marseille

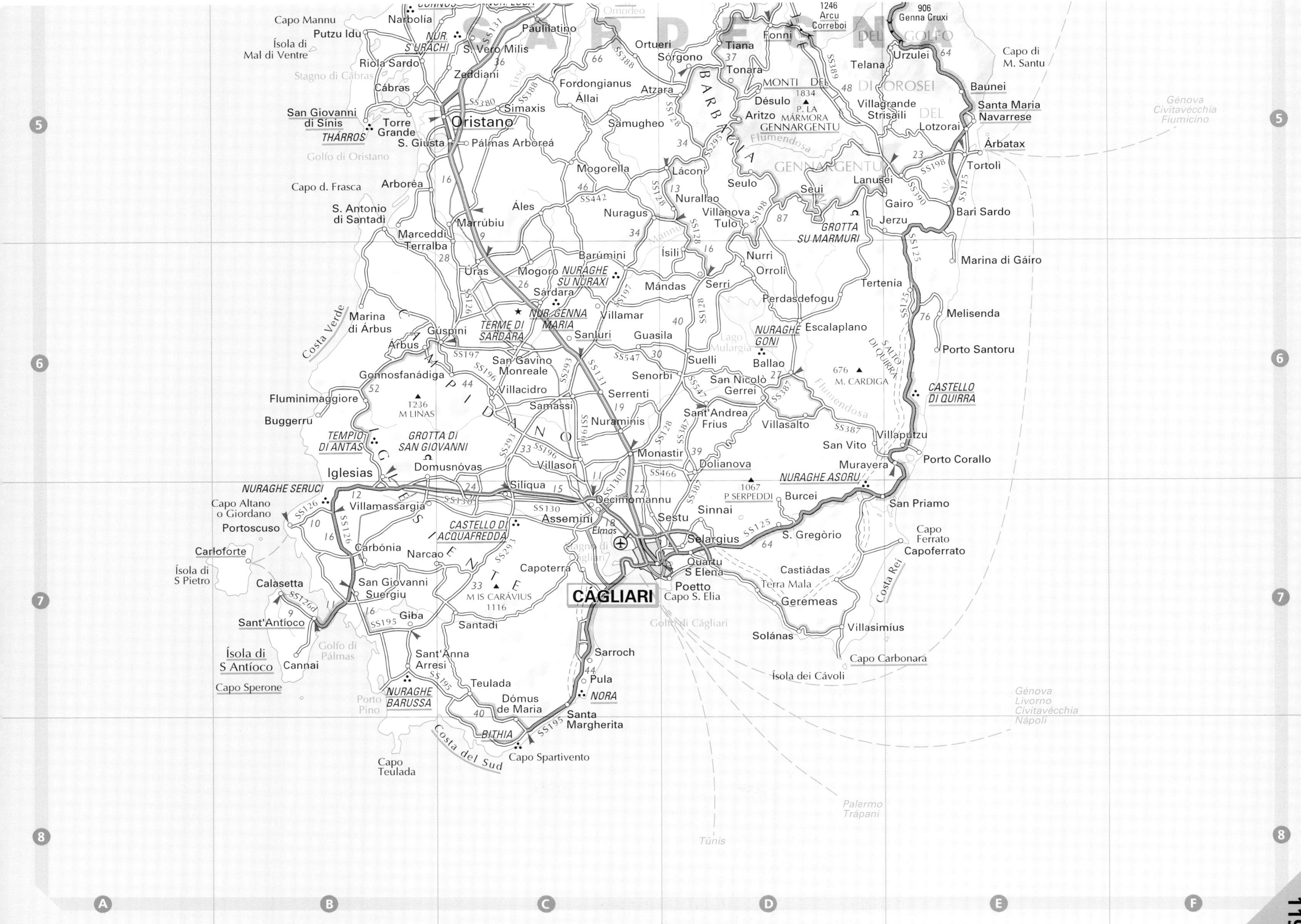

CÁGLIARI

Golfo di Cágliari

Capo Carbonàra
Isola dei Cávoli
Costa Rei
Golfo del

Capo Ferrato
Capoferrato
San Priamo
Porto Corallo
Porto Santoru
Melisenda
CASTELLO DI QUIRRA
Villaputzu
San Vito
Muravera
Villasalto
Villasìmius
Geremeas
Solànas
Castiàdas
Terra Mala
S. Gregòrio
Burcei
NURAGHE ASORU
M. CARDIGA
676
SALTO DI QUIRRA
Tertenia
Jerzu
Gàiro
Lanusei
Seui
GROTTA SU MARMURI
Marina di Gàiro
Bari Sardo
Árbatax
Tortolì
Lotzorai
Santa Maria Navarrese
Baunei
Capo di M. Santu

GOLFO DI OROSEI

Genna Cruxi
906
Arcu Correboi
1246
Fonni
Désulo
1834
P.LA MARMORA GENNARGENTU
MONTI DEL GENNARGENTU
Aritzo
Tonara
Tiana
Ollollai
Sòrgono
Ortueri
Atzara
Sámugheo
Fordongiànus
Àllai
Mogorella
Nuragus
Nurallao
Làconi
Villanova Tulo
Seùlo
Nurri
Orroli
Serri
Gèrrei
San Nicolò Gerrei
NURAGHE GONI
Ballao
Escalaplano
Perdasdefogu
Orroli
Ísili
Mándas
Serrenti
Nuràminis
Monastir
Sèstu
Selàrgius
Quartu
S. Elena
Póetto
Capo S. Elia
Sinnai
Dolianova
P. SERPEDDI
1067
Sant'Andrea Frius
Senòrbi
Suelli
Guasila
Villamar
Sanlùri
Barúmini
NURAGHE SU NURAXI
Villanovafranca
NUR. GENNA MARIA
San Gavino Monreale
Sárdara
TERME DI SÁRDARA
Pabillonis
Mogoro
Masùllas
Ales
Uras
Marrùbiu
Terralba
Arborèa
Marceddì
Pálmas Arboreá
Arbus
CASTELLO DI ACQUAFREDDA
M. LINAS
1236
Góni
Villacidro
Gonnosfanádiga
Guspini
Samàssi
Serramanna
Villasor
Decimomannu
Uta
Assèmini
Elmas
Capoterra
Sarroch
Pula
NORA
Santa Margherita
Domus de Maria
Teulada
BITHIA
Sant'Anna Arresi
Santadi
MIS CARÁVIUS
1116
Narcao
San Giovanni Suérgiu
Giba
NURAGHE BARUSSA
Carbònia
Villamassàrgia
Siliqua
Domusnovas
Iglesias
GROTTA DI SAN GIOVANNI
TEMPIO DI ANTAS
NURAGHE SERUCI
Fluminimaggiore
Buggerru
Marina di Árbus
Costa Verde
Carloforte
Ísola di S Pietro
Capo Altano o Giordano
Portoscuso
Calasetta
Cannai
Sant'Antìoco
Ísola di S Antìoco
Capo Sperone
Porto Pino
Golfo di Pálmas
Capo Teulada
Costa del Sud
Capo Spartivento
Dómus de Maria

Oristano
S. Vero Milis
Zeddiani
Simaxis
Villa Urbana
NUR. S'URACHI
Narbolia
Riola Sardo
Cábras
Torre Grande
San Giovanni di Sinis
THARROS
Stagno di Cábras
Capo Mannu
Ísola di Mal di Ventre
Putzu Idu
Golfo di Oristano
Capo d. Frasca
S. Giusta
S. Antonio di Santadi
Paulilàtino
Fordongiànus

BARBAGIA
SARDEGNA
PIDANO
NURAGHE
VENTE

Génova
Civitavécchia
Fiumicino

Génova
Livorno
Civitavécchia
Nápoli

Palermo
Tràpani

Tunis

Génova
Civitavécchia
Nápoli

SS125
SS198
SS389
SS128
SS131
SS130
SS126
SS195
SS196
SS197
SS293
SS466
SS547
SS387
SS128
SS388
SS442

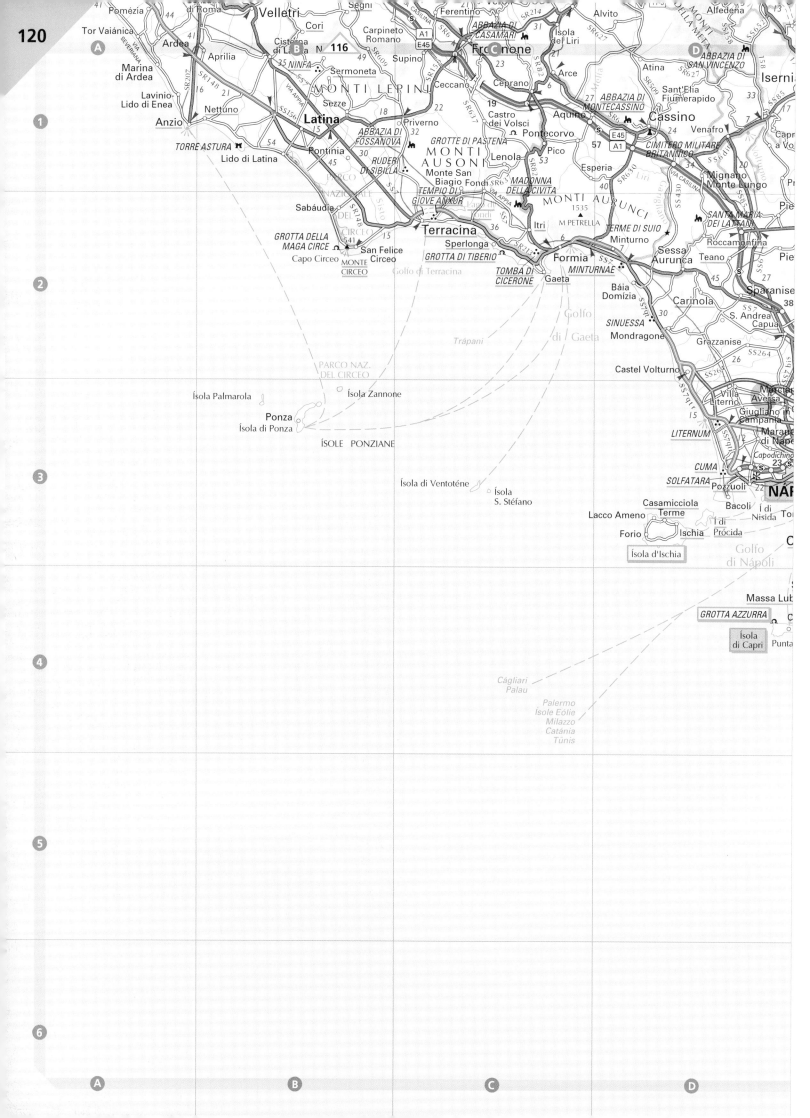

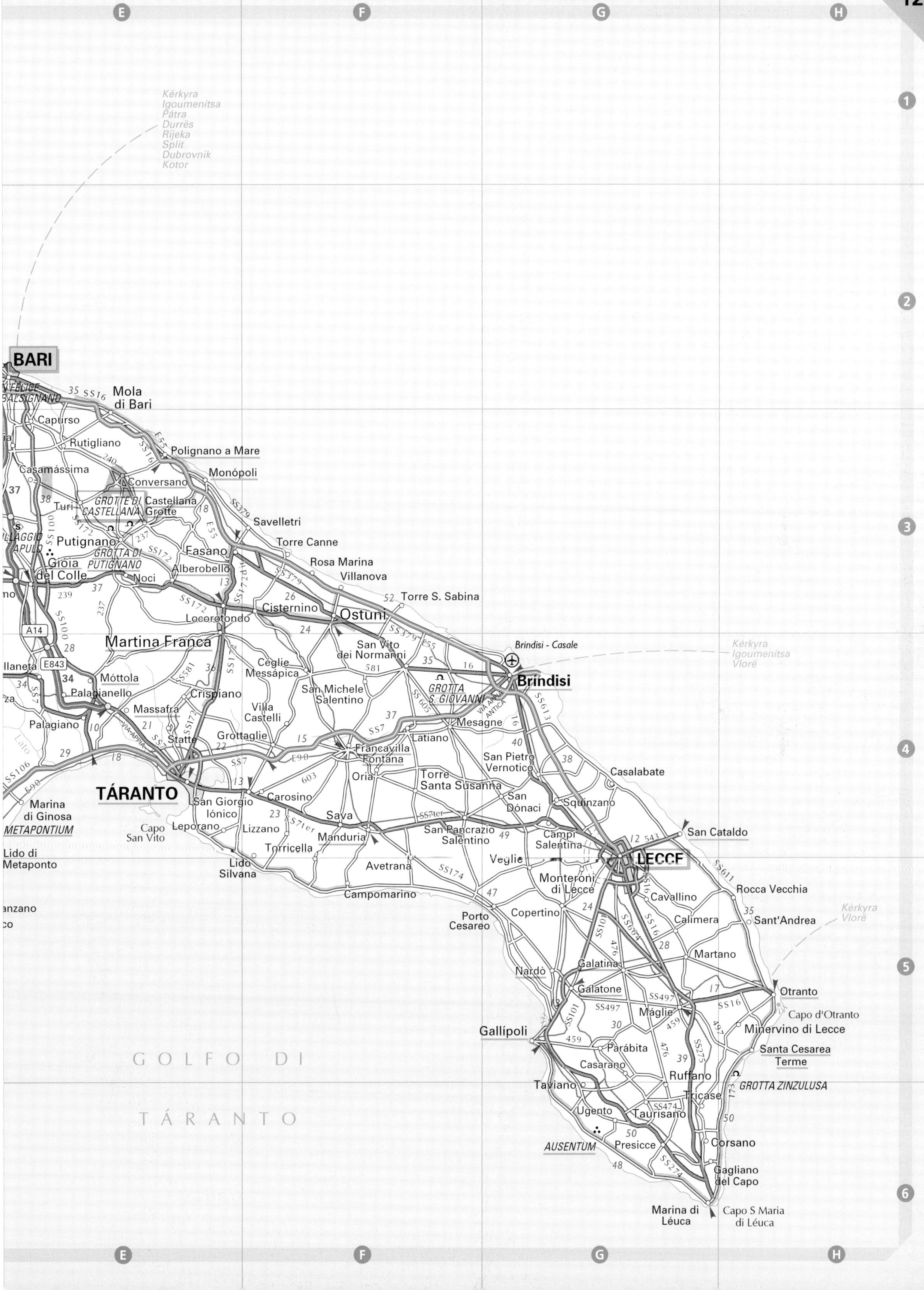

E F G H

1

2

Kérkyra
Igoumenítsa
Pátra
Durrës
Rijeka
Split
Dubrovnik
Kotor

3

BARI

SAN FELICE
A BALSIGNANO
35 SS16 Mola
di Bari
Capurso
Rutigliano Polignano a Mare
240 SS16
Casamássima Monópoli
Conversano
37 *GROTTE DI* Castellana
38 Turi *CASTELLANA* Grotte
VILLAGGIO SS172 Savelletri
APULO Putignano 237 SS172
Gióia *GROTTA DI* Fasano Torre Canne
del Colle *PUTIGNANO* Alberobello Rosa Marina
Noci Villanova
239 37 Locorotondo 26 52 Torre S. Sabina
Planeta 28 Martina Franca 24 Cisternino SS379
E843 San Vito Ostuni
34 Móttola dei Normanni *Brindisi - Casale*
Palagianello Cegle 581 35 16
Crispiano Messápica San Michele *GROTTA* **Brindisi**
Massafra Salentino *S. GIOVANNI* SS613
Palagiano Villa SS605 Mesagne 16
10 Statte Castelli 37 *VIA APPIA* SS16
29 18 Grottaglie 15 Francavilla Latiano 40
TÁRANTO 22 Fontana San Pietro 38
13 603 Oria Torre Vernotico Casalabate
Marina San Giorgio Carosino Santa Susanna San
di Ginosa Iónico 23 SS71ter Sava Dónaci Squinzano
METAPONTIUM Leporano Lizzano Manduria San Pancrazio 49 Campi 12 543 San Cataldo
Capo Torricella Salentino Salentina **LECCE**
Lido di San Vito Lido Avetrana SS174 Veglie SS611 Rocca Vecchia
Metaponto Silvana 47 Monteroni Cavallino 35 Sant'Andrea
Campomarino di Lecce 24 Calimera
Porto Copertino 28 Martano *Kérkyra*
Cesareo 476 *Vloré*
Nardò Galatina 17 Otranto
GOLFO *DI* Galatone SS497 SS16 Capo d'Otranto
Gallípoli SS101 SS497 Máglie 459 Minervino di Lecce
30 459 Santa Cesarea
TÁRANTO Parábita 39 SS275 Terme
459 Casarano Ruffano *GROTTA ZINZULUSA*
Taviano Tricase 50
Ugento SS474 Taurisano
AUSENTUM 50 Presicce Corsano
48 SS274 Gagliano
del Capo
Marina di Capo S Maria
Léuca di Léuca

4

5

6

E F G H

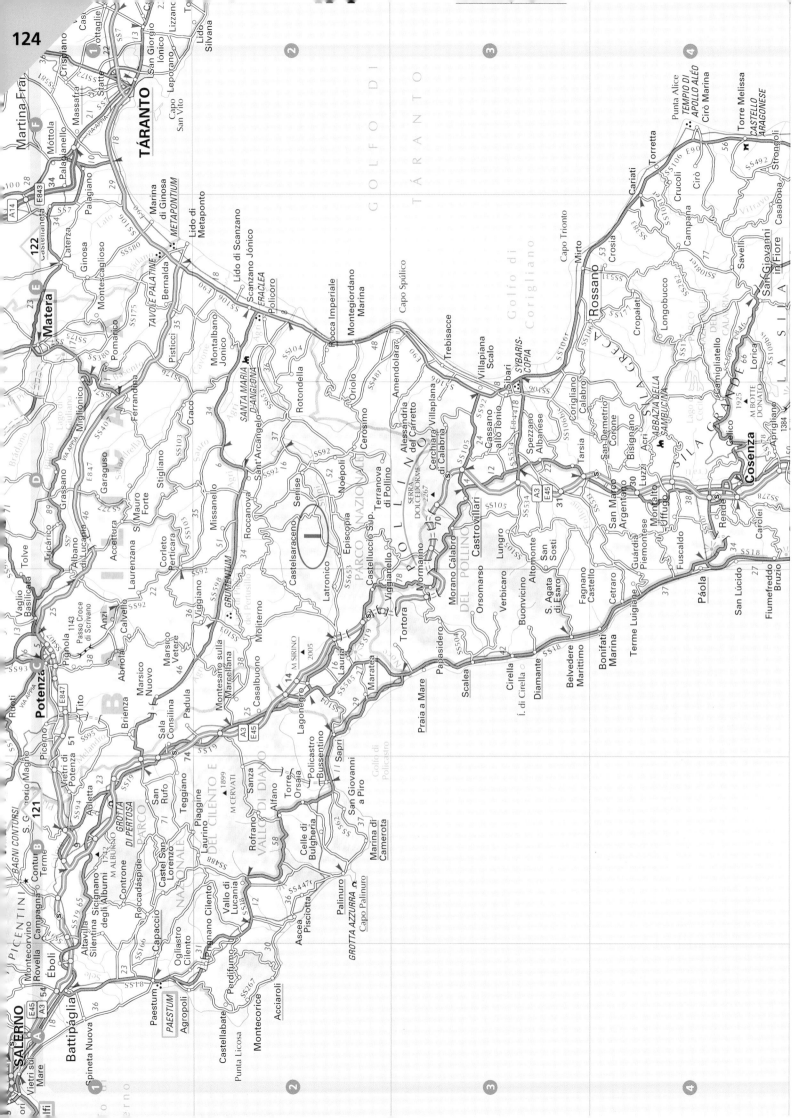

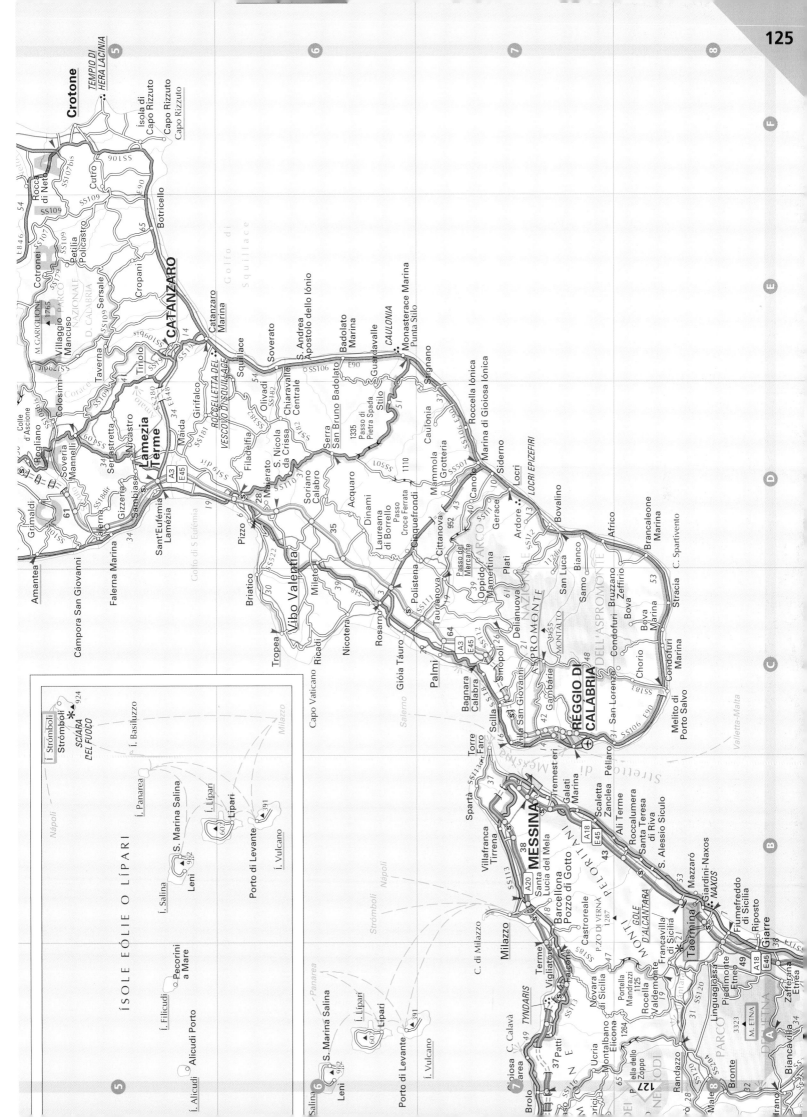

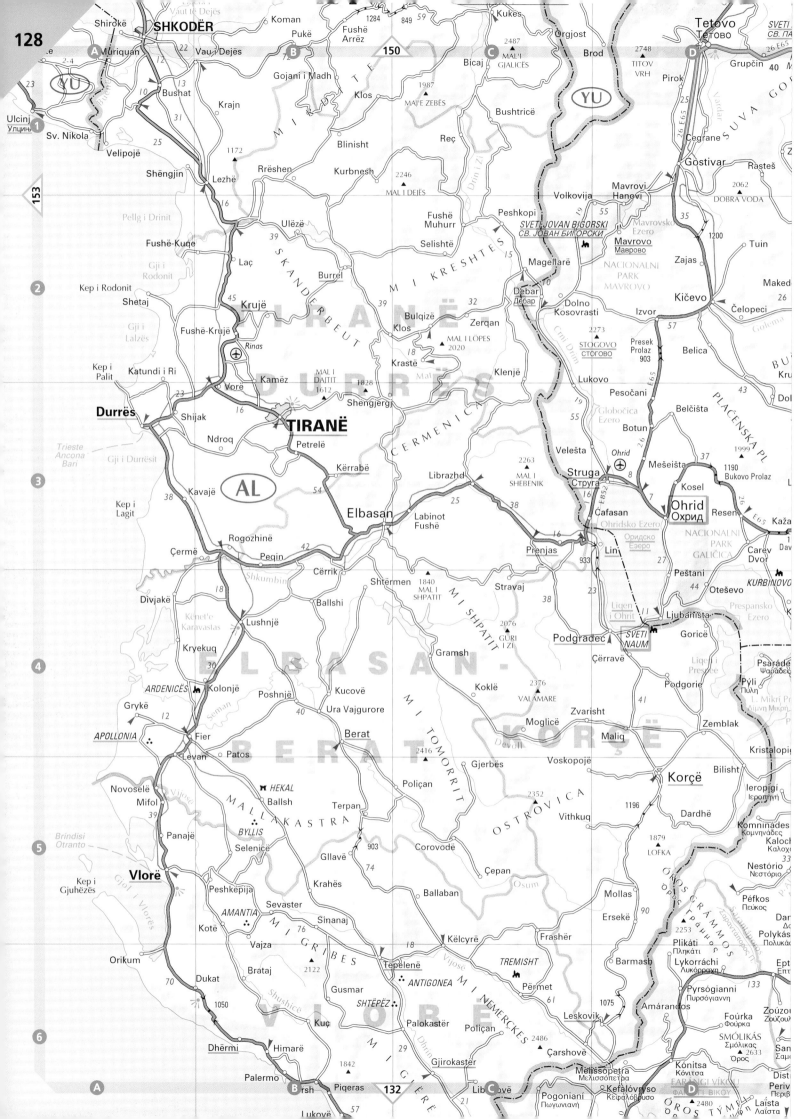

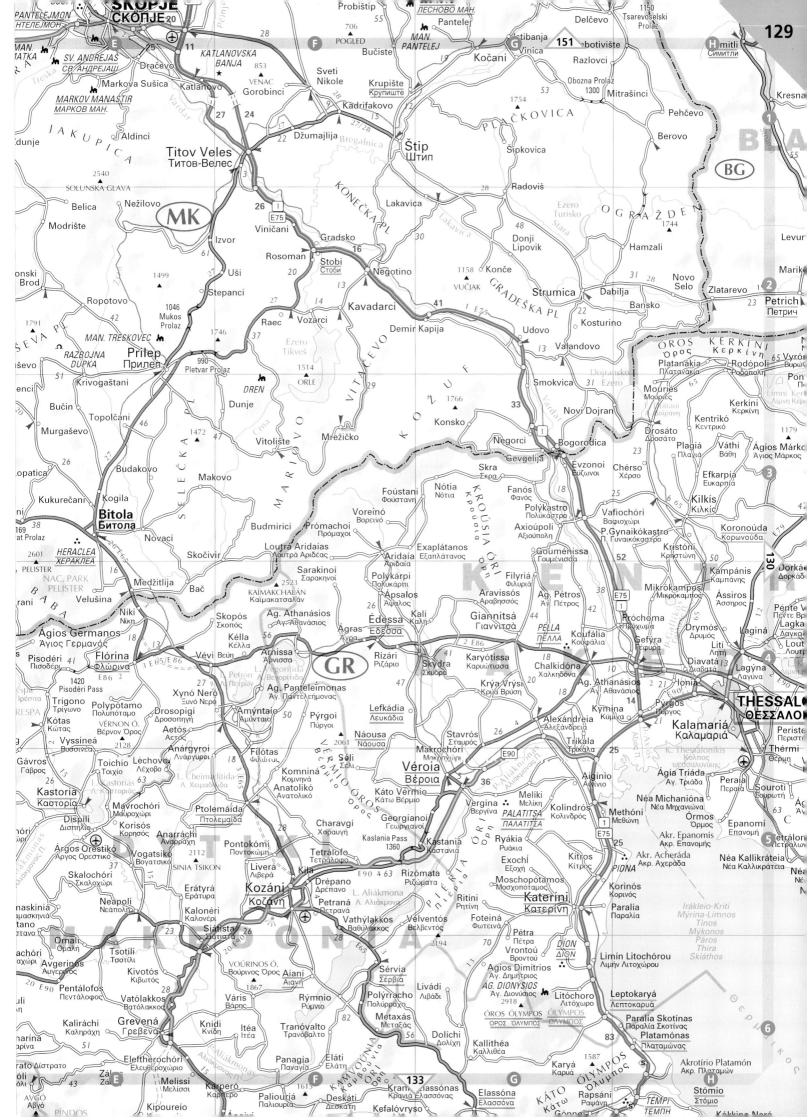

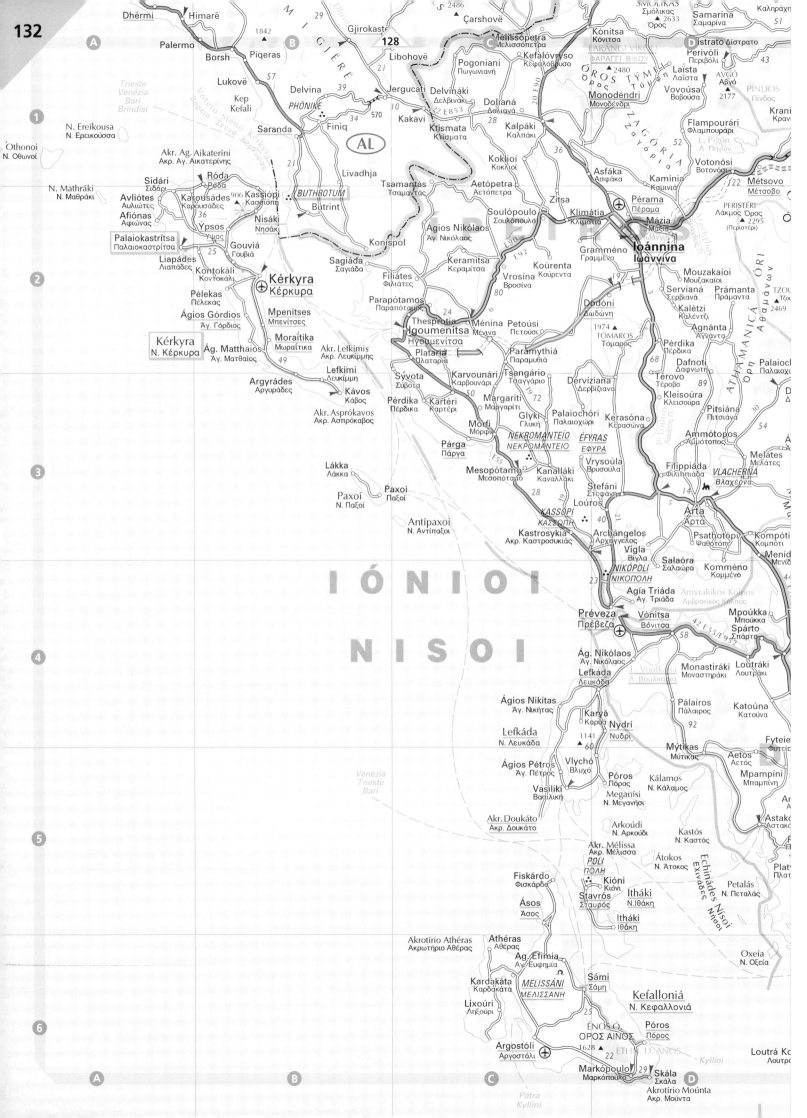

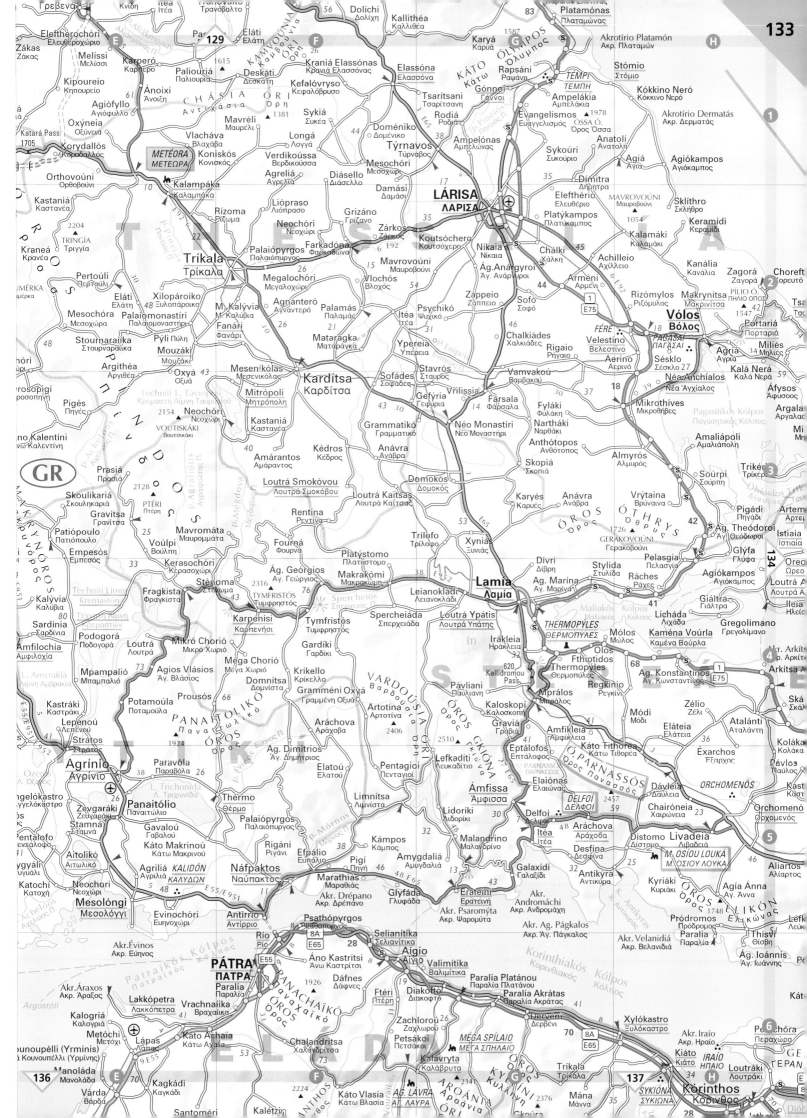

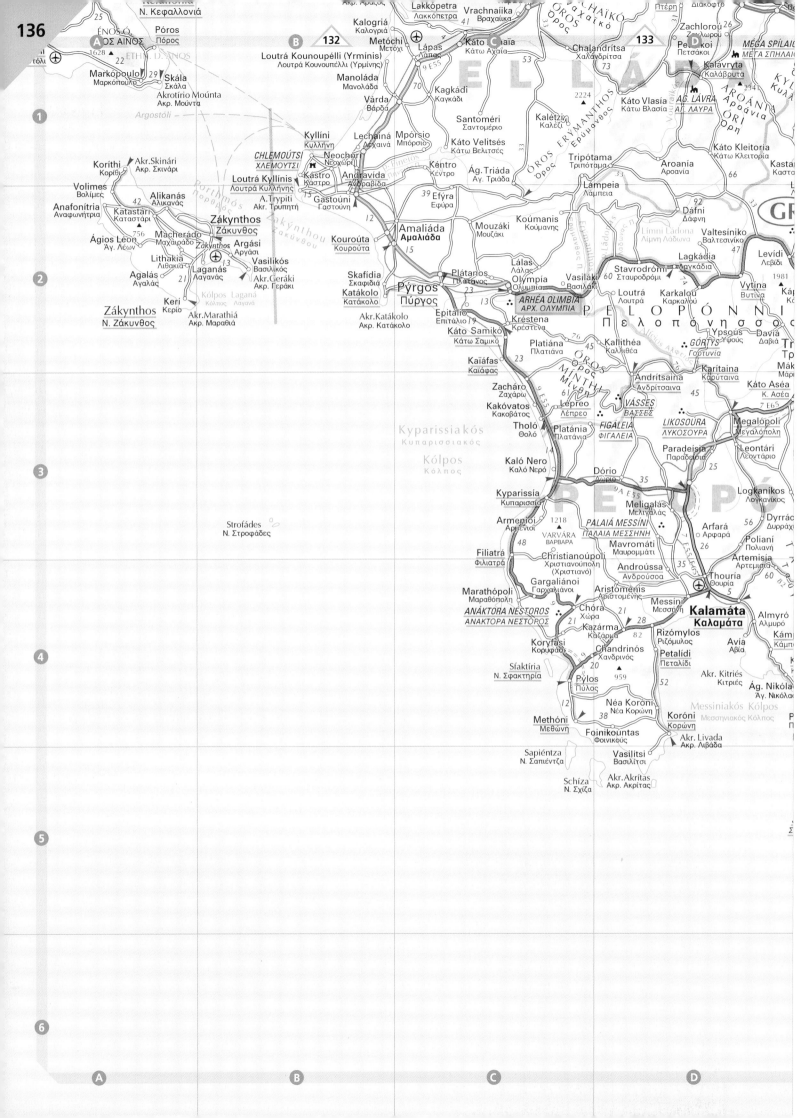

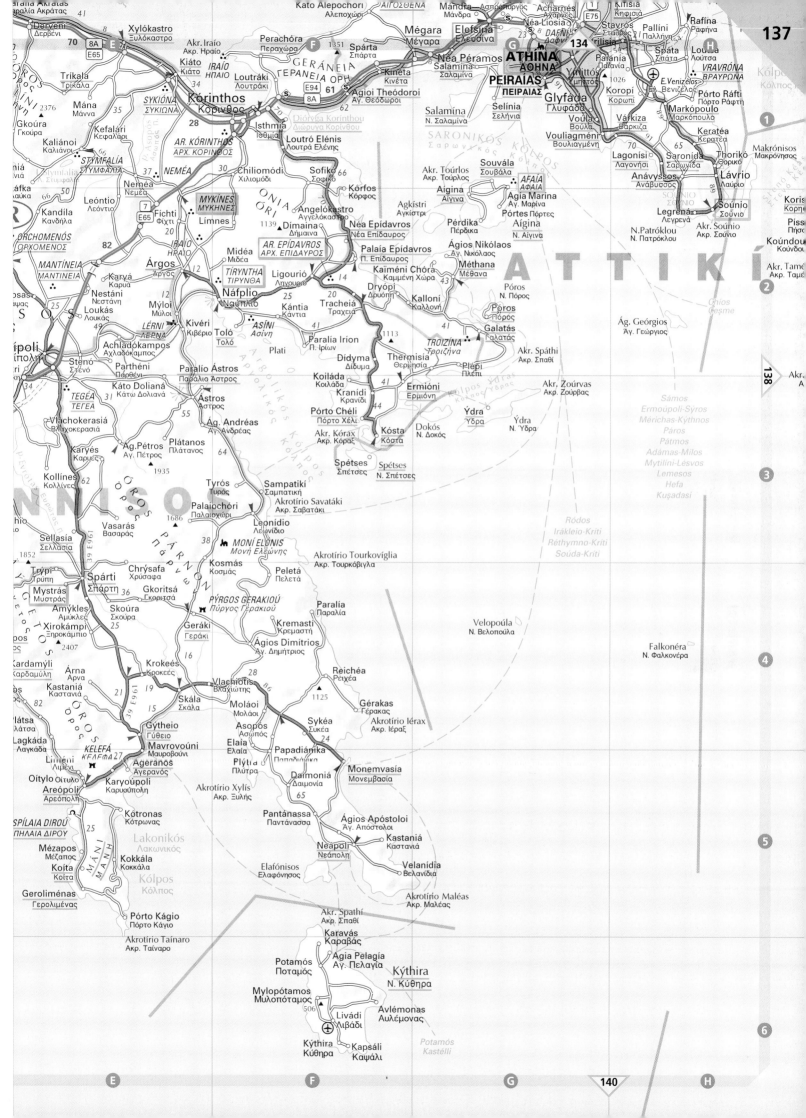

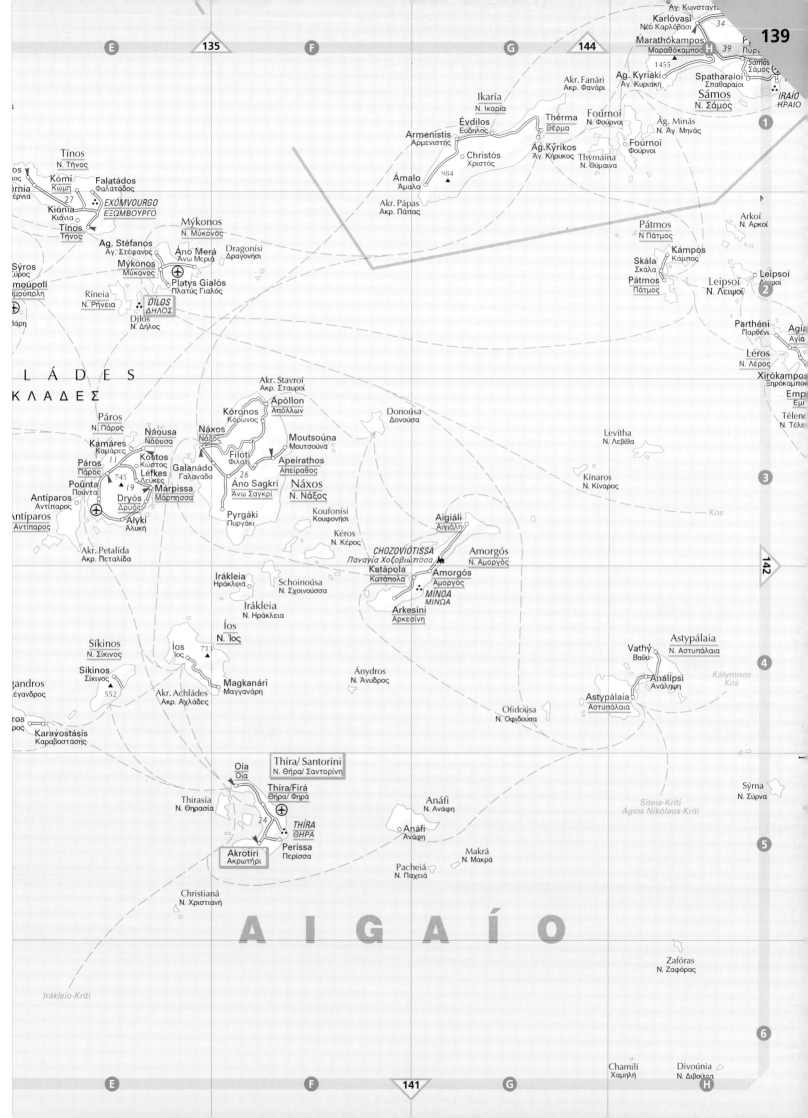

Ἀγ. Κωνσταντῖ
Karlóvasi
Néo Karlóvasi
Νέο Καρλόβασι   34
Marathókampos
Μαραθόκαμπος   39   Πύργ
1455   Sámos
Σάμος
Ag. Kyriakí
Αγ. Κυριακή   Spatharaíoi
Σπαθαραίοι   IRAÍO
ΗΡΑΙΟ
Sámos
Ν. Σάμος
Akr. Fanári
Ακρ. Φανάρι
Ikaría
Ν. Ικαρία   Fourní
Ν. Φούρνοι
Évdilos   Thérma   Àg. Minás
Armenístis   Εύδηλος   Θέρμα   Ν. Άγ. Μηνάς
Αρμενιστής   Fourní
Foúrnoi
Christós   Αγ. Κήρυκος   Φούρνοι
Χριστός   Ág. Kýrikos
Thymaína
Ámalo   984   Ν. Θύμαινα
Άμαλο

Akr. Pápas   Arkoí
Akr. Pápas   Ν. Αρκοί
Ακρ. Πάπας   Pátmos
Ν Πάτμος   Leipsoí
Kámpos   Ν. Λειψοί
Κάμπος   Leipsoí
Skála
Σκάλα
Pátmos   Parthéni   Agia
Πάτμος   Παρθένι   Αγία
Léros
Syros   Ν. Λέρος
Σύρος
μούπολι   Xirókampos
Ξηρόκαμπος   Emp
Εμ
Téle
Ν. Τέλε

Tínos
Ν. Τήνος
Kómi   Falatádos
Κώμη   Φαλατάδος
nia   27
ernia   Kiónia   EXÓMVOURGO
Κιόνια   ΕΞΩΜΒΟΥΡΓΟ   Mýkonos
Tínos   Ν. Μύκονος
Τήνος   Dragonísi
Ag. Stéfanos   Άνο Merá   Δραγονήσι
Αγ. Στέφανος   Άνω Μεριά
Mýkonos   Platýs Gialós
Μύκονος   Πλατύς Γιαλός
Syros   Ríneia
Σύρος   Ν. Ρήνεια   DÍLOS
μούπολι   ΔΗΛΟΣ
άρη   Dílos   LÁDES   Donoúsa
Ν. Δήλος   ΚΛΑΔΕΣ   Δονούσα   Levítha
Ν. Λεβίθα
Akr. Stavroí
Ακρ. Σταυροί
Páros   Kóronos   Apóllon   Kínaros
Ν. Πάρος   Κόρωνος   Απόλλων   Ν. Κίναρος
Náousa   Náxos   Kos
Kamáres   Νάουσα   Νάξος   Moutsoúna
Καμάρες   11   Filóti   Μουτσούνα
Páros   Kóstos   Φιλότι
Πάρος   745   Κώστος   Léfkes   Apeírathos
Roúnta   Galanádo   Απείραθος
Πούντα   19   Λεύκες   Γαλανάδο   26
Antíparos   Dryós   Márpissa   Áno Sagkrí   Náxos   Aigiáli
Αντίπαρος   Δρυός   Μάρπισσα   Άνω Σαγκρί   Ν. Νάξος   Αιγιάλη
Antíparos   Alykí   Pyrgáki   Koufonísi   Amorgós
Αντίπαρος   Αλυκή   Πυργάκι   Κουφονήσι   CHOZOVIÓTISSA   Ν. Αμοργός
Akr. Petalída   Panagía Χοζοβιώτισσα
Ακρ. Πεταλίδα   Kéros   Παναγία Χοζοβιώτισσα
Ν. Κέρος   Katápola   Amorgós
Κατάπολα   Αμοργός
Irákleia   MÍNOA
Ηράκλεια   Schoinoúsa   ΜΙΝΩΑ
Ν. Σχοινούσσα   Arkesíni
Irákleia   Αρκεσίνη
Ν. Ηράκλεια
Íos   Ánydros   Astypálaia
Ν. Ίος   Ν. Άνδρος   Vathý   Ν. Αστυπάλαια
Síkinos   Βαθύ
Ν. Σίκινος   Íos   713   Kálymnos
Ίος   Ofidoúsa   Kos
Síkinos   Ν. Οφιδούσα   Análipsi
Σίκινος   Magkanári   Ανάληψη
gandros   552   Μαγκανάρη   Astypálaia
έγανδρος   Akr. Achládes   Αστυπάλαια
Ακρ. Αχλάδες
ros   Karavostásis   Sýrna
Καραβοστάσις   Ν. Σύρνα

Thíra/ Santoríni
Oía   Ν. Θήρα/ Σαντορίνη
Οία   Siteía-Kríti
Thíra/Firá   Ágios Nikólaos-Kríti
Thirasía   Θήρα/ Φηρά   Anáfi
Ν. Θρασία   Ν. Ανάφη
24   THÍRA
ΘΗΡΑ   Anáfi   Makrá
Akrotíri   Períssa   Ανάφη   Ν. Μακρά
Ακρωτήρι   Περίσσα   Pacheiá
Ν. Παχειά
Christianá   Zafóras
Ν. Χριστιανή   Ν. Ζαφόρας

A I G A Í O

Irákleio-Kríti   Chamilí   Divoúnia
Χαμηλή   Ν. Διβούνια

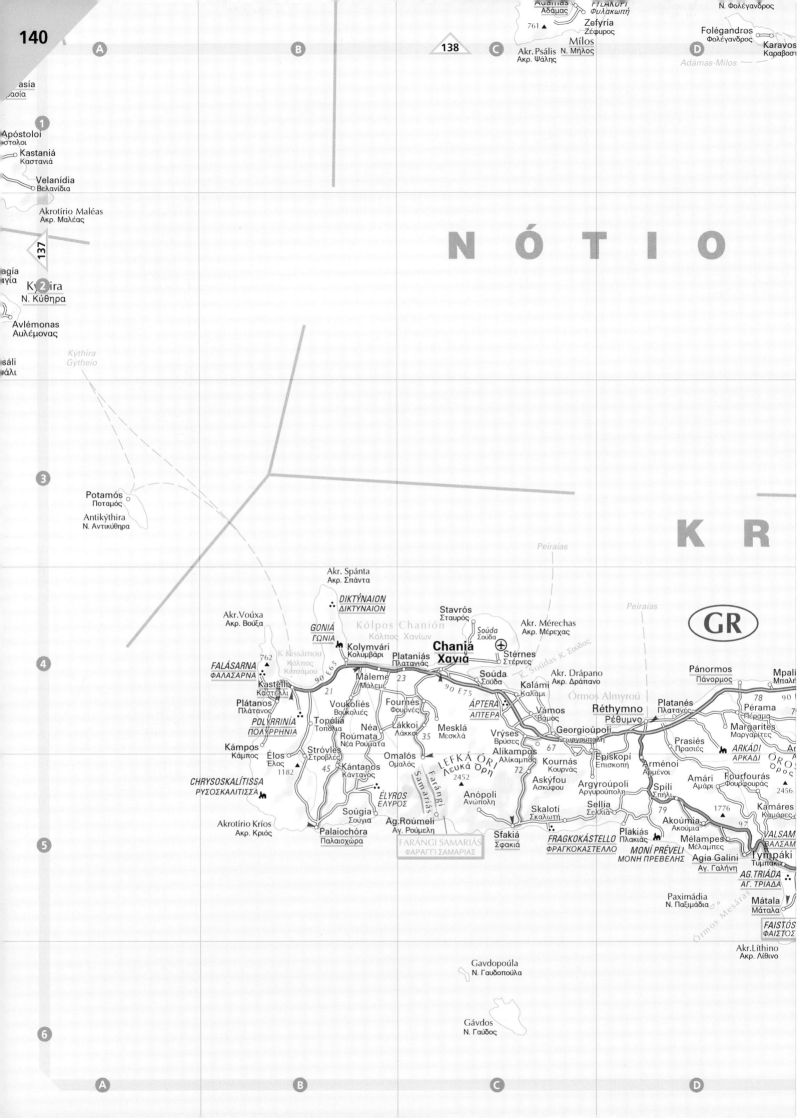

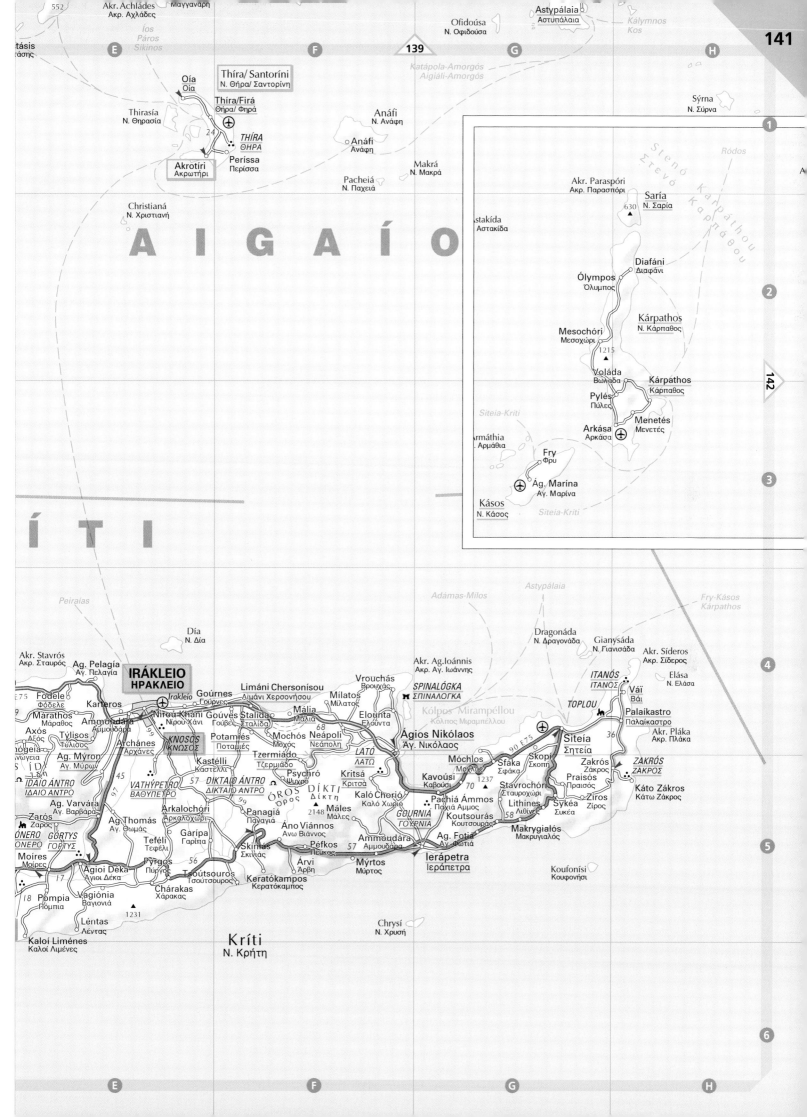

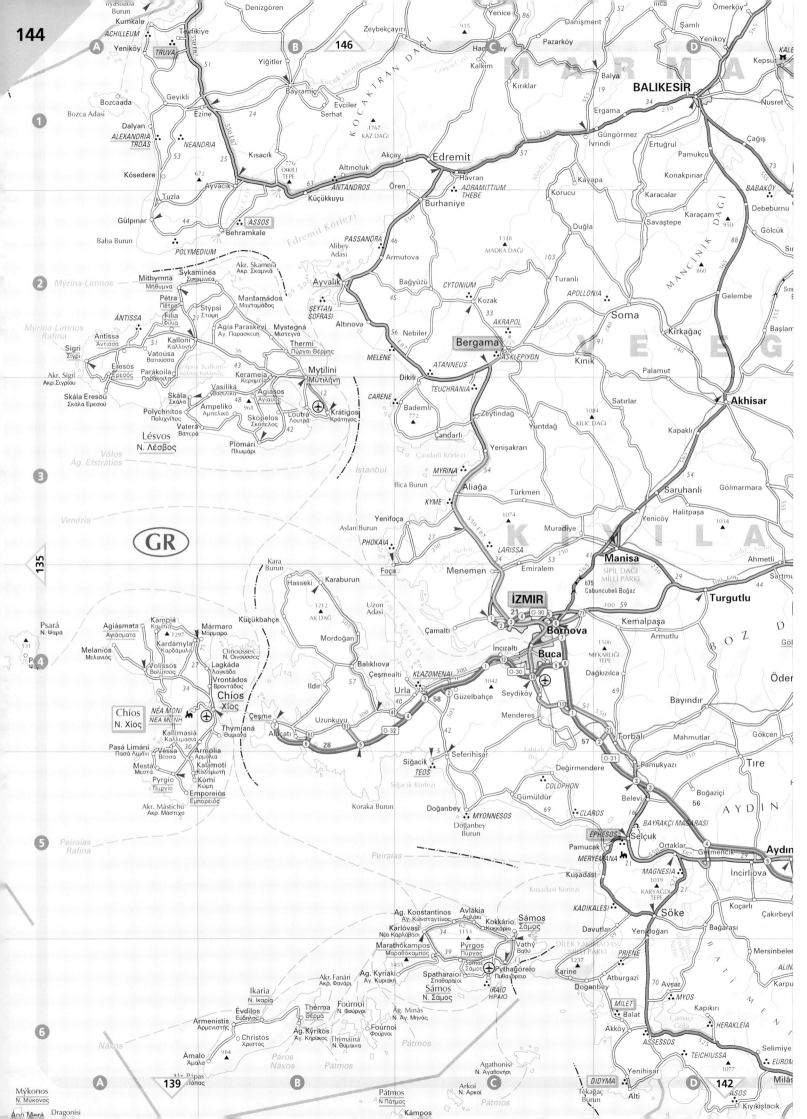

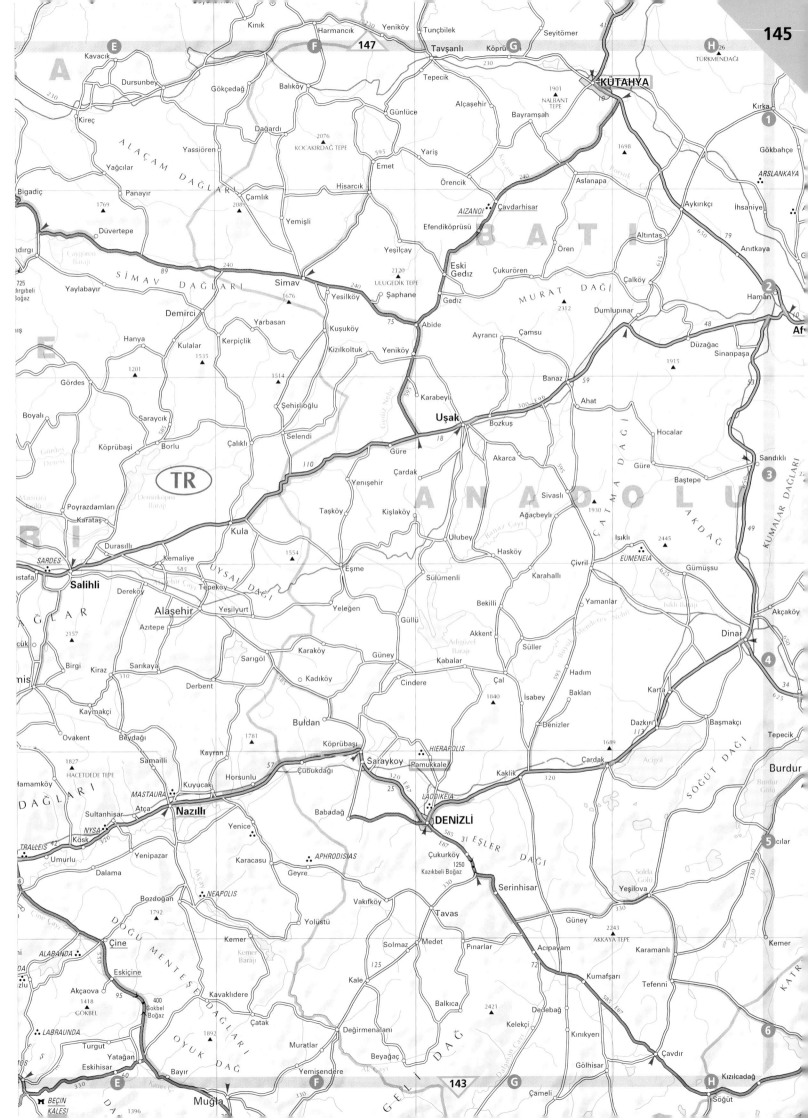

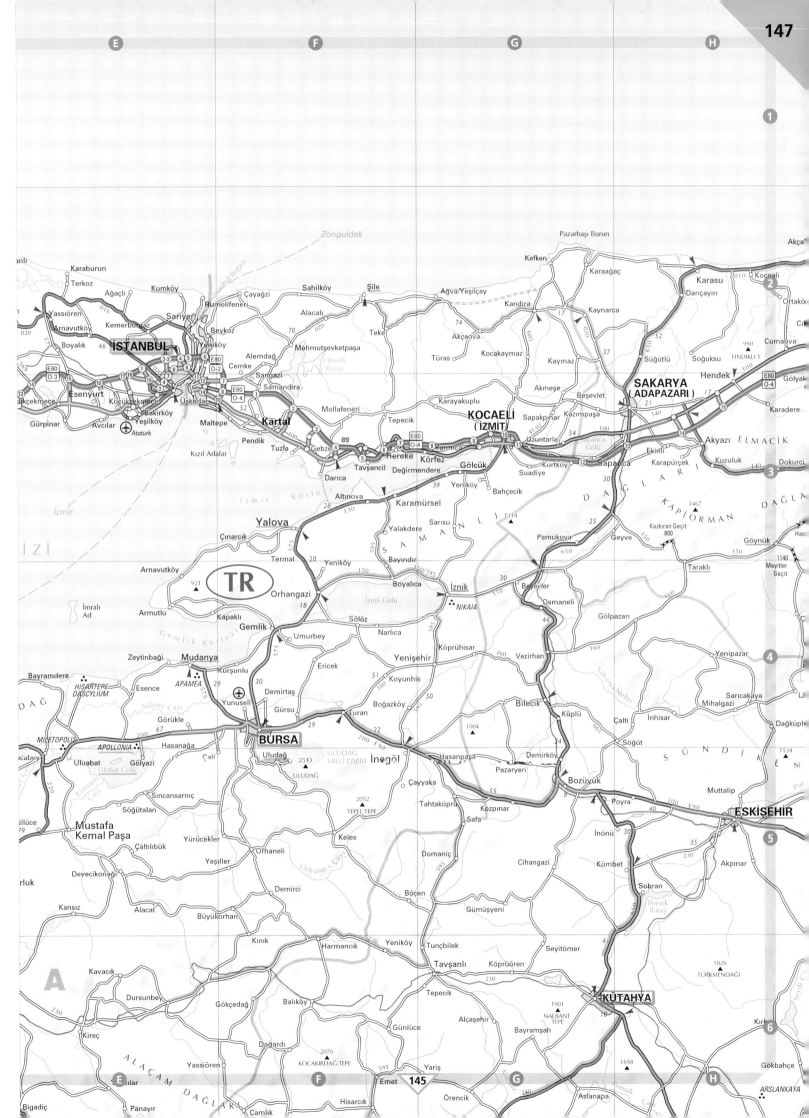

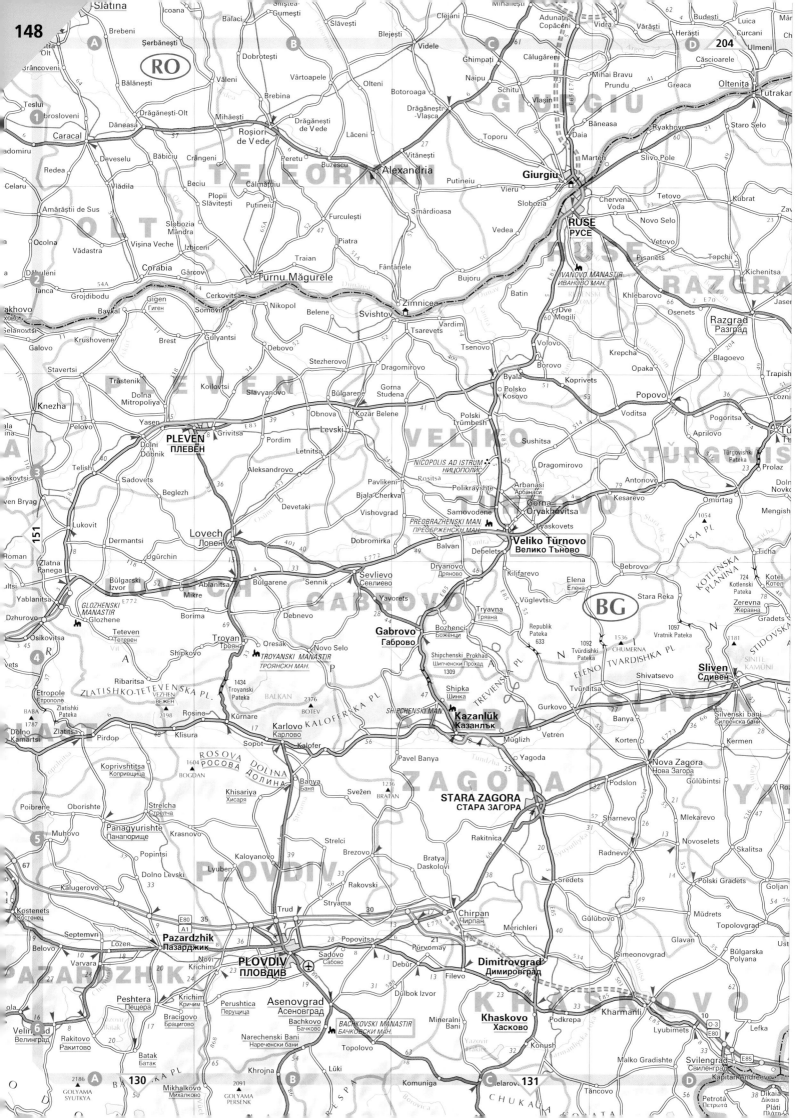

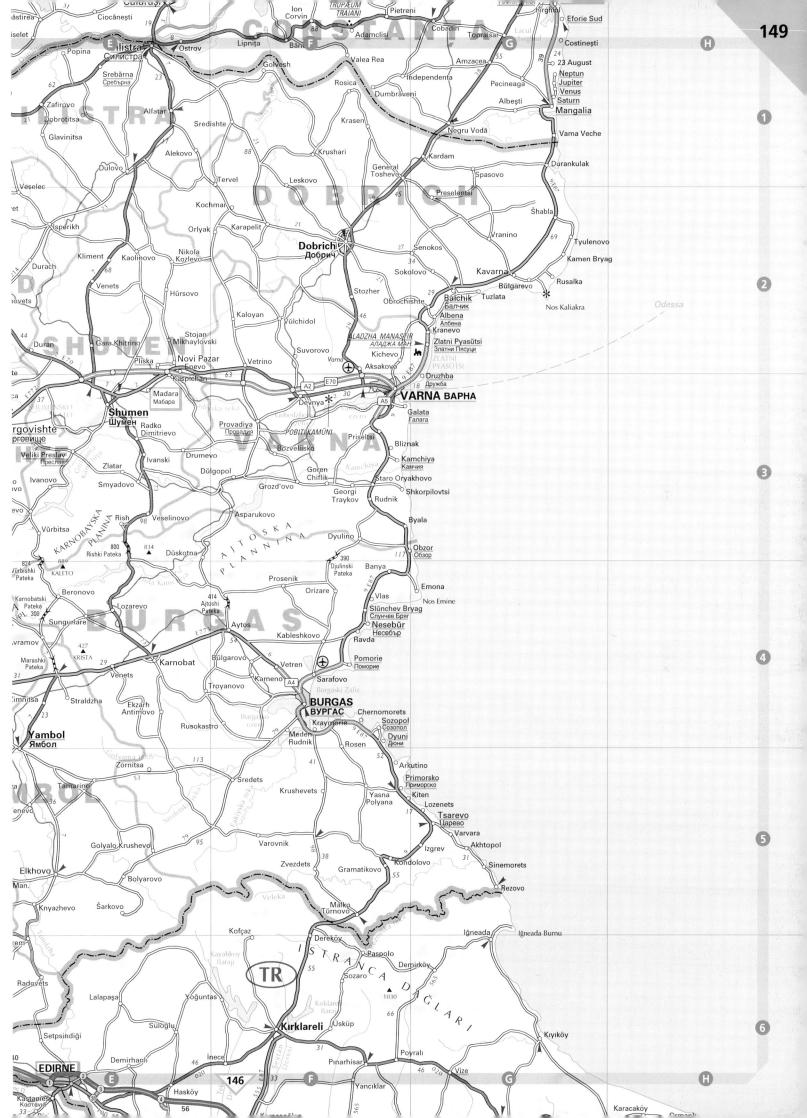

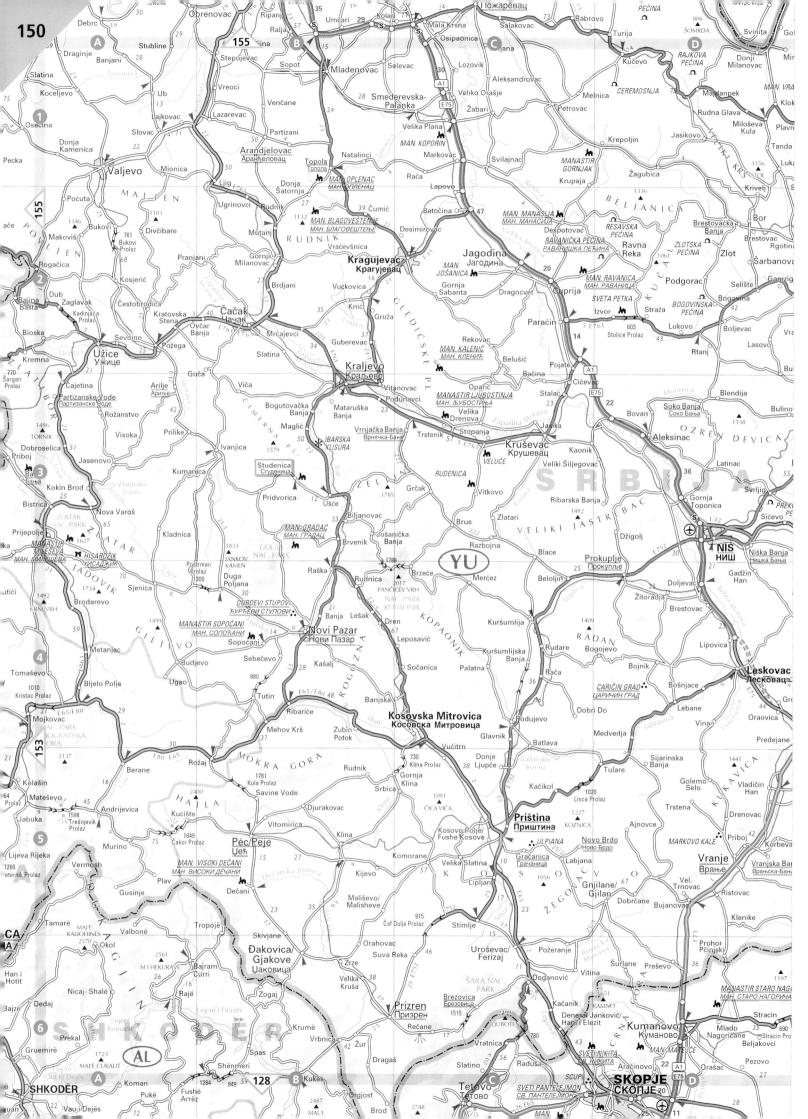

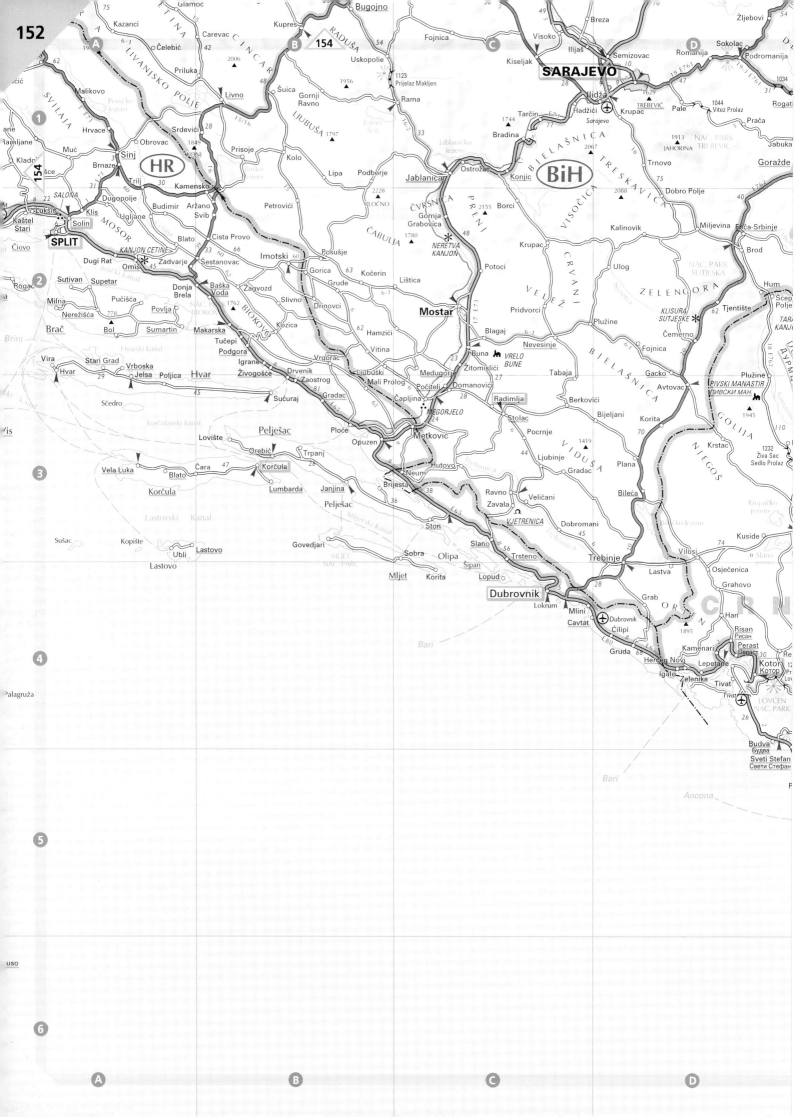

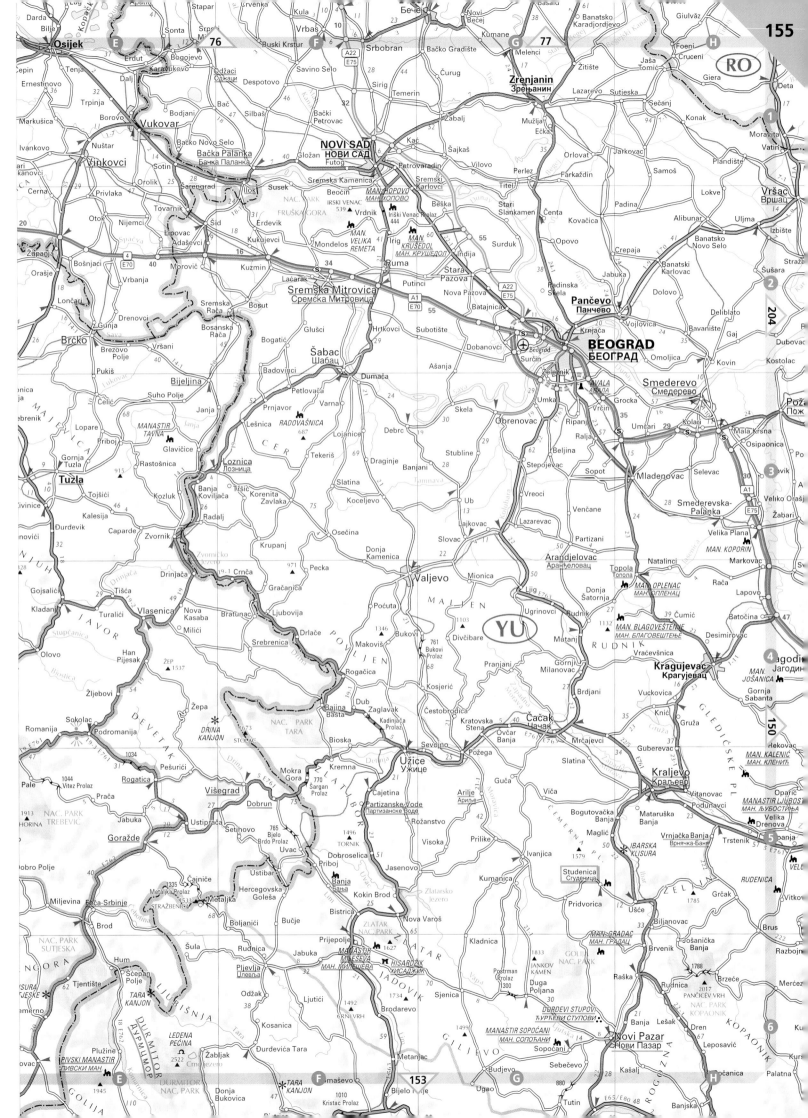

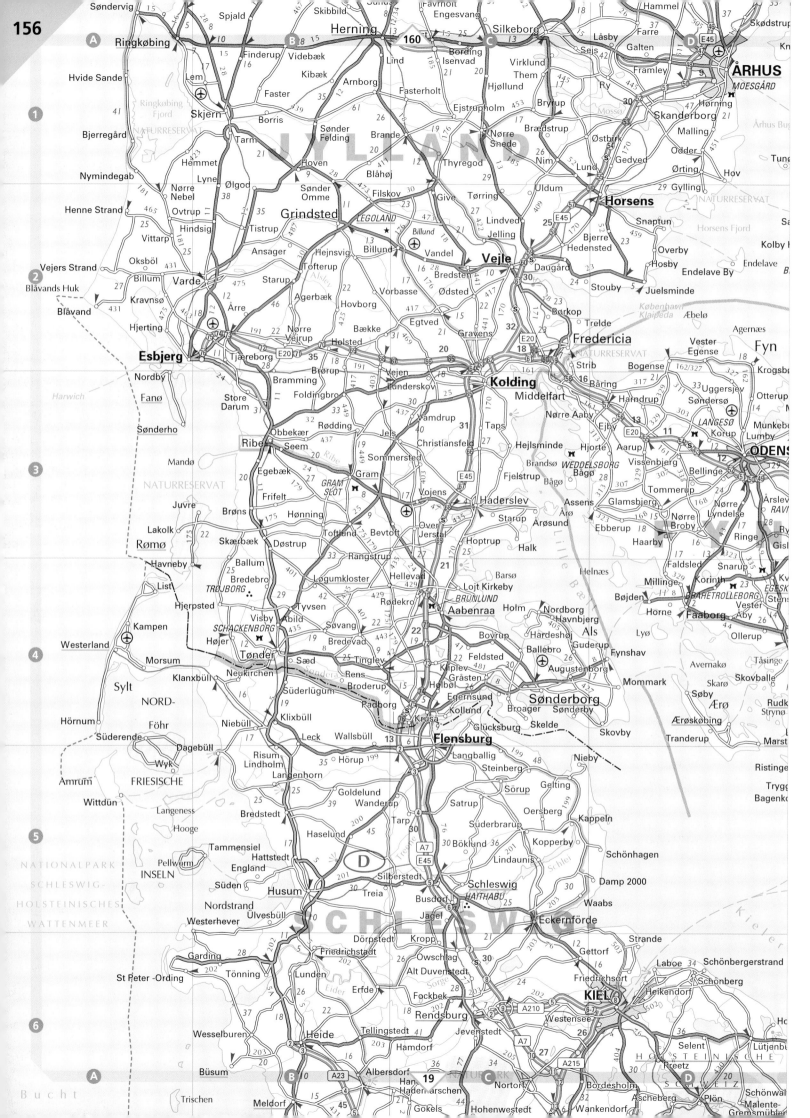

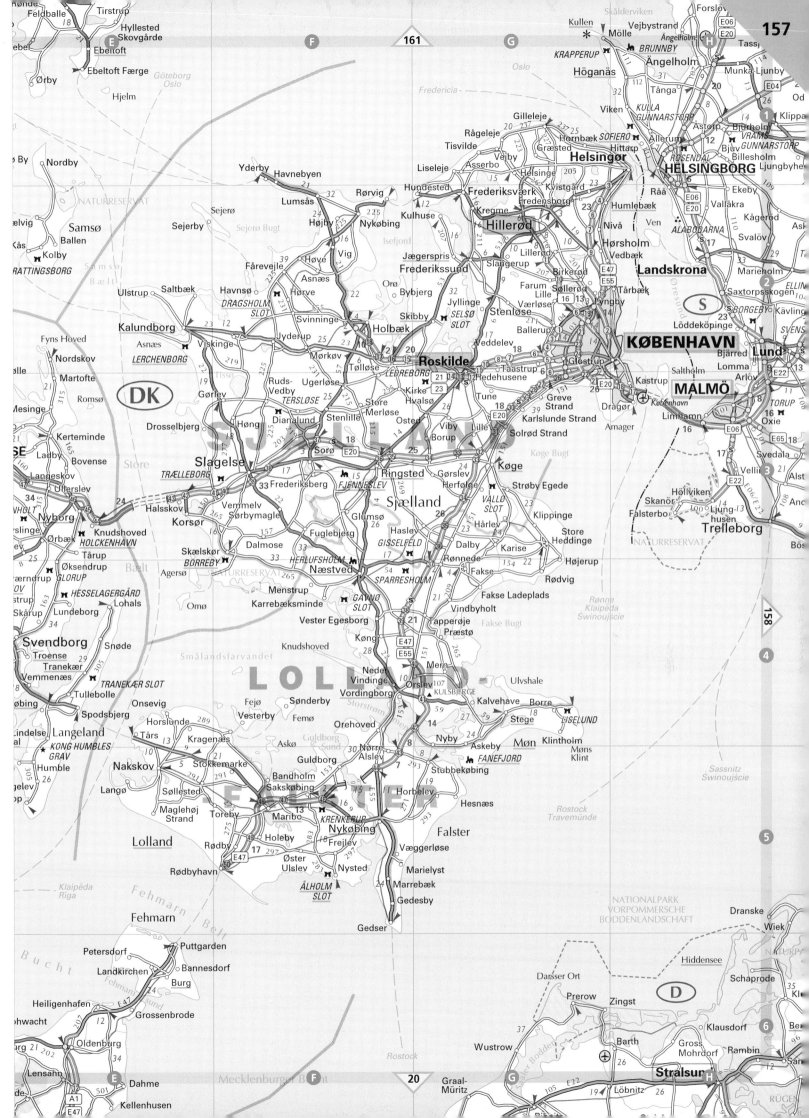

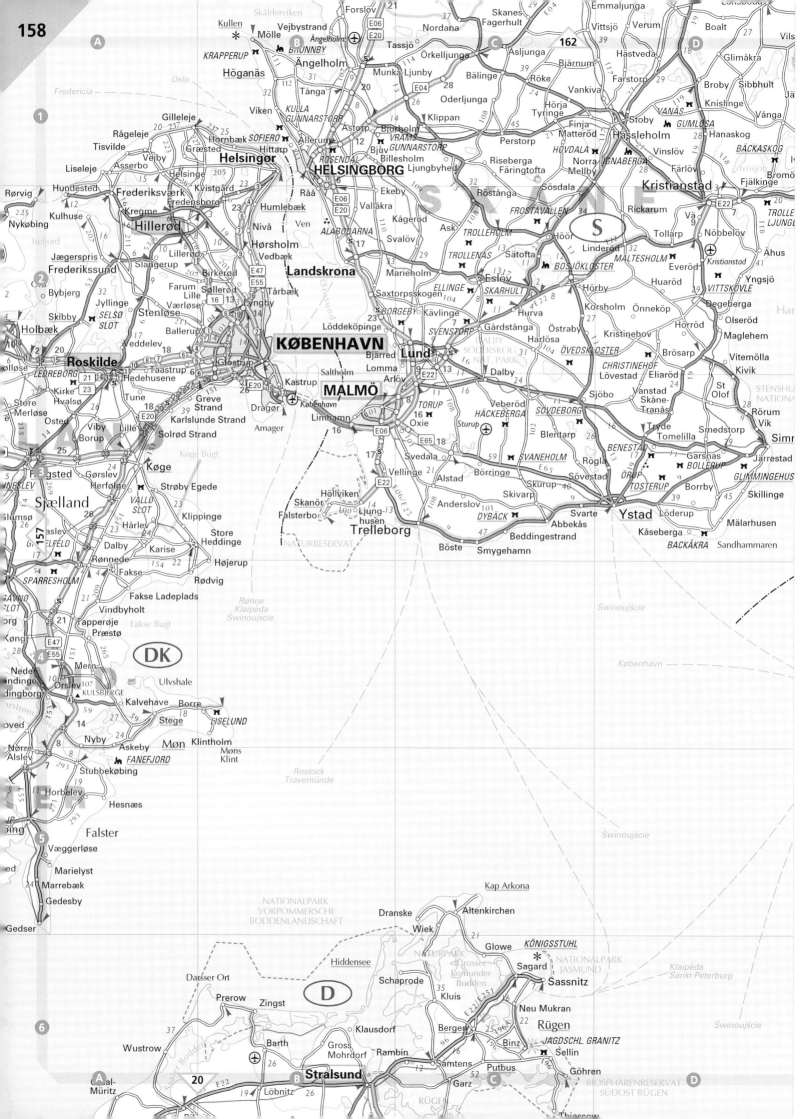

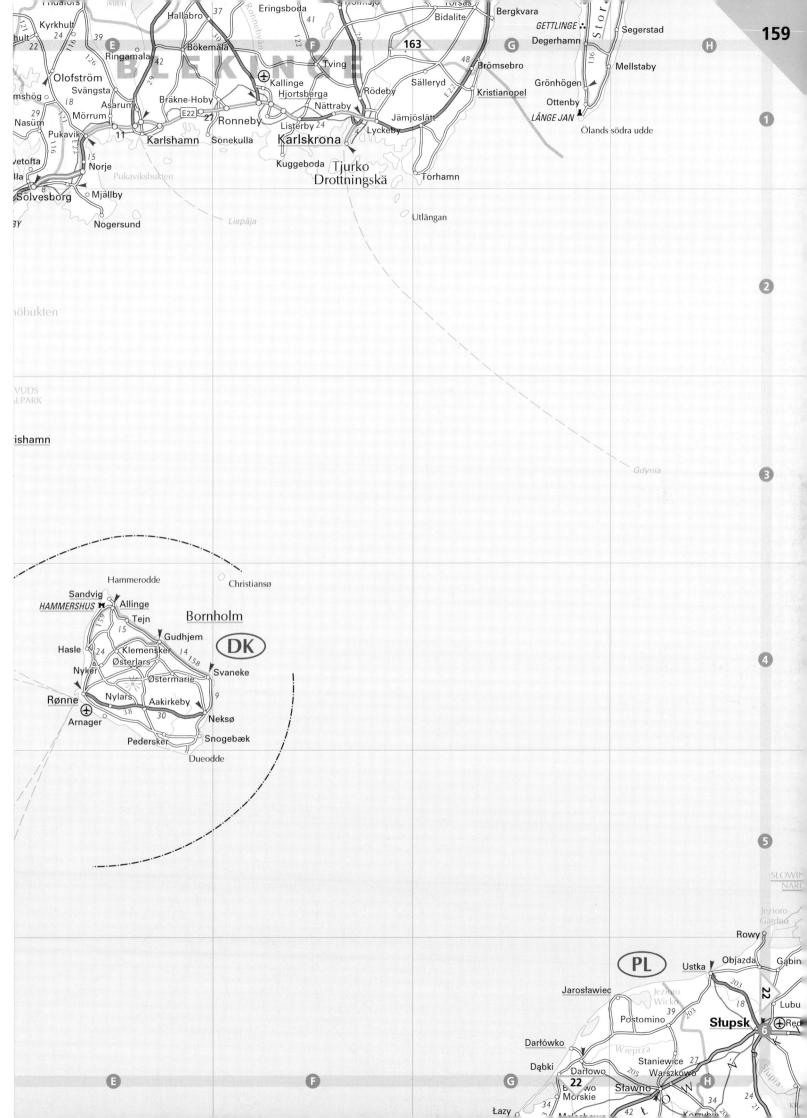

Thidalors · Mien
Kyrkhult · Hallabro · Eringsboda · Holmsjö · Torsas · Bergkvara
37 · 41
Kyrkhult · 24 · 116 · 39 · Bökemåla · 122 · 28 · Bidalite · **GETTLINGE** · Segerstad
22 · 126 · E · Ringamala · 42 · F · Tving · 163 · 48 · G · Degerhamn · H · Stor
Olofström · 29 · Kallinge · Sälleryd · Brömsebro · Grönhögen · 136 · Mellstaby
Svängsta · Hjortsberga · Rödeby · Kristianopel · Ottenby
mshög · 18 · Asarum · Bräkne-Hoby · E22 · Nättraby · E22 · **LÅNGE JAN**
Nasūm · 29 · Mörrum · E22 · 27 · Ronneby · Listerby · 24 · Jämjöslätt · Ölands södra udde
Pukavik · 11 · Karlshamn · Sonekulla · Karlskrona · Lyckeby · 4
etofta · 15 · Norje · Kuggeboda · Tjurko · Torhamn
Sölvesborg · Mjällby · **BLEKINGE**
BY · Nogersund · Pukaviksbukten · Liepäja · Utlängan

nöbukten

Gdynia

VUDS
ALPARK

ishamn

Hammerodde · Christiansø
Sandvig · Allinge
HAMMERSHUS · Tejn
159 · Bornholm
15 · Gudhjem
Hasle · 24 · Klemensker · 14 · 158 · **DK**
Nyker · Østerlars
Rønne · Østermarie · Svaneke
Nylars · 9
Arnager · 38 · Aakirkeby · Østermarie
Pedersker · Neksø
Dueodde · Snogebæk

SŁOWIN
NARO

Jezioro
Gardno
Rowy
PL · Ustka · Objazda · Gåbin
203
Jarosławiec · 22 · Lubu
Jezioro
Wicko
39 · 203 · 18
Postomino · Słupsk · Reg
Darłówko · Wieprza · 6
Dąbki · Darłowo · 205 · Staniewice · 27
22 · Warszkowo · H
Morskie · Sławno · W
Łazy

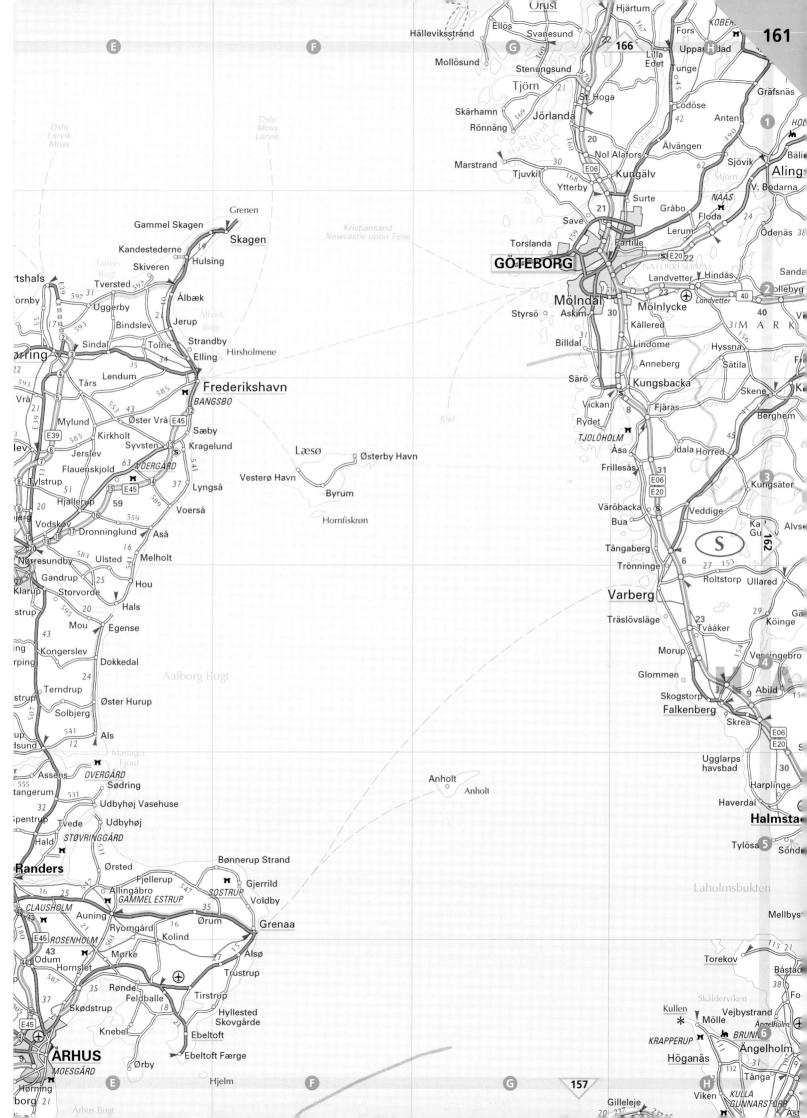

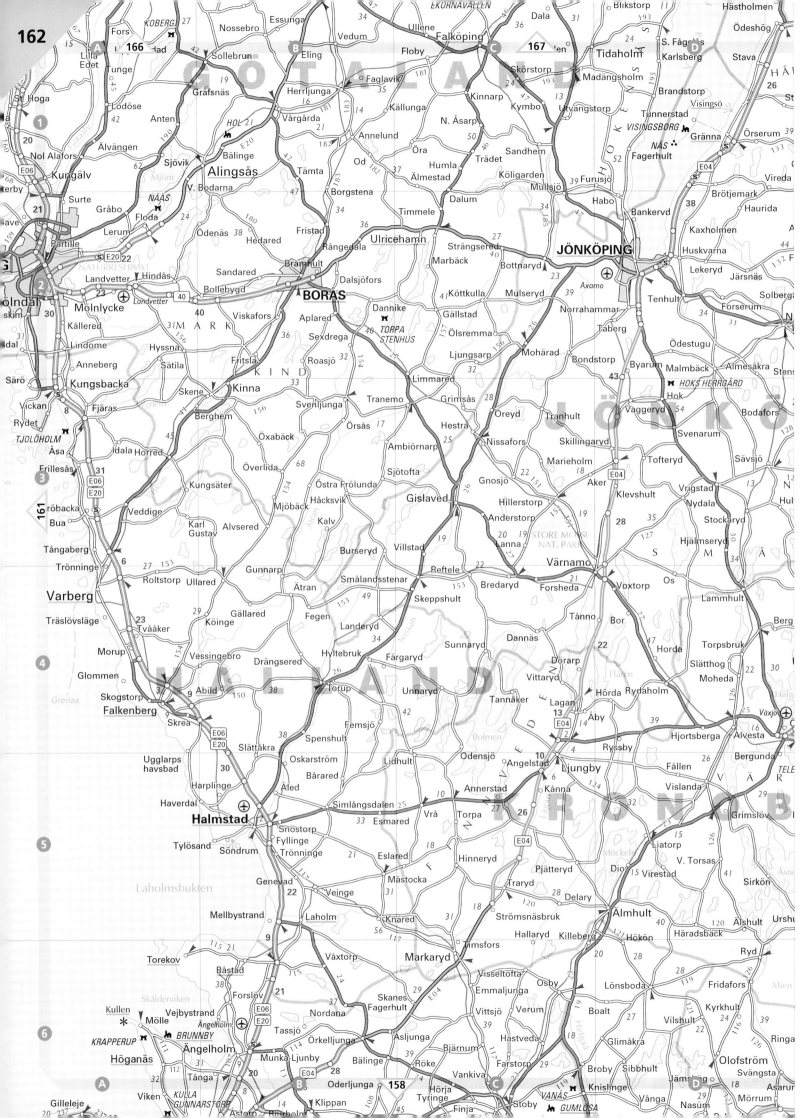

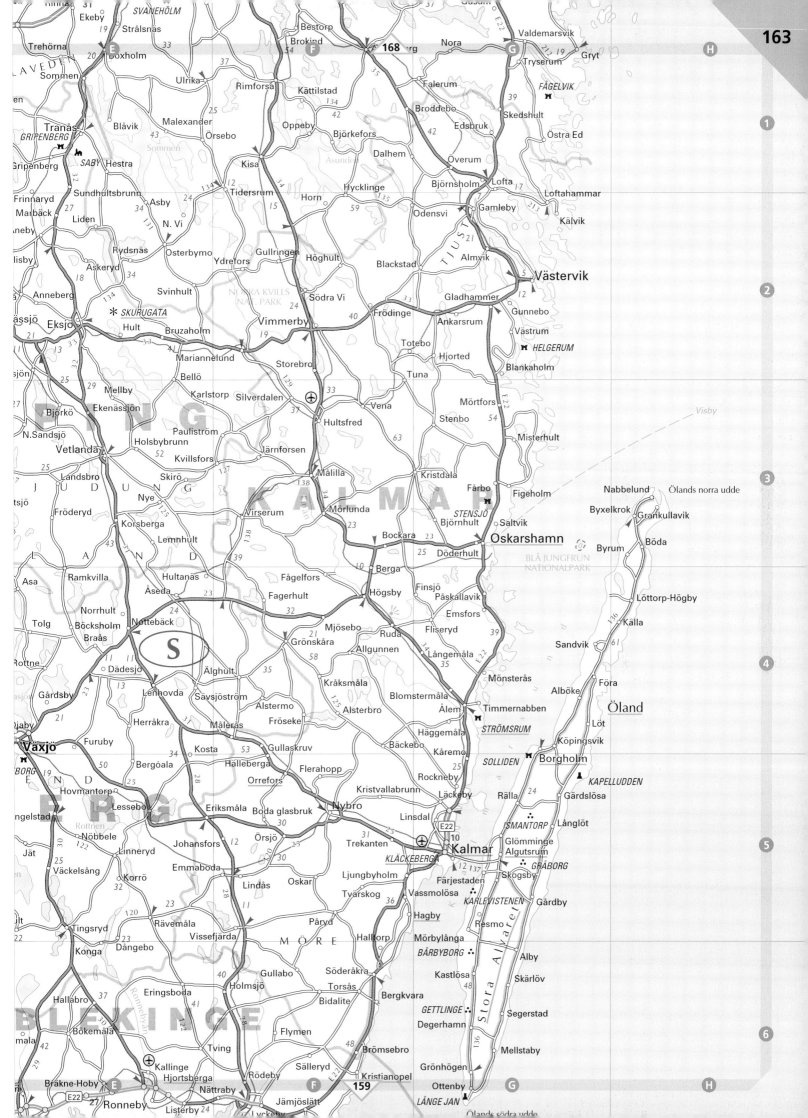

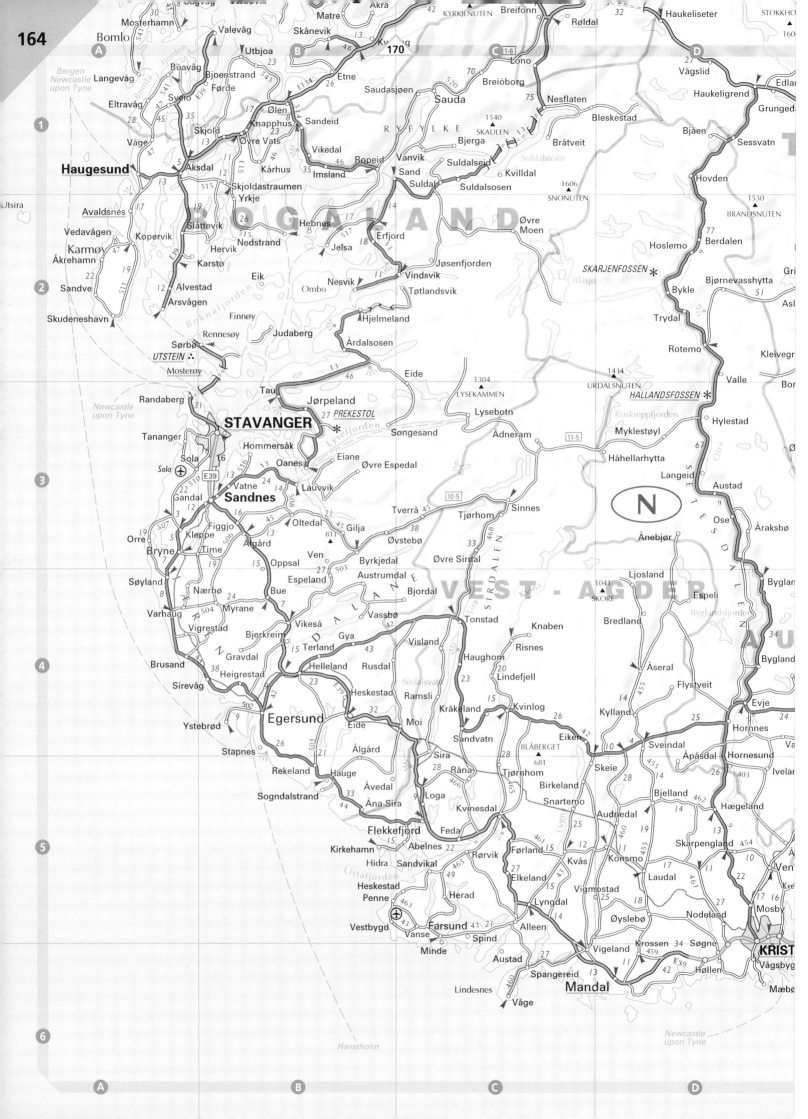

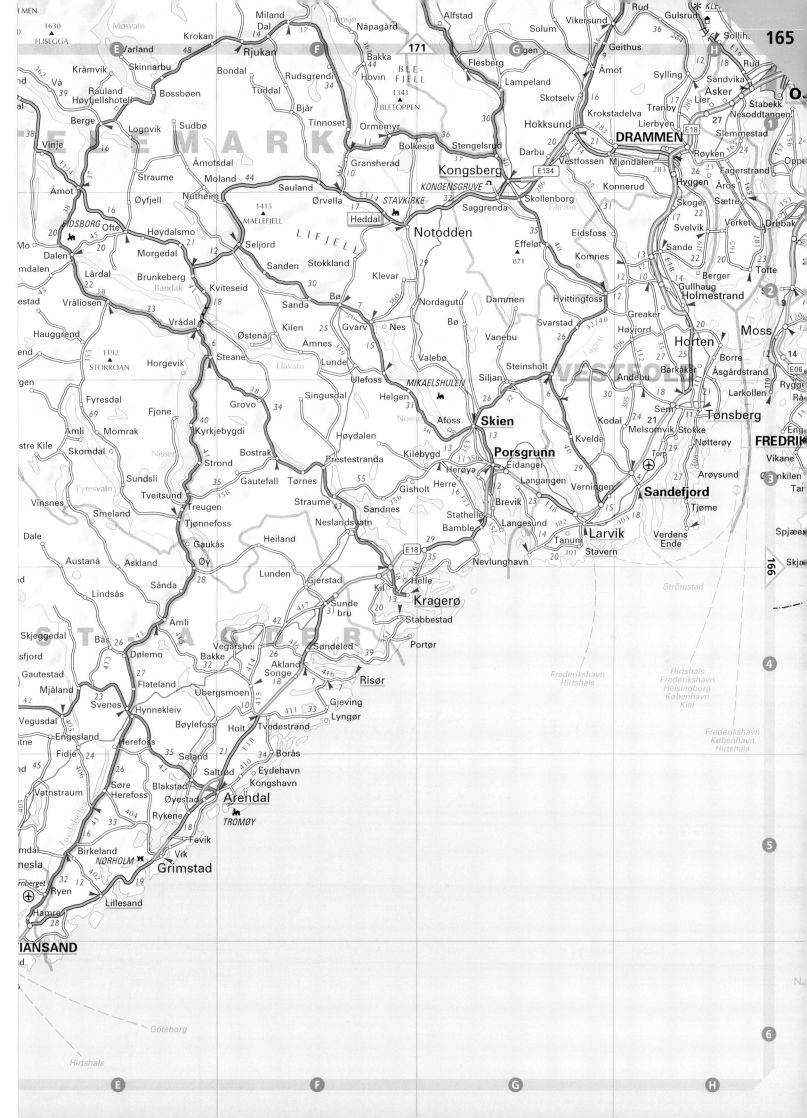

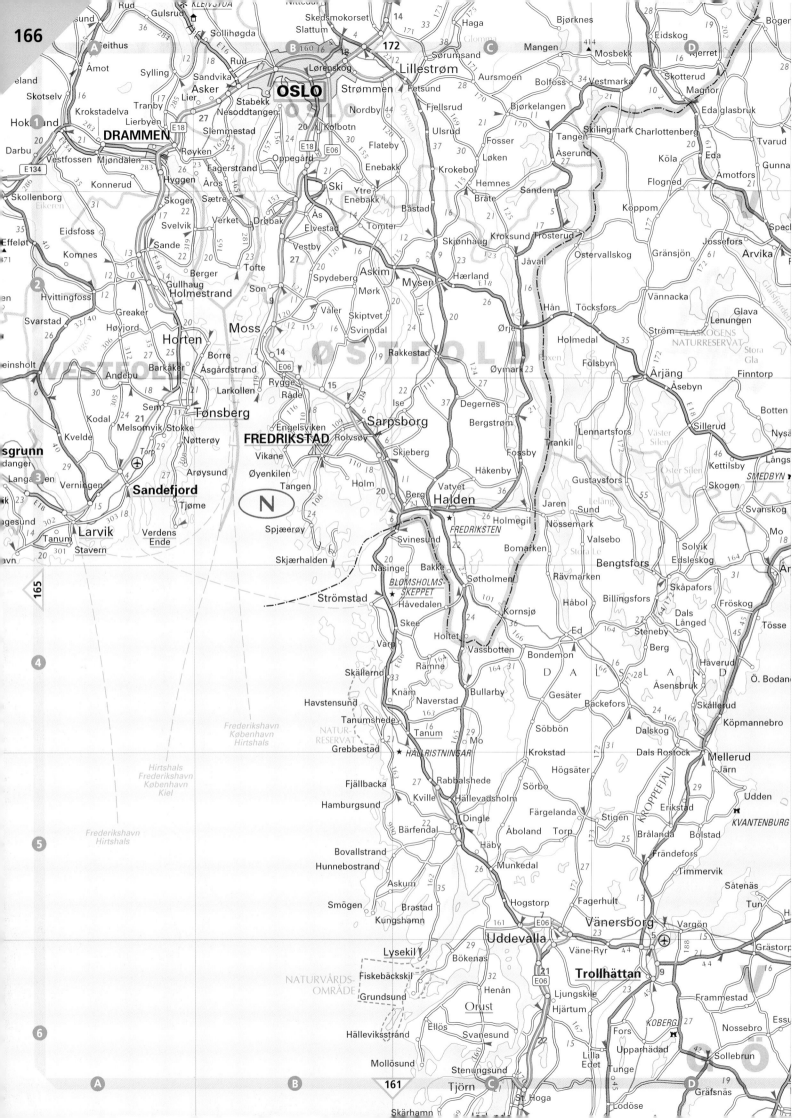

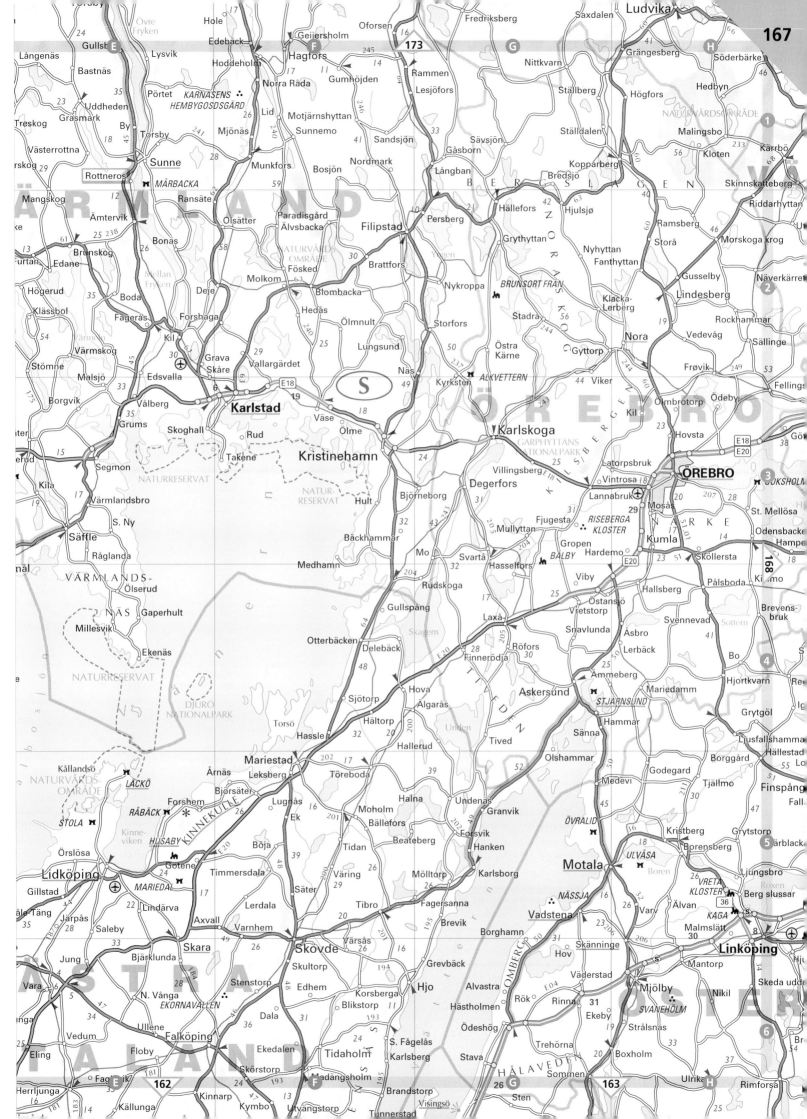

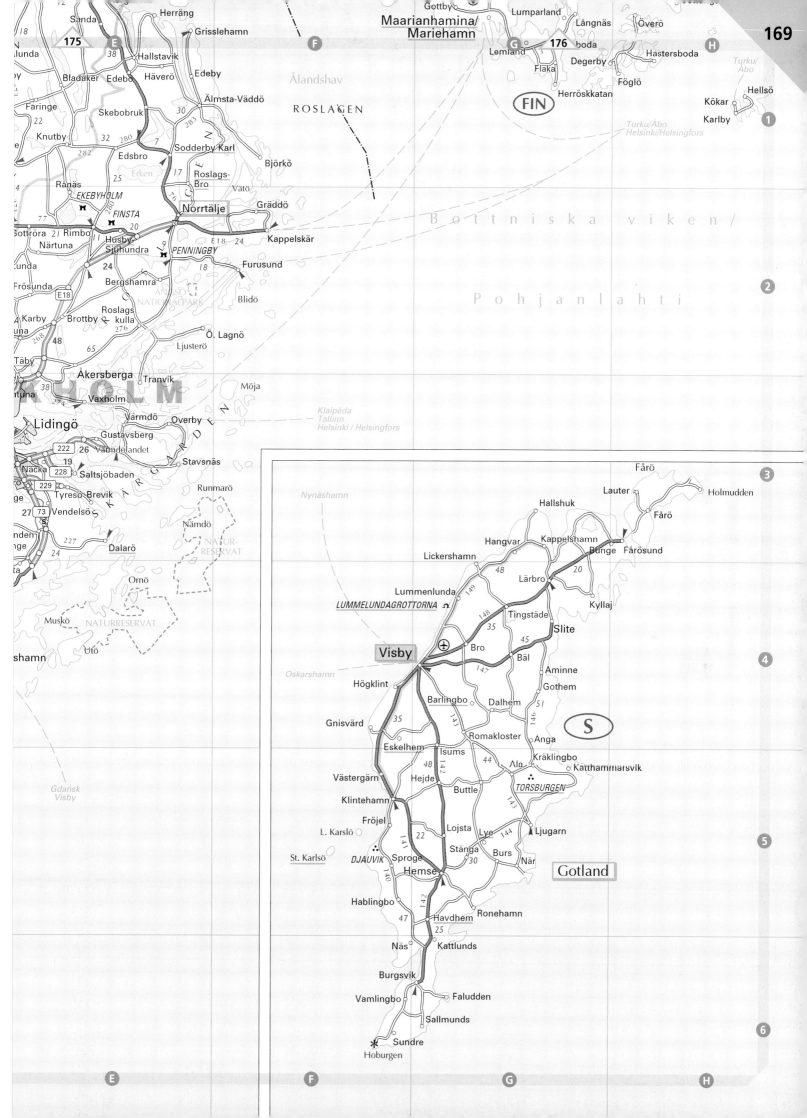

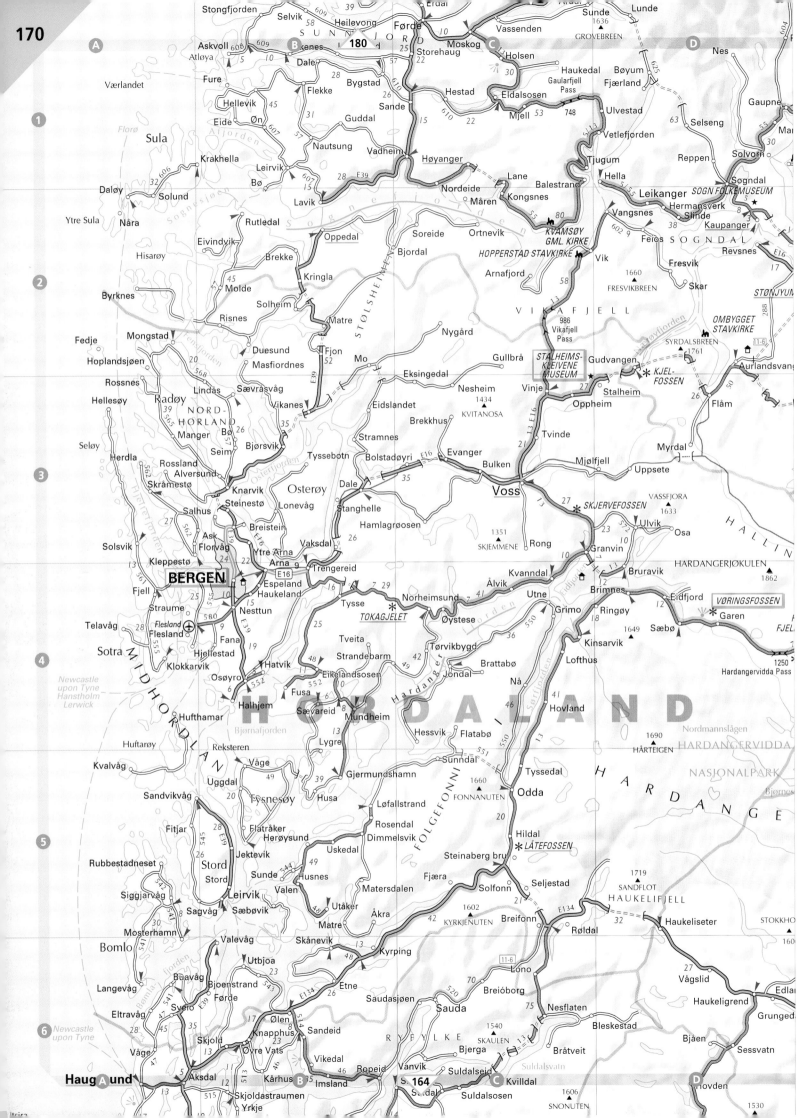

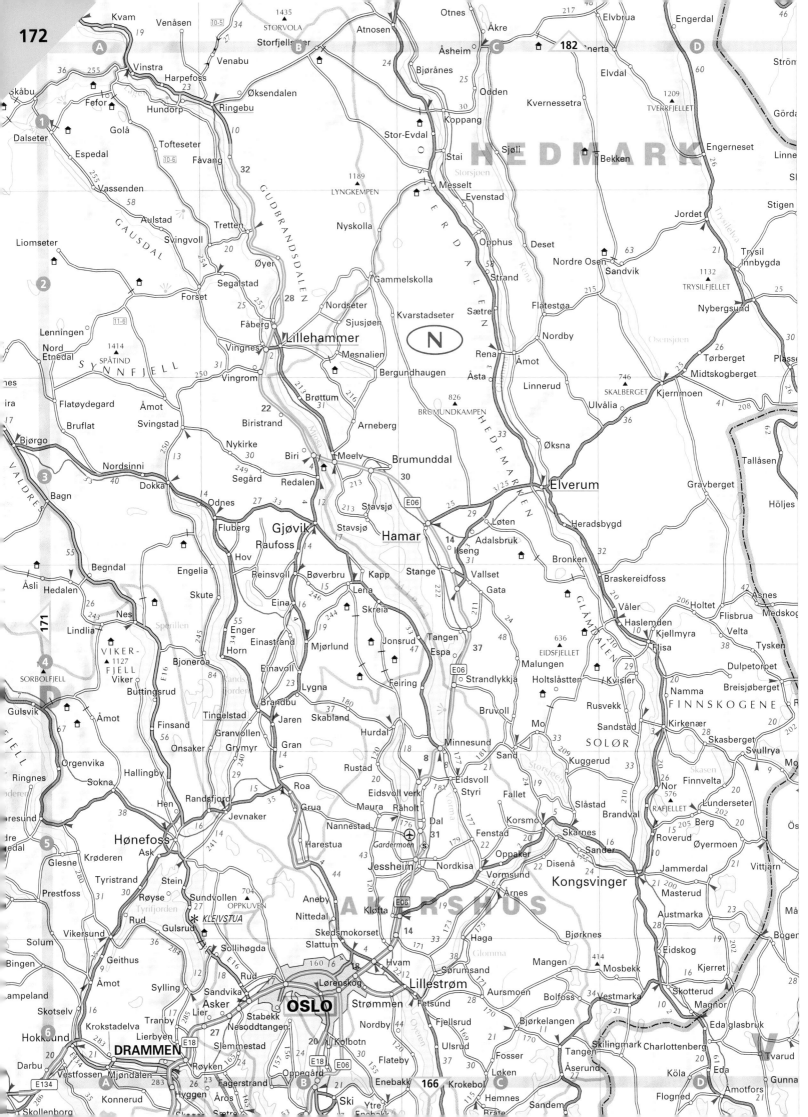

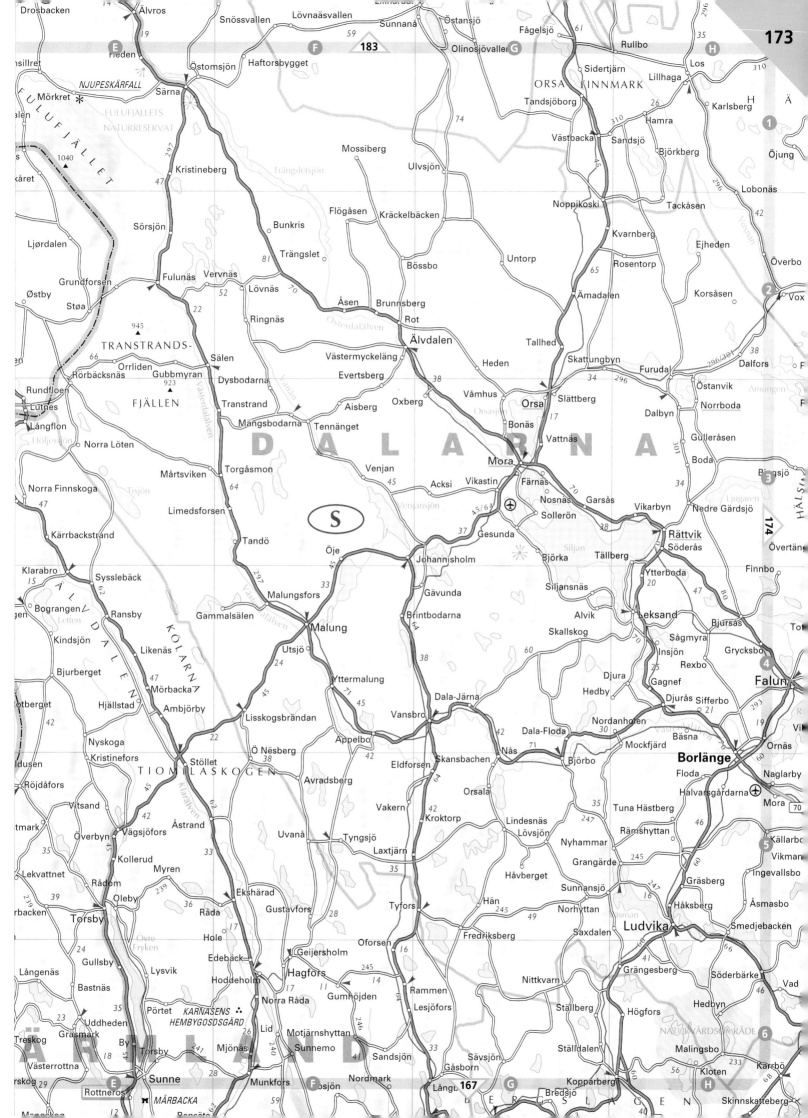

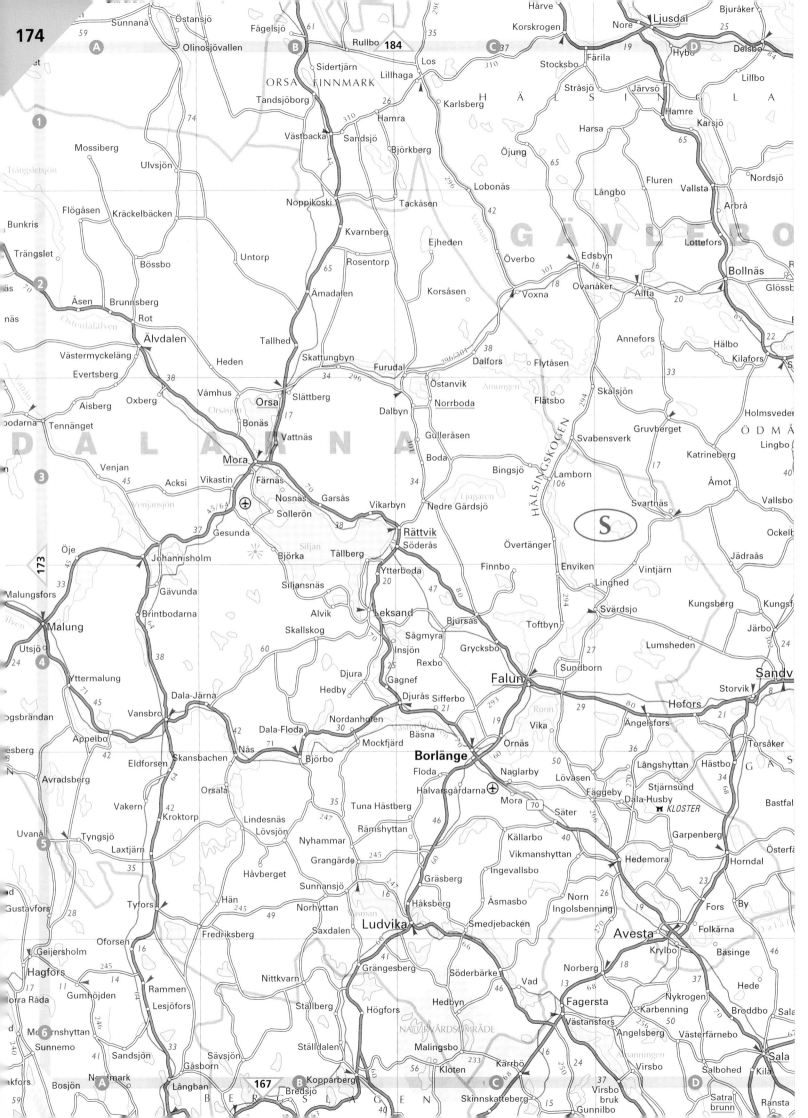

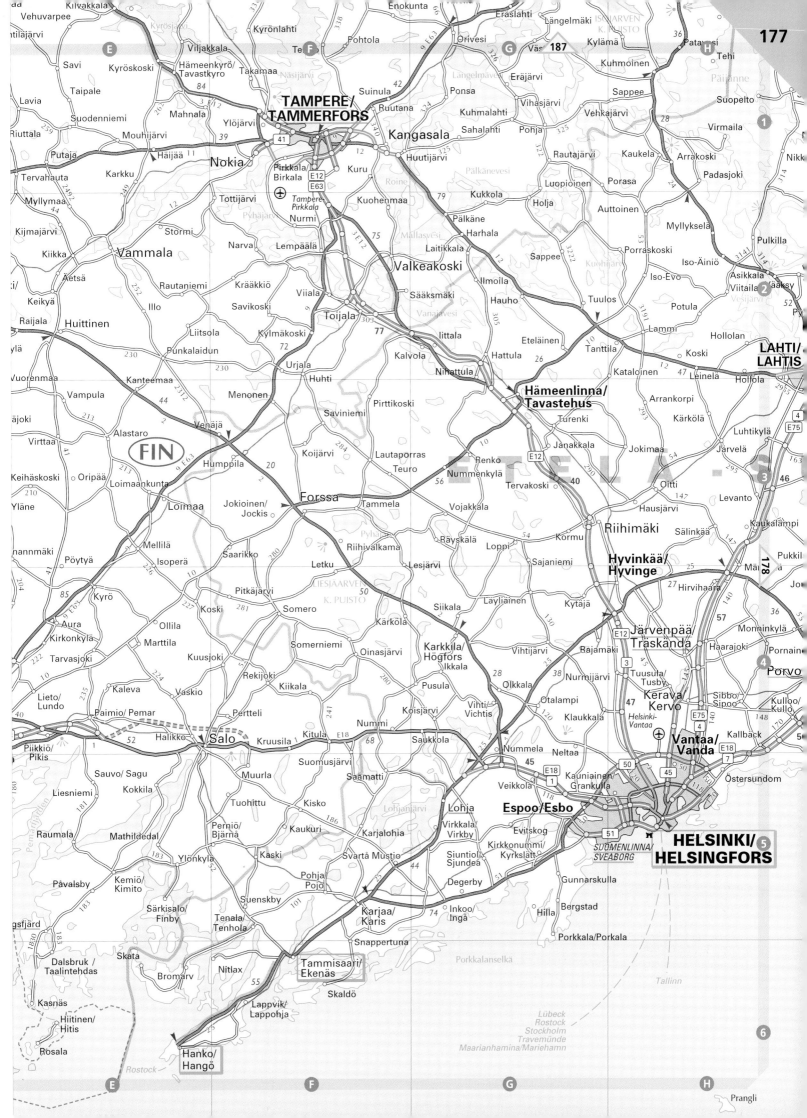

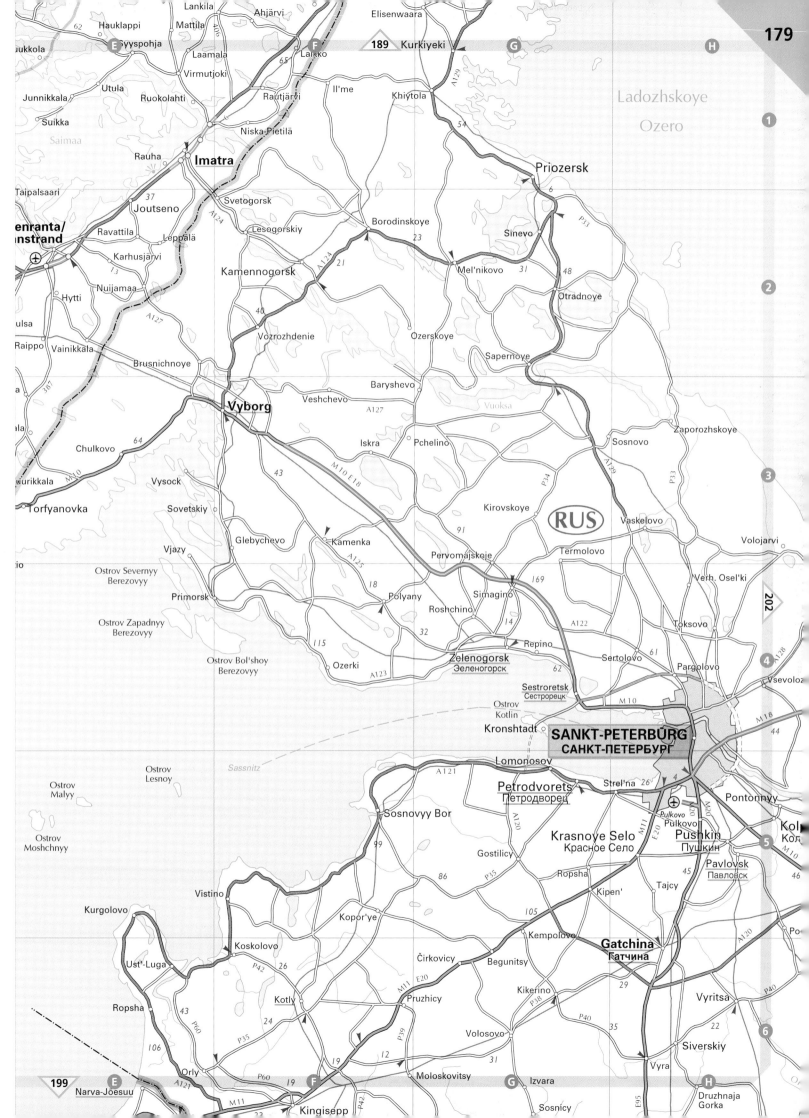

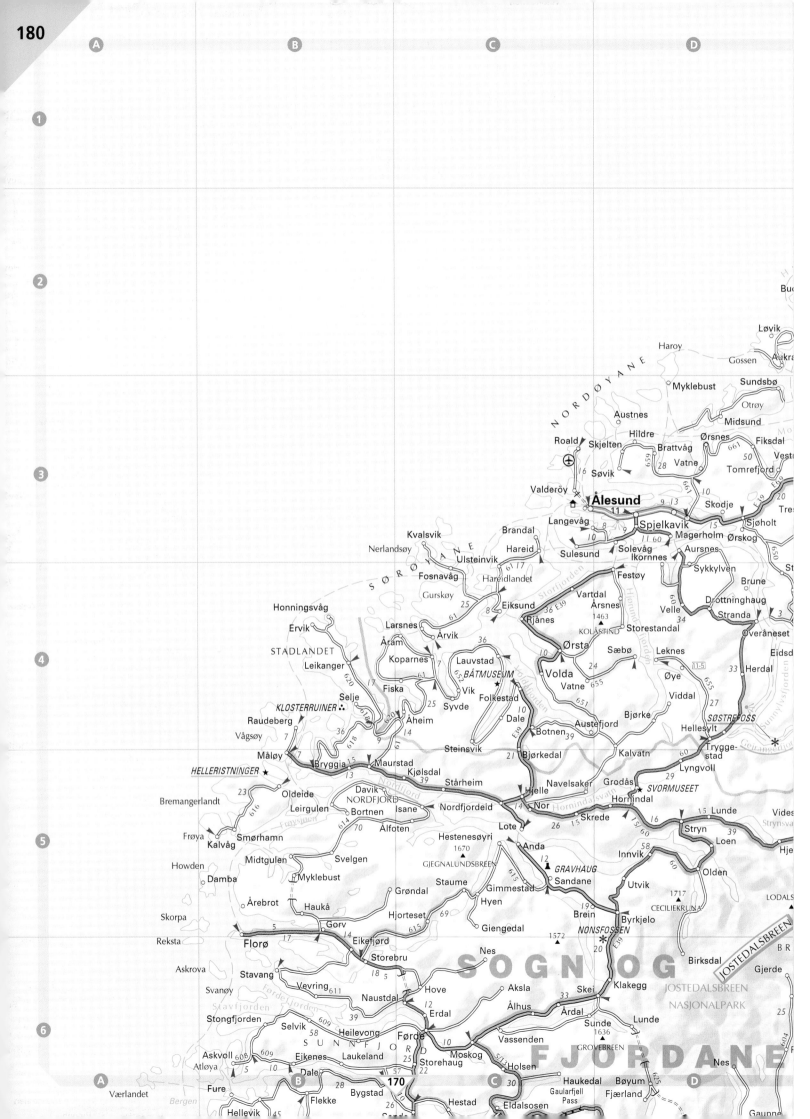

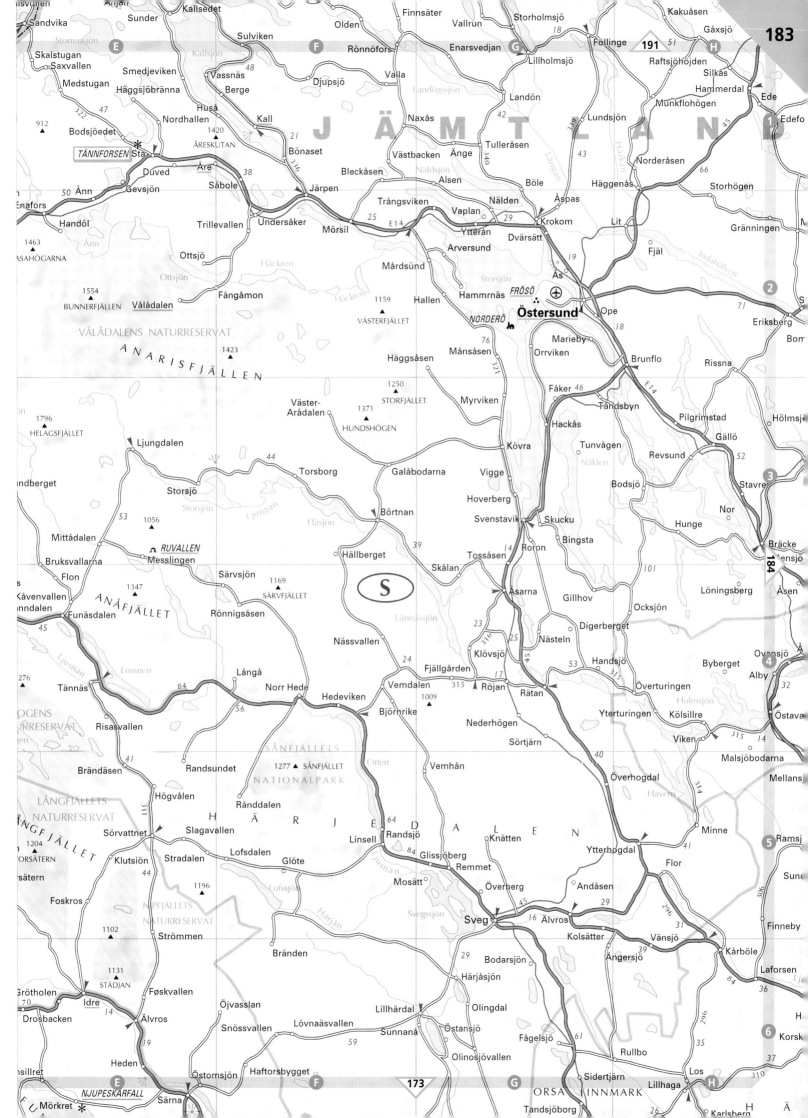

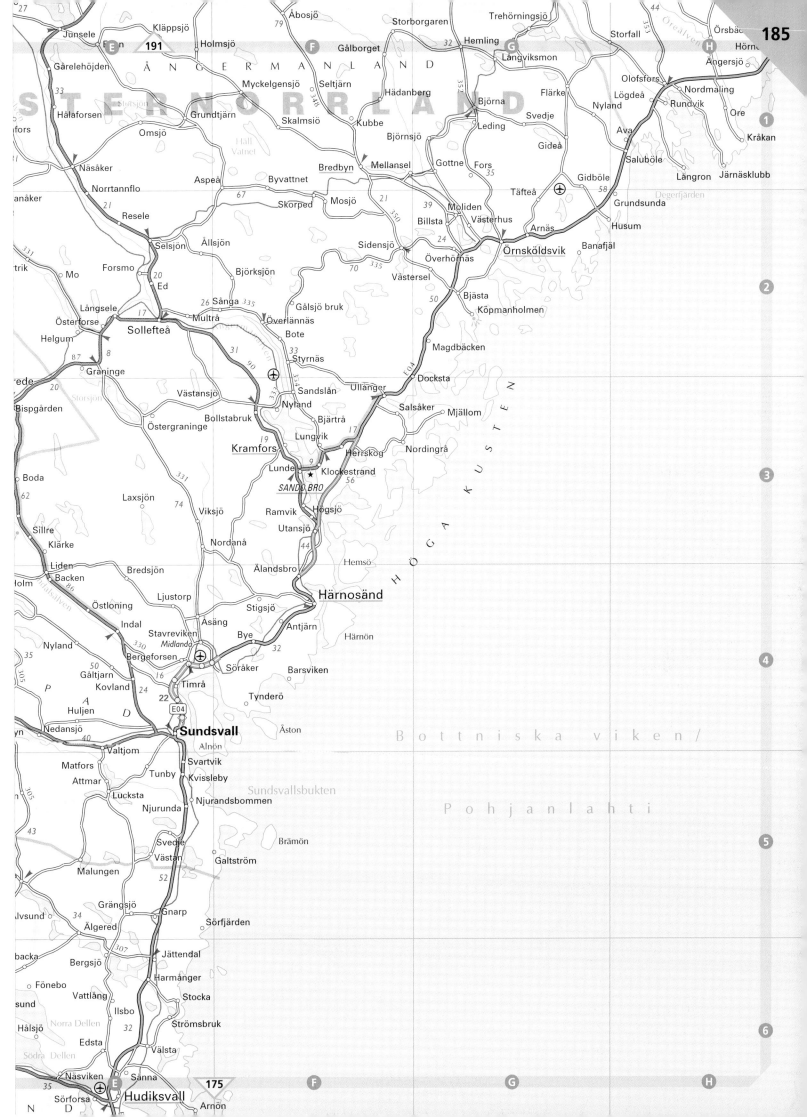

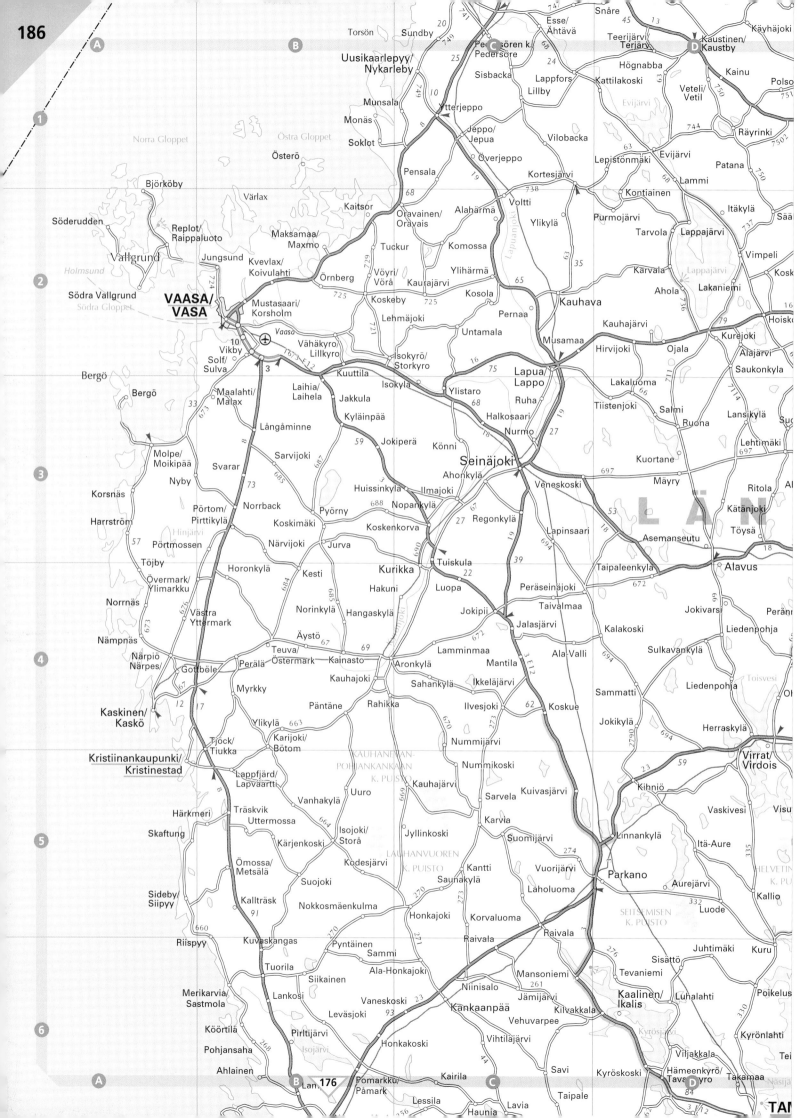

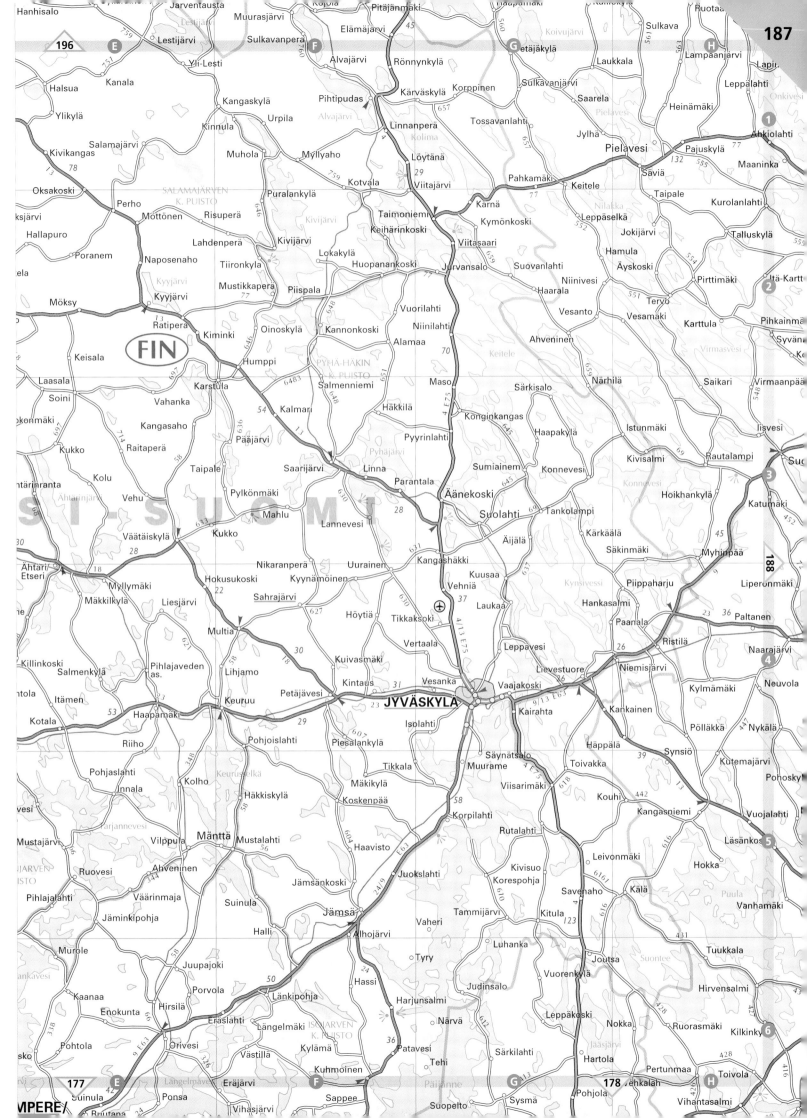

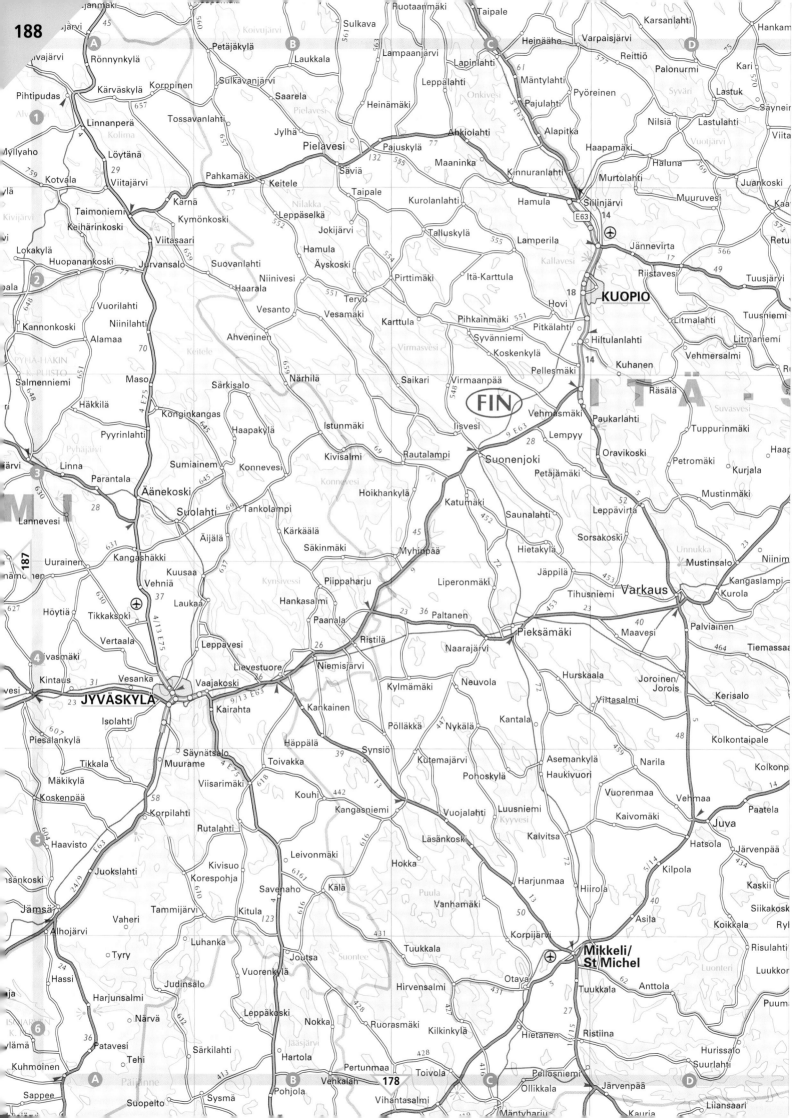

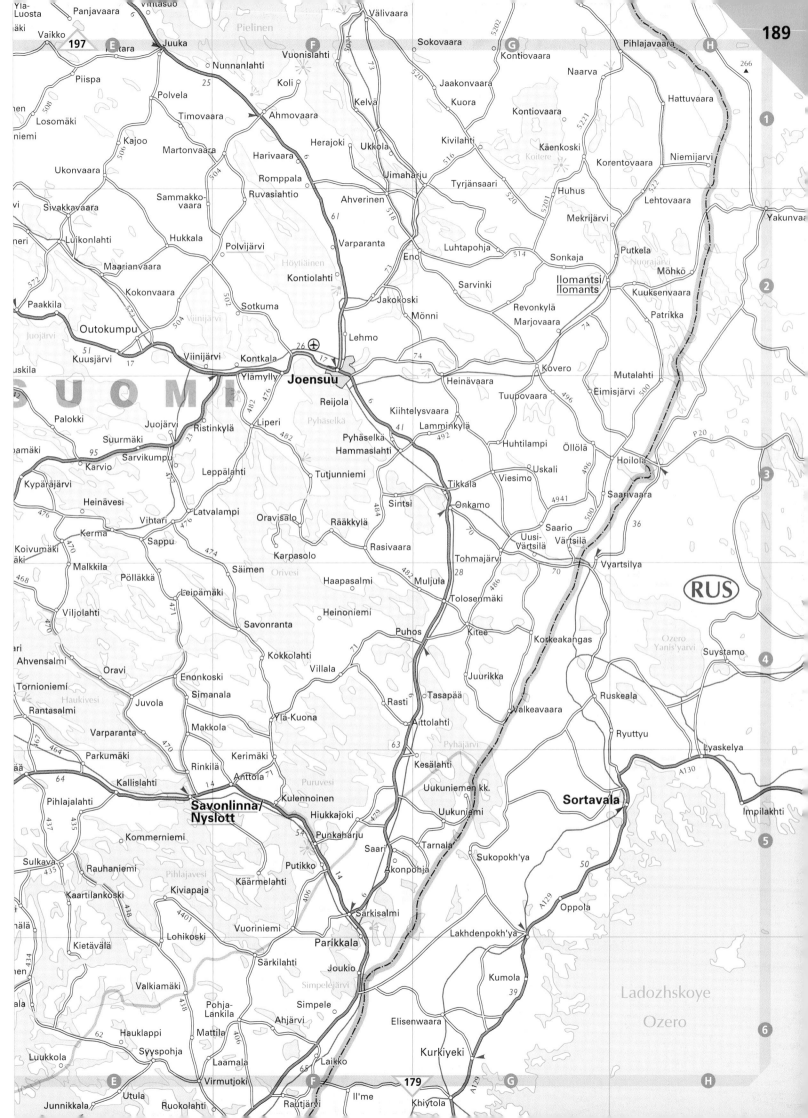

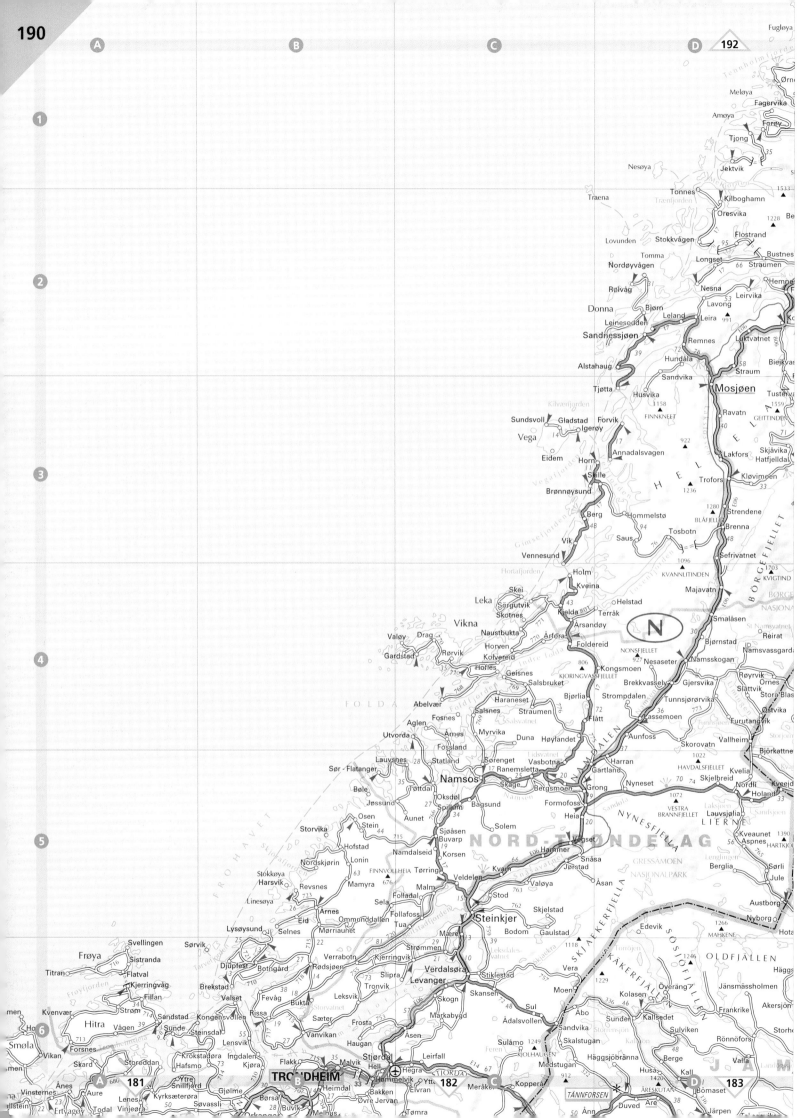

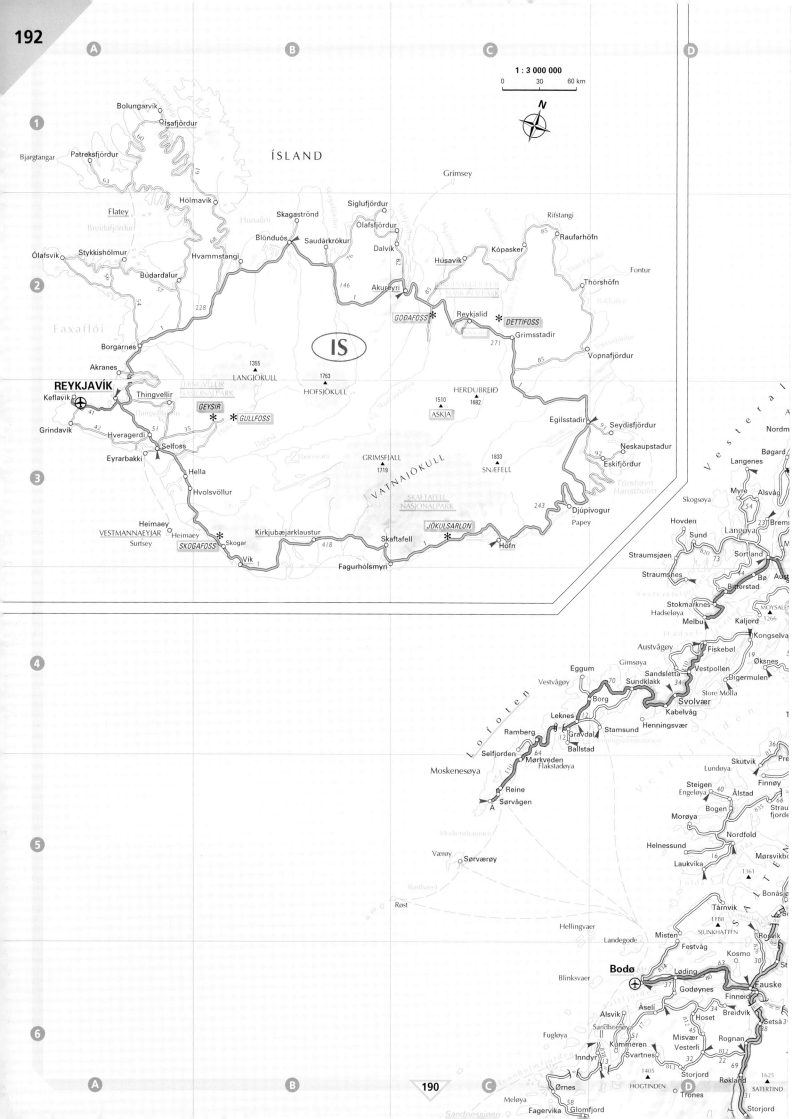

ÍSLAND

1 : 3 000 000

0   30   60 km

N

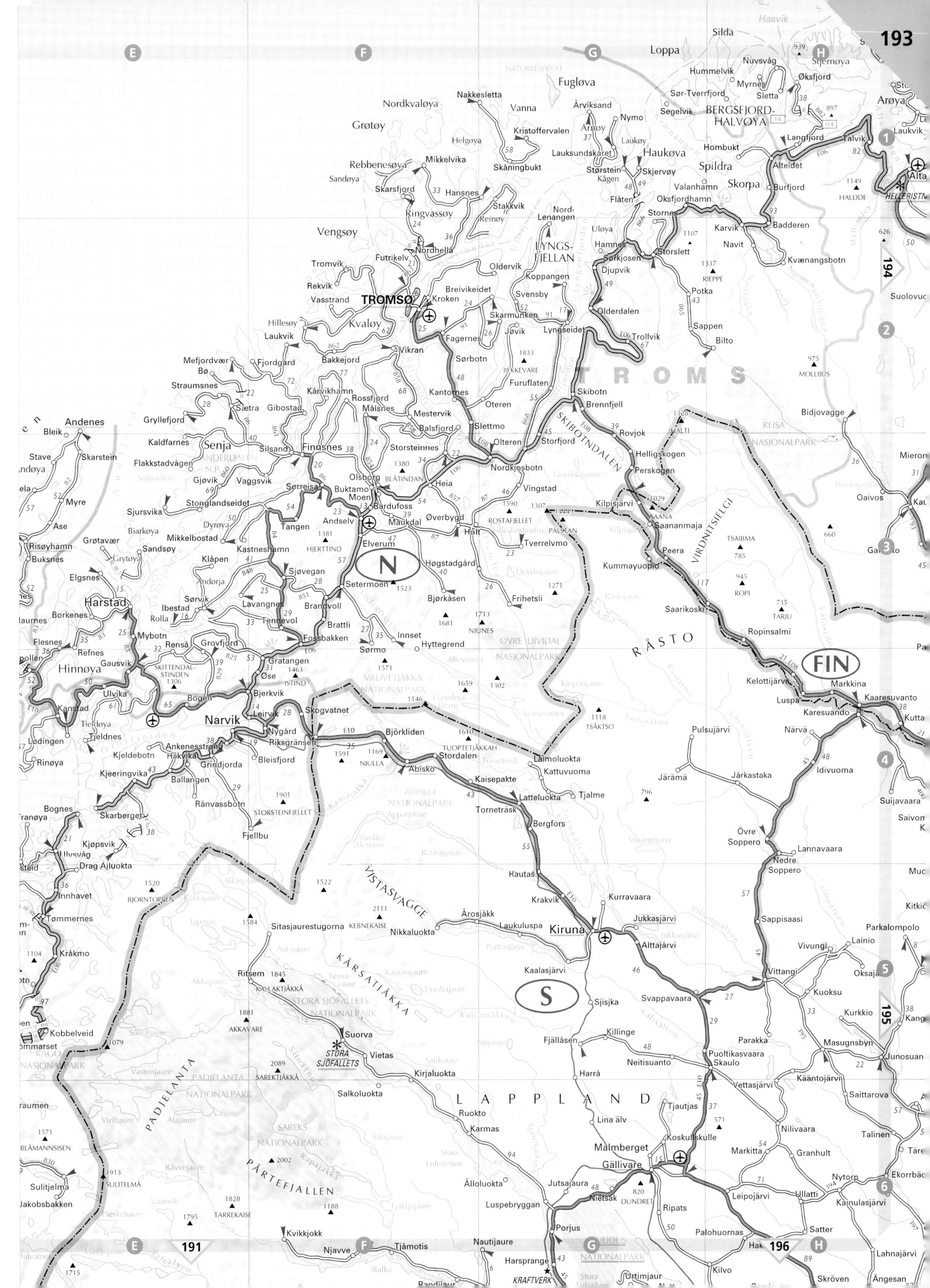
E
F
G
H
Loppa
Silda
Hasvik
Fugløva
Nordkvaløya
Grøtøy
Vanna
Nakkesletta
Nuvsvåg
Hummelvik
Myrnes
Sletta
Øksfjord
Sør-Tverrfjord
Segelvik
BERGSFJORD-HALVØYA
Arøya
Laukvik
Årviksand
Arnøy
Nymo
Kristoffervalen
Lauksundskaret
Laukøy
Haukøya
Hombukt
Langfjord
Talvik
Alta
Alteidet
Helgøya
Mikkelvika
Rebbenesøya
Sandøya
Skåningbukt
Størstein
Kågen
Skjervøy
Spildra
Skorpa
Burfjord
HALDDE
HELLERISTN.
Skarsfjord
Hansnes
Valanhamn
Oksfjordhamn
Fløten
Stakkvik
Reinøy
Ringvassøy
Nord-Lenangen
Stornes
Badderen
Vengsøy
Uløya
Hamnes
Karvik
Navit
Storslett
Nordhella
LYNGS-FJELLAN
Sørkjosen
Djupvik
Kvænangsbotn
Tromvik
Futrikelv
Oldervik
Koppangen
RIEPPE
Rekvik
Breivikeidet
Vasstrand
TROMSØ
Kroken
Svensby
Potka
Olderdalen
Suolovuo
Hillesøy
Kvaløy
Skarmunken
Jøvik
Lyngseidet
Laukvik
Fagernes
Trollvik
Sappen
Bilto
Vikran
Sørbotn
JIEKKEVARE
Mefjordvær
Bø
Fjordgård
Bakkejord
TROMS
MOLLIJUS
Straumsnes
Kårvikhamn
Kantornes
Furuflaten
Skibotn
Gibostad
Sætra
Rossfjord
Målsnes
Mestervik
Oteren
Brennfjell
Bidjovagge
Andenes
Bleik
Gryllefjord
Balsfjord
Slettmo
HALTI
REISA NASJONALPARK
Kaldfarnes
Senja
ANDERDALEN N.P.
Silsand
Finnsnes
Storsteinnes
Olteren
Storfjord
Rovjok
Stave
Skarstein
Flakkstadvågen
Helligskogen
Mieron
Gjøvik
Vaggsvik
Olsborg
BLÅTINDAN
Nordkjosbotn
SKIBOTNDALEN
Perskogen
Myre
Sørreisa
Buktamo
Heia
Vingstad
Oaivos
Stonglandseidet
Moen
Bardufoss
Kilpisjärvi
Sjursvika
Andselv
Øverbygd
ROSTAFJELLET
PALSTAN
SAANA
Saananmaja
Ase
Biarkøya
Dyrøya
Tangen
Maukdal
Holt
VIRDNITSIELGI
Risøyhamn
Grøtavær
Mikkelbostad
HJERTTIND
Elverum
Tverrelvmo
TSAIBMA
Buksnes
Sandsøy
Kastneshamn
Peera
Klåpen
N
Høgstadgård
Kummayuopio
Elgsnes
Sjøvegan
Andørja
Setermoen
ROPI
Harstad
Sørvik
Lavangnes
Brandvoll
Bjørkåsen
Frihetsli
Ibestad
Saarikoski
Borkenes
Rolla
Tennevol
NJUNES
TARJU
Brattli
RÅSTO
Ropinsalmi
Flesnes
Mybotn
Refnes
Rensa
Grovfjord
Fossbakken
Innset
Hyttegrend
ØVRE DIVIDAL NASJONALPARK
Hinnøya
Gausvik
SKITTENDAL-STINDEN
Gratangen
Sørmo
ISTIND
VADVETJÅKKA NATIONALPARK
FIN
Kelottijärvi
Markkina
Ulvika
Øse
Bjerkvik
Bogen
Luspa
Kaaresuvanto
Karesuando
Kanstad
Leirvik
Skogvatnet
TSÅKTSO
Kutta
Tieldøya
Narvik
Nygård
Riksgränsen
Björkliden
Pulsujärvi
Närvä
Lødingen
Tjeldnes
Ankenesstrand
Håkvika
Bleisfjord
TUOPTETJÅKKAH
Stordalen
Laimoluokta
Kattuvuoma
Idivuoma
Rinøya
Kjeldebotn
Grindjorda
NJULLA
Abisko
Järämä
Jårkastaka
Kjeeringvika
Ballangen
Kaisepakte
Tjalme
Suijavaara
ABISKO NATIONALPARK
Latteluokta
Torneträsk
Bognes
Skarberget
Rånvassbotn
STORSTEINFJELLET
Saivomuotka
Tranøya
Bergfors
Övre Soppero
Kjøpsvik
Ulvsvåg
Fjellbu
Lannavaara
Drag
Ajluokta
Nedre Soppero
Muonio
VISTASVAGGE
Kautas
Innhavet
BJORNTOPPEN
Krakvik
Kurravaara
Kitkiöjärvi
Tømmernes
Årosjäkk
Jukkasjärvi
Sappisaasi
Sitasjaurestugorna
KEBNEKAISE
Nikkaluokta
Laukuluspa
Kiruna
Parkalompolo
Alttajärvi
Lainio
Vivungi
Kråkmo
KÅRSATJÅKKA
Kaalasjärvi
Ritsem
KALLAKTJÅKKÅ
Vittangi
Oksajärvi
STORA SJÖFALLETS NATIONALPARK
S
Sjisjka
Svappavaara
Kuoksu
AKKAVARE
Kurkkio
Kobbelveid
Suorva
Killinge
Fjällåsen
Parakka
Masugnsbyn
Kangos
Rommarset
RAGO NASJONALPARK
STORA SJÖFALLETS
Vietas
Neitisuanto
Puoltikasvaara
Skaulo
Junosuando
PADJELANTA NATIONALPARK
SAREKTJÅKKÅ
Kirjaluokta
Harrå
Kääntöjärvi
Vettasjärvi
Saittarova
Straumen
Salkoluokta
LAPPLAND
Ruokto
Tjautjas
Lina älv
Karmas
Nilivaara
Talinen
BLÅMANNSISEN
SAREKS NATIONALPARK
Koskullskulle
Malmberget
Markitta
Granhult
Tärendö
Sulitjelma
SULITELMA
Gällivare
PÅRTEFJALLEN
Nytorp
Ekorrbäcken
Ållolukta
Jutsajaura
Nietsak
DUNDRET
Ullatti
Leipojärvi
Kainulasjärvi
Jakobsbakken
TARREKAISE
Luspebryggan
Ripats
Porjus
Kvikkjokk
Palohuornas
Satter
Njavve
Tjåmotis
Nautijaure
MUDDUS NATIONALPARK
Harsprange
KRAFTVERK
Kilvo
Lahnajärvi
Skröven
Ängesan
Urtimjaur
191
196
194
195

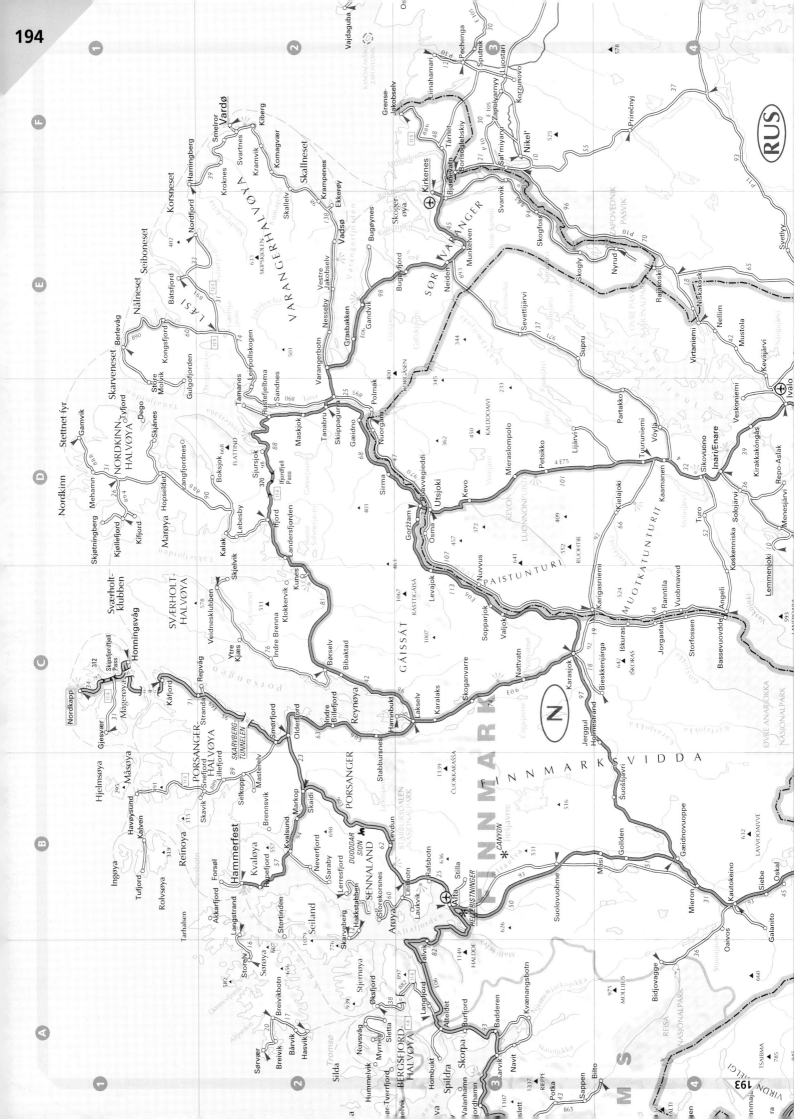

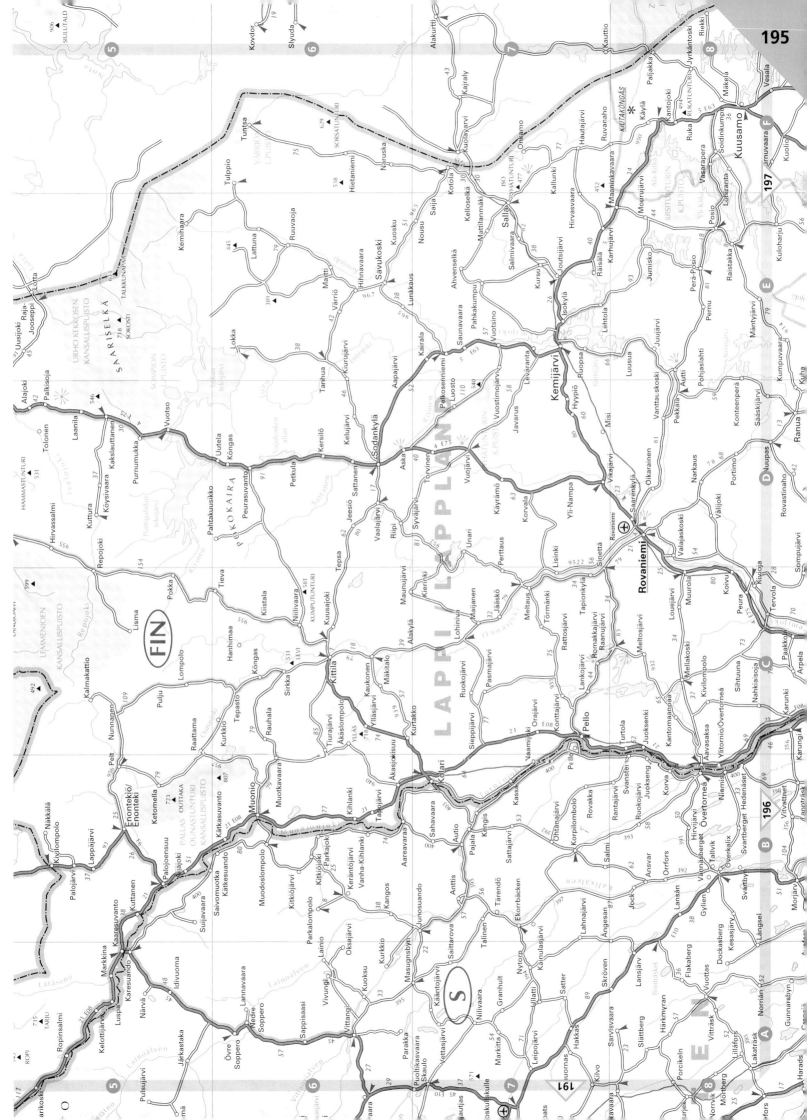

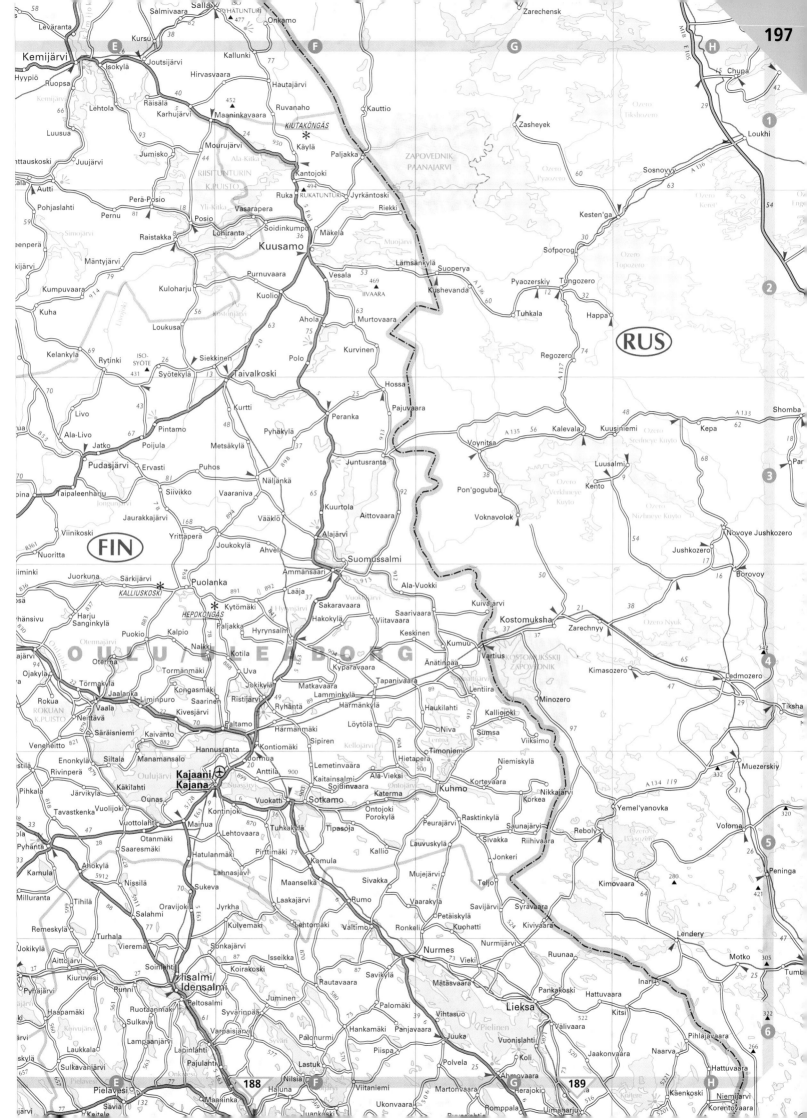

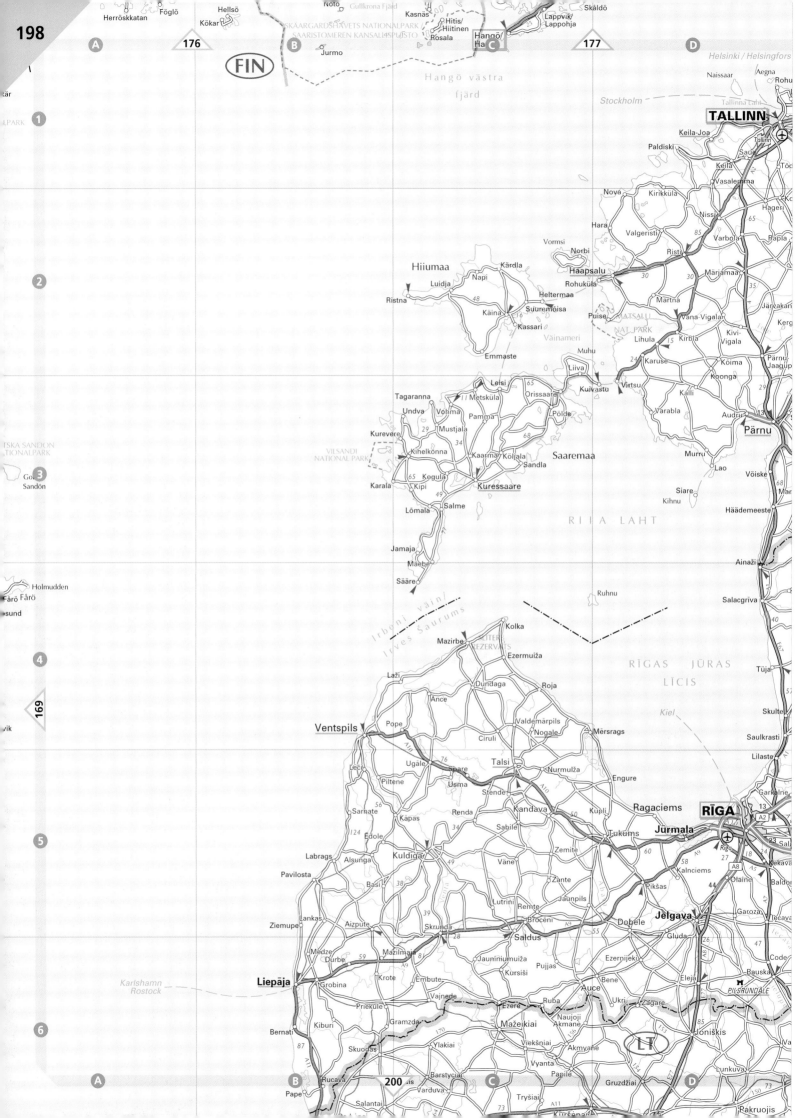

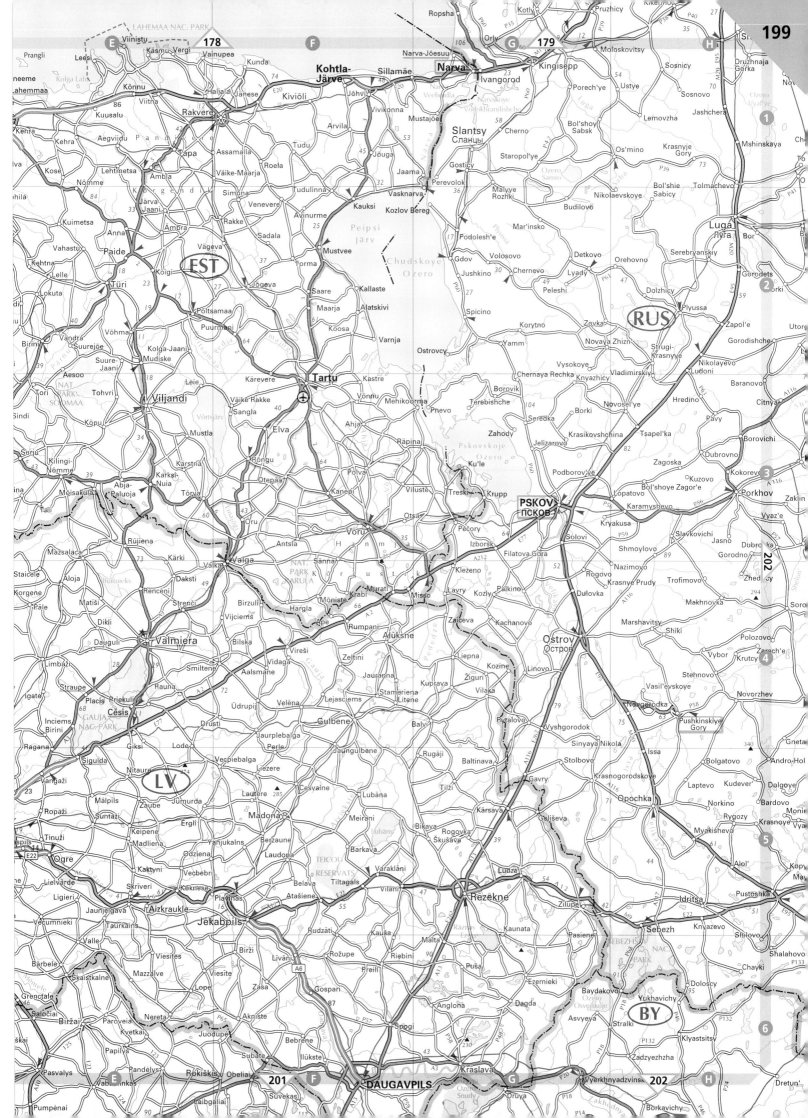

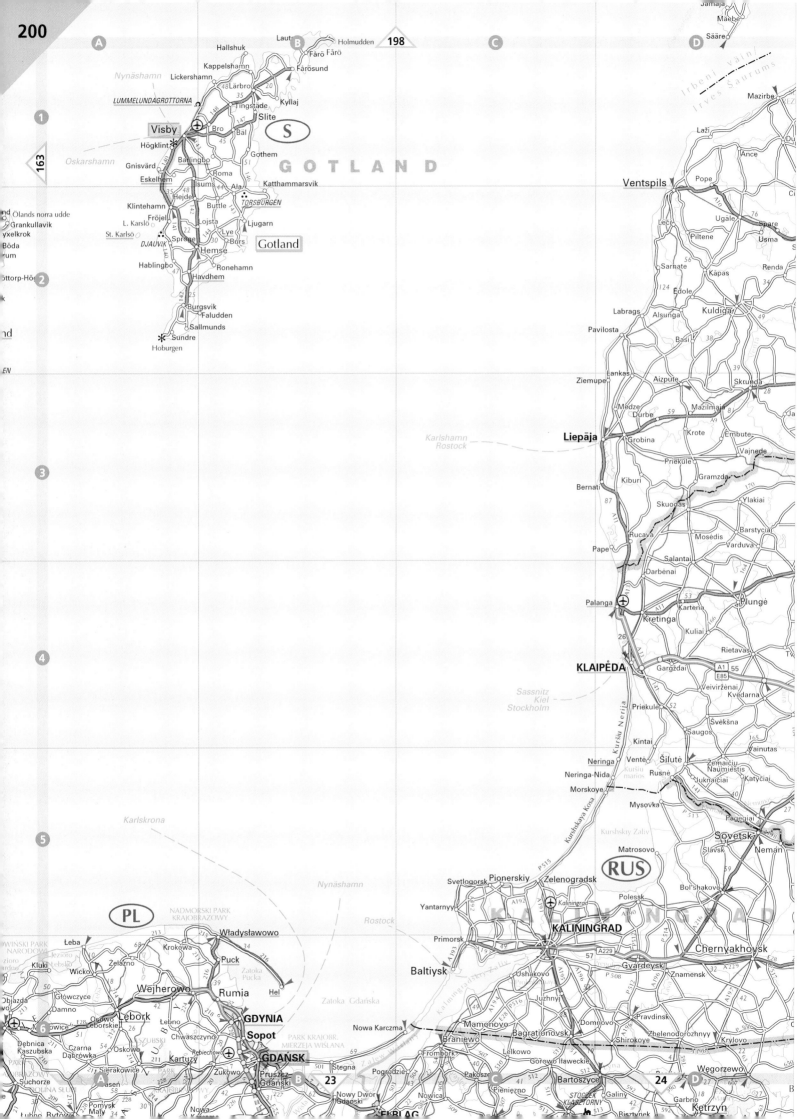

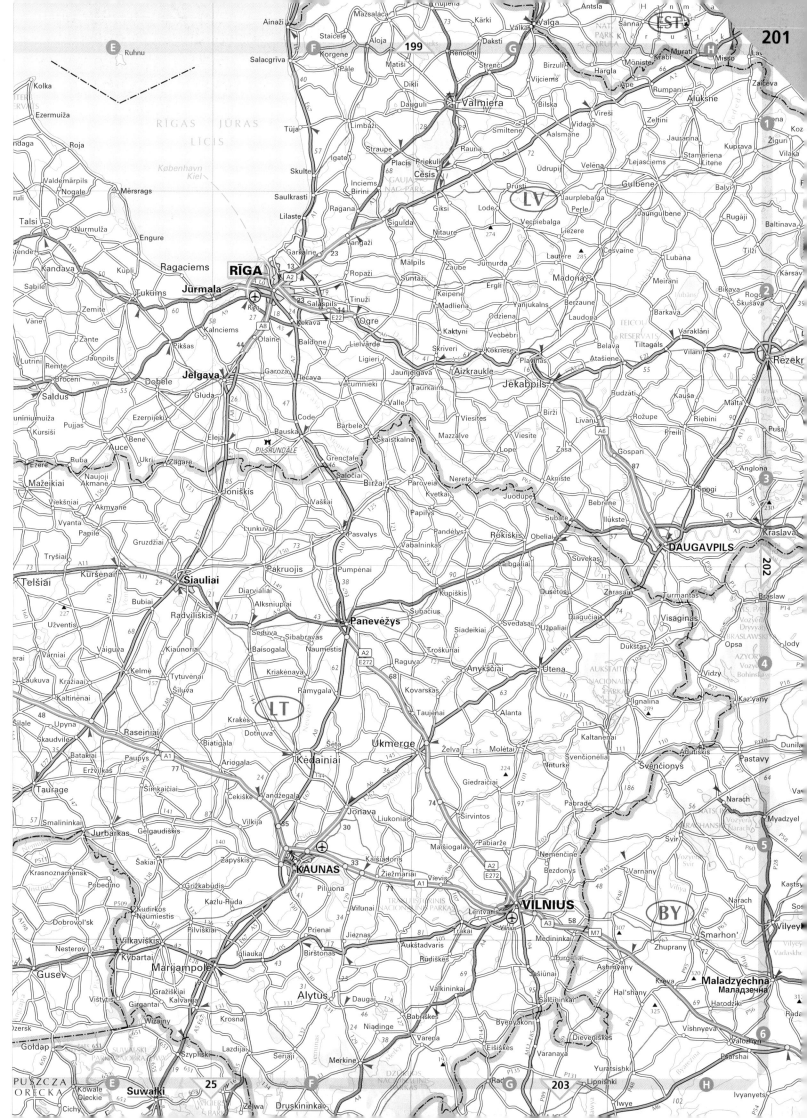

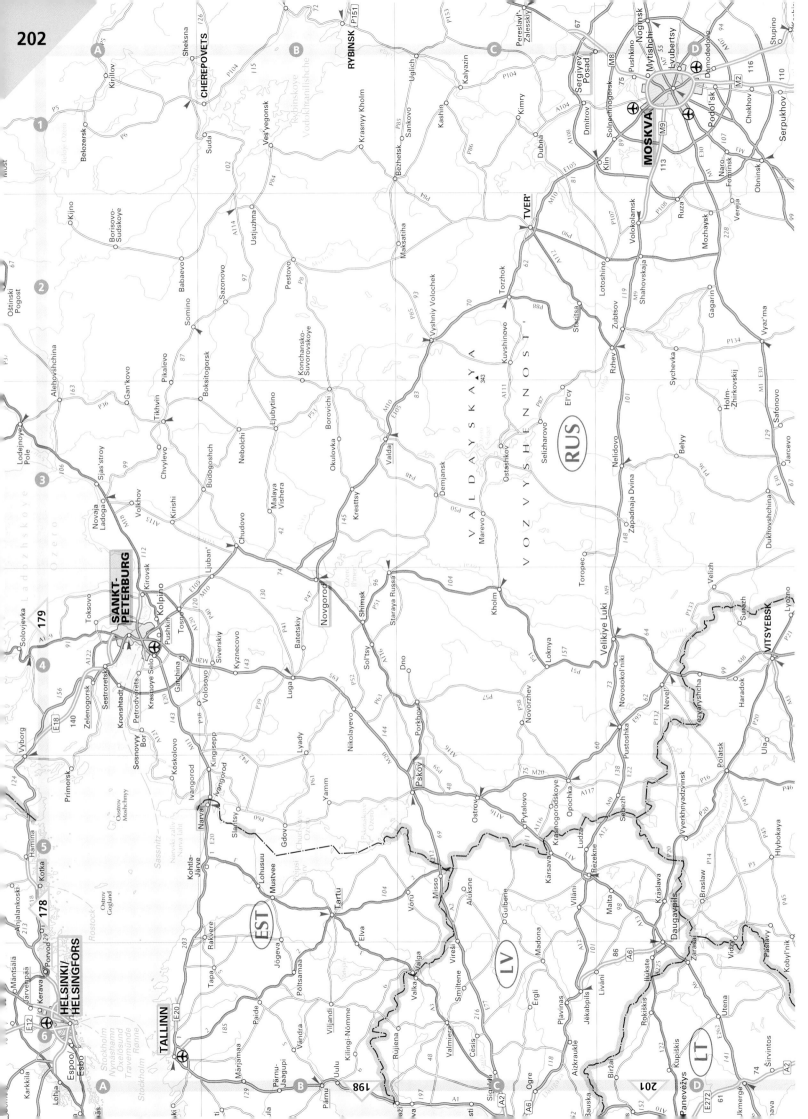

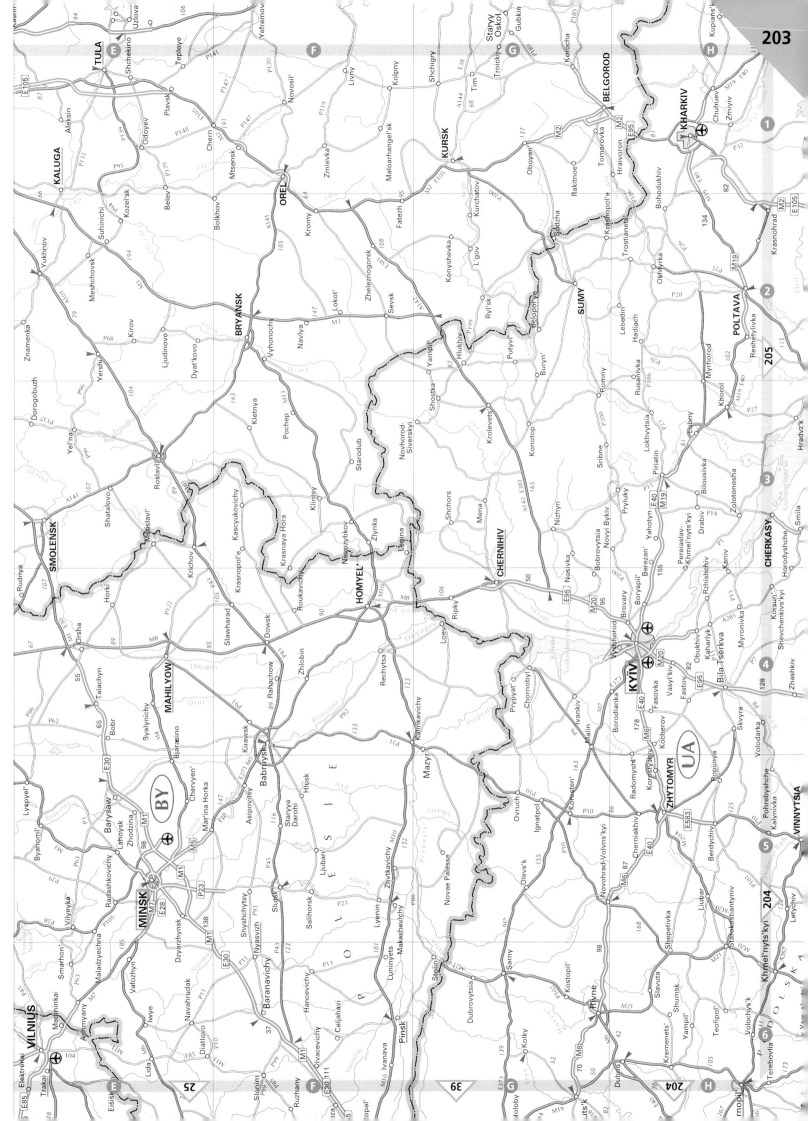

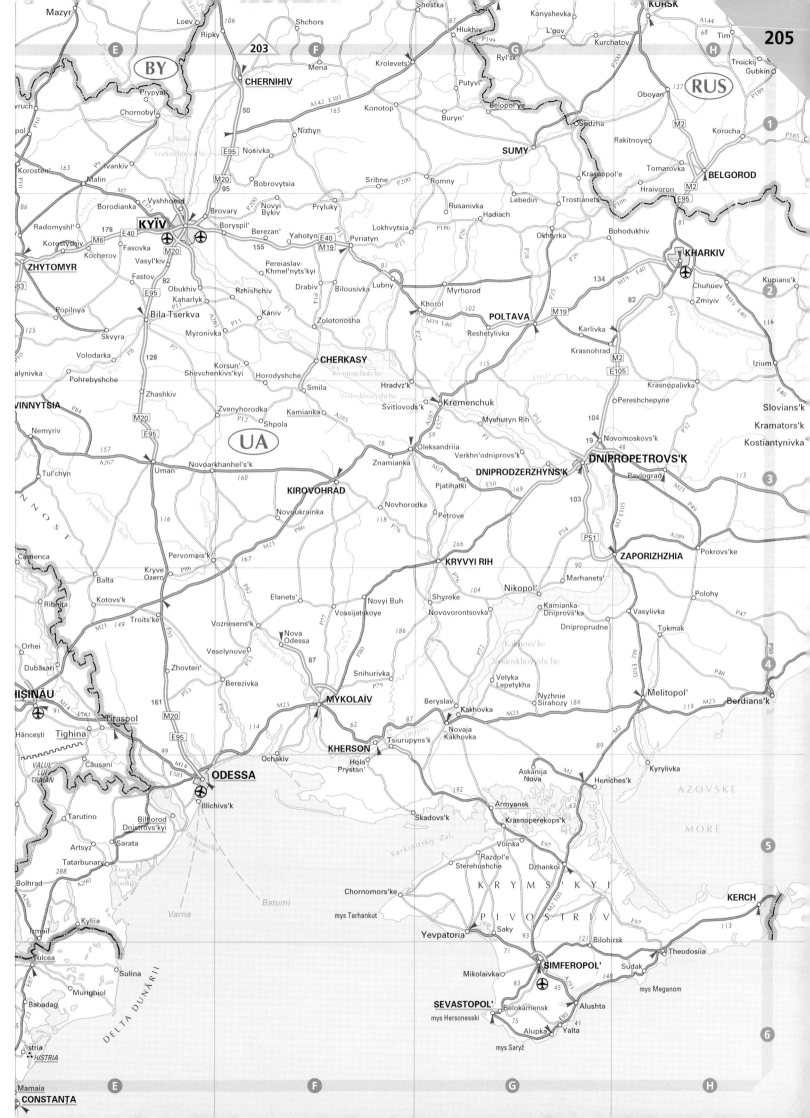

CITIES AND URBAN AREAS
CITTÀ E AREE URBANE
CIUDADES Y ÁREAS URBANAS
VILLES ET AIRES URBAINES
STÄDTE UND ZUFAHRTEN

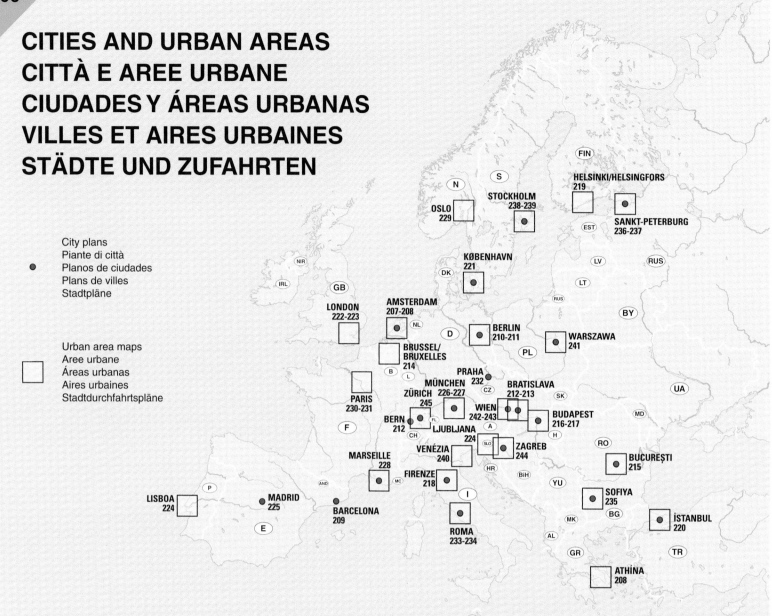

City plans
Piante di città
Planos de ciudades
Plans de villes
Stadtpläne

Urban area maps
Aree urbane
Áreas urbanas
Aires urbaines
Stadtdurchfahrtspläne

FIN
HELSINKI/HELSINGFORS 219
N   S   STOCKHOLM 238-239
OSLO 229   EST   SANKT-PETERBURG 236-237
LV   RUS
NIR   LT
IRL   KØBENHAVN 221
DK   BY
GB   RUS
LONDON 222-223   AMSTERDAM 207-208   BERLIN 210-211   WARSZAWA 241
NL   D   PL
BRUSSEL/ BRUXELLES 214   UA
B   L   PRAHA 232
MÜNCHEN 226-227   BRATISLAVA 212-213   MD
PARIS 230-231   ZÜRICH 245   CZ   SK
BERN 212   WIEN 242-243   BUDAPEST 216-217
F   CH   FL   A   RO
LJUBLJANA 224   SLO   ZAGREB 244   BUCUREȘTI 215
MARSEILLE 228   VENÉZIA 240   HR   BiH   YU
FIRENZE 218   SOFIYA 235
P   AND   MC   MK   BG   İSTANBUL 220
LISBOA 224   MADRID 225   I   AL   TR
E   BARCELONA 209   ROMA 233-234   GR
H   ATHÍNA 208
M

GB Legend	**I** Legenda	**E** Leyenda	**F** Légende	**D** Zeichenerklärung
Buildings	Caseggiati	Edificios	Immeubles	Gebäude
Monuments	Monumenti	Monumentos	Monuments	Denkmäler
Motorways, access points, service areas	Autostrade, caselli, stazioni di servizio	Autopista, accesos, stazioni di servizio	Autoroutes, accès, aires de service	Autobahnen, Anschlüsse, Tankstellen
Roads with motorway characteristics	Superstrade	Autovías	Routes-express	Autobahnähnliche Schnellstraßen
Through roads	Strade di attraversamento	Travesías	Routes de traversée	Hauptdurchfahrtsstraßen
Other roads	Altre strade	Otras carreteras	Autres routes	Sonstige Straßen
Numbering of motorway and national road	Numeri di autostrada e strada nazionale	Números de autopista y carretera nacional	Numéros d'autoroute et route nationale	Autobahnnummer, Staatsstraßennummer
Road in tunnel	Gallerie stradali	Túneles en carretera	Tunnels routiers	Straßentunnels
Directions	Direzioni	Direcciones	Directions	Richtungen
Railways and stations	Ferrovie e stazioni	Ferrocarriles y estaciones	Chemins de fer et gares	Eisenbahnen und Bahnhöfe
Gardens and parks; cemeteries	Giardini e parchi; cimiteri	Jardines y parques; cementerios	Jardins et parcs; cimetières	Gärten und Parks; Friedhöfe
Hospital	Ospedale	Hospital	Hôpital	Krankenhaus
Camping	Campeggio	Cámping	Camping	Campingplatz
Ferry route with car transportation	Trasporto auto su traghetto	Transbordador de automóviles	Bac pour autos	Autofähre
Panoramic view	Punto panoramico	Vista panorámica	Vue panoramique	Aussichtspunkt
Parking	Parcheggio	Aparcamiento	Parking	Parkplatz
Underground railway stations	Fermate della metropolitana	Estaciones del metro	Stations de métro	U-Bahnhöfe
Tourist information	Ufficio informazioni	Información turística	Informations touristiques	Touristische Auskünfte
Pedestrian areas	Aree pedonali	Áreas peatonales	Zones réservées aux piétons	Fußgängerzone

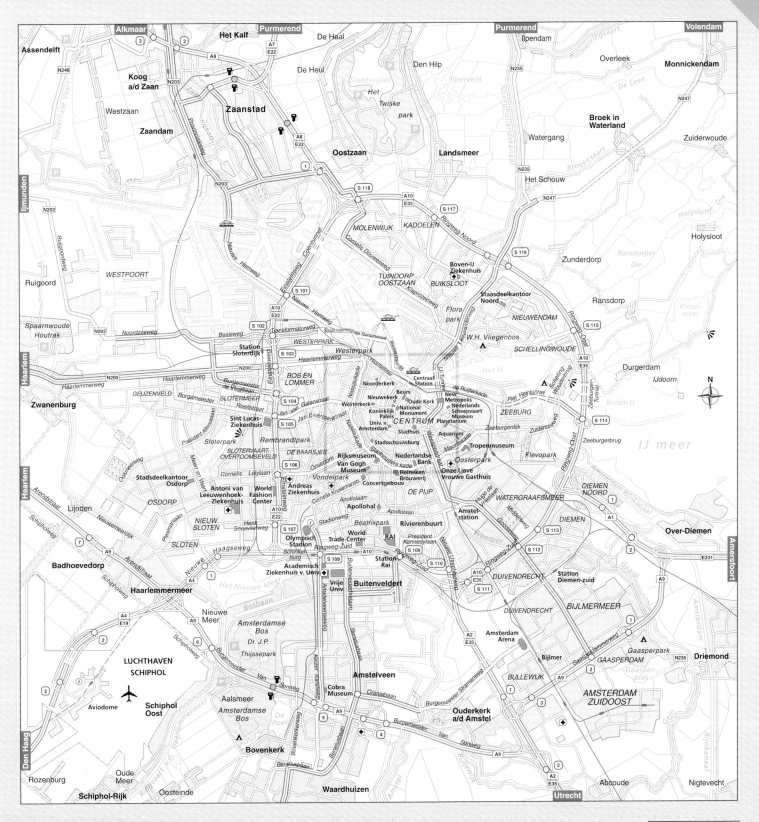

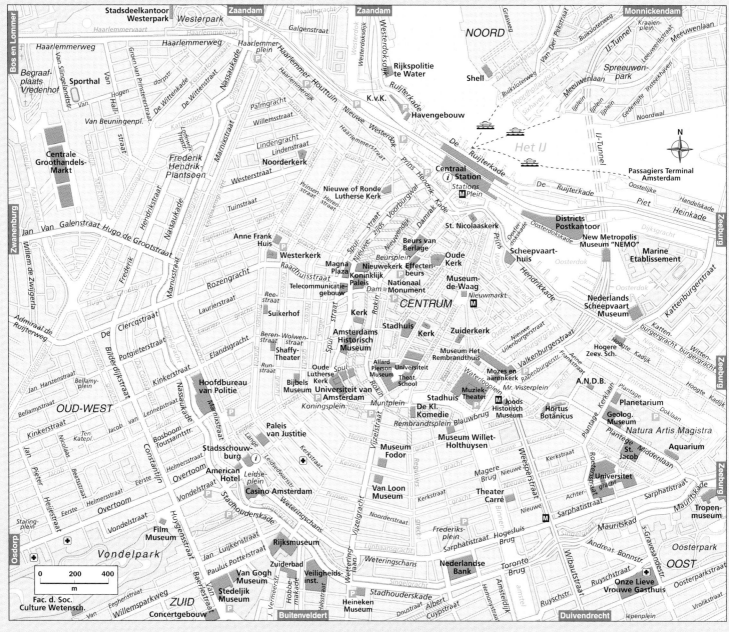

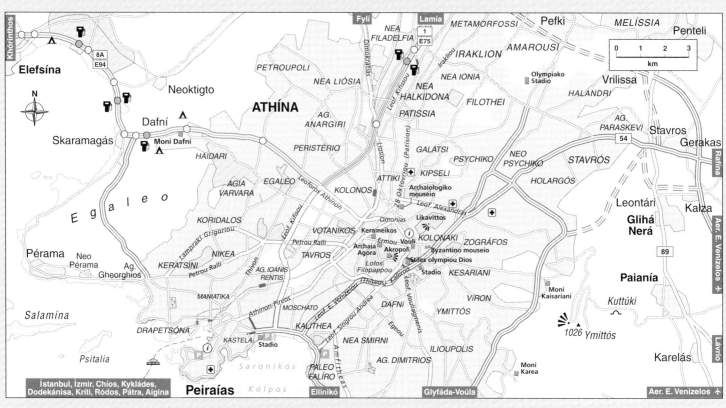

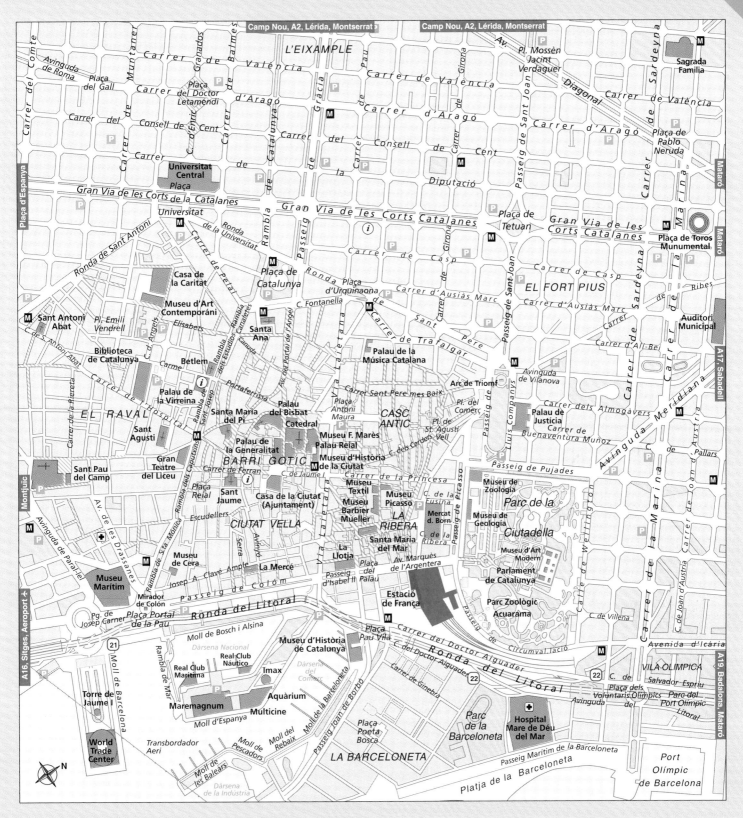

Camp Nou, A2, Lérida, Montserrat
Camp Nou, A2, Lérida, Montserrat

L'EIXAMPLE

Pl. Mossèn Jacint Verdaguer

Sagrada Familia

Carrer de Roma
Plaça del Gall
Carrer del Conte
Carrer de Balmes
Carrer Granados
Carrer de Muntaner
Carrer de València
Carrer de València
Carrer de València

Plaça del Doctor Letaméndi
Carrer del Doctor
d'Aragó
Carrer d'Aragó
Carrer d'Aragó
Carrer de Sardeyna
Carrer de Girona
Carrer de Sardeyna

Plaça de Pablo Neruda

Carrer del Consell de Cent
Carrer del Consell de Cent
Diagonal

Carrer de la Marina

Universitat Central Plaça
Gran Via de les Corts de la Catalanes
Diputació
Gran Via de les Corts Catalanes
Plaça de Tetuan
Gran Via de les Corts Catalanes

Plaça de Toros Munumental

Universitat
Ronda de la Universitat
Ronda de Sant Antoni

Rambla de Catalunya
Passeig de Gràcia
Plaça de Catalunya
Plaça d'Urquinaona
Carrer de Casp
Carrer de Casp
EL FORT PIUS

Casa de la Caritat
Carrer de Pelai
C. Fontanella

Museu d'Art Contemporáni
Carrer d'Ausiàs Marc
Carrer d'Ausiàs Marc

Sant Antoni Abat
Pl. Emili Vendrell
Santa Ana
Carrer de Trafalgar
Carrer d'Alt-Bei
Auditori Municipal

Biblioteca de Catalunya
Palau de la Música Catalana
Avinguda de Vilanova

Betlem
Carme
Portaferrissa
Arc de Triomf
Carrer dels Almogávers

EL RAVAL
Palau de la Virreina
Santa Maria del Pí
Palau del Bisbat
Plaça Antoni Maura
Carrer Sant Pere mes Baix
Pl. del Comerç
CASC ANTIC
Pl. de St. Agustí
Palau de Justicia
Carrer de Buenaventura Muñoz

Sant Agustí
Catedral
Museu F. Marès
Palau Reial
Pl. de St. Agustí Vell

Gran Teatre del Liceu
Palau de la Generalitat
BARRI GOTIC
Museu d'Història de la Ciutat
C. dels Carders
C. de Jaume I
Carrer de la Princesa
Museu de Zoologia
Parc de la
Passeig de Pujades

Sant Pau del Camp
Plaça Reial
Sant Jaume
Casa de la Ciutat (Ajuntament)
Museu Textil
Museu Picasso
C. de la Fusina
Museu de Geologia
Ciutadella

Museu de Cera
Escudellers
Serra
Avinyó
CIUTAT VELLA
Museu Barbier Mueller
LA RIBERA
Mercat d. Born
Museu d'Art Modern

Museu Marítim
Josep A Clavé Ample
La Mercé
La Llotja
Santa Maria del Mar
C. de la Ribera
Parlament de Catalunya

Mirador de Colón
Passeig de Colóm
Passeig d'Isabel II
Plaça del Palau
Av. Marquès de l'Argentera
Estació de França
Parc Zoológic Acuarama

Pg. de Josep Carner
Plaça Portal de la Pau
Ronda del Litoral
Plaça Pau Vila
Carrer del Doctor Aiguader
Ronda del Litoral

Moll de Bosch i Alsina
Museu d'Història de Catalunya
Carrer de Ginebra
VILA OLIMPICA

Dàrsena Nacional
Real Club Náutico
Dàrsena del Comerç
C. del Doctor Aiguader
Plaça dels Voluntaris Olímpics
Parc del Port Olímpic

Torre de Jaume I
Real Club Marítima
Imax
Carrer de Ginebra
Parc de la Barceloneta
Hospital Mare de Déu del Mar

Maremagnum
Aquàrium
Multicine
Plaça Poeta Bosca

World Trade Center
Transbordador Aeri
Moll d'Espanya
Moll del Rebaix
Moll de Pescadors
Passeig Joan de Borbó
LA BARCELONETA
Passeig Marítim de la Barceloneta
Port Olímpic de Barcelona

Moll de les Balears
Dàrsena de la Indústria
Platja de la Barceloneta

Plaça d'Espanya
Montjuïc
A16, Sitges, Aeroport
Mataró
A17, Sabadell
A19, Badalona, Mataró

0 100 200 300 400
m

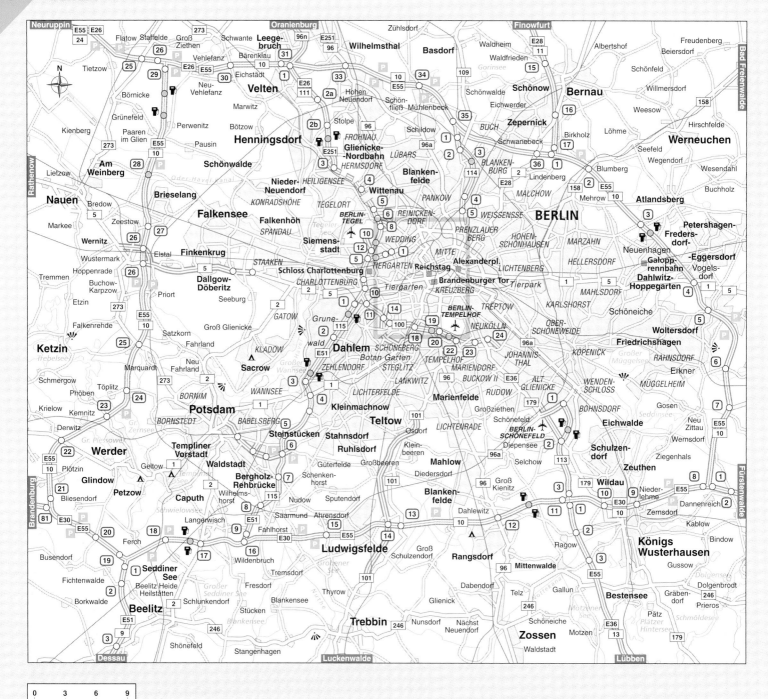

BERLIN

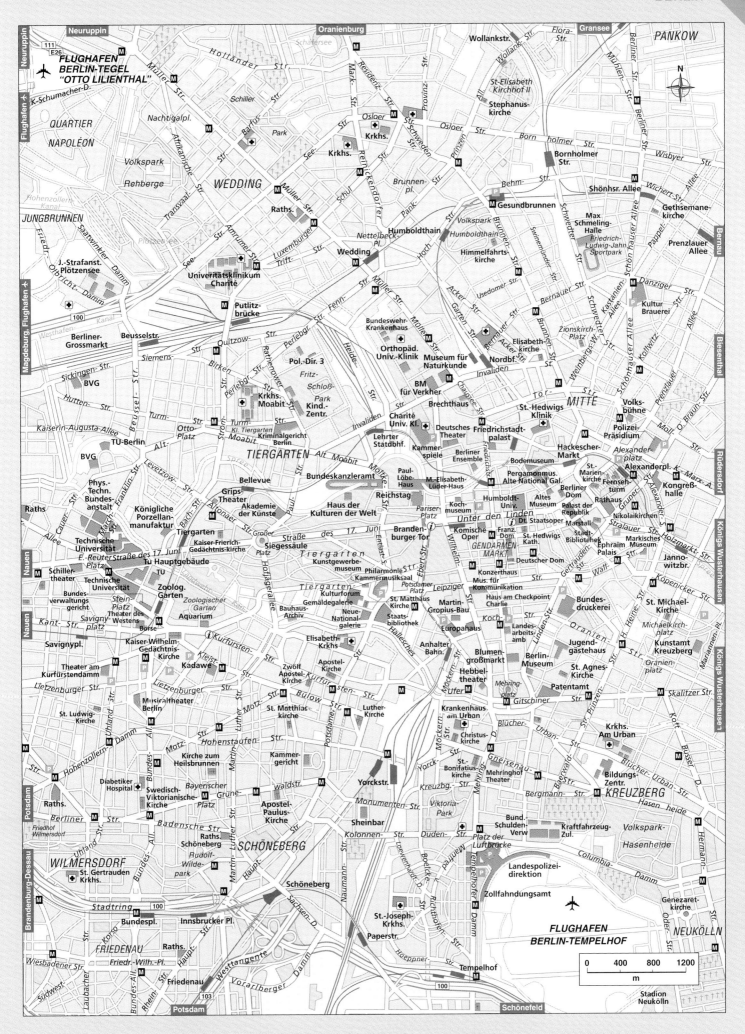

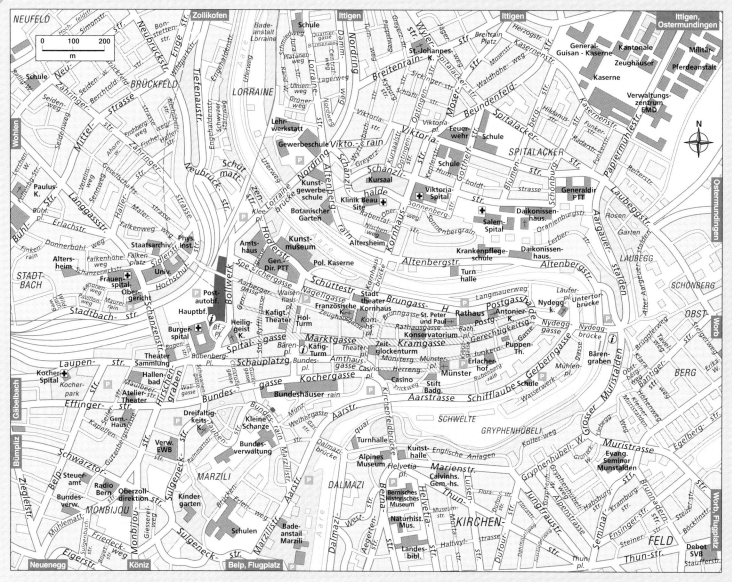

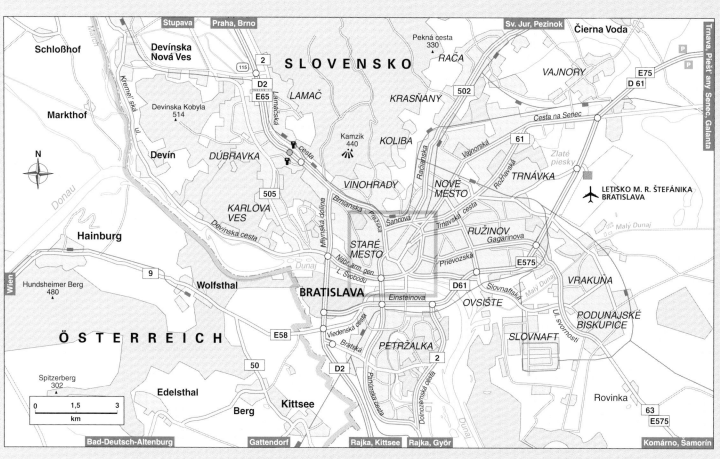

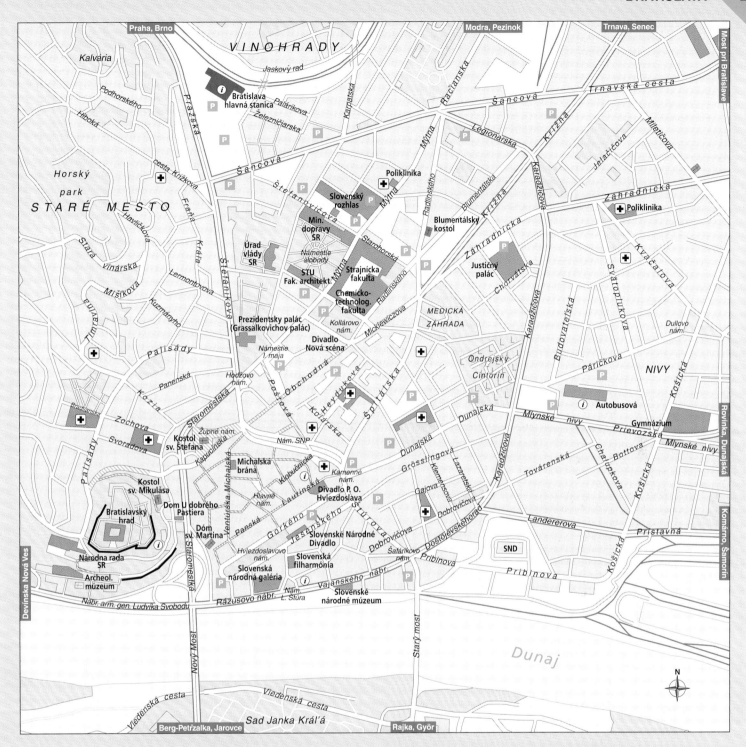

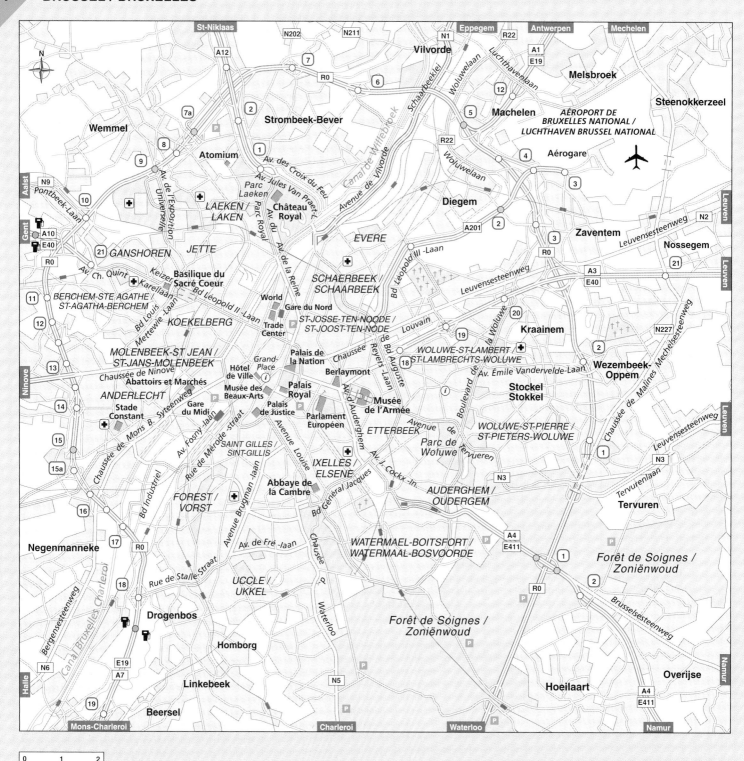

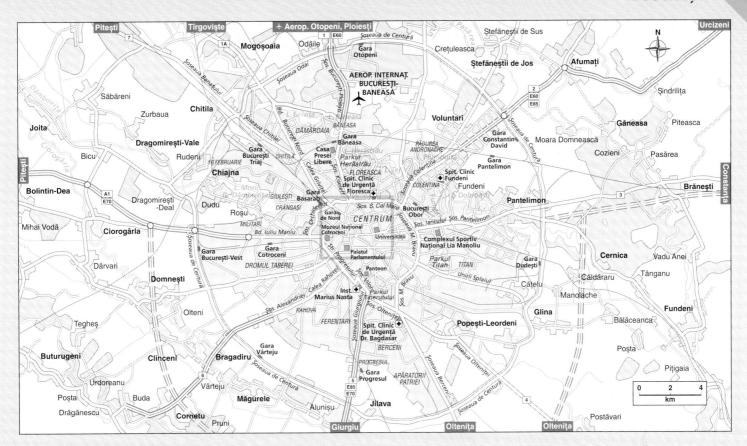

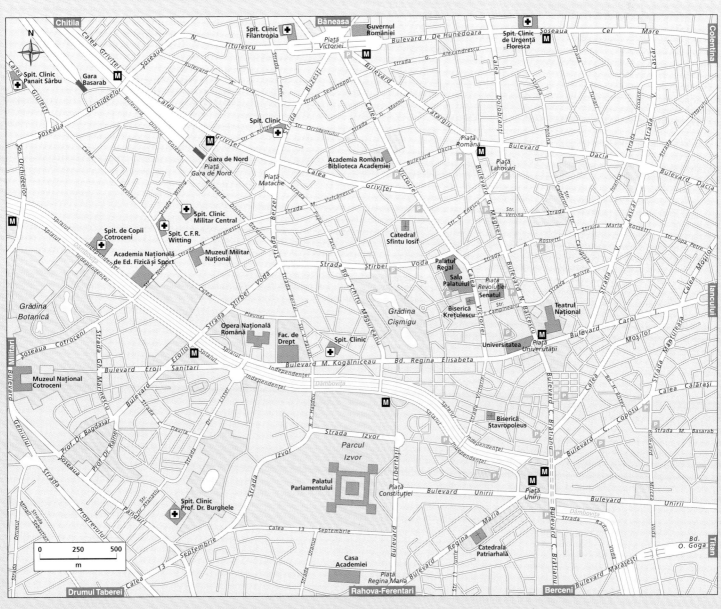

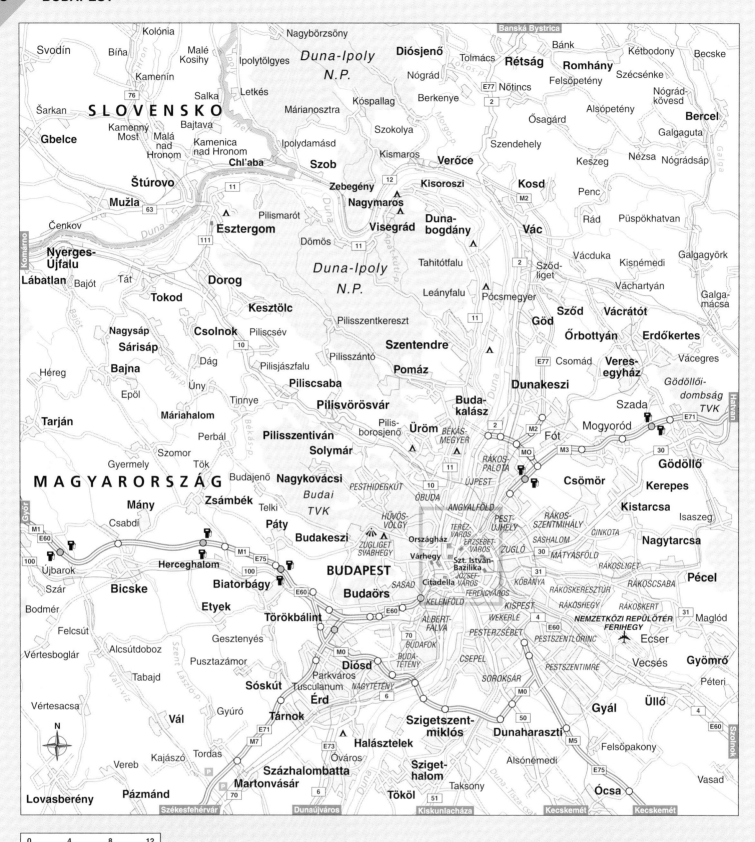

0   4   8   12

km

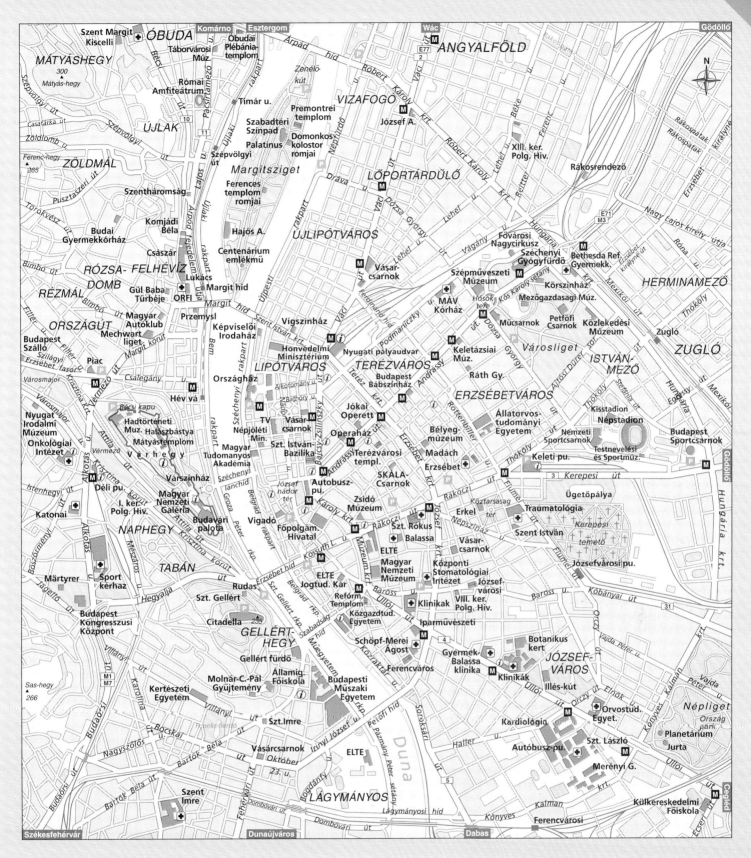

0   400   800
m

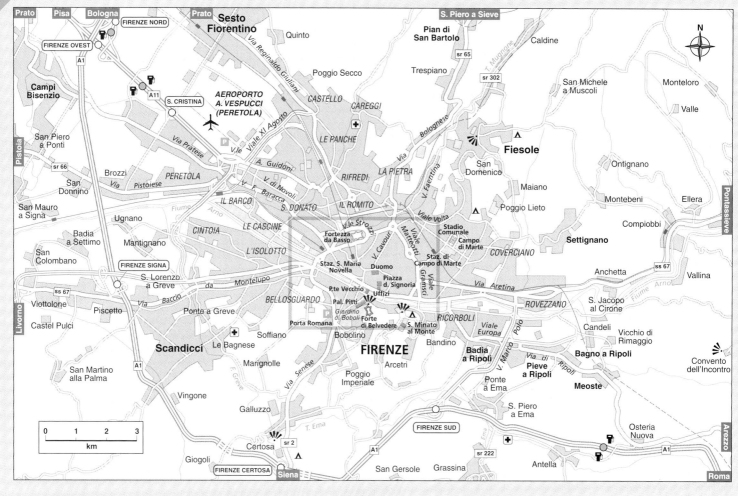

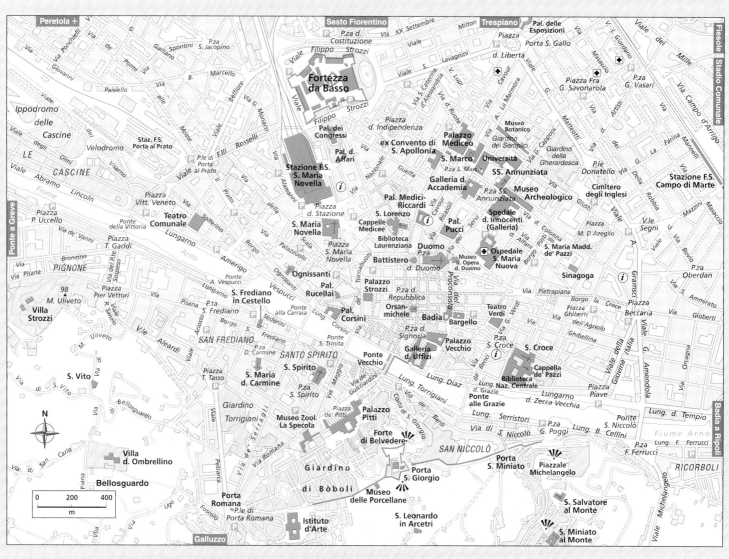

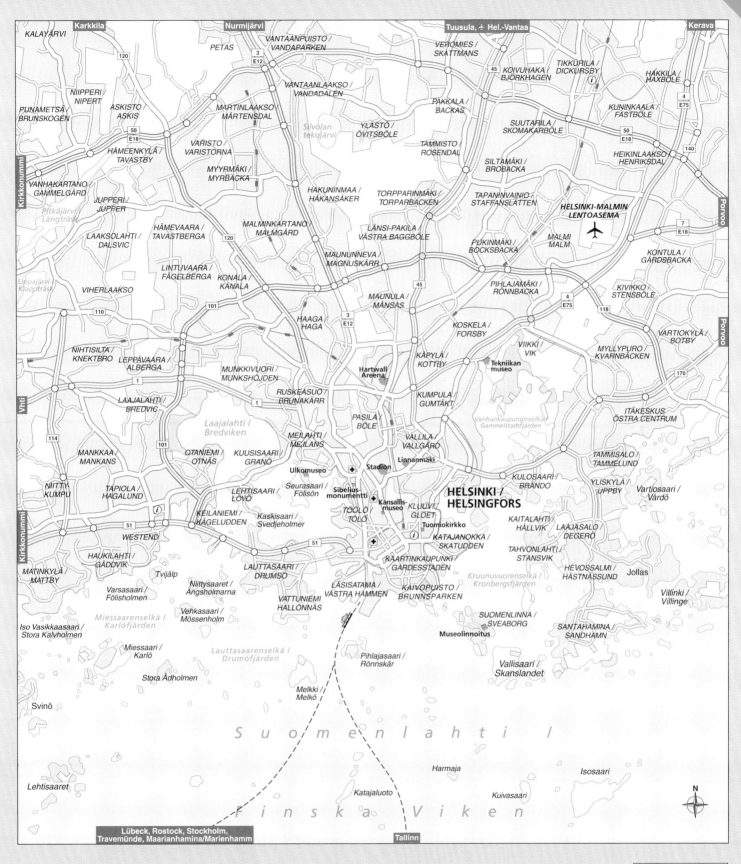

KALAYARVI

PETAS

VANTAANPUISTO / VANDAPARKEN

VEROMIES / SKATTMANS

TIKKURILA / DICKURSBY

HAKKILA / HAXBÖLE

NIIPPERI / NIPERT

VANTAANLAAKSO / VANDADALEN

KOIVUHAKA / BJÖRKHAGEN

PUNAMETSÄ / BRUNSKOGEN

ASKISTO / ASKIS

MARTINLAAKSO / MÄRTENSDAL

PAKKALA / BACKAS

SUUTARILA / SKOMAKARBÖLE

KUNINKAALA / FASTBÖLE

Silvolan tekojärvi

YLÄSTÖ / ÖVITSBÖLE

HÄMEENKYLÄ / TAVASTBY

VARISTO / VARISTORNA

TAMMISTO ROSENDAL

SILTAMÄKI / BROBACKA

HEIKINLAAKSO / HENRIKSDAL

VANHAKARTANO / GAMMELGÅRD

MYYRMÄKI / MYRBACKA

JUPPERI / JUPPER

Pitkäjärvi / Långträsk

HAKUNINMAA / HÅKANSÅKER

TORPPARINMÄKI / TORPARBACKEN

TAPANINVAINIO / STAFFANSLÄTTEN

HELSINKI-MALMIN LENTOASEMA

LAAKSOLAHTI / DALSVIC

HÄMEVAARA / TAVASTBERGA

MALMINKARTANO / MALMGÅRD

LÄNSI-PAKILA / VÄSTRA BAGGBÖLE

PUKINMÄKI / BÖCKSBACKA

MALMI MALM

KONTULA / GÅRDSBACKA

LINTUVAARA / FÅGELBERGA

MAUNUNNEVA / MAGNUSKÄRR

VIHERLAAKSO

KONALA / KÅNALA

PIHLAJAMÄKI / RÖNNBACKA

KIVIKKO STENSBÖLE

MAUNULA / MÅNSAS

NIHTISILTA / KNEKTBRO

HAAGA HAGA

KÄPYLÄ / KOTTBY

KOSKELA / FORSBY

VIIKKI / VIK

VARTIOKYLÄ / BOTBY

LEPPÄVAARA / ALBERGA

MUNKKIVUORI / MUNKSHÖJDEN

Tekniikan museo

MYLLYPURO / KVARNBÄCKEN

LAAJALAHTI / BREDVIG

RUSKEASUO / BRUNAKÄRR

Hartwall Areena

KUMPULA / GUMTÄKT

Laajalahti / Bredviken

PASILA / BÖLE

MEILAHTI / MEILANS

VALLILA / VALLGÅRD

Vanhankaupunginselkä Gammelstadsfjärden

ITÄKESKUS ÖSTRA CENTRUM

MANKKAA MANKANS

OTANIEMI OTNÄS

KUUSISAARI GRANÖ

Ulkomuseo

Stadion

Linnanmäki

TAMMISALO / TAMMELUND

NIITTY KUMPU

TAPIOLA / HAGALUND

LEHTISAARI / LÖVÖ

Seurasaari / Fölisön

Sibelius-monumentti

KULOSAARI / BRÄNDÖ

YLISKYLÄ UPPBY

Vartiosaari / Vårdö

HELSINKI / HELSINGFORS

WESTEND

KEILANIEMI / KÅGELUDDEN

Kaskisaari / Svedjeholmer

TÖÖLÖ TÖLÖ

Kansallis-museo

KLUUVI GLOET

KAITALAHTI / HÅLLVIK

LAAJASALO DEGERÖ

HAUKILAHTI / GÅDDVIK

Tuomiokirkko

KATAJANOKKA / SKATUDDEN

TAHVONLAHTI STANSVIK

MATINKYLÄ / MATTBY

Tvijälp

LAUTTASAARI / DRUMSÖ

KÄÄRTINKAUPUNKI / GARDESSTADEN

HEVOSSALMI / HÄSTNÄSSUND

Jollas

Varsasaari / Fölisholmen

Niittysaaret / Ängsholmarna

VATTUNIEMI HALLONNÄS

LÄNSISATAMA / VÄSTRA HAMMEN

KAIVOPUISTO / BRUNNSPARKEN

Kruunuvuorenselkä Kronbergsfjärden

Villinki Villinge

Iso Vasikkaasaari / Stora Kalvholmen

Vehkasaari / Mössenholm

Miessaarenselkä / Karlöfjärden

SUOMENLINNA / SVEABORG

SANTAHAMINA SANDHAMN

Miessaari / Karlö

Museolinnoitus

Stora Ådholmen

Lauttasaarenselkä / Drumöfjärden

Pihlajasaari / Rönnskär

Vallisaari / Skanslandet

Svinö

Melkki / Melkö

S u o m e n l a h t i /

Harmaja

Isosaari

Lehtisaaret

Katajaluoto

Kuivasaari

F i n s k a   V i k e n

N

Tallinn

0   1   2
Km

E12 / 3
E18 / 50
110
101
114
51
1
120
45
4 / E75
118
170
7 / E18
140
4 / E75
50 / E18

Kirkkonummi
Vihti
Porvoo

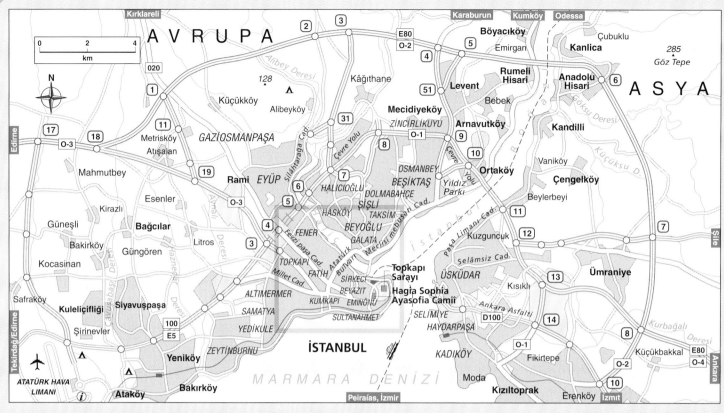

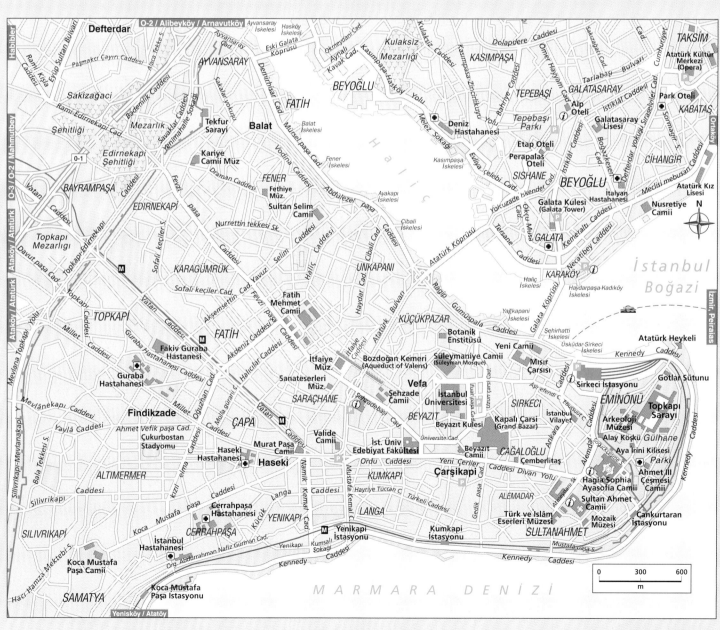

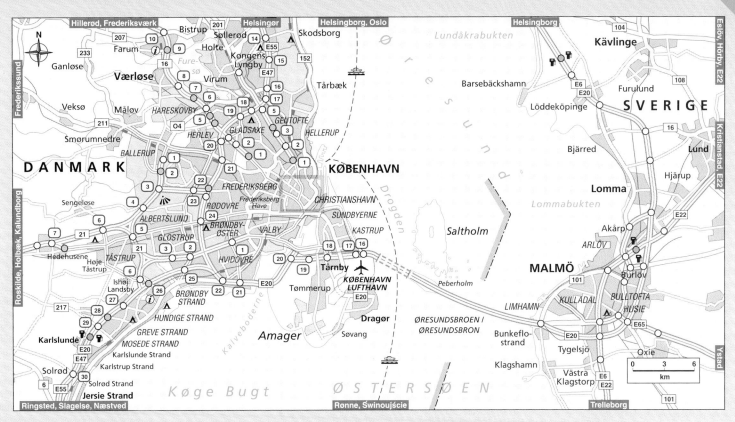

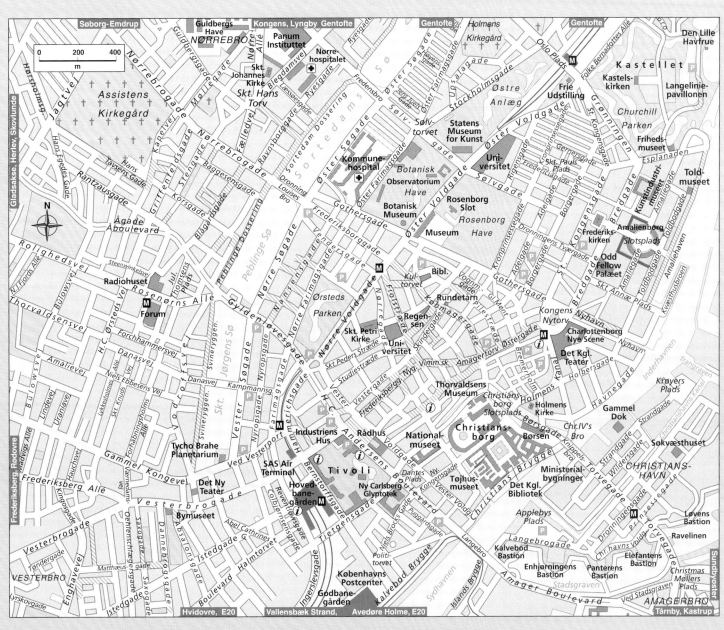

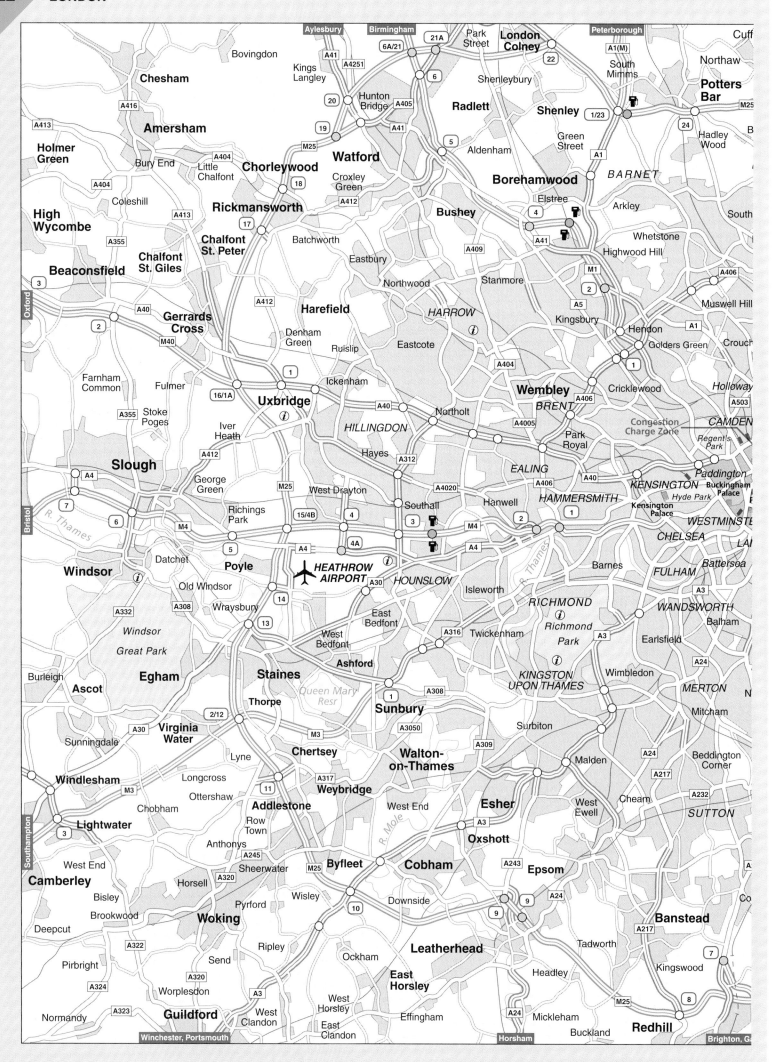

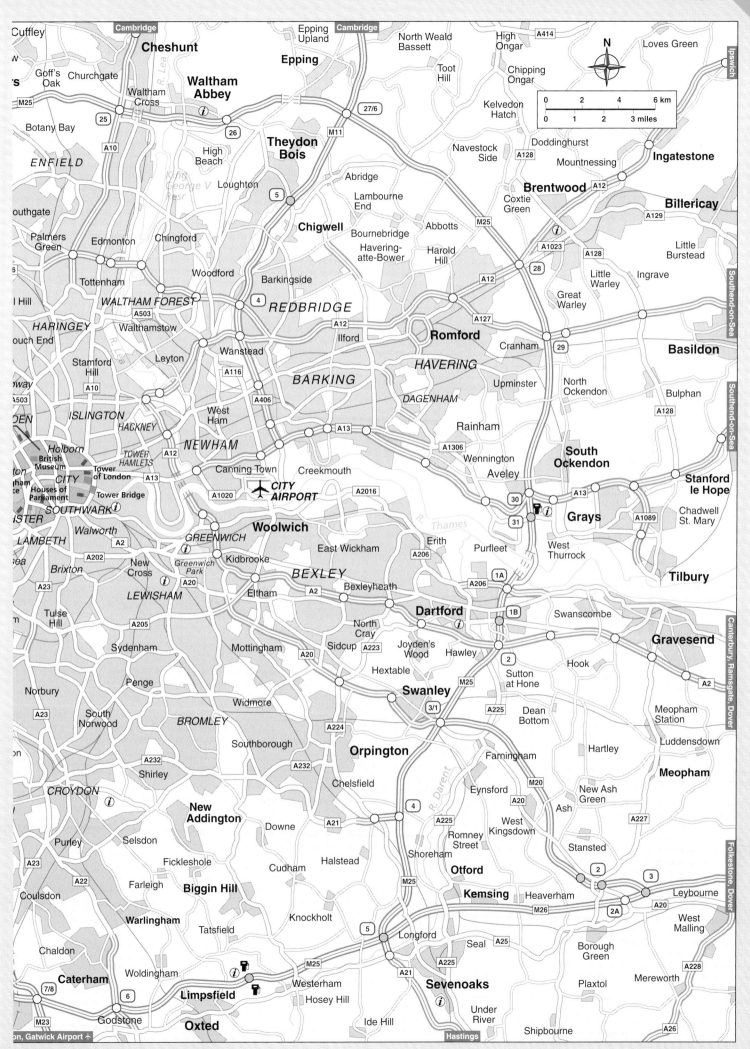

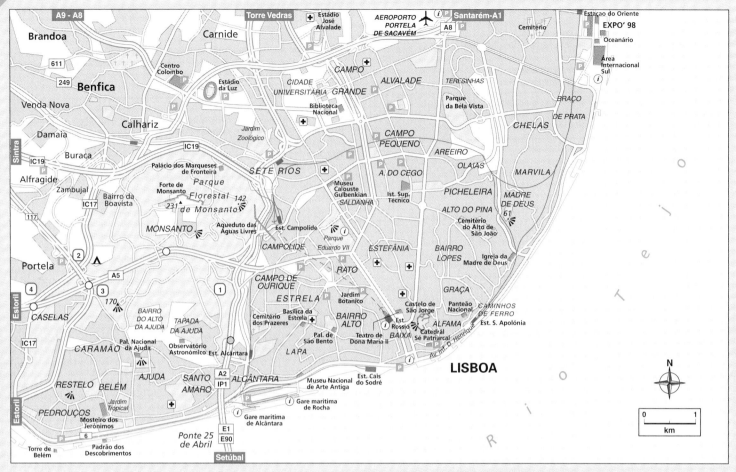

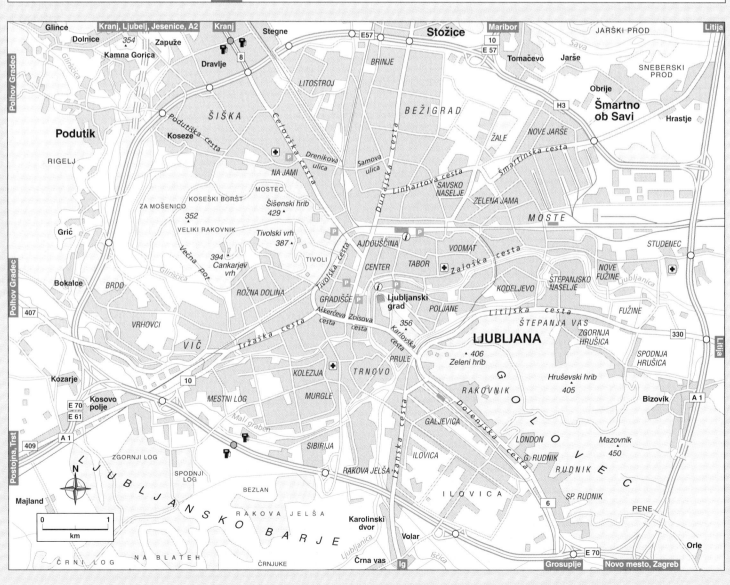

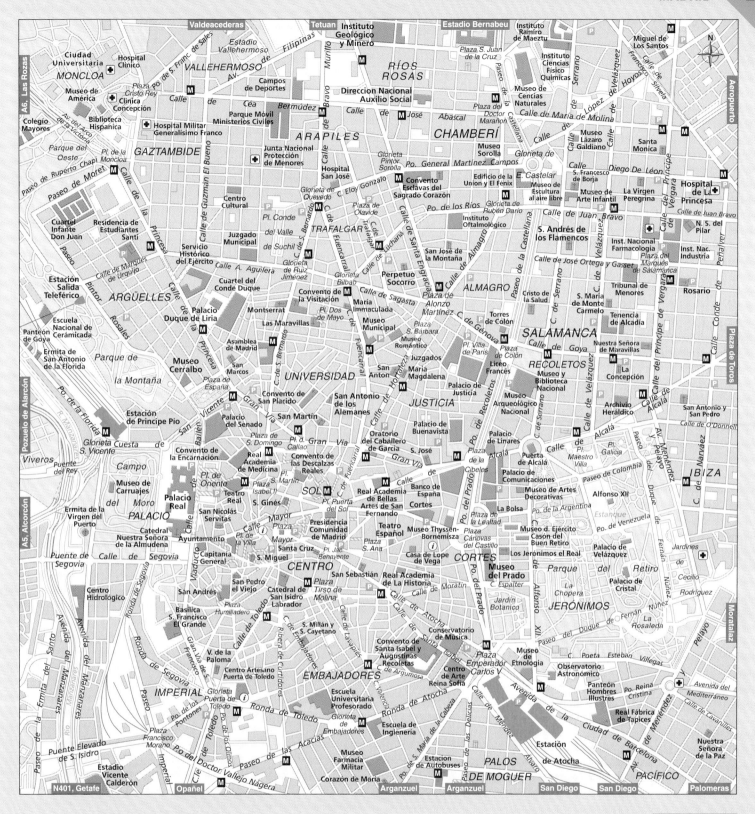

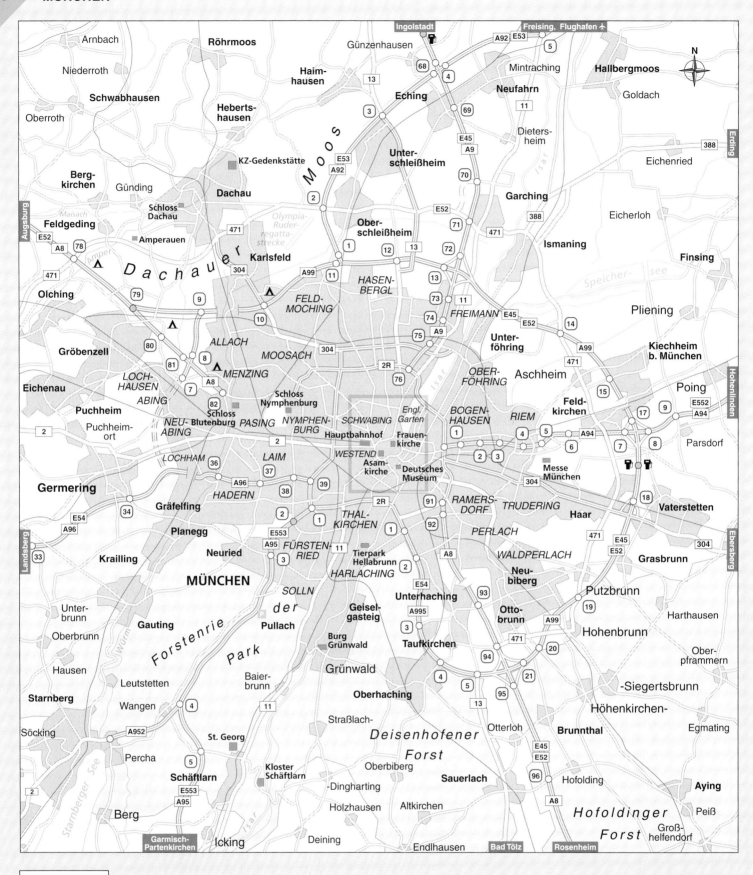

Ingolstadt
Freising, Flughafen ✈

N

Arnbach
Röhrmoos
Günzenhausen
Mintraching
Hallbergmoos

Niederroth
Haim-hausen
Eching
Neufahrn
Goldach

Schwabhausen
Heberts-hausen
KZ-Gedenkstätte
Unter-schleißheim
Dietersheim
Eichenried

Oberroth
Dachau
Garching
Eicherloh

Berg-kirchen
Schloss Dachau
Ober-schleißheim
Ismaning

Günding
Amperauen
HASEN-BERGL
Speicher-see
Pliening

Augsburg
Feldgeding
Maisach
Karlsfeld
FELD-MOCHING
Kiechheim b. München

Olching
Gröbenzell
MOOSACH
FREIMANN
Unter-föhring
Aschheim
Poing

Eichenau
LOCH-HAUSEN
MENZING
Schloss Nymphenburg
OBER-FÖHRING
Feld-kirchen
Parsdorf

Puchheim
ABING
NEU-ABING
Schloss Blutenburg
PASING
NYMPHEN-BURG
SCHWABING
Engl. Garten
BOGEN-HAUSEN
RIEM
Messe München

Puchheim-ort
Hauptbahnhof
Frauen-kirche
Hohenlinden

Germering
LOCHHAM
LAIM
WESTEND
Asam-kirche
Deutsches Museum
RAMERS-DORF
TRUDERING
Haar
Vaterstetten

Gräfelfing
HADERN
THAL-KIRCHEN
PERLACH

Planegg
FÜRSTEN-RIED
Tierpark Hellabrunn
WALDPERLACH
Grasbrunn

Landsberg
Krailling
Neuried
HARLACHING
Neu-biberg
Putzbrunn

MÜNCHEN
SOLLN
Geisel-gasteig
Otto-brunn
Hohenbrunn
Harthausen

Unter-brunn
Gauting
der
Pullach
Unterhaching
Ober-pframmern

Oberbrunn
Burg Grünwald
Taufkirchen
-Siegertsbrunn

Hausen
Forstenrie
Park
Baier-brunn
Grünwald
Höhenkirchen-

Starnberg
Leutstetten
Oberhaching
Brunnthal
Egmating

Söcking
Wangen
Straßlach-
Otterloh

Percha
St. Georg
Deisenhofener Forst
Sauerlach
Hofolding

Schäftlarn
Kloster Schäftlarn
Oberbiberg
Altkirchen
Hofoldinger Forst
Peiß

Berg
-Dingharting
Holzhausen
Groß-helfendorf

Garmisch-Partenkirchen
Icking
Deining
Endlhausen
Bad Tölz
Rosenheim

Starnberger See
Forstenrie
Würm

0   2   4
km

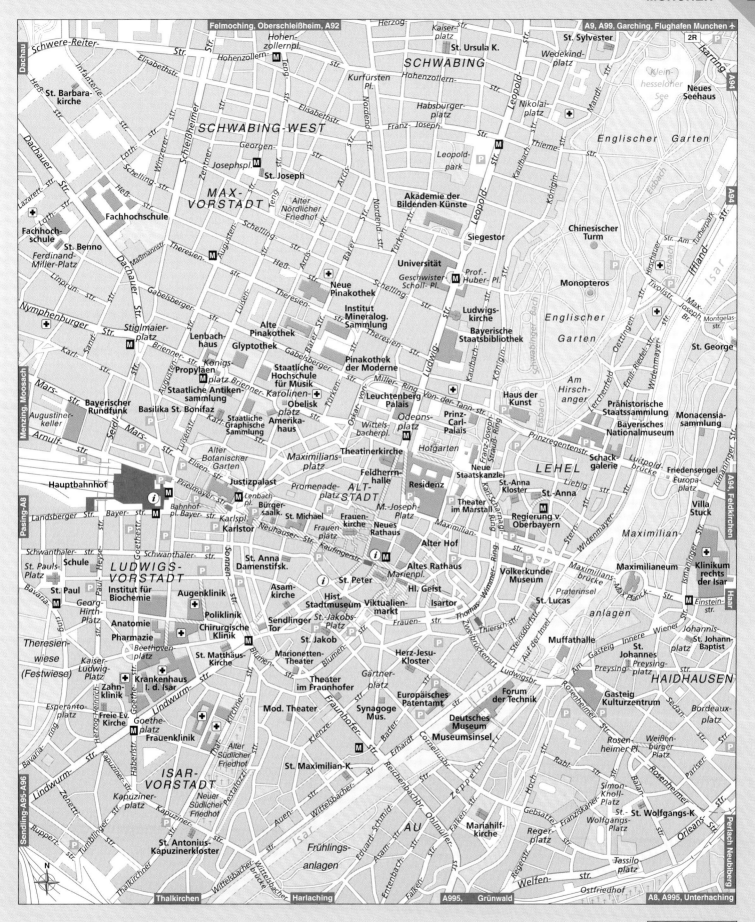

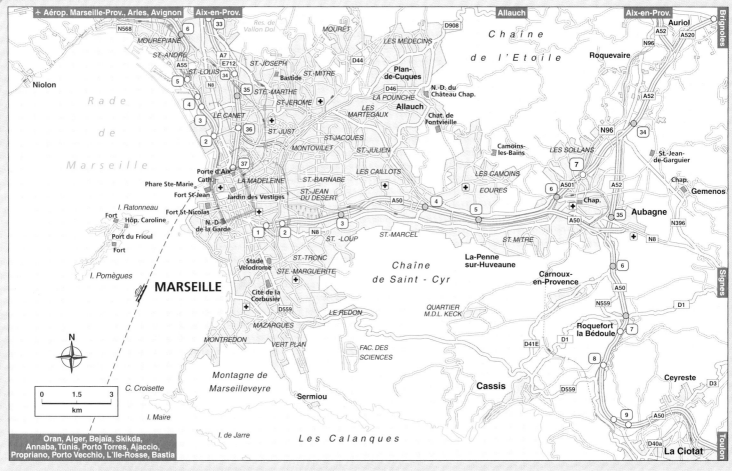

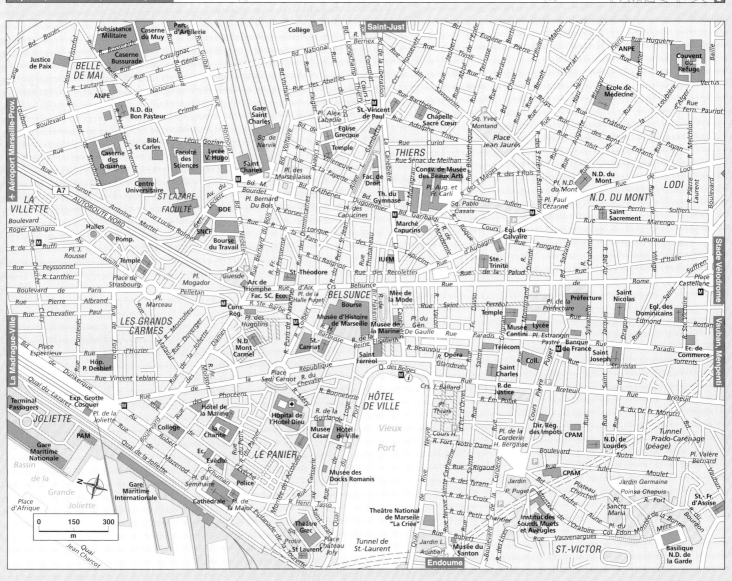

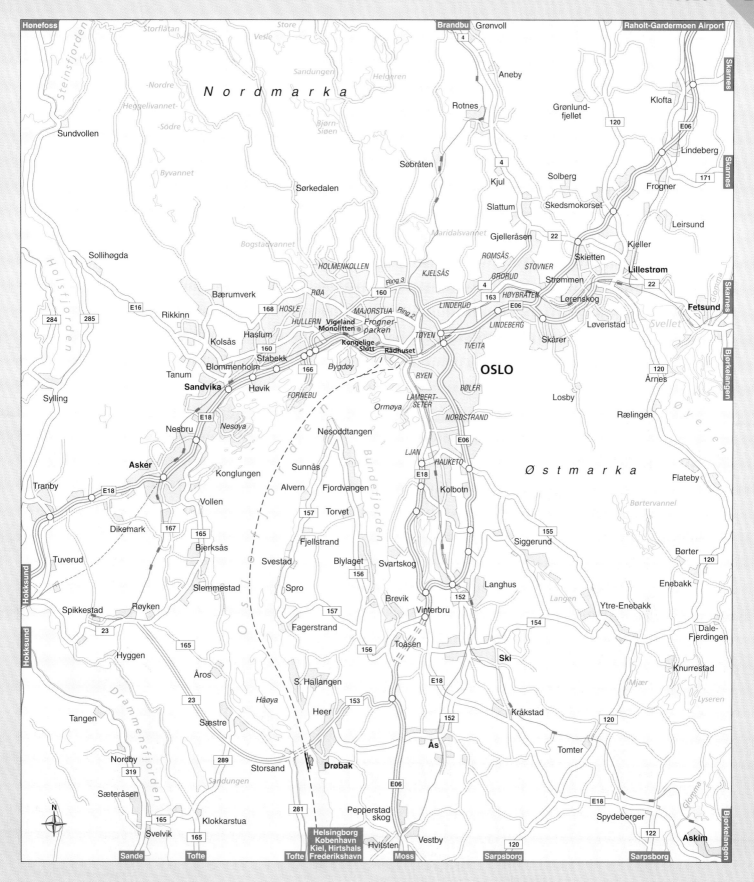

Grønvoll

Storflåtan
Store
Vesle
Sandungen
Helgeren

Aneby

Grønvoll

Klofta

Grønlund-
fjellet

Nordre
Heggelivannet
Södre
Bjørn-
Siøen

Rotnes

120

E06

Lindeberg

Skarnes

Sundvollen

N o r d m a r k a

Søbråten

4

Frogner

171

Byvannet

Sørkedalen

Kjul

Solberg

Skedsmokorset

Leirsund

Skarnes

Sollihøgda

Slattum

Maridalsvannet

Gjelleråsen

22

Kjeller

Steinsfjorden
Holsfjorden

HOLMENKOLLEN

Ring 3

KJELSÅS

ROMSÅS

STOVNER

Skjetten

Lillestrøm

Bærumverk

RØA

160

4

GRORUD

Strømmen

E16

Rikkinn

168 HOSLE

MAJORSTUA

Ring 2

LINDERUD

163

HØYBRÅTEN

E06

Lørenskog

22

Fetsund

284 285

HULLERN Vigeland
Monolitten

Frogner-
parken

TØYEN

LINDEBERG

Skårer

Svellet

Haslum

Kolsås

160

Kongelige
Slott

Rådhuset

TVEITA

Løvenstad

120

Stabekk

Bygdøy

RYEN

OSLO

Årnes

Tanum

Blommenholm

166

BØLER

Losby

Sandvika Høvik

FORNEBU

LAMBERT-
SETER

NORDSTRAND

Sylling

Nesøya

Ormøya

Rælingen

Bjørkelangen

E18

Nesbru

Nesoddtangen

E06

Ø s t m a r k a

Asker

Konglungen

Sunnås

LJAN

HAUKETO

Flateby

Tranby

Alvern

Fjordvangen

E18

Kolbotn

Børtervannet

E18

Vollen

157

Torvet

Dikemark

167

Bjerksås

Fjellstrand

Siggerund

155

Børter

Tuverud

165

Bundefjorden

Svestad

Blylaget

156

Svartskog

Langhus

120

Enebakk

Slemmestad

Spro

Brevik

152

Ytre-Enebakk

Spikkestad

Røyken

157

Vinterbru

154

Dale-
Fjerdingen

23

Fagerstrand

Langen

Ski

Hyggen

165

Toåsen

Knurrestad

Mjær

Åros

156

E18

Oslofjorden
Drammensfjorden

Håøya

153

Heer

152

Kråkstad

120

Lyseren

Tangen

23

S. Hallangen

Sæstre

Nordby

289

Storsand

Drøbak

Ås

Tomter

319

Sandungen

Sæteråsen

N

E06

E18

Klokkarstua

165

Pepperstad
skog

Spydeberger

122

Askim

Svelvik

165

Hvitsten

Vestby

120

281

0	2,5	5

km

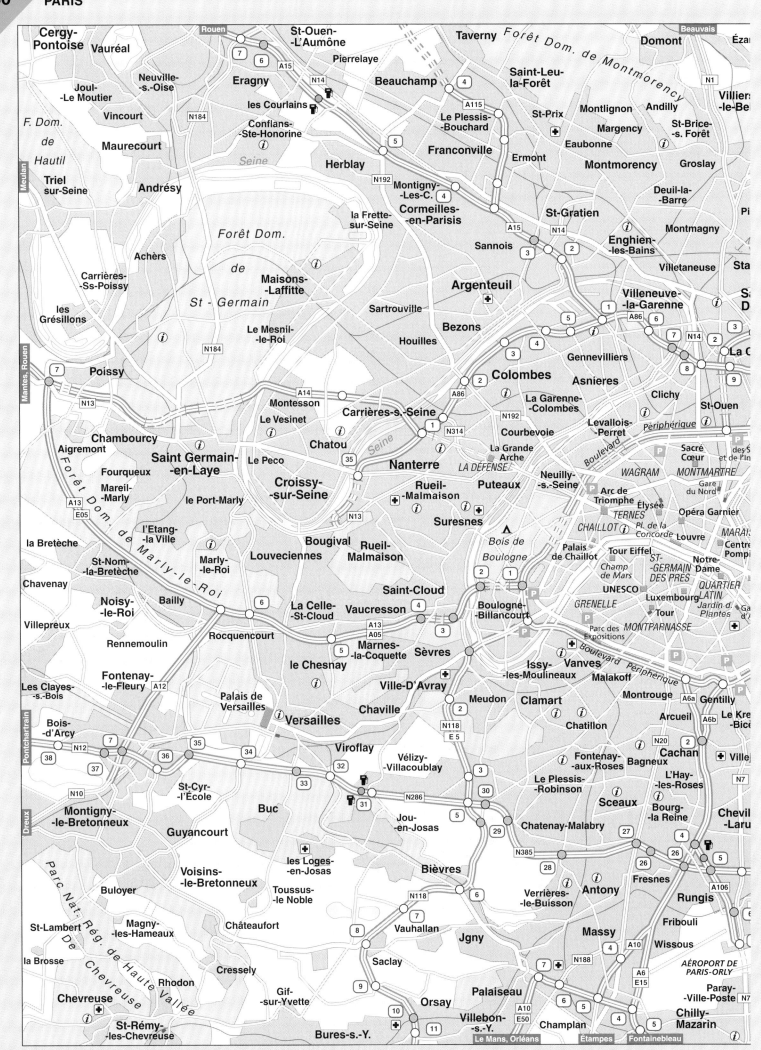

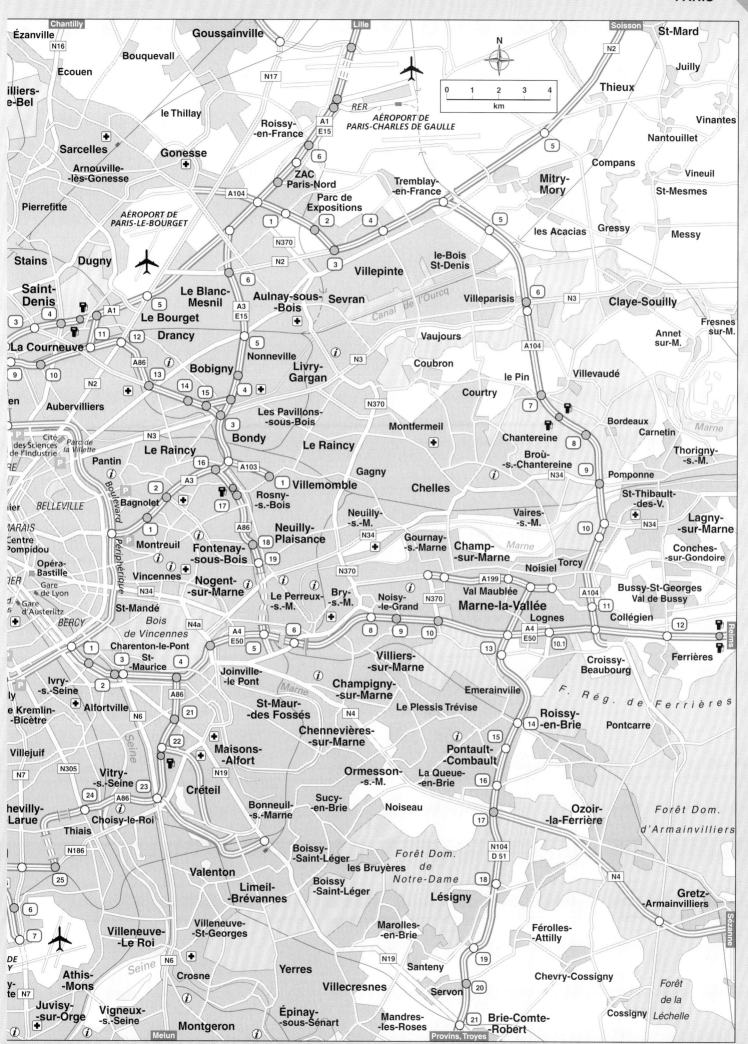

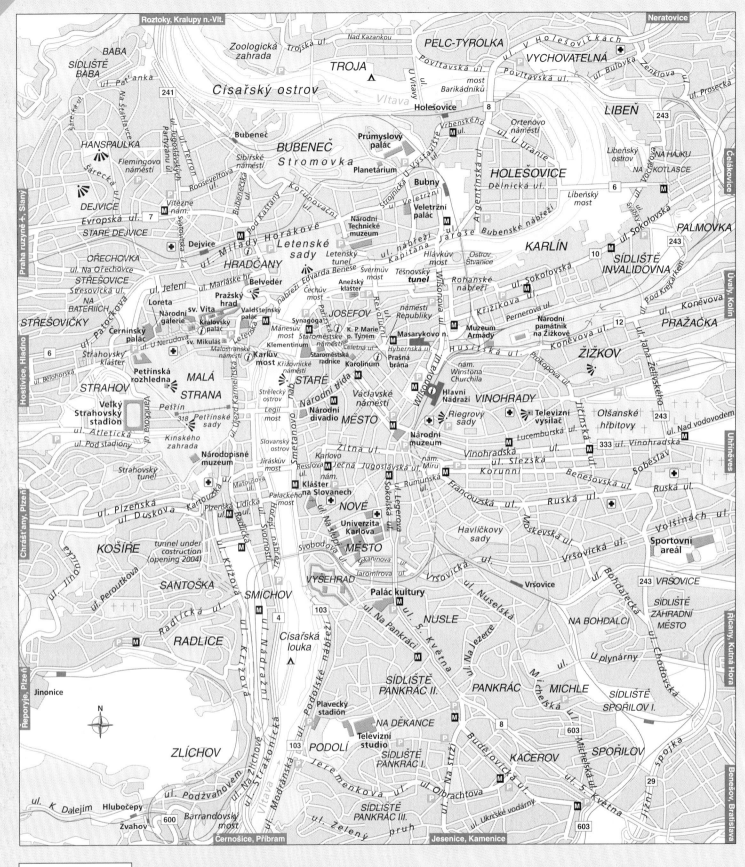

Neratovice

BABA
SÍDLIŠTĚ BABA

ul. Pať anka

Zoologická zahrada
Trojská ul.
Nad Kazankou

PELC-TYROLKA

ul. V Holešovičkách

VYCHOVATELNÁ

HANSPAULKA
Flemingovo náměstí

ul. Jugoslávských Partyzánů ul.
ul. Terron

Bubeneč

TROJA

Povltavská ul.
Povltavská ul.
ul. Buľovka
Zenklova

ul. Prosecká

Císařský ostrov
Vltava

most Barikádníků

Holešovice

8

LIBEŇ

243

Šárecka ul.
Na Šťáhlavce ul.

241

DEJVICE
STARÉ DEJVICE

Na Šárce ul.

Sibiřské náměstí
Bubenečská

Stromovka

Průmyslový palác

Planetárium

Vrbenského ul.

Ortenovo náměstí
ul. U Uranie

Libeňský ostrov

NA HÁJKU
NA KOTLASCE

 OŘECHOVKA
ul. Na Ořechovce
STŘEŠOVICE
Střešovická ul.
NA BATERIÍCH

Roseveltova ul.
Vítězné nám.
Evropská ul. 7
Svatovítská

Dejvice

Pod Kaštany

Korunovační ul.

Strojnická
ul.
Veletržní

Národní Technické muzeum

Veletržní palác

Bubny

Dělnická ul.

HOLEŠOVICE

Libeňský most

6
M

ul. Sokolovská

PALMOVKA

243

STŘEŠOVIČKY

ul. Patočkova

ul. Mlady Horákové

Letenské sady

Letenský tunel

ul. nábřeží Kapitána Jaroše
Bubenské nábřeží

KARLÍN

10

SÍDLIŠTĚ INVALIDOVNA

243

ul. Jelení

HRADČANY

Hlávkův most

Ostrov Štvanice

ul. Sokolovská

Pod Krejcárkem

6

Loreta
Národní galerie

Belvedér
sv. Víta
Pražský hrad
Královský palác

ul. Mariánské hr.
Chotkova

náměstí Edvarda Beneše
Švermův most
Čechův most
Anežský klášter

Těšnovský tunel
Rohanské nábřeží

Křižíkova ul.
Pernerova ul.

Národní památník na Žižkově

12

ul. Koněvova

PRAŽAČKA

ŽIŽKOV

ul. Jana Želivského

STŘEŠOVIČKY

Černínský palác

Valdštejnský palác

Mánesův most
Staroměstské náměstí

JOSEFOV
Synagóga
K. P. Marie p. Týnem

náměstí Republiky

Husitská ul.
Koněvova ul.

Národní muzeum

Strahovský klášter
ul. Bělohorská

U Nerudova
sv. Mikuláš

Klementinum
Malostranské náměstí
Karlův most

Celetná ul.
Staroměstská radnice
Karolinum

Masarykovo n.

Hybernská ul.

Muzeum Armády

Prokopova ul.

Prašná brána

nám. Winstona Churchila

Petřínská rozhledna

MALÁ STRANA

Strahovský tunel

Křižovnické náměstí
STARÉ

Petřín
318
Petřínské sady

Střelecký ostrov

Národní třída

Václavské náměstí

Hlavní Nádraží

VINOHRADY

Italská ul.

Olšanské hřbitovy

243

Velký Strahovský stadión

Vaníčkova ul.
ul. Atletická
ul. Pod stadióny

Legií most

Slovanský ostrov
Jiráskův most

Kinského zahrada

Národopisné muzeum

Národní divadlo

MĚSTO

Riegrovy sady

Národní muzeum

Televizní vysílač

Lucemburská ul.

ul. Nad vodovodem

Strahovský tunel

Resslova

Zítná ul.
Ječná Jugoslávská ul.

nám. Miru

Rumunská ul.

Vinohradská ul. Slezská

333 ul. Vinohradská

Sobĕsláv

Benešovská ul.

Ruská ul.

ul. Plzeňská
ul. Duskova

Kartouzská

Lidická ul.
Plzeňská

Matoušova
Radlická
Svornosti

Karlovo
Klášter na Slovanech
Palackého most

NOVÉ
MĚSTO

Univerzita Karlova
Na slupi

ul. Legerova

Sokolská ul.

Francouzská ul.

Moskevská ul.

Ruská ul.

Vršovická ul.

Volšinách ul.

KOŠÍŘE

tunnel under construction (opening 2004)

Křížová

Sekaninova
Jaromírova ul.

Havlíčkovy sady

Vršovická ul.

Sportovní areál

ul. Peroutkova
ul. Jinonická

SANTOŠKA

Radlická
Křížová ul.

VYŠEHRAD

Svobodova ul.

SMÍCHOV

Palác kultury

Vršovická ul.
ul. Nuselská

Vršovice

243 VRSOVICE

4
103

Císařská louka

ul. Na Pankráci
ul. 5. Května

NUSLE

Na Jezerce

NA BOHDALCI

SÍDLIŠTĚ ZAHRADNÍ MĚSTO

RADLICE

Podolské nábřeží
Strakonická

SÍDLIŠTĚ PANKRÁC II.

PANKRÁC

U plynárny

Michelská ul.

MICHLE

SÍDLIŠTĚ SPOŘILOV I.

Jinonice

Plavecký stadión

NA DĚKANCE

8

ul. Chodovská

ZLÍCHOV

103
PODOLÍ

Televizní studio

SÍDLIŠTĚ PANKRÁC I.

Budějovická ul.

603

Michelská ul.

SPOŘILOV

ul. Podzvahovem
ul. Na Zlíchově
Vltava
Modřanská

Jeremenkova ul.

SÍDLIŠTĚ PANKRÁC III.

KAČEROV

ul. 5. Května

Jižní spojka

29

ul. K Dalejím
Hlubočepy
Žvahov

600
Barrandovský most

ul. Zelený pruh

ul. Ukrčské vodárny

603

N

0   200   400
m

Praha ruzyně ↟, Slaný | Hostivice. Hladno | Chrášť any, Plzeň | Řeporyje, Plzeň | Úvaly, Kolín | Uhřineves | Říčany, Kutná Hora | Benešov, Bratislava

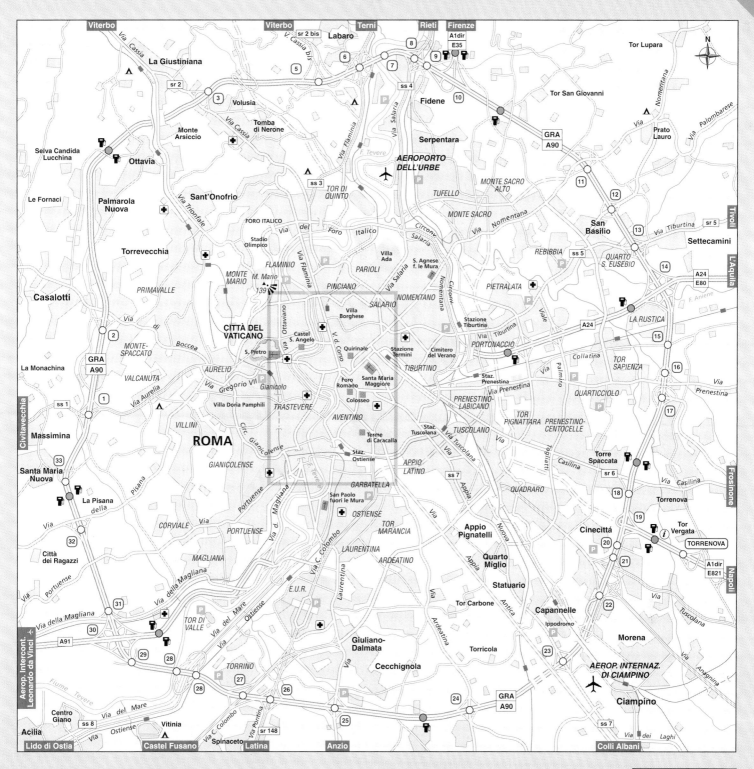

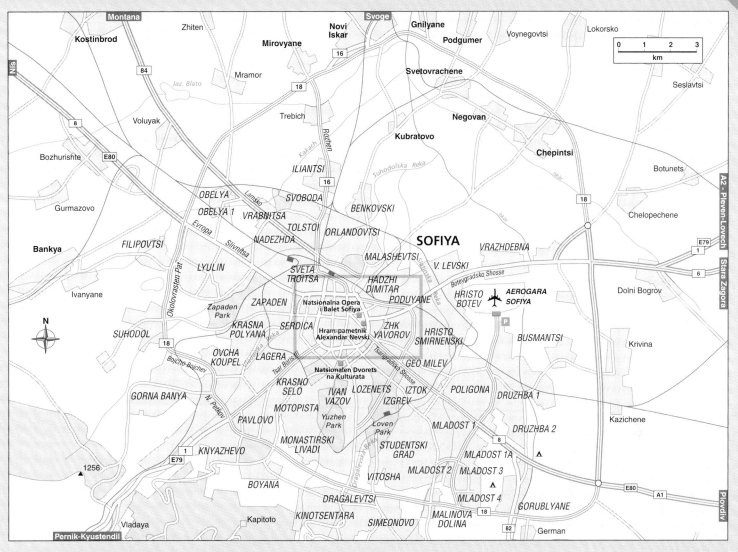

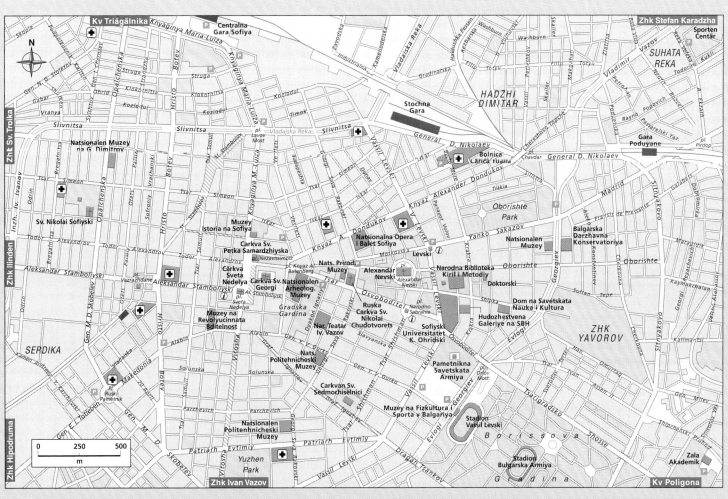

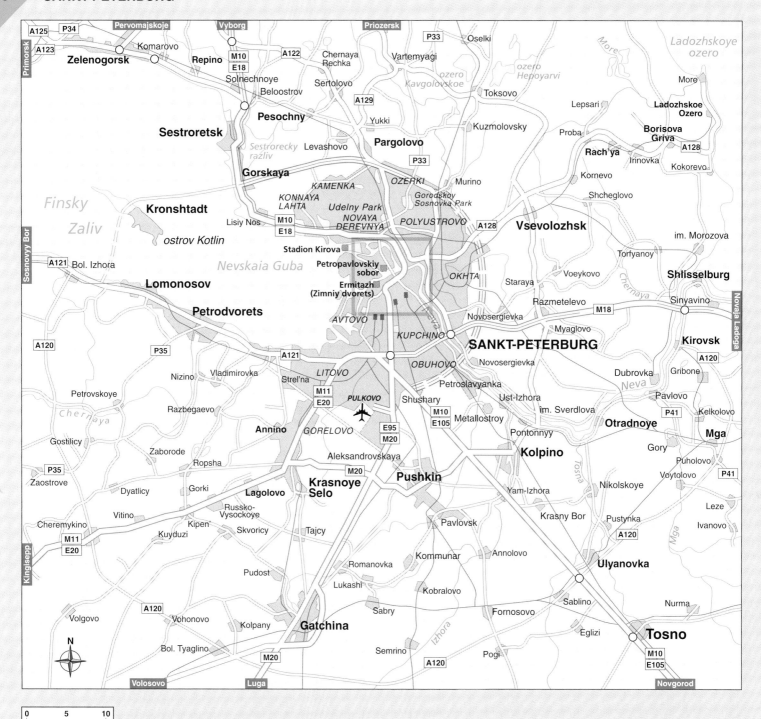

Zelenogorsk

Pervomajskoje | A125 | P34 | A123 | Primorsk

Komarovo

Repino

Vyborg

Priozersk

Oselki

P33

Chernaya Rechka

Vartemyagi

Sertolovo

Sestroretsk

Solnechnoye

Beloostrov

A122

M10 E18

A129

Yukki

Toksovo

ozero Kavgolovskoe

ozero Hepoyarvi

More

Lepsari

Proba

More

Ladozhskoe Ozero

Borisova Griva

A128

Pargolovo

Kuzmolovsky

Rach'ya

Irinovka

Kokorevo

Pesochny

Levashovo

P33

Murino

Kornevo

Gorskaya

Shcheglovo

KAMENKA

OZERKI

Gorodskoy Sosnovka Park

Ladozhskoye ozero

Finsky Zaliv

Kronshtadt

KONNAYA LAHTA

Udelny Park

NOVAYA DEREVNYA

POLYUSTROVO

Vsevolozhsk

Lisiy Nos

M10 E18

A128

im. Morozova

ostrov Kotlin

Stadion Kirova

Torfyanoy

Voeykovo

Sosnovyy Bor

Nevskaia Guba

Petropavlovskiy sobor

OKHTA

Staraya

Razmetelevo

Shlisselburg

A121

Bol. Izhora

Ermitazh (Zimniy dvorets)

Novosergievka

M18

Sinyavino

Lomonosov

AVTOVO

Myaglovo

Novaja Ladoga

Petrodvorets

KUPCHINO

SANKT-PETERBURG

Novosergievka

Neva

Kirovsk

A120

Dubrovka

A120

P35

A121

OBUHOVO

Petroslavyanka

Pavlovo

Gribone

Nizino

Vladimirovka

Strel'na

LITOVO

Shushary

Ust-Izhora

im. Sverdlova

Kelkolovo

Razbegaevo

M11 E20

PULKOVO

M10 E105

Metallostroy

Pontonnyy

P41

Petrovskoye

Chernaya

Annino

GORELOVO

E95 M20

Aleksandrovskaya

Otradnoye

Gory

Mga

Gostilicy

Zaborode

Ropsha

M20

Yam-Izhora

Krasny Bor

Nikolskoye

Puholovo

Voytolovo

P41

P35

Zaostrove

Dyatlicy

Gorki

Krasnoye Selo

Skvoricy

Tajcy

Pushkin

Pustynka

Leze

Ivanovo

Cheremykino

M11 E20

Vitino

Kipen'

Russko-Vysockoye

Kuyduzi

Lagolovo

Pavlovsk

Kommunar

Annolovo

Krasny Bor

Tosna

A120

Ulyanovka

Pudost

Romanovka

Lukashi

Kobralovo

Mga

Izhora

Sablino

Nurma

A120

Volgovo

Vohonovo

Kolpany

Gatchina

Sabry

Fornosovo

Eglizi

Tosno

Bol. Tyaglino

M20

Semrino

Pogi

A120

M10 E105

Volosovo | Luga | Novgorod

Kolpino

N

0 5 10
km

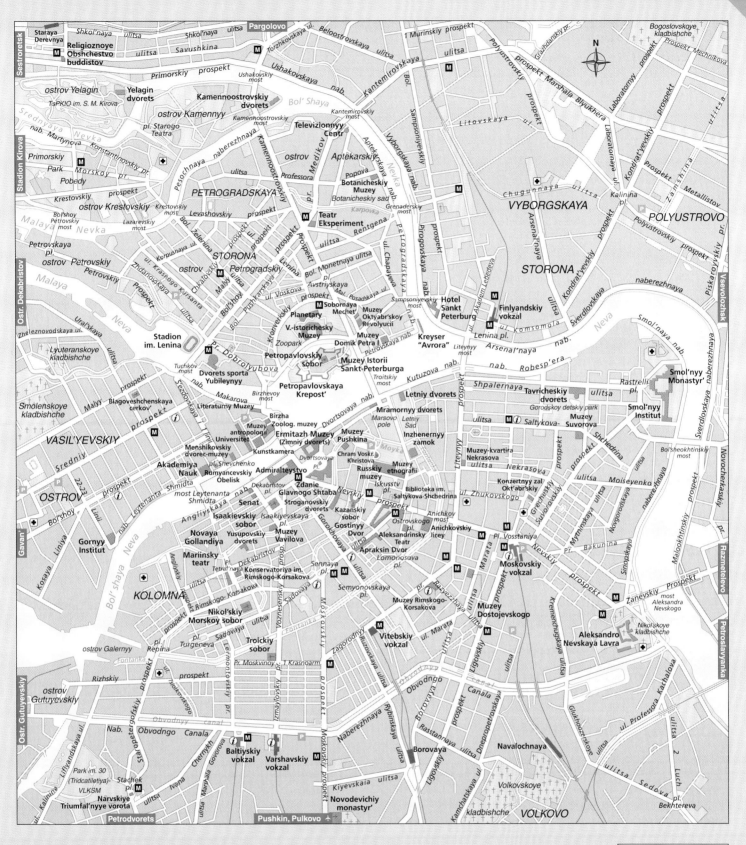

Pargolovo

Pushkin, Pulkovo

Staraya Derevnya
Shkol'naya ulitsa
Shkol'naya ulitsa
Savushkina
Torzhkovskaya ul.
Beloostrovskaya ulitsa
1 Murinskiy prospekt
Grazhdanskiy pr.
Bogoslovskoye kladbishche
Prospekt Mechnikova
Polyustrovskiy prospekt
Prospekt Marshala Blyukhera
Laboratornaya ul.
Laboratornyy prospekt

Religioznoye Obshchestvo buddistov
Primorskiy prospekt
Ushakovskaya nab.
Ushakovskiy most
Kantemirovskaya ulitsa
Sampsonievskiy prospekt
Litovskaya ul.
Kondrat'yevskiy prospekt
Metallistov
Kalinina pl.

ostrov Yelagin
TsPKiO im. S. M. Kirova
Yelagin dvorets
Kamenoostrovskiy dvorets
Bol' Shaya
Kamenoostrovskiy most
Kantemirovskiy most
VYBORGSKAYA
POLYUSTROVO

Srednaya Nevka
nab. Martynova
Konstantinovskiy pr.
ostrov Kamennyy
pl. Starogo Teatra
Televizionnyy Centr
Aptekarskiy pr.
Professora Popova
Chugunnaya ulitsa

Primorskiy Park Pobedy
Morskoy pr.
ostrov Medikov
ostrov
Botanicheskiy Muzey
Botanicheskiy sad
Grenaderskiy most
Arsenal'naya ul.
STORONA

Krestovskiy prospekt
Levashovskiy prospekt
PETROGRADSKAYA
Teatr Eksperiment
Rentgena
Karpovka
Pirogovskaya nab.
VYBORGSKAYA

ostrov Krestovskiy
Krestovskiy most
ulitsa
Ul. Chapayeva
STORONA

Bol'shoy Petrovskiy most
Lazarevskiy most
Lenina
STORONA
Bol. Monetnaya ulitsa
Hotel Sankt Peterburg
naberezhnaya

Petrovskaya pl.
ostrov Petrovskiy
Petrovskiy prospekt
PETROGRADSKIY
Bol. Posadskaya ulitsa
Avstriyskaya pl.
Samsonievskiy most
Finlyandskiy vokzal
Sverdlovskaya nab.

Malaya Nevka
Zhdanovskaya
Bol. Zelenina
ul. Krasnogo Kursanta
Bol'shoy prospekt
Voskova
Mal. Posadskaya ul.
Muzey Oktyabr'skoy Revolyucii
Akadem Lebedeva
Lenina pl.
ul. komsomola
Neva

ostrov Petrovskiy
Chkalovskiy pr.
Malyy prospekt
Sobornaya Mechet'
Planetary
V.-istorichesky Muzey
Zoopark
Muzey Domik Petra I
Kreyser "Avrora"
Arsenal'naya nab.
Smol'naya nab.

Ural'skaya ul.
Petrovskiy prospekt
Stadion im. Lenina
Tuchkov most
Petropavlovskiy sobor
Muzey Istorii Sankt-Peterburga
Petrovskaya nab.
Liteynyy pr.
nab. Robesp'era

Lyuteranskoye kladbishche
Pr. Dobrolyubova
Dvorets sporta Yubileynyy
Birzhevoy most
Petropavlovskaya Krepost'
Troitskiy most
Kutuzova nab.
Smol'nyy Monastyr'
Rastrelli pl.

Smolenskoye kladbishche
Makarova nab.
Dvortsovaya nab.
Shpalernaya ulitsa
Tavricheskiy dvorets
Smol'nyy Institut

VASIL'YEVSKIY
Malyy prospekt
Blagoveshchenskaya cerkov'
Literaturnyy Muzey
Birzha
Zoolog. muzey
Muzey antropologii
Letniy dvorets
Mramornyy dvorets
Marsovo pole
Letniy Sad
Gorodskoy detskiy park
Muzey Suvorova
Saltykova-Shchedrina
Sverdlovskaya naberezhnaya
Novocherkasskiy pr.

Srednyy prospekt
Universitet
Ermitazh Muzey (Zimnyy dvorets)
Muzey Pushkina
Inzhenernyy zamok
ulitsa

Menshikovskiy dvorec-muzey
Kunstkamera
Chram Voskr. Khristova
Muzey etnografii
Muzey-kvartira Nekrasova
Nekrasova ulitsa

OSTROV
22-23
Akademiya Nauk
Romyancevskiy Obelisk
Dvortsovaya
Russkiy muzey
Iskusstv pl.
Biblioteka im. Saltykova-Shchedrina
Konzertnyy zal Okt'abr'skiy
Moiseyenko ulitsa
Bol'sheokhtinskiy most

Bol'shoy prospekt
Shmidta
Admiralteystvo
Nevskiy prospekt
Grechskiy prospekt
Suvorovskiy prospekt

Kosaya Liniya
most Leytenanta Shmidta
Dekabristov pl.
Zdanie Glavnogo Shtaba
Kazanskiy sobor
Gostinyy Dvor
Aleksandrinskiy Teatr
Anichkov most
Aleksandrinskiy licey
Anichkovskiy
Ligovskiy prospekt
Pr. Bakunina
Novgorodskaya ulitsa

Gornyy Institut
Senat
Stroganovskiy dvorets
ul. Zhukovskogo
Maloohktinskiy pr.

Angliyskaya nab.
Isaakievskiy sobor
Isaakiyevskaya pl.
Apraksin Dvor
Lomonosova pl.
Pl. Vosstaniya
Moskovskiy vokzal

Novaya Gollandiya
Yusupovskiy dvorets
Muzey Vavilova
Gorokhovaya
Ostrovskogo pl.
Nevskiy prospekt
most Aleksandra Nevskogo

Mariinsky teatr
Tetral'naya pl.
Konservatoriya im. Rimskogo-Korsakova
Sennaya pl.
ulitsa
Semyonovskaya pl.
Marata
Nikol'skoye kladbishche

KOLOMNA
Pr. Rimskogo-Korsakova
Moskovskiy prospekt
Fontanka
Sadovaya
Voznesenskiy pr.
Muzey Rimskogo-Korsakova
Muzey Dostojevskogo
Aleksandro Nevskaya Lavra

Nikol'skiy Morskoy sobor
pl. Repina
pl. Turgeneva
Sadovaya
Vitebskiy vokzal
ul. Marata
Kremenchugskaya ulitsa

ostrov Galernyy
Troickiy sobor
Pr. Moskvinoy, 1 Krasnoarm.
Zagorodnyy
Ruzovskaya ulitsa
Dnepropetrovskaya ul.

ostrov Gutuyevskiy
Rizhskiy prospekt
Izmaylovskiy pr.
Obvodnyy Canala
Borovaya
Obvodngo Canala
Navalochnaya

Park im. 30 (Tridcatiletiya)-VLKSM
Nab. Obvodngo Canala
Baltiyskiy vokzal
Varshavskiy vokzal
Borovaya
Volkovskoye kladbishche

Stachek pl.
Narvskiye Triumfal'nye vorota
Novodevichiy monastyr'
Kiyevskaia ulitsa
VOLKOVO
pl. Bekhtereva

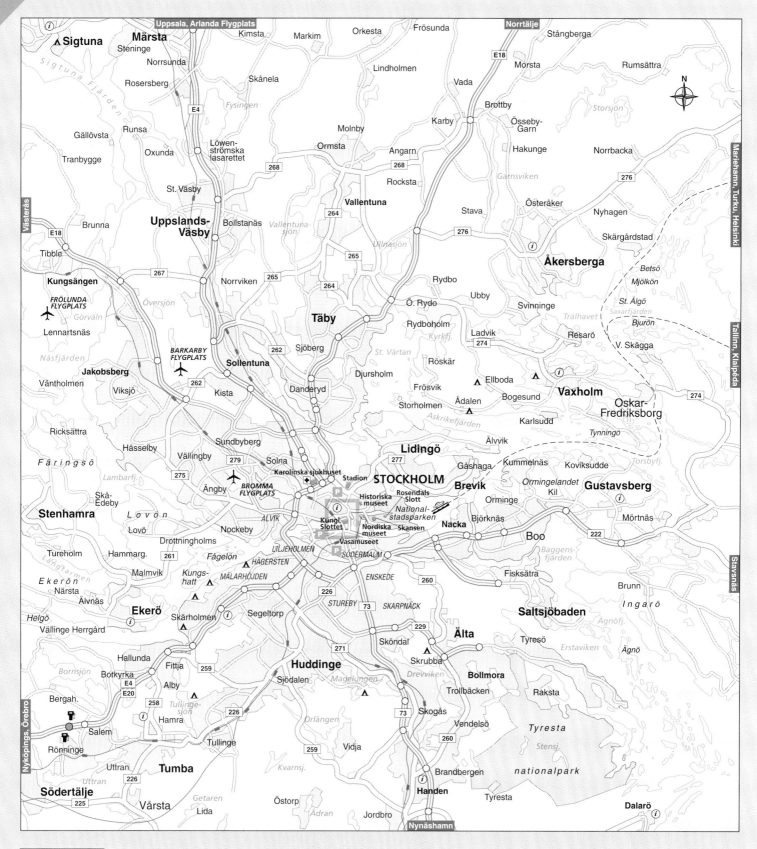

Sigtuna Märsta Kimsta Markim Orkesta Frösunda Stångberga

Steninge Lindholmen E18 Morsta Rumsättra

Norrsunda Skånela Vada

Rosersberg Molnby Brottby Össeby-Garn Storsjön

Gällövsta Runsa Ormsta Angarn Karby Hakunge Norrbacka

Oxunda Löwen-strömska lasarettet 268 Rocksta 268 276

Tranbygge St. Väsby Vallentuna Stava Österåker

Brunna Uppslands-Väsby Bollstanäs 264 Nyhagen

Tibble Vallentuna-sjön Skärgårdstad

Kungsängen 267 265 264 276 Åkersberga

FRÖLUNDA FLYGPLATS Norrviken 265 Rydbo Betsö

Översjön 264 Ubby Svinninge Mjölkön

Lennartsnäs Täby Ö. Rydo St. Älgö

Näsfjärden 262 Sjöberg Rydboholm Ladvik 274 Resarö Bjurön

BARKARBY FLYGPLATS St. Värtan 274 V. Skägga

Jakobsberg 262 Kista Danderyd Djursholm Röskär Vaxholm

Väntholmen Viksjö Frösvik Ådalen Bogesund Oskar-Fredriksborg

Ricksättra Sundbyberg Storholmen Karlsudd 274

Hässelby Vällingby 279 Solna Älvvik Tynningö

Färingsö 275 Lambarfj. Karolinska sjukhuset Stadion STOCKHOLM Gåshaga Kummelnäs Koviksudde

Skå-Edeby Ängby BROMMA FLYGPLATS Historiska museet Rosendals Slott Brevik Ormingelandet Kil Gustavsberg

Stenhamra Lovön Alvik Kungl. Slottet National-stadsparken Orminge Mörtnäs

Lovö Nockeby Nordiska museet Skansen Björknäs Boo 222

Drottningholms Vasamuseet Nacka

Tureholm Hammarg. 261 Fågelön LILJEHOLMEN SÖDERMALM Baggens-fjärden

Malmvik HÄGERSTEN Fisksätra Brunn

Ekerön Kungs-hatt MÄLARHÖJDEN ENSKEDE 260 Ingarö

Närsta STUREBY SKARPNÄCK Saltsjöbaden Agnöfj.

Helgö Älvnäs Skärholmen 226 73 229 Älta Tyresö Agnö

Vällinge Herrgård Ekerö Segeltorp Sköndal Erstaviken

Hallunda Fittja Skrubba Bollmora

Bornsjön Botkyrka 259 Huddinge Skogås Drevviken Trollbäcken Raksta

Bergah. E4 Alby Sjödalen Magelungen Tyresta

E20 258 Hamra 226 Vendelsö Tyresta nationalpark

Rönninge Salem Örlången 73 Skogås Stensj.

Uttran Tullinge 259 Vidja Brandbergen

Tumba 226 260

Södertälje Vårsta Getaren Östorp Handen Tyresta

225 Lida Ådran Jordbro Dalarö

Västerås E18 E4 Nyköpings, Örebro Mariehamn, Turku, Helsinki Tallinn, Klaipéda Stavsnäs

0 2,5 5
km

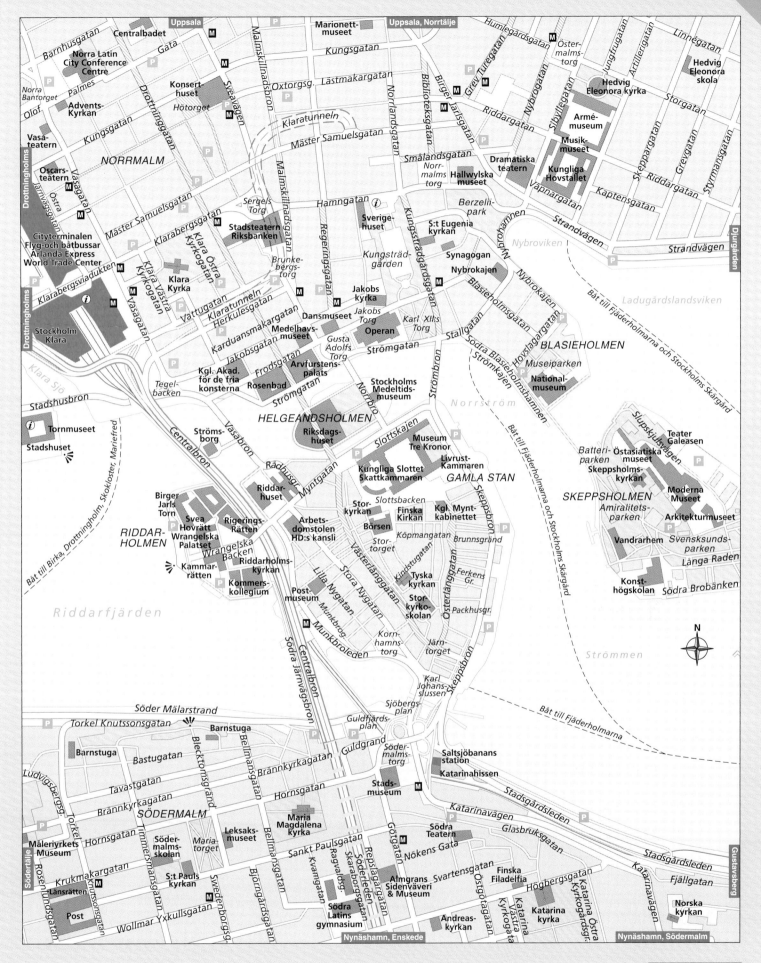

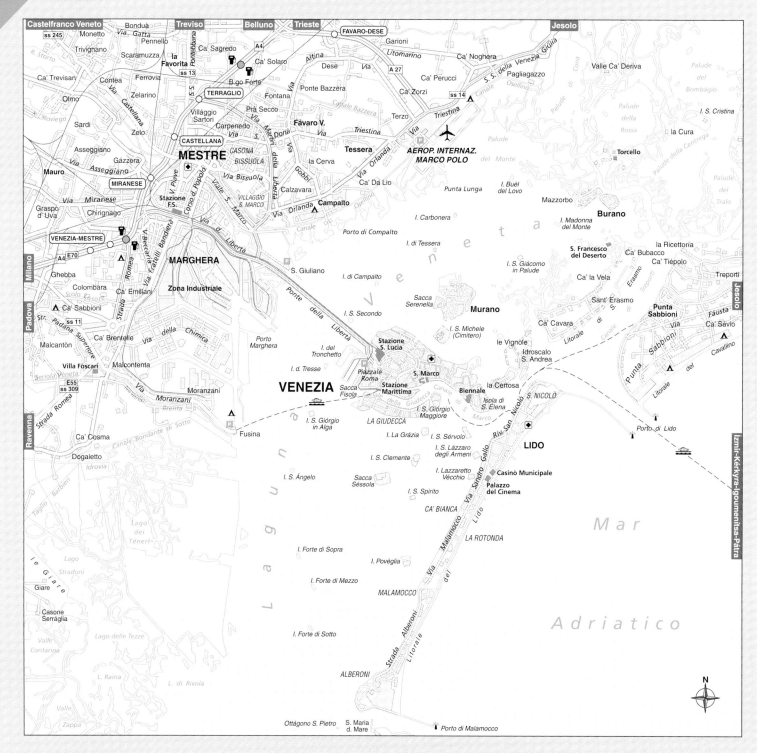

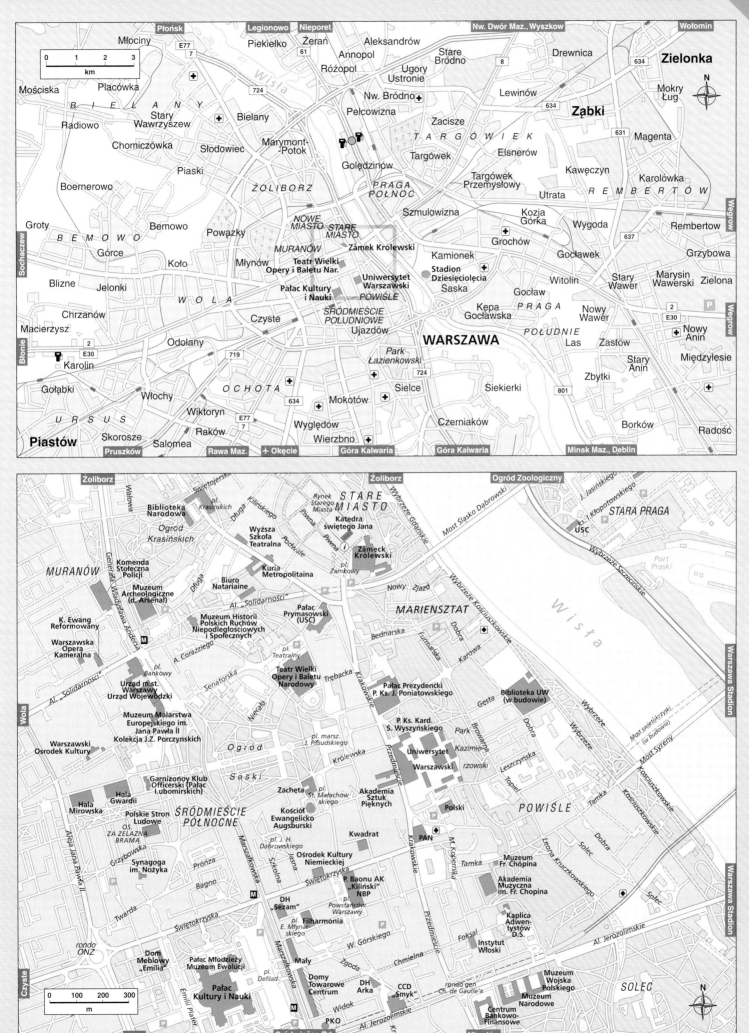

Untergrub
Lachsfeld
Kreuzstetten
Gaweinstal
Hohenruppersdorf

Eitzersthal
Viendorf
Weinsteig
Kleinharras

E59
Geitzendorf
Roseldorf
Karnabrunn
Bad Pirawarth
7

Obermallebern
Niederhollabrunn
Wollmannsberg
Linaberg 270
Großschweinbarth
220

Nieder-rußbach
Ober-hautzenthal
Sierndorf
303
Schleinbach
Kronberg
E461 Hochleiten-wald
Raggendorf
Matzen
Prottes

Seitzersdorf-Wolfpassing
E49
Hatzen-bach
Mollmannsdorf
Ulrichskirchen
Wolkersdorf
Ollersdorf

Gaisruck
Hausleiten
4
Stockerau
31
Harmannsdorf
Stetten
Bockfließ
Auersthal

Schmida
Leobendorf
Hagenbrunn
Großengersdorf
Strasshof a. d. Nordbahn
Gänserndorf

Perzendorf
3
3
30
28
26
6
Korneuburg
Seyring
E461
Deutsch--Wagram

Donau
22
E49
Hadersfeld
Bisamberg
7
Föhrenhain
Kapellerfeld
Safari-park

19
Zeiselmauer
E59
St. Andrä-Wördern
Klosterneuburg
16
Lang-enzersdorf
Gerasdorf b. Wien
Parbasdorf
Markgrafneusiedl

Tulln
14
Wolfpassing
Naturpark
3
A22
Oberlisse
Süssenbrunn
Obersiebenbrunn

Staasdorf
Königstetten
Eichenhain
10
14
FLORIDS-DORF
Aderklaa
Raasdorf
Glinzendorf

Tulbing
495
Tulbinger Kogel
7
6
DONAUSTADT
Pysdorf
Leopoldsdorf im Marchfelde

Judenau
Chorherrn
Kahlenberg
ASPERN
Groß-enzersdorf
Rutzendorf
Breitstetten
Fuchsenbig

Freundorf
GRINZING
4
STADLAU
ESSLING
Franzensdorf
Andlersdorf

Mauerbach
DÖBLING
3
3b
WIEN
Oberhausen
Wittau
Wagram an der Donau
3

Sieghartskirchen
Gablitz
HERNALS
1
National-park
Mühlleiten

Rappoltenkirchen
Troppberg 542
HADERSDORF
Alte Hofburg
Donau
Schönau a. d. Donau
Mannsdorf a. d. Donau
Orth an der Donau

Purkersdorf
PENZING
1
Schönbrunn
National-park Donau-Auen

Pressbaum
A1
9
HIETZING
MEIDLING
A23
SIMMERING
A4
Donau-Auen

44
Lainzer
FAVORITEN
8
13
E58
9

23
Wolfsgraben
Laab im Walde
Tiergarten
17
Zentral-friedhof
10a
19
E58
Bratislava

Breitenfurt bei Wien
13
Perchtoldsdorf
LIESING
224
A2
Schwechat
FLUGHAFEN WIEN-SCHWECHAT
Fischamend Markt

Steinplattl 649
36
Vösendorf
11
Rauchen-warth
10
E60
A4
Arbesthal

Klausen Leopoldsdorf
Grub
Sparbach
5
Lanzendorf
Zwölfaxing
Göttlesbrunn
32

Kaltenleutgeben
Höllensteinberg 645
32
A21 E60
7
16
Leopoldsdorf
Himberg
Achau
Enzersdorf an der Fischa
Györ

15
17
23
26
11
Maria Enzersdorf a. Gebirge
9
Schwadorf
Maria Ellend
Neusiedl a. See

15
Alland
Heiligenkreuz
Gaaden
Anninger 674
Hinterbrühl
Mödling
Wiener Neudorf
Velm
Trautmannsdorf an der Leitha

Groisbach
Raisenmarkt
210
Guntramsdorf
Gramatneusiedl
Götzendorf an der Leitha
Sarasdorf
Sommerein

Nöstach
Schwarzensee
Hoher Lindkogel 834
Trais-kirchen
Moosbrunn
Reisenberg
Kaiser-stein-bruch
Winde am See

Neuhaus
11
21
19
Baden
A3
60
Mannersdorf am Leithagebirge
Leitha Geb. Breitenbrunn

Weißenbach a. d. Triesing
18
Bad Vöslau
A2
210
14
Unterwalterdorf
15
Hof am Leithaberge

Pottenstein
E59
17
17
Oberwalterdorf
16
Ebreichsdorf
Deutsch Brodersdorf

0   3   6
km

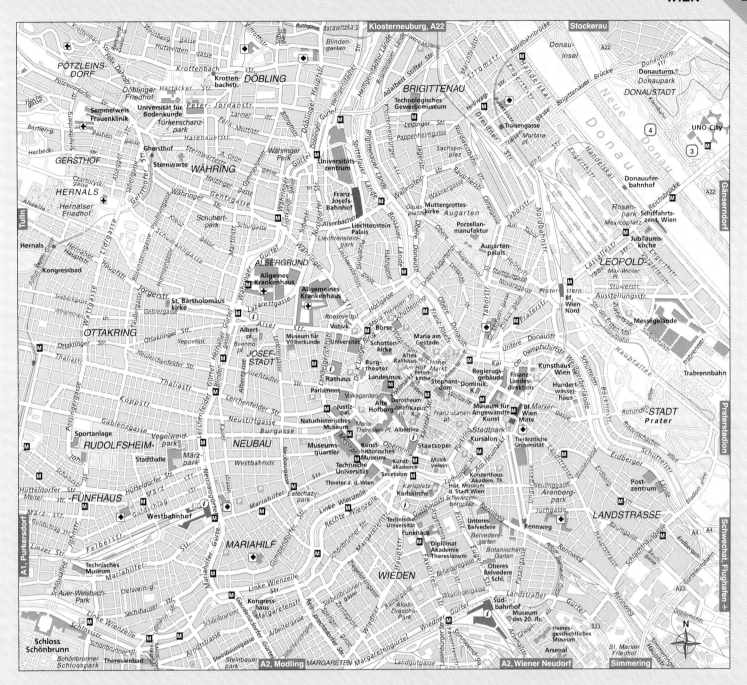

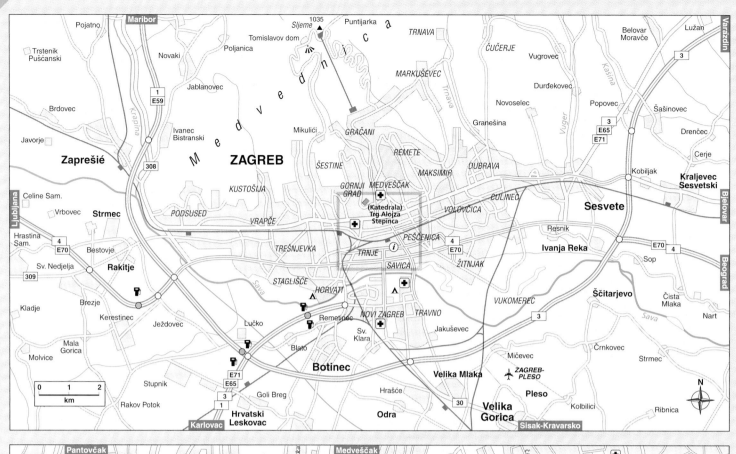

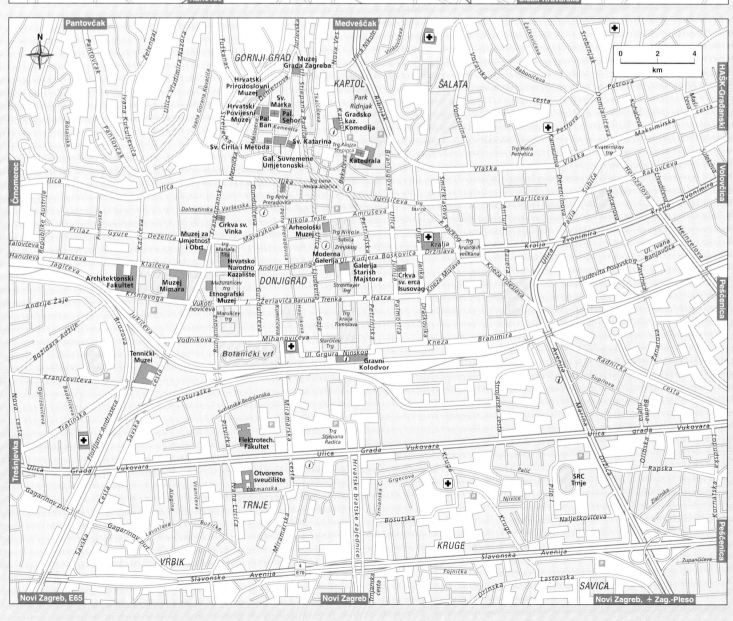

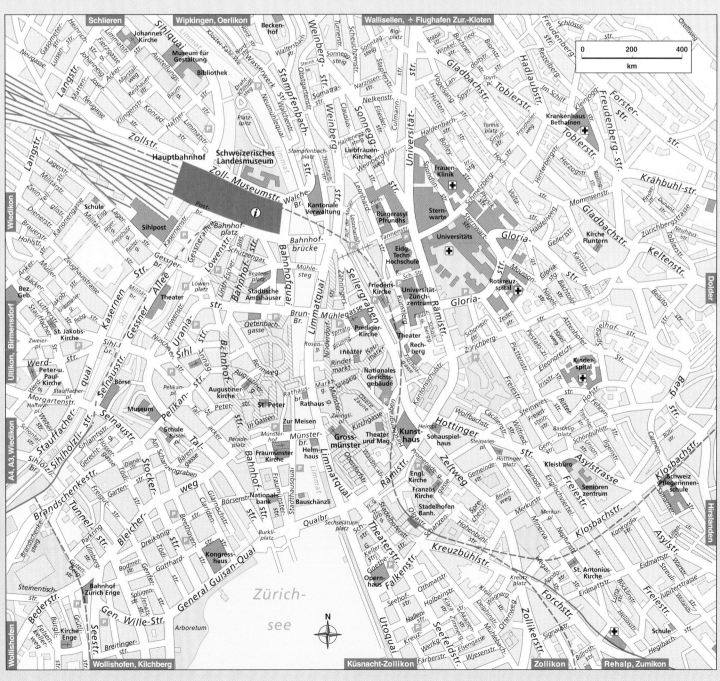

INDEX OF NAMES
INDICE DEI NOMI
ÍNDICE DE TOPÓNIMOS
INDEX DES NOMS
NAMENVERZEICHNIS

How to use the index • Avvertenze per la ricerca
Instrucciones para la consulta • Notices pour la recherche
Erläuterungen des Suchsystems

The index lists the place names, tourist sites, main tunnels and passes contained in the atlas, followed by the abbreviation of the country name to which they belong.
All names contained in two adjoining pages are referenced to the even page number.

L'indice elenca i toponimi dei centri abitati, dei siti turistici, dei principali tunnel e passi presenti nell'atlante, accompagnati dalla sigla della nazione di appartenenza.
Tutti i nomi contenuti in due pagine affiancate sono riferiti alla pagina di numero pari.

El índice presenta los topónimos de localidades, lugares turísticos, principales túneles y puertos de montaña que figuran en el atlas, seguidos de la sigla que indica el País de pertenencia. Todos los nombres contenidos en dos páginas juntas éstan referidos a la página de número par.

L'index récense les noms des localités, sites touristiques, principales tunnels et cols contenus dans l'atlas, suivis par le sigle qui indique le Pays d'appartenance.
Tous les noms contenus dans deux pages l'une à côté de l'autre sont rapportés à la page avec nombre pair.

Der Index enthält die im Atlas vorhandenen Ortsnamen, Sehenswürdigkeiten, wichtigsten Tunnels und Pässe, von dem zugehörigen Staatskennzeichen gefolgt.
Alle in zwei anliegenden Seiten enthaltenen Namen sind auf die Seite mit gerader Zahl bezogen.

Alb - Aro 247

Albaina [E] 82 G5
Alba Iulia [RO] 204 B5
Albaladejo [E] 96 G5
Albalate de Cinca [E] 90 G4
Albalate del Arzobispo [E] 90 E5
Albalate de las Nogueras [E] 98 B1
Albalate de Zorita [E] 98 A1
Alban [F] 106 C3
Albánchez [E] 102 H4
Albano di Lucania [I] 120 H4
Albano Laziale [I] 116 A6
Albaredo d'Adige [I] 110 F1
Albarella [I] 110 H2
Albares [E] 88 H6
Albarracín [E] 98 D1
Albarracín, Cuevas de- [E] 98 D1
Albatana [E] 104 C1
Albena [BG] 148 G2
Albenga [I] 108 G4
Albens [F] 70 A3
Albentosa [E] 98 E3
Alberga [S] 168 B3
Albergaria-a-Velha [P] 80 B5
Alberic [E] 98 E5
Albernoa [P] 94 D3
Alberobello [I] 122 E3
Alberoni [I] 110 H1
Albersdorf [D] 18 E2
Albert [F] 28 E4
Albertirsa [H] 76 D1
Albertville [F] 70 B3
Albeşti [RO] 148 G1
Albi [F] 106 B2
Albignasego [I] 110 G1
Albisola Marina [I] 108 H3
Albo [F] 114 C2
Albocácer / Albocàsser [E] 98 G2
Albocàsser / Albocácer [E] 98 G2
Alböke [S] 162 G4
Alboraia / Alboraya [E] 98 E4
Alboraya / Alboraia [E] 98 E4
Alborea [E] 98 C4
Albox [E] 102 H4
Albrechtice nad Vltavou [CZ] 48 F6
Albrechtsburg [A] 62 D4
Albufeira [P] 94 C5
Albujón [E] 104 C4
Albuñol [E] 102 E5
Albuñuelas [E] 102 D4
Alburquerque [E] 86 F5
Alby [S] 162 G6
Alby [S] 184 C4
Alcácer do Sal [P] 94 C1
Alcáçovas [P] 94 D2
Alcadozo [E] 98 B6
Alcafores [P] 86 G3
Alcaide [E] 102 H3
Alcalá de Chivert / Alcalà de Xivert [E] 98 G2
Alcalá de Guadaira [E] 94 G6
Alcalá de Henares [E] 88 G6
Alcalá de la Selva [E] 98 E2
Alcalá del Júcar [E] 98 C5
Alcalá de los Gazules [E] 100 G4
Alcalá del Río [E] 94 G6
Alcalá del Valle [E] 102 A3
Alcalà de Xivert / Alcalá de Chivert [E] 98 G2
Alcalá la Real [E] 102 D3
Álcamo [I] 126 C2
Alcanar [E] 92 A6
Alcanede [P] 86 C4
Alcanena [P] 86 C4
Alcañices [E] 80 G4
Alcañiz [E] 90 F6
Alcántara [E] 86 G4
Alcantara, Gole d'- [I] 124 A8
Alcantarilla [E] 104 C3
Alcaracejos [E] 96 C5
Alcaraz [E] 96 H6
Alcaria Ruiva [P] 94 D4
Alcarràs [E] 90 H5
Alçaşehir [TR] 144 G1
Alcaudete [E] 102 D2
Alcaudete de la Jara [E] 96 D1
Alcázar de San Juan [E] 96 G3
Alcobaça [P] 86 C3
Alcoba de los Montes [E] 96 D3
Alcobendas [E] 88 F5
Alcobertas [P] 86 C3
Alcocèber / Alcossebre [E] 98 G3
Alcocer [E] 90 A6
Alcochete [P] 86 B5
Alcoentre [P] 86 B4
Alcofra [P] 80 C6
Alcoi / Alcoy [E] 104 E1
Alcolea [E] 102 F5
Alcolea del Pinar [E] 90 B4
Alconchel [E] 94 F2
Alcora / l'Alcora [E] 98 F3
Alcorcón [E] 88 F6
Alcorisa [E] 90 F6
Alcossebre / Alcocèber [E] 98 G3
Alcoutim [P] 94 D5
Alcover [E] 92 C4
Alcoy / Alcoi [E] 104 E1
Alcubierre [E] 90 F3
Alcublas [E] 98 E3
Alcúdia [E] 104 F4
Alcuéscar [E] 86 H6
Aldeacentenera [E] 96 B1
Aldeadávila de la Ribera [E] 80 F5
Aldea del Cano [E] 86 H6
Aldea del Fresno [E] 88 E5
Aldea del Rey [E] 96 E5
Aldea de Trujillo [E] 96 B1
Aldealpozo [E] 90 C3
Aldeanueva de Ebro [E] 84 A5
Aldeaquemada [E] 96 F6
Aldeavieja [E] 88 E4
Aldeburgh [GB] 14 G3
Aldeia da Ponte [P] 86 G2
Aldeia do Bispo [P] 86 G2
Aldenhoven [D] 30 F4
Aldernäset [S] 190 F5
Aldershot [GB] 14 D4
Aldinci [MK] 128 E1
Aldtsier [NL] 16 F2
Åled [S] 162 B5
Aledo [E] 104 B3
Alegranza [E] 100 E5
Alehoyshchina [RUS] 202 D1
Alekovo [BG] 148 E1
Aleksandrovac [YU] 150 C1
Aleksandrovo [BG] 148 B3
Aleksandrów Kujawski [PL] 36 F1
Aleksandrów Łódzki [PL] 36 G4
Aleksin [RUS] 202 F5
Aleksinac [YU] 150 D3
Ålem [S] 162 G4
Alemdağ [TR] 146 F2
Ålen [N] 182 C3
Alençon [F] 26 F6
Alenquer [P] 86 B4
Aléria [F] 114 C4
Aléria [F] 114 C4
Alès [F] 106 F3
Ales [I] 118 C5
Aleşd [RO] 204 B4
Alessándria [I] 70 F6
Alessandria del Carretto [I] 122 D6
Alessándria della Rocca [I] 126 D3
Ålesund [N] 180 C3
Alexándreia [GR] 128 G4
Alexandria [RO] 148 B1
Alexandria Troas [TR] 130 H6
Alexandroúpoli [GR] 130 G3
Alexandrów [PL] 38 A3
Alf [D] 44 G2
Alfafar [E] 98 E5
Alfaites [P] 86 G2
Alfajarín [E] 90 E4
Alfambra [E] 98 E1
Alfambras [P] 94 B4
Alfândega [P] 80 F4
Alfano [I] 120 G5
Alfarela de Jales [P] 80 E4
Alfaro [E] 84 B5
Alfarràs [E] 90 H4
Alfas [E] 104 F2
Alfatar [BG] 148 E1
Alfedena [I] 116 D6
Alfeizerão [P] 86 B3
Alfeld [D] 46 H5
Alfeld [D] 32 F3
Alfena [P] 80 C4
Alfonsine [I] 110 G3
Alford [GB] 6 F6
Ålfoten [N] 180 C5
Alfreton [GB] 10 F5
Alfstad [N] 170 G5
Alfta [S] 174 D2
Algaida [E] 104 E5
Algajola [F] 114 B3
Algar [E] 100 G4
Algar [E] 104 H5
Ålgarås [S] 166 F4
Ålgård [N] 164 B3
Algård [N] 164 B5
Algarinejo [E] 102 D3
Algarra [E] 98 D3
Algatocín [E] 100 H4
Algeciras [E] 100 G5
Algemesí [E] 98 E5
Algered [S] 184 E5
Alghero [I] 118 B3
Alghult [S] 162 F4
Alginet [E] 98 E5
Algodonales [E] 100 H3
Algora [E] 90 A5
Algoso [P] 80 F4
Algsjö [S] 190 G5
Alguazas [E] 104 C3
Algutsrum [S] 162 G5
Algyő [H] 76 E4
Alhama de Aragón [E] 90 C4
Alhama de Granada [E] 102 D4
Alhama de Murcia [E] 104 B3
Alhambra [E] 96 G5
Alhaurín de la Torre [E] 102 B5
Alhaurín el Grande [E] 102 B4
Alhojärvi [FIN] 186 F5
Ålholm Slot [DK] 20 B1
Ålhus [N] 180 C6
Alía [E] 96 C2
Ália [I] 126 D3
Aliaga [E] 98 F1
Aliağa [TR] 144 C3
Aliártos [GR] 134 A5
Alibunar [YU] 154 H2
Alicante / Alacant [E] 104 E2
Alicudi Porto [I] 124 A5
Åliden [S] 196 A4
Alife [I] 120 E2
Alija del Infantado [E] 80 H3
Alijó [P] 80 E4
Alikámpos [GR] 140 C4
Alikanás [GR] 136 A2
Alikylä [FIN] 196 C6
Alimena [I] 126 E3
Alinda [TR] 142 D1
Alingsås [S] 162 B1
Alinyà [E] 92 D2
Aliseda [E] 86 G5
Alistráti [GR] 130 C3
Ali Terme [I] 124 B7
Alivéri [GR] 134 C5
Aljaraque [E] 94 E5
Aljezur [P] 94 B4
Aljubarrota [P] 86 C3
Aljucén [E] 86 G6
Aljustrel [P] 94 C3
Alkmaar [NL] 16 D3
Alkotz [E] 84 B3
Alkoven [A] 62 B4
Alksniupiai [LT] 200 F4
Alkvettern [S] 166 G2
Allai [I] 118 C5
Allaines [F] 42 E5
Allainville [F] 42 E4
Allan [F] 68 F6
Allanche [F] 68 C3
Alland [A] 62 E5
Allariz [E] 78 C5
Allauch [F] 108 B5
Alleen [N] 164 C5
Alleghe [I] 72 E4
Allejaur [S] 190 G3
Allemont [F] 70 A5
Allensbach [D] 58 G4
Allentsteig [A] 62 D3
Allepuz [E] 98 E1
Aller-Heiligen [D] 58 F1
Allersberg [D] 46 G6
Allershausen [D] 60 E3
Allerum [S] 156 H1
Alleuze, Château d'- [F] 68 C4
Allevard [F] 70 A4
Allgunnen [S] 162 F4
Allihies [IRL] 4 A5
Allingåbro [DK] 160 E5
Allinge [DK] 158 E4
Allo [E] 84 A4
Alloa [GB] 8 E3
Ålloluokta [S] 192 G6
Allonnes [F] 42 E5
Allonnes [F] 54 E2
Allonö [S] 168 B5
Allos [F] 108 D3
Alloue [F] 54 E5
Ållsjön [S] 184 E2
Allstedt [D] 34 B5
Almacelles [E] 90 H4
Almada [P] 86 B5
Almadén [E] 96 C4
Almadén de la Plata [E] 94 G5
Almadenejos [E] 96 D4
Almadrones [E] 90 A5
Almagreira [P] 100 E4
Almagro [E] 96 F4
Almandoz [E] 84 B3
Almansa [E] 98 D6
Almanza [E] 82 C4
Almaraz [E] 88 B6
Almargen [E] 102 B3
Almarza [E] 90 B2
Almås [N] 182 C2
Almassora / Almazora [E] 98 F3
Almazán [E] 90 B3
Almazora / Almassora [E] 98 F3
Almedina [E] 96 G5
Almeida [P] 80 E6
Almeida de Sayago [E] 80 G5
Almeirim [P] 86 C4
Almelo [NL] 16 G4
Almenar [E] 90 H4
Almenara [E] 102 B1
Almenara de Tormes [E] 80 G6
Almenar de Soria [E] 90 C3
Almendra [P] 80 E5
Almendral [E] 94 G2
Almendralejo [E] 94 G2
Almenno S. Salvatore [I] 70 H4
Almere [NL] 16 E4
Almería [E] 102 G5
Almerimar [E] 102 F6
Almesåkra [S] 162 D2
Almestad [S] 162 C1
Älmhult [S] 162 D5
Almodôvar [P] 94 C4
Almodóvar del Campo [E] 96 E4
Almodóvar del Pinar [E] 98 C3
Almodóvar del Río [E] 102 B1
Almogía [E] 102 C4
Almograve [P] 94 B3
Almoharín [E] 86 H6
Almonaster la Real [E] 94 F4
Almonte [E] 94 F6
Almoradí [E] 104 D3
Almorox [E] 88 E6
Almourol [P] 86 D4
Almsele [S] 190 F5
Älmsta [S] 168 E1
Älmsta-Väddö [S] 168 E1
Almudévar [E] 90 F3
Almuñécar [E] 102 D5
Almunge [S] 168 D1
Almuradiel [E] 96 F5
Almvik [S] 162 G2
Almyró [GR] 136 D4
Almyropótamos [GR] 134 D5
Almyrós [GR] 132 H3
Alness [GB] 6 E4
Alnwick [GB] 8 G5
Aloja [LV] 198 E4
Alol' [RUS] 198 H5
Alónnisos [GR] 134 C3
Álora [E] 102 B4
Alosno [E] 94 E5
Alost (Aalst) [B] 28 H2
Alp [E] 92 E2
Alpalhão [P] 86 E4
Alpbach [A] 60 E6
Alpedrinha [P] 86 F3
Alpen [D] 30 G2
Alpengarten [D] 60 D6
Alpera [E] 98 C5
Alphen-aan den Rijn [NL] 16 D5
Alpirsbach [D] 58 F2
Alpua [FIN] 196 D5
Alpuente [E] 98 D3
Alpullu [TR] 146 B2
Alqueva [P] 94 E3
Alquézar [E] 90 G3
Als [DK] 160 E4
Alsager [GB] 10 D5
Alsasua / Altsasu [E] 82 H5
Alsen [S] 182 G1
Alsenz [D] 46 B4
Alsfeld [D] 46 D1
Ålshult [S] 162 D5
Alsleben [D] 34 B4
Ålsø [DK] 160 F6
Alsótold [H] 64 D5
Ålstad [N] 192 D5
Alstad [S] 158 C3
Alstahaug [N] 190 D2
Alstätte [D] 16 G5
Alsterbro [S] 162 F4
Alstermo [S] 162 F4
Alston [GB] 8 F6
Alsvåg [N] 192 D3
Alsvik [N] 192 D6
Alta [N] 194 B3
Altafulla [E] 92 C5
Altamira, Cuevas de- [E] 82 E3
Altamura [I] 122 D3
Altarejos [E] 98 B2
Altaussee [A] 62 A6
Altavilla Silentina [I] 120 F4
Altdahn [D] 44 H4
Altdorf [CH] 58 F6
Altdorf [D] 46 G5
Altea [E] 104 F2
Alteidet [N] 192 H1
Altena [D] 32 C5
Altenahr [D] 30 G5
Altenau [D] 32 G4
Altenberg [D] 48 E2
Altenberge [D] 16 H5
Altenberger Dom [D] 30 H4
Altenburg [A] 62 D3
Altenburg [D] 34 C6
Altenglan [D] 44 H3
Altenhundem [D] 32 C5
Altenkirchen [D] 32 C6
Altenkirchen [D] 20 D1
Altenklingen [CH] 58 G4
Altenmarkt [A] 62 C6
Altenmarkt [D] 60 F5
Altenmarkt im Pongau [A] 72 H1
Altenstadt [D] 60 B4
Altenstadt [D] 60 D5
Altensteig [D] 58 G1
Altentreptow [D] 20 D4
Altenwalde [D] 18 D3
Alter do Chão [P] 86 E5
Alteren [N] 190 E2
Altheim [A] 60 H4
Althofen [A] 74 B2
Altimir [BG] 150 G3
Altinkum [TR] 142 C2
Altinoluk [TR] 144 B1
Altinova [TR] 144 B2
Altinova [TR] 146 F3
Altintaş [TR] 144 H2
Altinyayla [TR] 142 G2
Altipiani di Arcinazzo [I] 116 B6
Altkirch [F] 58 D4
Altlandsberg [D] 34 E2
Altmörbitz [D] 34 C6
Altmünster [A] 62 A5
Altnaharra [GB] 6 E3
Alto de los Leones de Castilla [E] 88 F4
Altomonte [I] 124 D3
Alton [GB] 14 D4
Altopascio [I] 110 E5
Altötting [D] 60 G4
Altrier [L] 44 F2
Alt Ruppin [D] 20 C6
Altsasu / Alsasua [E] 82 H5
Alt Schadow [D] 34 F3
Altshausen [D] 58 H3
Altstätten [CH] 58 H5
Alttajärvi [S] 192 G5
Altuna [S] 168 C1
Altura [E] 98 E3
Altwarp [D] 20 E4
Altwindeck [D] 58 F1
Alūksne [LV] 198 F4
Ålum [DK] 160 D5
Ålund [S] 196 A4
Alunda [S] 168 D1
Alupka [UA] 204 G6
Alushta [UA] 204 G6
Alvaiázere [P] 86 D3
Alvajärvi [FIN] 186 F1
Alvalade [P] 94 C3
Ålvan [S] 166 H5
Älvängen [S] 160 H1
Alvastra [S] 166 G6
Alvdal [N] 182 B5
Älvdalen [S] 172 F2
Alverca do Ribatejo [P] 86 B5
Alversund [N] 170 B3
Alvesta [S] 162 D4
Alvestad [N] 164 A2
Alvignac [F] 66 G4
Ålvik [N] 170 C4
Alvik [S] 172 G4
Ålvik [S] 196 B3
Alvito [I] 116 C6
Alvito [P] 94 D2
Älvkarleby [S] 174 E4
Alvor [P] 94 B5
Älvros [S] 182 E6
Älvros [S] 182 G5
Älvsbacka [S] 166 F2
Älvsbyn [S] 196 A3
Älvsered [S] 162 B3
Alvsund [S] 184 E5
Ålvundeid [N] 180 F3
Alykí [GR] 138 E3
Alykí [GR] 130 E4
Alykí [GR] 130 E4
Alytus [LT] 24 G2
Alzenau [D] 46 D3
Alzey [D] 46 B4
Alzira [E] 98 E5
Alzon [F] 106 E3
Alzonne [F] 106 B4
Åmådalen [S] 172 G2
Amadora [P] 86 B5
Åmål [S] 166 D4
Amalfi [I] 120 E4
Amaliáda [GR] 136 C2
Amaliápoli [GR] 132 H3
Amalo [GR] 138 G1
Amance [F] 58 B3
Amancey [F] 58 B5
Amandola [I] 116 C2
Amantea [I] 124 D5
Amantia [AL] 128 B5
Amarante [P] 80 C4
Amárantos [GR] 132 F3
Amărăştii de Sus [RO] 150 G2
Amareleja [P] 94 E3
Amári [GR] 140 D5
Amárynthos [GR] 134 C5
Amatrice [I] 116 C3
Amaxádes [GR] 130 E2
Amay [B] 30 E5
Ambarès [F] 66 D3
Ambazac [F] 54 G6
Ambelákia [GR] 130 H1
Amberg [D] 46 H5
Ambérieu-en-Bugey [F] 68 G2
Ambert [F] 68 D3
Ambiörnarp [S] 162 B3
Ambjörby [S] 172 E4
Ambla [EST] 198 E1
Amble [GB] 8 G5
Ambleside [GB] 10 D2
Amboise [F] 54 G2
Ämbra [EST] 198 E2
Ambrières [F] 26 E5
Åmdal [N] 164 D5
Ameixial [P] 94 C4
Amélia [I] 116 A3
Amélie-les-Bains [F] 92 F2
Amelinghausen [D] 18 F5
Amendolara [I] 122 D6
Amer [E] 92 F3
A Merca [E] 78 C5
Amerongen [NL] 16 E5
Amersfoort [NL] 16 E5
Amersham [GB] 14 E3
Amesbury [GB] 12 G4
A Mezquita [E] 78 E6
Amfiaréio [GR] 134 C5
Amfíkleia [GR] 132 G4
Amfilochía [GR] 132 D4
Amfípoli [GR] 130 C4
Amfissa [GR] 132 G5
Amiens [F] 28 E5
Åmilden [S] 190 H4
Aminne [S] 168 G4
Amiternum [I] 116 C4
Åmli [N] 164 E4
Amlwch [GB] 10 B3
Ammanford [GB] 12 E2
Ämmänsaari [FIN] 196 F4
Ammarnäs [S] 190 F2
Ammeberg [S] 166 G4
Ammoudára [GR] 140 E4
Ammoudára [GR] 140 F5
Åmnes [N] 164 F2
Amorbach [D] 46 D4
Amòreira, Acueducto de- [P] 86 E6
Amorgós [GR] 138 G4
Amorosi [I] 120 E2
Åmot [N] 164 E1
Åmot [N] 164 G1
Åmot [N] 170 G4
Åmot [N] 172 C2
Åmot [S] 174 D3
Åmotfors [S] 166 D1
Amótopos [GR] 132 D3
Åmotsdal [N] 164 E1
Amou [F] 84 D2
Ampelákia [GR] 132 G1
Ampelikó [GR] 134 H2
Ampelónas [GR] 132 G1
Ampezzo [I] 72 F4
Ampfing [D] 60 F4
Amphion [F] 70 B2
Amplepuis [F] 68 F2
Amposta [E] 92 A6
Ampudia [E] 82 C6
Ampuero [E] 82 F3
Ampuis [F] 68 F3
Ampus [F] 108 D4
Amriswil [CH] 58 H4
Åmsele [S] 190 H5
Amsteg [CH] 70 F1
Amsterdam [NL] 16 D4
Amstetten [A] 62 C4
Åmtervik [S] 166 E2
Amtoft [DK] 160 C4
Amurrio [E] 82 G4
Amvrosia [GR] 130 F2
Amygdaleónas [GR] 130 D3
Amygdaliá [GR] 132 G5
Amýkles [GR] 136 E4
Amýntaio [GR] 128 F4
Amzacea [RO] 148 G1
Anadia [P] 80 B6
Anáfi [GR] 138 F5
Anagni [I] 116 B6
Anáktora Néstoros [GR] 136 C4
Análipsi [GR] 138 H4
Anárgyroi [GR] 128 E5
Anarráchi [GR] 128 E5
Anascaul [IRL] 4 B4
Anäset [S] 196 A5
Åna-Sira [N] 164 B5
Anätinpää [FIN] 196 G4
Anatolí [GR] 132 G1
Anatolikó [GR] 128 F5
Anávyssos [GR] 136 H1
Anávra [GR] 132 G3
Anávra [GR] 132 F3
An Cabhán / Cavan [IRL] 2 E4
Ancenis [F] 40 G6
Ancerville [F] 44 C5
An Charraig / Carrick [IRL] 2 D2
Anchuras [E] 96 D2
Ancona [I] 112 C6
Ancy-le-Franc [F] 56 F2
Anda [N] 180 C5
An Daingean / Dingle [IRL] 4 A3
Andalo [I] 72 C4
Åndalsnes [N] 180 E3
Andåsen [S] 182 G5
Andau [A] 62 G6
Ändebol [S] 168 B4
Andebu [N] 164 H3
Andechs [D] 60 D5
Andelot [F] 44 D6
Andenes [N] 192 E2
Andenne [B] 30 D5
Andermatt [CH] 70 F1
Andernach [D] 30 H6
Andernos-les-Bains [F] 66 B3
Andersfors [S] 196 A5
Anderslov [S] 158 C3
Anderstorp [S] 162 C3
Andijk [NL] 16 E3
Andilla [E] 98 E3
Andocs [H] 76 A3
Andolsheim [F] 58 E3
Andorno Micca [I] 70 E4
Andorra [E] 90 F6
Andorra la Vella [AND] 84 H6
Andover [GB] 12 H4
Andrade, Castelo de- [E] 78 D2
Andravida [GR] 136 B1
Andrespol [PL] 36 G4
Andretta [I] 120 G3
Andrézieux-Bouthéon [F] 68 E3
Andria [I] 122 C2
Andrijevica [YU] 150 A5
Andritsaina [GR] 136 D3
Ándros [GR] 134 E6
Androússa [GR] 136 D4
Andrychów [PL] 50 G4
Andselv [N] 192 F3
Andújar [E] 102 D1
Anduze [F] 106 F3
Änebjør [N] 164 D3
Aneby [N] 172 B5
Aneby [S] 162 E2
Ånes [N] 180 F1
Anet [F] 42 E3
Anfo [I] 72 B5
Ånga [S] 168 G4
Ånge [S] 190 G2
Ånge [S] 182 G1
Ånge [S] 184 C4
Ångebo [S] 184 D6
Angeja [P] 80 B5
Ängelholm [S] 156 H1
Angeli [FIN] 194 C4
Angelókastro [GR] 136 F2
Angelókastro [GR] 132 E5
Angelsberg [S] 168 B1
Ängelsfors [S] 174 D4
Angelstad [S] 162 C5
Angenstein [CH] 58 E4
Anger [A] 74 E1
Ängersjö [S] 184 H1
Angermünde [D] 20 E6
Angern [A] 62 G4
Angers [F] 40 H6
Ängersjö [S] 182 G6
Angerville [F] 42 E5
Angesan [S] 194 B8
Ängesbyn [S] 196 B3
Anghelo Ruiu, Necropoli- [I] 118 B3
Anghiari [I] 110 G6
Angiari [I] 110 F1
Anglès [E] 92 F3
Angles-sur-l'Anglin [F] 54 F4
Anglet [F] 84 C2
Anglona [LV] 198 G6
Anglure [F] 44 A5
Ango, Manoir d'- [F] 28 C4
Angoulême [F] 66 E1
Angra do Heroísmo [P] 100 D3
Ångskär [S] 174 F4
Angsö [S] 168 C2
Angüés [E] 90 G3
Anguiano [E] 90 B1
Anguillara Sabazia [I] 114 H5
Anguillara Veneta [I] 110 G2
Angulo [E] 82 G4
Angvik [N] 180 F2
Anholt [DK] 160 G5
Aniane [F] 106 E4
Aniche [F] 28 F4
Anina [RO] 204 A6
Anıtkaya [TR] 144 H2
Anjala [FIN] 178 C3
Anjalankoski [FIN] 178 C3
Anjan [S] 190 D6
Anjos [P] 100 E3
Anjum [NL] 16 F1
Ankaran [SLO] 72 H6
Ankarede [S] 190 E4
Ankarsrum [S] 162 G2
Ankarvattnet [S] 190 E4
Ankenesstrand [N] 192 E4
Anklam [D] 20 D4
Ankum [D] 32 D1
Anlezy [F] 56 E4
Ånn [S] 182 E2
Anna [EST] 198 E2
Annaberg [A] 60 H6
Annaberg [A] 62 D5
Annaberg-Buchholz [D] 48 D2
Annadalsvagen [N] 190 D3
Annalong [NIR] 2 G4
Annan [GB] 8 E5
Anna Paulowna [NL] 16 D3
An Nás / Naas [IRL] 2 F6
Anndalsvågen [N] 190 D3
Anneberg [S] 160 H2
Anneberg [S] 162 E2
Annecy [F] 70 B3
Annefors [S] 174 D2
Annelund [S] 162 B1
Annemasse [F] 70 B2
Annenheim [A] 74 A3
Annerstad [S] 162 C5
Annestown [IRL] 4 E5
Annonay [F] 68 F4
Annopol [PL] 52 D1
Annot [F] 108 D3
Annweiler [D] 46 B5
Anógia [GR] 140 E4
Anoixi [GR] 132 E1
Áno Kalentíni [GR] 132 D3
Áno Kastritsi [GR] 132 F6
Áno Merá [GR] 138 E2
Anópoli [GR] 140 C5
Áno Sangkri [GR] 138 F3
Añover de Tajo [E] 96 F1
Áno Viánnos [GR] 140 F5
Áno Vrontoú [GR] 130 C2
Anquela del Ducado [E] 90 B5
An Rinn / Ring [IRL] 4 E5
Ans [DK] 160 D6
Ansager [DK] 156 B2
Ansbach [D] 46 F5
Anse [F] 68 F2
Ansedónia [I] 114 F4
Anseremme [B] 30 D6
Ansfelden [A] 62 B4
Ansó [E] 84 D4
An Spidéal / Spiddal [IRL] 2 B5
Anstad [N] 180 F5
Anstey [GB] 10 F6
Anstruther [GB] 8 F3
Ansvar [S] 194 B8
Antandros [TR] 134 H1
Antas [P] 80 D5
Antas, Tempio di- [I] 118 B6
Antegnate [I] 70 H5
Anten [S] 160 H1
Antequera [E] 102 C4
Anterselva / Antholz [I] 72 E2
Antey St. André [I] 70 D3
Anthéor [F] 108 E5
Anthí [GR] 130 B3
Antholz / Anterselva [I] 72 E2
Anthótopos [GR] 132 G3
Antibes [F] 108 E5
Antigonea [AL] 128 C6
Antigua [E] 100 E6
Antigua Bilbilis [E] 90 D4
Antikyra [GR] 132 H5
Antimáchia [GR] 142 B3
An Tinbhear Mór / Arklow [IRL] 4 G4
Antíparos [GR] 138 E3
Antírrio [GR] 132 F5
Antissa [GR] 134 G2
Ántissa [GR] 134 G2
Antjärn [S] 184 F4
Antnäs [S] 196 B3
Antonin [PL] 36 E5
Antoniów [PL] 52 D1
Antonovo [BG] 148 D3
Antopal' [BY] 38 H2
Antraigues [F] 68 E5
Antrain [F] 26 D5
Antrim [NIR] 2 G3
Antrodoco [I] 116 B4
Antsla [EST] 198 F3
Anttila [FIN] 196 F5
Anttis [S] 194 B7
Anttola [FIN] 188 D6
Anttola [FIN] 188 F5
Antwerpen (Anvers) [B] 30 C3
An Uaimh / Navan [IRL] 2 F5
Anundshögen [S] 168 C2
Anvers (Antwerpen) [B] 30 C3
Anvin [F] 28 E3
Anykščiai [LT] 200 G4
Anzi [I] 120 H4
Anzio [I] 120 A1
Aoiz / Agoitz [E] 84 C4
Aosta / Aoste [I] 70 D4
Aoste / Aosta [I] 70 D4
Apamea [TR] 146 E4
Apasdal [N] 164 D5
Apátfalva [H] 76 F4
Apatin [YU] 76 C6
Apchon [F] 68 B3
Ape [LV] 198 F4
Apécchio [I] 110 H6
Apeirathos [GR] 138 F3
Apeldoorn [NL] 16 F5
Apen [D] 18 C5
Apensen [D] 18 F4
Aphrodisias [TR] 144 F5
Apice [I] 120 F2
Apinac [F] 68 E3
Aplared [S] 162 B2
A Pobra de Brollón / Puebla del Brollón [E] 78 D4
A Pobra de Navia [E] 78 E4
A Pobra de Trives [E] 78 D5
Apoíkia [GR] 134 E6
Apolakkiá [GR] 142 D5
Apolda [D] 34 B6
Apollo Aléo, Tempio di- [I] 124 F4
Apóllon [GR] 138 F3
Apollonia [AL] 128 A4
Apollonía [GR] 138 D3
Apollonía [GR] 138 D4
Apollonía [GR] 130 B4
Apollonia [TR] 144 D2
Apollonia [TR] 146 E4
Apollonia [TR] 142 H4
A Pontenova [E] 78 E2
Apothicairerie, Grotte de l'- [F] 40 C5
Äppelbo [S] 172 F4
Appelhülsen [D] 16 H6
Appenweier [D] 44 H6
Appenzell [CH] 58 H5
Appiano / Eppan [I] 72 D3
Appingedam [NL] 16 H2
Appleby-in-Westmorland [GB] 10 E1
Apremont, Gorges d'- [F] 42 F5
Aprica [I] 72 B4
Apricena [I] 116 G6
Aprigliano [I] 124 D4
Aprilia [I] 116 A6
Aprilovo [BG] 148 D3
Ápsalos [GR] 128 F4
Apt [F] 108 B3
Áptera [GR] 140 C4
Áquila [CH] 70 G2
Aquileia [I] 72 G5
Aquilonia [I] 120 G3
Aquino [I] 120 C1
Arabba [I] 72 E3
Araburg [A] 62 E5
Araceli [E] 102 C3
Aracena [E] 94 F4
Aráchova [GR] 132 G5
Aráchova [GR] 132 F4
Aračinovo [MK] 128 E1
Arad [RO] 76 G4
Aragona [I] 126 D4
Arahal [E] 100 H2
Araksbø [N] 164 D3
Åram [N] 180 C4
Aramits [F] 84 D3
Araña, Cueva de la- [E] 98 D5
Aranda de Duero [E] 88 G2
Arandjelovac [YU] 150 B1
Aranjuez [E] 96 G1
Arantzazu [E] 82 H5
Aras de Alpuente [E] 98 D3
Aratos [GR] 130 F2
Aravaca [E] 88 F5
Aravissós [GR] 128 G4
Arazede [P] 80 B6
Arbanasi [BG] 148 C3
Arbatax [I] 118 E5
Arbesbach [A] 62 C3
Arbeteta [E] 90 B6
Arboga [S] 168 B3
Arbois [F] 58 A5
Arbon [CH] 58 H5
Arbøre [DK] 160 B4
Arboréa [I] 118 B5
Arbrå [S] 174 D2
Arbroath [GB] 8 F2
Arbúcies [E] 92 F3
Arbus [I] 118 B6
Arc, Pont d'- [F] 106 G2
Arcachon [F] 66 B3
Arcas [E] 98 B2
Arc de Berà [E] 92 C5
Arce [I] 120 C1
Arcen [NL] 30 F3
Arc-en-Barrois [F] 56 H2
Archánes [GR] 140 E5
Archángelos [GR] 142 D3
Archar [BG] 150 F2
Archena [E] 104 C2
Arches [F] 58 C2
Archiac [F] 66 D1
Archidona [E] 102 C3
Archivel [E] 104 A2
Arcidosso [I] 114 G2
Arcinazzo Romano [I] 116 B5
Arcis-sur-Aube [F] 44 B5
Arco [I] 72 C5
Arco de Baúlhe [P] 80 D3
Arcos de Jalón [E] 90 B4
Arcos de la Frontera [E] 100 G3
Arcos de la Sierra [E] 98 C1
Arcos de Valdevez [P] 78 B6
Ard [IRL] 2 B4
Ardagh [IRL] 4 C3
Årdal [N] 180 C6
Årdala [S] 168 C4
Ardales [E] 102 B4
Årdalsosen [N] 164 B2
Årdalstangen [N] 170 E2
Ardara [IRL] 2 E2
Ardea [I] 116 A6
Ardee [IRL] 2 F5
Arden [DK] 160 D4
Ardenicës [AL] 128 B4
Ardentes [F] 54 H4
Ardez [CH] 72 B2
Ardfert [IRL] 4 B3
Ardfinnan [IRL] 4 D4
Ardglass [NIR] 2 G4
Ardino [BG] 130 E1
Ardisa [E] 84 C6
Ardore [I] 124 D7
Ardres [F] 14 G6
Ardrossan [GB] 8 C3
Ardvasar [GB] 6 B5
Åre [S] 182 E1
Areatza [E] 82 G4
Arebrot [N] 180 B5
Arëhava [BY] 38 G4
Arenas [E] 82 D2
Arenas de San Pedro [E] 88 D5
Arendal [N] 164 F5
Arendonk [B] 30 D3
Arendsee [D] 20 A6
Arene / Arrankudiaga [E] 82 G4
Arenenberg [CH] 58 G4
Areños [E] 82 D3
Arenys de Mar [E] 92 F4
Arenzano [I] 108 H3
Areópoli [GR] 136 E5
Ares [E] 78 D2
Arès [F] 66 B3
Ares del Maestrat / Ares del Maestre [E] 98 F2
Ares del Maestre / Ares del Maestrat [E] 98 F2
Aréthousa [GR] 130 C4
Areti [GR] 130 B4
Aretxabaleta [E] 82 H4
Arevalillo [E] 88 C4
Arévalo [E] 88 E3
Arezzo [I] 114 G1
Arfará [GR] 136 D3
Årfora [N] 190 C4
Argalastí [GR] 134 A3
Argamasilla de Alba [E] 96 G4
Argamasilla de Calatrava [E] 96 E5
Argancy [F] 44 F4
Arganda del Rey [E] 88 G6
Arganil [P] 86 E2
Argási [GR] 136 B2
Argegno [I] 70 G3
Argelès-Gazost [F] 84 E4
Argelès-Plage [F] 92 G1
Argelès-sur-Mer [F] 92 G1
Argenta [I] 110 G3
Argentan [F] 26 F5
Argentat [F] 66 H3
Argentella [F] 114 A3
Argentera [I] 108 E2
Argentiera [I] 118 B3
Argentière [F] 70 C3
Argenton-Château [F] 54 D2
Argenton-sur-Creuse [F] 54 G4
Argentré [F] 26 E6
Argent-sur-Sauldre [F] 56 C2
Argés [E] 96 F2
Argirónta [GR] 142 B3
Argithéa [GR] 132 E3
Argomariz [E] 82 H5
Árgos [GR] 136 E2
Árgos Orestikó [GR] 128 E5
Argostóli [GR] 132 C6
Arguedas [E] 84 B5
Arguineguín [E] 100 C6
Arguis [E] 84 D6
Arguisuelas [E] 98 C3
Argy [F] 54 G3
Argyrádes [GR] 132 B3
Argyroúpoli [GR] 140 C5
Arhéa Olimbía [GR] 136 C2
Århus [DK] 156 D1
Ariano Irpino [I] 120 F2
Ariano nel Polésine [I] 110 H2
Aridaía [GR] 128 F3
Arieiro [P] 100 B3
Arilje [YU] 150 A3
Arinagour [GB] 6 A6
Ariño [E] 90 E5
Arinthod [F] 56 H6
Ariogala [LT] 200 F5
Aristoménis [GR] 136 D4
Aritzo [I] 118 D5
Ariza [E] 90 C4
Årjäng [S] 166 D2
Arjeplog [S] 190 G2
Arjona [E] 102 D1
Arkádi [GR] 140 D4
Arkadia [PL] 36 H3
Arkalochóri [GR] 140 E5
Arkása [GR] 140 H3
Arkesíni [GR] 138 F4
Arkítsa [GR] 134 A4
Arklow / An Tinbhear Mór [IRL] 4 G4
Arkösund [S] 168 C5
Arkutino [BG] 148 F5
Ärla [S] 168 C3
Arlanc [F] 68 D3
Arlberg Tunnel [A] 72 B1
Arlempdes [F] 68 D5
Arles [F] 106 G4
Arles-sur-Tech [F] 92 F2
Arlon [B] 44 E2
Arlöv [S] 156 H3
Armagh [NIR] 2 F4
Armação de Pera [P] 94 B5
Armémoi [GR] 140 D5
Arméniol [GR] 132 G2
Armenistís [GR] 138 G1
Armentières [F] 28 F3
Armilla [E] 102 E4
Armiñón [E] 82 G5
Armólia [GR] 134 G5
Armoy [NIR] 2 G2
Armuña de Tajuña [E] 88 H6
Armutlu [TR] 144 D4
Armutlu [TR] 146 E4
Armutova [TR] 144 B2
Armyansk [UA] 204 G5
Árna [GR] 136 E4
Årna [N] 170 B4
Arnac-Pompadur [F] 66 G2
Arnafjord [N] 170 C2
Arnage [F] 42 B5
Arnager [DK] 158 E4
Arnaía [GR] 130 C5
Arnäs [S] 184 G2
Arnäs [S] 166 F5
Arnavutköy [TR] 146 E2
Arnavutköy [TR] 146 E4
Arnay-le-Duc [F] 56 F4
Arnborg [DK] 156 B1
Arneberg [N] 172 B3
Arneburg [D] 34 C1
Arnedillo [E] 90 C1
Arnedo [E] 84 A5
Árnes [E] 90 G6
Årnes [N] 172 C5
Årnes [N] 190 B5
Årnes [N] 190 C4
Arnhem [NL] 16 F5
Árnissa [GR] 128 F4
Arnoldstein [A] 72 H3
Arnön [S] 174 E1
Arnsberg [D] 32 C4
Arnsburg [D] 46 D2
Arnschwang [D] 48 D6
Årnset [N] 190 B6
Arnstadt [D] 46 G1
Arnstein [D] 46 E3
Arnuera [E] 82 F3
Aroania [GR] 136 D1
Aroche [E] 94 E4
Arökto [H] 64 F5
Arolla [CH] 70 D3
Arolsen [D] 32 E5
Arona [I] 70 F4

Aronkylä [FIN] 186 B4
Åros [N] 164 H1
Arosa [CH] 70 H1
Årosjåkk [S] 192 F5
Årøsund [DK] 156 C3
Arouca [P] 80 C5
Årøysund [N] 164 H3
Arpajon [F] 42 F4
Arpela [FIN] 196 C2
Arquà Petrarca [I] 110 G1
Arquata del Tronto [I] 116 C3
Arquata Scrivia [I] 110 B2
Arquillinos [E] 102 F1
Arrabal / Oia [E] 78 A5
Arracourt [F] 44 F5
Arraiolos [P] 86 D6
Arrakoski [FIN] 176 H1
Arrankorpi [FIN] 176 H3
Arras [F] 28 F4
Arrasate o Mondragón [E] 82 H4
Arrate [E] 82 H4
Ärre [DK] 156 B2
Arreau [F] 84 F4
Arrecife [E] 100 E6
Årrenjarka [S] 190 G1
Arrens-Marsous [F] 84 E4
Arrentela [P] 86 B5
Arriate [E] 102 A4
Arriaundi [E] 82 H4
Arriba Fóssil [P] 86 A5
Arrifana [P] 94 B4
Arriondas [E] 82 C2
Arroba de los Montes [E] 96 D3
Arromanches-les-Bains [F] 26 F3
Arronches [P] 86 F5
Arroyo de la Luz [E] 86 G5
Arroyo de la Miel-Benalmádena Costa [E] 102 B5
Arroyo de San Serván [E] 94 G2
Arruda dos Vinhos [P] 86 B4
Årsandøy [N] 190 C4
Ars-en-Ré [F] 54 B4
Arsiè [I] 72 D5
Arsiero [I] 72 D5
Arslankaya [TR] 144 H1
Årslev [DK] 156 D3
Årsnes [N] 180 D4
Arsoli [I] 116 B5
Ars-sur-Moselle [F] 44 E4
Årsunda [S] 174 E4
Arsvågen [N] 164 A2
Arsy [F] 28 E6
Artá [E] 104 F5
Árta [GR] 132 D3
Artà, Coves d'- [E] 104 F5
Artajona [E] 84 B4
Artana [E] 98 F3
Artánd [H] 76 H2
Arta Terme [I] 72 G3
Arteixo [E] 78 C2
Artemare [F] 68 H3
Artemísia [GR] 136 D4
Artemísio [GR] 134 A3
Artemónas [GR] 138 D3
Artena [I] 116 B6
Artenay [F] 42 E5
Artern [D] 34 A5
Artesa de Segre [E] 92 C3
Arth [CH] 58 F6
Arth [D] 60 F3
Arthous, Ancient Prieure d'- [F] 84 C2
Arthurstown [IRL] 4 E5
Arties [E] 84 G5
Artix [F] 84 E3
Artjärvi / Artsjö [FIN] 178 B3
Artotína [GR] 132 F4
Artrik [S] 184 E2
Artsjö / Artjärvi [FIN] 178 B3
Artsyz [UA] 204 E5
A Rúa [E] 78 E5
Arucas [E] 100 C6
Arudy [F] 84 D3
Arundel [GB] 14 D5
Arva [E] 94 H6
Årvåg [N] 180 G1
Arvagh [IRL] 2 E4
Årversund [S] 182 G2
Árvi [GR] 140 F5
Arvidsjaur [S] 190 H3
Arvieux [F] 70 B6
Årvik [N] 180 C4
Arvika [S] 166 D2
Årviksand [N] 192 G1
Arvila [EST] 198 F1
Arville [F] 42 C5
Arzachena [I] 118 E2
Arzacq-Arraziguet [F] 84 E2
Aržano [HR] 152 B2
Arzberg [D] 48 C3
Arzignano [I] 72 D6
Arzl [A] 72 C1
Arzúa [E] 78 C3
As [B] 30 E4
Aš [CZ] 48 C3
Ås [N] 166 B2
Ås [N] 182 D2
Ås [S] 182 G2
Åså [DK] 160 E3
Åsa [N] 190 C5
Åsa [S] 160 H3
Åsa [S] 162 E4
Aşağıinova [TR] 146 C5
Aşağıtefen [TR] 144 F3
Asäng [S] 184 E4
Ašanja [YU] 154 G2
Åsarna [S] 182 G4
Åsarum [S] 158 E1
Åsbro [S] 166 H4
Asby [S] 162 E2
Ascain [F] 84 C2
Ascea [I] 120 F5
Ascha [D] 60 G2
Aschach [A] 62 B4
Aschaffenburg [D] 46 D3
Aschau [A] 72 E1
Aschau [D] 60 F5
Aschbach Markt [A] 62 C5
Ascheberg [D] 16 H6
Ascheberg [D] 18 G2
Aschendorf [D] 16 H3
Aschersleben [D] 34 B4
Asciano [I] 114 G1
Ascó [E] 90 H6
Asco [F] 114 B3
Ascoli Piceno [I] 116 C3
Ascoli Satriano [I] 120 G2
Ascona [CH] 70 F3
Åse [N] 192 E3
Åsebyn [S] 166 D3
Åseda [S] 162 E4
Åsele [S] 190 G5
Åseli [N] 192 D6
Asemankylä [FIN] 188 C5
Asemanseutu [FIN] 186 D3
Åsen [N] 190 C6
Åsen [S] 172 F2
Åsen [S] 182 G4
Åsen [S] 184 C4
Asendorf [D] 18 E6
Asenovgrad [BG] 148 B6
Åsensbruk [S] 166 D4
Åseral [N] 164 D4
Åserund [N] 166 C1
Asfáka [GR] 132 C1
Asfeld [F] 44 B2
Åsgårdstrand [N] 164 H2
Ashbourne [GB] 10 E5
Ashbourne [IRL] 2 F6
Åsheim [N] 182 C6
Ashford [GB] 14 F5
Ashington [GB] 8 G5
Ashmyany [BY] 200 H6
Ashton-under-Lyne [GB] 10 E4
Asiago [I] 72 D5
Asikkala [FIN] 176 H2
Äsila [FIN] 188 D5
Asíni [GR] 136 F2
Asipovitsy [BY] 202 B6
Ask [N] 170 H5
Ask [N] 170 B3
Ask [S] 158 C2
Aska [FIN] 194 D6
Askainen / Villnäs [FIN] 176 D4
Askanija Nova [UA] 204 G5
Askeaton [IRL] 4 C3
Askeby [DK] 156 G4
Asker [N] 164 H1
Askersund [S] 166 G4
Askeryd [S] 162 E2
Askim [N] 166 C2
Askim [S] 160 G2
Askland [N] 164 E3
Asklepiyon [TR] 144 C2
Askola [FIN] 178 B4
Asköping [S] 168 B3
Askós [GR] 130 B4
Askum [S] 166 B5
Askvoll [N] 170 B1
Askyfou [GR] 140 C5
Aslanapa [TR] 144 G1
Aslestad [N] 164 E2
Åsli [N] 170 G4
Åsljunga [S] 162 B6
Åsmasbo [S] 172 H5
Asmunti [FIN] 196 E2
Asnæs [DK] 156 F2
Åsnes [N] 172 D4
As Nogais [E] 78 E4
Asola [I] 110 E1
Asolo [I] 72 E5
Asopós [GR] 136 F4
Asoru, Nuraghe- [I] 118 D7
Asos [GR] 132 C5
Asotthalom [H] 76 D4
Aspa [S] 168 C4
Aspang Markt [A] 62 E6
Asparukovo [BG] 148 F3
Åspas [S] 182 G2
Aspe [E] 104 D2
Aspeå [S] 184 F1
Aspet [F] 84 G4
Aspnes [N] 190 D5
Aspö [S] 168 C2
As Pontes de García Rodríguez / Puentes de Garcá Rodríguez [E] 78 D2
Aspres-sur-Buëch [F] 108 C2
Asprópyrgos [GR] 134 B6
Asprováltа [GR] 130 C4
Aspsele [S] 190 G6
Assamalla [EST] 198 F1
Assel [D] 18 E4
Assé-le-Boisne [F] 26 F6
Assemini [I] 118 C7
Assen [NL] 16 G3
Assens [DK] 156 D3
Assens [DK] 160 E5
Asserbo [DK] 156 G1
Asserigi [I] 116 C4
Asseria [HR] 112 G5
Assesos [TR] 142 C1
Assiros [GR] 128 H4
Assisi [I] 116 A2
Assling [D] 60 F5
Assmannshausen [D] 46 B3
Assopía [GR] 134 B5
Assoro [I] 126 F3
Assos [TR] 134 H1
Åsta [N] 172 C3
Astaffort [F] 66 E6
Astakós [GR] 132 D5
Åstan [N] 180 H1
Asten [A] 62 B4
Asten [NL] 30 F3
Asti [I] 70 E6
Astorga [E] 78 G6
Åstorp [S] 156 H1
Åstrand [S] 172 E5
Ástros [GR] 136 E3
Astrup [DK] 160 D4
Astryna [BY] 24 G3
Astudillo [E] 82 D6
Astura, Torre- [I] 120 B1
Astypálaia [GR] 138 H4
Asvyeya [BY] 198 G6
Aszód [H] 64 D6
Aszófő [H] 76 A2
Atalaia [P] 86 B5
Atalánti [GR] 132 H4
Ataneuss [TR] 144 C2
Atapuerca [E] 82 E5
Atarfe [E] 102 E4
Atašiene [LV] 198 F5
Atburgazi [TR] 142 B1
Atça [TR] 144 E5
Ateca [E] 90 C4
Atella [I] 120 G3
Atessa [I] 116 E5
Ath [B] 28 G3
Athboy [IRL] 2 E5
Athea [IRL] 4 C3
Athenry [IRL] 2 C5
Athéras [GR] 132 C6
Athína [GR] 134 C6
Athleague [IRL] 2 D5
Athlone / Baile Átha Luain [IRL] 2 D5
Athy [IRL] 4 F3
Atienza [E] 90 A4
Atina [I] 116 C6
Atkár [H] 64 E6
Åtlo [N] 190 B6
Atnbrua [N] 180 H6
Atnosen [N] 182 B6
Atostugan [S] 190 E3
A Toxa [E] 78 B4
Atran [S] 162 B4
Äträsk [S] 190 H5
Atri [I] 116 D3
Atripalda [I] 120 F3
Atsalama [EST] 198 F1
Attáli [GR] 134 C4
Attel [D] 60 F4
Attendorn [D] 32 C5
Attersee [A] 60 H5
Attigny [F] 44 C2
Attleborough [GB] 14 G2
Attmar [S] 184 E5
Attnang-Puchheim [A] 62 A5
Attre [B] 28 G3
Attrup [DK] 160 D3
Åtvidaberg [S] 168 B6
Atzara [I] 118 D5
Atzendorf [D] 34 B4
Atzeneta del Maestrat [E] 98 F3
Au [A] 62 D6
Au [D] 60 E3
Aub [D] 46 E4
Aubagne [F] 108 B5
Aubange [B] 44 E3
Aubenas [F] 68 E6
Aubenton [F] 28 G6
Aubérive [F] 56 H2
Aubérive [F] 44 C3
Aubeterre-sur-Dronne [F] 66 E2
Aubiet [F] 84 G3
Aubigny [F] 54 B3
Aubigny-sur-Nere [F] 56 C2
Auboué [F] 44 E4
Aubrac [F] 68 C5
Aubusson [F] 68 B1
Auce [LV] 198 C6
Aucelon [F] 68 G6
Auch [F] 84 G2
Auchinleck [GB] 8 D4
Auchterarder [GB] 8 E2
Auchtermuchty [GB] 8 E2
Audelange [F] 56 H4
Audenge [F] 66 C3
Auderville [F] 26 D1
Audeux [F] 58 B4
Audierne [F] 40 A3
Audincourt [F] 58 C4
Audlem [GB] 10 D5
Audnedal [N] 164 D5
Audressein [F] 84 G5
Audru [EST] 198 D3
Audruicq [F] 14 H6
Audun-le-Roman [F] 44 E3
Aue [D] 48 D2
Auer / Ora [I] 72 D4
Auerbach [D] 46 H4
Auerbach [D] 48 C2
Auerbacher Schloss [D] 46 C4
Auffach [A] 60 F6
Augher [NIR] 2 F3
Aughnacloy [NIR] 2 F3
Aughrim [IRL] 4 G4
Augsburg [D] 60 D3
August [RO] 148 G1
Augusta [I] 126 G4
Augustenborg [DK] 156 C4
Augustów [PL] 24 E3
Augustusburg [D] 48 D1
Aukra [N] 180 D2
Aukštadvaris [LT] 24 G1
Auktsjaur [S] 190 H3
Auletta [I] 120 G4
Aulla [I] 110 C4
Aullène [F] 114 B5
Aulnay [F] 54 D5
Aulstad [N] 170 H2
Ault [F] 28 C4
Aulus-les-Bains [F] 84 H5
Auma [D] 48 B2
Aumale [F] 28 D5
Aumetz [F] 44 E3
Aumont-Aubrac [F] 68 C5
Aunay-sur-Odon [F] 26 E4
Auneau [F] 42 E4
Aunet [N] 190 B6
Aunet [N] 190 C5
Auneuil [F] 28 D6
Aunfoss [N] 190 D4
Auning [DK] 160 E5
Aups [F] 108 D4
Aura [FIN] 176 E4
Aurach [A] 60 F6
Aurach [D] 46 F5
Auray [F] 40 D4
Aurdal [N] 170 G3
Aure [N] 180 G1
Aurejärvi [FIN] 186 D5
Aurich [D] 18 B4
Aurignac [F] 84 G4
Aurillac [F] 68 B4
Auritz / Burguete [E] 84 C3
Aurland [N] 170 D2
Auron [F] 108 E3
Auronzo di Cadore [I] 72 F3
Aursmoen [N] 166 C1
Aursnes [N] 180 D3
Ausa Corno [I] 72 G5
Ausejo [E] 90 C1
Ausentum [I] 122 G6
Aussernbrünst [D] 60 H3
Austad [N] 164 C6
Austad [N] 164 D3
Austanå [N] 164 E3
Austbygda [N] 170 F5
Austbygdi [N] 170 F5
Austefjord [N] 180 C4
Austertana [N] 194 D2
Austmarka [N] 172 D5
Austnes [N] 180 D3
Austpollen [N] 192 E4
Austrått [N] 190 B6
Austrumdal [N] 164 B4
Auterive [F] 84 H4
Authon [F] 108 D3
Authon-du-Perche [F] 42 C5
Autio [S] 194 B7
Autol [E] 84 A5
Autti [FIN] 194 E8
Auttoinen [FIN] 176 H2
Autun [F] 56 F4
Auve [F] 44 C4
Auvers-s-Oise [F] 42 F3
Auvillers-les-Forges [F] 28 H5
Auxerre [F] 56 E2
Auxi-le-Château [F] 28 D4
Auxonne [F] 56 H4
Auzances [F] 56 B6
Auzon [F] 68 D3
Avå [FIN] 176 C4
Ava [S] 184 H1
Avafors [S] 196 B2
Availles-Limouzine [F] 54 F5
Aval, Falaise d'- [F] 26 G2
Avala [YU] 154 G3
Avaldsnes [N] 164 A2
Avallon [F] 56 E3
Ávas [GR] 130 G3
Avaträsk [S] 190 F5
Avaviken [S] 190 G3
Avcılar [TR] 146 E3
Ávdira [GR] 130 E3
Ávdira [GR] 130 E3
Ävedal [N] 164 B5
A Veiga [E] 78 E6
Aveiras de Cima [P] 86 C4
Aveiro [P] 80 B5
Avelengo / Hafling [I] 72 D3
Avellino [I] 120 F3
Aven Armand [F] 106 E2
Avenches [CH] 58 C6
Aven de Marzal [F] 106 G2
Aven d'Orgnac [F] 106 G2
Averbode [B] 30 D3
Aversa [I] 120 D3
Avesnes-le-Comte [F] 28 E4
Avesnes-sur-Helpe [F] 28 G4
Avesta [S] 174 D5
Avetrana [I] 122 F4
Avezzano [I] 116 C5
Avgerinós [GR] 128 E6
Avía [GR] 136 D4
Aviano [I] 72 F5
Aviemore [GB] 6 E5
Avigliana [I] 70 D5
Avigliano [I] 120 G3
Avigna [I] 72 D3
Avignon [F] 106 G3
Ávila [E] 88 E4
Avilés [E] 78 H3
Avinurme [EST] 198 F2
Avinyó [E] 92 E3
Avio [I] 72 C5
Avión [E] 78 C4
Avis [P] 86 D5
Avlákia [GR] 144 C5
Avlémonas [GR] 136 F6
Avlí [GR] 130 D3
Avliótes [GR] 132 A2
Avlóna [GR] 134 C5
Avlonári [GR] 134 C5
Avlum [DK] 160 C6
Avola [I] 126 G5
Avonmouth [GB] 12 F3
Avoriaz [F] 70 C2
Avradsberg [S] 172 F5
Avramov [BG] 148 E4
Avranches [F] 26 D4
Avşar [TR] 142 C1
Avtovac [BiH] 152 D3
Axat [F] 106 B5
Axel [NL] 28 H1
Axioúpoli [GR] 128 G3
Ax-les-Thermes [F] 106 A6
Axmarby [S] 174 E3
Axminster [GB] 12 F4
Axós [GR] 140 E4
Axvall [S] 166 F5
Ay [F] 44 B3
Ayagalip [TR] 130 G5
Ayamonte [E] 94 D5
Ayas [I] 70 D3
Aydın [TR] 144 D5
Aydıncık [TR] 130 G5
Ayerbe [E] 84 D6
Aykırıkçı [TR] 144 H2
Aylesbury [GB] 14 D3
Ayllón [E] 88 H3
Aylsham [GB] 14 G2
Ayna [E] 98 B6
Ayoó de Vidriales [E] 80 H3
Ayora [E] 98 D5
Ayr [GB] 8 C4
Ayrancı [TR] 144 G2
Äyskoski [FIN] 186 H2
Äystö [FIN] 186 B4
Aytos [BG] 148 F4
Ayvacık [TR] 134 H1
Ayvalık [TR] 144 B2
Azaila [E] 90 F5
Azambuja [P] 86 C4
Azannes-et-Soumazannes [F] 44 D3
Azanúy [E] 90 H3
Azaruja [P] 86 D6
Azay-le-Ferron [F] 54 G3
Azay-le-Rideau [F] 54 F2
Azinheira dos Barros [P] 94 C2
Azıtepe [TR] 144 E4
Aznalcóllar [E] 94 G5
Azpeitia [E] 82 H4
Azuaga [E] 96 A5
Azuara [E] 90 E5
Azuel [E] 96 D5
Azul, Cueva- [E] 104 E6
Azuqueca de Henares [E] 88 G5
Azur [F] 66 A6
Azyory [BY] 24 G4
Azzano Decimo [I] 72 F5
Azzurra, Grotta- [I] 120 F5
Azzurra, Grotta- [I] 120 D4

B

Baad [A] 60 B6
Baal [D] 30 F4
Baamonde [E] 78 D3
Baar [D] 60 D3
Baarle Nassau [NL] 30 D2
Baarn [NL] 16 E4
Babadag [RO] 204 E6
Babadağ [TR] 144 F5
Babaeski [TR] 146 B2
Babaevo [RUS] 202 E1
Babaköy [TR] 144 D2
Babenhausen [D] 60 C4
Babenhausen [D] 46 D3
Babiak [PL] 36 F3
Babiak [PL] 22 G3
Babica [PL] 52 D4
Babice [PL] 50 G4
Băbiciu [RO] 148 A1
Babięta [PL] 24 B4
Babigoszcz [PL] 20 F4
Babimost [PL] 36 A3
Babin Potok [HR] 112 G3
Babócsa [H] 74 G5
Babriškes [LT] 24 G2
Babruysk [BY] 202 C6
Babušnica [YU] 150 E4
Babylon [CZ] 48 D5
Babylón [CZ] 62 E2
Bač [MK] 128 E4
Bač [SLO] 74 A6
Bač [YU] 154 E1
Bača [SLO] 72 H4
Bacău [RO] 204 D5
Baccarat [F] 44 F6
Baceno [I] 70 F2
Bacharach [D] 46 B3
Bachkovo [BG] 148 B6
Bachórz [PL] 52 E4
Bačina [YU] 150 C3
Bačka Palanka [YU] 154 F1
Bačka Topola [YU] 76 D5
Bäckby [FIN] 196 C6
Backe [S] 190 F6
Bäckebo [S] 162 F4
Bäckefors [S] 166 D4
Backen [S] 184 E4
Backen [S] 184 D4
Bäckhammar [S] 166 F3
Bački Breg [YU] 76 C5
Bački Petrovac [YU] 154 F1
Backnang [D] 46 D6
Bačko Gradište [YU] 154 G1
Bačko Novo Selo [YU] 154 E1
Bačko Petrovo Selo [YU] 76 E6
Baćkowice [PL] 52 C1
Bacoli [I] 120 D3
Bacqueville-en-Caux [F] 28 B4
Bácsalmás [H] 76 D5
Bácsbokod [H] 76 C5
Baczyna [PL] 34 H1
Bad Abbach [D] 60 F2
Badacsonytomaj [H] 74 H3
Bad Aibling [D] 60 F5
Badajoz [E] 86 F6
Badalona [E] 92 E4
Bad Aussee [A] 62 A6
Bad Bederkesa [D] 18 D4
Bad Bentheim [D] 16 H5
Bad Bergzabern [D] 46 B5
Bad Berka [D] 46 H1
Bad Berleburg [D] 32 D5
Bad Berneck [D] 46 H3
Bad Bertrich [D] 44 G1
Bad Bevensen [D] 18 G5
Bad Bibra [D] 34 B5
Bad Blankenburg [D] 46 H2
Bad Brambach [D] 48 C3
Bad Bramstedt [D] 18 F3
Bad Breisig [D] 30 H5
Bad Brückenau [D] 46 E2
Bad Buchau [D] 60 A4
Badderen [N] 192 H2
Bad Deutsch-Altenburg [A] 62 G5
Bad Doberan [D] 20 B3
Bad Driburg [D] 32 E4
Bad Düben [D] 34 D4
Bad Dürkheim [D] 46 B4
Bad Dürrenberg [D] 34 C5
Bad Dürrheim [D] 58 F3
Bad Elster [D] 48 C3
Bademli [TR] 144 C3
Bad Ems [D] 46 B2
Baden [A] 62 F5
Baden [CH] 58 F4
Baden-Baden [D] 58 F1
Bad Endorf [D] 60 F5
Badenweiler [D] 58 E3
Baderna [HR] 112 D2
Bad Essen [D] 32 D2
Bad Frankenhausen [D] 34 A5
Bad Freienwalde [D] 34 F1
Bad Friedrichshall [D] 46 D5
Bad Gandersheim [D] 32 G3
Badgastein [A] 72 G2
Bad Gleichenberg [A] 74 E3
Bad Godesberg [D] 30 H5
Bad Goisern [A] 60 H6
Bad Gottleuba [D] 48 F1
Bad Grund [D] 32 G4
Bad Hall [A] 62 B5
Bad Harzburg [D] 32 H3
Bad Herrenalb [D] 58 F1
Bad Hersfeld [D] 32 F6
Bad Hofgastein [A] 72 G1
Bad Homburg [D] 46 C2
Bad Honnef [D] 30 H5
Bad Hönningen [D] 30 H5
Badia Polèsine [I] 110 F2
Badia Tedalda [I] 110 G6
Bad Iburg [D] 32 D2
Bad Ischl [A] 60 H5
Bad Kissingen [D] 46 E3
Bad Kleinen [D] 20 A4
Bad Kleinkirchheim [A] 72 H3
Bad König [D] 46 D4
Bad Königshofen [D] 46 F2
Bad Kösen [D] 34 B6
Bądkowo [PL] 36 F2
Bad Kreuznach [D] 46 B3
Bad Krozingen [D] 58 E3
Bad Laasphe [D] 32 D6
Bad Langensalza [D] 32 H6
Bad Lauchstädt [D] 34 B5
Bad Lausick [D] 34 D6
Bad Lauterburg [D] 32 G4
Bad Leonfelden [A] 62 B3
Bad Liebenstein [D] 46 F1
Bad Liebenwerda [D] 34 E5
Bad Liebenzell [D] 58 G1
Bad Lippspringe [D] 32 E3
Badljevina [HR] 154 C1
Bad Marienberg [D] 46 B1
Bad Meinberg [D] 32 E3
Bad Mergentheim [D] 46 E5
Bad Mitterndorf [A] 62 B6
Bad Münder [D] 32 F2
Bad Münster Ebernburg [D] 46 B3
Bad Münstereifel [D] 30 G5
Bad Muskau [D] 34 G5
Bad Nauheim [D] 46 C2
Bad Nenndorf [D] 32 F2
Bad Neuenahr [D] 30 G5
Bad Neustadt [D] 46 F2
Bad Oeynhausen [D] 32 E2
Badolato [I] 124 E6
Badolato Marina [I] 124 E6
Bad Oldesloe [D] 18 G3
Badonviller [F] 44 F6
Bad Orb [D] 46 D2
Badovinci [YU] 154 F2
Bad Peterstal [D] 58 F2
Bad Pirawarth [A] 62 F4
Bad Pyrmont [D] 32 E3
Bad Radkersburg [A] 74 E3
Bad Ragaz [CH] 58 H6
Bad Reichenhall [D] 60 G5
Bad Rippoldsau [D] 58 F2
Bad Rothenfelde [D] 32 D2
Bad Saarow-Pieskow [D] 34 F3
Bad Sachsa [D] 32 G4
Bad Säckingen [D] 58 E4
Bad Salzdetfurth [D] 32 G3
Bad Salzuflen [D] 32 E3
Bad Salzungen [D] 46 F1
Bad Schallerbach [A] 62 B4
Bad Schandau [D] 48 F1
Bad Schmiedeberg [D] 34 D4
Bad Schönau [A] 74 F1
Bad Schönborn [D] 46 C5
Bad Schussenried [D] 60 B4
Bad Schwalbach [D] 46 B2
Bad Schwartau [D] 18 G3
Bad Segeberg [D] 18 G3
Bad Sooden-Allendorf [D] 32 F5
Bad St. Leonhard [A] 74 C2
Bad Sülze [D] 20 C3
Bad Tatzmannsdorf [A] 74 F1
Bad Tennstedt [D] 32 H5
Bad Tölz [D] 60 E5
Badules [E] 90 D5
Bad Urach [D] 58 H2
Bad Vöslau [A] 62 F5
Bad Waldsee [D] 60 B4
Bad Wiessee [D] 60 E5
Bad-Wildungen [D] 32 E5
Bad Wilsnack [D] 20 B6
Bad Wimpfen [D] 46 D5
Bad Windsheim [D] 46 F5
Bad Wörishofen [D] 60 C4
Bad Wurzach [D] 60 B5
Bad Zwischenahn [D] 18 C5
Bække [DK] 156 B2
Bækmarksbro [DK] 160 B5
Baells [E] 90 H3
Baelo Claudia [E] 100 G5
Baena [E] 102 D2
Bæverfjord [N] 180 F2
Baeza [E] 102 F2
Bagà [E] 92 E2
Bağarası [TR] 144 D5
Bågede [S] 190 E5
Bagenalstown / Muine Bheag [IRL] 4 F4
Bagenkop [DK] 18 H1
Bagh a Chaisteil / Castlebay [GB] 6 A5
Bagheria [I] 126 D2
Bagn [N] 170 G3
Bagnacavallo [I] 110 G4
Bagnara Calabra [I] 124 C7
Bagnères-de-Bigorre [F] 84 F4
Bagnères-de-Luchon [F] 84 F5
Bagni Contursi [I] 120 F4
Bagni del Másino [I] 70 H3
Bagni di Bormio [I] 72 B3
Bagni di Craveggia [I] 70 F3
Bagni di Lucca [I] 110 E5
Bagni di Rabbi [I] 72 C3
Bagni di Salomone [I] 72 E2
Bagni di Vinadio [I] 108 E3
Bagno di Romagna [I] 110 G5
Bagnoles-de-l'Orne [F] 26 F5
Bagnoli di Sopra [I] 110 G1
Bagnolo Mella [I] 72 B6
Bagnolo Piemonte [I] 108 F1
Bagnolo San Vito [I] 110 E2
Bagnols-en-Forêt [F] 108 D5
Bagnols-les-Bains [F] 68 D6
Bagnols-sur-Cèze [F] 106 G3
Bagnone [I] 110 D4
Bagnoregio [I] 114 H3
Bagno Vignoni [I] 114 G2
Bågø [DK] 156 C3
Bagod [H] 74 F3
Bagolino [I] 72 B5
Bagrationovsk [RUS] 22 H2
Bagsund [N] 190 C5
Báguena [E] 90 D5
Bagunte [P] 80 B3
Bağyüzü [TR] 144 C2
Bahçecik [TR] 146 G3
Bahillo [E] 82 D5
Bàia delle Zagare [I] 116 H6
Bàia Domízia [I] 120 D2
Baia Mare [RO] 204 B4
Baiano [I] 120 E3
Baião [P] 80 C4
Bàia Sardínia [I] 118 E2
Baiersbronn [D] 58 F2
Baigneux-les-Juifs [F] 56 G3
Baile Átha Cliath / Dublin [IRL] 2 F6
Baile Átha Luain / Athlone [IRL] 2 D5
Băile Felix [RO] 76 H2
Bailén [E] 102 E1
Băile Tuşnad [RO] 204 C5
Bailieborough [IRL] 2 F4
Bailleul [F] 28 F2
Bailleul [F] 26 H2
Bain-de-Bretagne [F] 40 F5
Bains-les-Bains [F] 58 C2
Baio [E] 78 B2
Baiona [E] 78 A5
Bais [F] 26 E6
Baisogala [LT] 200 F4
Baix [F] 68 F5
Baixas [F] 92 G1
Baja [H] 76 C4
Bajánsenye [H] 74 F3
Bajina Bašta [YU] 154 F4
Bajmok [YU] 76 D5
Bajna [H] 64 B6
Bajram Curri [AL] 150 A6
Bajša [YU] 76 D6
Bajzë [AL] 152 E4
Bak [H] 74 G3
Bakacak [TR] 146 C5
Bakar [HR] 112 E1
Bakewell [GB] 10 E5
Bakio [E] 82 G3
Bakırköy [TR] 146 E3
Bakka [N] 164 F1
Bakke [N] 164 F4
Bakke [N] 166 C4
Bakkejord [N] 192 F2
Bakken [N] 192 H3
Bakko [N] 170 F5
Baklan [TR] 144 G4
Bakonygyepes [H] 74 H2
Bakonypéterd [H] 76 A1
Bakonyszántkány [H] 76 A1
Bakonyszombathely [H] 76 A1
Baks [H] 76 E3
Baksa [H] 76 A5
Baksjöliden [S] 190 G5
Baktakék [H] 64 F4
Baktsjaur [S] 190 H3
Bakum [D] 18 C6
Bakvattnet [S] 190 D6
Bål [S] 168 G4
Bala [GB] 10 C5
Balaguer [E] 92 B3
Balanegra [E] 102 F5
Bălăneşti [RO] 148 A1
Balassagyarmat [H] 64 C5
Balástya [H] 76 E4
Balat [TR] 142 B1
Balatonakali [H] 74 H2
Balatonalmádi [H] 76 A2
Balatonboglár [H] 74 H3
Balatonederics [H] 74 H3
Balatonföldvár [H] 76 A3
Balatonfüred [H] 76 A2
Balatonfűzfő [H] 76 A2
Balatonkenese [H] 76 A2
Balatonkeresztúr [H] 74 H3
Balatonlelle [H] 74 H3
Balatonszemes [H] 76 A3
Balazote [E] 98 B5
Balbigny [F] 68 E2
Balboa [E] 78 E4
Balbriggan [IRL] 2 F5
Bålby [S] 166 G3
Balchik [BG] 148 G2
Balcon de Europa [E] 102 D5
Baldenstein [CH] 70 H1
Balderschwang [D] 60 B6
Baldock [GB] 14 E3
Baldone [LV] 198 E5
Bale [HR] 112 D2
Baleines, Phare des- [F] 54 B4
Baleira [E] 78 E3
Baleizão [P] 94 D3
Balestrand [N] 170 C1
Balestrate [I] 126 C2
Balewo [PL] 22 F4
Balgviken [S] 168 B3
Balice [PL] 50 H3
Balıkesir [TR] 144 D1
Balıklıova [TR] 144 B4
Balıköy [TR] 144 F1
Bålinge [S] 168 D1
Bälinge [S] 158 C1
Bälinge [S] 162 B1
Balingen [D] 58 G2
Balinț [RO] 76 H5
Balio Chitarra [I] 126 B2
Baljvine [BiH] 154 B3
Balkány [H] 64 H5
Balkıca [TR] 142 F1
Balla [IRL] 2 C4
Ballaban [AL] 128 C5
Ballachulish [GB] 6 C6
Ballaghaderreen [IRL] 2 D4
Ballangen [N] 192 E4
Ballantrae [GB] 8 C4
Ballao [I] 118 D6
Ballater [GB] 6 E6
Ballebro [DK] 156 C4
Ballefors [S] 166 F5
Ballen [DK] 156 E2
Ballenstedt [D] 34 A4
Balleroy [F] 26 E3
Ballerup [DK] 156 G2
Ballı [TR] 146 B3
Ballina [IRL] 2 C6
Ballina [IRL] 2 C3
Ballinafad [IRL] 2 D4
Ballinagh [IRL] 2 E4
Ballinakill [IRL] 4 E3
Ballinamore [IRL] 2 E4
Ballinascarty [IRL] 4 C5
Ballinasloe [IRL] 2 D5
Ballindine [IRL] 2 C4
Ballindooly Castle [IRL] 2 C5
Balling [DK] 160 C5
Ballingarry [IRL] 4 C3
Ballingarry [IRL] 4 E4
Ballinhassig [IRL] 4 C5
Ballinrobe [IRL] 2 C4
Ballinskelligs [IRL] 4 A4
Ballinspittle [IRL] 4 C5
Ballintober, Abbey- [IRL] 2 C4
Ballintra [IRL] 2 E3
Ballivor [IRL] 2 E5
Ballobar [E] 90 G4
Ballon [F] 42 B4
Ballon [IRL] 4 F4
Ballsh [AL] 128 B5
Ballshi [AL] 128 B4
Ballstad [N] 192 C4
Ballstad [N] 192 D4
Ballum [DK] 156 B3
Ballybay [IRL] 2 F4
Ballybofey [IRL] 2 E2
Ballybunion [IRL] 2 B6
Ballycanew [IRL] 4 F4
Ballycastle [NIR] 2 G2
Ballycastle [IRL] 2 C3
Ballyclare [NIR] 2 G3
Ballyconneely [IRL] 2 B4
Ballycotton [IRL] 4 D5
Ballycumber [IRL] 2 D5
Ballydehob [IRL] 4 B5
Ballydesmond [IRL] 4 C4
Ballyduff [IRL] 4 D4
Ballyduff [IRL] 4 B3
Ballyemund [IRL] 4 F4
Ballyfarnan [IRL] 2 D4
Ballygawley [NIR] 2 F3
Ballyglass [IRL] 2 C4
Ballygowan [NIR] 2 G4
Ballyhaunis [IRL] 2 C4
Ballyheige [IRL] 4 B3
Ballyhillin [IRL] 2 F1
Ballyjamesduff [IRL] 2 E4
Ballykeeran [IRL] 2 D5
Ballylanders [IRL] 4 D4
Ballylongford [IRL] 2 B6
Ballylynan [IRL] 4 F3
Ballymacoda [IRL] 4 D5
Ballymahon [IRL] 2 D5
Ballymena [NIR] 2 G3
Ballymoe [IRL] 2 D4
Ballymoney [NIR] 2 G2
Ballymore [IRL] 2 E5
Ballymore Eustace [IRL] 4 F3
Ballymote [IRL] 2 D3
Ballynahinch [NIR] 2 G4
Ballyragget [IRL] 4 E3
Ballyronan [NIR] 2 G3
Ballyroon [IRL] 4 B5
Ballysadare [IRL] 2 D3
Ballyshannon [IRL] 2 E3
Ballyvaughan [IRL] 2 C5
Ballywalter [NIR] 2 H4
Balmaseda [E] 82 G4
Balmazújváros [H] 64 G6
Balme [I] 70 C5
Balmúccia [I] 70 E3
Balş [RO] 150 G1
Balsareny [E] 92 D3
Balsfjord [N] 192 F2
Balsicas [E] 104 C4
Balsjö [S] 190 H6
Balsorano [I] 116 C6
Bålsta [S] 168 D2
Balsthal [CH] 58 E5
Balta [UA] 204 E4
Baltanás [E] 88 F1
Baltar [E] 78 C6
Bălţi [MD] 204 D4
Baltimore [IRL] 4 B5
Baltinava [LV] 198 G5
Baltinglass [IRL] 4 F3
Baltiysk [RUS] 22 G1
Baltrum [D] 18 B3
Balugães [P] 78 A6
Balvan [BG] 148 C3
Balvi [LV] 198 G4
Balya [TR] 144 D1
Balzers [FL] 58 H6
Bamberg [D] 46 G4
Bamble [N] 164 G3
Bana [H] 64 A6
Banafjäl [S] 184 G2
Banagher [IRL] 2 D6
Banarli [TR] 146 C3
Banatski Karlovac [YU] 154 H2
Banatsko Aranđelovo [YU] 76 E5
Banatsko Karadjordjevo [YU] 76 F6
Banatsko Novo Selo [YU] 154 H2
Banaz [TR] 144 G3
Banbridge [NIR] 2 G4
Banbury [GB] 14 D2
Banchory [GB] 6 F6
Bande [E] 78 C5
Bandholm [DK] 156 F5
Bandırma [TR] 146 D4
Bandol [F] 108 B5
Bandon [IRL] 4 C5
Băneasa [RO] 148 C1
Banff [GB] 6 F5
Bångnäs [S] 190 E4
Bangor [F] 40 C5
Bangor [GB] 10 B4
Bangor [NIR] 2 H3
Bangor Erris [IRL] 2 C3
Bangsbo [DK] 160 E3
Bangsund [N] 190 C5
Banica [BG] 150 G3
Banie [PL] 20 F6
Banja [YU] 152 E2
Banja [YU] 150 B4
Banja Koviljača [YU] 154 E3
Banjaloka [SLO] 112 F1
Banja Luka [BiH] 154 C3
Banjani [YU] 150 A1
Banjska [YU] 150 C4
Bánk [H] 64 H6
Banka [SK] 64 A3
Bankervd [S] 162 D2
Bankja [BG] 150 F5
Bannalec [F] 40 C3
Bannesdorf [D] 20 A2
Bañolas / Banyoles [E] 92 F3
Banon [F] 108 C3
Baños de Alicún de las Torres [E] 102 F3
Baños de Cerrato [E] 88 F1
Baños de la Encina [E] 102 E1
Baños de la Fuensanta [E] 104 A3
Baños de Montemayor [E] 88 B4
Baños de Panticosa [E] 84 E5
Baños de Río Tobía [E] 82 G6
Bánov [CZ] 62 H2
Bánovce nad Bebravou [SK] 64 B3
Banovići [BiH] 154 D3
Bánréve [H] 64 E4
Bansin [D] 20 E3
Banská Bystrica [SK] 64 C3
Banská Štiavnica [SK] 64 C3
Bansko [BG] 130 B1
Bansko [MK] 128 H2
Banteer [IRL] 4 C4
Ban. Topola [YU] 76 F6
Bantry [IRL] 4 B5
Bantry House [IRL] 4 B5
Banya [BG] 148 B5
Banya [BG] 148 F4
Banya [BG] 148 D4
Banyeres de Mariola [E] 104 D1
Banyoles / Bañolas [E] 92 F3
Banyuls-sur-Mer [F] 92 G2
Banz [D] 46 G3
Bapaume [F] 28 F4
Bar [YU] 152 E5
Baradla [H] 64 E3
Barajas de Melo [E] 96 H1
Barakaldo [E] 82 G3
Baralla [E] 78 E4
Baranavichy [BY] 202 A6
Baránd [H] 76 G1
Baranowo [PL] 24 C5
Baranów Sandomierski [PL] 52 D2
Baraona [E] 90 B4
Baraqueville [F] 68 A6
Bårared [S] 162 B5
Barásoain [E] 84 B4
Barbadillo de Herreros [E] 90 A1
Barban [HR] 112 D2
Barbarano Vicentino [I] 72 D6
Barbaros [TR] 146 C3
Barba-Rossahöhle [D] 32 H5
Barbaste [F] 66 E5
Barbastro [E] 90 G3
Barbat [HR] 112 F3
Barbate [E] 100 F5
Bārbele [LV] 198 E6
Barberino Val D'Elsa [I] 110 F6
Barbezieux [F] 66 E2
Barbing [D] 60 F2
Barbizon [F] 42 F5
Barbotan-les-Thermes [F] 66 D6
Barby [D] 34 C3
Bärbyborg [S] 162 G6
Bârca [RO] 150 G2
Barcarrota [E] 94 F2

Bockum-Hovel [D] 32 C3
Bocognano [F] 114 B4
Bócsa [H] 76 D3
Bocsig [RO] 76 H4
Böda [S] 162 H3
Boda [S] 172 H3
Boda [S] 166 E2
Boda [S] 184 E3
Bodaanowice [PL] 50 F1
Bodaczów [PL] 52 F1
Bodafors [S] 162 D3
Boda glasbruk [S] 162 F5
Bodarsjön [S] 182 G6
Bodegraven [NL] 16 D5
Boden [S] 196 B3
Bodenmais [D] 48 D6
Bodenteich [D] 18 G6
Bodenwerder [D] 32 F3
Bodenwöhr [D] 48 C6
Bodjani [YU] 154 E1
Bodman [D] 58 G4
Bodmin [GB] 12 C4
Bodø [N] 192 D6
Bodom [N] 190 C5
Bodrogkeresztúr [H] 64 G4
Bodrum [TR] 142 C2
Bodsjö [S] 182 H3
Bodsjöedet [S] 182 E1
Bodträskfors [S] 196 A2
Bodzanów [PL] 36 H2
Bodzentyn [PL] 52 C1
Boëge [F] 70 B2
Boën [F] 68 E2
Bøgard [N] 192 D3
Bogarra [E] 98 A6
Bogatić [YU] 154 F2
Bogatovo [RUS] 22 G2
Bogatynia [PL] 48 G1
Boğaziçi [TR] 144 D5
Boğazköy [TR] 146 F4
Bogda [RO] 76 H5
Bogdaniec [PL] 34 H2
Bogen [D] 60 G2
Bogen [N] 192 E4
Bogen [N] 192 D5
Bogen [S] 172 D6
Bogense [DK] 156 D2
Bogetići [YU] 152 E4
Boggc [N] 100 F3
Böglosa [S] 168 C2
Bognanco [I] 70 E3
Bognes [N] 192 E4
Bognor Regis [GB] 14 D5
Bogojevo [YU] 154 E1
Bogojevo [YU] 150 D4
Bogoria [PL] 52 C2
Bogorodica [MK] 128 G3
Bogoroditsk [RUS] 202 F5
Bogovina [YU] 150 D2
Bogovinska Pećina [YU] 150 D2
Bograngen [S] 172 E4
Bogumiłowice [PL] 36 G6
Boguszów-Gorce [PL] 50 B2
Bogutovačka banja [YU] 150 B3
Bohain-en-Vermandois [F] 28 F5
Bohdalov [CZ] 50 A5
Boheeshil [IRL] 4 B4
Bohinjska Bistrica [SLO] 74 A4
Böhmenkirch [D] 60 B2
Bohmte [D] 32 D2
Bohodukhiv [UA] 204 G2
Bohonal [E] 96 D2
Bohonal de Ibor [E] 88 B6
Böhönye [H] 74 H4
Boialvo [P] 80 B6
Boichinovtsi [BG] 150 F3
Bois-du-Four [F] 68 B6
Boitzenburg [D] 20 D5
Bòixols [E] 92 C2
Boizenburg [D] 18 G5
Böja [S] 166 F5
Bojano [I] 120 E1
Bojanów [PL] 52 D2
Bojanowo [PL] 36 C4
Bøjden [DK] 156 D4
Bojnica [BG] 150 E2
Bojnik [YU] 150 D4
Bojtiken [S] 190 E3
Bokel [D] 18 F3
Bökemåla [S] 162 E6
Bökenäs [S] 166 C6
Bokinić [HR] 112 E3
Böklund [D] 18 F1
Boksitogorsk [RUS] 202 D2
Boksjok [N] 194 D2
Bol [HR] 152 A2
Bolaños de Calatrava [E] 96 F4
Bolayır [TR] 146 B4
Bolbec [F] 26 H3
Bolca [I] 72 C6
Boldekow [D] 20 D4
Boldva [H] 64 F4
Bøle [N] 190 B5
Böle [S] 182 G1
Bolekhiv [UA] 52 H6
Bolemin [PL] 34 H2
Bolesławiec [PL] 36 A6
Bolesławiec [PL] 36 E6
Bolesławów [PL] 50 C3
Boleszkowice [PL] 34 G2
Bolfiar [P] 80 B5
Bolfoss [N] 166 C1
Bolgatovo [RUS] 198 H5
Bolgheri [I] 114 E1
Bolhrad [UA] 204 D5
Boliden [S] 196 A4
Bolimów [PL] 38 A3
Bolinglanna [IRL] 2 B3
Boljanići [YU] 152 E2
Boljevac [YU] 150 D2
Bolkesjø [N] 164 G1
Bolkhov [RUS] 202 E5
Bolków [PL] 50 B1
Bollebygd [S] 162 B2
Bollène [F] 106 G2
Böllerkirche [D] 46 B3
Bollnäs [S] 174 D2
Bollstabruk [S] 184 F3
Bollullos de la Mitación [E] 94 G6
Bollullos Par del Condado [E] 94 F6
Bologna [I] 110 F3
Bologne [F] 44 C6
Bolótana [I] 118 C4
Bolotovo [RUS] 198 H4
Bolsena [I] 114 H3
Bol'shakovo [RUS] 200 D5
Bol'shie Sabicy [RUS] 198 H2
Bol'shoye Zagor'e [RUS] 198 H3
Bol'shoy Sabsk [RUS] 198 G1
Bolstad [S] 166 D5
Bolstadøyri [N] 170 C3
Bolstaholm [FIN] 176 A5
Bolsward [NL] 16 E2
Bolszewo [PL] 22 D2
Boltaña [E] 84 E5
Boltenhagen [D] 18 H3
Boltigen [CH] 70 D1
Bolton [GB] 10 E4
Bolungarvik [IS] 192 A1
Bóly [H] 76 B5
Bolyarovo [BG] 148 E5
Bolzano / Bozen [I] 72 D3
Bomarken [S] 166 C3
Bomarsund [FIN] 176 B5
Bomarzo [I] 114 H4
Bombarral [P] 86 B4
Bominago [I] 116 C4
Bom Jesus do Monte [P] 80 C3
Bomsund [S] 184 C2
Bonaduz [CH] 70 H1
Bonaguil, Château de- [F] 66 F5
Boñar [E] 82 C3
Bonar Bridge [GB] 6 E4
Bonares [E] 94 F6
Bonäs [S] 166 E2
Bonäs [S] 172 G3
Bönaset [S] 182 F1
Bonäsjøen [N] 192 D5
Bonassola [I] 110 C4
Bondal [N] 164 F1
Bondemon [S] 166 C4
Bondeno [I] 110 F2
Bondstorp [S] 162 C2
Bonefro [I] 116 F6
Bonete [E] 98 C6
Bonhomme, Col du- [F] 58 D2
Bonifacio [F] 114 B6
Bonifati Marina [I] 124 C4
Bonlieu [F] 70 A1
Bonn [D] 30 G5
Bonnat [F] 54 H5
Bonndorf [D] 58 F4
Bønnerup Strand [DK] 160 F5
Bonnesvalyn [F] 42 H3
Bonnétable [F] 42 C5
Bonneval [F] 42 D5
Bonneval-sur-Arc [F] 70 C4
Bonneville [F] 70 B2
Bonnières [F] 42 E3
Bonnieux [F] 106 H4
Bonnigheim [D] 46 D6
Bonny-sur-Loire [F] 56 D2
Bono [I] 118 D4
Bonorva [I] 118 C4
Bonport, Abbaye de- [F] 28 B6
Bonyhád [H] 76 B4
Boom [B] 30 C3
Boos [D] 30 G6
Boos [F] 28 C5
Booth of Toft [GB] 6 H3
Bootle [GB] 10 D4
Bopfingen [D] 60 C2
Boppard [D] 44 H1
Bor [CZ] 48 D4
Bor [RUS] 198 H2
Bor [S] 162 D4
Bor [YU] 150 D2
Borås [N] 164 F4
Borås [S] 162 B2
Borba [P] 86 E6
Borbona [I] 116 B4
Borchen [D] 32 E4
Borci [BiH] 152 C2
Borculo [NL] 16 G5
Bordány [H] 76 E4
Bordeaux [F] 66 C3
Bordeira [P] 94 A4
Bordères [F] 84 F4
Bordesholm [D] 18 F2
Bordighera [I] 108 F4
Bording [DK] 160 C6
Borek Wielkopolski [PL] 36 D4
Borello [I] 110 G5
Borensberg [S] 166 H5
Borg [N] 192 C4
Borgå / Porvoo [FIN] 178 B4
Borgafjäll [S] 190 E4
Borgarnes [IS] 192 A2
Borgen [N] 164 E3
Borgentreich [D] 32 E4
Börger [D] 18 B5
Borger [NL] 16 G3
Borggård [S] 166 H5
Borghamn [S] 166 G6
Borgholm [S] 162 G4
Borgholzhausen [D] 32 D2
Borghorst [D] 16 H5
Børglumkloster [DK] 160 D3
Borgo Callea [I] 126 D3
Borgoforte [I] 110 E2
Borgomanero [I] 70 F4
Borgonovo Val Tidone [I] 70 G6
Borgorose [I] 116 B5
Borgo San Dalmazzo [I] 108 F3
Borgo San Lorenzo [I] 110 F5
Borgosésia [I] 70 E4
Borgo Ticino [I] 70 F4
Borgo Tossignano [I] 110 F4
Borgo Val di Taro [I] 110 C3
Borgo Valsugana [I] 72 D4
Borgo Vercelli [I] 70 F5
Borgsjö [S] 190 G5
Borgsjö [S] 184 D4
Borgstena [S] 162 B1
Borgund [N] 170 E2
Borgvattnet [S] 184 C1
Borgvik [S] 166 E3
Borima [BG] 148 B4
Borisoglebskiy [RUS] 194 F3
Borisovo-Sudskoye [RUS] 202 E1
Borja [E] 90 D3
Börjelslandet [S] 196 B3
Borken [D] 32 E6
Borken [D] 16 G6
Borkenes [N] 192 E3
Borki [RUS] 198 G3
Børkop [DK] 156 C2
Borków [PL] 52 B1
Borkum [D] 16 G1
Borlänge [S] 172 H4
Borlaug [N] 170 E2
Børlia [N] 182 B3
Borlu [TR] 144 E3
Bormes-les-Mimosas [F] 108 D6
Bórmio [I] 72 B3
Borna [D] 34 C6
Bornhöved [D] 18 G3
Börnicke [D] 34 D1
Bornos [E] 100 G3
Bornova [TR] 144 C4
Borodianka [UA] 204 E2
Borodinskoye [RUS] 178 F2
Borová Lada [CZ] 62 A2
Borovan [BG] 150 G3
Borovany [CZ] 62 C2
Borovets [BG] 150 G5
Borovichi [RUS] 198 H3
Borovichi [RUS] 202 D2
Borovik [RUS] 198 G3
Borovo [HR] 154 E1
Borovoy [RUS] 196 H4
Borovtsi [BG] 150 F3
Borowa [PL] 36 D6
Borrby [S] 158 D3
Borre [DK] 156 G4
Borre [N] 164 H2
Borreby [DK] 156 F3
Borreda [E] 92 E2
Borremose [DK] 160 D4
Borriana / Burriana [E] 98 F3
Börringe [S] 158 C3
Borriol [E] 98 F3
Borris [DK] 156 B1
Borris [IRL] 4 F4
Borris-in-Ossory [IRL] 2 D6
Borrisokane [IRL] 2 D6
Borrisoleigh [IRL] 4 E3
Borrum [S] 168 C6
Borș [RO] 76 H2
Børsa [N] 182 B1
Borșa [RO] 204 C4
Børselv [N] 194 C2
Borsfa [H] 74 F4
Borsh [AL] 132 B1
Borsodnádasd [H] 64 E4
Börstil [S] 174 G5
Bort-les-Orgues [F] 68 B3
Börtnan [S] 182 F3
Bortnen [N] 180 B5
Borup [DK] 156 G3
Borynia [UA] 52 F6
Boryslav [UA] 52 G5
Boryspil' [UA] 204 F2
Borzechowo [PL] 22 D4
Borzone, Abbazia di- [I] 110 B3
Borzysław [PL] 22 B3
Bosa [I] 118 B4
Bosanci [HR] 112 G1
Bosanska Dubica [BiH] 154 B2
Bosanska Gradiška [BiH] 154 C2
Bosanska Krupa [BiH] 154 A2
Bosanska Rača [BiH] 154 F2
Bosanski Brod [BiH] 154 D2
Bosanski Novi [HR] 154 A2
Bosanski Petrovac [BiH] 154 A3
Bosanski Šamac [BiH] 154 D2
Bosansko Grahovo [BiH] 154 A4
Bošany [SK] 64 B3
Bösárkány [H] 62 G6
Bosco Chiesanuova [I] 72 C5
Bösel [D] 18 C5
Bosilegrad [YU] 150 E5
Bosiljevo [HR] 112 G1
Bosjön [S] 166 F1
Boskoop [NL] 16 D5
Boskovice [CZ] 50 C5
Bosna Klanac [BiH] 154 D4
Bošnjace [YU] 150 D4
Bošnjaci [HR] 154 E2
Bosque de Muniellos [E] 78 F4
Bosque de Oma [E] 82 H4
Bosruck Tunnel [A] 62 B6
Bössbo [S] 172 F2
Bossbøen [N] 164 E1
Bossea [I] 108 G3
Bossòst [E] 84 F5
Böste [S] 158 C3
Boston [GB] 10 G6
Bostrak [N] 164 F3
Bosut [YU] 154 F2
Bőszénfa [H] 76 A4
Bote [S] 184 F2
Botevgrad [BG] 150 G4
Boticas [P] 80 E3
Botinec [HR] 74 E6
Botnen [N] 180 C4
Botngård [N] 190 B6
Bótoa [E] 86 F6
Bötom / Karijoki [FIN] 186 B4
Botoroaga [RO] 148 C1
Botoșani [RO] 204 D4
Botricello [I] 124 E5
Botsmark [S] 196 A5
Botten [S] 166 D3
Bottheim [N] 180 G5
Bottidda [I] 118 D4
Bottnaryd [S] 162 C2
Bottrop [D] 30 G3
Botun [MK] 128 D3
Botunets [BG] 150 G4
Bouaye [F] 54 B1
Boudry [CH] 58 C6
Bouesse [F] 54 H4
Bouges-Le-Château [F] 54 H3
Bouguenais [F] 54 B1
Bouillon [B] 44 D2
Bouilly [F] 44 A6
Boulay-Moselle [F] 44 F4
Bouligny [F] 44 E3
Boulogne [F] 14 G6
Boulogne-sur-Gesse [F] 84 G3
Bouloire [F] 42 C5
Boumois, Château de- [F] 54 E2
Bouniagues [F] 66 E4
Bourbon-Lancy [F] 56 E5
Bourbon-l'Archambault [F] 56 D5
Bourbonne-les-Bains [F] 58 B2
Bourbourg [F] 14 H6
Bourbriac [F] 40 D2
Bourdeaux [F] 68 F6
Bourdeilles [F] 66 F2
Bourg [F] 66 D3
Bourg-Achard [F] 26 H3
Bourganeuf [F] 54 H6
Bourg-Argental [F] 68 F4
Bourg-de-Péage [F] 68 F5
Bourg-en-Bresse [F] 68 G2
Bourges [F] 56 C3
Bourg-et-Comin [F] 44 A2
Bourg-Lastic [F] 68 B2
Bourg-Madame [F] 92 E1
Bourgneuf-en-Retz [F] 54 B2
Bourgogne [F] 44 B3
Bourgoin-Jallieu [F] 68 G3
Bourg-St-Andéol [F] 106 G2
Bourg-St-Maurice [F] 70 C4
Bourgtheroulde-Infreville [F] 26 H4
Bourgueil [F] 54 E2
Bourideys [F] 66 C5
Bourmont [F] 58 B2
Bourne [GB] 10 G6
Bournemouth [GB] 12 G5
Bourneville [F] 26 H3
Bournezeau [F] 54 C3
Boussac [F] 56 B5
Boussens [F] 84 G4
Bouvignes [B] 30 D5
Bouvron [F] 40 F6
Bouxwiller [F] 44 G5
Bouzonville [F] 44 F3
Bova [I] 124 C8
Bovalino [I] 124 D7
Bovallstrand [S] 166 C5
Bova Marina [I] 124 C8
Bovan [YU] 150 D3
Bovec [SLO] 72 H4
Bóveda [E] 78 D4
Bòvegno [I] 72 B5
Bovense [DK] 156 E3
Boverbru [N] 172 B4
Bøverdal [N] 180 F6
Boves [I] 108 F3
Bović [HR] 112 H1
Bovik [FIN] 176 A5
Bovino [I] 120 G2
Bovolenta [I] 110 G1
Bovolone [I] 110 F1
Bovrup [DK] 156 C4
Boxberg [D] 46 E5
Boxholm [S] 166 G6
Boxmeer [NL] 16 F6
Boxtel [NL] 30 E2
Boyalı [TR] 144 E3
Boyalıca [TR] 146 F4
Boyalık [TR] 146 E2
Boyle [IRL] 2 D4
Bøylefoss [N] 164 F4
Bøyum [N] 170 D1
Božaj [YU] 152 E4
Božava [HR] 112 F5
Bozburun [TR] 142 D3
Bozcaada [TR] 130 H6
Bozdoğan [TR] 144 E5
Bozel [F] 70 B4
Bozen / Bolzano [I] 72 D3
Bozhenci [BG] 148 C4
Bozhurishte [BG] 150 F4
Božica [YU] 150 E5
Bozkuş [TR] 144 G3
Bozouls [F] 68 B5
Bozouls, Trou de- [F] 68 B5
Bozüyük [TR] 146 G5
Bozveliisko [BG] 148 F3
Bozyaka [TR] 142 G2
Bózzolo [I] 110 E1
Bra [B] 30 E6
Bra [I] 108 G2
Brå [N] 182 B1
Braås [S] 162 E4
Brabecke [D] 32 D5
Brabova [RO] 150 F1
Bracciano [I] 114 H5
Brachlewo [PL] 22 E4
Bracieux [F] 54 H2
Bracigovo [BG] 148 A6
Bräcke [S] 182 H3
Brackenheim [D] 46 C6
Brackley [GB] 14 D3
Bracknell [GB] 14 D4
Brackwede [D] 32 D3
Brad [RO] 204 B5
Bradford [GB] 10 E3
Bradina [BiH] 152 C1
Brae [GB] 6 G3
Brædstrup [DK] 156 C1
Braemar [GB] 6 E6
Braga [P] 80 C3
Bragança [P] 80 F3
Brahestad / Raahe [FIN] 196 C4
Brahetrolleborg [DK] 156 D4
Brail [CH] 72 B2
Brăila [RO] 204 D6
Braine [F] 44 A2
Braine-le-Comte [B] 28 H3
Braintree [GB] 14 F3
Brake [D] 18 D4
Brakel [B] 28 G3
Brakel [D] 32 E4
Bräkne-Hoby [S] 158 F1
Brålanda [S] 166 D5
Bram [F] 106 B4
Brämhult [S] 162 B2
Bramming [DK] 156 B2
Brampton [GB] 8 E5
Bramsche [D] 32 D2
Branč [SK] 62 H3
Branč [SK] 64 A4
Branca [I] 116 B1
Brancaleone Marina [I] 124 D8
Brancion [F] 56 G6
Brancoli, Pieve di- [I] 110 D5
Brâncoveni [RO] 150 G1
Brand [A] 72 A1
Brandal [N] 180 C3
Brändåsen [S] 182 E5
Brändbo [S] 184 D5
Brandbu [N] 170 H4
Brande [DK] 156 C1
Bränden [S] 182 F6
Brandenberg [A] 60 E6
Brandenburg [D] 34 D2
Brand-Erbisdorf [D] 48 E1
Brandhof [A] 62 D6
Brandis [D] 34 E4
Brändö [FIN] 176 C5
Brandomil [E] 78 B2
Brandon [F] 56 F6
Brandon [GB] 8 F6
Brandstorp [S] 162 D1
Brandval [N] 172 D5
Brandvoll [N] 192 F3
Brandýsek [CZ] 48 F3
Brandýs nad Labem Stará Boleslav [CZ] 48 G3
Braniewo [PL] 22 F2
Branišovice [CZ] 62 F2
Branitz, Schloss- [D] 34 F4
Brankovice [CZ] 50 D6
Brännäker [S] 190 F4
Brännberg [S] 196 A3
Branne [F] 66 D3
Brannenburg [D] 60 F5
Brännland [S] 190 H6
Brañosera [E] 82 D4
Brańsk [PL] 38 E1
Brantôme [F] 66 F2
Branzi [I] 70 H3
Bras-d'Asse [F] 108 C3
Braskereidfoss [N] 172 D4
Braslaw [BY] 200 H4
Braslaw [BY] 202 B4
Brașov [RO] 204 C5
Brassac [F] 106 C3
Brassac-les-Mines [F] 68 D3
Brasschaat [B] 30 D2
Bras-sur-Meuse [F] 44 D3
Brastad [S] 166 C5
Břasy [CZ] 48 E4
Brąszewice [PL] 36 F5
Brataj [AL] 128 B6
Bråte [N] 166 C1
Bratislava [SK] 62 G4
Bratków Dolny [PL] 36 F4
Brattabø [N] 170 C4
Brattåker [S] 190 F4
Brattbäcken [S] 190 F5
Bratten [S] 190 G5
Brattfors [S] 166 F2
Brattingsborg [DK] 156 E2
Brattli [N] 192 F3
Brattsele [S] 190 F6
Brattvåg [N] 180 D3
Bratunac [BiH] 154 F4
Bråtveit [N] 164 C1
Bratya Daskalovi [BG] 148 C5
Braubach [D] 46 B2
Braunau [A] 60 G4
Braunfels [D] 46 C2
Braunlage [D] 32 H4
Braunschweig [D] 32 H2
Braus, Col de- [F] 108 F4
Bravone [F] 114 C4
Bray / Bré [IRL] 4 G3
Bray-sur-Seine [F] 42 G5
Bray-sur-Somme [F] 28 E5
Brazatortas [E] 96 D5
Brbinj [HR] 112 F5
Brčko [BiH] 154 E2
Bré / Bray [IRL] 4 G3
Brebina [RO] 148 B1
Brécey [F] 26 D4
Brechin [GB] 8 F2
Brecht [B] 30 D2
Břeclav [CZ] 62 G3
Brecon [GB] 12 F2
Bred [S] 168 C2
Breda [NL] 16 D6
Bredaryd [S] 162 C4
Bredbyn [S] 184 F1
Bredebro [DK] 156 B4
Bredelar [D] 32 E4
Bredevad [DK] 156 B4
Bredland [N] 164 D4
Bredsel [S] 196 A3
Bredsjö [S] 166 G1
Bredsjön [S] 184 E4
Bredstedt [D] 18 E1
Bredsten [DK] 156 C2
Bredträsk [S] 190 G6
Bree [B] 30 E3
Bregana [HR] 74 E5
Breganze [I] 72 D5
Bregenz [A] 60 B6
Bregovo [BG] 150 E1
Bréhal [F] 26 D4
Brehna [D] 34 C5
Breidablik [N] 180 E5
Breidvik [N] 192 D6
Breifonn [N] 170 C5
Breil-sur-Roya [F] 108 F4
Brein [N] 180 C5
Breióborg [N] 164 C1
Breisach [D] 58 E3
Breisen [D] 34 D1
Breisjøberget [N] 172 D4
Breistein [N] 170 B3
Breitachklamm [D] 60 B6
Breite [CH] 58 F5
Breitenbrunn [D] 60 C4
Breitengussbach Hallstadt [D] 46 G4
Breivik [N] 194 A2
Breivikbotn [N] 194 A2
Breivikeidet [N] 192 G2
Brekke [N] 170 B2
Brekken [N] 182 D3
Brekkvasselv [N] 190 D4
Brekstad [N] 190 B6
Bremen [D] 18 D5
Bremerhaven [D] 18 D4
Bremervörde [D] 18 E4
Bremnes [N] 192 D3
Bremsnes [N] 180 E2
Breń [PL] 20 H6
Brenes [E] 94 H6
Brenna [N] 190 D3
Brenner Pass [Eur.] 72 D2
Brennfjell [N] 192 G2
Brennsvik [N] 194 B2
Breno [I] 72 B5
Brénod [F] 68 H2
Brentwood [GB] 14 F4
Brenzone [I] 72 C5
Brescello [I] 110 E2
Bréscia [I] 72 B6
Breskens [NL] 28 G1
Bresles [F] 28 D6
Bressanone / Brixen [I] 72 D3
Bressuire [F] 54 D3
Brest [BG] 148 A2
Brest [BY] 38 F3
Brest [F] 40 B2
Brestova [HR] 112 E2
Brestovac [YU] 150 C3
Brestovac [YU] 150 D2
Brestovačka Banja [YU] 150 D2
Brestovăț [RO] 76 H5
Breteau [F] 56 D2
Bretenoux [F] 66 H4
Bretesche, Château de la- [F] 40 E5
Breteuil [F] 28 D5
Breteuil [F] 26 H5
Bretten [D] 46 C6
Breuberg [D] 46 D4
Breuil-Cervinia [I] 70 D3
Breuna [D] 32 E4
Brevens Bruk [S] 166 H4
Brevik [N] 164 G3
Brevik [S] 168 E3
Brevik [S] 166 G5
Breza [BiH] 154 D4
Brežice [SLO] 74 D5
Breziški Grad [SLO] 74 D5
Breznica [HR] 74 F5
Breznica Đak. [HR] 154 D1
Březnice [CZ] 48 E5
Breznik [BG] 150 F5
Brezno [SK] 64 D3
Brézolles [F] 26 H5
Brezová [SK] 62 H3
Brezovica [SK] 52 C6
Brezovica [SLO] 74 B5
Brezovica [YU] 150 C6
Brezovo [BG] 148 B5
Brezovo Polje [BiH] 154 E2
Brezovo Polje [HR] 154 A2
Briançon [F] 70 B6
Briare [F] 56 D2
Briatico [I] 124 C6
Bribirske Mostine [HR] 112 H5
Briceni [MD] 204 D3
Bricquebec [F] 26 D2
Bridgnorth [GB] 10 D6
Bridgwater [GB] 12 F4
Bridlington [GB] 10 G3
Bridport [GB] 12 F5
Briec [F] 40 B3
Brie-Comte-Robert [F] 42 G4
Brielle [NL] 16 C5
Brienne-le-Château [F] 44 B5
Brienz [CH] 70 E1
Brienza [I] 120 G4
Brieskow-Finkenheerd [D] 34 G3
Brieves [E] 78 G3
Briey [F] 44 E3
Brig [CH] 70 E2
Brigg [GB] 10 G4
Brighton [GB] 14 E5
Brignogan-Plage [F] 40 B1
Brignoles [F] 108 C5
Brignoud [F] 68 H4
Brihuega [E] 88 H5
Brijesta [HR] 152 B3
Brilon [D] 32 D4
Brimnes [N] 170 D4
Brinches [P] 94 E3
Brindisi [I] 122 G4
Brinje [HR] 112 F2
Brinkum [D] 18 D5
Brinon [F] 56 E3
Brintbodarna [S] 172 F4
Briones [E] 82 G6
Brione Verzasca [CH] 70 F2
Brionne [F] 26 H4
Brioude [F] 68 D3
Brioux-sur-Boutonne [F] 54 D5
Briouze [F] 26 F5
Brisighella [I] 110 G4
Brissac-Quincé [F] 54 D1
Brissago [CH] 70 F3
Bristol [GB] 12 G3
Brive-la-Gaillarde [F] 66 G3
Briviesca [E] 82 F5
Brixen / Bressanone [I] 72 D3
Brixham [GB] 12 E5
Brixlegg [A] 60 E6
Brnaze [HR] 152 A1
Brněnec [CZ] 50 C5
Brno [CZ] 50 C6
Bro [S] 168 G4
Bro [S] 168 D2
Broadstairs [GB] 14 G5
Broager [DK] 156 C4
Broby [S] 158 D1
Brocēni [LV] 198 C5
Brock [D] 32 C2
Bröckel [D] 32 G2
Brockenhurst [GB] 12 G5
Brod [BiH] 152 D2
Brod [YU] 128 D1
Brodarevo [YU] 150 A4
Brodarica [HR] 112 H6
Broddbo [S] 168 B1
Broddebo [S] 162 F1
Brodenbach [D] 44 H1
Broderup [DK] 156 B4
Brodestorf [D] 20 B3
Brodick [GB] 8 C3
Brod na Kupi [HR] 112 F1
Brodnica [PL] 22 F5
Brody [PL] 34 G4
Brody [PL] 38 C6
Brody [PL] 36 A3
Brody [UA] 204 C2
Broglie [F] 26 G4
Brohl [D] 30 H6
Brojce [PL] 20 G3
Brok [PL] 38 C1
Brokind [S] 168 A6
Brolo [I] 124 B6
Bromarv [FIN] 176 E6
Brome [D] 32 H2
Bromma [N] 170 G4
Brommat [F] 68 B5
Bromölla [S] 158 E1
Brömsebro [S] 158 G1
Bromsgrove [GB] 12 H1
Bron [F] 68 G3
Brønderslev [DK] 160 E3
Broni [I] 70 G6
Bronikowo [PL] 20 H5
Bronken [N] 172 C4
Bronnbach [D] 46 E4
Brønnøysund [N] 190 C3
Brøns [DK] 156 B3
Bronte [I] 126 F3
Broons [F] 26 B5
Brørup [DK] 156 B2
Brösarp [S] 158 D2
Brossac [F] 66 E2
Brossasco [I] 108 F2
Brøstrud [N] 170 F4
Brötjemark [S] 162 D1
Broto [E] 84 E5
Brottby [S] 168 E2
Bröttem [N] 182 B2
Brotterode [D] 46 F1
Brøttum [N] 172 B3
Brou [F] 42 D5
Brouage [F] 54 C5
Brough [GB] 10 E2
Broughshane [NIR] 2 G3
Broughton in Furness [GB] 10 D2
Brouis, Col de- [F] 108 F4
Broumov [CZ] 50 B2
Brouvelieures [F] 58 C2
Brouwershaven [NL] 16 B5
Brovary [UA] 204 E2
Brovst [DK] 160 D3
Brownhills [GB] 10 E6
Brozas [E] 86 G4
Brseč [HR] 112 E2
Brtnice [CZ] 50 A6
Brua [N] 182 C5
Bruchhausen-Vilsen [D] 18 E6
Bruchhauser Steine [D] 32 D5
Bruchsal [D] 46 C5
Bruck [A] 72 F2
Bruck [D] 48 C6
Brück [D] 34 D3
Bruck an der Grossglocknerstrasse [A] 72 G1
Bruck an der Leitha [A] 62 G5
Bruck an der Mur [A] 74 D1
Brückl [A] 74 C3
Brudzeń Duży [PL] 36 G2
Brüel [D] 20 A4
Bruère-Allichamps [F] 56 C4
Bruff [IRL] 4 D4
Bruflat [N] 170 G3
Brugg [CH] 58 F4
Brugge [B] 28 G1
Brugnato [I] 110 C4
Bruhagen [N] 180 E2
Brühl [D] 30 G4
Brújula, Puerto de- [E] 82 F6
Bruksvallarna [S] 182 E3
Brûlon [F] 42 A5
Brumath [F] 44 H5
Brummen [NL] 16 F5
Brumov-Bylnice [CZ] 64 A2
Brumunddal [N] 172 B3
Brunau [D] 34 B1
Brune [N] 180 D4
Bruneck / Brunico [I] 72 E2
Brunehamel [F] 28 H5
Brunete [E] 88 F5
Brunflo [S] 182 H2
Brunheda [P] 80 E4
Brunico / Bruneck [I] 72 E2
Bruniquel [F] 66 G6
Brunkeberg [N] 164 E2
Brunlund [DK] 156 C4
Brunna [S] 168 D1
Brunnen [CH] 58 F6
Brunnsberg [S] 172 F2
Brunsbüttel [D] 18 E3
Brunskog [S] 166 E2
Brunsort Från [S] 166 G2
Brunssum [NL] 30 F4
Bruntál [CZ] 50 D4
Bruravik [N] 170 D4
Brus [YU] 150 C3
Brusand [N] 164 A4
Brušane [HR] 112 G4
Brusarci [BG] 150 F2
Brusasco [I] 70 E5
Brúsio [CH] 72 B4
Bruška [HR] 112 H5
Bruška Rodaljice [HR] 112 H5
Brusnichnoye [RUS] 178 E2
Brusník [SK] 64 D4
Brussel / Bruxelles [B] 30 C4
Brüssow [D] 20 E5
Brusy [PL] 22 C4
Bruvno [HR] 112 H4
Bruvoll [N] 172 C4
Bruxelles / Brussel [B] 30 C4
Bruyères [F] 58 C2
Bruzaholm [S] 162 E2
Bruzzano Zeffirio [I] 124 D8
Brvenik [YU] 150 B3
Brwinów [PL] 38 B3
Bryansk [RUS] 202 E6
Brydal [N] 182 C5
Bryggja [N] 180 B5
Bryne [N] 164 A3
Bryrup [DK] 156 C1
Brza Palanka [YU] 150 E1
Brzeće [YU] 150 C4
Brzeg [PL] 50 D1
Brzeg Dolny [PL] 36 C6
Brześć Kujawski [PL] 36 F2
Brzesko [PL] 52 B4
Brzeszcze [PL] 50 G4
Brzezie [PL] 36 E4
Brzezie [PL] 22 B4
Brzeziny [PL] 36 E5
Brzeziny [PL] 36 H4
Brzeźnica [PL] 52 D3
Brzeźnica [PL] 50 H4
Brzeźno [PL] 36 D3
Brzostek [PL] 52 D4
Brzóza [PL] 38 C4
Brzoza [PL] 22 D6
Brzozie Lubawskie [PL] 22 F5
Brzozów [PL] 52 E4
Bua [S] 160 H3
Buavåg [N] 164 A1
Buberget [S] 190 H5
Bubiai [LT] 200 E4
Bubry [F] 40 D3
Bubwith [GB] 10 F4
Buca [TR] 144 C4
Buçaco [P] 80 B6
Bučany [SK] 62 H4
Buccheri [I] 126 F4
Bucchianico [I] 116 D4
Buchach [UA] 204 C3
Buchen [D] 46 D4
Buchen [D] 18 G4
Buchenwald [D] 34 A6
Buchholz [D] 18 F5
Buchin Prohod [BG] 150 F4
Buchloe [D] 60 C4
Buchlov [CZ] 62 G2
Buchs [CH] 58 H6
Buchy [F] 28 C5
Bučin [MK] 128 E3
Búcine [I] 110 F6
Bučište [MK] 128 F1
Bučje [YU] 152 E2
Bučje [YU] 150 D2
Bückeburg [D] 32 E2
Bücken [D] 18 E6
Buckfastleigh [GB] 12 E5
Buckie [GB] 6 F5
Buckingham [GB] 14 D3
Buckow [D] 34 F2
Bučovice [CZ] 50 C6
Bucquoy [F] 28 E4
Bucsa [H] 76 F1
București [RO] 204 C6
Buczek [PL] 36 G5
Buczyna [PL] 52 F3
Bud [N] 180 E2
Budakovo [MK] 128 E3
Budaörs [H] 64 C6
Budapest [H] 64 C6
Búðardalur [IS] 192 A2
Buddusò [I] 118 D3
Bude [GB] 12 D4
Budești [RO] 204 C6
Budilovo [RUS] 198 G2
Budimci [HR] 154 D1
Budimlić Japra [BiH] 154 A2
Budimir [HR] 152 A2
Büdingen [D] 46 D2
Budišov nad Budišovkou [CZ] 50 D4
Budjevo [YU] 150 A4
Budmirici [MK] 128 F3
Budogoshch [RUS] 202 D2
Budomierz [PL] 52 G3
Budoni [I] 118 E3
Budowo [PL] 22 C2
Budrio [I] 110 F3
Budry [PL] 24 C2
Budva [YU] 152 D4
Budyně nad Ohří [CZ] 48 F3
Budziszewice [PL] 36 H4
Budzyń [PL] 36 C1
Bue [N] 164 B4
Bue Marino, Grotta del- [I] 118 E4
Bueña [E] 90 D6
Buen Amor, Castillo- [E] 80 H6
Buenavista del Norte [E] 100 B5
Buendia [E] 88 H6
Bufón de Arenillas [E] 82 D2
Buğdayli [TR] 146 D5
Bugeat [F] 68 A2
Buggerru [I] 118 B6
Bugojno [BiH] 154 C4
Bugøyfjord [N] 194 E3
Bugøynes [N] 194 E2
Bugyi [H] 76 C2
Bühl [D] 58 F1
Buhuși [RO] 204 D4
Băilești [RO] 150 F2
Builth Wells [GB] 12 F1
Buis-les-Baronnies [F] 108 B2
Buitenpost [NL] 16 F2
Buitrago [E] 88 G4
Bujalance [E] 102 D1
Bujanovac [YU] 150 D5
Bujanovac [YU] 150 D5
Bujaraloz [E] 90 F4
Buje [HR] 112 D1
Bujoru [RO] 148 C2
Buk [PL] 36 C3
Buk [PL] 20 E5
Bükkösd [H] 76 A5
Bukovi [YU] 150 A2
Bukovo, Manastir- [YU] 150 E1
Bukowiec [PL] 36 B3
Bukowina Tatrzańska [PL] 52 B6
Bukowo Morskie [PL] 22 A2
Bukowsko [PL] 52 E5
Buksnes [N] 192 E3
Bukta [N] 190 B6
Buktamo [N] 192 F3
Bülach [CH] 58 F4
Buldan [TR] 144 F4
Bŭlgarene [BG] 148 B3
Bŭlgarene [BG] 148 B4
Bŭlgarevo [BG] 148 G2
Bŭlgarovo [BG] 148 F4
Bŭlgarska Polyana [BG] 146 A1
Bŭlgarski Izvor [BG] 148 A4
Bulgnéville [F] 58 B2
Bulinovac [YU] 150 D3
Bulken [N] 170 C3
Bulkowo Wieś [PL] 36 H2
Bullarby [S] 166 C4
Bullas [E] 104 B2
Bulle [CH] 70 C1
Bulqizë [AL] 128 C2
Bultei [I] 118 D4
Buna [BiH] 152 C2
Bunclody [IRL] 4 F4
Buncrana [IRL] 2 F2
Bunde [D] 16 H2
Bünde [D] 32 E2
Bundoran [IRL] 2 D3
Bungay [GB] 14 G2
Bunge [S] 168 G3
Bunić [HR] 112 G3
Bunkris [S] 172 F2
Bunleix [F] 68 B2
Bunmahon [IRL] 4 E5
Bunnahowen [IRL] 2 B3
Bunnyconnellan [IRL] 2 C3
Buñol [E] 98 E4
Bunratty [IRL] 2 C6
Bunratty Castle [IRL] 2 C6
Buonalbergo [I] 120 F2
Buonconvento [I] 114 G2
Buonfornello [I] 126 D2
Buonvicino [I] 124 C3
Buoux, Fort de- [F] 108 B3
Bur [DK] 160 B5
Burano [I] 72 F6
Burbach [D] 32 C6
Burcei [I] 118 D7
Bureå [S] 196 A4
Bureå [S] 190 B3
Burela [E] 78 E2
Büren [CH] 58 D5
Büren [D] 32 D4
Burfjord [N] 192 H1
Burford [GB] 12 H3
Burg [D] 34 C3
Burg [D] 18 H2
Burg [D] 18 E3
Burgas [BG] 148 F4
Burgau [D] 60 C3
Burgau [P] 94 B5
Burgbernheim [D] 46 F5
Burgdorf [CH] 58 E5
Burgdorf [D] 32 G2
Burgebrach [D] 46 F4
Bürgel [D] 34 B6
Bürgeln [D] 58 E4
Burgelu / Elburgo [E] 102 B4
Burghaun [D] 46 E1
Burghausen [D] 60 G4
Burg Hessenstein [D] 32 E5
Burgh-Haamstede [NL] 16 B5
Búrgio [I] 126 C3
Burgistein [CH] 58 D6
Burgjoss [D] 46 E3
Burg Klam [A] 62 C4
Burgkunstadt [D] 46 G3
Burglengenfeld [D] 48 B6
Burg Metternich [D] 44 G1
Burgos [E] 82 E6
Burgsinn [D] 46 E3
Burg Stargard [D] 20 D5
Burgsvik [S] 168 G6
Burguete / Auritz [E] 84 C3
Burguillos [E] 94 G5
Burguillos del Cerro [E] 94 G3
Burg Vetschau [D] 34 F4
Burhaniye [TR] 144 C2
Burie [F] 54 D6
Burila Mare [RO] 150 E1

G

Gennep [NL] 16 F6
Gennes [F] 54 E2
Génolhac [F] 68 D6
Génova [I] 110 B3
Genshagen [D] 34 E3
Gent (Gand) [B] 28 G2
Genthin [D] 34 C2
Gentioux [F] 68 A2
Genzano di Lucánia [I] 120 H3
Genzano di Roma [I] 116 A6
Georgianoí [GR] 128 G5
Georgioúpoli [GR] 140 C4
Georgi Traykov [BG] 148 F3
Georgsheil [D] 18 B4
Geotermia, Museo della- [I] 114 F1
Gera [D] 48 C1
Geraardsbergen [B] 28 H3
Gerabronn [D] 46 E5
Gerace [I] 124 D7
Gerakarou [GR] 130 B4
Gérakas [GR] 136 F4
Geráki [GR] 136 E4
Gerakiní [GR] 130 B5
Gérardmer [F] 58 D2
Geras [A] 62 E3
Gerasdorf bei Wien [A] 62 F4
Gerbéviller [F] 44 F6
Gerbstedt [D] 34 B4
Gerchsheim [D] 46 E4
Geremeas [I] 118 D7
Gerena [E] 94 G5
Gerês [P] 78 B6
Geretsried [D] 60 E5
Gérgal [E] 102 G5
Gerlos [A] 72 E1
Germaringen [D] 60 C5
Germay [F] 44 D6
Germencik [TR] 144 D5
Germersheim [D] 46 B5
Gernika-Lumo [E] 82 H4
Gernrode [D] 34 A4
Gernrode [D] 34 B4
Gernsbach [D] 58 F1
Gernsheim [D] 46 C4
Gerola Alta [I] 70 H3
Geroliménas [GR] 136 E5
Gerolstein [D] 30 G6
Gerolzhofen [D] 46 F4
Gerona / Girona [E] 92 F3
Gerovo [HR] 112 F1
Gerri de la Sal [E] 92 C1
Gersfeld [D] 46 E2
Gersthofen [D] 60 D3
Gesäter [S] 166 C4
Gesäuse [A] 62 C6
Gescher [D] 16 G6
Geseke [D] 32 D4
Gestelnburg [CH] 70 E2
Gesualdo [I] 120 F3
Gesunda [S] 172 G3
Geta [FIN] 176 A5
Getafe [E] 88 F6
Getaria [E] 84 A2
Gettorf [D] 18 F2
Getxo [E] 82 G3
Gevgelija [MK] 128 G3
Gevrey-Chambertin [F] 56 G4
Gevsjön [S] 182 E1
Gex [F] 70 B2
Gey [D] 30 F5
Geyikli [TR] 130 H6
Geyre [TR] 144 F5
Geyser [IS] 20 96 C4
Geyve [TR] 146 G3
Gföhl [A] 62 D3
Ghalipsós [GR] 130 C4
Ghedi [I] 72 B6
Gheorghieni [RO] 204 C4
Ghilarza [I] 118 C4
Ghimpaţi [RO] 148 C1
Ghisonaccia [F] 114 C4
Ghisoni [F] 114 B4
Giáltra [GR] 132 H4
Giannitsá [GR] 128 G4
Giannoúli [GR] 130 H2
Giardinetto [I] 120 G2
Giardini-Naxos [I] 124 B8
Giarmata [RO] 76 G5
Giarratana [I] 126 F5
Giarre [I] 124 A8
Giat [F] 68 B2
Giba [I] 118 B7
Gibellina [I] 126 B2
Gibellina, Ruderi di- [I] 126 C2
Gibellina Vecchia [I] 126 C2
Gibilmanna, Santuario di- [I] 126 E2
Gibostad [N] 192 F2
Gibraleón [E] 94 E5
Gibraltar [GBZ] 100 G5
Gic [H] 74 H1
Gidböle [S] 184 G1
Gideå [S] 184 G1
Gideåkroken [S] 190 G5
Gide [PL] 50 G1
Gieboldehausen [D] 32 G4
Giedraičiai [LT] 200 G5
Gielas [S] 190 E3
Gielniów [PL] 38 A5
Gien [F] 56 C2
Giengen [D] 60 C3
Giens [F] 108 C6
Gieselwerder [D] 32 F4
Giessen [D] 46 C1
Gieten [NL] 16 G3
Giethoorn [NL] 16 F3
Gietrzwałd [PL] 22 G4
Giffoni [I] 120 F3
Gifhorn [D] 32 H2
Gigen [BG] 148 A2
Giglio Porto [I] 114 E4
Gignac [F] 106 E4
Gijón [E] 82 B1
Giksi [LV] 198 E4
Gilford [NIR] 2 G4
Gilja [N] 164 B3
Gilleleje [DK] 156 G1
Gillhov [S] 182 G4
Gillingham [GB] 12 G4
Gillstad [S] 166 E5
Gimat [F] 84 G2
Gimdalen [S] 184 C3
Gimel-les-Cascades [F] 66 H3
Gimmestad [N] 180 C5
Gimo [S] 174 F5
Gimont [F] 84 G3
Ginosa [I] 122 D4
Ginzling [A] 72 E2
Gióia del Colle [I] 122 E3
Gióia Táuro [I] 124 C6
Gioiosa Marea [I] 126 G1
Giornico [CH] 70 G2
Giove Anxur, Tempio di- [I] 120 C2
Giovinazzo [I] 122 D2
Giraltovce [SK] 52 D6
Girgantai [LT] 24 E2
Girifalco [I] 124 D5
Girolata [F] 114 A3
Giromagny [F] 58 C3
Girona / Gerona [E] 92 F3
Gironella [E] 92 E2
Girvan [GB] 8 C4
Gisholt [N] 164 F3
Gislaved [S] 162 C3
Gislev [DK] 156 E3
Gisors [F] 28 C6
Gisselås [S] 190 E6
Gisselfeld [DK] 156 F3
Gissi [I] 116 E5
Gisslarbo [S] 168 B2
Gistaín [E] 84 F5
Gistel [B] 28 F1
Gistrup [DK] 160 E4
Gittun [S] 190 G2
Giulianova [I] 116 D3
Giurgiţa [RO] 150 G2
Giurgiu [RO] 148 C1
Give [DK] 156 C2
Givet [F] 30 D6
Givors [F] 68 F3
Givry [B] 28 H4
Givry [F] 56 G5
Givry-en-Argonne [F] 44 C4
Giżalki [PL] 36 E3
Gizeux [F] 54 F2
Giżycko [PL] 24 C3
Gizzeria [I] 124 D5
Gjemnes [N] 180 F2
Gjerbës [AL] 128 C5
Gjerde [N] 180 D6
Gjermundshamn [N] 170 B5
Gjern [DK] 160 D6
Gjerrild [DK] 160 F5
Gjerstad [N] 164 F4
Gjersvik [N] 190 D4
Gjesvær [N] 194 C1
Gjeving [N] 164 F4
Gjirokastër [AL] 128 C6
Gjølga [N] 190 B6
Gjølme [N] 180 H1
Gjøra [N] 180 G3
Gjóv [FR] 160 B1
Gjøvik [N] 172 B3
Gjøvik [N] 192 E3
Gkoritsá [GR] 136 E4
Gkoúra [GR] 136 D1
Gla [GR] 134 A5
Gladbeck [D] 30 H2
Gladenbach [D] 32 D6
Gladhammer [S] 162 G2
Gladstad [N] 190 C3
Glamoč [BiH] 154 B4
Glåmos [N] 182 C3
Glamsbjerg [DK] 156 D3
Glandore [IRL] 4 B5
Glandorf [D] 32 D2
Glanmire [IRL] 4 C5
Glanworth [IRL] 4 D4
Glarus [CH] 58 G6
Glasgow [GB] 8 D3
Glashütte [D] 48 E1
Glashütten [A] 74 C3
Glastonbury [GB] 12 F4
Glauchau [D] 48 C1
Glava [S] 166 D2
Glavan [BG] 148 D5
Glavanovtsi [BG] 150 E4
Glavičice [BiH] 154 E3
Glavinitsa [BG] 148 E1
Glavnik [YU] 150 C4
Gleann Cholm Cille / Glencolumbkille [IRL] 2 D2
Gleichen [D] 46 G1
Gleina [D] 48 C1
Gleinalm Tunnel [A] 74 D1
Gleisdorf [A] 74 E2
Glenamaddy [IRL] 2 D4
Glenamoy [IRL] 2 C3
Glencolumbkille / Gleann Cholm Cille [IRL] 2 D2
Glendalough [IRL] 4 G3
Glenealy [IRL] 4 G4
Glengarriff [IRL] 4 B5
Glénic [F] 54 H5
Glenmore [IRL] 4 E4
Glenrothes [GB] 8 E3
Glenties [IRL] 2 E2
Glenville [IRL] 4 D5
Glesne [N] 170 G5
Gletsch [CH] 70 F2
Gletscher Garten [D] 60 G5
Glewitz [D] 20 C3
Glifádha [GR] 136 G1
Glimåkra [S] 158 D1
Glin [IRL] 4 C3
Glina [HR] 112 H1
Glinka [PL] 50 G5
Glinojeck [PL] 38 A1
Glinsce / Glinsk [IRL] 2 B4
Glinsk / Glinsce [IRL] 2 B4
Glissjöberg [S] 182 G5
Gliwice [PL] 50 F3
Gllavë [AL] 128 B5
Głodowa [PL] 22 B3
Gloggnitz [A] 62 E6
Głogoczów [PL] 50 H4
Glogovac [HR] 74 G5
Głogów [PL] 36 B5
Głogówek [PL] 50 E3
Głogów Małopolski [PL] 52 E3
Glomfjord [N] 190 E1
Glommen [S] 160 H4
Glommersträsk [S] 190 H4
Glömminge [S] 162 G5
Glorup [DK] 156 E4
Glóssa [GR] 134 B3
Glössbo [S] 174 E2
Glossop [GB] 10 E4
Glostrup [DK] 156 G2
Glöte [S] 182 F5
Gloucester [GB] 12 G2
Główczyce [PL] 22 C2
Glowe [D] 20 D2
Glöwen [D] 20 B6
Głowno [PL] 36 H4
Gložan [YU] 154 F1
Glozhene [BG] 150 G2
Glozhene [BG] 148 A4
Glozhenski Manastir [BG] 148 A4
Głubczyce [PL] 50 E3
Głuchołazy [PL] 50 D3
Glücksburg [D] 156 C4
Glückstadt [D] 18 E3
Gluda [LV] 198 D5
Glumsø [DK] 156 F3
Glušci [YU] 154 F2
Głuszyca [PL] 50 B2
Glyfa [GR] 132 H3
Glyfáda [GR] 132 F5
Glykí [GR] 132 C3
Glyngøre [DK] 160 C4
Gmünd [A] 72 H2
Gmünd [A] 62 C3
Gmund [D] 60 E5
Gmunden [A] 62 A5
Gnarp [S] 184 E5
Gnarrenburg [D] 18 E4
Gnesta [S] 168 D4
Gneux [F] 44 B3
Gniechowice [PL] 50 C1
Gniew [PL] 22 E4
Gniewkowo [PL] 36 E1
Gniezno [PL] 36 D2
Gnisvärd [S] 168 F4
Gnjilane [YU] 150 D5
Gnocchetta [I] 110 H2
Gnoien [D] 20 C3
Gnosjö [S] 162 C3
Göbel [TR] 146 D5
Goch [D] 16 F6
Göd [H] 64 C6
Godafoss [IS] 192 C2
Godalming [GB] 14 D5
Godby [FIN] 176 A5
Godech [BG] 150 F4
Godegard [S] 166 H5
Godelheim [D] 32 F4
Goderville [F] 26 G2
Godętowo [PL] 22 D2
Godkowo [PL] 22 G3
Gödöllő [H] 64 D6
Godovič [SLO] 74 B5
Godowa [PL] 52 D4
Gödre [H] 76 A4
Godziesze Wielkie [PL] 36 E5
Godzkzewo [PL] 22 F3
Goes [NL] 16 B6
Gogolin [PL] 50 E2
Gógolo [I] 72 C3
Göhren [D] 20 E2
Goirle [NL] 30 E2
Góis [P] 86 E2
Góito [I] 110 E1
Goizueta [E] 84 B3
Gojani i Madh [AL] 128 B1
Gojsalići [BiH] 154 E4
Gökçedağ [TR] 144 F1
Gökçen [TR] 144 D4
Gokels [D] 18 F2
Goksholm [S] 166 H3
Gol [N] 170 F3
Gola [HR] 74 G4
Golä [N] 170 H1
Gołąb [PL] 38 D5
Gołańcz [PL] 36 D1
Gölby [FIN] 176 A5
Golchen [D] 20 D4
Gölcük [TR] 146 G3
Gölcük [TR] 144 E4
Golçük [TR] 142 E2
Gölcük [TR] 144 D2
Golčův Jeníkov [CZ] 48 H4
Golczewo [PL] 20 F4
Gołdap [PL] 24 D2
Goldbach [D] 46 D3
Goldberg [D] 20 B4
Goldelund [D] 156 B5
Golden [IRL] 4 D4
Goldenstedt [D] 18 D6
Goleen [IRL] 4 B5
Golegã [P] 86 D4
Golema Crcorija [MK] 150 E6
Golemo Selo [YU] 150 D5
Goleniów [PL] 20 F5
Goleniowy [PL] 50 H2
Golfe-Juan [F] 108 E5
Golfo Aranci [I] 118 E2
Golfo di Sogno [F] 114 B6
Gölhisar [TR] 142 G1
Golina [PL] 36 E3
Goliševa [LV] 198 G5
Goljan Man. [BG] 148 D5
Gollden [N] 194 B4
Gollhofen [D] 46 F4
Golling [A] 60 G6
Gölmarmara [TR] 144 D3
Golmayo [E] 90 B3
Golnik [SLO] 74 B4
Gölpazarı [TR] 146 H4
Golpejas [E] 80 G6
Golspie [GB] 6 E4
Golssen [D] 34 E4
Golub Dobrzyń [PL] 22 E6
Golubinja [BiH] 154 D4
Golubovci [YU] 152 E4
Gołuchów [PL] 36 E4
Golvesh [BG] 148 F1
Golyalo Krushevo [BG] 148 E5
Gölyazi [TR] 146 E5
Gołymin-Ośrodek [PL] 38 B1
Golzow [D] 34 D3
Gómara [E] 90 C3
Gombasecká Jaskyňa [SK] 64 E3
Gombo [I] 110 D5
Gomes Aires [P] 94 C4
Gommern [D] 34 B3
Gomunice [PL] 36 G6
Gönc [H] 64 G3
Goncelin [F] 70 A4
Gondomar [P] 80 C4
Gondrecourt [F] 44 D5
Gondrin [F] 66 D6
Gönen [TR] 146 D5
Goni, Nuraghe- [I] 118 D6
Goniá [GR] 140 B4
Goniądz [PL] 24 E4
Gónnoi [GR] 132 G1
Gonnosfanádiga [I] 118 C6
Gönyu [H] 64 A6
Gonzaga [I] 110 E2
Gooik [B] 28 H3
Goole [GB] 10 F4
Goor [NL] 16 G5
Göpfritz [A] 62 D3
Goppenstein [CH] 70 E2
Göppingen [D] 60 B2
Góra [PL] 36 C5
Góra [PL] 36 H2
Góra Kalwaria [PL] 38 C3
Góra Puławska [PL] 38 D5
Góra Świętej Anny [PL] 50 E3
Goražde [BiH] 152 E1
Gördalen [S] 172 E1
Gordaliza del Pino [E] 82 B5
Gordes [F] 106 H3
Gördes [TR] 144 E2
Gördes [TR] 144 E3
Goren Chiflik [BG] 148 F3
Gorenja Vas [SLO] 74 B5
Goresbridge [IRL] 4 F4
Gorey [IRL] 4 F4
Gorgier [CH] 58 C6
Gorgonzola [I] 70 G5
Gorica [BiH] 152 B2
Gorica [HR] 112 F4
Goričan [HR] 74 F4
Goricë [AL] 128 D4
Gorinchem [NL] 16 D5
Gorino Veneto [I] 110 H3
Göritz [D] 20 E5
Gorízia [I] 72 H5
Gorki [RUS] 178 G5
Gørlev [DK] 156 F3
Gorlice [PL] 52 C5
Görlitz [D] 34 G6
Gormanston Castle [IRL] 2 F5
Gormund [CH] 58 F5
Gorna Kremena [BG] 150 G3
Gorna Oryakhovitsa [BG] 148 C3
Gorna Studena [BG] 148 C3
Gorni Tsibur [BG] 150 F2
Gornja Grabovica [BiH] 152 C2
Gornjak, Manastir- [YU] 150 C1
Gornja Kamenica [YU] 150 E3
Gornja Klina [YU] 150 B5
Gornja Ploča [HR] 112 G4
Gornja Radgona [SLO] 74 E3
Gornja Sabanta [YU] 150 C2
Gornja Toponica [YU] 150 D3
Gornja Tuzla [BiH] 154 E3
Gornji Lapac [HR] 112 H4
Gornji Milanovac [YU] 150 B2
Gornji Podgradci [BiH] 154 B2
Gornji Ravno [BiH] 152 B1
Górno [PL] 52 C1
Gorobinci [MK] 128 F1
Gorodets [RUS] 198 H2
Gorodno [RUS] 198 H3
Górowo [PL] 22 G2
Górowo Iławeckie [PL] 22 G2
Gorredijk [NL] 16 F2
Gorron [F] 26 E5
Gørslev [DK] 156 G3
Gort [IRL] 2 C5
Górtys [GR] 140 E5
Górtys [GR] 136 D2
Görükle [TR] 146 E4
Gorv [N] 180 B5
Görvik [S] 184 C1
Gorzanów [PL] 50 C3
Görzke [D] 34 C3
Gorzkowice [PL] 36 G6
Gorzków-Osada [PL] 38 F6
Górzna [PL] 22 B5
Górzno [PL] 22 F6
Górzno [PL] 36 E4
Gorzów Śląski [PL] 50 F1
Gorzów Wielkopolski [PL] 34 H2
Górzyca [PL] 34 G2
Gorzyń [PL] 36 B2
Gorżżam [N] 194 D3
Gosaldo [I] 72 E4
Gosau [A] 60 H6
Gošća [UA] 204 D2
Göschenen [CH] 70 F1
Goščino [PL] 20 G3
Goslar [D] 32 G3
Gošlice [PL] 36 H2
Gospari [LV] 198 F6
Gospić [HR] 112 G4
Gosport [GB] 12 H5
Gossau [CH] 58 H5
Gosselies [B] 30 C5
Gossensass / Colle Isarco [I] 72 D2
Gössl [A] 62 B6
Gössweinstein [D] 46 G4
Gosticy [RUS] 198 G1
Gostilicy [RUS] 178 G5
Gostivar [MK] 128 D1
Gostkow [PL] 36 F4
Göstling [A] 62 C5
Gostomia [PL] 22 A6
Gostycyn [PL] 22 C5
Gostyń [PL] 36 C4
Gostynin [PL] 36 G3
Goszczanowo [PL] 36 A2
Göteborg [S] 160 G2
Götene [S] 166 E5
Gotha [D] 32 H6
Gothem [S] 168 G4
Götlunda [S] 168 A3
Gotse Delchev [BG] 130 C1
Gottböle [FIN] 186 A4
Gottby [FIN] 176 A5
Gotthard Tunnel [CH] 70 F2
Göttingen [D] 32 F4
Gottne [S] 184 G1
Gottolengo [I] 110 D1
Gottröra [S] 168 E2
Göttweig [A] 62 D4
Götzis [A] 58 H5
Gouarec [F] 26 A5
Gouda [NL] 16 D5
Goules, Col des- [F] 68 C2
Gouménissa [GR] 128 G3
Goumois [CH] 58 C5
Gourdon [F] 66 G4
Gourin [F] 40 C3
Gournay-en-Bray [F] 28 C5
Goúrnes [GR] 140 E4
Gourniá [GR] 140 G5
Gourville [F] 54 D6
Gouveia [P] 80 D6
Goúves [GR] 140 F4
Gouviá [GR] 132 B2
Gouzon [F] 56 B6
Govedartsi [BG] 150 G6
Govedjari [HR] 152 B3
Gøvstad [N] 170 F5
Goworowo [PL] 24 C6
Gowran [IRL] 4 F4
Gózd [PL] 52 B1
Gózd [PL] 38 C5
Gozdnica [PL] 34 H5
Graal-Müritz [D] 20 B2
Grab [BiH] 152 D4
Grabaţ [RO] 76 F5
Graberje [HR] 154 A1
Gråbo [S] 160 H2
Gråborg [S] 162 G5
Grabow [D] 20 A5
Grabów [PL] 36 F3
Grabowiec [PL] 52 G1
Grabówka [PL] 24 F5
Grabownica Starzeńska [PL] 52 E4
Grabów n Prosną [PL] 36 E5
Grabowskie [PL] 24 D5
Gračac [HR] 112 H4
Gračanica [BiH] 154 D3
Gračanica [YU] 154 F4
Gračanica [YU] 150 C5
Graçay [F] 54 H3
Grächen [CH] 70 E2
Gračišće [HR] 112 D2
Gradac [BiH] 152 C3
Gradac [HR] 152 B3
Gradac, Manastir- [YU] 150 B3
Gradačac [BiH] 154 D2
Graddis [N] 190 F1
Gräddö [S] 168 G2
Gradec [BG] 150 E2
Gradefes [E] 82 C4
Graderas, Cueva de las- [E] 90 E6
Gradets [BG] 148 D4
Gradignan [F] 66 C3
Gradina [YU] 150 E4
Gradina [HR] 112 F3
Gradisca d'Isonzo [I] 72 H5
Grado [E] 78 G3
Grado [I] 72 G6
Gradsko [MK] 128 F2
Græsted [DK] 156 G1
Grafenau [D] 60 H2
Gräfenberg [D] 46 G4
Grafenegg [A] 62 E4
Gräfenhainichen [D] 34 C4
Grafenwöhr [D] 48 B4
Grafing [D] 60 E4
Grafrath [D] 60 D4
Gräfsnäs [S] 162 A1
Graglia, Santuário di- [I] 70 E4
Gragnano [I] 120 E3
Grahovo [YU] 152 D4
Graiguenamanagh [IRL] 4 F4
Grainetière, Abbaye de la- [F] 54 C3
Graja, Cueva de la- [E] 102 E2
Grajewo [PL] 24 D4
Gralhos [P] 80 D3
Gralla [A] 74 D3
Grallagh [IRL] 2 D4
Gram [DK] 156 B3
Gramada [BG] 150 E2
Gramat [F] 66 G4
Gramatikovo [BG] 148 F5
Grametten [A] 62 D2
Gramkow [D] 20 A3
Grammatikó [GR] 132 G3
Gramméni Oxyá [GR] 132 F4
Gramméno [GR] 132 C2
Grammichele [I] 126 F4
Gramsh [AL] 128 C4
Gram Slot [DK] 156 B3
Gramzda [LV] 198 B6
Gramzow [D] 20 E5
Gran [N] 172 B4
Granada [E] 102 E4
Granadilla de Abona [E] 100 B5
Granard [IRL] 2 E4
Granarolo dell'Emília [I] 110 F3
Granåsen [S] 190 F5
Granátula de Calatrava [E] 96 F4
Granberget [S] 190 F5
Granboda [FIN] 176 B6
Grancey [F] 56 G3
Grandas de Salime [E] 78 F3
Grandcamp-Maisy [F] 26 E2
Grand Chartreuse, Couvent de la- [F] 68 H4
Grand-Champ [F] 26 A6
Grande-Fougeray [F] 40 F5
Grandpré [F] 44 C3
Grandrieu [F] 68 D5
Grand Roc [F] 66 F3
Grandson [CH] 58 C6
Grand-St-Bernard, Col du- [Eur.] 70 C3
Grandvilliers [F] 28 D5
Grañén [E] 90 F3
Grangärde [S] 172 H5
Grange [IRL] 2 D3
Grange-Bleneau, Château de la- [F] 42 G4
Grange-le-Bocage [F] 42 H5
Grängesberg [S] 172 H6
Granges-sur-Vologne [F] 58 D2
Grängsjö [S] 184 E5
Granhult [S] 192 H6
Graninge [S] 184 E2
Granitola Torretta [I] 126 B3
Granitz, Jagdschloss- [D] 20 E2
Granja [P] 94 E3
Granja [P] 80 B4
Granja de Moreruela [E] 82 A6
Granja de Torrehermosa [E] 96 B5
Grankulla / Kauniainen [FIN] 176 H5
Grankullavik [S] 162 H3
Granlunda [S] 168 C1
Gränna [S] 162 D1
Grannäs [S] 190 F3
Grannes [N] 190 E3
Gränningen [S] 184 C2
Granollers [E] 92 E4
Granön [S] 190 H5
Granowo [PL] 36 C3
Gransee [D] 20 D6
Gränsgård [S] 190 G3
Gransherad [N] 164 F1
Gransjö [S] 196 A2
Gränsjön [S] 166 D2
Gran Tarajal [E] 100 E6
Grantham [GB] 10 F6
Grantown-on-Spey [GB] 6 E5
Granträsk [S] 190 G5
Granvik [S] 166 G5
Granvika [N] 182 C5
Granville [F] 26 D4
Granvin [N] 170 C3
Granvollen [N] 172 B4
Grao / el Grau [E] 98 F6
Grasbakken [N] 194 E2
Gräsberg [S] 172 H5
Gräsmark [S] 166 E1
Gräsmyr [S] 190 H6
Gräsö [S] 174 F5
Grassano [I] 122 C4
Grassau [D] 60 F5
Grasse [F] 108 E4
Grässjön [S] 184 C3
Gråsten [DK] 156 C4
Grästorp [S] 166 D6
Gratangen [N] 192 F4
Gråtanliden [S] 190 F4
Gratkorn [A] 74 D2
Gråträsk [S] 190 H3
Graulhet [F] 106 B3
Graus [E] 90 H3
Grava [S] 166 E2
Grávalos [E] 84 A5
Gravberget [N] 172 D3
Gravdal [N] 192 C4
Gravdal [N] 164 B4
Grave [NL] 16 E6
Gravedona [I] 70 G3
Gravelines [F] 14 H6
Gravellona-Toce [I] 70 F3
Gravens [DK] 156 C2
Gravesend [GB] 14 F4
Graviá [GR] 132 G4
Gravina in Púglia [I] 122 D3
Gravitsa [GR] 132 E3
Gravmark [S] 196 A5
Gravoúna [GR] 130 E3
Gray [F] 58 A4
Graz [A] 74 D2
Grazalema [E] 100 H4
Gražiškiai [LT] 24 E2
Grazzanise [I] 120 D2
Grazzano Visconti [I] 110 C2
Grčak [YU] 150 C3
Grdelica [YU] 150 D4
Greaca [RO] 148 D1
Greaker [N] 164 H2
Great Dunmow [GB] 14 F3
Great Malvern [GB] 12 G2
Great Torrington [GB] 12 D3
Great Yarmouth [GB] 14 H2
Grebbestad [S] 166 B4
Grebenstein [D] 32 F5
Grębocin [PL] 22 E6
Greding [D] 46 G6
Greencastle [NIR] 2 G5
Greenock [GB] 8 D3
Greenwich [GB] 14 F4
Greetsiel [D] 16 H1
Gregolímano [GR] 132 H4
Greifenburg [A] 72 G3
Greiffenberg [D] 20 E6
Greifswald [D] 20 D3
Greillenstein [A] 62 D3
Grein [A] 62 C4
Greiz [D] 48 C2
Grenaa [DK] 160 F5
Grenade [F] 66 C6
Grenade [F] 84 H2
Grenchen [CH] 58 D5
Grenoble [F] 68 H4
Grense-Jakobselv [N] 194 F3
Grenzland-Turm [CZ] 48 C4
Gréolières [F] 108 E4
Gréoux-les-Bains [F] 108 C4
Gressoney-la-Trinité [I] 70 E3
Gressoney-St-Jean [I] 70 E4
Gresten [A] 62 D5
Gretna Green [GB] 8 E5
Greussen [D] 32 H5
Greux [F] 44 D6
Grevbäck [S] 166 G6
Greve in Chianti [I] 110 F6
Greven [D] 32 C2
Grevená [GR] 128 E6
Grevenbroich [D] 30 G4
Grevenbrück [D] 32 C5
Grevenmacher [L] 44 F2
Grevesmühlen [D] 18 H3
Greve Strand [DK] 156 G3
Greyabbey [NIR] 2 H4
Greystones [IRL] 4 G3
Grez-en-Bouère [F] 40 H5
Grezzana [I] 72 C6
Grianan of Aileach [IRL] 2 F2
Gries-am-Brenner [A] 72 D2
Griesbach [D] 60 H3
Gries in Sellrain [A] 72 D1
Grieskirchen [A] 62 A4
Griffen [A] 74 C3
Grignan [F] 106 H2
Grignols [F] 66 D5
Grillby [S] 168 C2
Grimaldi [I] 124 D5
Grimaud [F] 108 D5
Grimdalen [N] 164 E2
Grimma [D] 34 D6
Grimmen [D] 20 D3
Grimo [N] 170 C4
Grimsås [S] 162 C3
Grimsbu [N] 180 H5
Grimsby [GB] 10 G4
Grimslöv [S] 162 D5
Grímsstaðir [IS] 192 C2
Grimstad [N] 164 E5
Grindaheim [N] 170 F2
Grindavík [IS] 192 A3
Grinde [N] 164 A1
Grindelwald [CH] 70 E2
Grindjorda [N] 192 E4
Grindsted [DK] 156 B2
Griñón [E] 88 F6
Grinzane Cavour [I] 108 G2
Gripenberg [S] 162 E1
Gripenberg [S] 162 E1
Grisignano di Zocco [I] 72 D6
Grisolles [F] 84 H2
Grisslehamn [S] 174 G6
Grivitsa [BG] 148 B3
Grizáno [GR] 132 F2
Grižkabūdis [LT] 200 E5
Grøa [N] 180 G3
Gröbers [D] 34 C5
Grobina [LV] 198 B6
Gröbming [A] 74 B1
Grocka [YU] 154 H3
Grodås [N] 180 D5
Grödek [PL] 38 G1
Gródek nad Dunajcem [PL] 52 C4
Gröditz [D] 34 E5
Gródki [PL] 52 F1
Grodków [PL] 50 D2
Grodno [PL] 50 B2
Grodzeń [PL] 36 G1
Grodziec [PL] 36 E4
Grodziec [PL] 36 A6
Grodzisk Mazowieki [PL] 38 B3
Grodzisk Wielkopolski [PL] 36 B3
Groenlo [NL] 16 G5
Groix [F] 40 C4
Grojdibodu [RO] 148 A2
Grójec [PL] 38 B4
Grójec [PL] 36 D3
Grömitz [D] 18 H3
Gromnik [PL] 52 C4
Gromo [I] 72 A4
Gromovo [RUS] 200 D5
Grøna [N] 180 F5
Gronau [D] 16 G5
Gronau [D] 32 F3
Grönbo [S] 196 A4
Grønbua [N] 180 F6
Grong [N] 190 C5
Grönhögen [S] 158 G1
Grønhøj [DK] 160 C5
Gröningen [D] 34 A3
Groningen [NL] 16 G2
Grønlia [N] 190 B6
Grønnes [N] 180 E3
Grönskåra [S] 162 F4
Grönsö [S] 168 C2
Gropen [S] 166 G3
Grósio [I] 72 B4
Grossarl [A] 72 G1
Grossbeeren [D] 34 E2
Grossbreitenbach [D] 46 G2
Grossburgwedel [D] 32 G2
Grossenbrode [D] 18 H2
Grossenhain [D] 34 E5
Grossenkneten [D] 18 C5
Grossenzersdorf [A] 62 F4
Grosseto [I] 114 F3
Gross-Gerau [D] 46 C3
Gross-Gerungs [A] 62 C3
Grosshabersdorf [D] 46 F5
Grossharras [A] 62 F3
Grosshöchstetten [CH] 58 E6
Gross Mohrdorf [D] 20 C2
Gross Oesingen [D] 32 H1
Gross-Pertholz [A] 62 C3
Grosspetersdorf [A] 74 F2
Grossraming [A] 62 C5
Gross Räschen [D] 34 F5
Gross Schönebeck [D] 34 E1
Gross-Siegharts [A] 62 D3
Gross-Umstadt [D] 46 D3
Grostenquin [F] 44 F4
Grosuplje [SLO] 74 C5
Grøtavær [N] 192 E3
Grötholen [S] 182 E6
Grotli [N] 180 E5
Grottaglie [I] 122 F4
Grottaminarda [I] 120 F2
Grottammare [I] 116 D2
Grotteria [I] 124 D7
Grouw [NL] 16 F2
Grövelsjön [S] 182 D5
Grovfjord [N] 192 E4
Grovo [N] 164 F3
Grozd'ovo [BG] 148 F3
Grožnjan [HR] 112 D1
Grua [N] 172 B5
Grubben [N] 190 E3
Grubišno Polje [HR] 74 G6
Gruda [HR] 152 D4
Grude [BiH] 152 B2
Grudusk [PL] 22 H6
Grudziądz [PL] 22 E5
Gruemirë [AL] 152 E5
Gruia [RO] 150 E1
Gruibingen [D] 60 B3
Gruissan [F] 106 D5
Grumentum [I] 120 H5
Grums [S] 166 E3
Grünau [A] 62 B5
Grünberg [D] 46 D1
Grünburg [A] 62 B5
Grundfors [S] 190 E4
Grundfors [S] 190 G4
Grundforsen [S] 172 E2
Grundlsee [A] 62 A6
Grundsel [S] 190 H3
Grundsjö [S] 190 F4
Grundsjö [S] 190 F5
Grundsjön [S] 184 C5
Grundsund [S] 166 C6
Grundsunda [S] 184 H2
Grundtjärn [S] 184 E1
Grünenplan [D] 32 F3
Grungedal [N] 164 E1
Grünheide [D] 34 F2
Grünstadt [D] 46 B4
Grunwald [PL] 22 G5
Grupčin [MK] 128 D1
Grüsch [CH] 58 H6
Gruvberget [S] 174 D3
Gruyères [CH] 70 C1
Gruža [YU] 150 B2
Grūzdžiai [LT] 200 E3
Grybów [PL] 52 C5
Gryckbo [S] 172 H4
Gryfice [PL] 20 G4
Gryfino [PL] 20 F5
Gryfów Śląski [PL] 48 H1
Grykë [AL] 128 A4
Gryllefjord [N] 192 E2
Grymyr [N] 170 H5
Gryt [S] 168 C4
Gryt [S] 168 C6
Gryta [N] 190 A6
Grytgöl [S] 166 H4
Grythyttan [S] 166 G2
Grytsjö [S] 190 E4
Grytstorp [S] 166 H5
Gryzy [PL] 24 D3
Grzmiąca [PL] 22 A4
Grzybno [PL] 22 F5
Gschnitz [A] 72 D2
Gschwend [D] 46 E6
Gstaad [CH] 70 D2
Gstadt [D] 60 F5
Gsteig [CH] 70 D2
Guadahortuna [E] 102 E3
Guadalajara [E] 88 G5
Guadalcanal [E] 94 H4
Guadalcázar [E] 102 B1
Guadalerzas [E] 96 F3
Guadalest [E] 104 E2
Guadalmez [E] 96 C4
Guadalmina [E] 102 A5
Guadalupe [E] 96 C2
Guadalupe, Monasterio de- [E] 96 C2
Guadalupe, Santuario de- [E] 102 F1
Guadamur [E] 96 E2
Guadarrama [E] 88 F5
Guadix [E] 102 F4
Guagno [F] 114 B4
Gualdo Tadino [I] 116 B2
Guarcino [I] 116 C6
Guarda [CH] 72 B2
Guarda [P] 86 G2
Guardamar del Segura [E] 104 D3
Guardavalle [I] 124 D6
Guardiagrele [I] 116 D5
Guardialfiera [I] 116 E6
Guardia Lombardi [I] 120 F3
Guardia Piemontese [I] 124 C4
Guardia Sanframondi [I] 120 E2
Guardo [E] 82 C4
Guareña [E] 94 H2
Guarromán [E] 96 E6
Guasila [I] 118 C6
Guastalla [I] 110 E2
Gubbhägen [S] 190 E5
Gúbbio [I] 116 A1
Gubbmyran [S] 172 E2
Gubbträsk [S] 190 G4
Guben [D] 34 G4
Guberevac [YU] 150 B2
Gubin [PL] 34 G4
Gubkin [RUS] 202 F7
Guča [YU] 150 B2
Gudavac [BiH] 154 A2
Guderup [DK] 156 C4
Gudhjem [DK] 158 E4
Gudow [D] 18 G4
Gudvangen [N] 170 D2
Guebwiller [F] 58 D3
Güéjar Sierra [E] 102 E4
Guémené-Penfao [F] 40 F5
Guémené-sur-Scorff [F] 40 D3
Guenange [F] 44 F3
Guer [F] 26 B6
Guérande [F] 40 D6
Guéret [F] 54 H6
Guérigny [F] 56 D4
Guethary [F] 84 C2
Gueugnon [F] 56 E5
Güglingen [D] 46 C6
Guglionesi [I] 116 F5
Gugny [PL] 24 E5
Guía de Isora [E] 100 B5
Guichen [F] 26 C6
Guidonia [I] 116 A5
Guíglia [I] 110 E3
Guignes [F] 42 G4
Guijuelo [E] 88 C4
Guildford [GB] 14 D4
Guillaumes [F] 108 E3
Guillena [E] 94 G5
Guillestre [F] 108 E2
Guilvinec [F] 40 B3
Güímar [E] 100 C5
Guimarães [P] 80 C3
Guimiliau [F] 40 C2
Guincho [P] 86 A5
Guînes [F] 14 G6
Guingamp [F] 26 A4
Guipry [F] 40 F4
Guisamo [E] 78 D2
Guisborough [GB] 10 G2
Guise [F] 28 G5
Guissény [F] 40 B1
Guissona [E] 92 C3
Guitiriz [E] 78 D2
Guîtres [F] 66 D3
Gujan-Mestras [F] 66 B3
Gulbene [LV] 198 F4
Guldborg [DK] 156 F5
Gulgofjorden [N] 194 D1
Gulla [N] 180 G2
Gullabo [S] 162 F6
Gullaskruv [S] 162 F4
Gulleråsen [S] 172 H3
Gullfoss [IS] 192 B3
Gullhaug [N] 164 H2
Gullringen [S] 162 F2
Gullsby [S] 172 E6
Gullspång [S] 166 F4
Gullstein [N] 180 F1
Güllü [TR] 144 F4
Güllüce [TR] 146 E5
Güllük [TR] 142 C2
Gülpınar [TR] 134 G1
Gulsele [S] 190 F6
Gulsrud [N] 170 H5
Gulsvik [N] 170 G4
Gülübintsi [BG] 148 D5
Gülübovo [BG] 148 D5
Gulyantsi [BG] 148 B2
Gumboda [S] 196 A5
Gumhöjden [S] 166 F1
Gumiel de Hizán [E] 88 G2
Gummersbach [D] 32 C5
Gumpoldskirchen [A] 62 F5
Gumtow [D] 20 B6
Gümüldür [TR] 144 C5
Gümüşpınar [TR] 146 D2
Gümüşsu [TR] 144 H4
Gümüşyeni [TR] 146 G5
Gümzovo [BG] 150 E2
Gundelfingen [D] 60 C3
Gundelsheim [D] 46 D5
Güney [TR] 144 G5
Güney [TR] 144 F4
Güngörmez [TR] 144 D1
Gunja [HR] 154 E2
Günlüce [TR] 144 F1
Gunnarn [S] 190 G4
Gunnarp [S] 162 B4
Gunnarsbyn [S] 196 B2
Gunnarskog [S] 166 D1
Gunnarskulla [FIN] 176 G5
Gunnarvattnet [S] 190 E5
Gunnebo [S] 162 G2
Gunnilbo [S] 168 B2
Gunten [CH] 70 E1
Güntersberge [D] 32 H4
Guntersblum [D] 46 C4
Guntersdorf [A] 62 E3
Guntertshausen [A] 60 G4
Guntín [E] 78 D3
Günzburg [D] 60 C3
Gunzenhausen [D] 46 F6
Güre [TR] 144 H3
Güre [TR] 144 F3
Güreci [TR] 146 B5
Gurgazu [F] 114 B6
Gurk [A] 74 B2
Gurkovo [BG] 148 C4
Gürpinar [TR] 146 E3
Gurrea de Gállego [E] 90 F3
Gürsu [TR] 146 F4
Gurtnellen [CH] 70 F1
Gusev [RUS] 24 D1
Gusinje [YU] 150 A5
Gusmar [AL] 128 B6
Gúspini [I] 118 C6

Gusselby [S] 166 H2
Güssing [A] 74 F2
Gustavberg [S] 190 H4
Gustavfors [S] 172 F5
Gustavs / Kustavi [FIN] 176 C4
Gustavsberg [S] 168 E3
Gustavsfors [S] 166 D3
Güstrow [D] 20 B4
Gusum [S] 168 B6
Gusvattnet [S] 190 E5
Gutcher [GB] 6 H3
Gutenstein [A] 62 E5
Gütersloh [D] 32 D3
Gutštejn [CZ] 48 D4
Guttannen [CH] 70 F1
Gützkow [D] 20 D3
Güzelbahçe [TR] 144 C4
Guzet-Neige [F] 84 H5
Gvardeysk [RUS] 24 B1
Gvarv [N] 164 F2
Gvozd [HR] 112 H1
Gvozd [YU] 152 E3
Gwatt [CH] 70 D1
Gwda Wielka [PL] 22 B4
Gy [F] 58 B4
Gya [N] 164 B4
Gyl [N] 180 F2
Gylien [S] 194 B8
Gylling [DK] 156 D2
Gýmeš [SK] 64 B4
Gymnó [GR] 134 C5
Gyomaendrőd [H] 76 F2
Gyömrő [H] 76 D1
Gyöngyös [H] 64 E5
Gyöngyöspata [H] 64 D5
Gyönk [H] 76 B3
Győr [H] 62 H6
Gysinge [S] 174 E5
Gýtheio [GR] 136 E4
Gyttorp [S] 166 G2
Gyueshevo [BG] 150 E6
Gyula [H] 76 G3
Gzy [PL] 38 B1

H

Häädemeeste [EST] 198 D3
Haag [A] 62 C4
Haag [D] 60 F4
Haag am Hausruck [A] 62 A4
Haaksbergen [NL] 16 G5
Haapajärvi [FIN] 196 D6
Haapajoki [FIN] 196 C4
Haapa-Kimola [FIN] 178 B3
Haapakylä [FIN] 186 G3
Haapala [FIN] 196 D3
Haapamäki [FIN] 188 D3
Haapamäki [FIN] 188 D1
Haapamäki [FIN] 186 E4
Haapamäki [FIN] 196 E6
Haapasalmi [FIN] 188 F4
Haapavesi [FIN] 196 D5
Haapsalu [EST] 198 D2
Haar [D] 60 E4
Haarajoki [FIN] 176 H4
Haarala [FIN] 186 G2
Haaraoja [FIN] 196 D4
Haarby [DK] 156 D3
Haaren [D] 32 E4
Haarlem [NL] 16 D4
Haavisto [FIN] 186 F5
Habartice [CZ] 48 G1
Habay [B] 44 E2
Hablingbo [S] 168 F5
Habo [S] 162 D2
Håbol [S] 166 D4
Habry [CZ] 48 H4
Häby [S] 166 C5
Hachdorf [D] 58 G2
Hachenburg [D] 46 B1
Hachmühlen [D] 32 F2
Hackås [S] 182 G3
Hacketstown [IRL] 4 F4
Hacksjö [S] 190 G5
Håcksvik [S] 162 B3
Hadamar [D] 46 B2
Hädanberg [S] 184 F1
Haddington [GB] 8 F3
Haderslev [DK] 156 C3
Haderup [DK] 160 C5
Hadiach [UA] 204 G2
Hadım [TR] 144 G4
Hadleigh [GB] 14 G3
Hadmersleben [D] 34 B3
Hadsten [DK] 160 D6
Hadsund [DK] 160 E4
Hadžići [BiH] 152 C1
Hægeland [N] 164 D5
Hærland [N] 166 C2
Hafsmo [N] 180 G1
Haftorsbygget [S] 172 F1
Haga [N] 172 C5
Hagafoss [N] 170 F3
Hagby [S] 162 F5
Hagby [S] 168 D2
Hagebro [DK] 160 C5
Hagen [D] 32 C4
Hagen [D] 18 D4
Hagenow [D] 18 H5
Hageri [EST] 198 D2
Hagetmau [F] 84 E2
Hagfors [S] 172 F6
Häggås [S] 190 F5
Häggemåla [S] 162 G4
Häggenås [S] 182 H1
Häggsjöbränna [S] 182 E1
Häggsjömon [S] 190 G5
Häggsjövik [S] 190 E6
Haglebu [N] 170 G4
Hagondange [F] 44 E4
Hagudi [EST] 198 E2
Haguenau [F] 44 H5
Håhellarhytta [N] 164 D3
Hahn [D] 18 C4
Hahnbach [D] 46 H5
Hahót [H] 74 G3
Haiger [D] 32 D6
Haigerloch [D] 58 G2
Häijää [FIN] 176 E1
Hailsham [GB] 14 E6
Hailuoto / Karlö [FIN] 196 D4
Haina [D] 32 E6
Hainburg [A] 62 G4
Hainfeld [A] 62 E5
Hainichen [D] 48 D1
Hainsbach [D] 60 F2
Haithabu [D] 18 F1
Hajdúböszörmény [H] 64 G6
Hajdúdorog [H] 64 G5
Hajdúhadház [H] 64 H5
Hajdúnánás [H] 64 G5
Hajdúsámson [H] 64 H6
Hajdúszoboszló [H] 64 G6
Hajdúszovát [H] 76 G1
Hajerdin [BG] 150 G3
Hajnówka [PL] 38 F1
Hajós [H] 76 C4
Håkafot [S] 190 E5
Håkenby [N] 166 C3
Hakkas [S] 194 A7
Hakkenpää [FIN] 176 D4
Häkkilä [FIN] 186 F3
Häkkiskylä [FIN] 186 F5
Hakkstabben [N] 194 B2
Hakokylä [FIN] 196 F4
Håksberg [S] 172 H5
Hakuni [FIN] 186 C4
Håkvika [N] 192 E4
Hålaforsen [S] 184 E1
Halámky [CZ] 62 C2
Halberstadt [D] 34 A3
Hälbo [S] 174 D2
Hald [DK] 160 E5
Halden [N] 166 C3
Haldensee [A] 60 C6
Haldensleben [D] 34 B2
Halenkov [CZ] 50 E6
Halesworth [GB] 14 G3
Håle-Täng [S] 166 D5
Hälgö [S] 168 C4
Halhjem [N] 170 B4
Halič [SK] 64 D4
Halich [UA] 204 C3
Halifax [GB] 10 E4
Halikarnassos [TR] 142 C3
Halikko [FIN] 176 E4
Halitpaşa [TR] 144 D3
Haljala [EST] 198 E1
Halk [DK] 156 C3
Halkosaari [FIN] 186 C3
Hälla [S] 190 F6
Hallabro [S] 162 E6
Hallandsfossen [N] 164 D3
Hallapuro [FIN] 186 E2
Hallaryd [S] 162 C6
Hällbacken [S] 190 F2
Hällberget [S] 182 F3
Halle [B] 28 H3
Halle [D] 34 C5
Halle [D] 32 D3
Hälleberga [S] 162 F5
Hällefors [S] 166 G2
Hälleforsnäs [S] 168 B3
Hallein [A] 60 G6
Hallen [S] 182 G2
Hallenberg [D] 32 D5
Hallerud [S] 166 G4
Hällesjö [S] 184 D3
Hällestad [S] 166 H5
Hällevadsholm [S] 166 C5
Hałlevik [N] 190 A6
Hälleviksstrand [S] 166 C6
Halli [FIN] 186 F5
Hallignicourt [F] 44 C5
Hallila [FIN] 178 B3
Hallingby [N] 170 H5
Hällingsåfallet [S] 190 E5
Hall in Tirol [A] 72 D1
Hällnäs [S] 190 H5
Hållnäs [S] 174 F4
Hällnäs [S] 190 G2
Hällristningar [S] 166 C4
Hallsberg [S] 166 H4
Hallshuk [S] 168 G3
Hållsta [S] 168 B3
Hallstahammar [S] 168 B2
Hallstatt [A] 62 A6
Hallstavik [S] 168 E1
Halltorp [S] 162 F6
Halluin [B] 28 F2
Hällvik [S] 190 G2
Hallviken [S] 190 E6
Halmstad [S] 162 B5
Halna [S] 166 F5
Halne Fjellstue [N] 170 E4
Hals [DK] 160 E4
Halsa [N] 180 F2
Hal'shany [BY] 200 H6
Hålsjö [S] 184 E6
Halsskov [DK] 156 E3
Halstead [GB] 14 F3
Halsteren [NL] 16 C6
Halsua [FIN] 186 E1
Haltdalen [N] 182 C3
Haltern [D] 30 H2
Hältorp [S] 166 F4
Haltwhistle [GB] 8 F5
Haluna [FIN] 188 D1
Halvarsgårdarna [S] 172 H5
Halver [D] 32 C5
Ham [F] 28 F5
Hamamköy [TR] 144 E5
Hamar [N] 172 C3
Hambergen [D] 18 D5
Hamburg [D] 18 F4
Hamburgsund [S] 166 B5
Hambye, Abbaye de- [F] 26 D4
Hamdibey [TR] 146 C6
Hamdorf [D] 18 F2
Hämeenkyrö / Tavastkyro [FIN] 176 E1
Hämeenlinna / Tavastehus [FIN] 176 G3
Hämeler Wald [D] 32 G2
Hameln [D] 32 F3
Hämelschenburg [D] 32 F3
Hamersleben [D] 34 A3
Hamidiye [TR] 146 B3
Hamilton [GB] 8 D3
Hamina / Fredrikshamn [FIN] 178 D3
Hamingberg [N] 194 F1
Hamlagrøosen [N] 170 C3
Hamm [D] 32 C3
Hammar [S] 166 G4
Hammarland [FIN] 176 A5
Hammarstrand [S] 184 D2
Hammaslahti [FIN] 188 F3
Hammel [DK] 160 D6
Hammelburg [D] 46 E3
Hammer [N] 190 C5
Hammer [N] 190 C6
Hammerbach [D] 46 D2
Hammerdal [S] 182 H1
Hammerfest [N] 194 B2
Hammershus [DK] 158 E4
Hamminkeln [D] 16 G6
Hammrnäs [S] 182 G2
Hamna [N] 190 A6
Hamnbukt [N] 194 C3
Hamnes [N] 192 G2
Hamningberg [N] 194 F1
Hamoir [B] 30 E5
Hampetorp [S] 168 A3
Hampovica [HR] 74 G5
Hamra [S] 172 H1
Hamrångefjärden [S] 174 E3
Hamre [N] 164 E5
Hamre [S] 174 D1
Hams, Coves dels- [E] 104 F5
Hamula [FIN] 188 C2
Hamula [FIN] 186 G2
Hamzali [MK] 128 H2
Hamzići [BiH] 152 C2
Hån [S] 166 C2
Hän [S] 172 G5
Han [YU] 152 D4
Hanaskog [S] 158 D1
Hanau [D] 46 D3
Hânceşti [MD] 204 D4
Hancevichy [BY] 202 A6
Handegg [CH] 70 F1
Handen [S] 168 E3
Handlová [SK] 64 B3
Handöl [S] 182 E2
Hanerau-Hademarschen [D] 18 E2
Hanestad [N] 182 C6
Hangaskylä [FIN] 186 B4
Hangö / Hanko [FIN] 176 E6
Hangvar [S] 168 G3
Hanhimaa [FIN] 194 C6
Hanhisalo [FIN] 196 C6
Han i Hotit [AL] 152 E4
Hankamäki [FIN] 196 F6
Hankasalmi [FIN] 186 H4
Hanken [S] 166 G5
Hankensbüttel [D] 32 H1
Hanko / Hangö [FIN] 176 E6
Hanna [PL] 38 F4
Hann-Münden [D] 32 F5
Hannover [D] 32 F2
Hannuit (Hannut) [B] 30 D4
Hannusranta [FIN] 196 F5
Hannut (Hannuit) [B] 30 D4
Hânova [RO] 150 E1
Han Pijesak [BiH] 154 E4
Hanskühnenburg [D] 32 G4
Hansnes [N] 192 G1
Hanstedt [D] 18 F5
Hanstholm [DK] 160 C3
Han-sur-Lesse [B] 30 D6
Han-sur-Nied [F] 44 F4
Hantháza [H] 76 D2
Hanušovce [SK] 64 G2
Hanušovice [CZ] 50 C4
Hanya [TR] 144 E2
Haparanda [S] 196 C2
Happa [RUS] 196 G2
Häppälä [FIN] 186 H4
Hapträsk [S] 196 A2
Hara [EST] 198 D2
Härad [S] 168 C3
Haradok [BY] 202 C4
Harads [S] 196 A2
Häradsbäck [S] 162 D5
Haraneset [N] 190 C4
Haras du Pin [F] 26 F5
Hårberg [N] 190 B6
Harbergsdalen [S] 190 E4
Harbo [S] 174 E6
Harburg [D] 60 C2
Harburg [D] 18 F4
Hardegg [A] 62 E3
Hardegsen [D] 32 F4
Hardelot-Plage [F] 28 D2
Hardemo [S] 166 H3
Hardenberg [NL] 16 G4
Harderwijk [NL] 16 E4
Hardeshøj [DK] 156 C4
Hardheim [D] 46 D4
Hardom [FIN] 178 B4
Hareid [N] 180 C3
Haren [D] 16 H3
Haren [NL] 16 G2
Harestua [N] 172 B5
Harfleur [F] 26 G3
Harg [S] 174 G5
Hargla [EST] 198 F4
Hargshamn [S] 174 G5
Harhala [FIN] 176 G2
Haría [E] 100 E5
Harivaara [FIN] 188 F1
Härjåsjön [S] 182 G6
Harjavalta [FIN] 176 D2
Harju [FIN] 196 E4
Harjula [FIN] 196 D3
Harjunmaa [FIN] 188 C5
Harjunsalmi [FIN] 186 F6
Harkány [H] 76 B5
Härkeberga [S] 168 C2
Härkmeri [FIN] 186 B5
Härkmyran [S] 194 A8
Harlech [GB] 10 B5
Hårlev [DK] 156 G3
Harlingen [NL] 16 E2
Harlösa [S] 158 C2
Harmancık [TR] 146 F6
Harmanec [SK] 64 C3
Harmanecká Jaskyňa [SK] 64 C3
Harmånger [S] 184 E6
Härmänkylä [FIN] 196 F4
Härmänmäki [FIN] 196 F4
Harndrup [DK] 156 D3
Härnösand [S] 184 F4
Haro [E] 82 G5
Harodz'ki [BY] 200 H6
Haroldswick [GB] 6 H3
Haroué [F] 44 E6
Harpefoss [N] 170 H1
Harpenden [GB] 14 E3
Harplinge [S] 162 B5
Harpstedt [D] 18 D6
Harrå [S] 192 G5
Harrachov [CZ] 48 H2
Harran [N] 190 D5
Harre [DK] 160 C4
Harrogate [GB] 10 F3
Harrsjöhöiden [S] 190 E5
Harrsjön [S] 190 E5
Harrström [FIN] 186 A3
Harsa [S] 174 D1
Harsefeld [D] 18 E4
Harsewinkel [D] 32 D3
Harsprange [S] 190 H1
Harstad [N] 192 E3
Harstad [N] 166 D1
Harste [D] 32 F4
Harsum [D] 32 G2
Harsvik [N] 190 B5
Harta [H] 76 C3
Hartberg [A] 74 E1
Hartha [D] 34 D6
Hartland [GB] 12 D3
Hartlepool [GB] 10 G2
Hartmannshain [D] 46 D2
Hartola [FIN] 186 G6
Hårve [S] 184 C6
Harwich [GB] 14 G3
Harzgerode [D] 34 A4
Hasanağa [TR] 146 E5
Hasanpaşa [TR] 146 G5
Haselund [D] 18 E1
Haselünne [D] 18 B6
Håsjö [S] 184 D3
Hasköy [TR] 146 B2
Hasköy [TR] 144 G3
Haslach [A] 62 B3
Haslach [D] 58 F2
Hasle [DK] 158 E4
Haslemden [N] 172 D4
Haslemere [GB] 14 D5
Haslev [DK] 156 G3
Hasparren [F] 84 C2
Hasseki [TR] 134 H4
Hassel [D] 18 E6
Hassela [S] 184 E5
Hasselfelde [D] 32 H4
Hasselfors [S] 166 G4
Hasselt [B] 30 E4
Hasselt [NL] 16 F4
Hassfurt [D] 46 F3
Hassi [FIN] 186 F6
Hasslach [D] 46 H3
Hassle [S] 166 F4
Hassleben [D] 20 D5
Hässleholm [S] 158 D1
Hästbo [S] 174 D5
Hästbo [S] 174 E4
Hastersboda [FIN] 168 H1
Hästholmen [S] 166 G6
Hastière-Lavaux [B] 30 D6
Hastings [GB] 14 F6
Hästveda [S] 158 D1
Hasvik [N] 194 A2
Hatě [CZ] 62 E3
Haţeg [RO] 204 B5
Hatfield [GB] 14 E3
Hatfjelldal [N] 190 E3
Hatsola [FIN] 188 D5
Hattem [NL] 16 F4
Hatten [N] 190 D2
Hattingen [D] 30 H3
Hattonchâtel [F] 44 E4
Hattstedt [D] 18 E1
Hattula [FIN] 176 G2
Hattuselkonen [FIN] 196 G5
Hattuvaara [FIN] 188 H1
Hattuvaara [FIN] 196 G6
Hatulanmäki [FIN] 196 E5
Hatvan [H] 64 D6
Hatvik [N] 170 B4
Haug [N] 170 E1
Haugan [N] 190 B6
Haugastøl [N] 170 E4
Haugbøen [N] 180 F3
Hauge [N] 164 B5
Haugesund [N] 164 A1
Hauggrend [N] 164 E2
Haughom [N] 164 C4
Haugsdorf [A] 62 E3
Haugsten [N] 170 G1
Hauho [FIN] 176 G2
Haukå [N] 180 B5
Haukeland [N] 170 B4
Haukeligrend [N] 164 D1
Haukeliseter [N] 170 D5
Haukilahti [FIN] 196 G4
Haukipudas [FIN] 196 D3
Haukivuori [FIN] 188 C5
Hauklappi [FIN] 188 E6
Haule [NL] 16 G2
Haunersdorf [D] 60 G3
Haunia [FIN] 176 D1
Haurida [S] 162 D2
Hausach [D] 58 F2
Hausen [D] 46 E3
Häusern [D] 58 F4
Hausham [D] 60 E5
Hausjärvi [FIN] 176 H3
Hautajärvi [FIN] 194 F7
Haut-Asco [F] 114 B3
Haut-Barr, Château du- [F] 44 G5
Hautecombe, Abbaye de- [F] 68 H3
Hautefort, Château de- [F] 66 G3
Haute-Nendaz [CH] 70 D2
Hauterive, Abbaye de- [CH] 58 D6
Hauteville-Lompnes [F] 68 H2
Hauteville Plage [F] 26 D3
Haut Koenigsbourg [F] 58 D2
Hautmont [F] 28 G4
Havant [GB] 14 D5
Håvberget [S] 172 G5
Havdhem [S] 168 G5
Håvedalen [S] 166 C4
Havelange [B] 30 D5
Havelberg [D] 34 C1
Haverdal [S] 162 B5
Haverfordwest [GB] 12 D1
Haverhill [GB] 14 F3
Håverö [S] 168 E1
Håverud [S] 166 D4
Havířov [CZ] 50 F4
Hävla [S] 168 B4
Havlíčkův Brod [CZ] 48 D4
Havlíčkův Brod [CZ] 48 H5
Havnäs [S] 190 F5
Havnbjerg [DK] 156 C4
Havneby [DK] 156 A4
Havnebyen [DK] 156 F1
Havnsø [DK] 156 F2
Havøysund [N] 194 B1
Havraň [CZ] 48 E2
Havran [TR] 144 C1
Havsa [TR] 146 B2
Havstensund [S] 166 B4
Hawick [GB] 8 E4
Hayange [F] 44 E3
Hayle [GB] 12 B5
Hay-on-Wye [GB] 12 F2
Hayrabolu [TR] 146 B3
Haywards Heath [GB] 14 E5
Hazebrouck [F] 28 E2
Hazlov [CZ] 48 C3
Hazmburk [CZ] 48 F3
Headford [IRL] 2 C4
Heathfield [GB] 14 E5
Hebnes [N] 164 B2
Heby [S] 168 C1
Hechingen [D] 58 G2
Hecho [E] 84 D4
Hechtel [B] 30 E3
Hed [S] 168 A2
Hedal [N] 170 G4
Hedared [S] 162 B2
Hedås [S] 166 F2
Hedburg [D] 46 G3
Hedby [S] 172 H4
Hedbyn [S] 166 H1
Heddal [N] 164 F2
Hédé [F] 26 C5
Hede [S] 168 B1
Hedehusene [DK] 156 G2
Hedemora [S] 174 D5
Heden [S] 172 E1
Heden [S] 172 G2
Hedenäset [S] 194 B8
Hedensted [DK] 156 C2
Hedesunda [S] 174 E5
Hedeviken [S] 182 F4
Hee [DK] 160 B6
Heek [D] 16 H5
Heemstede [NL] 16 D4
Heerde [NL] 16 F4
Heerenveen [NL] 16 F3
Heerlen [NL] 30 F4
Heeze [NL] 30 E3
Heggenes [N] 170 G2
Heglibister [GB] 6 G4
Hegra [N] 182 C1
Hegyeshalom [H] 62 G5
Hegyhátsál [H] 74 F2
Heia [N] 192 F3
Heia [N] 190 C5
Heidal [N] 180 G6
Heide [D] 18 E2
Heideck [D] 46 G6
Heidelberg [D] 46 C5
Heiden [D] 16 G6
Heidenau [D] 48 E1
Heidenheim [D] 60 C2
Heidenreichstein [A] 62 D2
Heigrestad [N] 164 B4
Heikendorf [D] 18 G2
Heiland [N] 164 F3
Heilbronn [D] 46 D5
Heilevong [N] 180 B6
Heiligenberg [D] 58 H4
Heiligenblut [A] 72 G2
Heiligenbösch-Kirche [D] 44 G2
Heiligenhafen [D] 18 H2
Heiligenkreuz [A] 74 F2
Heiligenkreuz [A] 62 E4
Heiligenkreuz [A] 62 E5
Heiligenroth [D] 46 B2
Heiligenstadt [D] 32 G5
Heiligkreuztal [D] 58 H3
Heilsbronn [D] 46 F5
Heimaey [IS] 192 A3
Heimdal [N] 182 B1
Heimertingen [D] 60 B4
Heinääho [FIN] 196 F6
Heinämaa [FIN] 178 B3
Heinämäki [FIN] 186 H1
Heinävaara [FIN] 188 G2
Heinävesi [FIN] 188 E3
Heinersdorf [D] 34 F2
Heino [NL] 16 F4
Heinola [FIN] 178 B2
Heinoniemi [FIN] 188 F4
Heinsberg [D] 30 F4
Heiterwang [A] 60 C6
Heituinlahti [FIN] 178 D2
Hejde [S] 168 G5
Hejlsminde [DK] 156 C3
Hejnice [CZ] 48 H1
Hejnsvig [DK] 156 B2
Hekal [AL] 128 B5
Hel [PL] 22 E2
Heldenberg [A] 62 E4
Heldrungen [D] 34 A5
Helechal [E] 96 B4
Helensburgh [GB] 8 D2
Helfenburk [CZ] 48 F6
Helfštýn [CZ] 50 D5
Helgen [N] 164 F3
Helgerum [S] 162 G2
Helgum [S] 184 E2
Hell [N] 182 C1
Hella [IS] 192 A3
Hella [N] 170 D1
Helland [N] 180 G1
Helle [N] 164 F4
Helleland [N] 164 B4
Hellendoorn [NL] 16 G4
Helleristninger [N] 194 B3
Hellesøy [N] 170 A3
Hellesylt [N] 180 D4
Hellevad [DK] 156 B4
Hellevik [N] 170 B1
Hellevoetsluis [NL] 16 C5
Helligskogen [N] 192 G3
Hellín [E] 104 B1
Hellsö [FIN] 168 H1
Helmond [NL] 30 E2
Helmsdale [GB] 6 E3
Helmsley [GB] 10 F3
Helmstedt [D] 34 A3
Helnessund [N] 192 D5
Helsa [D] 32 F5
Helsingborg [S] 156 H1
Helsinge [DK] 156 G1
Helsingfors / Helsinki [FIN] 176 H5
Helsingør [DK] 156 H1
Helsinki / Helsingfors [FIN] 176 H5
Helstad [N] 190 D4
Helston [GB] 12 B5
Heltermaa [EST] 198 C2
Helvia Recina [I] 116 C1
Hemau [D] 46 H6
Hemel Hempstead [GB] 14 E3
Hemer [D] 32 C4
Hèming [F] 44 G5
Hemling [S] 190 G6
Hemmet [DK] 156 A1
Hemmingen [S] 190 H4
Hemmingsmark [S] 196 A4
Hemmoor [D] 18 E3
Hemnes [N] 166 C2
Hemnesberget [N] 190 D2
Hemse [S] 168 G5
Hemsedal [N] 170 F3
Hemslingen [D] 18 F5
Hen [N] 170 H5
Henån [S] 166 C6
Hendaye [F] 84 B2
Hendek [TR] 146 H3
Hengelo [NL] 16 G5
Hengersberg [D] 60 G2
Heniches'k [UA] 204 G5
Hénin Beaumont [F] 28 F3
Henley-on-Thames [GB] 14 D4
Hennan [S] 184 D5
Henneberg [D] 46 F2
Hennebont [F] 40 C4
Hennef [D] 30 H5
Hennerhöle [A] 60 H6
Henne Strand [DK] 156 A2
Henningsvær [N] 192 D4
Henrichemont [F] 56 C3
Henriksfjäll [S] 190 E4
Henryków [PL] 50 C2
Henstedt-Ulzburg [D] 18 F3
Hepokönqäs [FIN] 196 E4
Hepola [FIN] 196 C3
Heppenheim [D] 46 C4
Heraclea [MK] 128 E3
Herad [N] 170 F3
Herad [N] 164 C5
Heradsbygd [N] 172 C3
Herajoki [FIN] 188 F1
Herakleia [TR] 142 C1
Hera Lacinia, Tempio di- [I] 124 F5
Hérault, Gorges de l'- [F] 106 E3
Herbault [F] 54 G1
Herberstein [A] 74 E2
Herbertingen [D] 58 H3
Herbertstown [IRL] 4 D4
Herbesthal [B] 30 F5
Herbeumont [B] 44 D2
Herbignac [F] 40 E5
Herbolzheim [D] 58 E2
Herborn [D] 46 C1
Herbrechtingen [D] 60 C3
Herby [PL] 50 F2
Herceg Novi [YU] 152 D4
Hercegovac [HR] 74 G6
Hercegovska Goleša [YU] 152 E2
Hercegszántó [H] 76 C5
Herdal [N] 180 D4
Herdberg [D] 32 D4
Herdla [N] 170 A3
Herdoniae [I] 120 G2
Hereford [GB] 12 G2
Herefoss [N] 164 E4
Héreg [H] 64 B6
Hereke [TR] 146 F3
Herencia [E] 96 G3
Herend [H] 74 H2
Herentals [B] 30 D3
Herfølge [DK] 156 G3
Herford [D] 32 E2
Hergiswil [CH] 58 F6
Héricourt [F] 58 C4
Heringsdorf [D] 20 E3
Herisau [CH] 58 H5
Hérisson [F] 56 C5
Herleshausen [D] 32 G6
Herlufsholm [DK] 156 F3
Hermagor [A] 72 G3
Hermannsburg [D] 18 F6
Hermanns-Denkmal [D] 32 E3
Hermansverk [N] 170 D2
Heřmanův Městec [CZ] 50 A4
Herment [F] 68 B2
Hermeskeil [D] 44 G3
Hermo [E] 78 F4
Hermsdorf [D] 48 B1
Hernani [E] 84 B2
Herne [D] 30 H3
Herne Bay [GB] 14 G5
Herning [DK] 160 C6
Hernstein [A] 62 E5
Heroldsberg [D] 46 G5
Herøya [N] 164 G3
Herøysund [N] 170 B5
Herråkra [S] 162 E4
Herräng [S] 174 G5
Herraskylä [FIN] 186 D4
Herre [N] 164 G3
Herrenberg [D] 58 G1
Herrenchiemsee [D] 60 F5
Herrera [E] 96 E4
Herrera [E] 102 B2
Herrera del Duque [E] 96 C3
Herrera de los Navarros [E] 90 D5
Herrera de Pisuerga [E] 82 D5
Herreruela [E] 86 G5
Herrgotts Kirche [D] 46 E5
Herrljunga [S] 162 B1
Herrnburg [D] 18 G3
Herrnhut [D] 48 G1
Herröskatan [FIN] 168 G1
Herrsching [D] 60 D4
Herrskog [S] 184 F3
Hersbruck [D] 46 H5
Herselt [B] 30 D3
Hertford [GB] 14 E3
Hervás [E] 88 B5
Hervik [N] 164 B2
Herzberg [D] 32 G4
Herzberg [D] 34 E4
Herzberg [D] 34 D1
Herzberg [D] 20 B4
Herzberg [D] 46 E1
Herzfeld [D] 32 D4
Herzfelde [D] 34 F2
Herzlake [D] 18 B6
Herzogenaurach [D] 46 G5
Herzogenburg [A] 62 E4
Herzsprung [D] 20 C6
Hesdin [F] 28 D3
Hesel [D] 18 C4
Heskestad [N] 164 C5
Heskestad [N] 164 B4
Hesnæs [DK] 20 B1
Hessel [DK] 160 C4
Hesselagergård [DK] 156 E4
Hessich-Lichtenau [D] 32 F5
Hess Oldendorf [D] 32 F2
Hessvik [N] 170 C4
Hestad [N] 170 C1
Hestenesøyri [N] 180 C5
Hestra [S] 162 C3
Hestra [S] 162 E1
Hetin [YU] 76 F6
Het Loo [NL] 16 F5
Hettange-Grande [F] 44 E3
Hettstedt [D] 34 B4
Hetvehely [H] 76 A5
Heustreu [D] 46 F2
Heves [H] 64 E6
Hévíz [H] 74 G3
Hevlín [CZ] 62 F3
Hexentanzplatz [D] 34 A4
Hexham [GB] 8 F6
Heyrieux [F] 68 G3
Hidasnémeti [H] 64 G3
Hıdırdıvani [TR] 144 F2
Hieflau [A] 62 C6
Hierapolis [TR] 144 G5
Hiersac [F] 54 D6
Hietakylä [FIN] 188 C3
Hietanen [FIN] 188 C6
Hietaniemi [FIN] 194 E8
Hietaniemi [FIN] 194 F6
Hietaperä [FIN] 196 F5
High Cross [IRL] 4 F3
High Wycombe [GB] 14 D4
Higuera, Torre de la- [E] 100 F2
Higuera de la Serena [E] 96 B4
Higuera de Vargas [E] 94 F2
Higuera la Real [E] 94 F3
Higueruela [E] 98 C5
Hihnavaara [FIN] 194 E6
Hiirola [FIN] 188 C5
Hiitinen / Hitis [FIN] 176 E6
Híjar [E] 90 F5
Hilchenbach [D] 32 C5
Hildal [N] 170 C5
Hildburghausen [D] 46 G2
Hilden [D] 30 G4
Hilders [D] 46 E2
Hildesheim [D] 32 G3
Hildre [N] 180 D3
Hilkerode [D] 32 G4
Hilla [FIN] 176 G5
Hille [S] 174 E4
Hillegom [NL] 16 D4
Hillerød [DK] 156 G2
Hillerstorp [S] 162 C3
Hillesøy [N] 192 F2
Hilliliä [FIN] 196 C5
Hillsand [S] 190 E5
Hillsborough [GB] 2 G4
Hillswick [GB] 6 G3
Hilltown [NIR] 2 G4
Hilmo [N] 182 C2
Hilpoltstein [D] 46 G6
Hilterfingen [CH] 70 E1
Hiltulanlahti [FIN] 188 C2
Hilvarenbeek [NL] 30 E2
Hilversum [NL] 16 E4
Himanka [FIN] 196 C5
Himankakylä [FIN] 196 C5
Himarë [AL] 128 B6
Himmelkoron [D] 46 H3
Himmelpforten [D] 18 E4
Himstein [CZ] 48 D3
Hinckley [GB] 10 E6
Hindås [S] 160 H2
Hindelang [D] 60 C6
Hinderburg [D] 34 C1
Hindsig [DK] 156 B2
Hinnerjoki [FIN] 176 D3
Hinnerup [DK] 160 D6
Hinneryd [S] 162 C5
Hinojal [E] 86 H4
Hinojosa del Duque [E] 96 C4
Hinojosa del Valle [E] 94 H3
Hinterbichl [A] 72 F2
Hinterrhein [CH] 70 G2
Hintersee [D] 20 E4
Hinterstoder [A] 62 B6
Hinterthal [A] 72 G1
Hintertux [A] 72 D1
Hinterweidenthal [D] 44 H4
Hinterzarten [D] 58 F3
Hlo [E] 78 B4
Hirnsdorf [A] 74 E2
Hirschaid [D] 46 G4
Hirschau [D] 48 B5
Hirschberg [D] 48 B2
Hirschegg [A] 60 B6
Hirschhorn [D] 46 C5
Hirsch-Stein [D] 48 B3
Hirsilä [FIN] 186 E6
Hirsingue [F] 58 D4
Hirson [F] 28 G5
Hîrşova [RO] 204 D6
Hirtshals [DK] 160 E2
Hirvaskoski [FIN] 196 E3
Hirvassalmi [FIN] 194 D5
Hirvasvaara [FIN] 194 E7
Hirvensalmi [FIN] 186 H6
Hirvihaara [FIN] 176 H4
Hirvijärvi [S] 194 B8
Hirvijoki [FIN] 186 D2
Hirvisalo [FIN] 178 B2
Hisarcık [TR] 144 F2
Hisardžik [YU] 150 A3
Hisartepe Dascylium [TR] 146 E4
Hissjön [S] 190 H6
Histria [RO] 204 E6
Hita [E] 88 H5
Hitchin [GB] 14 E3
Hitiaş [RO] 76 H6
Hitis / Hiitinen [FIN] 176 E6
Hitra [N] 190 A6
Hittarp [S] 156 H1
Hitterdal [N] 182 D4
Hitzacker [D] 18 H5
Hiukkajoki [FIN] 188 F5
Hjallerup [DK] 160 E3
Hjällstad [S] 172 E4
Hjälmseryd [S] 162 D3
Hjältanstorp [S] 184 D4
Hjartåsen [N] 190 E2
Hjärtum [S] 166 C6
Hjelle [N] 180 D5
Hjelle [N] 180 C5
Hjellestad [N] 170 A4
Hjelmeland [N] 164 B2
Hjelset [N] 180 E3
Hjerkinn [N] 180 G4
Hjerpsted [DK] 156 B4
Hjerting [DK] 156 A2
Hjo [S] 166 F6
Hjøllund [DK] 156 C1
Hjørring [DK] 160 E2
Hjorte [DK] 156 D3
Hjorted [S] 162 G2
Hjorteset [N] 180 C5
Hjortkvarn [S] 166 H4
Hjortsberga [S] 162 D4
Hjortsberga [S] 158 F1
Hjulsbro [S] 168 A6
Hjulsjø [S] 166 G2
Hlinsko [CZ] 50 B4
Hlohovec [SK] 62 H4
Hluboká nad Vltavou [CZ] 62 C2
Hlučín [CZ] 50 E4
Hluk [CZ] 62 H2
Hlukhiv [UA] 202 E7
Hlusk [BY] 202 B6
Hlybokaya [BY] 202 B4
Hmelnicki [UA] 204 D3
Hniezdne [SK] 52 B6
Hnilec [SK] 64 E2
Hnúšťa-Likier [SK] 64 D3
Hobermayer-Hofen [A] 74 E2
Hobro [DK] 160 D5
Hocalar [TR] 144 H3
Hoče [SLO] 74 D4
Hoces del Cabriel [E] 98 C4
Hoces del Duratón [E] 88 G3
Hoces del Riaza [E] 88 G2
Höchberg [D] 46 E4
Hochburg [A] 60 G4
Hochburg [D] 58 E2
Hochdonn [D] 18 E3
Hochdorf [CH] 58 F5
Höchenschwand [D] 58 F4
Hochfelden [F] 44 H5
Hochosterwitz [A] 74 B3
Hochspeyer [D] 46 B4
Höchst [D] 46 D4
Höchstädt [D] 60 C3
Höchstadt [D] 46 G4
Hockenheim [D] 46 C5
Hodal [N] 182 C4
Hodalen [N] 182 C4
Hoddeholm [S] 166 F1
Hodenhagen [D] 18 E6
Hodkovice nad Mohelkou [CZ] 48 G2
Hódmezővásárhely [H] 76 E4
Hodøl [N] 182 D4
Hodonín [CZ] 62 G2
Hodoš [SLO] 74 F3
Hodošan [HR] 74 F4
Hoedekenskerke [NL] 28 H1
Hoek van Holland [NL] 16 C5
Hof [D] 48 B3
Hof [D] 58 F1
Hofgeismar [D] 32 F4
Hofheim [D] 46 F3
Hofles [N] 190 C4
Höfn [IS] 192 C3
Hofors [S] 174 D4
Hofstad [N] 190 B5
Höganäs [S] 156 H1
Högerud [S] 166 E2
Högfors [S] 166 H1
Högfors / Karkkla [FIN] 176 G4
Höghult [S] 162 F2
Högklint [S] 168 F4
Höglunda [S] 184 D2
Högnabba [FIN] 186 D1
Högsäter [S] 166 D5
Högsby [S] 162 F4
Høgset [N] 180 E2
Högsjö [S] 184 F3
Høgstadgård [N] 192 G3
Hogstorp [S] 166 C5
Högvålen [S] 182 E5
Hőgyész [H] 76 B4
Hohenau [A] 62 G3
Hohenbachschlucht [A] 72 B1
Hohenberg [A] 62 E5
Hohenbrunn [D] 60 E4
Hohenburg [D] 46 H5
Hoheneck [D] 46 F5
Hohenems [A] 58 H5
Hohenfels [D] 46 B4
Hohenhewen [D] 58 G4
Höhenkirchen [D] 60 E4
Hohenlimburg [D] 32 C4
Hohenlinden [D] 60 F4
Hohenlockstedt [D] 18 F3
Hohenneuffen [D] 58 H2
Hohenpeissenberg [D] 60 D5
Hohenschwangau [D] 60 C6
Hohenstein [D] 46 B2
Hohensyburg [D] 32 C4
Hohentauern [A] 74 C1
Hohentwiel [D] 58 G4
Hohen Wehrda [D] 46 E1
Hohenwerfen [A] 60 G6
Hohenwestedt [D] 18 F2
Hohenzollern [D] 58 G2
Hohne [D] 32 G1
Hohneck [F] 58 D3
Hohrodberg [F] 58 D3
Hohwacht [D] 18 G2
Hoikhankylä [FIN] 186 H3
Hoilola [FIN] 188 H3
Hoisko [FIN] 186 D2
Højby [DK] 156 F2
Højer [DK] 156 B4
Højerup [DK] 156 G4
Højslev Stby [DK] 160 C5
Hojsova Straž [CZ] 48 D6
Hok [S] 162 D3
Hökåsen [S] 168 B2
Hökhuvud [S] 174 F5
Hokka [FIN] 186 H5
Hokksund [N] 164 G1
Hökön [S] 162 D6
Hoks Herrgård [S] 162 D3
Hokusukoski [FIN] 186 E4
Hol [N] 170 F3
Hol [S] 162 B1
Holand [N] 190 D5
Hola Prystan' [UA] 204 F5
Holbæk [DK] 156 F2
Holbeach [GB] 10 G6
Holbøl [DK] 156 C4
Holckenhavn [DK] 156 E3
Holdorf [D] 32 D1
Hole [S] 172 F5
Holeby [DK] 20 A1
Holešov [CZ] 50 D6
Holíč [SK] 62 G3
Holice [CZ] 50 B4
Hölick [S] 174 E1
Holja [FIN] 176 G2
Höljes [S] 172 E3
Hollabrunn [A] 62 E3
Hollád [H] 74 G3
Høllen [N] 164 D6
Hollenegg [A] 74 D3
Hollenstedt [D] 18 F4
Hollerath [D] 30 F5
Hollestein [A] 62 C5
Hollfeld [D] 46 G4
Hollingsholm [N] 180 E2
Hollola [FIN] 176 H2
Hollola [FIN] 178 A2
Hollum [NL] 16 F1
Höllviken [S] 156 H3
Holm [DK] 156 C4
Holm [FIN] 196 B6
Holm [N] 166 B3
Holm [N] 190 C4
Hólmavík [IS] 192 B2

Kremmen [D] 34 D1
Kremna [YU] 152 E1
Kremnica [SK] 64 C3
Krems [A] 62 E4
Kremsmünster [A] 62 B5
Krenkerup [DK] 20 B1
Křenov [CZ] 50 C5
Krepa [PL] 36 F4
Krepcha [BG] 148 D2
Krepoljin [YU] 150 D1
Kresna [BG] 130 B1
Kréstena [GR] 136 C2
Krestsy [RUS] 202 D2
Kretinga [LT] 200 D4
Kreuth [D] 60 E5
Kreuzenstein [A] 62 F4
Kreuzlingen [CH] 58 G4
Kreuztal [D] 32 C6
Kreva [BY] 200 H6
Kriakėnava [LT] 200 F4
Krichim [BG] 148 B6
Krichov [BY] 202 D5
Kriebstein [D] 34 D6
Krieglach [A] 62 D6
Kriezá [GR] 134 C5
Krikello [GR] 132 F4
Krikkovo [RUS] 178 F6
Krimml [A] 72 E1
Krimmler Wasserfälle [A] 72 E1
Krimpen aan den IJssel [NL] 16 D5
Křinec [CZ] 48 H3
Kringla [N] 170 B2
Krinides [GR] 130 D3
Kristall-Höhle [D] 46 C2
Kristalopig [GR] 128 E5
Kristberg [S] 166 H5
Kristdala [S] 162 G3
Kristianopel [S] 158 G1
Kristiansand [N] 164 D5
Kristianstad [S] 158 D2
Kristiansund [N] 180 F2
Kristiinankaupunki / Kristinestad [FIN] 186 A5
Kristineberg [S] 172 E1
Kristineborg [S] 190 G4
Kristinefors [S] 172 E5
Kristinehamn [S] 166 F3
Kristinehov [S] 158 D2
Kristinestad / Kristiinankaupunki [FIN] 186 A5
Kristoffervalen [N] 192 G1
Kristóni [GR] 128 H3
Kristvallabrunn [S] 162 F5
Kritinía [GR] 142 D5
Kritsá [GR] 140 F5
Kriva Feja [YU] 150 E5
Kriváň [SK] 64 D3
Kriva Palanka [MK] 150 E6
Krivelj [YU] 150 D2
Krivodol [BG] 150 F3
Krivogaštani [MK] 128 E3
Křivoklát [CZ] 48 E4
Křižanov [CZ] 50 B6
Križevci [HR] 74 F5
Krk [HR] 112 E2
Krka [SLO] 74 C5
Krnjača [YU] 154 G2
Krnjak [HR] 112 G1
Krnjeuša [BiH] 154 A3
Krnov [CZ] 50 D4
Krobia [PL] 36 C4
Kroczyce [PL] 50 G2
Krøderen [N] 170 G5
Krokan [N] 170 E6
Krokan [N] 192 F2
Krokebol [N] 166 C1
Krokeés [GR] 136 E4
Kroken [N] 190 E3
Kroknes [N] 194 F2
Krokom [S] 182 G2
Krokowa [PL] 22 D1
Kroksjö [S] 190 G5
Kroksjö [S] 196 A5
Krokstad [S] 166 C5
Krokstadelva [N] 164 G1
Krokstadøra [N] 180 H1
Krokstrand [N] 190 E2
Kroksund [N] 166 C2
Kroktorp [S] 172 G5
Krokvåg [S] 184 D2
Krolevets' [UA] 202 D7
Królewiec [PL] 38 A6
Królowy Most [PL] 24 F5
Kroměříž [CZ] 50 D6
Kromerowo [PL] 22 H4
Krompachy [SK] 64 F2
Kromy [RUS] 202 E6
Kronach [D] 46 H3
Kronoby / Kruunupyy [FIN] 196 C6
Kronshtadt [RUS] 178 G4
Kröpelin [D] 20 B3
Kropp [D] 18 F2
Kroppenstedt [D] 34 B3
Kropstädt [D] 34 D3
Krościenko [PL] 52 F5
Krościenko nad Dunajcem [PL] 52 B5
Krosna [LT] 24 F2
Krośniewice [PL] 36 G3
Krosno [PL] 52 D4
Krosno [PL] 22 F3
Krosno Odrzańskie [PL] 34 H3
Krossbu [N] 180 E6
Krossen [N] 164 D6
Krostiz [D] 34 C5
Krotoszyn [PL] 36 D4
Krouna [CZ] 50 B4
Krško [SLO] 74 D5
Krstac [YU] 152 D3
Kruiningen [NL] 28 H1
Kruisland [NL] 16 C6
Krujë [AL] 128 B2
Kruk [N] 170 G2
Krukowo [PL] 24 B5
Krumbach [A] 62 E6
Krumbach [D] 60 C4
Krumë [AL] 150 B6
Krumovgrad [BG] 130 F1
Krumpendorf [A] 74 B3
Krün [D] 60 D6
Krupá [CZ] 48 E3
Krupac [BiH] 152 D1
Krupac [BiH] 152 C2
Krupaja [YU] 150 C1
Krupa na Vrbasu [BiH] 154 B3
Krupanj [YU] 154 F3
Krupe [PL] 38 F6
Krupina [SK] 64 C4
Krupište [MK] 128 F1
Krupp [RUS] 198 G3
Kruså [DK] 156 C4
Krušedol, Manastir- [YU] 154 F2
Kruševac [YU] 150 C3
Kruševo [MK] 128 E2
Krushari [BG] 148 F1
Krushevets [BG] 148 F5
Krushovene [BG] 148 A2
Kruszwica [PL] 36 E2
Kruszyna [PL] 50 G1
Krutcy [RUS] 198 H4
Krute [YU] 152 E5
Krutneset [N] 190 E3
Krutvatn [N] 190 E3
Kruunupyy / Kronoby [FIN] 196 C6
Kruusila [FIN] 176 F4
Krya [TR] 142 F3
Kryakusa [RUS] 198 G3
Krýa Vrýsi [GR] 128 G4
Kryekuq [AL] 128 A4
Kryksæterøra [N] 180 G1
Krylbo [S] 174 D6
Kryle [DK] 160 B6
Krylovo [RUS] 24 C2
Krymne [UA] 38 H4
Krynica [PL] 52 C5
Krynica Morska [PL] 22 F2
Krynki [PL] 24 F5
Kryopigí [GR] 130 C6
Kryspinów [PL] 50 H4
Kryve Ozero [UA] 204 E4
Kryvyi Rih [UA] 204 G3
Krzęcin [PL] 20 G6
Krzeczów [PL] 36 F6
Krzelów [PL] 36 C5
Krzepice [PL] 50 F1
Krzeszów [PL] 52 E2
Krzeszów [PL] 50 B2
Krzeszyce [PL] 34 G2
Krzywe [PL] 24 B6
Krzynowłoga Mała [PL] 22 H6
Krzywiń [PL] 36 C4
Krzyż Wlkp. [PL] 36 B1
Ksar es-Seghir [MA] 100 G6
Książ [PL] 50 B1
Książ Wielki [PL] 52 A2
Ktísmata [GR] 132 C1
Kubbe [S] 184 F1
Küblis [CH] 72 A2
Kubrat [BG] 148 D2
Kuç [AL] 128 B6
Kučevo [YU] 150 D1
Kuchl [A] 60 G6
Kučište [YU] 150 A5
Kucovë [AL] 128 B4
Küçükbahçe [TR] 134 H4
Küçükçekmece [TR] 146 E3
Küçükkuyu [TR] 134 H1
Kuddby [S] 168 B5
Kudever' [RUS] 198 H5
Kudirkos Naumiestis [LT] 24 E1
Kudowa-Zdrój [PL] 50 B3
Kufstein [A] 60 F6
Kuggeboda [S] 158 F1
Kuggerud [N] 172 C5
Kuha [FIN] 196 E2
Kuhanen [FIN] 188 D2
Kühlungsborn [D] 20 B3
Kuhmalahti [FIN] 176 G1
Kuhmo [FIN] 196 G5
Kuhmoinen [FIN] 176 H1
Kuhsen [D] 18 G4
Kuhstedt [D] 18 E4
Kühtai [A] 72 C1
Kuimetsa [EST] 198 E2
Kuivajärvi [FIN] 196 G4
Kuivaniemi [FIN] 196 D3
Kuivanto [FIN] 178 B3
Kuivasjärvi [FIN] 186 C5
Kuivasmäki [FIN] 186 F4
Kuivastu [EST] 198 D3
Kukës [AL] 128 C1
Kukko [FIN] 186 E3
Kukkola [FIN] 176 G2
Kukkulankoski [FIN] 196 C2
Kuklin [PL] 22 H5
Kuks [CZ] 50 B3
Kukuj [RUS] 202 D2
Kukujevci [YU] 154 F2
Kukurečani [MK] 128 E3
Kula [BG] 150 E2
Kula [TR] 144 F3
Kula [YU] 76 D6
Kulalar [TR] 144 E2
Kulaši [BiH] 154 C3
Kulata [BG] 130 B2
Kuldīga [LV] 198 C5
Kuleli [TR] 146 B2
Kulennoinen [FIN] 188 F5
Kulen Vakuf [BiH] 112 H4
Kulhuse [DK] 156 G2
Kuliai [LT] 200 D4
Kullaa [FIN] 176 D1
Kulloo / Kulloo [FIN] 178 A4
Kullo / Kullo [FIN] 178 A4
Kullstedt [D] 32 G5
Kulmbach [D] 46 H3
Kuloharju [FIN] 196 E2
Kultaranta [FIN] 176 D4
Kulykiv [UA] 52 H3
Kulvemäki [FIN] 196 F5
Kumafşarı [TR] 142 G1
Kumane [YU] 76 E6
Kumanica [YU] 150 B3
Kumanovo [MK] 150 D6
Kumarlar [TR] 146 B5
Kumbağ [TR] 146 C3
Kümbet [TR] 146 H5
Kumburk [CZ] 48 H2
Kumkale [TR] 130 H5
Kumköy [TR] 146 E2
Kumla [S] 166 H3
Kumlinge [FIN] 176 B5
Kummayuopio [S] 192 G3
Kummeren [N] 192 D6
Kumo / Kokemäki [FIN] 176 D2
Kumola [RUS] 188 G6
Kumpuvaara [FIN] 196 E2
Kumrovec [HR] 74 E5
Kumuu [FIN] 196 G4
Kunda [EST] 198 F1
Kunes [N] 194 C2
Kunes [N] 194 C2
Kungälv [S] 160 G1
Kungsängen [S] 168 D2
Kungsäter [S] 160 H3
Kungsbacka [S] 160 H3
Kungsberg [S] 174 D4
Kungsfors [S] 174 D4
Kungshållet [S] 168 C3
Kungshamn [S] 166 B5
Kungsör [S] 168 B3
Kunhegyes [H] 76 F1
Kunmadaras [H] 76 F1
Kunovice [CZ] 62 H2
Kunów [PL] 52 C1
Kunowo [PL] 36 C4
Kunpeszér [H] 76 C2
Kunrau [D] 34 A2
Kunštát [CZ] 50 C5
Kunszentmárton [H] 76 E3
Kunszentmiklós [H] 76 C2
Kunžak [CZ] 48 H6
Künzelsau [D] 46 E5
Kuohatti [FIN] 196 G5
Kuohenmaa [FIN] 176 F2
Kuoksu [S] 192 H5
Kuolio [FIN] 196 F2
Kuoloyarvi [RUS] 194 F7
Kuona [FIN] 196 D6
Kuopio [FIN] 188 D2
Kuora [FIN] 188 G1
Kuortane [FIN] 186 D3
Kuosku [FIN] 194 E6
Kup [PL] 50 E2
Kupferberg [D] 46 H3
Kupferzell [D] 46 E5
Kupians'k [UA] 204 H2
Kupirovo [HR] 112 H4
Kupiškis [LT] 200 G4
Kupjak [HR] 112 F1
Kupkovo [RUS] 198 G2
Kupli [LV] 198 D5
Küplü [TR] 130 H2
Küplü [TR] 146 G4
Kuprava [LV] 198 G4
Kupres [BiH] 154 C4
Kurbinovo [MK] 128 D4
Kurbnesh [AL] 128 B1
Kurchatov [RUS] 202 E7
Kurd [H] 76 B4
Kŭrdzhali [BG] 130 F1
Kurejoki [FIN] 186 D2
Kuremäe [EST] 198 F1
Kurevere [EST] 198 C3
Kurgolovo [RUS] 178 E5
Kurianka [PL] 24 F4
Kurikka [FIN] 186 C4
Kurilo [BG] 150 F4
Kuřim [CZ] 50 B6
Kurjala [FIN] 188 D3
Kurkiyeki [RUS] 188 G6
Kurkkio [FIN] 194 C6
Kurkkio [S] 192 H5
Kurne [BG] 148 B4
Kurola [FIN] 188 D4
Kurolanlahti [FIN] 188 C2
Kurów [PL] 38 D5
Kurowice [PL] 36 H4
Kurozwęki [PL] 52 C2
Kurravaara [S] 192 G5
Kuršėnai [LT] 200 E4
Kursiši [LV] 198 C6
Kursk [RUS] 202 F7
Kursu [FIN] 194 E7
Kuršumlija [YU] 150 C4
Kuršumlijska Banja [YU] 150 C4
Kurşunlu [TR] 146 F4
Kurşunlu [TR] 146 D4
Kurtakko [FIN] 194 C6
Kurtköy [TR] 146 G3
Kurtti [FIN] 196 G4
Kuru [FIN] 186 D6
Kuru [FIN] 176 F1
Kurvinen [FIN] 196 F2
Kurzeszyn [PL] 38 A4
Kurzętnik [PL] 22 F5
Kuşadası [TR] 144 D5
Kusel [D] 44 H3
Kushevanda [RUS] 196 G2
Kuside [YU] 152 D3
Kusmark [S] 196 A4
Küssnacht [CH] 58 F6
Kustavi / Gustavs [FIN] 176 C4
Kuşuköy [TR] 144 F2
Kuta [YU] 152 E3
Kütahya [TR] 144 G1
Kutemajärvi [FIN] 186 H5
Kutina [HR] 154 A1
Kutjevo [HR] 154 D1
Kutná Hora [CZ] 48 H4
Kutno [PL] 36 G3
Kuttanen [FIN] 194 B5
Kuttura [FIN] 194 D5
Kúty [SK] 62 G3
Kuuksenvaara [FIN] 188 H2
Kuurtola [FIN] 196 F3
Kuusaa [FIN] 186 G4
Kuusaa [FIN] 196 D5
Kuusajoki [FIN] 194 C6
Kuusalu [EST] 198 E1
Kuusamo [FIN] 194 F8
Kuusankoski [FIN] 178 C3
Kuusiniemi [FIN] 196 H3
Kuusjärvi [FIN] 188 E2
Kuusjoki [FIN] 176 F4
Kuuttila [FIN] 186 B2
Kuvaskangas [FIN] 186 B6
Kuvshinovo [RUS] 202 E3
Kuyucak [TR] 144 E5
Kuzmin [YU] 154 F2
Kuźmina [PL] 52 E5
Kuźnia Raciborska [PL] 50 E3
Kuźnica [PL] 24 F4
Kuzovo [RUS] 198 H3
Kuzuluk [TR] 146 H3
Kvænangsbotn [N] 192 H2
Kværndrup [DK] 156 D4
Kvål [N] 182 B2
Kvaløyseter [N] 190 B5
Kvalsund [N] 194 B2
Kvalsvik [N] 180 C3
Kvalvåg [N] 180 F2
Kvalvåg [N] 170 A5
Kvam [N] 180 H6
Kvam [N] 190 C5
Kvammen [N] 180 G2
Kvanndal [N] 170 C4
Kvanne [N] 180 F2
Kvantenburg [S] 166 D5
Kvarnåsen [S] 190 H4
Kvarnberg [S] 172 G2
Kvarsebo [S] 168 C5
Kvarstadseter [N] 172 B2
Kvås [N] 164 C5
Kveaunet [N] 190 D5
Kvėdarna [LT] 200 D4
Kveejdet [N] 190 D5
Kveina [N] 190 C4
Kvelde [N] 164 G3
Kvelia [N] 190 D5
Kvenvær [N] 190 A6
Kvernessetra [N] 172 C1
Kvetkai [LT] 198 E6
Kwevlax / Koivulahti [FIN] 186 B2
Kvicksund [S] 168 B2
Kvikkjokk [S] 190 G1
Kvikne [N] 182 B4
Kvilldal [N] 164 C1
Kville [S] 166 C5
Kvillsfors [S] 162 F3
Kvinesdal [N] 164 C5
Kvinlog [N] 164 C4
Kvisler [N] 172 D4
Kvissleby [S] 184 E5
Kvisvik [N] 180 F2
Kviteseid [N] 164 E2
Kvitnes [N] 180 F2
Kvitten [N] 182 D4
Kwiatkowice [PL] 36 G4
Kwidzyn [PL] 22 E4
Kwilcz [PL] 36 B2
Kyaralu [RUS] 194 F7
Kybartai [LT] 24 E1
Kyburg [CH] 58 G5
Kycklingvattnet [S] 190 E5
Kyffhäuser-Denkmal [D] 34 A5
Kyïv [UA] 204 E2
Kyjov [CZ] 62 G2
Kyläinpää [FIN] 186 B3
Kylämä [FIN] 186 F6
Kylänlahti [FIN] 196 G6
Kylemore Abbey [IRL] 2 B4
Kyle of Lochalsh [GB] 6 C5
Kyliia [UA] 204 E5
Kyllaj [S] 168 G4
Kylland [N] 164 D4
Kyllburg [D] 44 F1
Kyllíni [GR] 136 B1
Kylmäkoski [FIN] 176 F2
Kylmälä [FIN] 196 E4
Kylmämäki [FIN] 186 H4
Kymbo [S] 162 C1
Kyme [TR] 144 C3
Kými [GR] 134 C4
Kýmina [GR] 128 H4
Kymönkoski [FIN] 186 G2
Kypäräjärvi [FIN] 188 E3
Kypärävaara [FIN] 196 F4
Kyparissía [GR] 136 C3
Kyriáki [GR] 132 H5
Kyritz [D] 20 B6
Kyrkhult [S] 162 D6
Kyrkjebygdi [N] 164 E3
Kyrkslätt / Kirkkonummi [FIN] 176 G5
Kyrkstad [S] 196 B5
Kyrksten [S] 166 G2
Kyrö [FIN] 176 E4
Kyrönlahti [FIN] 186 D6
Kyröskoski [FIN] 176 E1
Kyrping [N] 170 B6
Kyrylivka [UA] 204 H5
Kyšice [CZ] 48 F3
Kysucké Nové Mesto [SK] 50 F6
Kytäjä [FIN] 176 G4
Kýthira [GR] 136 F6
Kýthnos [GR] 138 C2
Kytömäki [FIN] 196 F4
Kyustendil [BG] 150 E6
Kyyjärvi [FIN] 186 E2
Kyynämöinen [FIN] 186 F4
Kyzikos [TR] 146 D4
Kyznecovo [RUS] 202 C2

L

Laa an der Thaya [A] 62 F3
Laage [D] 20 B3
Lääja [FIN] 196 F4
Laajoki [FIN] 176 D3
Laakajärvi [FIN] 196 F5
Laakirchen [A] 62 A5
La Alameda [E] 96 E5
La Alamedilla [E] 88 E4
La Alberca [E] 88 B4
La Alberca de Záncara [E] 98 A3
La Albuera [E] 94 G2
La Algaba [E] 94 G6
La Almarcha [E] 98 B3
La Almolda [E] 90 F4
La Almudena [E] 104 B2
La Almunia de Doña Godina [E] 90 D4
Laamala [FIN] 188 E6
Laanila [FIN] 194 D5
La Antilla [E] 94 E6
Laarbruch [D] 30 F2
Laàs [F] 84 D3
Laasala [FIN] 186 E3
La Azohía [E] 104 C4
Labajos [E] 88 E4
la Balme [F] 68 G5
La Baña [E] 78 F6
La Bañeza [E] 78 G6
La Barca de la Florida [E] 100 G4
La Barrela [E] 78 D4
La Bassée [F] 28 F3
la Bastide [F] 108 D4
Labastide-d'Armagnac [F] 66 D6
La Bastide-de-Sérou [F] 84 H5
Labastide-Murat [F] 66 G4
La Bastide-Puylaurent [F] 68 D6
Labastide-Rouairoux [F] 106 C4
La Bastie d'Urfé [F] 68 E2
La Bâtiaz [CH] 70 C2
La Bâtie-Neuve [F] 108 D2
La Baule [F] 40 E6
La Bazoche-Gouet [F] 42 D5
Łabędzie [PL] 20 H4
la Bégude-de-Mazenc [F] 68 F6
La Belle Etoile [F] 44 A5
Labenne [F] 66 A6
La Bérarde [F] 70 A5
L'Aber-Wrac'h [F] 40 B1
La Bien Aparecida [E] 82 F3
Labin [HR] 112 E2
Labinot Fushë [AL] 128 C3
La Bisbal de Falset [E] 90 H5
Łabiszyn [PL] 36 E1
Labjana [YU] 150 C5
Låbod [H] 74 H4
Laboe [D] 18 G2
Laborel [F] 108 C2
Labouheyre [F] 66 B5
La Bourboule [F] 68 C2
La Bóveda de Toro [E] 88 D2
Labrags [LV] 198 B5
Labraunda [TR] 142 D1
Labrède [F] 66 C3
La Bresse [F] 58 D3
La Brillanne [F] 108 C3
Labrit [F] 66 C5
Łabunie [PL] 52 G1
Läby [S] 174 F6
Laç [AL] 128 B2
La Cabrera [E] 88 G4
La Caillere-St-Hilaire [F] 54 C3
La Calahorra [E] 102 F4
La Calera [E] 100 B5
La Caleta [E] 100 C6
La Caleta [E] 100 E5
La Caletta [I] 118 E3
Lacalm [F] 68 C5
La Calzada de Calatrava [E] 96 E5
La Calzada de Oropesa [E] 88 C6
La Campana [E] 102 A2
La Campana [E] 104 B4
La Cañada de Cañepla [E] 102 H3
Lacanau [F] 66 C2
Lacanau-Océan [F] 66 B2
La Canonica [F] 114 C3
La Canonja [E] 92 C5
La Canourgue [F] 68 C6
La Capelle [F] 28 G5
Lacapelle-Marival [F] 66 H4
La Capte [F] 108 C6
Lačarak [YU] 154 F2
La Caridad [E] 78 F2
La Carlota [E] 102 B2
La Carolina [E] 96 E6
La Cartuja [E] 100 F3
Lacaune [F] 106 C3
La Cavalerie [F] 106 D3
Lacave [F] 66 G4
Lacco Ameno [I] 120 D3
Lacedonia [I] 120 G2
La Celle-Dunoise [F] 54 H5
Lăceni [RO] 148 B1
La Cerca [E] 82 F4
Lâces [I] 72 C3
La Chaise-Dieu [F] 68 D3
La Chambre [F] 70 B4
Lachamp [F] 68 C5
Lachanás [GR] 130 B3
Lachaniá [GR] 142 D5
La Chapelle [F] 68 F1
La Chapelle-d'Angillon [F] 56 C3
la Chapelle-en-Valgaudemar [F] 70 A6
La Chapelle-en-Vercors [F] 68 G5
La Chapelle-Glain [F] 40 G5
la-Chapelle-Laurent [F] 68 C4
La Charité-sur-Loire [F] 56 D3
La Chartre [F] 42 C6
La Châtaigneraie [F] 54 D3
La Châtre [F] 54 H5
La Chaux-de-Fonds [CH] 58 C5
la Chèze [F] 26 B5
Lachowo [PL] 24 D4
La Ciotat [F] 108 B5
La Ciudad Encantada [E] 98 C2
Łąck [PL] 36 G2
Läckö [S] 166 E5
La Clayette [F] 56 F6
la Clisse [F] 54 C6
La Clusaz [F] 70 B3
La Cluse [F] 68 H2
La Cluse-et-Mijoux [F] 58 B6
La Codosera [E] 86 F5
Lacona [I] 114 D3
La Concepción [E] 102 C4
Láconi [I] 118 D5
La Coquille [F] 66 G2
La Coronada [E] 96 B3
La Corrèze [F] 66 H3
La Coruña / A Coruña [E] 78 C2
La Côte-St-André [F] 68 G4
Lacourt [F] 84 G5
La Courtine [F] 68 B2
la Couvertoirade [F] 106 E3
Lacq [F] 84 D3
La Croisière [F] 54 G5
La Croixille [F] 26 D6
La Croix-Valmer [F] 108 D6
La Cueva Santa [E] 98 E3
La Cumbre [E] 96 B1
La Cure [F] 70 B1
Lad [H] 74 H5
Lad [PL] 36 E3
Ladapeyre [F] 54 H5
Ladbergen [D] 32 C2
Ladby [DK] 156 E3
Lądek-Zdrój [PL] 50 C3
Ládi [GR] 130 H1
Ladispoli [I] 114 H5
Ladoeiro [P] 86 F3
Ladon [F] 42 F6
Ladoye, Cirque de- [F] 58 A6
Ladushkin [RUS] 22 G2
La Encinilla y El Rubio [E] 100 G3
Lærdalsøyri [N] 170 E2
Laerma [GR] 142 D5
La Espina [E] 78 G3
La Estrella [E] 96 D1
La Fère [F] 28 F6
la Ferrière [F] 42 C6
la Ferrière [F] 70 A4
La Ferrière-en-Parthenay [F] 54 E3
Laferté [F] 58 B3
La Ferté-Bernard [F] 42 C5
La Ferté-Gaucher [F] 42 H4
la-Ferté-Loupière [F] 56 E1
La Ferté-Macé [F] 26 F5
La Ferté-Milon [F] 42 H3
La Ferté-sous-Jouarre [F] 42 H3
La Ferté-St-Aubin [F] 56 B1
La Ferté-Vidame [F] 26 H5
Laffrey [F] 68 H5
Láfka [GR] 136 E1
La Flèche [F] 42 B6
La Florida [E] 78 G3
La Flotte [F] 54 B4
La Font de la Figuera [E] 98 D6
la Foresta, Convento- [I] 116 B4
Laforsen [S] 182 H6
Lafortunada [E] 84 E5
Lafrançaise [F] 66 F6
La Fregeneda [E] 80 E5
La Frua [I] 70 F2
La Fuente de San Esteban [E] 80 F6
La Gacilly [F] 40 E5
Lagan [S] 162 C4
Laganás [GR] 136 B2
La Garde-Freinet [F] 108 D5
La Garriga [E] 92 E4
La Garrovilla [E] 94 G1
Lage [D] 32 E3
Łagiewniki [PL] 50 C2
Laginá [GR] 130 B4
La Gineta [E] 98 B5
Lagkáda [GR] 136 E4
Lagkáda [GR] 134 G4
Lagkadás [GR] 130 B4
Lagkádia [GR] 136 D2
Lagkadíkia [GR] 130 B4
Lagnieu [F] 68 G2
Lagnö [S] 168 C6
Lagny [F] 42 G3
Lagoa [P] 94 B5
Lagoa [P] 100 E3
Lagonegro [I] 120 G5
Lagonísi [GR] 136 H1
Lágos [GR] 130 F3
Lagos [P] 94 B5
Lagosanto [I] 110 H3
Łagów [PL] 52 C1
Łagów [PL] 34 H3
La Granada de Rio Tinto [E] 94 F4
la Granadella [E] 90 H5
La Grand-Combe [F] 106 F2
La Grande-Motte [F] 106 F4
La Granja [E] 88 F4
La Granjuela [E] 96 B5
Lagrasse [F] 106 C5
La Grave [F] 70 B5
Lägsta [S] 190 G6
La Guardia / A Guarda [E] 78 A5
La Guardia / A Guarda [E] 96 G2
Laguardia / Biasteri [E] 82 G6
La Guardia de Jaén [E] 102 E2
Laguarres [E] 90 H3
Laguarta [E] 84 E5
Laguépie [F] 66 H6
La Guerche [F] 56 D4
La Guerche-de-Bretagne [F] 40 G4
Laguiole [F] 68 B5
Laguna de Duero [E] 88 E2
Laguna del Marquesado [E] 98 C2
Laguna de Negrillos [E] 82 B5
Laguna de Santiago [E] 100 B5
Laguna Negra [E] 90 B2
Lagunas de Villafáfila [E] 82 A6
Lagýna [GR] 128 H4
La Haba [E] 96 B3
Lahane [F] 66 B5
la Haye [F] 28 C5
La Haye-du-Puits [F] 26 D2
Lahdenperä [FIN] 186 F2
Lahemmaa [EST] 198 D1
La Hermida [E] 82 D3
Laheycourt [F] 44 C4
Lahinch [IRL] 2 B5
Lahnajärvi [S] 194 B7
Lahnasjärvi [FIN] 196 F5
Lahnberg [A] 72 F2
Lahnstein [D] 30 H6
Laholm [S] 162 B5
Laholuoma [FIN] 186 C5
La Horra [E] 88 G2
Lahoysk [BY] 202 B5
La Hoz de la Vieja [E] 90 E6
Lahr [D] 58 E2
Lähteenkylä [FIN] 176 D2
Lahti / Lahtis [FIN] 178 B2
Lahtis / Lahti [FIN] 178 B2
La Hutte [F] 26 F6
Laibgaliai [LT] 200 G3
Laichingen [D] 60 B3
Laifour, Roches de- [F] 44 C1
L'Aigle [F] 26 G5
La Iglesuela del Cid [E] 98 F2
Laignes [F] 56 F2
Laiguéglia [I] 108 G4
L'Aiguillon [F] 54 B4
Laihela / Laihia [FIN] 186 B3
Laihia / Laihela [FIN] 186 B3
Laikko [FIN] 188 F6
Laïliás [GR] 130 C2
Laimbach [A] 62 D4
Laimoluokta [S] 192 G4
Lainate [I] 70 G4
Lainijaur [S] 190 G4
Lainio [S] 192 H5
Lairg [GB] 6 E3
Laisbäck [S] 190 F4
La Isla [E] 82 C2
Laissac [F] 68 B6
Laísta [GR] 132 D1
Laisvall [S] 190 F2
Laitikkala [FIN] 176 G2
Laitila [FIN] 176 D3
Laitineva [FIN] 196 D4
la-Jaille-Yvon [F] 40 H5
La Jana [E] 98 G2
Lajares [E] 100 E6
La Javie [F] 108 D3
Lajes [P] 100 D3
Lajes das Flores [P] 100 B4
Lajes do Pico [P] 100 C3
Lajkovac [YU] 150 A1
la Jonquera [E] 92 G2
Lajoskomárom [H] 76 B3
Lajosmizse [H] 76 D2
Lakaluoma [FIN] 186 D3
Lakaniemi [FIN] 186 D2
Łaka Prudnicka [PL] 50 D3
Lakatnik [BG] 150 F4
Lakaträsk [S] 194 A8
Lakaträsk [S] 194 A8
Lakavica [MK] 128 G2
Lakfors [N] 190 D3
Lakhdenpokh'ya [RUS] 188 G6
Lakitelek [H] 76 E3
Lákka [GR] 132 B3
Lakkí [GR] 142 B2
Lákkoi [GR] 140 C4
Lakkoma [GR] 130 G4
Lakkópetra [GR] 132 E6
Lakolk [DK] 156 A3
Laksåvik [N] 190 A6
Lakselv [N] 194 C3
Lakši [BiH] 154 C2
La Lantejuela [E] 102 B2
Lalapaşa [TR] 146 B1
Lalas [GR] 136 C2
l'Albagés [E] 90 H5
L'Albi [E] 92 B4
L'Alcúdia [E] 98 E5
l'Alcora / Alcora [E] 98 F3
L'Alcúdia (Ilice) [E] 104 D2
L'Alcúdia de Crespins [E] 98 E6
L'Aldea [E] 92 B5
l'Alguenya [E] 104 D2
La Lima [I] 110 E4
Lalín [E] 78 C4
Lalinde [F] 66 F4
La Línea de la Concepción [E] 100 H5
Lalm [N] 180 G6
La Loupe [F] 26 H6
Lalouvesc [F] 68 F4
La Louvière [B] 28 H4
L'Alpe-d'Huez [F] 70 A5
Lalueza [E] 90 F3
La Luisiana [E] 102 B2
Lam [D] 48 D6
La Machine [F] 56 D4
La Maddalena [I] 118 E2
Lama dei Peligni [I] 116 D5
La Magdalena [E] 78 G5
La Malène [F] 68 C6
Lamalou-les-Bains [F] 106 D4
La Manga del Mar Menor [E] 104 D4
Lamarche [F] 58 B2
Lamargelle [F] 56 G3
La Marina [E] 104 D3
Lamarosa [P] 86 C5
Lamarque [F] 66 C2
Lamas do Vouga [P] 80 B5
Lamastre [F] 68 F5
La Mata [E] 104 D3
La Matanza [E] 82 B5
La Maucarrière [F] 54 E3
Lambach [A] 62 B4
Lamballe [F] 26 B4
Lambesc [F] 106 H4
Lamborn [S] 174 C3
Lambrecht [D] 46 B5
Lamego [P] 80 D4
la-Melleraye-de-Bretagne [F] 40 F5
L'Ametlla de Mar [E] 92 B5
Lamezia Terme [I] 124 D5
Lamía [GR] 132 G4
Lammhult [S] 162 D4
Lammi [FIN] 176 H2
Lammi [FIN] 186 D1
Lamminaho [FIN] 196 D6
Lamminkylä [FIN] 188 G3
Lamminkylä [FIN] 196 F4
Lamminmaa [FIN] 186 C4
La Molina [E] 92 E2
La Mongie [F] 84 F4
La Mota [E] 102 D3
La Mothe-Achard [F] 54 B3
Lamotte-Beuvron [F] 56 B2
La Motte-Chalancon [F] 108 B2
la Motte-du-Caire [F] 108 C2
Lamouroux, Grottes de- [F] 66 G3
Lampaanjärvi [FIN] 186 H1
Lampaul [F] 40 A1
Lampaul-Plouarzel [F] 40 A1
Lámpeia [GR] 136 C1
Lampeland [N] 164 G1
Lamperila [FIN] 188 C2
Lampeter [GB] 10 B6
Lampinsaari [FIN] 196 D5
L'Ampolla [E] 92 B5
Lamppi [FIN] 176 C1
Lamprechtshausen [A] 60 G5
Lamprechtsofenloch [A] 60 G6
Lämsänkylä [FIN] 196 F2
Lamsfeld [D] 34 F4
Lamstedt [D] 18 E4
La Mudarra [E] 88 E1
La Muela [E] 90 E4
La Mure [F] 68 H5
Lamure-sur-Azergues [F] 68 F2
La Murta [E] 98 E6
Lana [I] 72 C3
Lanaja [E] 90 F4
La Napoule-Plage [F] 108 E5
Lanark [GB] 8 D4
La Nava de Ricomalillo [E] 96 D1
La Nava de Santiago [E] 86 G6
Lancaster [GB] 10 D2
Lanciano [I] 116 E5
Łańcut [PL] 52 E3
Landau [D] 60 G3
Landau [D] 46 B5
Landeck [A] 72 C1
Landedo [P] 80 F3
Landenclorf [A] 62 F3
Landerneau [F] 40 B2
Landersfjorden [N] 194 D2
Landeryd [S] 162 B4
Landesbergen [D] 32 E1
Landete [E] 98 D3
Landévennec [F] 40 B2
Landivisiau [F] 40 C2
Landivy [F] 26 D5
Landkirchen [D] 18 H2
Landön [S] 182 G1
Landquart [CH] 58 H6
Landrecies [F] 28 G4
Landsberg [D] 60 D4
Landsberg [D] 34 C5
Landsbro [S] 162 E3
Landshut [D] 60 F3
Landshut, Ruine- [D] 44 G2
Landskrona [S] 156 H2
Landštejn [CZ] 62 D2
Landstuhl [D] 44 H3
Landvetter [S] 160 H2
Lane [N] 170 C1
Lanersbach [A] 72 E1
Lanesborough [IRL] 2 D5
La Neuve-Lyre [F] 26 H5
La Neuveville [CH] 58 D5
Langå [DK] 160 D5
Långå [S] 182 F4
Langa de Duero [E] 88 H2
Långåminne [FIN] 186 B3
Langangen [N] 164 G3
Langballig [D] 156 C5
Långban [S] 166 G1
Långbo [S] 174 D2
Langdal [N] 180 E4
Langeac [F] 68 D4
Langeais [F] 54 F2
Langeid [N] 164 D3
Längelmäki [FIN] 186 F6
Langelsheim [D] 32 G3
Långemåla [S] 162 G4
Langen [A] 72 B1
Langen [D] 46 C3
Langen [D] 18 D4
Langenargen [D] 58 H4
Långenäs [S] 166 E1
Langenau [D] 60 B3
Langenburg [D] 46 E5
Langenes [N] 192 D3
Längenfeld [A] 72 C2
Langenfeld [D] 30 G4
Langenhahn [D] 46 B1
Langenhorn [D] 156 B5
Langenisarhofen [D] 60 G3
Langenlois [A] 62 E4
Langennaundorf [D] 34 E5
Langenselbold [D] 46 D3
Langenthal [CH] 58 E5
Langenwang [A] 62 E6
Langenzenn [D] 46 F5
Langeoog [D] 18 B3
Langeskov [DK] 156 E3
Langesø [DK] 156 D3
Langesund [N] 164 G3
Langevåg [N] 164 A1
Langevåg [N] 180 C3
Langewiese [D] 32 D5
Langfjord [N] 192 H1
Langfjordnes [N] 194 D1
Långflon [S] 172 E3
Langhirano [I] 110 D3
Langholm [GB] 8 E5
Långjöby [S] 190 F4
Långlöt [S] 162 G5
Långnäs [FIN] 176 B5
Langnau im Emmental [CH] 58 E6
Langø [DK] 156 E5
Langogne [F] 68 D5
Langoiran [F] 66 D3
Langon [F] 66 D4
Langquaid [D] 60 F2
Langres [F] 56 H2
Långron [S] 184 H1
Långsel [S] 194 A8
Långsele [S] 184 E2
Långsele [S] 190 F5
Långserud [S] 166 D3
Långshyttan [S] 174 D5
Langstrand [N] 194 B2
Långträsk [S] 196 A3
Långträsk [S] 190 H4
Languidou, Chapelle de- [F] 40 B3
Langula [D] 32 G5
Långvattnet [S] 190 H4
Langviken [S] 196 A4
Långviksmon [S] 184 G1
Langvind [S] 174 E2
Langwarden [D] 18 D4
Langwedel [D] 18 E6
Langweid [D] 60 D3
Langwies [CH] 70 H1
Lanhelas [P] 78 A5
Lanjarón [E] 102 E5
Lankas [LV] 198 B5
Lankila [FIN] 178 D3
Länkipohja [FIN] 186 F6
Lankojärvi [FIN] 194 C7
Lankosi [FIN] 186 B6
Lanleff, Temple de- [F] 26 A3
Lanmeur [F] 40 C1
Länna [S] 168 C3
Lanna [S] 162 C3
Lannabruk [S] 166 G3
Lannavaara [S] 192 H4
Lannemezan [F] 84 F4
Lannevesi [FIN] 186 F3
Lannilis [F] 40 B1
Lannion [F] 40 D1
Lanobre [F] 68 B3
La Noguera [E] 98 D1
Lanouaille [F] 66 G2
Lansån [S] 194 B8
Lansikylä [FIN] 186 D3
Länsi-Vuokka [FIN] 196 F6
Lansjärv [S] 194 A8
Lanškroun [CZ] 50 C4
Lanslebourg-Mont-Cenis [F] 70 C5
Lanšperk [CZ] 50 B4
Lantosque [F] 108 F4
Lanusei [I] 118 E5
Lanvollon [F] 26 A4
Lánycsók [H] 76 B5
Lanzá [E] 78 C2
Lanzendorf [A] 62 F5
Lanžhot [CZ] 62 G3
Lanzo d'Intelvi [I] 70 G3
Lanzo Torinese [I] 70 D5
Lao [EST] 198 D3
Laodíkeia [TR] 144 G5
La Oliva [E] 84 B5
La Oliva [E] 100 E6
Laon [F] 28 G6
La Orotava [E] 100 B5
La Paca [E] 104 B3
La Pacaudière [F] 68 E1
Lapalisse [F] 56 D6
La Pallice [F] 54 B4
La Palma del Condado [E] 94 F6
Lapalme [F] 106 D5
La Palmyre [F] 54 B6
La Palud-sur-Verdon [F] 108 D4
La Panouse [F] 68 D5
Lápas [GR] 132 E6
La Pelechaneta / Pelejaneta [E] 98 F3
La Peraleja [E] 98 B1
la Pèruse [F] 54 E6
La Petite-Pierre [F] 44 G5
Lapeyrade [F] 66 D5
Lapinjärvi / Lappträsk [FIN] 178 B3
Lapinlahti [FIN] 188 C1
Lapinsaari [FIN] 186 C3
La Plagne [F] 70 B4
La Plaza / Teverga [E] 78 G4
Laplume [F] 66 E5
la Pobla de Lillet [E] 92 E2
La Pobla de Massaluca [E] 90 G6
la Pobla de Segur [E] 92 C1
la Pobla de Vallbona [E] 98 E4
la Pobla Tornesa [E] 98 G3
La Pola de Gordón [E] 78 H5
La Portera [E] 98 D4
Lapoutroie [F] 58 D2
Lapovo [YU] 150 C2
Lappach / Lappago [I] 72 E2
Lappago / Lappach [I] 72 E2
Lappajärvi [FIN] 194 B5
Lappajärvi [FIN] 186 D2
Läppe [S] 168 B3
Lappeenranta / Villmanstrand [FIN] 178 E2
Lappfjärd / Lapväärtti [FIN] 186 B5
Lappfors [FIN] 186 C1
Lappi [FIN] 176 D3
Lappo [FIN] 176 C5
Lappo / Lapua [FIN] 186 C2

264 Mal - Mil

Målilla [S] 162 F3
Mali Lošinj [HR] 112 E4
Malin [IRL] 2 F1
Malin [UA] 204 E1
Malines (Mechelen) [B] 30 C3
Malingsbo [S] 166 H1
Maliniec [PL] 36 E3
Malin More [IRL] 2 D2
Malinska [HR] 112 E2
Mali Prolog [HR] 152 B3
Maliq [AL] 128 D4
Mališevo [YU] 150 B5
Maliskylä [FIN] 196 D5
Malix [CH] 70 H1
Maljovica [BG] 150 G6
Malkara [TR] 146 B3
Małkinia Górna [PL] 38 D1
Malkkila [FIN] 188 E3
Malko Gradishte [BG] 148 D6
Malko Tŭrnovo [BG] 146 C1
Mallaig [GB] 6 B5
Mallersdorf [D] 60 F2
Málles Venosta / Mals im Vinschgau [I] 72 B2
Malling [DK] 156 D1
Mallnitz [A] 72 G2
Mallow [IRL] 4 C4
Malm [N] 190 C5
Malmbäck [S] 162 D2
Malmberget [S] 192 G6
Malmédy [B] 30 F5
Malmesbury [GB] 12 G3
Malmköping [S] 168 C3
Malmö [S] 156 H3
Malmslätt [S] 166 H5
Malo [I] 72 D5
Maloarhangel'sk [RUS] 202 F6
Małogoszcz [PL] 52 B1
Maloja [CH] 70 H2
Malo-les-Bains [F] 14 H6
Malón [GR] 142 E5
Malónas [GR] 142 E5
Malonno [I] 72 B4
Małopolski [PL] 52 D3
Måløy [N] 180 B5
Malpartida de Cáceres [E] 86 G5
Malpartida de Plasencia [E] 88 B5
Malpica de Bergantiños [E] 78 C1
Mālpils [LV] 198 E5
Mälsåker [S] 168 D3
Malšice [CZ] 48 G6
Mals im Vinschgau / Málles Venosta [I] 72 B2
Malsjö [S] 166 E3
Malsjöbodarna [S] 182 H4
Målsnes [N] 192 F2
Malta [A] 72 H2
Malta [LV] 198 G6
Maltat [F] 56 E5
Maltepe [TR] 146 C5
Maltepe [TR] 146 F3
Malton [GB] 10 G3
Malu [RO] 150 G1
Malung [S] 172 F4
Malungen [N] 172 C4
Malungen [S] 184 E5
Malungsfors [S] 172 F4
Maluszyn [PL] 50 H1
Malveira [P] 86 B4
Malvik [N] 182 C1
Mały Płock [PL] 24 D5
Malyye Rozhki [RUS] 198 G1
Mamaia [RO] 204 D6
Mamarrosa [P] 80 B6
Mamers [F] 26 G6
Mammola [I] 124 D7
Mamone [I] 118 E3
Mamonovo [RUS] 22 G2
Mamyra [N] 190 B5
Mána [GR] 136 E1
Maňa [SK] 64 B4
Manacor [E] 104 F5
Manamansalo [FIN] 196 E4
Manasija [YU] 150 C2
Manasija, Manastir- [YU] 150 C2
Manastir Ozren [BiH] 154 D3
Manastir Stern [BiH] 154 C2
Manastir Tavna [BiH] 154 E3
Mancha Real [E] 102 E2
Manchester [GB] 10 E4
Manching [D] 60 E2
Manciano [I] 114 G3
Mancier [F] 66 D6
Mandal [N] 164 D6
Måndalen [N] 180 E3
Mándas [I] 118 D6
Mandelieu [F] 108 E5
Mandello del Lario [I] 70 G3
Manderscheid [D] 44 G1
Mandjelos [YU] 154 F2
Mándra [GR] 134 B6
Mándra [GR] 130 H2
Mandráki [GR] 142 C4
Mandrikó [GR] 142 D4
Manduria [I] 122 F4
Manerba del Garda [I] 72 B6
Manérbio [I] 72 A6
Manětín [CZ] 48 D4
Mánfa [H] 76 B5
Manfredónia [I] 120 H1
Mangalia [RO] 148 G1
Mångbyn [S] 196 B5
Mangen [N] 166 C1
Manger [N] 170 A3
Mangfall Brücke [D] 60 E5
Mångsbodarna [S] 172 F3
Mangskog [S] 166 E1
Mangualde [P] 80 C6
Manguilla [E] 96 A4
Máni [GR] 130 H1
Maniago [I] 72 F4
Manisa [TR] 144 D3
Manita Peć [HR] 112 G4
Mank [A] 62 D5
Månkarbo [S] 174 E5
Mańki [PL] 22 G4
Manlleu [E] 92 E3
Mannheim [D] 46 C4
Mano [F] 66 C4
Manoláda [GR] 136 B1
Manon [E] 78 E1
Manorhamilton [IRL] 2 D3
Manosque [F] 108 C4
Manresa [E] 92 D3
Månsarp [S] 162 D2
Månsåsen [S] 182 G2
Manschnow [D] 34 G2
Mansfeld [D] 34 B4
Mansfield [GB] 10 F5
Mansilla de las Mulas [E] 78 H6
Mansle [F] 54 E6
Manso [F] 114 A3
Mansoniemi [FIN] 186 C6
Mantamádos [GR] 134 H2
Manteigas [P] 86 F2
Mantes [F] 42 E3
Mantila [FIN] 186 C4
Mantíneia [GR] 136 E2
Mäntlahti [FIN] 178 D4
Mantorp [S] 166 H6
Mantoúdi [GR] 134 B4
Mantova [I] 110 E1
Mäntsälä [FIN] 178 A3
Mänttä [FIN] 186 F5
Mäntyharju [FIN] 178 C1
Mäntyjärvi [FIN] 194 E8
Mäntylahti [FIN] 188 C1
Mäntyluoto [FIN] 176 C1
Manyas [TR] 146 D5
Manzanares [E] 96 F4
Manzanares el Real [E] 88 F5
Manzaneda [E] 78 E5
Manzanera [E] 98 E3
Manzanilla [E] 94 F6
Manzat [F] 68 C1
Maó / Mahón [E] 104 H5
Maqueda [E] 88 E6
Maranchón [E] 90 B5
Maranello [I] 110 E3
Marano di Napoli [I] 120 D3
Marano Lagunare [I] 72 G5
Marans [F] 54 C4
Maratea [I] 120 G5
Marateca [P] 86 B6
Marathiás [GR] 132 F5
Marathókampos [GR] 144 C6
Marathónas [GR] 134 C6
Marathópoli [GR] 136 C4
Maráthos [GR] 140 E4
Maravillas, Cueva de las- [E] 94 F4
Marbach [D] 46 D6
Marbäck [S] 162 E2
Marbäck [S] 162 C3
Mårbacka [S] 166 E1
Mårbacken [S] 172 E5
Marbella [E] 102 B5
Marboz [F] 68 G1
Marburg [D] 32 D6
Marcali [H] 74 H3
Marčana [HR] 112 D2
Marceddí [I] 118 B5
March [GB] 14 F2
Marchaux [F] 58 B4
Marche-en-Famenne [B] 30 D6
Marchegg [A] 62 G4
Marchena [E] 102 A2
Marchenilla [E] 94 G6
Marcheprime [F] 66 C3
Marciac [F] 84 F3
Marciana Marina [I] 114 D2
Marcianise [I] 120 E3
Marcigny [F] 56 E6
Marcilla [E] 84 B5
Marcillac-Vallon [F] 68 B5
Marcillat [F] 56 C6
Marcilly-le-Hayer [F] 42 H5
Marcinowice [PL] 50 C1
Marciszów [PL] 50 B1
Marckolsheim [F] 58 E2
Mårdsele [S] 190 H4
Mårdsjö [S] 184 C2
Mårdsund [S] 182 G2
Marebbe / St Vigil [I] 72 E3
Máre de Déu de la Balma [E] 98 G1
Mare de Déu del Toro [E] 104 H4
Mårem [N] 170 F5
Måren [N] 170 C2
Marennes [F] 54 B5
Marettimo [I] 126 A2
Mareuil [F] 66 F2
Mareuil [F] 54 C3
Marevo [RUS] 202 D3
Margarites [GR] 140 D4
Margariti [GR] 132 C3
Margate [GB] 14 G5
Margecany [SK] 64 F2
Margherita di Savoia [I] 120 H2
Margonin [PL] 22 B6
Marhaň [SK] 52 D6
Marhanets' [UA] 204 G4
Marhet [B] 44 E1
María [E] 102 H3
Maria Birnbaum [D] 60 D3
Maria Dreierchen [A] 62 E3
Mariager [DK] 160 D5
Maria Laach [D] 30 H6
Marialva [P] 80 E5
Maria Martenthal [D] 30 G6
Mariannelund [S] 162 F2
Marianopoli [I] 126 E3
Marianos [P] 86 C4
Mariánské Lázně [CZ] 48 D4
Maria Saal [A] 74 B3
Mariastein [A] 60 F6
Maria Taferl [A] 62 D4
Maria Trost [A] 74 D2
Maria Wörth [A] 74 B3
Mariazell [A] 62 D5
Maribo [DK] 20 A1
Maribor [SLO] 74 E3
Marieby [S] 182 G2
Mariedal [S] 166 E5
Mariedamm [S] 166 H4
Mariefred [S] 168 C3
Mariehamn / Maarianhamina [FIN] 176 A5
Marieholm [S] 158 C2
Marieholm [S] 162 C3
Marielyst [DK] 20 B1
Mariëmont [B] 28 H4
Marienberg [D] 48 D2
Marienborn [D] 34 A3
Marienburg [D] 44 G2
Marienstatt [D] 32 C6
Marienthal [D] 32 C6
Mariestad [S] 166 F5
Marifjøra [N] 170 D1
Marignane [F] 106 H5
Marigny-le-Châtel [F] 44 A5
Marihn [D] 20 C4
Marija Bistrica [HR] 74 E5
Marijampolė [LT] 24 E1
Marikostinovo [BG] 130 B2
Marilles [B] 30 D4
Marín [E] 78 B4
Marina [EST] 198 E3
Marina [HR] 116 H1
Marina di Alberese [I] 114 F3
Marina di Àrbus [I] 118 B6
Marina di Ardea [I] 116 A6
Marina di Camerota [I] 120 G5
Marina di Campo [I] 114 D3
Marina di Caronia [I] 126 F2
Marina di Carrara [I] 110 D4
Marina di Castagneto-Donorático [I] 114 E1
Marina di Chiéuti [I] 116 F5
Marina di Gáiro [I] 118 E6
Marina di Ginosa [I] 122 E4
Marina di Gioiosa Iónica [I] 124 D7
Marina di Grosseto [I] 114 F3
Marina di Léuca [I] 122 G6
Marina di Massa [I] 110 D4
Marina di Pietrasanta [I] 110 D5
Marina di Pisa [I] 110 D5
Marina di Ragusa [I] 126 F5
Marina di Ravenna [I] 110 H3
Marina di San Vito [I] 116 E4
Marina di Vasto [I] 116 E5
Mar'ina Horka [BY] 202 B5
Marina Palmense [I] 116 D2
Marina Romea [I] 110 H3
Marine de Sisco [F] 114 C2
Marinella [I] 126 B3
Marineo [I] 126 D2
Marines [F] 42 F2
Maringues [F] 68 D2
Marinha Grande [P] 86 C3
Marinhais [P] 86 C5
Mar'insko [RUS] 198 G2
Mariotto [I] 122 D3
Maristella [I] 118 B3
Märjamaa [EST] 198 D2
Marjaniemi [FIN] 196 C4
Marjovaara [FIN] 188 G2
Markaryd [S] 162 C6
Markdorf [D] 58 H4
Market Deeping [GB] 14 E1
Market Drayton [GB] 10 D5
Market Harborough [GB] 14 E2
Markethill [NIR] 2 F4
Market Rasen [GB] 10 G5
Market Weighton [GB] 10 G4
Marki [PL] 38 B3
Markina-Xemein [E] 82 H4
Märkisch Buchholz [D] 34 E3
Markitta [S] 192 H6
Markkina [FIN] 192 H4
Markkina [FIN] 192 H4
Markleugast [D] 46 H3
Markneukirchen [D] 48 C3
Markop [N] 194 B2
Markópoulo [GR] 136 H1
Markópoulo [GR] 136 A1
Markovac [YU] 150 C1
Markova Sušica [MK] 128 E1
Markovci pri Ptuju [SLO] 74 E4
Markovo Manastir [MK] 128 E1
Markovo Kale [YU] 150 D5
Markranstädt [D] 34 C5
Marksburg [D] 46 B2
Markt Bibart [D] 46 F4
Marktbreit [D] 46 E4
Markt Erlbach [D] 46 F5
Marktheidenfeld [D] 46 E4
Markt-Indersdorf [D] 60 E3
Marktjärn [S] 184 D4
Marktl [D] 60 G4
Marktoberdorf [D] 60 C5
Marktredwitz [D] 48 C4
Markt St Florian [A] 62 B4
Markt St Martin [A] 62 F6
Marktzeuln [D] 46 G3
Markušica [HR] 154 E1
Marl [D] 30 H2
Marlborough [GB] 12 H3
Marle [F] 28 G5
Marlenheim [F] 44 G6
Marlens [F] 70 B3
Marlow [D] 20 C3
Marma [S] 174 E4
Marmande [F] 66 E4
Marmara [TR] 146 C4
Marmaraereğlisi [TR] 146 D3
Marmári [GR] 134 D6
Marmaris [TR] 142 E3
Mármaro [GR] 134 G4
Marmelete [P] 94 B4
Marmolejo [E] 102 D1
Marmore, Cascata delle- [I] 116 A3
Marmoutier [F] 44 G5
Marmuri, Grotta su- [I] 118 D5
Marnay [F] 58 A4
Marne [D] 18 E3
Marnitz [D] 20 B5
Maróneia [GR] 130 F3
Maroslele [H] 76 E4
Maróstica [I] 72 D5
Marotta [I] 112 C6
Marpíssa [GR] 138 E3
Marquartstein [D] 60 F5
Marquion [F] 28 F4
Marquise [F] 14 G6
Marradi [I] 110 F5
Marrasjärvi [FIN] 194 C7
Marrebæk [DK] 20 B1
Marsala [I] 126 B2
Marsberg [D] 32 E4
Marschlins [CH] 58 H6
Marsciano [I] 116 A2
Marseillan [F] 106 E4
Marseillan-Plage [F] 106 E5
Marseille [F] 106 H5
Marseille-en-Beauvaisis [F] 28 D5
Marshavitsy [RUS] 198 H4
Marsico Nuovo [I] 120 G4
Marsico Vetere [I] 120 H4
Marsiliana [I] 114 F3
Marsliden [S] 190 E4
Märsta [S] 168 D2
Marstal [DK] 156 D4
Marstrand [S] 160 G1
Märsylä [FIN] 196 C5
Marta [I] 114 G3
Martano [I] 122 G5
Martel [F] 66 G3
Martelange [B] 44 E2
Marten [BG] 148 D1
Marttiü [H] 76 E2
Marthon [F] 66 F1
Martigné-Ferchaud [F] 40 G5
Martigny [CH] 70 C2
Martigues [F] 106 H5
Martim Longo [P] 94 D4
Martin [SK] 64 C2
Martina / Martinsbruck [CH] 72 B2
Martina Franca [I] 122 E3
Martín de Yeltes [E] 88 B3
Martinniemi [FIN] 196 D3
Martíno [GR] 134 B5
Martinsbruck / Martina [CH] 72 B2
Martinsicuro [I] 116 D3
Mártis [I] 118 C3
Martjanci [SLO] 74 E3
Martna [EST] 198 D2
Martock [GB] 12 F4
Martofte [DK] 156 E3
Martonvaara [FIN] 188 F1
Martonvásár [H] 76 C1
Martorell [E] 92 D4
Martos [E] 102 D2
Mårtsviken [S] 172 E3
Martti [FIN] 194 E6
Marttila [FIN] 176 E4
Maruševec [HR] 74 E4
Marvão [P] 86 F5
Marvejols [F] 68 C5
Marwald [PL] 22 G5
Marxwalde [D] 34 F2
Marxzell [D] 46 B6
Marynin [PL] 38 F5
Maryport [GB] 8 D6
Marzabotto [I] 110 F4
Marzahna [D] 34 D3
Marzahne [D] 34 D2
Marzamemi [I] 126 G6
Marzocca [I] 112 C6
Maschen [D] 18 F5
Mas d'Azil, Grotte du- [F] 84 H4
Mas de Barberans [E] 92 A5
Mas de las Matas [E] 90 F6
Masegoso de Tajuña [E] 90 A5
Maser [I] 72 E5
Masevaux [F] 58 D3
Masi [N] 194 B4
Maside [E] 78 C4
Masi Torello [I] 110 G3
Maskjok [N] 194 D2
Masku [FIN] 176 D4
Maslenica [HR] 112 G4
Maslovare [BiH] 154 C3
Maso [FIN] 186 G3
Maspalomas [E] 100 C6
Massa [I] 110 D4
Massa Fiscaglia [I] 110 G3
Massafra [I] 122 E4
Massa Lubrense [I] 120 E4
Massamagrell [E] 98 F4
Massa Marittima [I] 114 F2
Massat [F] 84 H5
Massay [F] 56 B3
Masseret [F] 66 G2
Masseube [F] 84 G3
Massiac [F] 68 C3
Mastaura [TR] 144 E5
Masterelv [N] 194 B2
Mastergeehy [IRL] 4 A4
Masterud [N] 172 D5
Mas Thibert [F] 106 G4
Mastichári [GR] 142 B3
Mästocka [S] 162 B5
Masty [BY] 24 G4
Masugnsbyn [S] 192 H5
Maszewo [PL] 34 G3
Maszewo [PL] 20 G5
Matabuena [E] 88 G4
Matala [GR] 140 D5
Matalebreras [E] 84 A6
Matallana de Torío [E] 82 B5
Matara [FIN] 188 E1
Mataragka [GR] 132 F2
Mataró [E] 92 E4
Mataruška Banja [YU] 150 B3
Mätäsvaara [FIN] 196 G6
Matejče, Manastir- [MK] 150 D6
Matelica [I] 116 B2
Matera [I] 122 D4
Matersdalen [N] 170 B5
Mateševo [YU] 152 E3
Mátészalka [H] 204 B3
Matfors [S] 184 E5
Matha [F] 54 D5
Mathay [F] 58 C4
Mathildedal [FIN] 176 E5
Matignon [F] 26 B4
Matiši [LV] 198 E4
Matka [MK] 128 E1
Matka, Manastir- [MK] 128 E1
Matkavaara [FIN] 196 F4
Matlock [GB] 10 E5
Matos [P] 94 D3
Matosinhos [P] 80 B4
Matour [F] 56 F6
Mátrafüred [H] 64 E5
Mátraháza [H] 64 E5
Matre [N] 170 B5
Matre [N] 170 B2
Matrei am Brenner [A] 72 D1
Matrei in Osttirol [A] 72 F2
Matrosovo [RUS] 200 D5
Mattaur [S] 190 G2
Matteröd [S] 158 C1
Mattersburg [A] 62 F6
Mattighofen [A] 60 G4
Mattila [FIN] 188 E6
Mattilanmäki [FIN] 194 E7
Mattinata [I] 116 H6
Mattinen [FIN] 176 C4
Mattsee [A] 60 G5
Mättsund [S] 196 B3
Matulji [HR] 112 E1
Matyli [BY] 24 G3
Matzen [A] 60 E6
Matzen [A] 62 F4
Maubeuge [F] 28 G4
Maubourguet [F] 84 F3
Mauchline [GB] 8 D4
Mauerkirchen [A] 60 H4
Maukdal [N] 192 F3
Maula [FIN] 196 C2
Maulbronn [D] 46 C6
Mauléon [F] 54 D2
Mauléon-Licharre [F] 84 D3
Maulévrier [F] 54 D2
Maumtrasna [IRL] 2 B4
Maunujärvi [FIN] 194 C6
Maupas, Château de- [F] 56 C3
Maupertus-sur-Mer [F] 26 D2
Maura [N] 172 B5
Maure [F] 26 B6
Mauriac [F] 68 B3
Maurnes [N] 192 D3
Mauron [F] 26 B6
Maurs [F] 66 H5
Maurstad [N] 180 B5
Maurvangen [N] 170 F1
Maury [F] 106 C6
Mausoleo de Fabara [E] 90 G5
Mautern [A] 74 C1
Mauterndorf [A] 72 H2
Mauth [D] 62 A2
Mauthausen [A] 62 C4
Mauvezin [F] 84 G2
Mauvoisin [CH] 70 D3
Mauzé-sur-le-Mignon [F] 54 C4
Mavréli [GR] 132 F1
Mavrochóri [GR] 128 E5
Mavroklísi [GR] 130 H2
Mavroléfki [GR] 130 D3
Mavromáta [GR] 132 F3
Mavrommáti [GR] 136 D3
Mavrothálassa [GR] 130 C3
Mavrovi Hanovi [MK] 128 D2
Mavrovo [MK] 128 D2
Mavrovoúni [GR] 136 E5
Mavrovoúni [GR] 132 G2
Maximiliana [E] 102 C4
Maximilians-Grotte [D] 46 H5
Maxmo [FIN] 186 B2
Maybole [GB] 8 C4
Mayen [D] 30 H6
Mayenne [F] 26 E6
Mayet [F] 42 B6
Maynooth [IRL] 2 F6
Mayoralgo [E] 86 H5
Mayorga [E] 82 B5
Mayrhofen [A] 72 E1
Mäyry [FIN] 186 D3
Mazagón [E] 94 E6
Mazamet [F] 106 C4
Mazara del Vallo [I] 126 B3
Mazarrón [E] 104 B4
Mažeikiai [LT] 198 C6
Mazères [F] 106 A4
Mazerulles [F] 44 F5
Mázia [GR] 132 D2
Maziha [RUS] 198 G2
Mazıköy [TR] 142 D2
Mazilmaja [LV] 198 B6
Mazirbe [LV] 198 C4
Mazsalaca [LV] 198 E3
Mazurki [PL] 38 C4
Mazyr [BY] 202 B7
Mazzalve [LV] 198 E6
Mazzarino [I] 126 E4
Mazzarò [I] 124 B8
Mazzarrone [I] 126 F5
M. D. de la Salut [E] 92 F3
M. D. de Pinós [E] 92 D3
M. D. de Queralt [E] 92 D2
Mdzewo [PL] 22 G6
Mealhada [P] 80 B6
Méandre de Queuille [F] 68 C1
Meaux [F] 42 G3
Mechelen (Malines) [B] 30 C3
Mechernich [D] 30 G5
Mechowo [PL] 20 F4
Męcikal [PL] 22 C4
Meckenbeuren [D] 58 H4
Meda [P] 80 E5
Medak [HR] 112 G4
Mede [I] 70 F6
Medebach [D] 32 D5
Medelim [P] 86 F3
Medellín [E] 96 A3
Medelser Schlucht [CH] 70 G1
Medemblik [NL] 16 E3
Medena Selišta [BiH] 154 B4
Meden Rudnik [BG] 148 F4
Medenychi [UA] 52 H5
Medet [TR] 144 G6
Medevi [S] 166 G5
Medgidia [RO] 204 D6
Medgyesegyháza [H] 76 G3
Medhamn [S] 166 F3
Mediaș [RO] 204 C5
Medicina [I] 110 G3
Medina Azahara [E] 102 C1
Medinaceli [E] 90 B4
Medina del Campo [E] 88 E2
Medina de Pomar [E] 82 F4
Medina de Rioseco [E] 82 B6
Medina-Sidonia [E] 100 G4
Medininkai [LT] 200 G5
Medle [S] 196 A4
Médous, Grotte de- [F] 84 F4
Médousa [GR] 130 E2
Medskogen [S] 172 D4
Medstugan [S] 182 E1
Medugorje [BiH] 152 C2
Medulin [HR] 112 D3
Medvedja [YU] 150 D4
Medved'ov [SK] 62 H5
Medvida [HR] 112 H5
Medvode [SLO] 74 B5
Medyka [PL] 52 F4
Medzilaborce [SK] 52 E6
Medžitlija [MK] 128 E4
Meerane [D] 48 C1
Meersburg [D] 58 H4
Meeuwen [B] 30 E3
Mefjordvær [N] 192 E2
Méga Chorió [GR] 132 F4
Méga Déreio [GR] 130 G2
Méga Doukáto [GR] 130 F3
Megáli Vólvi [GR] 130 B4
Megalochóri [GR] 132 F2
Megálo Chorió [GR] 142 C4
Megálo Livádi [GR] 138 C3
Megalópoli [GR] 136 D3
Mégara [GR] 134 B6
Megara Hyblaea [I] 126 G4
Méga Spílaio [GR] 132 G6
Megève [F] 70 B3
Megísti [GR] 142 H4
Megístis Lávras, Moní- [GR] 130 D5
Megorjelo [BiH] 152 C3
Meg. Panagía [GR] 130 C5
Megyaszó [H] 64 F4
Mehadia [RO] 204 A6
Mehamn [N] 194 D1
Mehikoorma [EST] 198 G3
Mehov Krš [YU] 150 B4
Mehtäkylä [FIN] 196 C5
Mohun-sur-Yèvre [F] 56 B3
Meijel [NL] 30 F3
Meilen [CH] 58 F5
Meillant, Château de- [F] 56 C4
Meilleraye, Abbaye de- [F] 40 F5
Meina [I] 70 F4
Meine [D] 32 H2
Meinerzhagen [D] 32 C5
Meiningen [D] 46 F2
Meira [E] 78 E3
Meirāni [LV] 198 F5
Meiringen [CH] 70 E1
Meisenheim [D] 44 H3
Meisingset [N] 180 F2
Meissen [D] 34 E6
Meitingen [D] 60 D3
Męka [PL] 36 F5
Mekrijärvi [FIN] 188 H2
Mel [I] 72 E4
Mélampes [GR] 140 D5
Melaniós [GR] 134 G4
Meláties [GR] 132 D3
Melbeck [D] 18 G5
Melbu [N] 192 D4
Meldal [N] 180 H2
Meldola [I] 110 G4
Meldorf [D] 18 E2
Melegnano [I] 70 G5
Melenci [YU] 76 E6
Melene [TR] 144 B2
Melfi [I] 120 G3
Melgaço [P] 78 C5
Melgar de Arriba [E] 82 C5
Melgar de Fernamental [E] 82 D5
Melgarejo [E] 100 G3
Melhus [N] 182 B1
Melide [E] 78 D3
Melides [P] 94 B2
Meligalás [GR] 136 D3
Meliki [GR] 128 G5
Melilli [I] 126 G4
Melisenda [I] 118 E6
Mélisey [F] 58 C3
Melíssa [GR] 130 E3
Melissáni [GR] 132 C6
Melíssi [GR] 132 E1
Melissópetra [GR] 128 D6
Melissourgós [GR] 130 B4
Melito di Porto Salvo [I] 124 C8
Melitopol' [UA] 204 H4
Melívoia [GR] 130 E2
Melk [A] 62 D4
Melksham [GB] 12 G3
Mellakoski [FIN] 194 C8
Mellansel [S] 184 F1
Mellansjö [S] 184 C5
Mellanström [S] 190 G3
Mellau [A] 60 B6
Mellby [S] 162 E3
Mellbystrand [S] 162 B5
Melle [D] 32 D2
Melle [F] 54 D5
Mellendorf [D] 32 F1
Mellerud [S] 166 D5
Mellieha [M] 126 C6
Mellifont Abbey [IRL] 2 F5
Mellilä [FIN] 176 E3
Mellin [D] 34 A1
Mellrichstadt [D] 46 F2
Mellstaby [S] 158 G1
Melnica [YU] 150 C1
Melnik [BG] 130 B2
Mělník [CZ] 48 F3
Mel'nikovo [RUS] 178 G2
Melrose [GB] 8 F4
Melsomvik [N] 164 H3
Melsungen [D] 32 F5
Meltaus [FIN] 194 C7
Melton Mowbray [GB] 10 F6
Meltosjärvi [FIN] 194 C8
Melun [F] 42 G4
Melvich [GB] 6 E2
Mélykút [H] 76 D4
Melzo [I] 70 G5
Membrilla [E] 96 F4
Membrío [E] 86 F4
Memmingen [D] 60 B4
Mena [UA] 202 D7
Menággio [I] 70 G3
Menai Bridge [GB] 10 B4
Menasalbas [E] 96 E2
Menat [F] 56 C6
Mendavia [E] 82 H6
Mende [F] 68 C6
Menden [D] 32 C4
Menderes [TR] 144 C4
Mendig [D] 30 H6
Mendryka [CZ] 50 B4
Menec [F] 40 D5
Menemen [TR] 144 C4
Menen [B] 28 F2
Menesjärvi [FIN] 194 D4
Menetés [GR] 140 H3
Ménez Hom [F] 40 B2
Menfi [I] 126 C3
Ménfőcsanak [H] 62 H6
Menga, Cueva de- [E] 102 C4
Mengamuñoz [E] 88 D4
Mengen [D] 58 H3
Mengeš [SLO] 74 C4
Mengíbar [E] 102 E1
Mengishevo [BG] 148 E3
Menídi [GR] 132 D3
Ménina [GR] 132 C2
Menonen [FIN] 176 F3
Mens [F] 68 H6
Menstrup [DK] 156 F4
Menthon [F] 70 B3
Menton [F] 108 F4
Méntrida [E] 88 E6
Menyushi [RUS] 198 G1
Menz [D] 20 C6
Meppel [NL] 16 F3
Meppen [D] 16 H4
Mequinenza [E] 90 G5
Mequinenza, Castillo de- [E] 90 G5
Mer [F] 54 H1
Mera de Boixo [E] 78 D1
Meråker [N] 182 D1
Meran / Merano [I] 72 D3
Merano / Meran [I] 72 D3
Merate [I] 70 G4
Mercatale [I] 114 H1
Mercatino Conca [I] 110 H5
Mercato San Severino [I] 120 F3
Mercato Saraceno [I] 110 G5
Merćez [YU] 150 C4
Merdrignac [F] 26 B5
Méréville [F] 42 F5
Mergozzo [I] 70 F3
Méribel [F] 70 B4
Méribel-les-Allues [F] 70 B4
Meriç [TR] 130 H2
Mérichas [GR] 138 C2
Merichleri [BG] 148 C5
Mérida [E] 94 H2
Merijärvi [FIN] 196 C5
Merikarvia / Sastmola [FIN] 186 B6
Merimasku [FIN] 176 D4
Měřín [CZ] 50 A5
Mering [D] 60 D4
Merkendorf [D] 46 F6
Merkine [LT] 24 G2
Merklingen [D] 60 B3
Merlara [I] 110 F1
Merle, Tours de- [F] 66 H4
Merligen [CH] 70 E1
Mern [DK] 156 G4
Mernye [H] 76 A4
Mersch [D] 30 F4
Mersch [L] 44 F2
Merseburg [D] 34 C5
Mersinbeleni [TR] 144 D6
Mērsrags [LV] 198 C4
Merthyr Tydfil [GB] 12 F2
Mértola [P] 94 D4
Méru [F] 42 F2
Mervans [F] 56 G5
Merville [F] 28 E3
Méry [F] 44 A5
Meryemana [TR] 144 D5
Merzig [D] 44 F3
Mesagne [I] 122 F4
Mesão Frio [P] 80 D4
Mesariá [GR] 138 D1
Meschede [D] 32 D5
Meschers-sur-Gironde [F] 54 C6
Meseišta [MK] 128 D3
Mesenikólas [GR] 132 F3
Meshchovsk [RUS] 202 E5
Mési [GR] 130 F3
Mesinge [DK] 156 E3
Mesklá [GR] 140 C4
Meslay [F] 40 H5
Mesnalien [N] 172 B2
Mesnil-Val [F] 28 C4
Mesocco [CH] 70 G2
Mesochóra [GR] 132 E2
Mesochóri [GR] 132 F1
Mesola [I] 110 H2
Mesolóngi [GR] 132 E5
Mesón do Vento [E] 78 C2
Mesopótamo [GR] 132 C3
Mespelbrunn [D] 46 D3
Messdorf [D] 34 B1
Messelt [N] 172 C1
Messimvría [GR] 130 G3
Messina [I] 124 B7
Messines de Baixo [P] 94 C5
Messíni [GR] 136 D4
Messkirch [D] 58 G3
Messlingen [S] 182 E3
Messtetten [D] 58 G3
Mestá [GR] 134 G5
Mestanza [E] 96 E5
Městec Králové [CZ] 48 H3
Mestervik [N] 192 F2
Mestervik [N] 192 F2
Mésti [GR] 130 G3
Mestilä [FIN] 176 D3
Mestlin [D] 20 B4
Město Albrechtice [CZ] 50 D3
Město Libavá [CZ] 50 D5
Mestre [I] 72 E6
Mesvres [F] 56 F5
Mesztegnyő [H] 74 H4
Metabief [F] 58 B6
Metagkitsi [GR] 130 C5
Metajka [YU] 152 E2
Metamórfosi [GR] 130 C5
Metanjac [YU] 150 A4
Metapontium [I] 122 D4
Metaxádes [GR] 130 H1
Metaxás [GR] 128 F6
Metéora [GR] 132 E1
Méteren [F] 28 F2
Méthana [GR] 136 G2
Methóni [GR] 136 C4
Methóni [GR] 128 G5
Metković [HR] 152 C3
Metlika [SLO] 74 D6
Metnitz [A] 74 B2
Metóchi [GR] 132 E6
Metóchi [GR] 134 A3
Metsäkylä [FIN] 178 C3
Metsäkylä [FIN] 196 F3
Metsälä / Ömossa [FIN] 186 B5
Metsküla [EST] 198 C3
Métsovon [GR] 132 D1
Metten [D] 60 G2
Mettet [B] 30 C5
Mettingen [D] 32 C2
Mettlach [D] 44 F3
Mettmann [D] 30 G3
Metz [F] 44 E4
Metzervisse [F] 44 F3
Metzingen [D] 58 H2
Meulan [F] 42 F3
Meung-sur-Loire [F] 42 E6
Meuselwitz [D] 34 C6
Meux [B] 30 D5
Mevik [N] 190 D1
Mexilhoeira Grande [P] 94 B5
Meximieux [F] 68 G2
Meyenburg [D] 20 B5
Meymac [F] 68 B2
Meyrargues [F] 108 B4
Meyrueis [F] 106 E2
Meyzieu [F] 68 G3
Mézapos [GR] 136 E5
Mezdra [BG] 150 G4
Mèze [F] 106 E4
Mézel [F] 108 D3
Mężenin [PL] 24 D6
Mežica [SLO] 74 C4
Mézières [F] 54 F5
Mézières-en-Brenne [F] 54 G4
Mézilhac [F] 68 E5
Mézin [F] 66 D6
Mezőberény [H] 76 G3
Mezőcsát [H] 64 F5
Mezőhegyes [H] 76 F4
Mezőhék [H] 76 E5
Mezőkeresztes [H] 64 F5
Mezőkovácsháza [H] 76 F4
Mezőkövesd [H] 64 F5
Mezőnyárád [H] 64 F5
Mezőörs [H] 64 A6
Mézos [F] 66 B5
Mezőszilas [H] 76 B3
Mezőtúr [H] 76 F2
Mezquita de Jarque [E] 90 E6
Mezzojuso [I] 126 D2
Mezzolombardo [I] 72 C4
Mgarr [M] 126 C5
Miączyn [PL] 52 G1
Miajadas [E] 86 H6
Miami Platja [E] 90 H6
Mianowice [PL] 22 C2
Miasteczko Śląskie [PL] 50 F2
Miastko [PL] 22 B3
Michałkowo [PL] 24 B2
Michalovce [SK] 64 H2
Michałów [PL] 38 C6
Michałowo [PL] 24 F6
Micheldorf [A] 62 B5
Michelstadt [D] 46 D4
Michendorf [D] 34 D3
Michów [PL] 38 D5
Middelburg [NL] 16 B6
Middelfart [DK] 156 C3
Middelharnis [NL] 16 C5
Middelkerke-Bad [B] 28 F1
Middlesbrough [GB] 10 F2
Middlewich [GB] 10 D4
Midhurst [GB] 14 D5
Midleton [IRL] 4 D5
Midlum [D] 18 D3
Midsland [NL] 16 E1
Midstkogberget [N] 172 D2
Midsund [N] 180 D3
Midtgulen [N] 180 B5
Miechów [PL] 50 H3
Mieders [A] 72 D1
Miedes [E] 90 D4
Międzdroje [PL] 20 F3
Miedźno [PL] 50 G1
Międzybórz [PL] 36 D5
Międzybrodzie Bialskie [PL] 50 G4
Międzychód [PL] 36 B2
Międzygórze [PL] 50 C3
Międzylesie [PL] 50 C3
Międzyrzec Podlaski [PL] 38 E3
Międzyrzecz [PL] 36 A2
Miedzywodzie [PL] 20 F3
Miehikkälä [FIN] 178 D3
Miejsce Piastowe [PL] 52 D5
Miejska Górka [PL] 36 C5
Miélan [F] 84 F3
Mielec [PL] 52 D3
Mielno [PL] 20 H3
Mieluskylä [FIN] 196 D5
Mierasjärvi [FIN] 194 D3
Mieraslompolo [FIN] 194 D3
Miercurea Ciuc [RO] 204 C5
Mieres [E] 78 H4
Mierkenis [S] 190 F1
Mieron [N] 194 B4
Mieroszów [PL] 50 B2
Miersig [RO] 76 H2
Mierzyno [PL] 22 D1
Miesbach [D] 60 E5
Mieścisko [PL] 36 D2
Mieste [D] 34 B2
Miesterhorst [D] 34 A2
Mieszkowice [PL] 34 G1
Mietoinen [FIN] 176 D4
Mifol [AL] 128 A5
Migennes [F] 42 H6
Migliarino [I] 110 G3
Migliarino [I] 110 D5
Migliónico [I] 122 D4
Mignano Monte Lungo [I] 120 D1
Miguel Esteban [E] 96 G3
Mihăești [RO] 148 B1
Mihai Bravu [RO] 148 C1
Mihajlovac [YU] 150 E1
Mihalgazi [TR] 146 H4
Mihla [D] 32 G6
Mijas [E] 102 B5
Mijoux [F] 70 A1
Mikaelshulen [N] 164 G3
Mikhaylovo [BG] 150 G3
Mikkelbostad [N] 192 E3
Mikkeli / St Michel [FIN] 188 C6
Mikkelvika [N] 192 F1
Mikolaivka [UA] 204 G6
Mikołajki [PL] 24 C4
Mikołajki Pomorskie [PL] 22 F4
Mikolin [PL] 50 D2
Mikołów [PL] 50 F3
Mikre [BG] 148 A4
Mikró Chorió [GR] 132 F4
Mikró Déreio [GR] 130 G2
Mikrókampos [GR] 128 H4
Mikrópoli [GR] 130 C3
Mikrothíves [GR] 132 H3
Mikstat [PL] 36 E5
Mikulčice [CZ] 62 G3
Mikulov [CZ] 62 F3
Mikulovice [CZ] 50 D3
Miłakowo [PL] 22 G3
Miland [N] 170 F5
Milano [I] 70 G5
Milano Marittima [I] 110 H4
Milanovac [HR] 76 A6
Milanówek [PL] 38 B3
Milâs [TR] 142 D2
Milatos [GR] 140 F4
Milazzo [I] 124 B7
Mildenhall [GB] 14 F2
Milejczyce [PL] 38 F2
Milejewo [PL] 22 F3
Milena [I] 126 D3
Mileševa, Manastir- [YU] 150 A3
Mileševo [YU] 150 A3
Miloševo [YU] 76 E6
Milet [TR] 142 B1
Miletići [HR] 112 G4
Mileto [I] 124 D6
Miletopolis [TR] 146 E4
Milevsko [CZ] 48 F5
Milford [IRL] 2 F2
Milford Haven [GB] 12 D2
Milići [BiH] 154 E4
Milicz [PL] 36 D5
Miliés [GR] 134 A2
Milín [CZ] 48 F5
Milína [GR] 134 A3
Militello in Val di Catania [I] 126 F4
Miljevina [BiH] 152 D2
Millares [E] 98 E5
Millares, Cueva de los- [E] 102 G5
Millas [F] 92 F1
Millau [F] 106 D2
Millbay [GB] 2 H3
Millesimo [I] 108 G3
Millesvik [S] 166 E4
Millevaches [F] 68 B2
Millinge [DK] 156 D4
Millom [GB] 10 D2
Millstatt [A] 72 H3
Millstreet [IRL] 4 C4
Milltown [IRL] 4 B4

Milltown Malbay [IRL] 2 B6
Milluranta [FIN] 196 E5
Milmarcos [E] 90 C5
Milmersdorf [D] 20 D6
Milna [HR] 152 A2
Miločer [YU] 152 D4
Miłomłyn [PL] 22 G4
Milos [GR] 138 D4
Miłosavci [BiH] 154 C2
Miloševa Kula [YU] 150 D1
Miłosław [PL] 36 D3
Milow [D] 20 A5
Milówka [PL] 50 G5
Milreu [P] 94 C5
Milseburg [D] 46 E2
Milštejn [CZ] 48 G1
Miltach [D] 60 D4
Miltenberg [D] 46 D4
Milton Keynes [GB] 14 E3
Milyutino [RUS] 198 H2
Mimizan [F] 66 B4
Mimizan-Plage [F] 66 B4
Mimoň [CZ] 48 G2
Mina de São Domingos [P] 94 D4
Minas de Riotinto [E] 94 F5
Minateda, Cuevas de– [E] 104 B1
Minateda-Horca [E] 104 B1
Minaya [E] 98 B4
Minde [N] 164 C5
Mindelheim [D] 60 C4
Minden [D] 32 E2
Mindin [D] 40 E6
Mindszent [H] 76 E3
Minehead [GB] 12 E3
Mineo [I] 126 F4
Mineralni Bani [BG] 148 C6
Minerbio [I] 110 F3
Minervino di Lecce [I] 122 H5
Minervino Murge [I] 120 H2
Minervio [F] 114 C2
Minglanilla [E] 98 C4
Mingorría [E] 88 E4
Miničevo [YU] 150 E3
Minne [S] 182 H5
Minnesund [N] 172 C4
Mínoa [GR] 138 G4
Minozero [RUS] 196 G4
Minsen [D] 18 C3
Minsk [BY] 202 B5
Mińsk Mazowiecki [PL] 38 C3
Minturnae [I] 120 D2
Minturno [I] 120 D2
Miočić [HR] 154 A5
Miokovićevo [HR] 74 H6
Mionica [YU] 150 A1
Mira [E] 110 H1
Mira [E] 98 D3
Mira [I] 72 E6
Mira [P] 80 B6
Mirabel [E] 86 H4
Mirabella Imbáccari [I] 126 F4
Mirabello [I] 110 F2
Miradolo Terme [I] 70 G6
Mirador del Fito [E] 82 C2
Miraflores [E] 82 E6
Miraflores [E] 96 E4
Miraflores de la Sierra [E] 88 F4
Miramar [F] 108 E5
Miramar [I] 112 B5
Miramare, Castello di– [I] 72 H6
Miramas [F] 106 G4
Mirambeau [F] 66 D2
Miramont-de-Guyenne [F] 66 E4
Miranda [E] 84 B4
Miranda de Ebro [E] 82 G5
Miranda do Corvo [P] 86 D2
Miranda do Douro [P] 80 G4
Mirande [F] 84 F3
Mirandela [P] 80 E4
Mirándola [I] 110 F2
Mirano [I] 72 E6
Mirantes [E] 78 G5
Miravet [E] 90 H6
Mirebeau [F] 54 E3
Mirebeau [F] 56 H3
Mirecourt [F] 44 E6
Mirepoix [F] 106 B5
Miróbriga [P] 94 B4
Mirosławiec [PL] 20 H5
Mirošov [CZ] 48 E5
Mirovice [CZ] 48 F5
Mirovo [BG] 150 G5
Mirów [PL] 50 G2
Mirow [PL] 50 G2
Mirsk [PL] 48 H1
Mirto [I] 124 E3
Mirueña [E] 88 D4
Misi [FIN] 194 D7
Misilmeri [I] 126 D2
Miskolc [H] 64 F4
Miskolctapolca [H] 64 F5
Mislata [E] 98 E4
Mislinja [SLO] 74 D4
Misso [EST] 198 F4
Mistelbach [A] 62 F3
Misten [N] 192 D5
Misterbianco [I] 126 G3
Misterhult [S] 162 G3
Mistretta [I] 126 F2
Misurina [I] 72 E3
Misvær [N] 192 D6
Miszewo [PL] 22 D2
Mitchelstown [IRL] 4 D4
Mitchelstown Caves [IRL] 4 D4
Míthymna [GR] 134 G2
Mitrašinci [MK] 128 G1
Mitrópoli [GR] 132 F3
Mittådalen [S] 182 E3
Mittelberg [A] 72 B1
Mittelberg [A] 60 B6
Mittelberg [D] 60 D6
Mittenwald [D] 60 D6
Mittenwalde [D] 20 D5
Mittenwalde [D] 34 E3
Mittersill [A] 72 F1
Mitterteich [D] 48 C4
Mittet [N] 180 E3
Mittewald [A] 72 F3
Mittweida [D] 48 D1
Mitwitz [D] 46 G3
Mizhiria [UA] 204 B3
Mizil [RO] 204 D5
Miziya [BG] 150 G2
Mjåland [N] 164 E4
Mjällby [S] 158 E2
Mjällom [S] 184 G3
Mjell [N] 170 C1
Mjöbäck [S] 162 B3

Mjölby [S] 166 H6
Mjølfjell [N] 170 D3
Mjölkbäcken [S] 190 E2
Mjölkvattnet [S] 190 D6
Mjönäs [S] 166 F1
Mjøndalen [N] 164 G1
Mjønes [N] 180 H1
Mjørlund [N] 172 B4
Mjösebo [S] 162 F4
Mjösjöby [S] 190 G6
M. Kalývia [GR] 132 F2
Mladá Boleslav [CZ] 48 G3
Mladá Vožice [CZ] 48 G5
Mladé Buky [CZ] 50 A2
Mladečské Jeskyně [CZ] 50 C5
Mladenovac [YU] 150 B1
Mlado Nagoričane [MK] 150 D6
Mława [PL] 22 G6
Mleczno [PL] 36 B5
Mlekarevo [BG] 148 D5
Mlini [HR] 152 C4
Młodasko [PL] 36 B2
Młogoszyn [PL] 36 G3
Mnary [PL] 22 F3
Młynarze [PL] 24 C6
Mnich [CZ] 48 G6
Mnichovice [CZ] 48 G4
Mnichovo Hradiště [CZ] 48 G2
Mnichów [PL] 52 B2
Mniów [PL] 52 B2
Mníšek pod Brdy [CZ] 48 F4
Mniszek [PL] 38 B5
Mo [N] 172 C4
Mo [N] 180 D4
Mo [N] 164 D2
Mo [S] 184 E2
Mo [S] 166 G3
Mo [S] 166 D3
Mo [S] 174 E2
Mo [S] 166 C4
Moaña [E] 78 B4
Moate [IRL] 2 D4
Moča [SK] 64 B5
Mocejón [E] 96 F1
Móchlos [GR] 140 G4
Mochós [GR] 140 F4
Mochowo [PL] 36 G1
Mochy [PL] 36 B3
Möckern [D] 34 C3
Mockfjärd [S] 172 H4
Möckmühl [D] 46 D5
Moclín [E] 102 D3
Modane [F] 70 B5
Modave [B] 30 D5
Módena [I] 110 E3
Módi [GR] 132 H4
Módica [I] 126 F5
Modigliana [I] 110 G4
Modliborzyce [PL] 52 E1
Mödling [A] 62 F5
Modliszewki [PL] 36 D2
Mönchengladbach [D] 30 G3
Mönchhof [A] 62 G4
Mónchio delle Corti [I] 110 D3
Monchique [P] 94 B4
Monclova [E] 102 B2
Moncofa [E] 98 F4
Moncontour [F] 26 B5
Moncoutant [F] 54 D3
Mondaríz [E] 78 B4
Mondaríz-Balneario [E] 78 B5
Mondaye, Abbaye de– [F] 26 E3
Mondéjar [E] 88 G6
Mondello [I] 126 C1
Mondim de Basto [P] 80 D4
Mondolfo [I] 112 C6
Mondoñedo [E] 78 E2
Mondorf-les-Bains [L] 44 F3
Mondoubleau [F] 42 C5
Mondoví [I] 108 G3
Mondragone [I] 120 D2
Mondsee [A] 60 H5
Monéglia [I] 110 C4
Monegrillo [E] 90 F4
Monemvasía [GR] 136 F5
Monesi [I] 108 F3
Monesterio [E] 94 G4
Monestier-de-Clermont [F] 68 G5
Monétier-Allemont [F] 108 C2
Moneygall [IRL] 2 D6
Moneymore [NIR] 2 F3
Monfalcone [I] 72 H5
Monfarracinos [E] 80 H5
Monfero [E] 78 D2
Monflanquin [F] 66 F5
Monforte [P] 86 E6
Monforte da Beira [P] 86 F4
Monforte de Lemos [E] 78 D4
Mongstad [N] 170 A2
Monguelfo / Welsberg [I] 72 E3
Monheim [D] 60 D2
Monheim [D] 30 G4
Mónichkirchen [A] 62 E6
Moní Eleónis [GR] 136 F3
Möniste [EST] 198 F4
Monistrol-d'Allier [F] 68 D4
Monistrol de Montserrat [E] 92 D4
Monistrol-sur-Loire [F] 68 E4
Monívea [IRL] 2 C5
Mónki [PL] 24 E5
Monmouth [GB] 12 G2
Mönni [FIN] 188 F2
Monnickendam [NL] 16 D4
Monninkylä [FIN] 178 A4
Monodéndri [GR] 132 C1
Monódryo [GR] 134 C4
Monólithos [GR] 142 D5
Monópoli [I] 122 E3
Monor [H] 76 D1
Monóvar / Monòver [E] 104 D2
Monóver / Monòvar [E] 104 D2
Monpazier [F] 66 F4
Monplaisir [F] 42 C5
Monreal [E] 96 G2
Monreal / Elo [E] 84 B4
Monreal del Campo [E] 90 D6
Monreale [I] 126 C2
Monroy [E] 86 H5
Monroyo [E] 98 G1
Mons (Bergen) [B] 28 G4
Monsanto [P] 86 G3
Monsaraz [P] 94 E3
Monschau [D] 30 F5
Monségur [F] 66 E4
Monsélice [I] 110 G1
Monsheim [D] 46 B4
Mønsted [DK] 160 D5
Mönsterås [S] 162 G4
Monsummano Terme [I] 110 E5
Montabaur [D] 46 B2

Molfetta [I] 122 D2
Montagnana [I] 110 F1
Montaigu [F] 54 C2
Montaigu-de-Quercy [F] 66 F5
Montaigut [F] 56 C6
Montaione [I] 110 E6
Montalbán [E] 96 E2
Montalbán [P] 94 E4
Montalbano Elicona [I] 124 A6
Montalbano Jónico [I] 122 D5
Montalcino [I] 114 F2
Montalegre [P] 78 C6
Montalieu [F] 68 G3
Montalivet-les-Bains [F] 66 C1
Montallegro [I] 126 C4
Montalto delle Marche [I] 116 C2
Montalto di Castro [I] 114 G4
Montalto Ligure [I] 108 G4
Montalto Uffugo [I] 124 D4
Montalvo [P] 94 C1
Montamarta [I] 80 H4
Montana [BG] 150 F3
Montana [CH] 70 D2
Montañana [E] 90 E4
Montánchez [E] 86 H6
Montanejos [E] 98 F3
Montaren [F] 106 G3
Montargil [P] 86 D5
Montargis [F] 42 F6
Montastruc la-Conseillère [F] 106 A3
Montauban [F] 66 F6
Montauban [F] 26 C5
Montbard [F] 56 F2
Montbazens [F] 66 H5
Montbazon [F] 54 F2
Montbéliard [F] 58 C4
Montbenoît [F] 58 C5
Montblanc [E] 92 C4
Mont-Blanc, Tunnel du– [Eur.] 70 C3
Montbonnot [F] 68 H4
Montbrison [F] 68 E3
Montbron [F] 66 F1
Montbrun-les-Bains [F] 108 B3
Montceau-les-Mines [F] 56 F5
Montchanin [F] 56 F5
Montcornet [F] 28 G6
Montcuq [F] 66 F5
Mont-de-Marsan [F] 66 C6
Montdidier [F] 28 E5
Mont-Dol [F] 26 C4
Monte [I] 100 B3
Montealegre [E] 82 C6
Montealegre del Castillo [E] 98 C6
Monte Arábi, Cueva de– [E] 98 C6
Montebelluna [I] 72 E5
Montebourg [F] 26 D2
Montebruno [I] 110 B3
Monte-Carlo [MC] 108 F4
Montecassino, Abbazia di– [I] 120 D1
Montecatini-Terme [I] 110 E5
Montécchio [I] 112 B5
Montécchio Emilia [I] 110 D3
Montécchio Maggiore [I] 72 E6
Montech [F] 66 F6
Montechiaro, Castello di– [I] 126 D4
Montecorice [I] 120 F5
Montecorvino Rovella [I] 120 F4
Monte da Pedra [P] 86 E4
Montefalco [I] 116 A2
Montefalcone nel Sannio [I] 116 D6
Montefiascone [I] 114 H3
Montefiorentino, Convento di– [I] 110 H6
Montefiorino [I] 110 E4
Monteforte Irpino [I] 120 E3
Montefrío [E] 102 D3
Montegabbione [I] 114 H2
Montegiordano Marina [I] 122 D5
Monte Gordo [P] 94 D5
Montegrotto Terme [I] 110 G1
Montehermoso [E] 86 H3
Monte Isola [I] 72 A5
Montejícar [E] 102 E3
Montelavar [P] 86 B5
Montel-de-Gelat [F] 68 C2
Montélimar [F] 68 F6
Montella [I] 120 F3
Montellano [E] 100 H3
Montemaggiore Belsito [I] 126 D2
Monte Maria, Abbazia di– / Marienberg, Kloster– [I] 72 B2
Montemiccioli, Torre di– [I] 114 F1
Montemolín [E] 94 G4
Montemor-o-Novo [P] 86 C6
Montemor-o-Velho [P] 86 D2
Montemurlo [I] 110 F5
Montendre [F] 66 D2
Montenegro de Cameros [E] 90 B2
Montenero di Bisáccia [I] 116 E5
Monte Oliveto Maggiore, Abbazia di– [I] 114 G2
Montepulciano [I] 114 G2
Montereale [I] 116 B4
Montereale Valcellina [I] 72 F4
Montereau [F] 56 C1
Monte Redondo [P] 86 C2
Monterenzio [I] 110 F4
Monteriggioni [I] 114 F1
Monteroda [P] 32 G5
Monteroni d'Árbia [I] 114 G1
Monteroni di Lecce [I] 122 G5
Monterosso al Mare [I] 110 C4
Monterosso Almo [I] 126 F5
Monterosso Grana [I] 108 F2
Monterotondo [I] 116 A5
Monterotondo Maríttimo [I] 114 E2
Monterroso [E] 78 D3
Monterrubio de la Serena [E] 96 B4
Monte San Biagio [I] 120 C1
Montesano sulla Marcellana [I] 120 G5
Monte San Savino [I] 114 G1
Monte Sant' Ángelo [I] 116 H6
Monte Santiago [E] 82 G4
Montesárchio [I] 120 E2
Montescaglioso [I] 122 D4
Monte Senario, Convento– [I] 110 F5

Montesilvano Marina [I] 116 D4
Montesinos, Los [E] 96 G5
Montesquieu-Volvestre [F] 84 H4
Montesquiou [F] 84 F3
Montevarchi [I] 110 F6
Monteverde [I] 120 G3
Monte Vergine, Santuario di– [I] 120 E3
Montfaucon-en-Velay [F] 68 E4
Montferrat [F] 108 D5
Montfort [F] 66 B6
Montfort [F] 26 C6
Montfort [F] 42 E3
Montgat [E] 92 E4
Mont Gargan [F] 66 H2
Montgenèvre [F] 70 B6
Montgenèvre, Col de– [Eur.] 70 B6
Montgiscard [F] 106 A3
Montguyon [F] 66 D2
Monthermé [F] 44 C1
Monthey [CH] 70 C2
Monthois [F] 44 C3
Monthureaux-sur-Saône [F] 58 B2
Monti [I] 118 D3
Monticelli Terme [I] 110 D3
Montichiari [I] 72 B6
Monticiano [I] 114 F2
Montier-en-Der [F] 44 C5
Montiers [F] 44 D4
Montijo [E] 94 G1
Montijo [P] 86 B5
Montilla [E] 102 C2
Monti-Sion, Santuari de– [E] 104 E5
Montivilliers [F] 26 G3
Montizón [E] 96 G6
Montlieu-la-Garde [F] 66 D2
Mont-Louis [F] 92 E1
Montluçon [F] 56 C5
Montluel [F] 68 G3
Montmajour, Abbaye de– [F] 106 G4
Montmarault [F] 56 C6
Montmédy [F] 44 D3
Montmélian [F] 70 A4
Montmeyan [F] 108 C4
Montmirail [F] 42 C5
Montmirail [F] 42 H4
Montmirey [F] 56 H4
Montmoreau-St-Cybard [F] 66 E2
Montmorillon [F] 54 F4
Montmort [F] 44 A4
Montoire-sur-le-Loir [F] 42 C6
Montoito [P] 94 E3
Montório al Vomano [I] 116 C3
Montoro [E] 102 D1
Montpellier [F] 106 E4
Montpezat-Le-Vieux [F] 106 E2
Montpezat [F] 66 G6
Montpon-Ménéstérol [F] 66 E3
Montpont-en-Bresse [F] 56 G6
Montréal [F] 106 D6
Montréal [F] 106 B4
Montréal [F] 84 F2
Montredon-Labassonnie [F] 106 C3
Montréjeau [F] 84 G3
Montrésor [F] 54 G3
Montresta [I] 118 B4
Montret [F] 56 G5
Montreuil [F] 28 D3
Montreuil-Bellay [F] 54 E2
Montreux [CH] 70 C1
Montrevault [F] 54 C1
Montrevel [F] 68 G1
Montrichard [F] 54 G2
Montroi / Montroy [E] 98 E5
Mont-roig del Camp [E] 90 H6
Montrond-les-Bains [F] 68 E3
Montrose [GB] 8 F2
Montroy / Montroi [E] 98 E5
Montsalvy [F] 68 B4
Montsauche-les-Settons [F] 56 F3
Montseny [E] 92 E3
Montserrat [E] 92 D4
Montsoreau [F] 54 E2
Mont-sous-Vaudrey [F] 56 H5
Monts-s-Guesnes [F] 54 E3
Mont-Ste-Odile [F] 44 G6
Montsûrs [F] 26 E6
Montuenga [E] 88 E3
Monturque [E] 102 C2
Monza [I] 70 G4
Monze [F] 106 C5
Monzón [E] 90 G3
Monzón de Campos [E] 82 D6
Monzuno [I] 110 F4
Moordorf [D] 18 D3
Moordorf [D] 18 F6
Moosburg [D] 60 F3
Moosbkk [N] 166 D1
Mosby [N] 164 D5
Moscavide [P] 86 B5
Moščenica [HR] 154 A1
Moščenice [HR] 112 G2
Moščenička Draga [HR] 112 G2
Moschendorf [A] 74 F2
Moschopótamos [GR] 128 G5
Moscufo [I] 116 D4
Mosédis [LT] 200 D3
Mosina [PL] 36 C3
Mosjö [S] 184 F2
Mosjøen [N] 190 D3
Moškanjci [SLO] 74 E4
Moskog [N] 180 C6
Moskosel [S] 190 H3
Moskva [RUS] 202 F3
Moslavina [HR] 76 A6
Mosonmagyaróvár [H] 62 G5
Mosqueruela [E] 98 F2
Moss [N] 166 B2
Mossberga [S] 172 F1
Mössingen [D] 58 G2
Most [CZ] 48 E2
Mosta [M] 126 C6
Mostar [BiH] 152 C2
Mosteiros [P] 80 E3
Mosterhamn [N] 170 A4
Mostki [PL] 52 C2
Móstoles [E] 88 F6
Mostowo [PL] 22 A3
Mostys'ka [UA] 52 F4
Mosty [PL] 38 F4
Mostyn [GB] 10 C4
Mosvik [N] 190 C6

Mostys'ka [UA] 52 F4
Mosune [HR] 112 F2
Moszczanka [PL] 38 D4
Mota, Cast. de la– [E] 88 E2
Mota del Cuervo [E] 96 H3
Mota del Marqués [E] 88 D1
Motala [S] 166 G5
Motala [S] 166 G5
Motherwell [GB] 8 D3
Motilla del Palancar [E] 98 B3
Motjärnshyttan [S] 166 F1
Motko [RUS] 196 H6
Motovun [HR] 112 E1
Motril [E] 102 E5
Motta di Livenza [I] 72 F5
Motta Visconti [I] 70 F6
Motte-Glain, Château de la– [F] 40 G6
Móttola [I] 122 E4
Möttönen [FIN] 186 E2
Mou [DK] 160 E4
Mouchard [F] 58 A5
Moudon [CH] 70 C1
Moúdros [GR] 130 F6
Mougins [F] 108 E5
Mouhijärvi [FIN] 176 E1
Moulihérne [F] 54 E1
Moulins [F] 56 D5
Moulins-Engilbert [F] 56 E4
Moulins-la-Marche [F] 26 G5
Mountallen [IRL] 2 D4
Mount Bellew [IRL] 2 D5
Mount Charles [IRL] 2 D6
Mountmellick [IRL] 2 E6
Mountrath [IRL] 2 D6
Mountshannon [IRL] 2 C6
Moura [P] 94 E4
Mourão [P] 94 E2
Mouriés [GR] 128 H3
Mouros, Castelo dos– [P] 86 A5
Mouruyärvi [FIN] 194 E8
Mouruyärvi [FIN] 194 E8
Moustiers-Ste-Marie [F] 108 D4
Mouthe [F] 58 B6
Mouthier [F] 58 B5
Mouthoumet [F] 106 C5
Moutier [CH] 58 D5
Moutier-d'Ahun [F] 54 H6
Moûtiers [N] 70 B4
Moûtiers [F] 54 B3
Mouton-Rothschild [F] 66 C2
Moutsoúna [GR] 138 F3
Mouy [F] 28 D6
Mouzakaíoi [GR] 132 D2
Mouzáki [GR] 136 C2
Mouzáki [GR] 132 E2
Mouzon [F] 44 D2
Moville [IRL] 2 F2
Moy [NIR] 2 F3
Moynalty [IRL] 2 F5
Moyne Abbey [IRL] 2 C3
Moyuela [E] 90 E5
Moyvore [IRL] 2 E5
Mozháysk [RUS] 202 E4
Mozia [I] 126 B2
Mozirje [SLO] 74 C4
Mozyr' [RUS] 196 H5
Mozyr' [RUS] 24 C2
Mpalí [GR] 140 D4
Mpampíni [GR] 132 E4
Mpampíni [GR] 132 D5
Mpatsí [GR] 134 E6
Mpórsio [GR] 136 C1
Mpoúkka [GR] 132 C4
Mpráios [GR] 132 D4
Mragowo [PL] 24 B4
Mrakovica [BiH] 154 B2
Mrazovac [BiH] 112 H2
Mrčajevci [YU] 150 B2
Mrežičko [MK] 128 F3
Mrkonjić-Grad [BiH] 154 B3
Mrkopalj [HR] 112 F1
Mrocza [PL] 22 C5
Mroczeń [PL] 36 E6
Mrzeżyno [PL] 20 G3
Mrzygłód [PL] 52 E4
Mšeno [CZ] 48 G3
Mshinskaya [RUS] 198 H1
Mstislavl' [BY] 202 D5
Mstów [PL] 50 H1
Mszana Dolna [PL] 52 A5
Mszczonów [PL] 38 B4
Mt-Dauphin [F] 108 E1
Mt. Melleray Monastery [IRL] 4 D4
Mt. St. Joseph Abbey [IRL] 2 D6
Mtsensk [RUS] 202 F5
Muć [HR] 152 A1
Múccia [I] 116 B2
Much [D] 30 H4
Mücheln [D] 34 B5
Muchówka [PL] 52 B4
Muciélagos, Cava de los– [E] 102 ...
Muckross [IRL] 4 B4
Muckross House [IRL] 4 B4
Mudanya [TR] 146 E4
Mudau [D] 46 D4
Mudela, Castillo de– [E] 96 F5
Müden [D] 18 F6
Mudiske [EST] 198 E2
Müdrets [BG] 148 C4
Muel [E] 90 E4
Muelas del Pan [E] 80 H4
Muezerskiy [RUS] 196 H5
Muff [IRL] 2 F2
Muge [P] 86 C4
Mügeln [D] 34 D6
Muggendorf [D] 46 G4
Múggia [I] 72 H6
Muğla [TR] 142 E2
Müglizh [BG] 148 C4
Mugnano [I] 114 H2
Mugron [F] 66 C6
Mühlacker [D] 46 C6
Mühlbach [A] 72 G1
Mühlberg [D] 34 E5
Mühldorf [D] 60 F3
Mühlhausen [D] 32 G5
Mühlhausen [D] 46 G5
Mühlig-Hofmann-fjella [Ant.] ...
Muhniemi [FIN] 178 B3
Muhos [FIN] 196 D4
Muhovo [BG] 148 A5
Muine Bheag / Bagenalstown [IRL] 4 F4
Muiños [E] 78 C6
Muir of Ord [GB] 6 D5
Mujejärvi [FIN] 196 G5
Mukacheve [UA] 204 B3
Mula [E] 104 B3
Mulazzo [I] 110 C4
Mulba [E] 94 H5
Mulegns [CH] 70 H2

Mülheim [D] 44 G2
Mülheim [D] 30 G3
Müllheim [D] 58 D3
Mujjula [FIN] 188 G4
Müllheim [D] 58 D3
Mullinavat [IRL] 4 E4
Mullingar [IRL] 2 E5
Mullrose [D] 34 G3
Mullsjö [S] 162 C2
Mullyfan [S] 166 G3
Mullyttan [S] 166 G3
Mulseryd [S] 162 C2
Multia [FIN] 186 F4
Multrå [S] 184 E2
Muñana [E] 88 D4
München [D] 48 B3
Müncheberg [D] 34 F2
München [D] 60 B4
Münchhausen [D] 32 D6
Münchhausen [D] 34 E4
Munderkingen [D] 60 B4
Mundheim [N] 170 B4
Munera [E] 96 H5
Mungia [E] 82 G3
Muñico [E] 88 D4
Muniesa [E] 90 E5
Munka-Ljunby [S] 156 H1
Munkebo [DK] 156 E3
Munkedal [S] 166 C5
Munkelven [N] 194 E3
Munkflohögen [S] 182 H1
Munkfors [S] 166 F1
Münnerstadt [D] 46 F3
Munsala [FIN] 186 C1
Münsingen [CH] 58 D6
Münsingen [D] 58 H2
Munsö [S] 168 D3
Münster [CH] 70 E2
Münster [D] 32 C3
Munster [D] 18 F6
Münster [D] 58 D3
Münstertal [D] 58 E3
Münzenberg [D] 46 C2
Münzkirchen [A] 62 A3
Muodoslompolo [S] 194 B6
Muonio [FIN] 194 B6
Muotkalahti [RUS] 194 F6
Muotkavaara [FIN] 194 B6
Muotkavaara [FIN] 194 B6
Muradiye [TR] 144 C4
Murakeresztúr [H] 74 G4
Murán [SK] 64 E3
Murano [I] 72 E6
Muras [E] 78 E2
Murat [F] 68 C4
Muratlar [TR] 142 E1
Muratlı [TR] 146 C2
Murato [F] 114 C3
Murat-sur-Vèbre [F] 106 D3
Murau [A] 74 B2
Muravera [I] 118 E6
Murazzano [I] 108 G2
Murça [P] 80 E4
Mürchevo [BG] 150 F3
Murchin [D] 20 E3
Murcia [E] 104 C3
Murciélagos, Cueva de los– [E] 102 C2
Murciélagos, Cueva de los– [E] 102 E5
Mur–de–Barrez [F] 68 B4
Mur-de-Bretagne [F] 26 A5
Mureck [A] 74 E3
Mürefte [TR] 146 C2
Muret [F] 84 H3
Murgados [E] 78 D1
Murgaševo [MK] 128 E3
Murgia / Murguía [E] 82 G5
Murg-Kraftwerk [D] 58 F1
Murgula / Murgia [E] 82 G5
Muri [CH] 58 F5
Murias de Paredes [E] 78 G4
Murieta [E] 82 H6
Murighiol [RO] 204 E6
Murino [YU] 150 A5
Muriqan [AL] 128 A1
Murjek [S] 196 H2
Murjek [S] 196 H2
Murlo [I] 114 F2
Murnau [D] 60 D5
Muro [E] 104 E4
Muro de Alcoy / Muro del Comtat [E] 104 E1
Muro del Comtat / Muro de Alcoy [E] 104 E1
Murole [FIN] 186 E6
Muro Lucano [I] 120 G3
Muros [E] 78 B3
Murowana Goślina [PL] 36 C2
Mürren [CH] 70 E2
Murrhardt [D] 46 D6
Murrisk Abbey [IRL] 2 B4
Murru [EST] 198 D3
Mursalevo [BG] 150 F6
Murska Sobota [SLO] 74 E3
Mursko Središče [HR] 74 F4
Murta [RO] 150 G2
Murten [CH] 58 D6
Murter [HR] 112 G5
Murtinheira [P] 80 A6
Murtolahti [FIN] 188 D1
Murtosa [P] 80 B5
Murtovaara [FIN] 196 F2
Murtovaara [FIN] 196 F2
Murvica [HR] 112 G5
Mürzsteg [A] 62 D6
Mürzzuschlag [A] 62 E6
Musamaa [FIN] 186 C2
Mussalo [FIN] 178 C4
Musselkanaal [NL] 16 H3
Mussidan [F] 66 E3
Mussomeli [I] 126 D3
Mussy [F] 56 G2
Mustafa Kemal Paşa [TR] 146 E5
Müstair [CH] 72 B3
Mustajärvi [FIN] 186 E5
Mustajõe [EST] 198 G1
Mustalahti [FIN] 186 F5
Mustasaari / Korsholm [FIN] 186 B2
Mustér / Disentis [CH] 70 G1
Mustikkaperä [FIN] 186 F2
Mustinmäki [FIN] 188 D3
Mustinsalo [FIN] 188 D3
Mustla [EST] 198 E3
Mustola [FIN] 194 D4
Mustvee [EST] 198 F2
Muszaki [PL] 22 H5
Muszyna [PL] 52 C5
Muszynka [PL] 52 C5

Mutalahti [FIN] 188 H3
Mutanj [YU] 150 B2
Mutriku [E] 82 H4
Muttalip [TR] 146 H5
Mutterstadt [D] 46 B5
Murame [FIN] 186 G5
Muurasjärvi [FIN] 196 D6
Muurikkala [FIN] 178 D3
Muurla [FIN] 176 F5
Muurola [FIN] 178 D3
Muurola [FIN] 194 C8
Muuruvesi [FIN] 188 D2
Muxia [E] 78 B2
Múzeum Oravskej Dediny [SK] 50 H6
Muzillac [F] 40 E5
Mužla [SK] 64 B5
Mužlja [YU] 154 G1
Myakishevo [RUS] 198 H5
Mybotn [N] 192 E3
Myckelgensjö [S] 184 F1
Myczków [PL] 52 E5
Myhinpää [FIN] 186 H3
Myjava [SK] 62 H3
Mykines [GR] 136 E2
Myking [N] 170 F4
Myklebust [N] 180 D3
Myklebust [N] 180 B5
Myklestøyl [N] 164 D3
Mykolaiv [UA] 204 F4
Mykolaiv [UA] 52 H5
Mykonos [GR] 138 E2
Myllyaho [FIN] 186 F1
Myllykoski [FIN] 178 C3
Myllykselä [FIN] 176 H2
Myllymaa [FIN] 176 E2
Myllymäki [FIN] 186 E4
Myloi [GR] 136 E2
Mylopótamos [GR] 136 F6
Mylund [DK] 160 E3
Mynämäki [FIN] 176 D4
Myndos [TR] 142 C2
Myonnesos [TR] 144 C5
Myos [TR] 142 C1
Myrane [N] 164 B4
Myrås [S] 190 G3
Myrdal [N] 170 D3
Myre [N] 192 D3
Myre [N] 192 E3
Myren [S] 172 E5
Myrhrod [UA] 204 G2
Myrina [GR] 130 F6
Myrina [TR] 144 C3
Myrkky [FIN] 186 B4
Myrmoen [N] 182 D3
Myrnes [N] 192 H1
Myronivka [UA] 204 F2
Myrskylä / Mörskom [FIN] 178 B3
Myrtiés [GR] 142 B3
Myrtos [GR] 140 F5
Myrvika [N] 190 C4
Myrviken [S] 182 G3
Mysen [N] 166 C2
Myšenec [CZ] 48 F6
Myshall [IRL] 4 F4
Myshuryn Rih [UA] 204 G3
Myślenice [PL] 50 H4
Myślibórz [PL] 34 G1
Myślice [PL] 22 F4
Mysłowice [PL] 50 G3
Mysovka [RUS] 200 D5
Mystegná [GR] 134 H2
Mystrás [GR] 136 E4
Myszków [PL] 50 G2
Myszyniec [PL] 24 C5
Mytikas [GR] 132 D5
Mytilíni [GR] 134 H2
Mytishchi [RUS] 202 F4
Myto [BY] 24 H3
Mýto [CZ] 48 E4
Mzurki [PL] 36 G5

N

Nå [N] 170 C4
Naamijoki [FIN] 194 B7
Naantali / Nådendal [FIN] 176 D4
Naarajärvi [FIN] 188 C4
Naarajärvi [FIN] 196 G6
Naarden [NL] 16 E4
Naarva [FIN] 188 G1
Nääs [S] 160 H2
Naas / An Nás [IRL] 2 F6
Näätämö [FIN] 194 E3
Nabaskoze / Navascués [E] 84 C4
Nabbelund [S] 162 H3
Nabburg [D] 48 C5
Náchod [CZ] 50 B3
Nacka [S] 168 E3
Nădab [RO] 76 G3
Nadarzyn [PL] 38 B3
Nadăş [RO] 76 H4
Naddvik [N] 170 E2
Nadela [E] 78 E3
Nådend / Naantali [FIN] 176 D4
Nădlac [RO] 76 F4
Nadrin [B] 30 E6
Nádudvar [H] 76 G1
Nærbo [N] 164 A4
Næstved [DK] 156 F4
Näfels [CH] 58 G6
Náfpaktos [GR] 132 F5
Náfplio [GR] 136 F2
Naggen [S] 184 D5
Naglarby [S] 174 C5
Nagłowice [PL] 52 A2
Nagold [D] 58 G2
Nagu / Nauvo [FIN] 176 D5
Nagyatád [H] 74 H4
Nagybajom [H] 74 H4
Nagybaracska [H] 76 C5
Nagycenk [H] 62 F6
Nagycserkesz [H] 64 G5
Nagydorog [H] 76 B3
Nagygyimót [H] 74 H1
Nagyhalász [H] 64 H4
Nagyigmánd [H] 64 A6
Nagyiván [H] 64 F6
Nagykálló [H] 64 H5
Nagykanizsa [H] 74 G4
Nagykáta [H] 76 D1
Nagykónyi [H] 76 B3
Nagykőrös [H] 76 D2
Nagylak [H] 76 F4
Nagylóc [H] 64 D5
Nagymágocs [H] 76 F3
Nagymaros [H] 64 C5
Nagyoroszi [H] 64 C5
Nagyszénás [H] 76 F3
Nagyvázsony [H] 74 H2
Naharros [E] 98 B2
Nahe [D] 18 F3
Nahkiaisoja [FIN] 194 C8
Naila [D] 46 H3
Nailloux [F] 106 A4
Nailsworth [GB] 12 G3
Naipu [RO] 148 C1
Nairn [GB] 6 E5
Najac [F] 66 H6
Nájera [E] 82 G6
Näkkälä [FIN] 194 B5
Nakkesletta [N] 192 G1
Nakkila [FIN] 176 D2
Naklo [SLO] 74 B4
Nakło nad Notecią [PL] 22 C6
Nakovo [YU] 76 F5
Nakskov [DK] 156 E5
Nälden [S] 182 G2
Nałęczów [PL] 38 D5
Nálepkovo [SK] 64 F2
Näljänkä [FIN] 196 F3
Nalkki [FIN] 196 E4
Nalzen [F] 106 A5
Nalžovské Hory [CZ] 48 E6
Nambroca [E] 96 F2
Namdalseid [N] 190 C5
Náměšť nad Oslavou [CZ] 50 B6
Námestovo [SK] 50 G5
Namma [N] 172 D4
Nämpnäs [FIN] 186 A4
Namsos [N] 190 C5
Namsskogan [N] 190 D4
Namsvassgardån [N] 190 D4
Namur [B] 30 D5
Namysłów [PL] 36 D6
Nanclares de la Oca / Langraiz Oka [E] 82 G5
Nancy [F] 44 E5
Nangis [F] 42 G4
Nannestad [N] 172 B5
Nans-les-Pins [F] 108 C5
Nant [F] 106 E3
Nantes [F] 40 F6
Nanteuil-le-Haudouin [F] 42 G3
Nantiat [F] 54 G6
Nantua [F] 68 H2
Nantwich [GB] 10 D5
Naours, Grottes de- [F] 28 E4
Náousa [GR] 138 E3
Náousa [GR] 128 F4
Näpagård [N] 170 F6
Naples [TR] 146 C3
Nápoli [I] 120 E3
Na Pomezí [CZ] 50 C3
Naposenaho [FIN] 186 E2
När [S] 168 G5
Nåra [N] 170 A2
Narach [BY] 200 H5
Naraio, Castelo de- [E] 78 D2
Narberth [GB] 12 D1
Narbolia [I] 118 C5
Narbonne [F] 106 D5
Narbonne-Plage [F] 106 D5
Narbuvollen [N] 182 C4
Narcao [I] 118 B7
Nardis, Cascata di- [I] 72 C4
Nardò [I] 122 G5
Narechenski Bani [BG] 148 B6
Narew [PL] 24 F6
Närhilä [FIN] 186 G3
Narila [FIN] 188 D5
Narjordet [N] 182 C4
Narkaus [FIN] 194 D8
Narlıca [TR] 146 F4
Narni [I] 116 A4
Naro [I] 126 D4
Naro-Fominsk [RUS] 202 F4
Narol [PL] 52 G2
Narón [E] 78 D4
Närpes / Närpiö [FIN] 186 A4
Närpiö / Närpes [FIN] 186 A4
Narta [HR] 74 G6
Narthaki [GR] 132 G3
Närtuna [S] 168 E2
Naruska [FIN] 194 F6
Narva [EST] 198 G1
Narva [FIN] 176 F2
Närvä [FIN] 186 G6
Närvä [S] 192 H4
Narva-Jõesuu [EST] 198 G1
Närvijoki [FIN] 186 B3
Narvik [N] 192 E4
Näs [S] 172 G5
Näs [S] 166 G2
Näs [S] 168 F6
Näs [S] 162 D1
Näsåker [S] 184 E1
N. Åsarp [S] 162 C1
Năsăud [RO] 204 C4
Nasbinals [F] 68 C5
Nascimiento del Río Cuervo [E] 98 C1
Näset [S] 184 D4
Näshulta [S] 168 B3
Našice [HR] 154 D1
Nasielsk [PL] 38 B2
Näsinge [S] 166 C4
Näsland [S] 190 H5
Naso [I] 124 B4
Na Špičáku [CZ] 50 D3
Nassau [D] 46 B2
Nassereith [A] 72 C1
Nässja [S] 166 G5
Nässjö [S] 184 D1
Nässjö [S] 162 D2
Nasswald [A] 62 E6
Nästansjö [S] 190 F4
Nastazin [PL] 20 G5
Nästeln [S] 182 G4
Nästi [FIN] 176 D3
Nastola [FIN] 178 B3
Näsum [S] 158 E1
Näsviken [S] 190 E6
Näsviken [S] 174 E1
Natalinci [YU] 150 B1
Nattavaara [S] 196 A1
Nättraby [S] 158 F1
Nattvatn [N] 194 C3
Naturno / Naturns [I] 72 C3
Naturns / Naturno [I] 72 C3
Nauders [A] 72 B2
Nauen [D] 34 D2
Naujoji Akmenė [LT] 198 C6
Naul [IRL] 2 F5
Naumburg [D] 34 B6
Naumestis [LT] 200 F4
Naunhof [D] 34 D5
Nausta [S] 190 H2
Naustbukta [N] 190 C4
Naustdal [N] 180 C6
Nauste [N] 180 F3
Nautijaure [S] 190 H1
Nautsi [RUS] 194 E4
Nautsung [N] 170 B1
Nauvo / Nagu [FIN] 176 D5
Nava [E] 82 C2
Navacelles, Cirque de- [F] 106 E3
Navacerrada [E] 88 F4
Nava de la Asunción [E] 88 E3
Nava del Rey [E] 88 D2
Navahermosa [E] 96 E2
Navahrudak [BY] 202 A5
Navalcán [E] 88 C6
Navalcarnero [E] 88 F6
Navaleno [E] 90 A2
Navalguijo [E] 88 C5
Navalmanzano [E] 88 F3
Navalmoral [E] 88 D5
Navalmoral de la Mata [E] 88 B6
Navalón [E] 98 D6
Navalperal de Pinares [E] 88 E5
Navalvillar de Pela [E] 96 B3
Navan / An Uaimh [IRL] 2 F5
Nävårdalen [N] 182 B3
Navarredonda de Gredos [E] 88 C5
Navarrenx [F] 84 D3
Navarrés [E] 98 E5
Navarrete [E] 82 G6
Navàs [E] 92 E3
Navascués / Nabaskoze [E] 84 C4
Navas del Madroño [E] 86 G4
Navas del Rey [E] 88 E5
Navas de Oro [E] 88 E3
Navas de San Juan [E] 102 F1
Navatalgordo [E] 88 D5
Navekvaren [S] 168 C5
Navelli [I] 116 C4
Navelsaker [N] 180 C5
Nave Redonda [P] 94 B4
Näverkärret [S] 166 H2
Naverstad [S] 166 C4
Naveta des Tudons [E] 104 G4
Navia [E] 78 F2
Navilly [F] 56 G5
Navit [N] 192 H2
Navlya [RUS] 202 E6
Naxås [S] 182 F1
Náxos [GR] 138 E3
Naxos [I] 124 B8
Nazaré [P] 86 C3
Nazilli [TR] 144 E5
N.-D. de Clausis [F] 108 E2
N.-D. de Kerdevot [F] 40 B3
N.-D. de la Salette [F] 68 H5
N.-D. de Lure [F] 108 C3
N.-D. de Miracles [F] 108 E4
N.-D.-du-Haut [F] 58 C3
N.-D. du Mai [F] 108 C6
Ndroq [AL] 128 B3
Néa Anchíalos [GR] 132 H3
Néa Artáki [GR] 134 B5
Néa Epídavros [GR] 136 F2
Néa Fókaia [GR] 130 B6
Néa Kallikráteia [GR] 130 B5
Néa Karváli [GR] 130 D3
Néa Koróni [GR] 136 D4
Neale [IRL] 2 C4
Néa Liosia [GR] 134 C6
Néa Mádytos [GR] 130 C4
Néa Mákri [GR] 134 C6
Néa Michanióna [GR] 128 H5
Néa Moní [GR] 134 G4
Néa Moudaniá [GR] 130 B5
Neamţ, Mănăstirea- [RO] 204 C4
Neandria [TR] 130 H6
Néa Péramos [GR] 130 D3
Néa Péramos [GR] 134 B6
Néa Plágia [GR] 130 B5
Neapoli [GR] 136 F5
Neápoli [GR] 140 F4
Neápoli [GR] 128 E5
Neapolis [TR] 144 E5
Néa Poteídaia [GR] 130 B5
Néa Róda [GR] 130 C5
Néa Roúmata [GR] 140 B4
Néa Sánta [GR] 130 G2
Néa Skióni [GR] 130 C6
Néa Stýra [GR] 134 D5
Neath [GB] 12 E2
Néa Triglia [GR] 130 B5
Neauvic [F] 66 E3
Néa Výssa [GR] 130 H1
Néa Zíchni [GR] 130 C3
Nebiler [TR] 144 C2
Nebolchi [RUS] 202 D2
Nebra [D] 34 B5
Nechanice [CZ] 50 A3
Neckarelz [D] 46 D5
Neckargemünd [D] 46 C5
Neckargerach [D] 46 D5
Neckarsteinach [D] 46 C5
Neckarsulm [D] 46 D5
Neckenmarkt [A] 62 F6
Neda [E] 78 D1
Nedansjö [S] 184 E4
Neded [SK] 64 A5
Nedelišće [HR] 74 F4
Nederhögen [S] 182 G4
Nedervetil / Alaveteli [FIN] 196 C6
Neder Vindinge [DK] 156 F4
Nedre Eggedal [N] 170 G5
Nedre Gärdsjö [S] 172 H3
Nedre Soppero [S] 192 H4
Nedstrand [N] 164 B2
Nędza [PL] 50 E3
Neede [NL] 16 G5
Neermoor [D] 18 B4
Negorci [MK] 128 G3
Negotin [YU] 150 E1
Negotino [MK] 128 F2
Negovanovci [BG] 150 E2
Negrar [I] 72 C6
Negreira [E] 78 B3
Negren-Tino [CH] 70 G2
Négrondes [F] 66 F2
Negru Vodă [RO] 148 G1
Neheim-Hüsten [D] 32 C4
Nehoiu [RO] 204 C5
Neiden [N] 194 E3
Neitisuanto [S] 192 G5
Neittävä [FIN] 196 E4
Nejdek [CZ] 48 D3
Nekromanteío [GR] 132 C3
Neksø [DK] 158 E4
Nelas [P] 80 C6
Nelidovo [RUS] 202 D4
Nellim [FIN] 194 E4
Nellimö [FIN] 194 E4
Nellingen [D] 60 B3
Neltaa [FIN] 176 G4
Neman [RUS] 200 D5
Nembro [I] 70 H4
Neméa [GR] 136 E1
Neméa [GR] 136 E1
Nemenčinė [LT] 200 G5
Nemesszalók [H] 74 G1
Németkér [H] 76 C3
Nemours [F] 42 G5
Nemšová [SK] 64 A2
Nemti [H] 64 D5
Nemyriv [UA] 52 G3
Nemyriv [UA] 204 E3
Nenagh [IRL] 2 D6
Nendeln [FL] 58 H5
Neochóri [GR] 136 B1
Neochóri [GR] 132 E5
Neochóri [GR] 132 E3
Neochóri [GR] 134 A2
Neochóri [GR] 134 C5
Neochóri [GR] 132 F2
Néo Monastíri [GR] 132 G3
Néo Petrítsi [GR] 130 B2
Néos Marmarás [GR] 130 C6
Nepi [I] 114 H4
Nepomuk [CZ] 48 E5
Neptun [RO] 148 G1
Nérac [F] 66 E5
Neratovice [CZ] 48 G3
Néré [F] 54 D5
Neresheim [D] 60 C2
Nereta [LV] 198 E6
Nereto [I] 116 D3
Neretva Kanjon [BiH] 152 C2
Nerezine [HR] 112 E3
Nerežišća [HR] 152 A2
Neringa [LT] 200 D5
Neringa-Nida [LT] 200 D5
Néris-les-Bains [F] 56 C6
Nerja [E] 102 D5
Nerja, Cueva de- [E] 102 D5
Nérondes [F] 56 C4
Nerpio [E] 102 H2
Nerpio, Cuevas de- [E] 102 H2
Nersingen [D] 60 B3
Nerskogen [N] 180 H3
Nerva [E] 94 F5
Nervesa della Battaglia [I] 72 E5
Nervi [I] 110 B3
Nerviano [I] 70 G4
Nes [N] 170 H4
Nes [N] 170 D1
Nes [N] 164 F2
Nes [NL] 16 F1
Nesactium [HR] 112 D2
Nesaseter [N] 190 D4
Nesbyen [N] 170 G4
Nesebŭr [BG] 148 F4
Nesflaten [N] 164 C1
Neskaupstaður [IS] 192 D3
Neslandsvatn [N] 164 F3
Nesle [F] 28 F5
Nesna [N] 190 D2
Nesoddtangen [N] 166 B1
Nespereira [P] 80 C3
Nesseby [N] 194 E2
Nesselwang [D] 60 C5
Nestáni [GR] 136 E2
Nestavoll [N] 180 H4
Nesterov [RUS] 24 D1
Nestório [GR] 128 D5
Nesttun [N] 170 B4
Nesvik [N] 164 A6
Netolice [CZ] 62 B2
Netretić [HR] 112 G1
Netta [PL] 24 E4
Nettancourt [F] 44 C4
Nettetal [D] 30 F3
Nettuno [I] 120 B1
Nettuno, Grotta di- [I] 118 B3
Neubeckum [D] 32 D3
Neuberg [A] 74 E1
Neuberg an der Mürz [A] 62 D6
Neubrandenburg [D] 20 D4
Neubukow [D] 20 A3
Neubulach [D] 58 G1
Neuburg [D] 60 H3
Neuburg [D] 60 D2
Neuchâtel [CH] 58 C5
Neu Darchau [D] 18 G5
Neudorf [D] 46 C5
Neudorf [D] 34 A4
Neudorf-Platendorf [D] 32 H2
Neuenburg [D] 58 E3
Neuenbürg [D] 46 C6
Neuenburg [D] 18 C4
Neuenhaus [D] 16 G4
Neuenkirchen [D] 18 F5
Neuenstein [D] 32 F6
Neuenstein [D] 46 D5
Neuenstein [D] 46 D5
Neuenwalde [D] 18 D3
Neufahrn [D] 60 F3
Neuf-Brisach [F] 58 E3
Neufchâteau [B] 44 D2
Neufchâteau [F] 44 D6
Neufchâtel [F] 44 B2
Neufchâtel-en-Bray [F] 28 C5
Neufelden [A] 62 B3
Neuffen [D] 58 H2
Neugersdorf [D] 48 G1
Neuhaus [D] 46 H4
Neuhaus [D] 46 G2
Neuhaus [D] 60 H3
Neuhaus [D] 18 E3
Neuhaus [D] 32 F4
Neuhaus [D] 18 H5
Neuhausen am Rheinfall [CH] 58 F4
Neuhof [D] 34 E3
Neuhofen an der Krems [A] 62 B4
Neuillé Port-Pierre [F] 54 F1
Neuilly-l'Évêque [F] 58 A3
Neuilly-St-Front [F] 42 H3
Neu-Isenburg [D] 46 C3
Neukalen [D] 20 C4
Neukirch [D] 34 F6
Neukirchen [A] 72 F1
Neukirchen [A] 60 G4
Neukirchen [D] 156 B4
Neukloster [D] 20 A3
Neulengbach [A] 62 E4
Neulingen [D] 46 C6
Neu Lübbennau [D] 34 F3
Neum [BiH] 152 C3
Neumarkt [A] 74 B2
Neumarkt [A] 60 H5
Neumarkt [D] 46 H5
Neumarkt / Egna [I] 72 D4
Neumarkt-St Veit [D] 60 F4
Neu-Moresnet [B] 30 F5
Neumorschen [D] 32 F6
Neu Mukran [D] 20 D2
Neumünster [D] 18 F3
Neunagelberg [A] 62 C3
Neunburg [D] 48 C5
Neung-sur-Beuvron [F] 56 B2
Neunkirchen [A] 62 E6
Neunkirchen [D] 44 G3
Neuötting [D] 60 G4
Neupölla [A] 62 D3
Neuruppin [D] 20 C6
Neuschwanstein [D] 60 C6
Neusiedl am See [A] 62 G5
Neuss [D] 30 G3
Neustadt [D] 32 E6
Neustadt [D] 60 E2
Neustadt [D] 46 G2
Neustadt [D] 48 B1
Neustadt [D] 58 F3
Neustadt [D] 34 F6
Neustadt [D] 18 H3
Neustadt [D] 34 C1
Neustadt [D] 46 E3
Neustadt am Rübenberge [D] 32 F2
Neustadt an der Aisch [D] 46 F5
Neustadt an der Waldnaab [D] 48 C4
Neustadt an der Weinstrasse [D] 46 B5
Neustadt-Glewe [D] 20 A5
Neustift [A] 72 D1
Neustrelitz [D] 20 C5
Neu-Ulm [D] 60 B3
Neuves-Maisons [F] 44 E5
Neuvic [F] 68 B3
Neuville [F] 68 F2
Neuville [F] 54 E3
Neuville-aux-Bois [F] 42 E5
Neuvola [FIN] 186 H4
Neuvy [F] 54 H4
Neuvy-Bouin [F] 54 D3
Neuvy-sur-Barangeon [F] 56 C3
Neuwied [D] 30 H6
Neuzelle [D] 34 G3
Neveklov [CZ] 48 G4
Nevel' [RUS] 202 C4
Neverfjord [N] 194 B2
Nevers [F] 56 D4
Nevesinje [BiH] 152 C2
Nevlunghavn [N] 164 G3
Nevossuo [FIN] 178 C3
New Alresford [GB] 12 H4
Newark-on-Trent [GB] 10 F5
Newbiggin-by-the-Sea [GB] 8 G5
Newbliss [IRL] 2 F4
Newbridge / Droichead Nua [IRL] 2 E6
Newburgh [GB] 8 E2
Newbury [GB] 12 H4
Newcastle [NIR] 2 G4
Newcastle Emlyn [GB] 10 A6
Newcastle-under-Lyme [GB] 10 E5
Newcastle upon Tyne [GB] 8 G6
Newcastle West [IRL] 4 C3
New Galloway [GB] 8 D5
Newgrange [IRL] 2 F5
Newhaven [GB] 14 E6
Newinn [IRL] 4 D4
Newmarket [GB] 14 F3
Newmarket [IRL] 4 C4
Newmarket-on-Fergus [IRL] 2 C6
Newport [GB] 12 H5
Newport [GB] 10 D5
Newport [GB] 12 F3
Newport [IRL] 2 C3
Newport [IRL] 4 D3
Newport-on-Tay [GB] 8 F2
Newquay [GB] 12 C4
New Romney [GB] 14 F5
New Ross [IRL] 4 F4
Newry [NIR] 2 F4
Newton Abbot [GB] 12 E5
Newtonmore [GB] 6 D6
Newton Stewart [GB] 8 C5
Newtown [GB] 10 C6
Newtownabbey [GB] 2 G3
Newtownards [NIR] 2 G3
Newtown Butler [NIR] 2 E4
Newtownhamilton [NIR] 2 F4
Newtownmountkennedy [IRL] 4 G3
Newtownstewart [NIR] 2 F3
Nexon [F] 66 G2
Nežilovo [MK] 128 E2
Niadinge [LT] 24 G2
Niana [I] 70 E4
Nianfors [S] 174 E1
Niaux, Grotte de- [F] 84 H5
Nibe [DK] 160 D4
Nicaj-Shalë [AL] 150 A6
Nicastro [I] 124 D5
Nice [F] 108 E4
Nickelsdorf [A] 62 G5
Nicknoret [S] 190 H4
Nicolosi [I] 126 G3
Nicopolis ad Istrum [BG] 148 C3
Nicosia [I] 126 F3
Nicotera [I] 124 C6
Nidderau [D] 46 D2
Nideck, Château du- [F] 44 G6
Nidzica [PL] 22 G5
Niebla [E] 94 F5
Nieborow [PL] 36 H3
Niebüll [D] 156 B4
Nieby [D] 156 C5
Niechorze [PL] 20 G3
Niedalino [PL] 20 H3
Niederalteich [D] 60 G3
Niederau [A] 60 F6
Niederaula [D] 46 E1
Niederbronn-les-Bains [F] 44 H5
Niederelsungen [D] 32 E5
Niederkleen [D] 46 C2
Niederkrüchten [D] 30 F3
Niederoderwitz [D] 48 G1
Nieder Stotzingen [D] 60 C3
Niederwinkling [D] 60 G2
Nieder-Wöllstadt [D] 46 C2
Niedrzwica Duża [PL] 38 E6
Niemce [PL] 38 E5
Niemcza [PL] 50 C2
Niemegk [D] 34 D3
Niemica [PL] 22 A3
Niemijarvi [FIN] 188 H1
Niemis [S] 194 B8
Niemisel [S] 196 B2
Niemisjärvi [FIN] 186 H4
Niemiskylä [FIN] 196 G5
Niemodlin [PL] 50 D2
Nienburg [D] 32 F1
Nienhagen [D] 20 B3
Niepołomice [PL] 52 B4
Nieppe [F] 28 F3
Nierstein [D] 46 C3
Niesky [D] 34 G5
Nieszawa [PL] 36 F1
Nietsak [S] 192 G6
Nieuil [F] 54 E6
Nieuweschans [NL] 16 H2
Nieuwpoort [B] 28 F1
Nigrán [E] 78 B5
Nigrita [GR] 130 B3
Nihattula [FIN] 176 G2
Niilivaara [FIN] 194 C6
Niinilahti [FIN] 186 G2
Niinimäki [FIN] 188 D3
Niinisalo [FIN] 186 C6
Niinivesi [FIN] 186 G2
Niittumaa [FIN] 176 C2
Nijar [E] 102 G5
Nijemci [HR] 154 E2
Nijkerk [NL] 16 E5
Nijmegen [NL] 16 E6
Nijverdal [NL] 16 G4
Nikaia [GR] 132 G2
Nikaia [TR] 146 G4
Nikaranperä [FIN] 186 F3
Nikel' [RUS] 194 F3
Niki [GR] 128 E4
Nikiá [GR] 142 C4
Nikifóros [GR] 130 D3
Nikil [S] 166 H6
Nikisiani [GR] 130 D3
Nikitas [GR] 130 C5
Nikkajärvi [FIN] 196 G5
Nikkaluokta [S] 192 F5
Nikkaroinen [FIN] 178 A1
Nikolaevskoye [RUS] 198 H2
Nikola Kozlevo [BG] 148 E2
Nikolayevo [RUS] 198 H2
Nikopol [BG] 148 B2
Nikopol' [UA] 204 G4
Nikópoli [GR] 132 D4
Nikšić [YU] 152 E3
Nilivaara [S] 192 H6
Nilsiä [FIN] 188 D1
Nim [DK] 156 C1
Nîmes [F] 106 F3
Nin [HR] 112 G4
Ninfa [I] 116 B6
Ninove [B] 28 H3
Niort [F] 54 D4
Niquidetto [I] 70 D5
Niroú Cháni [GR] 140 E4
Niš [YU] 150 D3
Nisa [P] 86 E4
Nisáki [GR] 132 B2
Niscemi [I] 126 F4
Niška Banja [YU] 150 D3
Niskakoski [RUS] 194 E4
Niskos-Pietilä [FIN] 178 F1
Nisko [PL] 52 E2
Nissafors [S] 162 C3
Nissi [EST] 198 D2
Nissilä [FIN] 196 E5
Nissoria [I] 126 F3
Nitaure [LV] 198 E5
Nitlax [FIN] 176 F6
Nitra [SK] 64 A4
Nitrianske Pravno [SK] 64 B2
Nitrianske Rudno [SK] 64 B3
Nitry [F] 56 F2
Nittedal [N] 172 B5
Nittenau [D] 48 C6
Nittendorf [D] 60 F2
Nittkvarn [S] 166 G1
Nivå [DK] 156 G2
Niva [FIN] 196 G4
Nivala [FIN] 196 D5
Nivelles [B] 28 H3
Niversac [F] 66 F3
Nixhöhle [A] 62 D5
Nizhyn [UA] 202 D7
Nižná [SK] 50 H6
Nižná Boca [SK] 64 D2
Nižná Slaná [SK] 64 E3
Nizy-le-Comte [F] 28 G6
Nizza Monferrato [I] 108 H2
Njavve [S] 190 G1
Njegoševo [YU] 76 D6
Njetsavare [S] 190 H1
Njivice [HR] 112 E2
Njupeskärfall [S] 172 E1
Njurandsbommen [S] 184 E5
Njurunda [S] 184 E5
Njutånger [S] 174 E1
N. Kerdýllia [GR] 130 C4
Noailles [F] 28 D6
Noain (Elorz) [E] 84 B4
Noale [I] 72 E6
Noasca [I] 70 D4
Nöbbele [S] 162 E5
Nöbbelöv [S] 158 D2
Noceda [E] 78 F5
Nocera [I] 120 E3
Nocera Umbra [I] 116 B2
Noceto [I] 110 D2
Noci [I] 122 E3
Nocito [E] 84 D6
Nodeland [N] 164 D5
Nods [F] 58 B5
Noé [F] 84 H4
Noépoli [I] 122 C5
Noeux [F] 28 E3
Nogales [E] 94 G2
Nogara [I] 110 F1
Nogaro [F] 84 F2
Nogarole Rocca [I] 110 E1
Nogent [F] 56 H2
Nogent-le-Roi [F] 42 E4
Nogent-le-Rotrou [F] 26 G6
Nogent-sur-Seine [F] 42 H5
Nogersund [S] 158 E2
Noginsk [RUS] 202 F4
Nohfelden [D] 44 G3
Noia [E] 78 B3
Noirétable [F] 68 E2
Noirmoutier-en-l'Île [F] 54 A2
Noja [E] 82 F3
Nokia [FIN] 176 F1
Nokia [FIN] 186 H6
Nokkamäki [FIN] 196 F6
Nokkosmäenkulma [FIN] 186 B5
Nol [S] 160 H1
Nola [I] 120 E3
Nol Alafors [S] 160 H1
Nolay [F] 56 F4
Noli [I] 108 H3
Nomeny [F] 44 E5
Nomexy [F] 44 E6
Nõmme [EST] 198 E2
Nonancourt [F] 26 H5
Nonant-le-Pin [F] 26 G5
Nonantola [I] 110 F3
Nonaspe [E] 90 G5
Nonnenhorn [D] 58 H4
Nontron [F] 66 F2
Nonza [F] 114 C2
Noordwijk aan Zee [NL] 16 C4
Noormarkku / Norrmark [FIN] 176 D1
Nopankylä [FIN] 186 B3
Noppikoski [S] 172 G2
Nor [N] 172 D5
Nor [N] 180 C5
Nor [S] 182 H3
Nora [I] 118 C7
Nora [S] 168 B6
Nora [S] 166 H2
Nørager [DK] 160 D4
Norberg [S] 168 B1
Norchia [I] 114 G4
Norcia [I] 116 B3
Nordagutu [N] 164 F2
Nordanå [S] 184 E3
Nordana [S] 162 B6
Nordanåker [S] 184 D2
Nordanås [S] 190 G3
Nordanås [S] 190 F3
Nordanas [S] 190 G5
Nordanholen [S] 172 H4
Nordankäl [S] 184 D1
Nordansjö [S] 190 F4
Nordausques [F] 14 H6
Nordberg [N] 180 F5
Nordborg [DK] 156 C4
Nordby [DK] 156 E1
Nordby [DK] 156 A3
Nordby [N] 166 B1
Nordby [N] 172 C2
Norddeich [D] 16 H1
Nordeide [N] 170 C1
Norden [D] 16 H1
Norden [S] 190 H2
Nordenham [D] 18 D4
Norderåsen [S] 182 H1
Norderney [D] 18 B3
Norderö [S] 182 G2
Norderstedt [D] 18 F4
Nordeste [P] 100 E3
Nord Etnedal [N] 170 G2
Nordfjord [N] 194 E1
Nordfjordeid [N] 180 C5
Nordfold [N] 192 D5
Nordhalben [D] 46 H2
Nordhallen [S] 182 E1
Nordhausen [D] 32 H5
Nordhella [N] 192 F2
Nordhorn [D] 16 H4
Nordingrå [S] 184 F3
Nordkapp [N] 194 C1
Nordkirchen [D] 32 C3
Nordkisa [N] 172 C5
Nordkjosbotn [N] 192 G3
Nordli [N] 190 D5
Nördlingen [D] 60 C2
Nordmaling [S] 184 H1
Nordmark [S] 166 F1
Nordmela [N] 192 E3
Nordøyvågen [N] 190 D2
Nordre Osen [N] 172 D2
Nordsinni [N] 170 H3
Nordsjö [S] 174 D1
Nordskjørin [N] 190 B5
Nordskov [DK] 156 E2
Nordvik [N] 180 G2
Nordvika [N] 180 F1
Nordwalde [D] 16 H5
Nore [S] 184 D6
Noresund [N] 170 G5
Norg [NL] 16 G2
Norgravsjö [S] 190 G5
Norheimsund [N] 170 C4
Nørholm [N] 164 E5
Norhyttan [S] 172 G5
Norinkylä [FIN] 186 B4
Norje [S] 158 E1
Norkino [RUS] 198 H5
Norma [I] 116 B6
Normjöle [S] 190 H6
Norn [S] 174 C5
Norra Finnskoga [S] 172 E3
Norrahammar [S] 162 D2
Norraker [S] 190 E5
Norrala [S] 174 E2
Norra Löten [S] 172 E3
Norra Mellby [S] 158 C1
Norra Tresund [S] 190 F4
Norrback [FIN] 186 B3
Norrbäck [S] 190 G4
Norrberg [S] 190 F4
Norrboda [S] 174 G5
Norrboda [S] 172 H3
Norrby [FIN] 196 C6
Norrby [S] 190 G4
Nørre Aaby [DK] 156 D3
Nørre Alslev [DK] 156 F5
Norre Bergnäss [S] 190 G2
Nørre Broby [DK] 156 D3
Nørre Lyndelse [DK] 156 D3
Nørre Nebel [DK] 156 A2
Nørre Snede [DK] 156 C1
Nørresundby [DK] 160 D3
Nørre Vejrup [DK] 156 B2
Nørre Vorupør [DK] 160 B4
Norrfjärden [S] 196 B3
Norrfors [S] 190 H6
Norr Hede [S] 182 F4
Norrhult [S] 162 E4
Norriån [S] 194 A8
Norrköping [S] 168 B5
Norrmark / Noormarkku [FIN] 176 D1
Norrnäs [FIN] 186 A4
Norrskedika [S] 174 G5
Norrsunda [S] 168 D2
Norrsundet [S] 174 E3
Norrtälje [S] 168 E2
Norrtannflo [S] 184 E2
Norrvik [S] 196 A2
Nors [DK] 160 C3
Norsholm [S] 168 B5
Norsjö [S] 190 H4
Norsjövallen [S] 190 H4
Nort [F] 40 F6
Nörten-Hardenberg [D] 32 G4
Northallerton [GB] 10 F2
Northam [GB] 12 D3
Northampton [GB] 14 D2
North Berwick [GB] 8 F3
Northeim [D] 32 G4
Northleach [GB] 12 H2
North Walsham [GB] 14 G2
Northwich [GB] 10 D4
Nortorf [D] 18 F2
Norwich [GB] 14 G2
Nosivka [UA] 204 F1
Nosnäs [S] 172 G3
Nossa Senhora da Conceição [P] 94 C2
Nossa Senhora da Serra [P] 80 F3
Nossa Senhora de Taúde [P] 80 C5
Nossa Senhora do Cabo [P] 86 A6
Nossebro [S] 166 D6
Nössemark [S] 166 C3
Nossen [D] 34 E6
Nótia [GR] 128 G3
Nötö [FIN] 176 D6
Noto [I] 126 G5
Noto Antica [I] 126 G5
Notodden [N] 164 F2
Notre-Dame de Consolation [F] 58 C5
Notre-Dame de-la-Roquette [F] 108 D5
Notre-Dame des Fontaines [F] 108 F3
Nottebäck [S] 162 E4
Nøtterøy [N] 164 H3
Nottingham [GB] 10 F5
Nottuln [D] 16 H6
Nouan-le-Fuzelier [F] 56 B2
Nouans-les-Fontaines [F] 54 G3
Nousu [FIN] 194 E7
Nouvaillé-Maupertuis [F] 54 E4
Nouvion [F] 28 D4
Nova [EST] 198 D2
Nova [H] 74 F3
Nová Baňa [SK] 64 B4
Nová Bystrica [SK] 50 C6
Nová Bystřice [CZ] 62 D2
Novacella / Neustift [I] 72 D2
Novachene [BG] 150 G4
Novaci [MK] 128 E3
Nova Crnja [YU] 76 F6
Novae Palesse [BY] 202 B7
Novafeltria [I] 110 H5
Nova Gorica [SLO] 72 H5
Nova Gradiška [HR] 154 C1
Novaja Kakhovka [UA] 204 G4
Novaja Ladoga [RUS] 202 D1
Novajidrány [H] 64 G4
Nova Kasaba [BiH] 154 E4
Nováky [SK] 64 B3
Novalesa, Abbazia di- [I] 70 C5
Nova Levante / Welschnofen [I] 72 D3
Novalja [HR] 112 F4
Nova Odessa [UA] 204 F4
Nová Paka [CZ] 48 H2
Nova Pazova [YU] 154 G2
Novara [I] 70 F5
Novara di Sicilia [I] 124 A7
Novate Mezzola [I] 70 H3
Nova Topola [BiH] 154 C2
Nova Varoš [YU] 150 A3
Novaya Zhizn' [RUS] 198 G2
Nova Zagora [BG] 148 D5
Nové Hrady [CZ] 62 C3
Novelda [E] 104 D2
Novellara [I] 110 E2
Nové Město nad Metují [CZ] 50 B3
Nové Mesto nad Váhom [SK] 64 A3
Nové Město na Moravě [CZ] 50 B5
Noventa Vicentina [I] 110 G1
Novés [E] 88 E6
Noves [F] 106 G3
Nové Sady [SK] 64 A4
Nové Strašecí [CZ] 48 E3
Nové Zámky [SK] 64 B5
Novgorod [RUS] 202 C2
Novgorodka [RUS] 198 H4
Novhorodka [UA] 204 F3
Novhorod-Siverskyi [UA] 202 D6
Novi Bečej [YU] 76 E6
Novi di Modena [I] 110 E2
Novi Dojran [MK] 128 H3
Novi Grad [BiH] 154 D2
Novigrad [HR] 112 G5
Novigrad [HR] 112 D1
Novigrad Podravski [HR] 74 G5
Novi Han [BG] 150 G5
Novi Kazarci [YU] 76 F5
Novi Kneževac [YU] 76 E5
Novi Krichim [BG] 148 B6
Novi Ligure [I] 110 A2
Novi Marof [HR] 74 F5
Novion-Porcien [F] 28 H6
Novi Pazar [BG] 148 E2
Novi Pazar [YU] 150 B4
Novi Sad [YU] 154 F1
Novi Senkovac [HR] 74 H6
Novi Travnik [BiH] 154 C4
Novi Vinodolski [HR] 112 F2
Novoarkhanhel's'k [UA] 204 E3
Novo Brdo [YU] 150 C5
Novohrad-Volyns'kyi [UA] 204 D2
Novo mesto [SLO] 74 D6
Novo Miloševo [YU] 76 E6
Novomoskovsk [RUS] 202 F5
Novomoskovs'k [UA] 204 G3
Novorzhev [RUS] 198 H4
Novosady [PL] 24 F6
Novoselë [AL] 128 A5
Novoselets [BG] 148 D5
Novo Selo [BG] 150 E1
Novo Selo [BG] 148 D2
Novo Selo [BG] 148 B4
Novo Selo [MK] 128 H2
Novosel'ye [RUS] 198 H3
Novosil' [RUS] 202 F6
Novosokol'niki [RUS] 202 C4
Novoukraïnka [UA] 204 F3
Novoukraïnka [UA] 52 H2
Novovolyns'k [UA] 52 H1
Novovorontsovka [UA] 204 G4
Novo Zvečevo [HR] 154 C1
Novozybkov [RUS] 202 D6
Novska [HR] 154 B1
Nový Bohumín [CZ] 50 F4
Nový Bor [CZ] 48 G2
Nový Bydžov [CZ] 50 C6
Nový Hrad [CZ] 50 C6
Novyi Buh [UA] 204 F4
Novyi Bykiv [UA] 204 F2
Nový Jičín [CZ] 50 E5
Nový Knín [CZ] 48 F4
Nowa Brzeźnica [PL] 36 G6
Nowa Cerekwia [PL] 50 E4

Rødberg [N] 170 F5
Rødby [DK] 20 A1
Rødbyhavn [DK] 20 A1
Rødding [DK] 156 B3
Rødding [DK] 160 C5
Rödeby [S] 158 F1
Rodeiro [E] 78 C4
Rødekro [DK] 156 C4
Roden [NL] 16 G2
Rodenkirchen [D] 18 D4
Rodewald [D] 32 F1
Rodewisch [D] 48 C2
Rodez [F] 68 B6
Rødhus Klit [DK] 160 D3
Rodiá [GR] 132 G1
Rodi Garganico [I] 116 G5
Roding [D] 48 C6
Rødkærsbro [DK] 160 D5
Rodolívos [GR] 130 C3
Rodópoli [GR] 128 H2
Ródos [GR] 142 E4
Rodrigatos de la Obispalía [E] 78 G5
Rodrigo, Castelo- [P] 80 E6
Rødsjøen [N] 190 B6
Rødvig [DK] 156 G4
Roela [EST] 198 F1
Roermond [NL] 30 F3
Roeselare (Roulers) [B] 28 F2
Rœulx [B] 28 H3
Roflaschlucht [CH] 70 G2
Röfors [S] 166 G4
Rofrano [I] 120 G5
Rogač [HR] 154 A6
Rogačica [YU] 154 F4
Rogalice [PL] 50 D1
Rogalin [PL] 36 C3
Rogaška Slatina [SLO] 74 D4
Rogatec [SLO] 74 E4
Rogatica [BiH] 152 E1
Rogätz [D] 34 B2
Rogil [P] 94 B4
Rögla [S] 158 C3
Rogliano [F] 114 C2
Rogliano [I] 124 D5
Rognac [F] 106 H5
Rognan [N] 192 D6
Rogne [N] 170 G2
Rognes [N] 182 B2
Rogovo [RUS] 198 G4
Rogowo [PL] 36 D2
Rogozhinë [AL] 128 B3
Rogoznica [HR] 116 H1
Rogoźno [PL] 36 C2
Rohan [F] 26 A5
Rohatec [CZ] 62 G2
Rohatyn [UA] 204 C2
Rohrbach [A] 62 B3
Rohrbach-lès-Bitche [F] 44 G4
Rohrberg [D] 34 A1
Rohr i. Niederb. [D] 60 F2
Rohuküla [EST] 198 D2
Rohuneeme [EST] 198 D1
Roisel [F] 28 F5
Roja [LV] 198 C4
Röjan [S] 182 G4
Rojão Grande [P] 80 C6
Röjdåfors [S] 172 E5
Roiştea [RO] 150 G1
Rök [S] 166 G6
Röka [S] 190 G4
Röke [S] 158 C1
Rokiciny [PL] 36 H4
Rokietnica [PL] 52 F4
Rokiškis [LT] 200 G3
Rokity [PL] 22 C2
Rökkum [N] 180 F2
Røkland [N] 190 E1
Roknäs [S] 196 A3
Roknäs [S] 196 A3
Rokua [FIN] 196 E4
Rokycany [CZ] 48 E4
Rolandstorp [S] 190 E4
Rold [DK] 160 D4
Røldal [N] 170 C5
Rolle [CH] 70 B1
Rolltorp [S] 160 H4
Rølvåg [N] 190 D2
Rolvsøy [N] 166 B3
Roma [I] 116 A5
Roma [S] 168 G4
Romagnano Sésia [I] 70 E4
Romakkajärvi [FIN] 194 C7
Roman [BG] 150 G3
Roman [RO] 204 D4
Romangordo [E] 88 B6
Romanija [BiH] 152 D1
Romanshorn [CH] 58 H4
Romans-sur-Isère [F] 68 F5
Rombas [F] 44 E4
Rom By [DK] 160 B5
Romena, Castello di- [I] 110 G5
Romena, Pieve di- [I] 110 G5
Romeral [E] 96 G2
Romfartuna [S] 168 B2
Romilly-sur-Seine [F] 44 A5
Romny [UA] 204 G1
Romont [CH] 70 C1
Romorantin-Lanthenay [F] 54 H2
Romppala [FIN] 188 F1
Romsey [GB] 12 H4
Romtemplom [H] 64 C6
Røn [N] 170 G2
Roncade [I] 72 E6
Roncadelle [I] 72 A6
Roncal / Erronkari [E] 84 C4
Roncegno [I] 72 D4
Roncesvalles [E] 84 C3
Ronchamp [F] 58 C3
Ronchi dei Legionari [I] 72 H5
Ronciglione [I] 114 H4
Ronco Canavese [I] 70 D4
Roncofreddo [I] 110 H5
Ronco Scrivia [I] 110 B3
Ronda [E] 102 A4
Rønde [DK] 160 E6
Ronehamn [S] 168 G5
Rong [N] 170 C3
Rõngu [EST] 198 F3
Ronkeli [FIN] 196 G5
Rönnäng [S] 160 G1
Rønne [DK] 158 E4
Ronneburg [D] 48 C1
Ronneby [S] 158 F1
Rønnede [DK] 156 G4
Rönnigsåsen [S] 182 F4
Rönnliden [S] 190 H3
Rönnöfors [S] 190 D6
Rönnskär [S] 196 A4
Rönnynkylä [FIN] 186 F1
Rönö [S] 168 C5
Ronse (Renaix) [B] 28 G3
Roodeschool [NL] 16 G1
Roonah Quay [IRL] 2 B3
Roosendaal [NL] 16 C6
Roosky [IRL] 2 D4
Ropa [PL] 52 C5
Ropaži [LV] 198 E5
Ropczyce [PL] 52 D3
Ropeid [N] 164 B1
Ropinsalmi [FIN] 192 H3
Ropotovo [MK] 128 E2
Ropsha [RUS] 178 E6
Roque, Pointe de la- [F] 26 G3
Roquebillière [F] 108 F4
Roquebrune-Cap-Martin [F] 108 F4
Roquefort [F] 66 C5
Roquefort-sur-Soulzon [F] 106 D3
Roquemaure [F] 106 G3
Roquesteron [F] 108 E4
Roquetaillade, Château de- [F] 66 D4
Roquetas de Mar [E] 102 F5
Roquetes [E] 92 A5
Røra [N] 190 C6
Rörbäcksnäs [S] 172 E3
Rore [BiH] 154 B4
Roron [S] 182 G3
Røros [N] 182 C4
Rorschach [CH] 58 H5
Rörum [S] 158 D3
Rørvig [DK] 156 F2
Rørvik [N] 190 C4
Rørvik [N] 182 B1
Rørvik [N] 164 C5
Ros' [BY] 24 G5
Rosais [P] 100 C3
Rosala [FIN] 176 E6
Rosal de la Frontera [E] 94 E3
Rosa Marina [I] 122 F3
Rosans [F] 108 B2
Rosapenna [IRL] 2 E1
Rosarno [I] 124 C6
Rosas / Roses [E] 92 G2
Rosbach [D] 46 C2
Rosche [D] 18 G6
Rościszewo [PL] 36 H1
Roscoff [F] 40 C1
Roscommon [IRL] 2 D5
Roscrea [IRL] 2 D6
Rosdorf [D] 32 F4
Rosegg [A] 74 B3
Roselle [I] 114 F2
Roselle Módica [I] 126 G6
Rosen [BG] 148 F4
Rosenberg [D] 46 E6
Rosenburg [A] 62 E3
Rosendal [N] 170 B5
Rosenheim [D] 60 F5
Rosenhof [A] 62 C3
Rosenholm [DK] 160 E6
Rosentorp [S] 172 H2
Rosersberg [S] 168 D2
Roses / Rosas [E] 92 G2
Roseto degli Abruzzi [I] 116 D3
Roseto Valfortore [I] 120 F2
Roshchine [RUS] 178 G4
Rosica [BG] 148 F1
Rosice [CZ] 50 B6
Rosignano-Marittimo [I] 110 D6
Rosignano Solvay [I] 114 E1
Rosino [BG] 148 B4
Roşiori [RO] 76 H1
Roşiori de Vede [RO] 148 B1
Rosith [M] 8 E3
Roskilde [DK] 156 G2
Rosko [PL] 36 B1
Roslags-Bro [S] 168 E1
Roslags kulla [S] 168 E2
Roslavl' [RUS] 202 D5
Roslev [DK] 160 C4
Rosli [N] 180 G5
Rosmaninhal [P] 86 F4
Rosnowo [PL] 22 A3
Rosolina Mare [I] 110 H2
Rosolini [I] 126 G5
Rosoman [MK] 128 F2
Rosporden [F] 40 C3
Ross Abbey [IRL] 2 C4
Rossano [I] 124 E4
Rossas [P] 80 C5
Ross Carberry [IRL] 4 C5
Rosscor [NIR] 2 E3
Rosserk Abbey [IRL] 2 C3
Rosses Point [IRL] 2 D3
Rosslyn [N] 192 F2
Rosshaupten [D] 60 C5
Rossiglione [I] 108 H2
Rossio [P] 86 D4
Rossla [D] 34 A5
Rosslare Harbour [IRL] 4 F5
Rosslau [D] 34 C4
Rosslea [NIR] 2 F4
Rossnes [N] 170 A3
Rossön [S] 190 F6
Ross-on-Wye [GB] 12 G2
Rossosz [PL] 38 F4
Rossoszyca [PL] 36 F4
Røssvassbukt [N] 190 E3
Röstånga [S] 158 C2
Rostassac [F] 66 F5
Roštejn [CZ] 50 A6
Roštejn [CZ] 48 H6
Rostock [D] 20 B3
Rostrenen [F] 40 D3
Rostrevor [NIR] 2 G4
Röström [S] 190 F5
Rostvollen [N] 182 D5
Røsvik [N] 192 D5
Rosvik [S] 196 B3
Röszke [H] 76 E4
Roszki-Wodżki [PL] 24 E6
Rot [S] 172 F2
Rota [E] 100 F3
Rotberget [N] 172 D4
Rotemo [N] 164 D2
Rotenburg [D] 32 F6
Rotenburg [D] 18 E5
Rotenfels [D] 46 B3
Rotgülden [A] 72 H2
Roth [D] 46 G5
Rötha [D] 34 C6
Rothemühl [D] 20 E4
Rothenburg [D] 34 G5
Rothenburg, Ruine- [D] 46 G5
Rothenburg ob der Tauber [D] 46 E5
Rothéneuf [F] 26 C4
Rothenstein [D] 60 D2
Rotherham [GB] 10 F4
Rothes [GB] 6 E5
Rothesay [GB] 8 C3
Rotondella [I] 122 D5
Rótova [E] 98 E6
Rotsjö [S] 184 D3
Rott [D] 60 D5
Rott [D] 60 F5
Rottach [D] 60 E5
Rötteln [D] 58 E4
Rottenbach [D] 46 G2
Rottenbuch [D] 60 D5
Rottenburg [D] 60 F3
Rottenburg [D] 58 G2
Rottenmann [A] 62 B6
Rotterdam [NL] 16 C5
Rotthalmünster [D] 60 H4
Röttingen [D] 46 E5
Rottne [S] 162 E4
Rottneros [S] 166 E1
Rottweil [D] 58 G3
Rotvoll [N] 182 D2
Rötz [D] 48 C5
Roubaix [F] 28 F3
Rouchovany [CZ] 62 E2
Roudnice nad Labem [CZ] 48 F3
Rouen [F] 28 B5
Rouffach [F] 58 D3
Rouffignac, Grotte de- [F] 66 F3
Rougé [F] 40 F5
Rougemont [F] 58 C4
Rougemont [F] 58 D3
Rouillac [F] 54 D6
Roujan [F] 106 D4
Roulers (Roeselare) [B] 28 F2
Roundstone [IRL] 2 B4
Roundwood [IRL] 4 G3
Roússa [GR] 130 G2
Roussillon [F] 106 H4
Rouvres-en-Xaintois [F] 44 E6
Rovakka [S] 194 B7
Rovaniemi [FIN] 194 D8
Rovastinaho [FIN] 196 D2
Rovato [I] 72 A6
Roverbella [I] 110 E1
Rovereto [I] 72 C5
Röverhagen [D] 20 B3
Roverud [N] 172 D5
Roviés [GR] 134 B4
Rovigo [I] 110 G2
Rovinj [HR] 112 D2
Roviŝće [HR] 74 F5
Rovjok [N] 192 G3
Rów [PL] 20 F6
Rowy [PL] 22 B1
Royan [F] 54 B6
Royat [F] 68 C2
Royaumont, Abbaye de- [F] 42 F3
Roybon [F] 68 G4
Roye [F] 28 E5
Royère-de-Vassivière [F] 68 A1
Royken [N] 164 H1
Røyrvik [N] 190 D4
Røyse [N] 170 H5
Røysheim [N] 180 F6
Royston [GB] 14 E3
Röyttä [FIN] 196 C3
Roza [BG] 148 D5
Rožaj [YU] 150 B5
Różan [PL] 24 C6
Różanki [PL] 34 H1
Rožanstvo [YU] 150 A3
Rozay-en-Brie [F] 42 G4
Rožmberk nad Vltavou [CZ] 62 B3
Rožmitál pod Třemšínem [CZ] 48 E5
Rožňava [SK] 64 E3
Rožnov pod Radhoštěm [CZ] 50 E5
Rożnów [PL] 52 B4
Rozogi [PL] 24 C5
Rozoy [F] 28 G6
Rozprza [PL] 36 H5
Roztoky [CZ] 48 F3
Rožupe [LV] 198 F6
Rozvadov [CZ] 48 C4
Rozzano [I] 70 G5
Rrëshen [AL] 128 B1
Rtanj [YU] 150 D2
Ru [E] 78 D3
Rubbestadneset [N] 170 A5
Rubena [E] 82 E6
Rubielos de Mora [E] 98 E2
Rubiera [I] 110 E3
Rucava [LV] 200 D3
Ruciane-Nida [PL] 24 C4
Rud [N] 170 H5
Hud [N] 164 H1
Rud [S] 166 F3
Ruda [S] 162 F4
Ruda Maleniecka [PL] 38 A6
Rudare [YU] 150 C4
Rudawica [PL] 34 H5
Rudawka [PL] 24 F3
Rudelsburg [D] 34 B6
Rudenica [YU] 150 C3
Rudersdorf [D] 34 F2
Rüdersdorf [D] 34 F2
Rüdesheim [D] 46 B3
Rūdiškės [LT] 24 H1
Rudka [PL] 38 E1
Rudkøbing [DK] 156 E4
Rudna [PL] 36 B5
Rudna [PL] 22 C5
Rudna Glava [YU] 150 D1
Rudnica [YU] 152 E2
Rudnica [YU] 150 B4
Rudnik [BG] 148 F3
Rudnik [PL] 50 E3
Rudnik [YU] 150 B5
Rudnik [YU] 150 B2
Rudniki [PL] 50 F1
Rudnik nad Sanem [PL] 52 E2
Rudno [PL] 22 E4
Rudno [PL] 38 E4
Rudnya [RUS] 202 C5
Rudolphstein [D] 46 H2
Rudolstadt [D] 46 H1
Rudozem [BG] 130 E1
Rudsgrendi [N] 164 F1
Rudsjön [S] 190 F6
Rudskoga [S] 166 G4
Ruds-Vedby [DK] 156 F3
Rudy [PL] 50 F3
Rudzāti [LV] 198 F5
Rue [F] 28 D3
Rueda [E] 88 E2
Rueda, Monasterio de- [E] 90 F5
Rueda de Jalón [E] 90 D3
Ruelle-sur-Touvre [F] 66 E1
Ruffano [I] 122 G6
Ruffec [F] 54 E5
Ruffieux [F] 70 A3
Rugāji [LV] 198 G5
Rugby [GB] 14 D2
Rugeley [GB] 10 E6
Rugldalen [N] 182 C3
Rugles [F] 26 H5
Ruha [FIN] 186 C3
Ruhällen [S] 168 C1
Rühen [D] 32 H2
Ruhland [D] 34 F5
Ruhmannsfelden [D] 60 G2
Ruhpolding [D] 60 G5
Ruidera [E] 96 G4
Ruinas Romanas [E] 96 D1
Ruínas Romanas [P] 94 D2
Rūjiena [LV] 198 E3
Ruju, Nuraghe- [I] 118 D3
Ruka [FIN] 194 F8
Rukajärvi [FIN] 194 F8
Rullbo [S] 182 H6
Rülzheim [D] 46 B5
Rum [H] 74 G2
Ruma [YU] 154 F2
Rumburk [CZ] 48 G1
Rumelifeneri [TR] 146 E2
Rumia [PL] 22 D2
Rumigny [F] 28 H5
Rumilly [F] 70 A3
Rummen [B] 30 D4
Rumo [FIN] 196 F5
Rumont [F] 44 D4
Rumpani [LV] 198 F4
Runcorn [GB] 10 D4
Rundfloen [N] 172 E3
Rundvik [S] 184 H1
Runni [FIN] 196 E6
Ruokojärvi [FIN] 194 C7
Ruokojärvi [S] 194 B8
Ruokolahti [FIN] 178 E1
Ruokto [S] 192 F6
Ruona [FIN] 186 D3
Ruopsa [FIN] 194 E7
Ruorasmäki [FIN] 186 H6
Ruotaanmäki [FIN] 196 E6
Ruoti [I] 120 G3
Ruotsinpyhtää Strömfors [FIN] 178 C4
Ruovesi [FIN] 186 E5
Rupa [HR] 112 E1
Rupea [RO] 204 C5
Rupt [F] 58 C3
Rus [E] 102 F1
Rusalka [BG] 148 G2
Rusanivka [UA] 204 G2
Rúscio [I] 116 B3
Rusdal [N] 164 B4
Ruse [BG] 148 C2
Rusele [S] 190 G4
Ruševo [HR] 154 D1
Rusfors [S] 190 G4
Rush [IRL] 2 F6
Rushden [GB] 14 E2
Rusiec [PL] 36 F5
Rusinowo [PL] 22 A6
Ruskeala [RUS] 188 G4
Ruski Krstur [YU] 76 D6
Ruskila [FIN] 188 D2
Ruskeand [S] 190 F6
Ruskele [S] 190 G4
Rusksele [S] 190 G4
Rusné [LT] 200 D5
Rusokastro [BG] 148 F4
Rüsselsheim [D] 46 C3
Russenes [N] 194 C2
Russi [I] 110 G4
Russliseter [N] 180 G6
Rust [A] 62 F5
Rust [D] 58 E2
Rustad [N] 172 B5
Rustefjelbma [N] 194 D2
Rusvekk [N] 172 D4
Ruswil [CH] 58 E6
Ruszów [PL] 34 H5
Rutalahti [FIN] 186 G5
Rute [E] 102 C3
Rutenbrock [D] 16 H3
Rüthen [D] 32 D4
Ruthin [GB] 10 C4
Rüti [CH] 58 G5
Rüti [CH] 58 G6
Rutigliano [I] 122 E3
Rutka-Tartak [PL] 24 E2
Rutledal [N] 170 B2
Rutvik [S] 196 B3
Ruukki [FIN] 196 D4
Ruunaa [FIN] 196 G6
Ruurlo [NL] 16 F5
Ruutana [FIN] 176 F1
Ruutana [FIN] 196 E6
Ruuvaoja [FIN] 194 E6
Ruvallen [S] 182 E3
Ruvanaho [FIN] 194 F7
Ruvasiahtio [FIN] 188 F2
Ruvo di Puglia [I] 122 D2
Ruwer [D] 44 G2
Ruza [RUS] 202 E4
Ruzhany [BY] 24 H6
Ruzhintsi [BG] 150 E3
Růžkovy Lhotice [CZ] 48 G5
Ružomberok [SK] 64 C2
Ry [DK] 156 D1
Ryå [DK] 160 D3
Ryakhovo [BG] 148 D1
Ryákia [GR] 128 G5
Rybarzowice [PL] 50 G5
Rybinsk [RUS] 202 F2
Rybnik [PL] 50 F4
Rybník [SK] 64 E3
Ryboły [PL] 24 F6
Rychliki [PL] 22 F3
Rychnburk [CZ] 50 B4
Rychnov nad Kněžnou [CZ] 50 B3
Rychnowo [PL] 22 G4
Rychtal [PL] 36 E6
Rychwał [PL] 36 E3
Ryczywół [PL] 38 C4
Ryd [S] 162 D6
Rydaholm [S] 162 D4
Ryde [GB] 12 H5
Rydland [N] 182 B6
Rydsnäs [S] 162 E2
Rydułtowy [PL] 50 F4
Rydzyna [PL] 36 C4
Rye [GB] 14 F5
Ryen [N] 164 E5
Ryfoss [N] 170 F2
Rygge [N] 166 B2
Rygozy [RUS] 198 H5
Ryhälä [FIN] 188 E5
Ryhäntä [FIN] 196 F4
Rykene [N] 164 E5
Ryki [PL] 38 D4
Ryl'sk [RUS] 202 E7
Rymań [PL] 20 G3
Rymanów [PL] 52 D5
Rýmařov [CZ] 50 D4
Rymättylä / Rimito [FIN] 176 D5
Rýmnio [GR] 128 F6
Ryn [PL] 24 C3
Rynarzewo [PL] 22 D6
Ryomgård [DK] 160 E5
Rypefjord [N] 194 B2
Rypin [PL] 22 F6
Ryslinge [DK] 156 D3
Ryssby [S] 162 D4
Rysum [D] 16 H2
Rytel [PL] 22 C4
Rytinki [FIN] 196 E2
Rytkynkylä [FIN] 196 D5
Rytro [PL] 52 B5
Ryuttyu [RUS] 188 H4
Ryzmberk [CZ] 48 D5
Rzeczenica [PL] 22 B4
Rzeczyca [PL] 38 A5
Rzęgnowo [PL] 22 H6
Rzemień [PL] 52 D3
Rzepin [PL] 34 G3
Rzeszów [PL] 52 E3
Rzewnowo [PL] 20 F3
Rzgów [PL] 36 G4
Rzhev [RUS] 202 E4
Rzhishchiv [UA] 204 F2

S

Sääksjärvi [FIN] 186 D2
Sääksmäki [FIN] 176 F2
Saal [D] 60 F2
Saalbach [A] 72 F1
Saalburg [D] 46 C2
Saales [F] 44 G6
Saalfeld [D] 46 H2
Saalfelden [A] 60 G6
Saamatti [FIN] 176 F5
Saananmaja [FIN] 192 G3
Saanen [CH] 70 D1
Saarbrücken [D] 44 G4
Saarburg [D] 44 F3
Saare [EST] 198 F2
Saarela [FIN] 196 G5
Saarela [FIN] 186 G1
Saarenkylä [FIN] 194 D8
Saarenmaa [FIN] 176 D2
Saaresmäki [FIN] 196 E5
Saari [FIN] 188 F5
Saarijärvi [FIN] 186 F3
Saarikko [FIN] 176 F3
Saarikoski [FIN] 192 G3
Saarinen [FIN] 196 F4
Saario [FIN] 188 G3
Saarivaara [FIN] 188 G3
Saariväära [FIN] 196 G4
Saarlouis [D] 44 F3
Saas Almagell [CH] 70 E3
Saas-Fee [CH] 70 E3
Saas Grund [CH] 70 E3
Sääskijärvi [FIN] 196 E2
Šababurg [D] 32 F4
Šabac [YU] 154 F2
Sabadell [E] 92 E4
Sabaro [E] 82 C4
Sabáudia [I] 120 B2
Sabbioneta [I] 110 E2
Sabbucina [I] 126 E3
Sabile [LV] 198 C5
Sabiñánigo [E] 84 D5
Sabinosa [E] 100 A5
Sabinov [SK] 52 C6
Sabiote [E] 102 F2
Sables-d'Or-les-Pins [F] 26 B4
Sablé-sur-Sarthe [F] 42 A5
Såbole [S] 182 F1
Saborsko [HR] 112 G2
Sabres [F] 66 C5
Sabrosa [P] 80 D4
Sabugal [P] 86 G2
Šaby [S] 162 E1
Šaca [SK] 64 G3
Săcălaz [RO] 76 G5
Sacavém [P] 86 B5
Sacecorbo [E] 90 B5
Sacedón [E] 88 H6
Saceruela [E] 96 D4
Cacile [I] 72 F5
Sacra di San Michele [I] 70 C5
Sádaba [E] 84 B5
Sadala [EST] 198 F2
Sadikov Bunar [YU] 150 E4
Sadki [PL] 22 C6
Sadova [RO] 150 G2
Sadovets [BG] 148 A3
Sadovo [BG] 148 B6
Sądów [PL] 34 G3
S. Adriano [I] 110 G4
Sadská [CZ] 48 G3
Sädvaluspen [S] 190 F2
Sæbø [N] 170 D4
Sæbø [N] 180 D4
Sæbøvik [N] 170 B5
Sæby [DK] 160 E3
Sæd [DK] 156 B4
Saelices [E] 96 H2
Sælvig [DK] 156 E2
Saepinum [I] 120 E1
Saerbeck [D] 32 C2
Sæter [N] 190 B6
Sætra [N] 192 E2
Sætre [N] 172 C2
Sætre [N] 164 H2
Sætteråsen [N] 190 B6
Saeul [L] 44 E2
Sævareid [N] 170 B4
Sævråsvåg [N] 170 B3
Safa [TR] 146 G5
Safara [P] 94 E3
Säffle [S] 166 E3
Saffron Walden [GB] 14 F3
Safonovo [RUS] 202 D4
Sagard [D] 20 D2
S'Agaró [E] 92 G4
S. Agata di Esaro [I] 124 C3
Sagiáda [GR] 132 B2
Sågmyra [S] 172 H4
Sagone [F] 114 A4
Sagres [P] 94 A5
Şagu [RO] 76 G5
Sagu / Sauvo [FIN] 176 E5
Sagunt / Sagunto [E] 98 F4
Sagunto / Sagunt [E] 98 F4
Sagvåg [N] 170 A5
Ságvár [H] 76 A3
Sahagún [E] 82 C5
Sahalahti [FIN] 176 G1
Sahankylä [FIN] 186 C4
Sahavaara [S] 194 B7
Sahilköy [TR] 146 F2
Şahin [TR] 146 B3
Şahrajärvi [FIN] 186 F4
Šahy [SK] 64 C5
Saignelégier [CH] 58 D5
Saija [FIN] 194 E7
Saikari [FIN] 186 H3
Saillagouse [F] 92 E1
Saillans [F] 68 G6
Säimen [FIN] 188 F4
Sains [F] 28 G5
Saint Albain [F] 56 G6
Sainte-Lucie-de-Tallano [F] 114 B5
Sainte-Marie-Siché [F] 114 B5
Saintes [F] 54 C6
Saintfield [NIR] 2 G4
Saint Hilaire de la Côte [F] 68 G4
Saint-Jacques [I] 70 D3
Sairinen [FIN] 176 D4
Saissac [F] 106 B4
Saittarova [S] 192 H6
Saivomuotka [S] 194 B5
Sajaniemi [FIN] 176 G3
Sajenek [PL] 24 E3
Šajkaš [YU] 154 G1
Sajószentpéter [H] 64 F4
Sakaravaara [FIN] 196 F4
Šakiai [LT] 200 E5
Säkinmäki [FIN] 186 H3
Sakskøbing [DK] 20 B1
Saky [UA] 204 G5
Säkylä [FIN] 176 D3
Sala [S] 168 C1
Šal'a [SK] 64 A4
Salaberg [A] 62 C5
Salacgrīva [LV] 198 D4
Sala Consilina [I] 120 G4
Saladamm [S] 168 C1
Salahmi [FIN] 196 E5
Sálakos [GR] 142 D4
Salamajärvi [FIN] 186 E1
Salamanca [E] 80 H6
Salamina [GR] 134 B6
Salantai [LT] 200 D4
Salaóra [GR] 132 D4
Salar [E] 102 D4
Sălard [RO] 76 H1
Salardú [E] 84 G5
Salas [E] 78 G3
Salas de los Infantes [E] 88 H1
Salaspils [LV] 198 E5
Salau [F] 84 G5
Salaŭš [YU] 150 E2
Salbohed [S] 168 B1
Šalbris [F] 56 B2
Šalčininkai [LT] 200 G6
Salcombe [GB] 12 D5
Sălcuţa [RO] 150 F1
Saldaña [E] 82 C5
Salduba [E] 90 E3
Saldus [LV] 198 C5
Sale [I] 70 F6
Saleby [S] 166 E5
Salem [D] 58 H4
Salema [P] 94 A5
Salemi [I] 126 B2
Sälen [S] 172 E2
Salernes [F] 108 D4
Salerno [I] 120 F4
Salers [F] 68 B4
S. Alessio Siculo [I] 124 B8
Saletta [I] 70 C5
Salgótarján [H] 64 D4
Salhus [N] 170 B3
Sali [HR] 112 F5
Salice [F] 114 B4
Salice Terme [I] 70 F6
Salies-de-Béarn [F] 84 D2
Salies-du-Salat [F] 84 G4
Salignac-Eyvigues [F] 66 G4
Salihli [TR] 144 E4
Salihorsk [BY] 202 B6
Salinas [E] 78 H3
Salinas [E] 104 D2
Salinas de Pinilla [E] 96 H5
Saline di Volterra [I] 114 F1
Sälinkää [FIN] 176 H3
Salins [F] 58 B5
Salins-les-Bains [F] 58 A5
Salir [P] 94 C5
Salisbury [GB] 12 G4
Salka [SK] 64 C5
Salkoluokta [S] 192 F6
Salla [FIN] 194 E7
Sallanches [F] 70 B3
Sallent de Gállego [E] 84 D4
Sälleryd [S] 158 G1
Salles [F] 66 C4
Salles [F] 106 A4
Salles-Curan [F] 106 D2
Sällinge [S] 166 H2
Sallmunds [S] 168 G6
Salme [EST] 198 C3
Salmenkylä [FIN] 186 E4
Salmenniemi [FIN] 186 F2
Salmerón [E] 90 A6
Salmi [FIN] 186 D3
Salmi [S] 194 B7
Salmivaara [FIN] 194 E7
Salmivaara [FIN] 194 E7
Sal'miyarvi [RUS] 194 F3
Salmoral [E] 88 D4
Salo [FIN] 176 E4
Salò [I] 72 B6
Salobreña [E] 102 D5
Salociai [LT] 198 E6
Saloinen [FIN] 196 C4
Salon [F] 44 B5
Salona [HR] 152 A2
Salon-de-Provence [F] 106 H4
Salonta [RO] 76 H3
Salorino [E] 86 F5
Salou [E] 92 C5
Salovci [SLO] 74 F3
Salsåker [S] 184 F3
Salsbruket [N] 190 C4
Salse di Nirano [I] 110 E3
Salses-le-Château [F] 106 C6
Salsnes [N] 190 C4
Salsomaggiore Terme [I] 110 D2
Salsta [S] 168 D1
Salt [E] 92 F3
Saltash [GB] 12 D5
Saltbæk [DK] 156 E2
Saltrød [N] 164 F5
Saltsjöbaden [S] 168 E3
Saltum [DK] 160 D3
Saltvik [FIN] 176 B5
Saltvik [S] 162 G3
Saluböle [S] 184 H1
Saluzzo [I] 108 F2
Salvacañete [E] 98 D2
Salvada [P] 94 D3
Salvagnac [F] 106 B2
Salvarola, Terme di- [I] 110 E3
Salvaterra de Magos [P] 86 C5
Salvaterra de Miño [E] 78 B5
Salvatierra [E] 96 E5
Salvatierra / Agurain [E] 82 H5
Salvatierra de los Barros [E] 94 G2
Salviac [F] 66 G4
Salzburg [A] 60 G5
Salzburg [D] 46 F2
Salzgitter-Bad [D] 32 G3
Salzgitter-Lebenstedt [D] 32 G3
Salzhausen [D] 18 F5
Salzkotten [D] 32 D4
Salzwedel [D] 18 H6
Salzweg [D] 60 H3
Sama de Grado [E] 78 H4
Samadet [F] 66 C6
Samadet [F] 84 E2
Samailli [TR] 144 E5
Samandıra [TR] 146 F3
Samarina [GR] 128 D6
Samassi [I] 118 C6
Samatan [F] 84 G3
Samate [LV] 198 B5
Sambiase [I] 124 D5
Sambir [UA] 52 G5
Sambuca di Sicilia [I] 126 C3
Sambucheto [I] 116 B3
Sambuci [I] 116 B5
Sambucina, Abbazia della- [I] 124 D4
Samedan [CH] 72 A3
Samer [F] 28 D2
Sámi [GR] 132 C6
Samitier [E] 84 E6
Şamlı [TR] 146 D6
Sammakkola [FIN] 196 F6
Sammakkovaara [FIN] 188 E2
Sammatti [FIN] 186 D4
Sammi [FIN] 186 B6
Samnaun [CH] 72 B2
Samo [I] 124 C7
Samobor [HR] 74 E6
Samoëns [F] 70 C3
Samokov [BG] 150 G5
Šamorín [SK] 62 G5
Samos [E] 78 E4
Sámos [GR] 144 C5
Samoš [YU] 154 H1
Samos, Monasterio de- [E] 78 E4
Samostan Pleterje [SLO] 74 D6
Samothráki [GR] 130 F4
Samovodene [BG] 148 C3
Sampatikí [GR] 136 F3
Samper de Calanda [E] 90 F5
Sampéyre [I] 108 F2
Samtens [D] 20 D2
Samugheo [I] 118 C5
Saná [GR] 130 B5
San Adrián [E] 84 A5
San Agustín [E] 98 C3
San Andrés [E] 78 D1
San Anton Leitza [E] 84 B3
Sanary-sur-Mer [F] 108 C6
San Asensio [E] 82 G6
San Augustín [E] 100 C6
San Bartolomé de las Abiertas [E] 96 D1
San Bartolomé de la Torre [E] 94 E5
San Bartolomeo in Galdo [I] 120 F1
San Benedetto dei Marsi [I] 116 C5
San Benedetto del Tronto [I] 116 D2
San Benedetto in Alpe [I] 110 G5
San Benedetto Po [I] 110 E2
San Bernardino [CH] 70 G2
San Bernardino, Tunnel del- [Eur.] 70 G2
San Biagio di Callalta [I] 72 F6
San Biágio Plátani [I] 126 D3
San Bonifácio [I] 110 F1
San Bruzio [I] 114 F3
San Calogero [I] 126 C3
San Candido / Innichen [I] 72 E3
San Carlos del Valle [E] 96 G5
San Casciano dei Bagni [I] 114 G2
San Casciano in Val di Pesa [I] 110 F6
San Cataldo [I] 126 E3
San Cataldo [I] 122 G4
Sancergues [F] 56 D3
Sancerre [F] 56 D3
Sancey-le-Grand [F] 58 C5
Sanchidrián [E] 88 E4
San Cipirello [I] 126 C2
San Claudio al Chienti [I] 116 C1
San Clemente [E] 98 A4
San Clemente a Casuria [I] 116 D4
San Clemente al Vomano [I] 116 D3
San Clodio, Monasteiro de- [E] 78 C4
Sancoins [F] 56 D4
San Cosme (Barreiros) [E] 78 E2
San Cristóbal de la Laguna [E] 100 C5
San Cristóbal de la Vega [E] 88 E3
Sancti Esperitus, Convent de- [E] 98 F4
Sancti-Spiritus [E] 96 C3
Sancti Spiritus [E] 88 A3
Sand [N] 164 B1
Sand [N] 172 C4
Sanda [N] 164 F2
Sånda [N] 164 E4
Sanda [S] 174 G6
San Damiano d'Asti [I] 70 E6
Sandane [N] 180 C5
San Daniele del Friuli [I] 72 G4
San Daniele Po [I] 110 D2
Sandanski [BG] 130 B2
Sandared [S] 162 B2
Sandarne [S] 174 E2
Sandau [D] 34 C1
Sandaucourt [F] 44 E6
Sandbach [GB] 10 D5
Sande [D] 18 C4
Sande [N] 164 H2
Sande [N] 170 C1
Sandefjord [N] 164 H3
Sandeid [N] 164 B1
Sandem [N] 166 C2
San Demetrio Corone [I] 124 D4
Sanden [N] 164 F2
Sander [N] 172 C5
Sandhem [S] 162 C1
Sandias [E] 78 C5
Sandıklı [TR] 144 H3
Sand in Taufers / Campo Tures [I] 72 E2
Sandizell [D] 60 D3
Sandl [A] 62 C3
Sandnäset [S] 184 D4
Sandnes [N] 164 B3
Sandnes [N] 194 D2
Sandnes [N] 164 C3
Sandness [GB] 6 G3
Sandnessjøen [N] 190 D2
Sando [E] 80 G6
Sandö Bro [S] 184 F3
Sandomierz [PL] 52 D2
San Dónaci [I] 122 G4
San Doná di Piave [I] 72 F6
San Donato Milanese [I] 70 G5
Sandøreng [N] 190 E3
Sándorfalva [H] 76 E4
Sandown [GB] 12 H5
S. Andrea [I] 120 D2
S. Andrea Apostolo dello Iónio [I] 124 E6
Sandrigo [I] 72 D6
Šandrovac [HR] 74 G5
Sandsbraten [N] 170 G5
Sandsjö [S] 172 G1
Sandsjö [S] 190 G5
Sandsjön [S] 166 F1
Sandsjönäs [S] 190 G4
Sandslån [S] 184 F3
Sandsletta [N] 192 D4
Sandsøy [N] 192 E3
Sandstad [N] 190 A6
Sandstad [N] 172 D4
Sandstedt [D] 18 D4
Sandur [FR] 160 A2
Sandvatn [N] 164 C4
Sandve [N] 164 A2
Sandvig [DK] 158 E4
Sandvik [S] 162 G4
Sandvika [N] 164 H1
Sandvika [N] 190 C6
Sandvika [N] 190 D2
Sandvikal [N] 164 C5
Sandviken [S] 190 D6
Sandviken [S] 174 E4
Sandvikvåg [N] 170 A5
Sandwich [GB] 14 G5
San Emiliano [E] 78 G4
San Esteban [E] 84 B3
San Esteban de Gormaz [E] 88 H3
San Fele [I] 120 G3
San Felice Circeo [I] 120 B2
San Felice in Balsignano [I] 122 D2
San Felice sul Panaro [I] 110 F2
San Ferdinando di Puglia [I] 120 H2
San Fernando [E] 100 F4
San Francisco [E] 82 B6
San Fratello [I] 126 F2
San Fruttuoso [I] 110 B3
Sånga [S] 184 F2
San Galgano, Abbazia di- [I] 114 F2
Sangarcía [E] 88 E4
San Gavino Monreale [I] 118 C6
Sangazi [TR] 146 F3
San Gemini [I] 116 A3
San Gemini Fonte [I] 116 A3
Sangerhausen [D] 34 B5
San Germano [I] 70 E5
San Gimignano [I] 110 E6
San Ginés de la Jara, Monasteiro de- [E] 104 C4
San Ginesio [I] 116 C2
Sanginkylä [FIN] 196 E4
San Giorgio di Livenza [I] 72 F6
San Giórgio di Nogaro [I] 72 G5
San Giorgio Iónico [I] 122 F4
San Giovanni, Grotta- [I] 122 F4
San Giovanni, Grotta di- [I] 118 D6
San Giovanni al Mavone [I] 116 C4
San Giovanni di Sínis [I] 118 B5
San Giovanni in Croce [I] 110 D2
San Giovanni in Fiore [I] 124 E4
San Giovanni in Persiceto [I] 110 F3
San Giovanni in Venere [I] 116 E4
San Giovanni Lupatoto [I] 110 F1
San Giovanni Rotondo [I] 116 G6
San Giovanni Suergiu [I] 118 B7
San Giovanni Valdarno [I] 110 F6
San Giovenale [I] 114 H4
Sangis [S] 196 C2
Sangis [S] 196 C2
San Giuliano Terme [I] 110 D5
San Giuseppe Jato [I] 126 C2
San Giustino [I] 110 G6
San Giusto [I] 116 B2
Sangla [EST] 198 F3
Sangüesa / Zangoza [E] 84 C5
Sanguinet [F] 66 B4
Sáni [GR] 130 B6
San Ignacio de Loiola [E] 82 H4
Sanitz [D] 20 C3
San Javier [E] 104 D4
San José [E] 102 G6
San José / Sant Josep [E] 104 C5
San José del Valle [E] 100 G4
San Juan de Alicante / Sant Joan d'Alacant [E] 104 E2
San Juan del Olmo [E] 88 D4
San Juan de los Terreros [E] 104 B4
San Juan del Puerto [E] 94 E6
San Juan de Muskiz [E] 82 G3
San Juan de Ortega [E] 82 F6
Sankovo [RUS] 202 F3
Sankt Magdalena / Santa Maddalena Vallalta [I] 72 E2
Sankt-Michaelisdonn [D] 18 E3
Sankt-Peterburg [RUS] 178 H4
Sankt Valentin auf der Haide / San Valentino alla Muta [I] 72 B2
San Lazzaro di Savena [I] 110 F3
San Leo [I] 110 H5

Sommerfeld [D] 34 D1
Sommersted [DK] 156 C3
Sommesous [F] 44 B4
Sommières [F] 106 F3
Somo [E] 82 F3
Somogyszob [H] 74 G4
Somogyvár [H] 74 H3
Somosierra [E] 88 G4
Somosierra, Puerto de- [E] 88 G4
Somovit [BG] 148 B2
Sompolno [PL] 36 F2
Sompuis [F] 44 B5
Sompujärvi [FIN] 196 D2
Son [N] 166 B2
Son Bou [E] 104 H4
Sonceboz [CH] 58 D5
Soncillo [E] 82 E4
Soncino [I] 70 H5
Sóndalo [I] 72 B3
Sondby [FIN] 178 B4
Søndeled [N] 164 F4
Sønder Balling [DK] 160 C5
Sønderborg [DK] 156 C4
Sønderby [DK] 156 C4
Sønderby [DK] 160 B6
Sønderby [DK] 156 F4
Sønder Dråby [DK] 160 C4
Sønder Felding [DK] 156 B1
Sønderho [DK] 156 A3
Sønder Omme [DK] 156 B1
Sondershausen [D] 32 H5
Søndersø [DK] 156 D3
Søndervig [DK] 160 B6
Søndervika [N] 182 D4
Sondrio [I] 70 H3
Söndrum [S] 162 B5
Sonekulla [S] 158 E1
Songe [N] 164 F4
Songesand [N] 164 B3
Sonka [FIN] 194 C8
Sonkaja [FIN] 188 G2
Sonkajärvi [FIN] 196 E6
Sonnansjö [S] 184 D4
Sonneberg [D] 46 G2
Sonntagberg [A] 62 C5
Sonogno [CH] 70 F2
Sonsbeck [D] 30 G2
Sonseca [E] 96 F2
Sonta [YU] 76 C6
Sonthofen [D] 60 B6
Sontra [D] 32 F6
Son Xoriguer [E] 104 G4
Söörmarkku [FIN] 176 D1
Sopeira [E] 84 F6
Sopela [E] 82 G3
Sophienhöhle [D] 46 H4
Sopočani [YU] 150 B4
Sopočani [YU] 150 B4
Soponya [H] 76 B2
Sopot [BG] 148 B4
Sopot [PL] 22 E2
Sopot [YU] 150 B1
Sopparjok [N] 194 C3
Sopron [H] 62 F6
Sora [I] 116 C6
Soragna [I] 110 D2
Söråker [S] 184 F4
Sorano [I] 114 G3
Sorbas [E] 102 H5
Sorbie [GB] 8 C5
Sørbø [N] 164 B2
Sörbo [S] 166 C5
Sørbymagle [DK] 156 F3
Sore [F] 66 C4
Söréd [H] 76 B1
Søre Herefoss [N] 164 E5
Sørenget [N] 190 C5
Soresina [I] 70 H5
Sörfjärden [S] 184 E5
Sør-Flatanger [N] 190 B5
Sörfors [S] 190 H6
Sörforsa [S] 174 E1
Sórgono [I] 118 D5
Sorgues [F] 106 G3
Sörgutvik [N] 190 C4
Soria [E] 90 B3
Soriano Calabro [I] 124 D6
Soriano nel Cimino [I] 114 H4
Sorica [SLO] 74 B4
Sorihuela del Guadalimar [E] 102 G1
Sorita [E] 98 G1
Sørkjosen [N] 192 G2
Sorkwity [PL] 24 B4
Sørli [N] 190 D5
Sørli [N] 190 D5
Sörmjöle [S] 190 H6
Sørmo [N] 192 F3
Sorø [DK] 156 F3
Soroca [MD] 204 D3
Soroní [GR] 142 D4
Sorpe [E] 84 G5
Sørreisa [N] 192 F3
Sorrento [I] 120 E4
Sorsakoski [FIN] 188 D3
Sorsele [S] 190 G3
Sörsjön [S] 172 E2
Sorso [I] 118 C3
Sort [E] 84 G6
Sortavala [RUS] 188 H5
Sortino [I] 126 G4
Sörtjärn [S] 182 G4
Sortland [N] 192 D3
Sør-Tverrfjord [N] 192 H1
Sørumsand [N] 166 C1
Sorunda [S] 168 D4
Sörup [D] 156 C5
Sørup [DK] 160 D4
Sørvær [N] 194 A2
Sørværøy [N] 192 C5
Sørvågen [N] 192 C5
Sørvágur [FR] 160 A1
Sörvattnet [S] 182 E5
Sõrve [EST] 198 C4
Sørvik [N] 190 B6
Sörviken [S] 184 D1
Sørvollen [N] 182 C5
Sösdala [S] 158 C2
Sos del Rey Católico [E] 84 C5
Soses [E] 90 H5
Sošice [HR] 74 D6
Sośnica [PL] 50 G2
Sośnicowice [PL] 50 F3
Sosnicy [RUS] 198 G5
Sosnovo [RUS] 178 G3
Sosnovo [RUS] 198 H1
Sosnovyy [RUS] 196 H1
Sosnovyy Bor [RUS] 178 F5
Sosnowica [PL] 38 F5
Sosnowiec [PL] 50 G3
Sospel [F] 108 F4
Sossano [I] 110 F1
Sóstis [GR] 130 F2
Sostrup [DK] 160 F5
Sotaseter [N] 180 E5
Soteska [SLO] 74 C6
Søtholmen [N] 166 C4
Sotillo de la Adrada [E] 88 E5
Sotillo de las Palomas [E] 88 D6
Sotin [HR] 154 E1
Sotkamo [FIN] 196 F5
Sotkuma [FIN] 188 F2
Sotobañado y Priorato [E] 82 D5
Soto del Barco [E] 78 H3
Soto del Real [E] 88 F5
Sotos [E] 98 C2
Sotresgudo [E] 82 D5
Sotrondio / San Martín del Rey Aurelio [E] 78 H4
Sotta [F] 114 B6
Sottomarina [I] 110 H1
Sottrum [D] 18 E5
Sottunga [FIN] 176 B5
Sotuélamos [E] 96 H4
Soúda [GR] 140 C4
Souesmes [F] 56 C2
Soufflenheim [F] 46 B6
Souflí [GR] 130 H2
Soúgia [GR] 140 B5
Souillac [F] 66 G4
Souilly [F] 44 D4
Soulac-sur-Mer [F] 54 B6
Soulaines-Dhuys [F] 44 C6
Soulópoulo [GR] 132 C2
Soultz [F] 58 D3
Soultz [F] 44 H5
Soumoulou [F] 84 E3
Soúnio [GR] 136 H2
Souppes-sur-Loing [F] 42 G5
Sourdeval [F] 26 E4
Sourdon [F] 28 E5
Soure [P] 86 D2
Sournia [F] 92 F1
Souroti [GR] 130 B5
Soúrpi [GR] 132 H3
Sousceyrac [F] 66 H4
Sousel [P] 86 E6
Soustons [F] 66 A6
Soutelo [E] 78 C4
Southampton [GB] 12 H5
Southend-on-Sea [GB] 14 F4
South Molton [GB] 12 E4
Southport [GB] 10 D3
South Shields [GB] 8 G6
Southwold [GB] 14 H3
Soutomaior, Cast. de- [E] 78 B4
Souvála [GR] 136 G1
Souvigny [F] 56 D5
Søvang [DK] 156 B4
Sövassli [N] 180 H1
Sovata [RO] 204 C5
Sover [I] 72 D4
Soverato [I] 124 E6
Soveria Mannelli [I] 124 D5
Sövestad [S] 158 D3
Sovetsk [RUS] 200 D5
Sovetskiy [RUS] 178 F3
Søvik [N] 180 D3
Sovinec [CZ] 50 D4
Sowia Góra [PL] 36 B2
Sowiniec [PL] 20 G6
Soyen [D] 60 F4
Søyland [N] 164 A4
Sozaro [TR] 146 C1
Sozopol [BG] 148 F4
Spa [B] 30 E5
Spacco della Regina [I] 114 F4
Spaichingen [D] 58 G3
Spakenburg [NL] 16 E4
Spalding [GB] 10 G6
Spálené Poříčí [CZ] 48 E5
Spalt [D] 46 G6
S. Pancrázio [I] 72 C3
Spandau [D] 34 E2
Spangenberg [D] 32 F5
Spangereid [N] 164 C6
Španovica [HR] 154 C1
S.Pantaleón de Losa [E] 82 F4
Sparanise [I] 120 D2
Spare [LV] 198 C5
Sparreholm [S] 168 C4
Sparresholm [DK] 156 F4
Spárta [GR] 134 B6
Spartà [I] 124 B7
Spárti [GR] 136 E4
Spárto [GR] 132 D4
Spas [AL] 150 B6
Spasovo [BG] 148 G1
Spáta [GR] 134 C6
Spatharaíoi [GR] 138 H1
Spean Bridge [GB] 6 C6
Specke [S] 166 D2
S. Pedro de Cardeña [E] 82 E6
S. Pedro de Teverga [E] 78 G4
Speinshart [D] 48 B4
Spello [I] 116 A2
Spenge [D] 32 D2
Spennymoor [GB] 10 F1
Spenshult [S] 162 B4
Spentrup [DK] 160 E5
Spercheiáda [GR] 132 F4
Sperlonga [I] 120 C2
Spétses [GR] 136 F3
Speyer [D] 46 C5
Spezzano Albanese [I] 124 D3
Spicino [RUS] 198 G2
Spiddal / An Spidéal [IRL] 2 B5
Spiegelau [D] 60 H2
Spiekeroog [D] 18 C3
Spielfeld [A] 74 D3
S. Pietro al Natisone [I] 72 H4
Spiez [CH] 70 E1
Spijkenisse [NL] 16 C5
Spílaia Diroú [GR] 136 E5
Spíli [GR] 140 D5
Spilimbergo [I] 72 F4
Spilja Hrustovača [BiH] 154 B3
Spina, Necropoli di- [I] 110 G3
Spinalógka [GR] 140 F4
Spinazzola [I] 120 H3
Spincourt [F] 44 E3
Spind [N] 164 C5
Špindlerův-Mlýn [CZ] 50 A2
Spineta Nuova [I] 120 F4
Špionica Donja [BiH] 154 D3
Spišić Bukovica [HR] 74 G5
Spiss [A] 72 B2
Spišská Belá [SK] 52 B6
Spišská Nová Ves [SK] 64 E2
Spišské Podhradie [SK] 64 F2
Spišský Hrad [SK] 64 F2
Spišský Štvrtok [SK] 64 E2
Spital am Pyhrn [A] 62 B6
Spittal an der Drau [A] 72 H3
Spitz [A] 62 D4
Spjærøy [N] 166 B3
Spjald [DK] 160 B6
Spjelkavik [N] 180 D3
Spjutsund [FIN] 178 B4
Split [HR] 152 A2
Splügen [CH] 70 G2
Spodsbjerg [DK] 156 E4
Špogi [LV] 198 F6
Spoleto [I] 116 B3
Spoltore [I] 116 D4
Spotorno [I] 108 H3
Spøttrup [DK] 160 C4
Sprakensehl [D] 32 H1
Spręcowo [PL] 22 G4
Spremberg [D] 34 F5
Spresiano [I] 72 E5
Springe [D] 32 F2
Sproge [S] 168 F5
Spychowo [PL] 24 C4
Spydeberg [N] 166 C2
Spytkowice [PL] 50 H5
Squillace [I] 124 E6
Squinzano [I] 122 G4
Srahmore [IRL] 2 C3
Srbac [BiH] 154 C2
Srbica [YU] 150 C5
Srbobran [YU] 76 E6
Srđevići [BiH] 152 B1
Srebărna [BG] 148 E1
Srebrenica [BiH] 154 F4
Srebrenik [BiH] 154 D3
Sredets [BG] 148 C5
Sredets [BG] 148 F5
Središče ob Dravi [SLO] 74 F4
Sredishte [BG] 148 F1
Srednogortsi [BG] 130 E1
Šrem [PL] 36 C3
Sremska Kamenica [YU] 154 F1
Sremska Mitrovica [YU] 154 F2
Sremska Rača [YU] 154 F2
Sremski Karlovci [YU] 154 F2
Sribne [UA] 204 F1
Šroda Slaska [PL] 36 C6
Šroda Wielkopolska [PL] 36 D3
Srokowo [PL] 24 C3
Srpska Crnja [YU] 76 F6
Srpski Miletić [YU] 76 C6
S. Salvador de Leyre [E] 84 C4
S. Silvestre de Guzmán [E] 94 E5
S. Stefano d'Aveto [I] 110 C3
Sta [S] 182 E1
Staaken [D] 34 E2
Sta. Ana, Monasterio de- [E] 104 C2
Staatz [A] 62 F3
Stabbestad [N] 164 F4
Stabbursnes [N] 194 C2
Stabekk [N] 166 B1
Sta. Casilda [E] 82 F5
Stachy [CZ] 48 E6
Sta. Coloma de G. [E] 92 E4
Sta Comba Dão [P] 80 C6
Sta. Cristina de Lena [E] 78 H4
Stade [D] 18 E4
Stadra [S] 166 G2
Stadskanaal [NL] 16 H3
Stadt Allendorf [D] 32 E6
Stadthagen [D] 32 F2
Stadtilm [D] 46 G1
Stadtkyll [D] 30 F6
Stadtlauringen [D] 46 F3
Stadtlohn [D] 16 G5
Stadtoldendorf [D] 32 F3
Stadtroda [D] 48 B1
Stadtsteinach [D] 46 H3
St Aegyd [A] 62 D5
Sta. Elena [E] 84 E5
Sta. Espina, Monasterio de- [E] 88 E1
Stäfa [CH] 58 G5
Staffarda, Abbazia di- [I] 108 F2
Staffelstein [D] 46 G3
Stafford [GB] 10 E5
St-Affrique [F] 106 D3
Stágeira [GR] 130 C4
St-Agnant [F] 54 C5
St-Agrève [F] 68 E5
Stahle [D] 32 F3
Stai [N] 172 C1
Staicele [LV] 198 E4
St-Aignan [F] 40 G5
St-Aignan [F] 54 H2
Staigue Fort [IRL] 4 B4
Stainach [A] 62 B6
Staines [GB] 14 E4
Stainville [F] 44 D5
Stainz [A] 74 D2
Stakčín [SK] 64 H2
Stakenjokk [S] 190 E4
Stalać [YU] 150 C3
St-Alban [F] 68 C5
St Albans [GB] 14 E3
Stalden [CH] 70 E2
Stalheim [N] 170 D3
Stalheims-Kleivene Museum [N] 170 C3
Stalída [GR] 140 F4
Stall [A] 72 G2
Stallarholmen [S] 168 C3
Ställberg [S] 166 G1
Ställdalen [S] 166 G1
Stalon [S] 190 F4
Stalowa Wola [PL] 52 E2
St-Amand-en-Puisaye [F] 56 D2
St-Amand-les-Eaux [F] 28 G3
St-Amand-Longpré [F] 42 C6
St-Amand-Montrond [F] 56 C4
St-Amans [F] 68 C5
St-Amant-Roche-Savine [F] 68 D3
Sta. Maria da Real [E] 78 C4
Sta. Maria de Bellpuig de Les Avellanes [E] 92 B2
Sta. Maria de Conxo [E] 78 C3
Sta. Maria de la Vega [E] 88 D2
Sta. Maria de Lebeña [E] 82 D3
Sta. Maria de Melque [E] 96 E2
Sta. Maria de Mezonzo [E] 78 D3
Sta. Maria la Real [E] 82 D4
Sta. Maria la Real [E] 84 A6
St-Ambroix [F] 106 F2
St-Amé [F] 58 C3
Stameriena [LV] 198 F4
Stamford [GB] 14 E1
Stamná [GR] 132 E5
St-Amour [F] 56 H6
Stams [A] 72 C1
Stamsele [S] 190 F6
Stamsund [N] 192 D4
St Andrä [A] 74 C3
St-André [F] 42 D3
St Andreasberg [D] 32 G4
St-André-de-Cubzac [F] 66 D3
St-André-les-Alpes [F] 108 D3
St Andrews [GB] 8 F2
Stånga [S] 168 G5
Stange [N] 172 C4
Stangerum [DK] 160 E5
Stanghelle [N] 170 B3
Staniewice [PL] 22 B2
Stanišić [YU] 76 C5
Stanisławów [PL] 38 C3
Štanjel [SLO] 72 H5
Staňkov [CZ] 48 D5
St Annaparochie [NL] 16 F2
Stanós [GR] 130 C4
Stans [CH] 58 F6
Stansstad [CH] 58 F6
St-Anthème [F] 68 E3
St-Antoine [F] 68 G4
St.-Antoine, Chapelle- [F] 84 D3
St Anton [A] 72 B1
St-Antonin-Noble-Val [F] 66 G6
St.-Antonino [F] 114 B3
Stany [PL] 52 D2
Stanzach [A] 60 C6
St-Août [F] 54 H4
Stapar [YU] 76 C6
Stapnes [N] 164 B4
Stąporków [PL] 38 B6
Stara Cerlev [SLO] 74 C6
Starachowice [PL] 38 B6
Stará Ľubovňa [SK] 52 C6
Stara Moravica [YU] 76 D5
Stara Novalja [HR] 112 F3
Stara Pazova [YU] 154 G2
Stara Reka [BG] 148 D4
Stara Wrona [PL] 38 B2
Staraya Russa [RUS] 202 C2
Stara Zagora [BG] 148 C5
Stare [PL] 24 E5
Stare Czarnowo [PL] 20 F5
Stare Dębno [PL] 20 H4
Staré Město [CZ] 50 C4
Staré Město [CZ] 62 H2
Staré Město pod Sněžníkem [CZ] 50 C3
Stare Osieczno [PL] 20 H6
Stargard-Szczeciński [PL] 20 F5
Stårheim [N] 180 C5
Starigrad [HR] 112 F3
Stari Grad [HR] 152 A2
Stari Gradac [HR] 74 G5
Starigrad Paklenica [HR] 112 G4
Stari Mikanovci [HR] 154 D1
Stari Slankamen [YU] 154 G2
Staritsa [RUS] 202 E3
Starjak [HR] 74 E6
Starkov [CZ] 50 B5
Starnberg [D] 60 D4
Starodub [RUS] 202 D6
Starogard [PL] 20 G4
Starogard Gdański [PL] 22 E3
Starokostiantyniv [UA] 204 D2
Staromieście [PL] 50 H2
Staro Nagoričane [MK] 150 D6
Staro Nagoričane, Manastir- [MK] 150 D6
Staro Oryakhovo [BG] 148 F3
Staropol'ye [RUS] 198 G1
Staro Selo [BG] 148 D1
Starożreby [PL] 36 H2
Starup [DK] 156 B2
Starup [DK] 156 C3
Starý Bernštejn [CZ] 48 G2
Stary Borek [PL] 52 E4
Stary Dzierzgoń [PL] 22 F4
Stary Gózd [PL] 38 B5
Starý Hrozenkov [CZ] 64 A2
Staryi Sambir [UA] 52 F5
Starý Plzenec [CZ] 48 E5
Stary Sącz [PL] 52 B5
Starý Smokovec [SK] 52 B6
Stary Szelków [PL] 38 B1
Starý Vestec [CZ] 48 G3
Stary Wieś [PL] 38 E6
Staryya Darohi [BY] 202 B6
Staryy Oskol [RUS] 202 F7
Starzyny [PL] 50 H2
St-Astier [F] 66 F3
Staszów [PL] 52 C2
Stat. Angistis [GR] 130 C3
Stathelle [N] 164 G3
Statland [N] 190 C5
Statte [I] 122 E4
St-Aubane [F] 108 E4
St-Auban-sur-l'Ouvèze [F] 108 B2
St-Aubin-d'Aubigné [F] 26 C5
St-Aubin-du-Cormier [F] 26 D5
St-Aubin-sur-Mer [F] 26 F3
St.-Augustin, Château de- [F] 56 D4
St-Aulaye [F] 66 E2
Staume [N] 180 C5
Staupitz [D] 34 E5
St Austell [GB] 12 C5
Stava [S] 162 D1
Stavang [N] 180 B6
Stavanger [N] 164 B3
Stavaträsk [S] 196 A4
Stave [N] 192 E3
Staveley [GB] 10 F5
Stavelot [B] 30 E5
Stavenisse [NL] 16 C6
Staveren [NL] 16 E3
Stavern [N] 164 G3
Stavertsi [BG] 148 A3
Stavkirke [N] 164 F2
St-Avold [F] 44 F4
Stavre [S] 182 H3
Stavreviken [S] 184 E4
Stavrochóri [GR] 140 G5
Stavrodrómi [GR] 136 D2
Stavrós [GR] 134 C6
Stavrós [GR] 132 C5
Stavrós [GR] 130 C4
Stavrós [GR] 140 C4
Stavrós [GR] 134 B4
Stavrós [GR] 132 G3
Stavrós [GR] 128 G4
Stavroúpoli [GR] 130 E2
Stavsjø [N] 172 B3
Stavsjø [N] 172 B3
Stavsnäs [S] 168 E3
Stawiguda [PL] 22 G4
Stawiski [PL] 24 D5
Stawiszyn [PL] 36 E4
St-Aygulf [F] 108 D5
St-Bard [F] 68 B1
St. Barthélemy [CH] 70 C1
St. Bartholomä [D] 60 G6
St-Béat [F] 84 F5
St-Beauzély [F] 106 D2
St-Benin [F] 56 D4
St-Benoît [F] 54 G5
St-Benoît-sur-Loire [F] 56 C1
St-Bertrand-de-Comminges [F] 84 F4
St.-Blaise [F] 106 G5
St Blasien [D] 58 F4
St-Blin [F] 44 D6
St-Bonnet [F] 68 H6
St-Bonnet-de-Joux [F] 56 F6
St-Bonnet-en-Champsaur [F] 70 A6
St-Bonnet-le-Château [F] 68 E3
St-Brevin-les-Pins [F] 40 E6
St-Brice-en-Coglès [F] 26 D5
St-Brieuc [F] 26 B4
St-Calais [F] 42 C5
St-Cast-le-Guildo [F] 26 B4
St-Céré [F] 66 H4
St-Cergue [CH] 70 B1
St-Cernin [F] 68 B4
St-Chamas [F] 106 H4
St-Chamond [F] 68 F3
St-Chély-d'Apcher [F] 68 C5
St-Chély-d'Aubrac [F] 68 B5
St-Chinian [F] 106 D4
St Christina / Santa Cristina [I] 72 D3
St Christoph [A] 72 B1
St.Christophe-en-Oisans [F] 70 A5
St-Ciers [F] 66 D2
St-Cirq-Lapopie [F] 66 G5
St.-Clair [F] 26 F3
St-Clar [F] 66 E6
St-Claud [F] 54 E6
St-Claude [F] 70 A1
St Clears [GB] 12 D2
St-Clément-sur-Durance [F] 108 E2
St-Côme-d'Olt [F] 68 B5
St-Cyprien [F] 66 F4
St-Cyprien-Plage [F] 92 G1
St David's [GB] 12 D1
St-Denis [F] 42 F3
St-Denis-d'Oléron [F] 54 B5
St-Denis-d'Orques [F] 42 A5
St-Didier-en-Velay [F] 68 E4
St-Dié [F] 58 D2
St-Dizier [F] 44 C5
St-Donat-sur-l'Herbasse [F] 68 F4
St. Doulagh's Church [IRL] 2 F6
Steane [N] 164 E2
Ste-Anne-d'Auray [F] 26 A6
Ste-Anne-la-Palud [F] 40 B2
Ste.-Barbe [F] 40 C3
Stechelberg [CH] 70 E2
Štěchovice [CZ] 48 F4
Steckborn [CH] 58 G4
Ste-Croix [CH] 58 C6
Ste-Croix-Volvestre [F] 84 G4
Steeg [A] 72 B1
Steenbergen [NL] 16 C6
Ste.-Engrâce [F] 84 D4
Ste-Enimie [F] 68 C6
Steenvoorde [F] 28 E2
Steenwijk [NL] 16 F3
Stefáni [GR] 132 D3
Štefanikova Mohyla [SK] 62 H3
Stefaniná [GR] 130 C4
Ste-Foy-la-Grande [F] 66 E3
Stegaros [N] 170 E5
Ste-Gauburge-Ste-Colombe [F] 26 G5
Stege [DK] 156 G4
Stegeborg [S] 168 B5
Stegersbach [A] 74 E2
Stegna [PL] 22 E2
St-Egrève [F] 68 H4
Ste-Hélène [F] 66 C3
Ste-Hermine [F] 54 C3
Stehnovo [RUS] 198 H4
Steigen [N] 192 D5
Steilwände [D] 60 B5
Stein [A] 62 D4
Stein [D] 46 G5
Stein [N] 190 B5
Stein [N] 170 H5
Steinaberg bru [N] 170 C5
Steinach [A] 72 D2
Stein am Rhein [CH] 58 G4
Steinau [D] 46 E2
Steinbach [D] 46 H2
Steinberg [D] 156 C5
Steinestø [N] 170 B3
Steinfeld [A] 72 G3
Steinfeld [D] 32 D1
Steinfeld [D] 30 G5
Steinfurt [D] 16 H5
Steingaden [D] 60 D5
Steinhagen [D] 20 C3
Steinhausen [D] 60 B4
Steinheim [D] 32 E3
Steinhorst [D] 32 G1
Steinibach [CH] 58 G6
Steinkjer [N] 190 C5
Steinløysa [N] 180 E2
Stein Pass [Eur.] 60 G6
Steinsåsen [N] 182 D4
Steinsberg [D] 46 C5
Steinsburg [D] 46 F2
Steinsholt [N] 164 G2
Steinsøynes [N] 180 F1
Steinsvik [N] 180 C4
Ste.-Jalle [F] 108 B2
Ste-Livrade-sur-Lot [F] 66 E5
Stellendam [NL] 16 C5
St-Eloy-les-Mines [F] 56 C6
Ste-Marie-aux-Mines [F] 58 D2
Ste-Marie-de-Campan [F] 84 F4
Ste-Maure-de-Touraine [F] 54 F3
Ste-Maxime [F] 108 D5
Ste-Menehould [F] 44 C4
Ste-Mère-du-Mont [F] 26 E2
Ste-Mère-Eglise [F] 26 E2
St-Emilion [F] 66 D3
Stemó [GR] 136 E2
Sten [S] 162 D1
Stenay [F] 44 D3
Stenbjerg [DK] 160 B4
Stenbo [S] 162 G3
Stendal [D] 34 C2
Stende [LV] 198 C5
Steneby [S] 166 D4
Stengelsrud [N] 164 G1
St Englmar [D] 60 G2
Stenhammar [S] 168 B4
Stení [GR] 134 C4
Steninge [S] 168 D2
Stenlille [DK] 156 F3
Stenløse [DK] 156 G2
Stennäs [S] 190 G6
Sténoma [GR] 132 F4
Stensele [S] 190 F4
Stensjö [S] 162 G3
Stensjön [S] 162 E2
Stenstorp [S] 166 F6
Stensträsk [S] 190 H4
Stenstrup [DK] 156 D4
Stensund [S] 190 G2
Stensund [S] 190 G3
Stenträsk [S] 190 H2
Stenudden [S] 190 G2
Stenungsund [S] 160 G1
Steornabhagh / Stornoway [GB] 6 C2
Stepanci [MK] 128 E2
Stepnica [PL] 20 F4
Stepojevac [YU] 150 B1
Sterdyń-Osada [PL] 38 D2
Sterehushche [UA] 204 G5
Stern / la Villa [I] 72 E3
Stérna [GR] 130 D2
Šternberg [D] 20 B4
Šternberk [CZ] 50 D5
Šternberk [CZ] 48 H6
Stérnes [GR] 140 C4
Stérnia [GR] 138 E1
Sterzing / Vipiteno [I] 72 D2
Ste-Sévère [F] 56 B5
Stes-Maries-de-la-Mer [F] 106 F5
St. Estèphe [F] 66 C2
Ste-Suzanne [F] 42 A4
Stęszew [PL] 36 C3
Štětí [CZ] 48 F2
St-Étienne [F] 108 C3
St-Étienne [F] 68 E3
St-Étienne-de-Baïgorry [F] 84 C3
St-Étienne-de-St-Geoirs [F] 68 G4
St-Étienne-de-Tinée [F] 108 E3
St-Étienne-les-Orgues [F] 108 C3
Ste-Tulle [F] 108 C4
Stevenage [GB] 14 E3
Stewarton [GB] 8 D3
Steyerberg [D] 32 E1
Steyersberg [A] 62 E6
Steyr [A] 62 B5
Steyr-Durchbruch [A] 62 B5
Stezherovo [BG] 148 B2
St-Fargeau [F] 56 D2
St.-Fiacre [F] 40 C3
St-Firmin [F] 68 H6
St-Florent [F] 114 C3
St-Florent [F] 40 G6
St-Florent [F] 56 B3
St.-Florent-des-Bois [F] 54 C3
St-Florentin [F] 56 E1
St. Florian [A] 60 H4
St-Flour [F] 68 C4
St-Fort-sur-Gironde [F] 66 D1
St-Fulgent [F] 54 C2
St Gallen [A] 62 C6
St Gallen [CH] 58 H5
St Gallenkirch [A] 72 B1
St-Galmier [F] 68 E3
St. Gangolf [D] 44 F3
St-Gaudens [F] 84 G4
St-Gaultier [F] 54 G4
St-Geniez-d'Olt [F] 68 B6
St-Genis-de-Saintonge [F] 66 D1
St-Genix-sur-Guiers [F] 68 H3
St.George [CH] 70 B1
St Georgen [A] 74 C2
St Georgen [A] 60 H5
St Georgen [D] 58 F3
St-Georges [F] 40 G6
St-Georges-de-Didonne [F] 54 C6
St. Georges-on-Couzan [F] 68 E2
St-Geours-de-Maremne [F] 66 B6
St-Germain [F] 66 G2
St-Germain [F] 42 F3
St-Germain-de-Joux [F] 68 H2
St-Germain-des-Fossés [F] 56 D6
St-Germain-des-Vaux [F] 26 D1
St-Germain-du-Bois [F] 56 G5
St-Germain-du-Plain [F] 56 G5
St-Germain-Laval [F] 68 E2
St-Germain-Lembron [F] 68 C3
St-Germain-l'Herm [F] 68 D3
St-Germain-Plage [F] 26 D3
St-Germer-de-Fly [F] 28 D6
St-Gervais [F] 106 D3
St-Gervais-d'Auvergne [F] 68 C1
St-Gervais-les-Bains [F] 70 C3
St-Géry [F] 66 G5
St-Gildas-des-Bois [F] 40 E5
St Gilgen [A] 60 H5
St-Gilles [F] 106 G4
St-Gilles-Croix-de-Vie [F] 54 B2
St Gingolph [CH] 70 C2
St-Girons [F] 84 G5
St-Girons-en-Marensin [F] 66 B5
St-Girons-Plage [F] 66 A5
St Goar [D] 46 B2
St Goarshausen [D] 46 B2
St-Gobain [F] 28 F6
St-Gorgon-Main [F] 58 B5
St-Guénolé [F] 40 B3
St-Guilhem-le-Desert [F] 106 E3
St Helens [GB] 10 D4
St-Helier [GBJ] 26 C3
St. Hilaire Cottes [F] 28 E3
St-Hilaire-de-Villefranche [F] 54 C5
St-Hilaire-du-Harcouët [F] 26 D5
St-Hippolyte [F] 58 C5
St-Hippolyte-du-Fort [F] 106 F3
St. Hoga [S] 160 G1
St-Honoré [F] 56 E4
St-Hubert [B] 44 D1
Stia [I] 110 G5
Stìcciano Scalo [I] 114 F2
Stiefern [A] 62 E3
Stiens [NL] 16 F2
Stift Zwettl [A] 62 D3
Stigen [N] 172 E2
Stigen [S] 166 D5
Stigliano [I] 122 C4
Stigliano, Bagni di- [I] 114 H5
Stignano [I] 124 D7
Stigsjö [S] 184 F4
Stigtomta [S] 168 C4
Stiklestad [N] 190 C6
Stilla [N] 194 B3
Stilo [I] 124 D6
St-Imier [CH] 58 D5
Stimlje [YU] 150 C5
St Ingbert [D] 44 G4
Stintino [I] 118 B2
Štip [MK] 128 F1
Stirling [GB] 8 E3
Štirovača [HR] 112 F3
Štitary [CZ] 62 E2
Štíty [CZ] 50 C4
St Ives [GB] 12 B5
St Ives [GB] 14 F2
Stixenstein [A] 62 E6
St-Jacut [F] 26 C4
St. Jakob [A] 72 F2
St Jakob im Rosental [A] 74 B3
St-James [F] 26 D5
Stjärnsund [S] 174 D5
Stjärnsund [S] 166 G4
St-Jean-Brévelay [F] 26 A6
St-Jean-Cap-Ferrat [F] 108 F4
St-Jean-d'Angély [F] 54 D5
St-Jean-de-Bournay [F] 68 G3
St-Jean-de-Losne [F] 56 H4
St-Jean-de-Luz [F] 84 B2
St-Jean-de-Maurienne [F] 70 B5
St-Jean-de-Monts [F] 54 A2
St-Jean-du-Bruel [F] 106 E3
St-Jean-du-Gard [F] 106 F2
St-Jean-du-Liget, Chapelle- [F] 54 G3
St-Jean-en-Royans [F] 68 G5
St-Jean-le-Thomas [F] 26 D4
St-Jean-Pied-de-Port [F] 84 C3
St. Jeans-d' Arves [F] 70 B5
St-Jeoire [F] 70 B2
St. Joan de Penyagolosa [E] 98 F2
St Johann am Tauern [A] 74 C1
St Johann im Pongau [A] 72 G1
St Johann in Tirol [A] 60 F6
St Johnstown [IRL] 2 F2
Stjørdal [N] 182 C1
St-Jorioz [F] 70 B3
St-Jory [F] 84 H3
St-Jouan-de-l'Isle [F] 26 B5
St-Jouin-de-Marnes [F] 54 E3
St-Juéry [F] 106 C2
St-Julien [F] 56 H6
St-Julien [F] 84 G4
St-Julien-Chapteuil [F] 68 E4
St-Julien-de-Vouvantes [F] 40 G5
St-Julien-en-Beauchêne [F] 68 G6
St-Julien-en-Genevois [F] 70 B2
St-Julien-l'Ars [F] 54 F4
St-Junien [F] 54 F6
St Just [GB] 12 B5
St-Just-en-Chaussée [F] 28 E6
St-Just-en-Chevalet [F] 68 E2
St-Justin [F] 66 D5
St Lambrecht [A] 74 B2
St-Lary-Soulan [F] 84 F5
St-Laurent [F] 66 G1
St-Laurent [F] 26 E3
St-Laurent-en-Grandvaux [F] 70 B1
St-Laurent-les-Bains [F] 68 D6
St-Laurent-Médoc [F] 66 C2
St-Leger [F] 56 F4
St.-Léon, Chapelle- [F] 44 G5
St-Léonard-de-Noblat [F] 66 H1
St Leonhard [A] 62 D4
St-Leu-d'Esserent [F] 42 F2
St-Lizier [F] 84 G4
St-Lô [F] 26 E3
St Lorenzen [A] 72 F3
St-Louis [F] 58 E4
St-Loup-sur-Semouse [F] 58 C3
St-Luc [CH] 70 D2
St-Lunaire [F] 26 C4
St-Lys [F] 84 H3
St-Macaire [F] 66 D4
St-Maclou [F] 26 G3
St-Maixent-l'Ecole [F] 54 D4
St.Malm [S] 168 B4
St-Malo [F] 26 C4
St-Mamest [F] 66 F3
St. Marcel [F] 70 B4
St-Marcellin [F] 68 G4
St. Marcellin-en-Forez [F] 68 E3
St. Märgen [D] 58 F3
St. Maria [D] 46 E6
St. Maria zu den Engeln [CH] 58 G5
St-Mars-la-Jaille [F] 40 G6
St. Martin [F] 40 E5
St-Martin-d'Auxigny [F] 56 C3
St-Martin-de-Londres [F] 106 E3
St. Martin-d' Entraunes [F] 108 E3
St-Martin-de-Ré [F] 54 B4
St-Martin-du-Canigou [F] 92 F1
St-Martin-Vésubie [F] 108 F3
St-Martory [F] 84 G4
St-Mathieu [F] 66 F1
St.-Mathieu, Pointe de- [F] 40 A2
St-Mathieu-de-Tréviers [F] 106 E3
St.Maurice [CH] 70 C2
St.Maurice la Souterraine [F] 54 G5
St-Maurice-Navacelles [F] 106 E3
St Maurice-sur-Moselle [F] 58 C3
St Mawes [GB] 12 C5
St-Maximin-la-Ste-Baume [F] 108 C5
St-Méen [F] 26 B5
St. Meinrad [CH] 58 G5
St. Mellösa [S] 166 H3
St Michael [A] 72 H2
St Michael [A] 74 C1
St Michael [A] 74 F2
St Michel / Mikkeli [FIN] 188 C6
St.-Michel-de Cuxa [F] 92 F1
St-Michel-de-Maurienne [F] 70 B5
St.Michel de Rieufret [F] 66 C4
St-Michel-en-Grève [F] 40 D1
St-Michel-en-l'Herm [F] 54 C4
St-Michel-Mont-Mercure [F] 54 C3
St-Mihiel [F] 44 D4
St. Miquel del Fai [E] 92 E3
St-Morand [F] 58 D4
St Moritz [CH] 70 H2
St-Nazaire [F] 40 E6
St-Nectaire [F] 68 C2
St Neots [GB] 14 E2
St.-Nicodème [F] 26 A5
St-Nicolas [F] 40 E5
St Nicolas-de-Port [F] 44 E5
St-Nicolas-du-Pélem [F] 26 A4
St-Niklaas [B] 28 H2
St Niklaus [CH] 70 E2
St Nikolai [A] 74 B1
Støa [N] 172 E2
Stobi [MK] 128 F2
Stoby [S] 158 D1
Stocka [S] 184 E6
Stockach [D] 58 G4
Stockaryd [S] 162 D3
Stockbridge [GB] 12 H4
Stöcke [S] 196 A6
Stockelsdorf [D] 18 G3
Stockerau [A] 62 F4
Stockheim [D] 46 G3
Stockholm [S] 168 D3
Stockport [GB] 10 E4
Stocksbo [S] 174 C1
Stockton on Tees [GB] 10 F2
Stoczek Klasztorny [PL] 22 H3
Stoczek Łukowski [PL] 38 D3
Stod [CZ] 48 D5
Stod [N] 190 C5
Stöde [S] 184 D4
Stødi [N] 190 E1
Stødi [N] 190 E1
St Oedenrode [NL] 30 E2
Stojan Mikhaylovski [BG] 148 E2
Stoke-on-Trent [GB] 10 E5
Stokke [N] 164 H3
Stokkemarke [DK] 156 F5
Stokkland [N] 164 F2
Stokkvågen [N] 190 D2
Stokkvågen [N] 190 D2
Stokmarknes [N] 192 D4
Štoky [CZ] 48 H5
Stola [S] 166 E5
Stolac [BiH] 152 C3
Stolberg [D] 30 F4
Stolbovo [RUS] 198 G5
Stolin [BY] 202 A7
Stollberg [D] 48 D2
Stöllet [S] 172 E5
Stolno [PL] 22 E5
St Olof [S] 158 D3
Stolpe [D] 34 E2
Stolpe [D] 20 E6
Stolpen [D] 34 F6
Stołpie [PL] 38 F5
Stolzenau [D] 32 E1
St-Omer [F] 28 E2
Stómio [GR] 132 G1
Stömne [S] 166 E2
Ston [HR] 152 C3
Stonařov [CZ] 48 H6
Stone [GB] 10 E5
Stonehaven [GB] 8 G1
Stongfjorden [N] 180 B6
Stonglandseidet [N] 192 E3
Stopanja [YU] 150 C3
Stopnica [PL] 52 C2
Stora [PL] 36 H6
Storå [S] 166 H2
Storå / Isojoki [FIN] 186 B5
Stora Blåsjön [S] 190 E4
Storås [N] 180 H2
Stora Sjöfallet [S] 192 F5
Storbäck [S] 190 F4
Storbergvika [N] 190 D5
Storborgaren [S] 190 G6
Storby [FIN] 174 H5
Stord [N] 170 B5
Stordal [N] 180 D4
Stordalen [S] 192 F4
Storebro [S] 162 F2
Storebru [N] 180 B6
Store Darum [DK] 156 B3
Storehaug [N] 170 C1
Store Heddinge [DK] 156 G3
Storekorsnes [N] 194 B2
Storelv [N] 194 A2
Storelvavoll [N] 182 D3
Store Merløse [DK] 156 F3
Store Molvik [N] 194 D1
Støren [N] 182 B2
Storestølen [N] 170 E3
Stor-Evdal [N] 172 C1
Storfall [S] 190 H6
Storfjellseter [N] 182 B6
Storfjord [N] 192 G3
Storfjord [N] 192 G3
Storfors [S] 166 G2
Storforshei [N] 190 E2
Storfossen [N] 194 C4
Storhallaren [N] 190 A6
Storhögen [S] 182 H2
Storholmsjö [S] 190 E6
Storjola [S] 190 E4
Storjord [N] 192 D6
Storjord [N] 190 E1
Storjorda [N] 190 E1
Storkow [D] 34 F3
Storkyro / Isokyrö [FIN] 186 B2
Storlægda [N] 182 C5
Storli [N] 180 G3
Storlien [S] 182 D2
Stormi [FIN] 176 E2
Stormyren [S] 190 G3
Störnäset [S] 190 F5
Stornes [N] 192 G2
Stornorrfors [S] 190 H6
Stornoway / Steornabhagh [GB] 6 C2
Storo [I] 72 B5
Storoddan [N] 180 G1
Storsätern [S] 182 D5
Storsävarträsk [S] 190 H5
Storsjö [S] 182 E3
Storslett [N] 192 G2
Størstein [N] 192 G1
Storsteinnes [N] 192 F3
Storsund [S] 196 A3
Stortinden [N] 194 B2
Storuman [S] 190 F4
Storvallen [S] 182 D2
Storvik [S] 174 D4
Storvika [N] 190 B5
Storvorde [DK] 160 E4
Storvreta [S] 168 D1
Stössen [D] 34 B6
St Oswald [A] 62 C3
St.-Oswald [F] 44 F3
Stotel [D] 18 D4
Sto. Toribio de Liébana [E] 82 D3
Stotternheim [D] 32 H6
St. Ottilien [D] 60 D4

Teck [D] 58 H2
Tecklenburg [D] 32 C2
Tecuci [RO] 204 D5
Teerijärvi / Terjärv [FIN] 196 C6
Teféli [GR] 140 E5
Tefenni [TR] 142 H1
Tegéa [GR] 136 E3
Tegelen [NL] 30 F3
Tegelträsk [S] 190 G6
Tegernsee [D] 60 E5
Teggiano [I] 120 G4
Téglás [H] 64 H5
Teglio [I] 72 A4
Teguise [E] 100 E6
Tehi [FIN] 176 H1
Teichel [D] 46 H1
Teichiussa [TR] 142 C1
Teignmouth [GB] 12 E5
Teillay [F] 40 F5
Teillet [F] 106 C3
Teisendorf [D] 60 G5
Teisko [FIN] 186 E6
Teixeiro [E] 78 D2
Tejeda [E] 100 C6
Tejn [DK] 158 E4
Teke [TR] 146 F2
Tekeriš [YU] 154 F3
Tekirdağ [TR] 146 C3
Tekovské Lužany [SK] 64 B5
Telana [I] 118 E5
Telavåg [N] 170 A4
Telč [CZ] 48 H6
Telde [E] 100 C6
Teleborg [S] 162 E5
Telese Terme [I] 120 E2
Telford [GB] 10 D6
Telfs [A] 72 C1
Telgte [D] 32 C3
Telheiro [P] 94 B3
Telish [BG] 148 A3
Teljo [FIN] 196 G5
Tellingstedt [D] 18 E2
Tellskap [CH] 58 F6
Telmessos [TR] 142 G3
Telšiai [LT] 200 E4
Telti [I] 118 D3
Tembleque [E] 96 G2
Temerin [YU] 154 F1
Temmes [FIN] 196 D4
Temnata Dupka [BG] 150 F4
Témpio Pausánia [I] 118 D3
Templemore [IRL] 4 E3
Templetouhy [IRL] 4 E3
Templin [D] 20 D6
Templom [H] 64 C5
Temse [B] 28 H2
Temska [YU] 150 E3
Tenala / Tenhola [FIN] 176 F5
Tenby [GB] 12 D2
Tence [F] 68 E4
Tenda, Colle di- / Tende, Col de- [Eur.] 108 F3
Tende [F] 108 F3
Tendilla [E] 88 H6
Tenebrón [E] 88 A3
Tenevo [BG] 148 E5
Tenhola / Tenala [FIN] 176 F5
Tenhult [S] 162 D2
Tenja [HR] 154 E1
Tenk [H] 64 E6
Tennänget [S] 172 F3
Tennevol [N] 192 F3
Tenterden [GB] 14 F5
Tentudia, Mon. de- [E] 94 G4
Teo / Ramallosa [E] 78 C3
Teofipol' [UA] 204 D2
Teolo [I] 110 G1
Teos [TR] 144 C5
Tepasto [FIN] 194 C6
Tepecik [TR] 144 G1
Tepecik [TR] 146 F3
Tepeköy [TR] 144 E4
Tepelenë [AL] 128 B6
Teplá [CZ] 48 D4
Teplice [CZ] 48 E2
Teplice nad Metují [CZ] 50 B2
Teploye [RUS] 202 F5
Tepsa [FIN] 194 C6
Téramo [I] 116 C3
Ter Apel [NL] 16 H3
Teratyn [PL] 38 G6
Terebin' [PL] 52 G1
Terebishche [RUS] 198 G3
Terebovlia [UA] 204 C3
Terehovo [RUS] 198 H4
Teremia Mare [RO] 76 F5
Terespol [PL] 38 F3
Terezín [CZ] 48 F2
Terezino Polje [HR] 74 H5
Tergnier [F] 28 F6
Terjärv / Teerijärvi [FIN] 196 C6
Terkoz [TR] 146 E2
Terland [N] 164 B4
Terlizzi [I] 122 D2
Termal [TR] 146 F3
Termas de Monfortinho [P] 86 G3
Terme di Lurisia [I] 108 F3
Terme di Valdieri [I] 108 F3
Terme Luigiane [I] 124 C4
Termes-d'Armagnac [F] 84 F2
Terme S. Lucia [I] 116 C2
Terme Vigliatore [I] 126 D4
Términi Imerese [I] 126 D2
Terminillo [I] 116 B4
Terminón [E] 82 E5
Térmoli [I] 116 F5
Termolovo [RUS] 178 G3
Termonfeckin [IRL] 2 F5
Terndrup [DK] 160 E4
Terneuzen [NL] 28 H1
Terni [I] 116 A3
Ternitz [A] 62 E6
Ternopil' [UA] 204 C2
Térovo [GR] 132 D2
Terpan [AL] 128 B5
Terpezita [RO] 150 F1
Terpní [GR] 130 B3
Terracina [I] 120 C2
Terradillos de los Templarios [E] 82 C5
Terråk [N] 190 D4
Terralba [I] 118 C5
Terra Mala [I] 118 D7
Terra Mitica [E] 104 E2
Terranova di Pollino [I] 122 C6
Terrassa / Tarrasa [E] 92 E4
Terrasson-la-Villedieu [F] 66 G3
Terrateig [E] 98 E6
Terrazos [E] 82 F5
Terriente [E] 98 D2
Terskanperä [FIN] 196 D5
Tersløse [DK] 156 F3
Tertenía [I] 118 E6
Teruel [E] 98 E2
Tervahauta [FIN] 176 E1
Tervakoski [FIN] 176 G3
Tervel [BG] 148 F1
Tervo [FIN] 186 H2
Tervola [FIN] 196 C2
Tervuren [B] 30 C4
Terz [A] 62 D5
Terzaga [E] 90 C6
Tesejerague [E] 100 D6
Teslić [BiH] 154 C3
Teslui [RO] 150 G1
Tessin [D] 20 C3
Tessy-sur-Vire [F] 26 E4
Tét [H] 62 H6
Tetbury [GB] 12 G3
Teterow [D] 20 C4
Teteven [BG] 148 A4
Tetovo [BG] 148 D2
Tetovo [MK] 128 D1
Tetrálofo [GR] 128 F5
Tettnang [D] 58 H4
Teuchrania [TR] 144 C3
Teufelshöhle [D] 46 H4
Teufen [CH] 58 H5
Teulada [E] 104 F2
Teulada [I] 118 C7
Teupitz [D] 34 E3
Teurnia [A] 72 H3
Teuro [FIN] 176 F3
Teuva / Östermark [FIN] 186 B4
Tevaniemi [FIN] 186 D6
Tevel [H] 76 B4
Tevfikiye [TR] 130 H5
Tewkesbury [GB] 12 G2
Tewli [BY] 38 G2
Texeiro [E] 78 E3
Thal [A] 72 F3
Thale [D] 34 A4
Thalfang [D] 44 G2
Thalheim [D] 48 D2
Thalmässing [D] 46 G6
Thalwil [CH] 58 F5
Thame [GB] 14 D3
Thann [F] 58 D3
Thannhausen [D] 60 C3
Tharandt [D] 48 E1
Thárros [I] 118 B5
Thásos [GR] 130 E4
Thatcham [GB] 12 H4
Thaumiers [F] 56 C4
Theessen [D] 34 C3
Them [DK] 156 C1
Themar [D] 46 F2
Thénezay [F] 54 E3
Thenon [F] 66 G3
Theodosiia [UA] 204 H6
Theológos [GR] 130 E4
Theológos [GR] 134 A4
Théoule [F] 108 E5
Thera [TR] 142 E2
Thérma [GR] 138 G1
Thermá [GR] 130 G4
Thérmi [GR] 130 B4
Thermí [GR] 134 H2
Thermisía [GR] 136 G2
Thérmo [GR] 132 F5
Thermopíles [GR] 132 G4
Thermopýles [GR] 132 G4
Thernberg [A] 62 E6
Thérouanne [F] 28 E2
Thespies [GR] 134 A5
Thessaloníki [GR] 130 A4
Thetford [GB] 14 G2
The Turoe Stone [IRL] 2 C5
Theuley [F] 58 B3
Theux [B] 30 E5
Thevet-St-Julien [F] 56 B4
Theze [F] 84 E3
Thiaucourt-Regniéville [F] 44 E4
Thiberville [F] 26 G4
Thiélbemont-Farémont [F] 44 C5
Thiendorf [D] 34 E5
Thiene [I] 72 D5
Thiers [F] 68 D2
Thiersee [A] 60 F6
Thiersheim [D] 48 C3
Thiesi [I] 118 C3
Thiessow [D] 20 E2
Thimariá [GR] 130 H3
Thingeyri [IS] 20 96 C1
Thingvellir [IS] 192 A3
Thionville [F] 44 E3
Thíra [GR] 138 F5
Thíra / Fira [GR] 138 F5
Thirette [F] 68 H1
Thirsk [GB] 10 F3
Thisted [DK] 160 C4
Thísvi [GR] 132 H5
Thíva [GR] 134 B5
Thivars [F] 42 D4
Thiviers [F] 66 F2
Thizy [F] 68 F2
Tho, Pieve del- [I] 110 G4
Thoissey [F] 68 G1
Tholey [D] 44 G3
Tholó [GR] 136 C3
Thomasberg [A] 62 E6
Thomas Street [IRL] 2 D5
Thomastown [IRL] 4 E4
Thônes [F] 70 B3
Thonon [F] 70 B2
Thonon-les-Bains [F] 70 B2
Thorens-Glières, Château de- [F] 70 B3
Thorikó [GR] 136 H1
Thörl [A] 62 D6
Thornbury [GB] 12 G3
Thorney [GB] 14 F2
Thornhill [GB] 8 D4
Thoronet, Abbaye du- [F] 108 D5
Thors [F] 44 C6
Thórshöfn [IS] 192 C2
Thouarcé [F] 54 D2
Thouars [F] 54 E2
Thouría [GR] 136 D4
Thoúrio [GR] 130 H1
Thueyts [F] 68 E5
Thuin [B] 28 H4
Thuir [F] 92 G1
Thum [D] 48 D2
Thun [CH] 70 D1
Thuret [F] 68 D2
Thürkow [D] 20 C4
Thurles / Durlas [IRL] 4 E3
Thurnau [D] 46 H3
Thurn Pass [A] 72 F1
Thurso [GB] 6 F2
Thury-Harcourt [F] 26 F4
Thusis [CH] 70 H1
Thyborøn [DK] 160 B4
Thymianá [GR] 134 G5
Thyregod [DK] 156 C1
Tiana [I] 118 D5
Tibaes [P] 80 C3
Tibarrié [F] 106 C3
Tibava [SK] 64 H2
Tiberio, Grotta di- [I] 120 C2
Tibro [S] 166 F5
Ticha [BG] 148 D3
Tidaholm [S] 166 F6
Tidan [S] 166 F5
Tidersrum [S] 162 F1
Tidö [S] 168 B2
Tiefenbronn [D] 58 G1
Tiefencastel [CH] 70 H2
Tiefensee [D] 34 F2
Tiel [NL] 16 E5
Tielt [B] 28 G2
Tiemassaari [FIN] 188 D4
Tienen [B] 30 D4
Tiengen [D] 58 F4
Tiercé [F] 40 H6
Tierga [E] 90 D3
Tiermas [E] 88 H3
Tierp [S] 174 F5
Tieva [FIN] 194 C6
Tighina [MD] 204 E4
Tigkáki [GR] 142 C3
Tignes [F] 70 C4
Tihany [H] 76 A2
Tihilä [FIN] 196 E5
Tihusniemi [FIN] 188 D4
Tihuţa, Pasul- [RO] 204 C4
Tiironkyla [FIN] 186 F2
Tiistenjoki [FIN] 186 D3
Tijarafe [E] 100 A4
Tikhvin [RUS] 202 D1
Tikkakoski [FIN] 186 G4
Tikkala [FIN] 186 F5
Tikkala [FIN] 188 G3
Tilberga [S] 168 C2
Tilburg [NL] 30 E2
Tilbury [GB] 14 F4
Til-Châtel [F] 56 H3
Tiltagals [LV] 198 F5
Tiltrem [N] 190 B5
Tilži [LV] 198 G5
Tim [RUS] 202 F7
Timahoe [IRL] 4 F3
Time [N] 164 A3
Timişoara [RO] 76 G5
Timmel [D] 18 B4
Timmele [S] 162 C2
Timmendorfer Strand [D] 18 H3
Timmernabben [S] 162 G4
Timmersdala [S] 166 F5
Timmervik [S] 166 D5
Timoleague [IRL] 4 C5
Timoniemi [FIN] 196 G5
Timovaara [FIN] 188 E1
Timrå [S] 184 E4
Timsfors [S] 162 C6
Tinahely [IRL] 4 F4
Tinajo [E] 100 E5
Tinca [RO] 76 H3
Tinchebray [F] 26 E4
Tindaya [E] 100 E6
Tineo [E] 78 G3
Tingelstad [N] 170 H4
Tinglev [DK] 156 B4
Tingsryd [S] 162 E5
Tingstad [S] 168 B5
Tingstäde [S] 168 G4
Tingvoll [N] 180 F2
Tinnoset [N] 164 F1
Tínos [GR] 138 E2
Tiñosillos [E] 88 E4
Tintern Abbey [IRL] 4 F5
Tinuži [LV] 198 E5
Tiobraid Árann / Tipperary [IRL] 4 D4
Tione di Trento [I] 72 C4
Tipasjoki [FIN] 196 F5
Tipasoja [FIN] 196 F5
Tipperary / Tiobraid Árann [IRL] 4 D4
Tiranë [AL] 128 B3
Tirano [I] 72 B4
Tiraspol [MD] 204 E4
Tire [TR] 144 D5
Tirgo [E] 82 G6
Tiriolo [I] 124 E5
Tirmo [FIN] 178 B4
Tirol / Tirolo [I] 72 C3
Tirolo / Tirol [I] 72 C3
Tirrénia [I] 110 D6
Tirschenreuth [D] 48 C4
Tirstrup [DK] 160 E6
Tíryntha [GR] 136 F2
Tišća [BiH] 154 E4
Tiscar-Don Pedro [E] 102 F2
Tismana, Mănăstirea- [RO] 204 B6
Tisno [HR] 112 G6
Tišnov [CZ] 50 B6
Tisovec [SK] 64 D3
Tistrup [DK] 156 B2
Tisvilde [DK] 156 G1
Tiszaalpár [H] 76 E3
Tiszabábolna [H] 64 F6
Tiszacsege [H] 64 F6
Tiszaföldvár [H] 76 E2
Tiszafüred [H] 64 F6
Tiszakécske [H] 76 E2
Tiszalök [H] 64 G5
Tiszalúc [H] 64 F5
Tiszaörs [H] 64 F6
Tiszaroff [H] 76 E1
Tiszaszőlős [H] 64 F6
Tiszaújváros [H] 64 F5
Tiszavasvári [H] 64 G5
Titel [YU] 154 G1
Titisee [D] 58 F3
Tito [I] 120 G4
Tito Bustillo, Cueva de- [E] 82 C2
Titova Spilja [BiH] 154 A3
Titov Veles [MK] 128 F1
Titran [N] 190 A6
Tittling [D] 60 H3
Tittmoning [D] 60 G4
Titz [D] 30 F4
Tiuccia [F] 114 A4
Tiukka / Tjöck [FIN] 186 B4
Tiurajärvi [FIN] 194 C6
Tivat [YU] 152 D4
Tived [S] 166 G4
Tiverton [GB] 12 E4
Tivoli [I] 116 B5
Tizzano [F] 114 A6
Tjæreborg [DK] 156 B2
Tjällmo [S] 166 H5
Tjalme [S] 192 G4
Tjämotis [S] 190 G1
Tjautjas [S] 192 G6
Tjeldnes [N] 192 E4
Tjele [DK] 160 D5
Tjelle [N] 180 F3
Tjentište [BiH] 152 D2
Tjöck / Tiukka [FIN] 186 B4
Tjolmen [N] 190 E3
Tjolöholm [S] 160 H3
Tjøme [N] 164 H3
Tjong [N] 190 D1
Tjønnefoss [N] 164 E3
Tjørhom [N] 164 C3
Tjørnhom [N] 164 C5
Tjørnuvík [FR] 160 A1
Tjøtta [N] 190 D3
Tjuvkil [S] 160 G1
Tkon [HR] 112 G5
Tleń [PL] 22 D4
Tlmače [SK] 64 B4
Tlos [TR] 142 G3
Tłuchowo [PL] 36 G1
Tłuszcz [PL] 38 C2
Tobarra [E] 98 B6
Tobercurry [IRL] 2 D3
Tobermory [GB] 6 B6
Toblach / Dobbiaco [I] 72 E3
Tocha [P] 80 A6
Tocina [E] 94 H5
Töcksfors [S] 166 C2
Todalen [N] 180 G3
Todi [I] 116 A3
Todorići [BiH] 154 B4
Tødsø [DK] 160 C4
Todtmoos [D] 58 E4
Todtnau [D] 58 E3
Tõdva [EST] 198 D1
Toftbyn [S] 174 C4
Tofte [N] 164 H2
Tofterup [DK] 156 B2
Tofteryd [S] 162 D3
Tofteseter [N] 170 H1
Toftesetra [N] 180 G5
Toftir [FR] 160 B2
Toftlund [DK] 156 B3
Togher [IRL] 2 D5
Tohmajärvi [FIN] 188 G3
Toholampi [FIN] 196 C6
Tohvri [EST] 198 E3
Toichío [GR] 128 E5
Toijala [FIN] 176 F2
Toikkala [FIN] 178 C2
Toikkala [FIN] 178 D2
Toirano, Grotte di- [I] 108 G3
Toitz [D] 20 C3
Toivakka [FIN] 186 G5
Toivola [FIN] 178 C1
Töjby [FIN] 186 A4
Tojšići [BiH] 154 E3
Tokagjelet [N] 170 B4
Tokaj [H] 64 G4
Tokari [PL] 36 F4
Tokarnia [PL] 50 H4
Tokarnia [PL] 52 B2
Tokary [PL] 38 F2
Tokmak [UA] 204 H4
Toksovo [RUS] 178 H4
Tolcsva [H] 64 G4
Toledo [E] 96 F1
Tolentino [I] 116 C2
Tolfa [I] 114 G4
Tolfta [S] 174 F5
Tolg [S] 162 E4
Tolga [N] 182 C4
Tolkis / Tolkkinen [FIN] 178 B4
Tolkkinen / Tolkis [FIN] 178 B4
Tolkmicko [PL] 22 F2
Tollarp [S] 158 D2
Tølløse [DK] 156 F3
Tolmachevo [RUS] 198 H1
Tolmezzo [I] 72 G4
Tolmin [SLO] 72 H4
Tolna [H] 76 C4
Tolne [DK] 160 E2
Toló [GR] 136 F2
Tolob [GB] 6 G4
Tolonen [FIN] 194 D5
Tolosa [E] 84 B3
Tolosa [P] 86 E4
Tolosenmäki [FIN] 188 G4
Tolox [E] 102 B4
Tolva [FIN] 194 F8
Tolve [I] 120 H4
Tomar [P] 86 D3
Tomarovka [RUS] 202 F7
Tomaševo [YU] 150 A4
Tomaszów Lubelski [PL] 52 G2
Tomaszów Mazowiecki [PL] 36 H5
Tomatin [GB] 6 E5
Tombebœuf [F] 66 E4
Tomelilla [S] 158 D3
Tomelloso [E] 96 G4
Tomintoul [GB] 6 E5
Tømmernes [N] 192 E5
Tommerup [DK] 156 D3
Tømmervåg [N] 180 F2
Tommola [FIN] 178 C1
Tompa [H] 76 D4
Tomra [N] 180 D3
Tømra [N] 182 C2
Tomter [N] 166 B2
Tona [E] 92 E3
Tonara [I] 118 D5
Tonbridge [GB] 14 E5
Tondela [P] 80 C6
Tønder [DK] 156 B4
Tongeren (Tongres) [B] 30 E4
Tongres (Tongeren) [B] 30 E4
Tongue [GB] 6 E2
Tonnay-Boutonne [F] 54 C5
Tonnay-Charente [F] 54 C5
Tonneins [F] 66 E5
Tonnerre [F] 56 F2
Tonnes [N] 190 D1
Tönning [D] 18 E2
Tonquédec, Château de- [F] 40 D1
Tønsberg [N] 164 H3
Tonstad [N] 164 C4
Toomyvara [IRL] 2 D6
Toourmakeady [IRL] 2 C4
Topares [E] 102 H3
Topchii [BG] 148 D2
Töpchin [D] 34 E3
Topczewo [PL] 24 E6
Topli Dol [YU] 150 E3
Toplița [RO] 204 C4
Toplou [GR] 140 G4
Topo [P] 100 C3
Topola [YU] 150 B1
Topolčani [MK] 128 E3
Topoľčany [SK] 64 B3
Topoľčianský hrad [SK] 64 A3
Topólia [GR] 140 B4
Topolovățu Mare [RO] 76 H5
Topolovgrad [BG] 146 A1
Topolovica [HR] 74 G6
Topolovo [BG] 148 B6
Toporu [RO] 148 C1
Topusko [HR] 112 H1
Toques [E] 78 D3
Torà [E] 92 D3
Toral de los Vados [E] 78 F5
Torbalı [TR] 144 D4
Tørberget [N] 172 D2
Torbole [I] 72 C5
Torcello [I] 72 F6
Tordera [E] 92 F4
Tordesillas [E] 88 E2
Tordesilos [E] 90 C6
Töre [S] 196 B2
Töreboda [S] 166 F5
Toreby [DK] 20 A1
Torekov [S] 160 H6
Torelló [E] 92 E3
Toreno [E] 78 F5
Toresund [S] 168 C3
Torfyanovka [RUS] 178 E3
Torgåsmon [S] 172 F3
Torgau [D] 34 D5
Torgelow [D] 20 E4
Torgiano [I] 116 A2
Torhamn [S] 158 G1
Torhout [B] 28 F2
Tori [EST] 198 E3
Torigni-sur-Vire [F] 26 E3
Torija [E] 88 H5
Toril [E] 98 D2
Torino [I] 70 D5
Torino di Sangro [I] 116 E5
Torino di Sangro Marina [I] 116 E5
Torla [E] 84 E5
Torma [EST] 198 F2
Tormac [RO] 76 H6
Törmäkylä [FIN] 196 E4
Törmänen [FIN] 194 D5
Törmänki [FIN] 194 C7
Törmänmäki [FIN] 196 E4
Törmäsjärvi [FIN] 194 C8
Tormos [E] 84 D6
Tornal'a [SK] 64 E4
Tornavacas [E] 88 B5
Tornby [DK] 160 E2
Torneå / Tornio [FIN] 196 C2
Tørnes [N] 180 E2
Tørnes [N] 164 F3
Torneträsk [S] 192 G4
Tornio / Torneå [FIN] 196 C2
Tornioniemi [FIN] 188 E4
Tornjoš [YU] 76 E5
Toro [E] 88 D1
Törökszentmiklós [H] 76 E2
Toróni [GR] 130 C6
Torony [H] 74 F2
Toropec [RUS] 202 D3
Toros de Guisando [E] 88 E5
Torp [FIN] 174 H5
Torp [S] 166 C5
Torpa [S] 162 C5
Torpa Stenhus [S] 162 B2
Torpo [N] 170 F3
Torpoint [GB] 12 D5
Torpsbruk [S] 162 D4
Torpshammar [S] 184 D4
Torquay [GB] 12 E5
Torquemada [E] 82 D6
Torralba [E] 90 B4
Torralba [E] 96 F4
Torrão [P] 94 D2
Torre [E] 102 D5
Torre Annunziata [I] 120 E3
Torre Beretti [I] 70 F6
Torre Beretti [I] 70 F6
Torreblanca [E] 98 G3
Torrecaballeros [E] 88 F4
Torrecampo [E] 96 D5
Torre Canne [I] 122 F3
Torrechiara, Castello di- [I] 110 D3
Torrecilla [E] 98 C1
Torrecillas de la Tiesa [E] 96 B1
Torreciudad, Santuario de- [E] 90 H3
Torre de D. Chama [P] 80 F3
Torre de Juan Abad [E] 96 G5
Torre de la Higuera [E] 100 F2
Torre del Bierzo [E] 78 F5
Torre del Compte [E] 102 E2
Torre del Greco [I] 120 E3
Torre del Lago Puccini [I] 110 D5
Torre dell'Impiso [I] 126 B1
Torre del Mar [E] 102 C5
Torredembarra [E] 92 C5
Torre de Moncorvo [P] 80 E5
Torre de' Pàsseri [I] 116 D4
Torre de Santa María [E] 86 H6
Torredonjimeno [E] 102 D2
Torre Faro [I] 124 C7
Torrefarrera [E] 90 H4
Torregamones [E] 80 G4
Torre Grande [I] 118 B5
Torreguadiaro [E] 100 H5
Torreira [P] 80 B5
Torrejoncillo [E] 86 H4
Torrejón de Ardoz [E] 88 G6
Torrejón de la Calzada [E] 88 F6
Torrejón del Rey [E] 88 G5
Torrejón el Rubio [E] 88 A6
Torrelaguna [E] 88 G4
Torrelapaja [E] 90 C3
Torrelavega [E] 82 E3
Torrelobatón [E] 88 E1
Torrelodones [E] 88 F5
Torremaggiore [I] 116 F6
Torremejía [E] 94 H2
Torre Melissa [I] 124 F4
Torremocha [E] 86 H6
Torremolinos [E] 102 B5
Torremormojón [E] 82 C6
Torrenostra [E] 98 G3
Torrent [E] 98 E5
Torrente de Cinca [E] 90 G5
Torrenueva [E] 102 E5
Torre Orsaia [I] 120 G5
Torre-Pacheco [E] 104 C4
Torre Pellice [I] 70 C6
Torreperogil [E] 102 F2
Torrequemada [E] 86 H5
Torre Santa Susanna [I] 122 F4
Torres Cabrera [E] 102 C1
Torres Novas [P] 86 C4
Torre S. Sabina [I] 122 F3
Torres Vedras [P] 86 B4
Torretta [I] 124 F4
Torrette di Fano [I] 112 C6
Torre Vã [P] 94 C3
Torrevieja [E] 104 D3
Torricella [I] 122 F5
Torri del Benaco [I] 72 C6
Torríglia [I] 110 B3
Torrijas [E] 98 E3
Torrijos [E] 96 E1
Tørring [DK] 156 C2
Torrita di Siena [I] 114 G2
Torroella de Montgrí [E] 92 G3
Torrox [E] 102 D5
Torsåker [S] 174 D4
Torsåker [S] 168 D4
Torsås [S] 162 F6
Torsborg [S] 182 F3
Torsburgen [S] 168 G5
Torsby [S] 166 E1
Torsby [S] 172 E5
Torsfjärden [S] 190 E5
Torshälla [S] 168 B3
Tórshavn [FR] 160 B2
Torslanda [S] 160 G2
Torsminde [DK] 160 B5
Törtel [H] 76 E2
Tortinmäki [FIN] 176 E4
Tórtola de Henares [E] 88 H5
Tórtoles de Esgueva [E] 88 G2
Tortoli [I] 118 E5
Tortona [I] 110 B2
Tortora [I] 120 H6
Tortoreto [I] 116 D3
Tortoreto Lido [I] 116 D3
Tortorici [I] 126 F2
Tortosa [E] 92 A5
Tortosendo [P] 86 F2
Toruń [PL] 22 E6
Torup [S] 162 B4
Torup Strand [DK] 160 C3
Tõrva [EST] 198 E3
Tor Vaiánica [I] 116 A6
Torvikbukt [N] 180 F2
Tørvikbygd [N] 170 C4
Torvinen [FIN] 194 D7
Torvinen [FIN] 194 D7
Torvsjö [S] 190 F5
Torzhok [RUS] 202 E3
Torzym [PL] 34 H3
Tosbotn [N] 190 D3
Toscolano Maderno [I] 72 B5
Tösens [A] 72 C2
Toses, Collado de- [E] 92 E2
Tosno [RUS] 202 C1
Tossa de Mar [E] 92 F4
Tossåsen [S] 182 G3
Tossavanlahti [FIN] 186 G1
Tösse [S] 166 D4
Tostedt [D] 18 F5
Tószeg [H] 76 E2
Toszek [PL] 50 F3
Totana [E] 104 B3
Totebo [S] 162 F2
Tôtes [F] 28 B5
Tótkomlós [H] 76 F4
Tøtlandsvik [N] 164 C2
Totnes [GB] 12 E5
Tøttdal [N] 190 C5
Tottijärvi [FIN] 176 F2
Toucy [F] 56 E2
Touffou [F] 54 F4
Toul [F] 44 E5
Toulon [F] 108 C6
Toulon sur Allier [F] 56 D5
Toulon-sur-Arroux [F] 56 F5
Toulouse [F] 84 H3
Tourcoing [F] 28 F3
Tourmalet, Col du- [F] 84 E4
Tournai (Doornik) [B] 28 G3
Tournan [F] 42 G4
Tournay [F] 84 F4
Tournon [F] 68 F5
Tournon-d'Agenais [F] 66 F5
Tournon-St-Martin [F] 54 G4
Tournus [F] 56 G6
Tours [F] 54 F2
Tourves [F] 108 C5
Toury [F] 42 E5
Toutes Aures, Col de- [F] 108 D4
Toužim [CZ] 48 D3
Tovarnik [HR] 154 E2
Tøvik [N] 180 E2
Tövsala / Taivassalo [FIN] 176 C4
Tovste [UA] 204 C3
Towcester [GB] 14 D2
Töysä [FIN] 186 D3
Trabada [E] 78 F2
Trabadelo [E] 78 E5
Trabanca [E] 80 G5
Traben-Trarbach [D] 44 G2
Trabia [I] 126 D2
Trabotivište [MK] 128 H1
Trabuc, Grottes de- [F] 106 F3
Tracheiá [GR] 136 F2
Trachíli [GR] 134 C5
Tracino [I] 126 A5
Trädet [S] 162 C1
Trælleborg [DK] 156 F3
Trættia [N] 190 C6
Trafaria [P] 86 A5
Trafoi [I] 72 B3
Tragacete [E] 98 C1
Traian [RO] 148 B2
Traiguera [E] 92 A6
Traisen [A] 62 D5
Traiskirchen [A] 62 F5
Traismauer [A] 62 E4
Trajano [E] 100 G3
Trakai [LT] 24 H1
Trakošćan [HR] 74 E4
Tralee / Trá Lí [IRL] 4 B3
Trá Lí / Tralee [IRL] 4 B3
Tralleis [TR] 144 E5
Tramariglio [I] 118 B3
Tramelan [CH] 58 D5
Tramonti di Sopra [I] 72 F4
Tramore [IRL] 4 E5
Tranås [S] 162 E1
Tranby [N] 164 H1
Trancoso [P] 80 D6
Tranderup [DK] 156 D4
Tranekær [DK] 156 E4
Tranekær Slot [DK] 156 E4
Tranemo [S] 162 C3
Trångmon [S] 190 E4
Trängslet [S] 172 F2
Trångsviken [S] 182 G2
Tranhult [S] 162 C3
Trani [I] 122 D2
Trankil [S] 166 C3
Tranóvalto [GR] 128 F6
Tranøya [N] 192 E4
Transtrand [S] 172 F3
Tranum Strand [DK] 160 D3
Tranvik [S] 168 E3
Trápani [I] 126 B2
Trapishte [BG] 148 D3
Trappe d'Aiguebelle, Monastère de la- [F] 68 F6
Trappes [F] 42 F4
Traryd [S] 162 C5
Träskända / Järvenpää [FIN] 176 H4
Träskvik [FIN] 186 B5
Träslövsläge [S] 160 H4
Trasmiras [E] 78 D6
Trassem [D] 44 F3
Trästenik [BG] 148 A3
Tratzberg [A] 60 E6
Traun [A] 62 B4
Traunkirchen [A] 62 A5
Traunreut [D] 60 F5
Traunstein [D] 60 G5
Trautenfels [A] 62 B6
Trautmannsdorf [A] 62 F5
Travemünde [D] 18 H3
Travers [CH] 58 C6
Travnik [BiH] 154 C4
Travo [F] 114 B5
Trazo [E] 78 C2
Trbovlje [SLO] 74 C5
Trèban [F] 56 D5
Trebatsch [D] 34 F3
Trebbin [D] 34 E3
Třebechovice pod Orebem [CZ] 50 B3
Třebenice [CZ] 48 F2
Trébeurden [F] 40 D1
Třebíč [CZ] 50 A6
Trebinje [BiH] 152 D3
Trebisacce [I] 122 D6
Trebišov [SK] 64 G3
Trebnje [SLO] 74 C5
Třeboň [CZ] 62 C2
Tréboul [F] 40 B3
Třebovice [CZ] 50 B4
Trebujena [E] 100 F3
Trecastagni [I] 126 G3
Trecate [I] 70 F5
Trecenta [I] 110 F2
Trecesson, Château de- [F] 26 B6
Treffurt [D] 32 G5
Tregaron [GB] 10 B6
Trégastel [F] 40 D1
Tregnago [I] 72 C6
Tréguier [F] 26 A3
Trehörna [S] 162 E1
Trehörningsjö [S] 190 G6
Treia [D] 18 E1
Treibach [A] 74 B3
Treignac [F] 66 H2
Treis [D] 44 H1
Trekanten [S] 162 F5
Trelde [DK] 156 C2
Trelleborg [S] 158 C3
Tremês [P] 86 C4
Tremestieri [I] 124 B7
Tremezzo [I] 70 G3
Tremisht [AL] 128 C6
Třemošná [CZ] 48 E4
Tremp [E] 92 C2
Trenčianska Turná [SK] 64 A2
Trenčianske Bohuslavice [SK] 64 A3
Trenčín [SK] 64 A2
Trend [DK] 160 C4
Trendelburg [D] 32 F4
Trengereid [N] 170 B4
Trent [CH] 70 C3
Trento [I] 72 C4
Treppeln [D] 34 G3
Trept [F] 68 G3
Tres Cantos [E] 88 F5
Trescore Balneario [I] 70 H4
Tresenda [I] 72 B4
Tresfjord [N] 180 E3
Tresigallo [I] 110 G2
Treski [EST] 198 G3
Treskog [S] 166 D1
Treskovec, Manastir- [MK] 128 E2
Tresnurághes [I] 118 B4
Trespaderne [E] 82 F5
Třešť [CZ] 48 H6
Tresta [GB] 6 H3
Trets [F] 108 B5
Tretten [N] 170 H2
Treuchtlingen [D] 60 D2
Treuenbrietzen [D] 34 D3
Treugen [N] 164 E3
Treveles [E] 102 E4
Tréveray [F] 44 D5
Trevi [I] 116 B3
Treviglio [I] 70 H5
Trevignano Romano [I] 114 H4
Treviño [E] 82 G5
Treviso [I] 72 E6
Trévoux [F] 68 F2
Trezelles [F] 56 D6
Trezzano sul Naviglio [I] 70 G5
Trezzo sull'Adda [I] 70 G4
Trgovište [YU] 150 E5
Trhové Sviny [CZ] 62 C2
Triaize [F] 54 C4
Triánta [GR] 142 E4
Triaucourt-en-Argonne [F] 44 D4
Tribanj Kruščica [HR] 112 G4
Triberg [D] 58 F3
Tribsees [D] 20 C3
Tricárico [I] 120 H4
Tricase [I] 122 G6
Tricesimo [I] 72 G4
Trichiana [I] 72 E4
Trie [F] 84 F3
Trieben [A] 62 C6
Trier [D] 44 F2
Trieste [I] 72 H6
Trifels [D] 46 B5
Trignac [F] 40 E6
Trígono [GR] 128 E4
Trigueros [E] 94 F5
Tríkala [GR] 128 G4
Tríkala [GR] 132 F2
Tríkala [GR] 136 E1
Trikéri [GR] 134 A3
Trilj [HR] 152 A1
Trillevallen [S] 182 F2
Trillo [E] 90 A5
Trílofo [GR] 132 G3
Trim [IRL] 2 F5
Trimburg [D] 46 E3
Trindade [P] 94 D3
Trindade [P] 80 E4
Třinec [CZ] 50 F5
Trinidad [E] 84 A4
Trinita d'Agultu [I] 118 D2
Trinitápoli [I] 120 H2
Trinité, Ermitage de la- [F] 114 B6
Trino [I] 70 E5
Triollo [E] 82 D4
Triora [I] 108 F4
Trípoli [GR] 136 E2
Triponzo [I] 116 B3
Tripótama [GR] 136 D1
Triptis [D] 48 B1
Trisanna-Brücke [A] 72 B1
Trisulti, Abbazia di- [I] 116 C6
Trittau [D] 18 G4
Trittenheim [D] 44 G2
Trivento [I] 116 E6
Trnava [CZ] 50 B6
Trnava [SK] 62 H4
Trnovo [BiH] 152 D1
Troarn [F] 26 F3
Trocnov [CZ] 62 C2
Trodje [S] 174 E3
Troense [DK] 156 E4
Trofaiach [A] 74 C1
Trofimovo [RUS] 198 H4
Trofors [N] 190 D3
Trogir [HR] 116 H1
Tróia [I] 120 G2
Tróia [P] 86 B6
Troickij [RUS] 202 F7
Troina [I] 126 F3
Troisdorf [D] 30 H5
Trois Fontaines, Abbaye des- [F] 44 C5
Trois-Ponts [B] 30 E5
Troits'ke [UA] 204 E4
Troizína [GR] 136 G2
Trojane [SLO] 74 C4
Trøjborg [DK] 156 B4
Trolla [N] 182 B1
Trollhättan [S] 166 D6
Trollvik [N] 192 G2
Tromello [I] 70 F5
Tromøy [N] 164 F5
Tromsø [N] 192 F2
Tromvik [N] 192 F2
Tronco [P] 80 E3
Trondheim [N] 182 B1
Trones [N] 190 E1
Trönninge [S] 160 H3
Trönninge [S] 162 B5
Tronvik [N] 190 B6
Trôo [F] 42 C6
Troon [GB] 8 C3
Tropea [I] 124 C6
Tropfstein-Höhle [A] 74 C3
Tropojë [AL] 150 B5
Trosa [S] 168 D4
Troškūnai [LT] 200 G4
Trosky [CZ] 48 H2
Trossingen [D] 58 G3
Tröstau [D] 48 B3
Trostberg [D] 60 F4
Trosterud [N] 166 C2
Trostianets' [UA] 204 G2
Trouville [F] 26 G3
Trowbridge [GB] 12 G3
Troyan [BG] 148 B4
Troyanovo [BG] 148 E4
Troyanski Manastir [BG] 148 B4
Troyanski Pateka [BG] 148 B4
Troyen [N] 182 B2
Troyes [F] 44 B6
Trpanj [HR] 152 B3
Trpinja [HR] 154 E1
Tršić [YU] 154 F3
Trstena [SK] 50 H6
Trstena [YU] 150 D5
Trstenik [HR] 150 C3
Trsteno [HR] 152 C3
Trstín [SK] 62 H3
Trubia [E] 78 H3
Truchas [E] 78 F6
Truchtersheim [F] 44 H5
Trud [BG] 148 B5
Trujillo [E] 96 B1
Trulben [D] 44 H4
Trŭn [BG] 150 E4
Trun [CH] 70 G1
Trun [F] 26 F4
Truro [GB] 12 C5
Truskavets' [UA] 52 G5
Trustrup [DK] 160 F6
Trutnov [CZ] 50 B2
Trutnowy [PL] 22 E3
Truva [TR] 130 H5
Tryavna [BG] 148 C4
Trydal [N] 164 D2
Tryde [S] 158 D3
Tryggelev [DK] 156 E5
Tryggestad [N] 180 D4
Tryńcza [PL] 52 E3
Trýpi [GR] 136 E4
Trypití [GR] 130 C5
Tryserum [S] 162 G1
Tryškiai [LT] 200 E3
Tryszczyn [PL] 22 D5
Trzcianka [PL] 22 A6
Trzciel [PL] 36 B3
Trzcinna [PL] 34 H1
Trzcińsko Zdrój [PL] 20 F6
Trzebiatów [PL] 20 G3
Trzebiel [PL] 34 G5
Trzebież [PL] 20 F4
Trzebinia [PL] 50 G3
Trzebnica [PL] 36 C6
Trzemeszno [PL] 36 E2
Trzepowo [PL] 22 D3
Tržič [SLO] 74 B4
Trzin [SLO] 74 C5
Tsagkaráda [GR] 134 A2
Tsamandás [GR] 132 C1
Tsampíka, Moní- [GR] 142 E4
Tsangário [GR] 132 C3
Tsapel'ka [RUS] 198 H3
Tsarevets [BG] 148 C2
Tsarevo [BG] 148 G5
Tsarítsani [GR] 132 G1
Tschernitz [D] 34 G5
Tschierv [CH] 72 B3

Tsenovo [BG] 148 C2
Tsiurupyns'k [UA] 204 F4
Tsotíli [GR] 128 E6
Tsoútsouros [GR] 140 F5
Tua [N] 190 C5
Tua [P] 80 E4
Tuaim / Tuam [IRL] 2 C4
Tuam / Tuaim [IRL] 2 C4
Tubilla del Agua [E] 82 E5
Tübingen [D] 58 G2
Tubre / Taufers [I] 72 B3
Tučepi [HR] 152 B2
Tuchan [F] 106 C5
Tüchen [D] 20 B6
Tuchola [PL] 22 D4
Tuchomie [PL] 22 C3
Tuchów [PL] 52 C4
Tuckur [FIN] 186 B2
Tuczno [PL] 20 H6
Tuddal [N] 164 F1
Tudela [E] 84 B6
Tudela de Duero [E] 88 E2
Tudu [EST] 198 F1
Tudulinna [EST] 198 F2
Tuffé [F] 42 C5
Tufjord [N] 194 B1
Tuhkakylä [FIN] 196 F5
Tui [E] 78 B5
Tuin [MK] 128 D2
Tuineje [E] 100 E6
Tuiskula [FIN] 186 C3
Tuixén [E] 92 D2
Tūja [LV] 198 D4
Tukums [LV] 198 D5
Tula [RUS] 202 F5
Tulare [YU] 150 D5
Tuławki [PL] 22 H3
Tulca [RO] 76 H3
Tulcea [RO] 204 E6
Tul'chyn [UA] 204 E3
Tuliszków [PL] 36 E3
Tulla [IRL] 2 C6
Tullamore [IRL] 2 E6
Tulle [F] 66 H3
Tullebølle [DK] 156 E4
Tulleråsen [S] 182 G1
Tullgarn [S] 168 D4
Tullinge [S] 168 D3
Tullins [F] 68 G4
Tulln [A] 62 E4
Tullow [IRL] 4 F4
Tułowice [PL] 50 D2
Tulppio [FIN] 194 F6
Tulsk [IRL] 2 D4
Tum [PL] 36 G3
Tumba [S] 168 D3
Tumulus de Gavrinis [F] 40 D5
Tun [S] 166 D5
Tuna [S] 162 F3
Tunaberg [S] 168 C5
Tuna Hästberg [S] 172 H5
Tunbridge Wells [GB] 14 E5
Tunby [S] 184 E5
Tunçbilek [TR] 146 G6
Tune [DK] 156 G3
Túnel del Cadí [E] 92 E2
Túnel de Viella [E] 84 F5
Tunge [S] 160 H1
Tungelsta [S] 168 E4
Tungozero [RUS] 196 G2
Tunhovd [N] 170 F4
Tunnerstad [S] 162 D1
Tunnsjørørvika [N] 190 D4
Tunø By [DK] 156 D1
Tuntsa [FIN] 194 F6
Tunvågen [S] 182 G3
Tuohikotti [FIN] 178 C2
Tuohittu [FIN] 176 F5
Tuomioja [FIN] 196 D4
Tuorila [FIN] 186 B6
Tuornoel, Château de- [F] 68 C2
Tupadły [PL] 36 E2
Tuplice [PL] 34 G4
Tuppurinmäki [FIN] 188 D3
Tura [H] 64 D6
Turalići [BiH] 154 E4
Turan [TR] 146 F4
Turanlı [TR] 144 C2
Turany [SK] 50 G6
Türas [TR] 146 G2
Turbe [BiH] 154 C4
Turčianske Teplice [SK] 64 C2
Turckheim [F] 58 D3
Turda [RO] 204 B4
Turégano [E] 88 F3
Turek [PL] 36 F1
Turenki [FIN] 176 G3
Turenne [F] 66 G3
Turgeliai [LT] 200 G6
Tŭrgovishte [BG] 148 D3
Turgut [TR] 142 D1
Turgutbey [TR] 146 C2
Turgutlu [TR] 144 D4
Turgutreis [TR] 142 C3
Turhala [FIN] 196 E6
Türi [EST] 198 E2
Turi [I] 122 E3
Turiis'k [UA] 38 H5
Turís / Torís [E] 98 E5
Turka [UA] 52 F6
Türkeli [TR] 146 C4
Túrkeve [H] 76 F2
Türkheim [D] 60 C4
Türkmen [TR] 144 C3
Turku / Åbo [FIN] 176 D4
Turleque [E] 96 F2
Turlough [IRL] 2 C4
Turmantas [LT] 200 H4
Turňa nad Bodvou [SK] 64 F3
Turnberry [GB] 8 C4
Turnhout [B] 30 D3
Türnitz [A] 62 D5
Turnov [CZ] 48 H2
Turnu Măgurele [RO] 148 B2
Turnu Roşu, Pasul- [RO] 204 B5
Turo [FIN] 194 D4
Turobin [PL] 52 F1
Túrony [H] 76 B5
Turośl [PL] 24 C5
Turów [PL] 38 E4
Turrach [A] 74 A2
Turre [E] 102 H5
Turriff [GB] 6 F5
Turtagrø [N] 170 E1
Turtel [MK] 128 G1
Turtola [FIN] 194 C8
Turunç [TR] 142 E3
Turzovka [PL] 50 F5
Tusa [I] 126 E2
Tusby / Tuusula [FIN] 176 H4
Tuscánia [I] 114 G4
Tušilovic [HR] 112 G1
Tustervatnet [N] 190 D3
Tuszów Narodowy [PL] 52 D2
Tuszyn [PL] 36 G5
Tutin [YU] 150 B4
Tutjunniemi [FIN] 188 F3
Tutrakan [BG] 148 D1
Tutrakan [BG] 204 D6
Tuttlingen [D] 58 G3
Tútugi [E] 102 G3
Tutzing [D] 60 D5
Tützpatz [D] 20 D4
Tuukkala [FIN] 186 H6
Tuukkala [FIN] 188 C6
Tuulos [FIN] 176 G2
Tuupovaara [FIN] 188 G3
Tuuruniemi [FIN] 194 D4
Tuusjärvi [FIN] 188 D2
Tuuski [FIN] 178 C4
Tuusniemi [FIN] 188 E2
Tuusula / Tusby [FIN] 176 H4
Tuv [N] 170 F3
Tuvaltnet [S] 190 E6
Tuvnes [N] 190 A6
Tuzi [YU] 152 E4
Tuzla [BiH] 154 E3
Tuzla [TR] 146 F3
Tuzla [TR] 134 G1
Tuzlata [BG] 148 G2
Tvååker [S] 160 H4
Tväråbäck [S] 190 H5
Tvärålund [S] 190 H5
Tvärträsk [S] 190 G4
Tvärskog [S] 162 F5
Tvarud [S] 166 D1
Tvede [DK] 160 E5
Tvedestrand [N] 164 F4
Tveita [N] 170 B4
Tveitsund [N] 164 E3
Tver' (Kalinin) [RUS] 202 E3
Tverai [LT] 200 D4
Tverrå [N] 164 C3
Tverrå [N] 190 E2
Tverrelvmo [N] 192 G3
Tversted [DK] 160 E2
Tvindehaugen [N] 170 F1
Tving [S] 158 F1
Tvinno [N] 170 C3
Tvis [DK] 160 C5
Tvøroyri [FR] 160 A3
Tvorozhkovo [RUS] 198 G2
Tvrdošovce [SK] 64 A5
Tv-Torony [H] 74 G3
Tvŭrditsa [BG] 148 D4
Twann-Schlucht [CH] 58 D5
Twardogóra [PL] 36 D5
Twimberg [A] 74 C2
Twist [D] 16 H4
Twistringen [D] 18 D6
Tworków [PL] 50 E4
Tworóg [PL] 50 F2
Tychowo [PL] 22 A4
Tychy [PL] 50 G3
Tyczyn [PL] 52 E4
Tyfjord [N] 194 D1
Tyfors [S] 172 G5
Tyhkola [RUS] 196 G2
Tyholland [NIR] 2 F4
Tyin [N] 170 F2
Tyinosen [N] 170 E2
Tykocin [PL] 24 E5
Tylawa [PL] 52 D5
Tylisos [GR] 140 E4
Tylldal [N] 182 B5
Tylösand [S] 162 B5
Tylstrup [DK] 160 E3
Tymfristós [GR] 132 F4
Tympáki [GR] 140 D5
Tyndaris [I] 124 A7
Tynderö [S] 184 F4
Tyndrum [GB] 8 D2
Tynemouth [GB] 8 G6
Tyngsjö [S] 172 F5
Tyniec [PL] 50 H4
Tyniště nad Orlicí [CZ] 50 B3
Tynkä [FIN] 196 C5
Týn nad Vltavou [CZ] 48 F6
Tynnelsö [S] 168 C3
Tynset [N] 182 B4
Typpö [FIN] 196 C5
Tyrävaara [FIN] 196 F3
Tyresö [S] 168 E3
Tyringe [S] 158 C1
Tyrislöt [S] 168 C6
Tyristrand [N] 170 H5
Tyrjänsaari [FIN] 188 G1
Tyrnävä [FIN] 196 D4
Týrnavos [GR] 132 G1
Tyrós [GR] 136 F3
Tyřov [CZ] 48 E4
Tyrrellspass [IRL] 2 E5
Tyry [FIN] 186 F6
Tysken [N] 172 D4
Tysse [N] 170 B4
Tyssedal [N] 170 C5
Tystberga [S] 168 C4
Tyszki-Nadbory [PL] 24 D6
Tytuvėnai [LT] 200 E4
Tyulenovo [BG] 148 G2
Tyvsen [DK] 156 B4
Tywyn [GB] 10 B5
Tzermiádo [GR] 140 F5
Tzummarum [NL] 16 F2

U

Ub [YU] 150 A1
Úbeda [E] 102 F2
Ubergsmoen [N] 164 F4
Überlingen [D] 58 G4
Ubli [HR] 152 A3
Ubrique [E] 100 H4
Uccellina, Torre dell'- [I] 114 F3
Uchanie [PL] 38 G6
Uchorowo [PL] 36 C2
Uchte [D] 32 E1
Uckange [F] 44 E3
Uckfield [GB] 14 E5
Uclés [E] 96 H2
Ucria [I] 124 A7
Udbina [HR] 112 H4
Udbyhøj [DK] 160 E5
Udbyhøj Vasehuse [DK] 160 E5
Uddel [NL] 16 F4
Udden [S] 166 D5
Uddevalla [S] 166 C5
Uddheden [S] 166 E1
Uden [NL] 16 E6
Udine [I] 72 G5
Udovo [MK] 128 G2
Üdrupij [LV] 198 F4
Udvar [H] 76 B5
Ueckermünde [D] 20 E4
Uelsen [D] 16 G4
Uelzen [D] 18 G6
Uetersen [D] 18 F4
Uetze [D] 32 G2
Uffenheim [D] 46 F5
Uga [E] 100 E6
Ugāle [LV] 198 C5
Ugao [YU] 150 A4
Ugao-Miraballes [E] 82 G4
Ugento [I] 122 G6
Ugerløse [DK] 156 F3
Uggdal [N] 170 B5
Uggerby [DK] 160 E2
Uggerslev [DK] 156 D3
Ugglarpshavsbad [S] 160 H4
Ugíjar [E] 102 F5
Ugine [F] 70 B3
Uglich [RUS] 202 F3
Ugljan [HR] 112 F5
Ugljane [HR] 152 A2
Ugrinovci [YU] 150 B2
Ugŭrchin [BG] 148 A4
Uğurlutepe [TR] 130 G5
Uherse Mineralne [PL] 52 E5
Uherské Hradiště [CZ] 62 H2
Uherský Brod [CZ] 62 H2
Uherský Ostroh [CZ] 62 H2
Uhlířské Janovice [CZ] 48 G4
Uhříněves [CZ] 48 G4
Uhrovský Hrad [SK] 64 B3
Uhyst [D] 34 G5
Uig [GB] 6 B4
Újhartyán [H] 76 D2
Uimaharju [FIN] 188 G1
Uimila [FIN] 178 B2
Uithoorn [NL] 16 D4
Uithuizen [NL] 16 G1
Ujazd [PL] 50 E3
Ujazd [PL] 36 H5
Ujazd [PL] 52 C2
Újfehértó [H] 64 H5
Ujma [PL] 36 F2
Ujście [PL] 22 B6
Újszász [H] 76 E1
Ujué [E] 84 B5
Ukk [H] 74 G2
Ukkola [FIN] 188 F1
Ukmergė [LT] 200 G5
Ukonjärvi [FIN] 194 D4
Ukonvaara [FIN] 188 E1
Ukri [LV] 198 D6
Ukta [PL] 24 C4
Ula [BY] 202 C4
Ula [TR] 142 E2
Ul'anka [SK] 64 C3
Ulan Majorat [PL] 38 E4
Ulanów [PL] 52 E2
Ulbjerg [DK] 160 D5
Ulcinj [YU] 152 E5
Uldum [DK] 156 C2
Uleåborg / Oulu [FIN] 190 D4
Ulefoss [N] 164 F2
Uleila del Campo [E] 102 H5
Ulëzë [AL] 128 B2
Ulfborg [DK] 160 B5
Ulhówek [PL] 52 G2
Ulibice [CZ] 48 H3
Ulinia [PL] 22 C1
Uljanik [HR] 154 B1
Uljma [YU] 154 H2
Ullapool [GB] 6 D3
Ullared [S] 162 B4
Ullatti [S] 192 H6
Ullava [FIN] 196 C6
Ulldecona [E] 92 A6
Ulldemolins [E] 90 H5
Ullene [S] 166 E6
Ullerslev [DK] 156 E3
Üllés [H] 76 E4
Ullisjaur [S] 190 F4
Üllő [H] 76 D1
Ulm [D] 60 B3
Ulme [P] 86 D4
Ulmen [D] 44 G1
Ulmeni [RO] 148 D1
Ulnes [N] 170 G2
Ulog [BiH] 152 D2
Ulpiana [YU] 150 C5
Ulpia Traiana [RO] 204 B5
Ulricehamn [S] 162 C2
Ulrika [S] 162 E1
Ulriksfors [S] 190 E6
Ulsberg [N] 180 H3
Ulsrud [N] 166 C1
Ulsted [DK] 160 E4
Ulsteinvik [N] 180 C4
Ulstrup [DK] 156 E2
Ulstrup [DK] 160 D5
Uluabat [TR] 146 E5
Ulubey [TR] 144 G3
Uludağ [TR] 146 F5
Ulvåla [N] 172 D3
Ulvåsa [S] 166 H5
Ulverston [GB] 10 D2
Ülvesbüll [D] 18 E1
Ulvestad [N] 170 D1
Ulvik [N] 170 D3
Ulvika [N] 192 E4
Ulvila / Ulvsby [FIN] 176 D2
Ulvsby / Ulvila [FIN] 176 D2
Ulvsjön [S] 172 G1
Ulvsvåg [S] 192 E4
Umag [HR] 112 D1
Uman' [UA] 204 E3
Umasjö [S] 190 E2
Umbertide [I] 116 A1
Umbukta [N] 190 E2
Umčari [YU] 154 H3
Umeå [S] 196 A6
Umfors [S] 190 E2
Umfors [S] 190 E2
Umgransele [S] 190 G4
Umhausen [A] 72 C1
Umka [YU] 154 G3
Umurbey [TR] 146 B5
Umurbey [TR] 146 F4
Umurlu [TR] 144 E5
Uña [E] 98 C2
Unaja [FIN] 176 C3
Unari [FIN] 194 D7
Unbyn [S] 196 B3
Uncastillo [E] 84 C5
Undenäs [S] 166 G5
Undersåker [S] 182 F2
Úněšov [CZ] 48 D4
Ungheni [MD] 204 D4
Unhošť [CZ] 48 F3
Unichowo [PL] 22 C3
Uničov [CZ] 50 C4
Uniejów [PL] 36 F4
Unirea [RO] 150 F1
Unisław [PL] 22 D6
Unna [D] 32 C4
Unnaryd [S] 162 C4
Unserfrau / Madonna di Senales [I] 72 C2
Unset [N] 182 C5
Unsholtet [N] 182 C3
Untamala [FIN] 186 C2
Unterach [A] 60 H5
Unterlüss [D] 18 G6
Unter Pfaffenhofen [D] 60 D4
Unterradlberg [A] 62 E4
Unterschächen [CH] 70 G1
Unter-Schleissheim [D] 60 E4
Unteruhldingen [D] 58 H4
Unterwasser [CH] 58 H5
Unterweissenbach [A] 62 C4
Unterwössen [D] 60 F5
Untorp [S] 172 G2
Uors [CH] 70 G1
Úpice [CZ] 50 B2
Uppad [S] 166 D6
Upper Largo [GB] 8 F3
Upplands Väsby [S] 168 D2
Uppsala [S] 168 D1
Upyna [LT] 200 E4
Urachi, Nuraghe s'- [I] 118 C5
Uras [I] 118 C6
Ura Vajgurore [AL] 128 B4
Urbânia [I] 110 H6
Urbino [I] 112 B6
Urbise [F] 56 E6
Urçay [F] 56 C5
Urda [E] 96 F3
Urdaibai [E] 82 H3
Urdos [F] 84 D4
Uriage-les-Bains [F] 68 H5
Uriz / Arze-Arce [E] 84 C4
Urjala [FIN] 176 F2
Urk [NL] 16 E3
Urla [TR] 144 C4
Urlingford [IRL] 4 E3
Urnäsch [CH] 58 H5
Urnes [N] 170 D1
Uroševac [YU] 150 C6
Urpila [FIN] 188 F1
Urroz [E] 84 B4
Urshult [S] 162 E5
Ursus [PL] 38 B3
Urtimjaur [S] 196 A1
Ururi [I] 116 F6
Ury [F] 42 F5
Urzędów [PL] 38 D6
Urzelina [P] 100 C3
Urziceni [RO] 204 D6
Urzicuța [RO] 150 F2
Urzulei [I] 118 E5
Usagre [E] 94 H3
Uşak [TR] 144 G3
Ušće [YU] 150 B3
Uście Gorlickie [PL] 52 C5
Usedom [D] 20 E4
Ushakovo [RUS] 22 G2
Uši [MK] 128 F2
Usingen [D] 46 C2
Uskali [FIN] 188 G3
Uskedal [N] 170 B5
Uskoplje [BiH] 152 B1
Üsküdar [TR] 146 E3
Üsküp [TR] 146 C1
Uslar [D] 32 F4
Usmate Velate [I] 70 G4
Úsov [CZ] 50 C4
Ussé [F] 54 F2
Usseglio [I] 70 C5
Ussel [F] 68 B2
Ussel [I] 70 D4
Usseln [D] 32 D5
Usson-du-Poitou [F] 54 F5
Usson-les-Bains [F] 106 B6
Ustaoset [N] 170 E4
Ustaritz [F] 84 C2
Úštěk [CZ] 48 F2
Uster [CH] 58 G5
Ustibar [BiH] 152 E2
Ústí nad Labem [CZ] 48 F2
Ústí nad Orlicí [CZ] 50 B4
Ustiprača [BiH] 152 E1
Ustjuzhna [RUS] 202 E2
Ustka [PL] 22 B2
Ust'-Luga [RUS] 178 E6
Ustrem [BG] 146 A1
Ustroń [PL] 50 F5
Ustronie Morskie [PL] 20 H3
Ustrzyki Dolne [PL] 52 F5
Ustrzyki Górne [PL] 52 F6
Ustye [RUS] 198 H1
Ustyluh [UA] 38 G6
Ususău [RO] 76 H5
Utajärvi [FIN] 196 E4
Utåker [N] 170 B5
Utansjö [S] 184 F3
Utbjoa [N] 164 B1
Utebo [E] 90 E3
Utena [LT] 200 G4
Uthlede [D] 18 D4
Utiel [E] 98 D4
Utne [N] 170 C4
Utrecht [NL] 16 D5
Utrera [E] 100 G2
Utrillas [E] 90 E6
Utrine [YU] 76 E5
Utsjö [S] 172 F4
Utsjoki [FIN] 194 D3
Utstein [N] 164 A2
Uttendorf [A] 72 F1
Uttendorf [A] 60 G4
Uttermossa [FIN] 186 B5
Uttersberg [S] 168 A2
Utti [FIN] 178 C3
Utting [D] 60 D4
Uttoxeter [GB] 10 E5
Utula [FIN] 178 E1
Utvalnäs [S] 174 E4
Utvängstorp [S] 162 C1
Utvik [N] 180 D5
Utvorda [N] 190 C4
Uukuniemi [FIN] 188 G5
Uukuniemi [FIN] 188 G5
Uurainen [FIN] 186 F4
Uuro [FIN] 196 G6
Uuro [FIN] 186 B5
Uusijoki [FIN] 194 E5
Uusikaarlepyy / Nykarleby [FIN] 186 C1
Uusikaupunki / Nystad [FIN] 176 C3
Uusikylä [FIN] 178 B3
Uusi-Värtsilä [FIN] 188 G3
Uutela [FIN] 194 D6
Uva [FIN] 196 F4
Uvac [BiH] 152 E1
Úvaly [CZ] 48 G4
Uvanå [S] 172 F5
Uvdal [N] 170 F4
Uyeasound [GB] 6 H3
Uzdowo [PL] 22 G5
Uzel [F] 26 A5
Uzerche [F] 66 G2
Uzès [F] 106 G3
Uzeste [F] 66 D4
Uzhorod [UA] 204 B3
Užice [YU] 150 A2
Užokski, pereval- [UA] 52 F6
Užpaliai [LT] 200 G4
Üzümlü [TR] 142 G3
Uzunköprü [TR] 146 B3
Uzunkuyu [TR] 144 B4
Uzuntarla [TR] 146 G3
Užventis [LT] 200 E4

V

Vå [N] 164 E1
Vä [S] 158 D2
Vaajakoski [FIN] 186 G4
Vääkiö [FIN] 196 F3
Väkkiö [FIN] 196 F3
Vääksy [FIN] 178 A2
Vaala [FIN] 196 E4
Vaalajärvi [FIN] 194 D6
Vaalimaa [FIN] 178 D3
Vaarakylä [FIN] 196 F5
Vaaraniva [FIN] 196 F3
Väärinmaja [FIN] 186 E5
Vaas [F] 42 B6
Vaasa / Vasa [FIN] 186 B2
Vaassen [NL] 16 F4
Väätäiskylä [FIN] 186 E3
Vabalninkas [LT] 200 F3
Vác [H] 64 C5
Vacha [D] 46 F1
Váchartyán [H] 64 C6
Väckelsång [S] 162 E5
Vad [S] 168 A1
Väderstad [S] 166 G6
Vadheim [N] 170 C1
Vado Ligure [I] 108 H3
Vadsø [N] 194 E2
Vadstena [S] 166 G5
Vaduz [FL] 58 H6
Væggerløse [DK] 20 B1
Vafeika [GR] 130 E3
Vafiochóri [GR] 128 G3
Vág [H] 74 G1
Vågaholmen [N] 190 D1
Vågåmo [N] 180 G5
Vagan [BiH] 154 B4
Våge [N] 164 C6
Våge [N] 170 B5
Vage [N] 180 E3
Våge [N] 164 A1
Vägeva [EST] 198 E2
Vaggeryd [S] 162 D3
Vaggsvik [N] 192 F3
Vágia [GR] 134 B5
Vagiónia [GR] 140 E5
Vaglio Basilicata [I] 120 H4
Vagnhärad [S] 168 D4
Vagos [P] 80 B5
Vågsbygd [N] 164 D6
Vägsele [S] 190 G5
Vägsjöfors [S] 172 E5
Vågslid [N] 164 D1
Vágur [FR] 160 A3
Vähäkyro / Lillkyro [FIN] 186 B2
Vahanka [FIN] 186 E3
Vahastu [EST] 198 E2
Vaheri [FIN] 186 G5
Vái [GR] 140 H4
Vaiano [I] 110 F5
Vaiges [F] 40 H5
Vaiguva [LT] 200 E4
Vaihingen [D] 46 C6
Väike-Maarja [EST] 198 F1
Väike Rakke [EST] 198 F3
Vaikko [FIN] 196 F6
Vailly [F] 56 C2
Vailly [F] 44 A2
Vainikkala [FIN] 178 E2
Vainutas [LT] 200 D5
Vaison-la-Romaine [F] 106 H3
Vajmat [S] 190 H2
Vajont [I] 72 F4
Vajszló [H] 76 A5
Vajza [AL] 128 B5
Vakarel [BG] 150 G5
Vakern [S] 172 F5
Vakıfköy [TR] 144 F5
Vakıflar [TR] 146 C2
Vakijaur [S] 190 H1
Vaksdal [N] 170 B3
Valaajärvi [FIN] 194 D6
Välådalen [S] 182 E2
Valajanaapa [FIN] 196 D2
Valajaskoski [FIN] 194 D8
Valandovo [MK] 128 G2
Valanhamn [N] 192 G1
Valanída [GR] 132 F1
Valareña [E] 84 B6
Valaská Belá [SK] 64 B2
Valašská Polanka [CZ] 50 E6
Valašské Klobouky [CZ] 50 E6
Valašské Meziříčí [CZ] 50 E5
Valbella [CH] 70 H1
Valberg [F] 108 E3
Valberg [S] 166 E3
Valbiska [HR] 112 E2
Valbo [S] 174 E4
Valbondione [I] 72 A4
Valbonë [AL] 150 A5
Valbonnais [F] 68 H5
Valcarlos / Luzaide [E] 84 C3
Val-Claret [F] 70 C4
Valcum [H] 74 G3
Valdagno [I] 72 D6
Valdahon [F] 58 B5
Valdaj [RUS] 202 D3
Valdalen [N] 182 D5
Valdecaballeros [E] 96 C2
Valdecabras [E] 98 C2
Valdecarros [E] 88 C3
Valdedios [E] 82 C2
Valdeganga [E] 98 C5
Valdelacas de Tajo [E] 96 C1
Val del Charco del Agua Amarga, Cueva de la- [E] 90 F6
Valdeltormo [E] 90 G6
Valdemārpils [LV] 198 C4
Valdemarsvik [S] 168 C6
Valdemorillo [E] 88 F5
Valdemoro [E] 88 F6
Valdemoro Sierra [E] 98 C2
Valdenoceda [E] 82 F4
Valdepeñas [E] 96 F5
Valdepeñas de Jaén [E] 102 E3
Valdepolo [E] 82 C4
Valderas [E] 82 B5
Valderice [I] 126 B2
Valderöy [N] 180 C3
Valderrobres [E] 98 G1
Val d'Esquières [F] 108 D5
Valdeverdeja [E] 96 C1
Valdieri [I] 108 F3
Val d'Isère [F] 70 C4
Val-d'Izé [F] 26 D6
Valdobbiádene [I] 72 E5
Valdoviño [E] 78 D1
Valdštejn [CZ] 48 H2
Valea lui Mihai [RO] 204 B4
Valea Rea [RO] 148 F1
Valebø [N] 164 F2
Valečov [CZ] 48 G2
Vale de Açor [P] 94 D3
Vale de Cambra [P] 80 C5
Vale de Lobos [P] 94 C5
Vale do Arco [P] 86 D4
Vale do Côa, Parque Arqueológico do- [P] 80 E5
Vale do Poço [P] 94 D4
Válega [P] 80 B5
Váleggio sul Mincio [I] 110 E1
Valença do Minho [P] 78 B5
Valençay [F] 54 H3
Valence [F] 66 E6
Valence [F] 66 F6
Valence [F] 68 F5
Valence d'Albigeois [F] 106 C2
Valencia [E] 98 E4
Valencia de Alcántara [E] 86 F5
Valencia de Don Juan [E] 82 B5
Valencia de las Torres [E] 94 H3
Valencia del Ventoso [E] 94 G3
Valencia de Mombuey [E] 94 F3
Valenciennes [F] 28 G4
Văleni [RO] 148 B1
Vălenii de Munte [RO] 204 C6
Valensole [F] 108 C4
Valentano [I] 114 G3
Valentigney [F] 58 C4
Valenza [I] 70 F6
Våler [N] 166 B2
Våler [N] 172 D4
Valeria [E] 98 B3
Valevåg [N] 170 B6
Valfàbbrica [I] 116 A2
Valga [EST] 198 F4
Valgeristi [EST] 198 D2
Valgrisenche [I] 70 C4
Valguarnera Caropepe [I] 126 F3
Välijoki [FIN] 194 D8
Välijoki [FIN] 178 D2
Välikylä [FIN] 196 C6
Valimítika [GR] 132 G6
Välivaara [FIN] 196 G6
Valjevo [YU] 150 A1
Valjimena [E] 88 C4
Valjok [N] 194 C3
Valka [LV] 198 F4
Valkeakoski [FIN] 176 F2
Valkeala [FIN] 178 C2
Valkeavaara [FIN] 188 G4
Valkenburg [NL] 30 F4
Valkenswaard [NL] 30 E3
Valkiamäki [FIN] 188 E5
Valkininkai [LT] 24 H2
Valko / Valkom [FIN] 178 B4
Valkom / Valko [FIN] 178 B4
Valla [S] 182 F1
Valla [S] 184 D3
Vallada [E] 78 F4
Valladolid [E] 88 E2
Vallåkra [S] 156 H2
Vallargärdet [S] 166 F2
Vallata [I] 120 F3
Vallbona de les Monges [E] 92 C4
Valldal [N] 180 E4
Valldemossa [E] 104 E4
Valle [LV] 198 E6
Valle [N] 164 D2
Valle de Abdalajís [E] 102 B4
Valle de Cabuérniga [E] 82 E3
Valle dei Templi [I] 126 D4
Valle de la Serena [E] 96 A3
Valle de los Caidos [E] 88 F5
Valle de Matamoros [E] 94 F3
Valledoria [I] 118 C2
Vallehermoso [E] 100 B5
Vallelunga Pratameno [I] 126 D3
Vallen [S] 184 D1
Vallenhove [NL] 16 F3
Vallentuna [S] 168 E2
Valleraugue [F] 106 E2
Vallet [F] 54 C2
Valletta [M] 126 C6
Vallfogona de Ripollès [E] 92 E2
Vallheim [N] 190 D4
Vallo di Lucania [I] 120 F5
Valloire [F] 70 B5
Valloires, Abbaye de- [F] 28 D3
Vallombrosa [I] 110 F5
Vallon-en-Sully [F] 56 C5
Vallon-Pont-d'Arc [F] 68 E6
Vallorbe [CH] 58 B6
Vallorcine [F] 70 C3
Vallø Slot [DK] 156 G3
Vallouise [F] 70 B6
Vallrun [S] 190 E6
Valls [E] 92 C4
Vallsbo [S] 174 D3
Vallset [N] 172 C4
Vallsta [S] 174 D1
Vallter 20 [E] 92 E2
Vallvig [S] 174 E2
Valmadrid [E] 90 E4
Valmiera [LV] 198 E4
Valmigère [F] 106 C5
Valmojado [E] 88 E6
Valmontone [I] 116 B6
Valmorel [F] 70 B4
Val Moutier [CH] 58 D5
Valö [S] 174 F5
Valognes [F] 26 D2
Valongo [P] 80 C4
Valoria la Buena [E] 88 F1
Valøy [N] 190 C4
Valozhyn [BY] 200 H6
Valpaços [P] 80 E3
Valpelline [I] 70 D3
Valporquero de Torío [E] 78 H5
Valpovo [HR] 76 B6
Valras-Plage [F] 106 D5
Valréas [F] 106 H2
Vals [CH] 70 G2
Valsamónero [GR] 140 E5
Valsebo [S] 166 C3
Valset [N] 190 B6
Valsjöbyn [S] 190 E5
Valsjön [S] 184 D5
Valskog [S] 168 B3
Vals-les-Bains [F] 68 E6
Valsøybotn [N] 180 G2
Välsta [S] 184 E6
Val-Suzon [F] 56 G3
Valtesíniko [GR] 136 D2
Val Thorens [F] 70 B5
Valtiendas [E] 88 G3
Valtierra [E] 84 B5
Valtimo [FIN] 196 F5
Valtjom [S] 184 E4
Valtola [FIN] 178 C2
Váltos [GR] 130 H1
Valtournenche [I] 70 D3
Valul lui Traian [MD] 204 E5
Valvanera, Monasterio de- [E] 90 B1
Valverde [E] 100 A5
Valverde, Santuario di- [I] 118 B3
Valverde de Cervera [E] 84 A6
Valverde de Júcar [E] 98 B3
Valverde del Camino [E] 94 F5
Valverde de Leganés [E] 94 F2
Valverde del Fresno [E] 86 G3
Vama Veche [RO] 148 G1
Vamberk [CZ] 50 B3
Vamdrup [DK] 156 C3
Våmhus [S] 172 G3
Vamlingbo [S] 168 F6
Vammala [FIN] 176 E2
Vámos [GR] 140 C4
Vámosmikola [H] 64 C5
Vámospércs [H] 64 H6
Vámosszabadi [H] 62 H6
Vampula [FIN] 176 E3
Vamvakoú [GR] 132 G2
Vana-Vigala [EST] 198 D2
Vanda / Vantaa [FIN] 176 H4
Vandel [DK] 156 C2
Vandellós [E] 90 H6
Vandenesse [F] 56 E4
Vandoies / Vintl [I] 72 E2
Vändra [EST] 198 E2
Vandžegala [LT] 200 F5
Väne [LV] 198 C5
Vanebu [N] 164 G2
Vänersborg [S] 166 D5
Väne-Ryr [S] 166 D6
Vaneskoski [FIN] 186 C6
Vånga [S] 158 D1
Vangaži [LV] 198 E5
Vängel [S] 190 F6
Vangshylla [N] 190 C6
Vangsnes [N] 170 D2
Vanha-Kihlanki [S] 194 B6
Vanhakylä [FIN] 186 B5
Vanhamäki [FIN] 188 C5
Vänjaurbäck [S] 190 G5
Vänjaurträsk [S] 190 G5
Vânju Mare [RO] 150 E1
Vankiva [S] 158 D1
Vännacka [S] 166 D2
Vännäs [S] 190 H6
Vännäsberget [S] 194 B8
Vännäsby [S] 190 H6
Vannes [F] 40 D5
Vansbro [S] 172 G4
Vanse [N] 164 C5
Vänsjö [S] 182 H6
Vanstad [S] 158 D3
Vantaa / Vanda [FIN] 176 H4
Vanttauskoski [FIN] 194 D8
Vanvik [N] 164 C1
Vanvikan [N] 190 B6
Vanyarc [H] 64 D5
Vaplan [S] 182 G2
Vara [S] 166 E6
Varabla [EST] 198 D3
Varades [F] 40 G6
Varages [F] 108 C4
Varakļāni [LV] 198 F5
Varallo [I] 70 E4
Varanava [BY] 200 G6
Varangerbotn [N] 194 E2
Varaždin [HR] 74 F4
Varaždinske Toplice [HR] 74 F4
Varazze [I] 108 H3
Varberg [S] 160 H4
Varbola [EST] 198 D2
Varces [F] 68 H5
Várda [GR] 136 B1
Varde [DK] 156 B2
Vardim [BG] 148 C2
Vårdö [FIN] 176 B5
Vardø [N] 194 F2
Vardomb [H] 76 C4
Vårdsberg [S] 168 A5
Varduva [LT] 200 D3
Varel [D] 18 C4
Varellaíoi [GR] 134 D5
Varena [LT] 24 G2
Varengeville-sur-Mer [F] 28 C4
Varenna [I] 70 G3
Varennes-en-Argonne [F] 44 D3
Varennes-sur-Allier [F] 56 D6
Vareš [BiH] 154 D4
Varese [I] 70 F4
Varese Ligure [I] 110 C3
Vårgårda [S] 162 B1
Vargön [S] 166 D5
Vargträsk [S] 190 G5
Varhaug [N] 164 A4
Vårhus [N] 182 C3
Vári [GR] 138 D2
Varilhes [F] 84 H5
Varín [SK] 50 F6
Våring [S] 166 F5
Váris [GR] 128 F6
Varjakka [FIN] 196 D4
Varjisträsk [S] 190 H2
Varkaus [FIN] 188 D4
Várkiza [GR] 136 H1
Varland [N] 164 E1
Värmdö [S] 168 E3
Värmlandsbro [S] 166 E3
Varmo [I] 72 G5
Värmskog [S] 166 E2
Varna [BG] 148 F3
Varna [YU] 154 F3
Varna (Vahrn) [I] 72 D2
Värnamo [S] 162 D4
Varnany [BY] 200 H5
Varnhem [S] 166 F5
Varniai [LT] 200 E4
Varnja [EST] 198 F2
Varnsdorf [CZ] 48 G1
Varntresk [N] 190 E3
Väröbacka [S] 160 H3
Városföld [H] 76 D3
Varoška Rijeka [BiH] 112 H2
Varovnik [BG] 148 F5
Varp [S] 166 C4
Varpaisjärvi [FIN] 196 F6
Várpalota [H] 76 B2
Varpanen [FIN] 178 C1
Varparanta [FIN] 188 E4
Varparanta [FIN] 188 F2
Varpsjö [S] 190 F5
Várpslöd [H] 74 H2
Värriö [FIN] 194 E6
Vars [F] 108 E2
Vărşand [RO] 76 G3
Värsås [S] 166 F6
Varsi [I] 110 C3
Varsseveld [NL] 16 F6
Vartdal [N] 180 C4
Vartius [FIN] 196 G4
Vârtoapele [RO] 148 B1
Vârtopu [RO] 150 F1
Värtsilä [FIN] 188 G3
Varv [S] 166 H5
Varvara [BG] 148 A6
Varvara [BG] 148 G5
Varvára [GR] 130 C4
Varzi [I] 110 B2
Varzy [F] 56 E3
Vasa / Vaasa [FIN] 186 B2
Vasalemma [EST] 198 D1
Vasankari [FIN] 196 C5
Vasarapera [FIN] 194 F8
Vasarás [GR] 136 E3
Vásárosnamény [H] 204 B3
Vasbotna [N] 190 C5
Väse [S] 166 F3
Vasiláki [GR] 136 C2
Vasil'evskoye [RUS] 198 H4
Vasiliká [GR] 134 G2
Vasiliká [GR] 134 B3
Vasiliká [GR] 130 B5
Vasilikí [GR] 132 C5
Vasilikó [GR] 134 B5
Vasilikós [GR] 136 B2
Vasilishki [BY] 24 H3
Vasilitsi [GR] 136 D5
Vaškai [LT] 198 D6
Vaskelovo [RUS] 178 H3
Vaskelovo [RUS] 198 H6
Vaskio [FIN] 176 E4
Vaskivesi [FIN] 186 D5
Vasknarva [EST] 198 G2
Vasles [F] 54 E4
Vaslui [RO] 204 D5
Vassbø [N] 164 B4
Vassbotten [S] 166 C4
Vassenden [N] 180 C6
Vassenden [N] 170 G1
Vasses [GR] 136 D3
Vassli [N] 180 G1
Vassmolösa [S] 162 F5
Vassnäs [S] 182 E1
Vasstrand [N] 192 F2
Vassy [F] 26 E4
Västan [S] 184 E5
Västansfors [S] 168 A1
Västansjö [S] 190 G5
Västansjö [S] 190 E3
Västansjö [S] 190 F4
Västansjön [S] 184 E5
Västbacka [S] 172 G1
Västbacken [S] 182 F1
Västemyrriset [S] 190 G5
Västeråker [S] 168 D2
Väster-Arådalen [S] 182 F3
Västerås [S] 168 B2
Västerby [S] 168 D4
Västerfärnebo [S] 168 B1
Västergärn [S] 168 F5
Västerhaninge [S] 168 E3
Västerhus [S] 184 G2
Västermyckeläng [S] 172 F2
Västerrottna [S] 166 E1
Västersel [S] 184 G2
Västervik [S] 162 G2
Vastila [FIN] 178 C3
Västilä [FIN] 186 F6
Västland [S] 174 F5
Vasto [I] 116 E5
Västra Yttermark [FIN] 186 A4
Västrum [S] 162 G2
Vasvár [H] 74 G2
Vasylivka [UA] 204 H4
Vasyl'kiv [UA] 204 E2
Vát [H] 74 G1
Vatan [F] 54 H3
Vaterá [GR] 134 G3
Váthi [GR] 128 H3
Vathiý [GR] 134 B5
Vathý [GR] 144 C6
Vathý [GR] 138 H4
Vathýlakkos [GR] 130 D2
Vathýlakkos [GR] 128 F5
Vathýpetro [GR] 140 E5
Vathýpetrou [GR] 140 E5
Vatland [N] 164 C5
Vatne [N] 164 D4
Vatne [N] 180 D3
Vatne [N] 180 C4
Vatne [N] 164 B3
Vatnstraum [N] 164 E5
Vatólakkos [GR] 128 E6
Vatopedíou, Moní- [GR] 130 D5
Vatoúsa [GR] 134 G2
Vatra Dornei [RO] 204 C4
Vatta [H] 64 F5
Vattlång [S] 184 E6
Vattnäs [S] 172 G3
Vatvet [N] 166 C3
Vau [P] 94 B5
Vaucelles, Abbaye de- [F] 28 F4
Vauclaix [F] 56 E3
Vaucouleurs [F] 44 D5
Vaudoy en Brie [F] 42 G4
Vau i Dejës [AL] 128 B1

5th edition October 2004

© GEOnext - ISTITUTO GEOGRAFICO DE AGOSTINI, Novara and
© Automobile Association Developments Limited

Ordnance Survey®   This product includes mapping data licensed from
Ordnance Survey® with the permission of the Controller of Her Majesty's
Stationery Office. © Crown copyright 2003. All rights reserved.
Licence number 399221

Northern Ireland mapping reproduced by permission of the Director and Chief
Executive, Ordnance Survey of Northern Ireland, acting on behalf of the Controller
of Her Majesty's Stationery Office. © Crown copyright 2003. Permit No. 1674

Republic of Ireland mapping based on Ordnance Survey Ireland.
Permit No. MP0003403 © Ordnance Survey Ireland and Government of Ireland

Published by GEOnext - ISTITUTO GEOGRAFICO DE AGOSTINI, Novara
and Automobile Association Developments Limited whose registered
office is Millstream, Maidenhead Road, Windsor, Berkshire SL4 5GD.
Registered number 1878835

ISBN 0 7495 3852 X (flexibound)
ISBN 0 7495 3851 1 (wire bound)

A CIP catalogue record for this book is available from The British Library.

Printed in Italy by Canale & C. S.p.A., Torino

ROAD DISTANCES
DISTANZE STRADALI
DISTANCIAS KILOMÉTRICAS
DISTANCES ROUTIÈRES
STRASSENENTFERNUNGEN

Frankfurt am Main-Ljubljana = 804 km

From \ To	Amsterdam	Athína	Barcelona	Belfast	Beograd	Berlin	Bern	Birmingham	Bordeaux	Bratislava	Brussel/Bruxelles	Bucureşti	Budapest	Dublin	Edinburgh	Frankfurt am Main	Genève	Göteborg	Hamburg	Helsinki/Helsingfors	İstanbul	København	Köln	Kyïv	Lisboa	Ljubljana	London	Luxembourg	Madrid
Athína	2760																												
Barcelona	1557	2520																											
Belfast	1312	3520	2265																										
Beograd	1718	1044	1981	2816																									
Berlin	655	2288	1863	1868	1247																								
Bern	838	1971	944	1725	1363	922																							
Birmingham	738	3285	1691	582	2244	1295	1152																						
Bordeaux	1091	3049	552	1815	2007	1634	852	1241																					
Bratislava	1225	1618	1866	2324	577	671	938	1750	1879																				
Brussel/Bruxelles	206	2568	1355	1148	1673	763	637	574	883	1181																			
Bucureşti	2181	1106	2597	3279	619	1646	1893	2706	2613	977	2136																		
Budapest	1398	1429	1897	2497	388	864	1111	1923	2053	194	1353	788																	
Dublin	1088	3455	2041	164	2594	1644	1502	358	1585	2101	925	3057	2274																
Edinburgh	1190	3557	2143	305	2695	1746	1603	460	1686	2203	1026	3159	2376	468															
Frankfurt am Main	445	2323	1323	1545	1281	565	423	971	1150	788	400	1744	961	1321	1422														
Genève	908	2372	778	1683	1331	1072	165	1109	687	1088	706	1946	1261	1457	1561	573													
Göteborg	1178	3131	2479	2412	2090	823	1637	1839	2185	1514	1307	2490	1708	2187	2290	1214	1787												
Hamburg	463	2602	1763	1696	1561	294	910	1123	1470	985	591	1961	1178	1471	1574	487	1059	728											
Helsinki/Helsingfors	2580	3590	3788	3792	2641	1959	2847	3220	3551	2208	2687	2483	2252	3567	3670	2489	2996	982	2192										
İstanbul	2649	1092	2913	3748	935	2179	2294	3175	2929	1509	2605	681	1320	3522	3626	2213	2261	3022	2493	3164									
København	920	2873	2220	2153	1832	564	1378	1580	1927	1255	1048	2231	1449	1928	2031	955	1528	269	469	1123	2764								
Köln	265	2506	1342	1352	1464	575	585	778	1062	972	208	1928	1145	1126	1230	192	735	1141	425	2500	2396	882							
Kyïv	2016	1994	3093	3228	1322	1398	2190	2655	2988	1251	2123	888	1123	3003	3106	1884	2340	2211	1681	1595	1569	1952	1935						
Lisboa	2296	3787	1237	3019	3188	2838	2150	2446	1202	3090	2095	3804	3103	2793	2897	2355	1989	3397	2681	4764	4119	3138	2273	4199					
Ljubljana	1241	1572	1455	2294	530	999	836	1721	1471	435	1153	1146	443	2069	2173	804	803	1916	1203	2623	1462	1656	987	1565	2661				
London	533	2910	1486	766	2039	1090	947	193	1030	1546	370	2502	1719	541	645	766	905	1634	918	3015	2970	1375	574	2450	2243	1537			
Luxembourg	386	2355	1149	1355	1469	762	431	782	946	1010	213	1965	1183	1129	1233	240	500	1326	610	2687	2401	1066	188	2081	2159	956	582		
Madrid	1800	3145	614	2523	2573	2343	1535	1950	706	2458	1599	3189	2489	2298	2402	1859	1374	2901	2185	4268	3505	2642	1778	3684	619	2046	1750	1662	
	868	3415	1821	461	2374	1425	1282	138	1365	1881	705	2837	2054	310	339	1101	1240	1969	1253	3350	3305	1710	909	2785	2578	1872	323	911	2082
	1236	2567	505	2003	1526	1541	623	1429	654	1419	1034	2141	1441	1778	1881	1003	422	2158	1442	3467	2457	1899	1025	2564	1711	999	1230	832	1096
	1077	1218	977	1963	1026	1033	350	1390	985	919	876	1642	942	1737	1841	662	317	1833	1120	2959	1958	1574	823	2064	2182	499	1190	669	1568
	1742	2448	2878	2955	1513	1124	1938	2381	2714	1178	1850	1341	1125	2729	2833	1620	2088	1938	1408	1183	2023	1678	1662	557	3927	1593	2181	1817	3432
	2449	2864	3584	3661	2084	1830	2644	3088	3420	1885	2556	1758	1831	3435	3539	2326	2794	2643	2114	1116	2440	2385	2368	871	4364	2300	2888	2523	4138
	827	1990	1370	1880	949	585	442	1297	1278	466	739	1421	639	1655	1759	390	591	1502	789	2511	1880	1242	573	1718	2576	435	1107	521	1961
	1859	597	1555	2746	1483	1693	1132	2173	1704	1376	1658	2099	1399	2521	2624	1444	1085	2586	1874	3563	2415	2327	1606	2521	2761	956	1973	1476	2146
	1490	3443	2790	2723	2402	1134	1949	2150	2497	1826	1618	2801	2019	2498	2601	1525	2098	315	1039	1030	3333	580	1446	2522	3710	2248	1950	1636	3214
	525	2465	1039	1248	1800	1068	592	659	583	1340	324	2295	1513	1023	1126	604	529	1626	910	2993	2732	1367	502	2428	1796	1287	475	407	1300
	2094	4028	1076	2818	2986	2637	1948	2244	1000	2889	1893	3602	2902	2592	2696	2153	1788	3196	2480	4563	3918	2936	2072	3997	300	2459	2044	1956	531
	891	1946	1709	2045	904	341	769	1471	1601	328	902	1304	522	1820	1923	510	919	1186	657	2178	1836	927	693	1389	2814	664	1272	731	2300
	1618	2807	2825	2830	1766	996	1885	2257	2590	1333	1725	1676	1378	2604	2708	1527	2035	1760	1230	962	2357	1501	1537	1029	3803	1748	2057	1724	3307
	1658	1190	1354	2545	1282	1493	932	1972	1503	1175	1457	1898	1198	2320	2423	1243	884	2386	1673	3363	2214	2126	1405	2321	2560	755	1772	1275	1945
	2180	3190	3388	3393	2241	1558	2447	2819	3152	1809	2288	2084	1853	3167	3271	2089	2597	2284	1793	387	2765	2063	2099	1196	4365	2223	2619	2286	3869
	1727	1121	1990	2826	303	1389	1372	2252	2007	707	1682	824	539	2600	2704	1290	1339	2402	1644	2791	1113	2143	1474	1601	3196	539	2052	1478	2581
	2277	3998	998	3000	2957	2838	1919	2427	1183	2842	2076	3573	2873	2775	2878	2299	1759	3378	2662	4763	3889	3119	2255	4068	403	2430	2227	2128	510
	2139	654	2402	3237	424	1668	1783	2664	2418	998	2094	598	809	3012	3115	1702	1750	2512	1982	3061	781	2253	1885	1485	3608	951	2464	1890	2993
	2095	735	2358	3193	380	1624	1739	2620	2375	954	2050	372	765	2968	3071	1658	1707	2468	1938	2854	555	2209	1841	1259	3564	907	2420	1846	2949
	1534	3488	2835	2768	2446	1175	1993	2195	2541	1870	1663	2846	2064	2543	2646	1570	2143	481	1084	505	3378	624	1497	2566	3755	2293	1995	1681	3259
	1920	3105	3127	3132	2063	1298	2187	2559	2892	1631	2027	1973	1675	2907	3011	1829	2337	2062	1533	90	2654	1803	1839	1326	4105	2046	2359	2026	3609
	2333	454	2597	3432	619	1862	1978	2858	2613	1193	2288	656	1004	3207	3310	1896	1945	2707	2177	3139	642	2447	2080	1543	3802	1145	2658	2085	3188
	2103	735	2366	3201	606	1765	1748	2628	2383	1083	2058	886	915	2976	3163	1666	1715	2778	2020	3167	1069	2518	1849	1773	3572	915	2428	1854	2957
	3071	4692	4371	4304	3743	2715	3529	3731	4078	3311	3199	3586	3355	4114	4182	3106	3679	1949	2620	1360	4267	2160	3033	2698	5291	3829	3531	3217	4795
	1897	3363	363	2603	2322	2202	1283	2030	803	2206	1695	2937	2237	2378	2482	1663	1123	2819	2103	4128	3253	2560	1686	3433	894	1795	1830	1492	342
	1636	2550	2776	2849	1509	1018	1836	2275	2608	1077	1744	1384	1121	2623	2727	1518	1986	1733	1203	1142	2066	1474	1555	738	3821	1492	2075	1715	3325
	1202	2097	2342	2414	1056	584	1402	1841	2174	643	1309	1240	668	2189	2293	1084	1552	1397	868	1566	1922	1138	1121	815	3387	1057	1641	1281	2891
	1148	1664	1789	2246	622	629	861	1673	1802	66	1103	1022	240	2021	2125	711	1010	1473	943	2246	1554	1214	895	1319	3016	378	1473	933	2380
	1326	1435	1586	2424	394	988	968	1852	1603	417	1281	1009	347	2199	2302	889	936	2001	1243	2604	1325	1741	1073	1470	2793	135	1647	1074	2177